C PROGRAM DESIGN FOR ENGINEERS

Jeri R. Hanly
UNIVERSITY OF WYOMING

Elliot B. Koffman
TEMPLE UNIVERSITY

with

Joan C. Horvath
Jet Propulsion Laboratory
CALIFORNIA INSTITUTE OF TECHNOLOGY

**Addison-Wesley
Publishing
Company**

Reading, Massachusetts
Menlo Park, California
New York
Don Mills, Ontario
Wokingham, England
Amsterdam
Bonn
Sydney
Singapore
Tokyo
Madrid
San Juan
Milan
Paris

Lynne Doran Cote *Sponsoring Editor*
Helen M. Wythe *Production Editor*
Maite Suarez-Rivas *Assistant Editor*
Sandra Rigney *Production Services*
Lisa Delgado *Text Designer*
Tech-Graphics *Illustrations*
Eileen Hoff *Cover Design Supervisor*
Leslie Haimes *Cover Design*
Roy Logan *Senior Manufacturing Manager*

Library of Congress Cataloging-in-Publication Data
Hanly, Jeri R.
    C program design for engineers / Jeri R. Hanly, Elliot B. Koffman,
Joan C. Horvath.
      p.   cm.
    Includes index.
    ISBN 0-201-59064-6
    1. C (Computer program language)   2. Engineering—Data Processing.
I. Koffman, Elliot B.   II. Horvath, Joan C.   III. Title.
QA76.73.C15H362   1995
005.13'3--dc20   94-6971
                                                    CIP

2 3 4 5 6 7 8 9 10–CRW–97969594

This textbook teaches a disciplined approach to solving problems and to applying widely accepted software engineering methods to design program solutions as cohesive, readable, reusable modules. We present as an implementation vehicle for these modules a subset of ANSI C—a standardized, industrial-strength programming language known for its power and portability. Our examples and programming projects are based on problems drawn from a wide range of engineering disciplines. Many of these applications address current issues such as cellular telephone network deployment, space exploration, DNA mapping, and image enhancement. This text can be used for a first course in programming: It assumes no prior knowledge of computers or programming. The text also introduces implementations of basic numerical and statistical methods commonly used by engineers.

C PROGRAMMING FOR THE ENGINEERING MAJOR

Teaching a first course in programming for engineering majors is a special challenge because of the enormous range of computing backgrounds typically found among the students in a single class. It is difficult to hold the attention of class members who have already studied another programming language without overwhelming the true novices in the class. Our text's thorough, simple coverage of the basic control structures presented in Chapters 2–5 enables the instructor to move quickly through the early material, knowing that novice programming students who take time to read the text's examples and to work the many exercises will quickly catch up with classmates who have some programming experience. From Chapter 6 to the end of the text, the average difficulty of the programming projects rises steadily. Chapter 6 presents a program for finding a root of a mathematical function. Selected numerical and statistical methods whose implementations depend on arrays are presented in Chapters 7 and 8: computation of standard deviation in Chapter 7, and plotting functions, performing vector and matrix operations, and implementing Gaussian elimination for solving systems of linear equations in Chapter 8. Chapter 12 presents further discussion of root-finding techniques and introduces linear regression and correlation, numerical differentiation, numerical integration, and techniques for solving first-order ordinary differential equations.

USING C TO TEACH PROGRAM DEVELOPMENT

Two of our goals—teaching program design and teaching C—may be seen by some as contradictory. C is widely perceived as a language to be tackled only after one has learned the fundamentals of programming in some other, friendlier language. The perception that C is excessively difficult is traceable to the history of the language. Designed as a vehicle for programming the UNIX operating system, C found its original clientele among programmers who understood the complexities of the operating system and the underlying machine and who considered it natural to exploit this knowledge in their programs. Therefore, it is not surprising that textbooks whose primary goal is to teach C typically expose the student to program examples requiring an understanding of machine concepts that are not in the syllabus of a standard introductory programming course.

In this text, we are able to teach both a rational approach to program development and an introduction to ANSI C because we have chosen the first goal as our primary one. One might fear that this choice would lead to a watered-down treatment of ANSI C. On the contrary, we find that the blended presentation of programming concepts and of the implementation of these concepts in C captures a focused picture of the power of ANSI C as a high-level programming language, a picture that is often blurred in texts whose foremost objective is the coverage of all of ANSI C. Even following this approach of giving program design precedence over discussion of C language features, we have arrived at a coverage of the essential constructs of C that is quite comprehensive. Indeed, the subset of C presented is carefully chosen so as to be broad enough to allow a student who takes only this one programming course to acquire sufficient background for writing respectable scientific programs.

POINTERS AND THE ORGANIZATION OF THE BOOK

The order in which C language topics are presented is dictated by our view of the needs of the beginning programmer rather than by the structure of the C programming language. The reader may be surprised to discover that there is no chapter entitled "Pointers." This missing chapter title follows from our treatment of C as a high-level language, not from a lack of awareness of the critical role of pointers in C.

Whereas other high-level languages have separate language constructs for output parameters and arrays, C openly folds these concepts into its notion of a pointer, drastically increasing the complexity of learning the language. We simplify the learning process by discussing pointers from these separate perspectives at the points where such topics normally arise when teaching programming using other languages, thus allowing a student to absorb the intricacies of pointer usage a little at a time. Our approach makes possible the presentation of fundamental concepts using traditional high-level language terminology—output parameter, array, array subscript, string—and makes it easier for students without prior assembly-language background to master the many facets of pointer usage.

Therefore this text has not one, but six chapters that present aspects of pointers. Chapter 2 gives a brief introduction to file pointers, Chapter 6 discusses the use of pointers as simple output and input/output parameters, Chapter 7 deals with one-dimensional arrays and strings, Chapter 8 presents multidimensional arrays, Chapter 9 introduces record structure output parameters, and Chapter 10 teaches text file pointers in detail.

SOFTWARE ENGINEERING CONCEPTS

The book presents many aspects of software engineering. Some are explicitly discussed, and others are taught only by example. The connection between good problem-solving skills and effective software development is established early in Chapter 1 with a section that discusses the art and science of problem solving. The five-phase software development method presented in Chapter 1 is used in Chapter 2 to solve the first case study and is applied subsequently to case studies throughout the text. Major program style issues are highlighted in special displays, and the coding style used in examples is based on guidelines followed in segments of the C software industry. There are sections in several chapters that discuss algorithm tracing, program debugging, and testing.

Chapter 3 introduces procedural abstraction through parameterless void functions and selected C library functions. Chapter 6 completes the study of functions that have simple parameters. The chapter includes sections for functions returning a value, void functions, input parameters, and output parameters.

Case studies in Chapters 6 and 9 introduce by example the concepts of data abstraction and of encapsulation of a data type and operators. Chapter 11 presents C's facilities for formalizing procedural and data abstraction in personal libraries defined by separate header and implementation files.

The use of visible function interfaces is emphasized throughout the text. We do not mention the possibility of using a global variable until Chapter 11, and then we carefully describe both the dangers and the value of global variable usage.

PEDAGOGICAL FEATURES

We employ several pedagogical features to enhance the usefulness of this book as a teaching tool. Some of these features are discussed next.

End-of-Section Exercises   Most sections end with a number of self-check exercises. These include exercises that require analysis of program fragments as well as short programming exercises. Answers to selected self-check exercises appear at the back of the book; answers to the rest of the exercises are provided in the instructor's manual.

End-of-Chapter Exercises   A set of quick-check exercises with answers follows each chapter review. There are also review exercises whose solutions appear in the instructor's manual.

End-of-Chapter Projects   Each chapter ends with a set of programmlng projects. Answers to selected projects appear in the instructor's manual.

Examples and Case Studies   The book contains a wide variety of programming examples. Whenever possible, examples contain complete programs or functions rather than incomplete program fragments. Each chapter contains one or more substantial case studies that are solved following the software development method. Numerous case studies give the student glimpses of important engineering applications of computing. Table P.1 lists by discipline the relevant examples, exercises, and projects.

Syntax Display Boxes   The syntax displays describe the syntax and semantics of new C features and provide examples.

Program Style Displays   The program style displays discuss major issues of good programming style.

Error Discussions and Chapter Review   Each chapter concludes with a section that discusses common programming errors. Each chapter review includes a table of new C constructs.

Table P.1   Engineering and Science Applications

Aeronautical Engineering
Projectile flight, PP 3-2, p. 122
Aircraft type determination, Sec. 4.4, #2, p. 151
Mars Observer orbit adjustment, Sec. 5.1 and 5.2, p. 171–183; Fig. 5.1, p. 173;
    Fig. 5.2, p. 174
Drag calculation, PP 6-6, p. 325
Spacecraft tracking station, Ex. 7.8, p. 345
Aircraft database, PP 10-2, p. 533
Automated air traffic control, PP 10-6, p. 536
Aircraft maintenance scheduling system, PP 11-3, p. 587

(continued)

Table P.1   (continued)

Astronomy/Astrophysics
Telescope detector array, PP 8-1, p. 445
Planet database, Ex. 9.1, p. 451; Ex. 9.2, p. 454; Ex. 9.3, p. 457; Sec. 11.2, p. 547
Cepheid variables, PP 12-5, p. 637

Atmospheric Science
Wind speed categorization, Sec. 4.4, #3, p. 151
Doppler weather radar, PP 5-5, p. 238
Rainfall statistics, PP 7-5, p. 392
Meteorological database, PP 9-4, p. 492
Adiabatic lapse rate, PP 12-11, p. 641

Biology
Insect population, PP 2-10, p. 81
Fruit fly population, Ex. 4.8, 139
Bald eagle sightings, Ex. 5.5, p. 208
Game of Life, PP 8-3, p. 446

Biotechnology
Heart beat calculation, PP 2-5, p. 80
Noise loudness perception, Ex. 4.12, p. 146
Antibiotic testing, PP 4-1, p. 167
DNA nucleotide sequences, Sec. 7.8, p. 381
Neural network modeling, PP 10-4, p. 534; PP 10-5, p. 536

Civil Engineering
Road warning sign controller, Ex. 4.14, p. 148
Compass headings for surveyors, Sec. 4.5, p. 151
Concrete water channel design, PP 5-9, p. 240
Land boundary survey, Sec. 10.2, p. 503
Hydroelectric dam feasibility study, PP 12-9, p. 639

Chemical Engineering
Pipeline leak detection system, Ex. 7.11, p. 359
Color and opacity testing, PP 7-3, p. 392
Hydroxide identification, PP 7-6, p. 393
Periodic table database, PP 9-2, p. 491
Chemical elements database, PP 10-1, p. 533
Surface coatings application, PP 12-8, p. 638

Computer Science and Engineering
Input validation, Fig. 5.17, p. 213; Table 5.4, p. 215, Fig. 5.19, p. 218
Number separation into components, Sec. 6.3, p. 276
Implementing multiplication, Ex. 6.7, p. 293
Bubble sort, Sec. 7.6, p. 364
Array search, PP 7-2, 391
Computer keyboard design for programmers, PP 7-4, p. 392
Merge sort, PP 7-7, p. 393
Binary search, PP 7-8, p. 394

(continued)

Table P.1 (continued)

(continued)

Table P.1 (continued)

....

Column design, PP 6-4, p. 324
Molecular simulation, PP 6-9, p. 326
Metals database, Sec.10.4, p. 519
Heat transfer function library, PP 11-4, p. 588
Force on car brakes, Fig. 12.14, p. 613; Self-Check 1, p. 615
Heat sink design, PP 12-12, p. 642
Ship deceleration, PP 12-10, p. 641

Numerical Methods

Bisection method, Sec. 6.6, p. 301
Plotting functions, Ex. 7.13, p. 374; Fig. 8.13, p. 418; PP 8-4, 8-5, 8-6, all p. 447
Matrix-vector multiplication, Fig. 8.19, p. 427
Matrix multiplication, Fig. 8.21, p. 429; PP 8-7, p. 447
Gaussian elimination, Figs. 8.25–8.28, p. 435, 437, 439, 440; PP 8-8, p. 448
Gaussian elimination with complex coefficients, PP 9-6, p. 493
Inverting a matrix, PP 8-9, p. 448
Newton's method, Figs. 12.3–12.5, p. 595–600; PP 12-1,12-2, 12-3, p. 636
Simpson's rule, Fig. 12.18, p. 620; PP 12-14, p. 644

Petroleum Engineering

Tank monitoring, Ex. 5.3, p. 195

Physics

Fahrenheit to Celsius conversion, PP 2-1, p. 80; Fig. 5.9, p. 188
Cyclist deceleration, PP 3-6, p. 123
Electron emission calculation, PP 3-7, 124
Universal measurement conversion, Sec. 9.5, p. 476

Robotics and Automation

Quality control in manufacturing flat washers, Sec. 3.3, p. 102
Robot hand force controller, PP 4-3, p. 167
Actuator controller, PP 6-10, p. 327
Ornament-box-filling robot, Sec. 8.1, p. 397
Robot coordinate system transformations, PP 8-2, p. 445
Robot force control, PP 12-4, p. 636

Statistics

Failure risk probability, Ex. 6.2, p. 249
Student grades, PP 6-8, p. 326
Mean and standard deviation, Fig. 7.2, p. 336; Fig. 7.3, p. 340; Ex. 7.10, p. 354
Survey results analysis, PP 7-9, p. 394
Linear regression, Fig. 12.10, p. 606
Correlation, Fig. 12.12, p. 608

System Engineering

Cellular telephone network design, Sec 8.2, p. 403
Global positioning system (GPS) earth station design, PP 11-2, p. 586
Boat failure mode analysis, Sec. 12.2, PP 1, p. 609

KEY: PP = programming project, Sec. = case studies/exercises in sections, Fig. = figure, Ex. = example

APPENDIXES, COMPILERS, AND SUPPLEMENT

A reference table of ANSI C constructs appears on the inside covers of the book, and the first two appendixes are character set tables and an alphabetized list of information about selected C library functions. Because this text covers only a subset of ANSI C, the remaining appendixes play an especially vital role in increasing the value of the book as a reference. Appendix C gives a table showing the precedence and associativity of all ANSI C operators; the operators not previously defined are explained in this appendix. The only C numeric types used in the text are `int` and `double`; Appendix D discusses the range of numeric types available in ANSI C, and Appendix E presents how to define an enumerated data type. Throughout the book, array referencing is done with subscript notation; Appendix F is the only coverage of pointer arithmetic. Appendix G lists all ANSI C reserved words.

The availability of inexpensive, high-quality C compilers for computers of all sizes, the popularity of UNIX-based workstations, and the growth of commercial C software libraries have all contributed to increased use of C among academic and industrial computer users in many areas. Most C++ programming environments include ANSI C compilers, and there are even public domain C compilers available over the Internet. A catalogue of free compilers and interpreters is available via ftp from idiom.berkeley.ca.us. The catalogue is two directories down the path pub/compilers-list.

An instructor's manual with accompanying program disk is available for this book. To order it from your Addison-Wesley sales representative, use the reference number 0-201-93860-X. The instructor's manual is also available online. To receive more information send mail to CEng@aw.com.

ACKNOWLEDGMENTS

Many people participated in the development of this book. We especially thank Dr. Stephen C. Unwin of the California Institute of Technology Astronomy Department and Dr. John H. Rowland and Dr. Michael J. Magee of the University of Wyoming Computer Science Department for their assistance in creating and critiquing examples. We also express our appreciation to Karl Schneider and to many other people at the Jet Propulsion Laboratory, California Institute of Technology, who assisted in finding photographs or gave helpful suggestions during the book's preparation. We are grateful for the help of Thayne Routh, Masoud Kermani, and Samantha Besler, University of Wyoming graduate students who helped to verify the programming examples and to provide answer keys for the host of exercises.

The principal reviewers were enormously helpful in suggesting improvements and in finding errors. They include Alvin L. Day, Iowa State University; Marion Hagler, Texas Tech University; Jerzy Rozenblit, University of Arizona; Dr. Harry W. Tyrer, University of Missouri–Columbia; and Israel Urieli, Ohio University .

We also thank those who assisted in producing the photos used in our flat washer and image enhancement case studies: Steven L. Miller, University of Wyoming botany professor, for the original mushrooms photo; and Thayne Routh, Bruce Henry, and the Western Research Institute of Laramie, Wyoming, for the processed images.

It has been a pleasure to work with the Addison-Wesley team in this endeavor. The sponsoring editor, Lynne Doran Cote, was responsible for initiating the project and provided much guidance and encouragement throughout all phases of manuscript preparation. Her assistant, Maite Suarez-Rivas, coordinated the review process and the preparation of the instructor's manual and handled a great variety of other details. Helen Wythe supervised the design and production of the book, while Tom Ziolkowski developed the marketing campaign. Sandra Rigney coordinated the conversion of the manuscript to a finished book.

J.R.H.
E.B.K.
J.C.H.

CONTENTS

7. Arrays 328

8. Multidimensional Arrays 396

INTRODUCTION TO COMPUTERS AND PROGRAMMING

From the 1940s to the present—a period of only 50 years—the computer's development has spurred the growth of technology into realms only dreamed of at the turn of the century. Today engineers depend on computers to design and build machines of all types, to send rockets into space, and to model the impact of oil spills and other accidents with environmental consequences. Engineers also use computers to simulate experiments that either could not be conducted safely or could not be completed in a reasonable length of time. The computer program's role in this technology is essential; without a list of instructions to follow, the computer is virtually useless. Programming languages allow us to write those programs and thus to control computers.

You are about to begin the study of computer programming using one of the most versatile programming languages available today: the C language. This chapter introduces the computer and its components, the major categories of programming languages, and some of the software tools that you will use when developing a program. In this chapter we also outline a strategy for solving problems, and we look at the steps required to convert these solutions into executing computer programs.

1.1 ELECTRONIC COMPUTERS THEN AND NOW

It is difficult to live in today's society without having some contact with computers. Computers are used to provide instructional material in schools, find library books, send out bills, reserve airline and concert tickets, play games, send and receive electronic mail, and control microwave ovens. Engineers and scientists interact with computers even more than do most members of society. For example, consider the work of engineers in the automobile industry. First, they use computers to design an automobile (see Fig. 1.1). Next, an engineer calls on the computer to test the structural viability of the design and to predict the automobile's behavior under various conditions. If the engineer approves the design, the computer can then prepare instructions for other computers that drive the robots and machine tools that build the car (see Fig. 1.2). Small computers are also used as automobile components to control the vehicle's ignition, fuel, and transmission systems.

Computers were not always so pervasive in our society. Just a short time ago, computers were fairly mysterious devices that only a small percentage of the population knew much about. Computer know-how spread when advances in solid-state electronics led to cuts in the size and the cost of electronic computers. In the mid-1970s, a computer with the computational power of one of today's personal computers would have filled a 9-by-12-foot room and cost

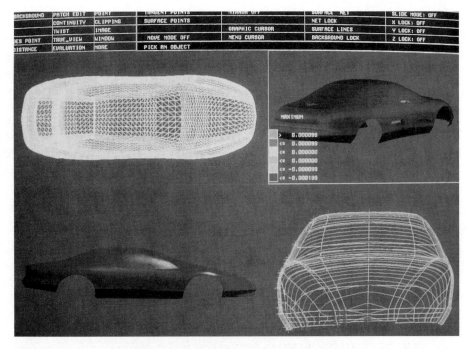

Figure 1.1 **Computer-Aided Design of an Automobile** (Courtesy of North American Operations [NAO], General Motors Corporation.)

$100,000. Today an equivalent personal computer costs less than $2000 and sits on a desktop.

If we take the literal definition for *computer* as "a device for counting or computing," then we could consider the abacus to be the first computer. The first electronic digital computer was constructed in the late 1930s by Dr. John Atanasoff and Clifford Berry at Iowa State University. Atanasoff designed his computer to perform mathematical computations for graduate students.

The first large-scale, general-purpose electronic digital computer, called the ENIAC, was built in 1946 at the University of Pennsylvania. Its design was funded by the U.S. Army, and it was used to compute ballistics tables, predict the weather, and make atomic energy calculations. The ENIAC weighed 30 tons and occupied a 30-by-50-foot space (see Fig. 1.3).

Although we are often led to believe otherwise, today's computers cannot reason as we do. Basically, computers are devices that perform computations at incredible speeds (more than one million operations per second) and with great accuracy. However, to accomplish anything useful, a computer must be *programmed,* that is, given a sequence of explicit instructions (*a program*) to perform.

Figure 1.2   Using Robots in Automobile Manufacturing (Courtesy of Ford Motor Company.)

To program the ENIAC, engineers had to connect hundreds of wires and arrange thousands of switches in a certain way. In 1946, Dr. John von Neumann of Princeton University proposed the concept of a *stored-program computer*—a computer whose program was stored in computer memory rather than being set by wires and switches. Von Neumann knew programmers could easily change the contents of computer memory, so he reasoned that the stored-program concept would greatly simplify programming a computer. Von Neumann's design was a success and is the basis of the digital computer as we know it today.

Brief History of Computing

Table 1.1 lists some of the milestones along the path from the abacus to modern-day computers and programming languages. The entries before 1890 list some of the earlier attempts to develop mechanical computing devices. In 1890, the first special-purpose computer that used electronic sensors was designed; this inven-

Figure 1.3   The ENIAC Computer Built in 1946 (Courtesy of Unisys Corporation.)

tion eventually led to the formation of the computer industry giant called International Business Machines Corporation (IBM).

As we look at the table from 1939 on, we see a variety of new computers introduced. The computers prior to 1975 were all very large, general-purpose computers called mainframes. The computers listed in the table after 1975 are all smaller computers. A number of important events in the development of programming languages and environments are also listed in the table. These include Fortran (1957), CTSS (1965), C (1972), VisiCalc (1978), and Windows (1989).

We often use the term *first generation* to refer to electronic computers that used vacuum tubes (1939–1958). The *second generation* began in 1958 with the changeover to transistors. The *third generation* began in 1964 with the introduction of integrated circuits, and the *fourth generation* began in 1975 with the advent of large-scale integration.

Table 1.1   Milestones in Computer Development

Date	Event
2000 B.C.	The abacus is first used for computations.
1642 A.D.	Blaise Pascal creates a mechanical adding machine for tax computations. It is unreliable.
1670	Gottfried von Leibniz creates a more reliable adding machine. It adds, subtracts, multiplies, divides, and calculates square roots.
1842	Charles Babbage designs an analytical engine to perform general calculations automatically. Ada Augusta (aka Lady Lovelace) is a programmer for this machine.
1890	Herman Hollerith designs a system to record census data. The information is stored on cards as holes that are interpreted by machines with electrical sensors. Hollerith starts a company that will eventually become IBM.
1939	John Atanasoff, with graduate student Clifford Berry, designs and builds the first electronic digital computer. His project is funded by a grant for $650.
1946	J. Presper Eckert and John Mauchly design and build the ENIAC computer. It uses 18,000 vacuum tubes and costs $500,000 to build.
1946	John von Neumann proposes that a program be stored in a computer in the same way that data are stored. His proposal (called "von Neumann architecture") is the basis of modern computers.
1951	Eckert and Mauchly build the first general-purpose commercial computer, the UNIVAC.
1957	An IBM team designs the first successful programming language, Fortran, for solving engineering and science problems.
1957	John Backus and his team at IBM complete the first Fortran compiler.
1958	IBM introduces the first computer to use the transistor as a switching device, the IBM 7090.
1958	Seymour Cray builds the first fully transistorized computer, the CDC 1604, for Control Data Corporation.
1964	IBM announces the first computer using integrated circuits, the IBM 360.
1965	The CTSS (Compatible Time-Sharing System) operating system is introduced. The system allows several users to use or share a single computer simultaneously.
1971	Nicklaus Wirth designs the Pascal programming language as a language for teaching structured programming concepts.
1972	Dennis Ritchie of AT&T Bell Laboratories designs the programming language C as the implementation language for the UNIX® operating system.
1975	The first microcomputer, the Altair, is introduced.
1975	The first supercomputer, the Cray-1, is announced.
1976	Digital Equipment Corporation introduces its popular minicomputer, the VAX 11/780™.
1977	Steve Wozniak and Steve Jobs found Apple Computer.
1978	Dan Bricklin and Bob Frankston develop the first electronic spreadsheet, VisiCalc, for the Apple computer.

(continued)

Table 1.1 (continued)

Date	Event
1981	IBM introduces the IBM PC.
1982	Sun Microsystems introduces its first workstation, the Sun 100.
1984	Apple introduces the Macintosh, the first widely available computer with a "user-friendly" graphical interface using icons, windows, and a mouse device.
1989	Microsoft Corporation introduces Windows, a Macintosh-like user interface for IBM computers.
1989	ANSI (the American National Standards Institute) publishes its first standard for the C programming language.
1990s	The international network Internet expands rapidly as home and business computer users join researchers and academicians using electronic mail and a myriad of other on-line services.

Categories of Computers

Modern-day computers are classified according to their size and performance. The three major categories of computers are microcomputers, minicomputers, and mainframes.

Many of you have seen or used *microcomputers* such as the IBM PC. Microcomputers are also called *personal computers* (PCs) or *desktop computers* because they are used by one person at a time and are small enough to fit on a desk. The smallest general-purpose microcomputers are often called *notebooks* or *laptops* because they are small enough to fit into a briefcase and are often used on one's lap in an airplane. The largest microcomputers, called *workstations,* are commonly used by engineers to produce engineering drawings and to assist in the design and development of new products.

Minicomputers are larger than microcomputers; they generally operate at faster speeds and can store larger quantities of information. Minicomputers can serve several different users simultaneously. The computer that you will use to solve problems for the course you are taking might well be a minicomputer, such as a VAX computer from Digital Equipment Corporation. A small- or medium-sized company might use a minicomputer to perform payroll computations and to keep track of its inventory. Engineers often use minicomputers to control a chemical plant or a production process.

The largest computers are called *mainframes*. A large company might have one or more mainframes at its central computing facility for performing business-related computations. Mainframes are also used as *number crunchers* to generate solutions to systems of equations that characterize an engineering or scientific problem. A mainframe can solve in seconds equations that might take hours to solve on a minicomputer or even days on a microcomputer. The largest mainframes, called *supercomputers,* are used to solve the most complex systems of equations.

In the late 1950s, mainframe computers could perform only 50 instructions per second. Now we commonly see much smaller workstations that can perform over 20 million instructions per second. It is obvious that in a relatively short time there have been tremendous changes in the speed and size of computers.

1.2 COMPONENTS OF A COMPUTER

Despite large variations in cost, size, and capabilities, modern computers are remarkably similar to one another in a number of ways. Basically, a computer consists of the components shown in Fig. 1.4. The arrows connecting the com-

**Figure 1.4
Components of
a Computer**

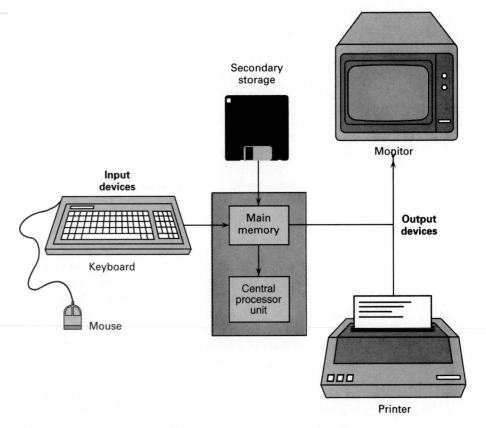

puter components show the direction of information flow. These computer components are called *hardware*.

All information that is to be processed by a computer must first be entered into the computer's *main memory* via an *input device*. The information in main memory is manipulated by the *central processor unit* (CPU), and the results of this manipulation are stored in main memory. Information in main memory can be displayed through an *output device*. *Secondary storage* is often used for storing large quantities of information in a semipermanent form.

Computer Memory

A computer's main memory stores information of all types: instructions, numbers, names, lists, and pictures. Think of a computer's memory as an ordered sequence of storage locations called *memory cells*. To be able to store and then *retrieve* or access information, we must have some way to identify the individual memory cells. Each memory cell has a unique *address* associated with it. The address indicates the cell's relative position in memory. The sample computer memory in Fig. 1.5 consists of 1000 memory cells, with addresses 0 through 999 (most computers have memories that consist of millions of individual cells).

The information stored in a memory cell is called its *contents*. Every memory cell always contains some information, although we may have no idea what that information is. Whenever new information is placed in a memory cell, any information already there is destroyed and cannot be retrieved. In Fig. 1.5, the

**Figure 1.5
A Computer
Memory with
1000 Cells**

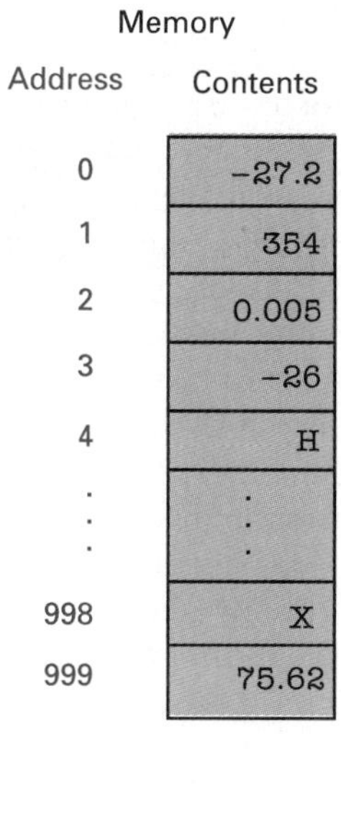

Memory

Address	Contents
0	−27.2
1	354
2	0.005
3	−26
4	H
⋮	⋮
998	X
999	75.62

contents of memory cell 3 is the number −26, and the contents of memory cell 4 is the letter H.

The memory cells shown in Fig. 1.5 are actually collections of smaller units called *bytes*. (The number of bytes in a memory cell varies from computer to computer.) A byte is the amount of storage required to store a single character and is composed of a sequence of even smaller units of storage called *bits*, which are single binary digits (0 or 1). Generally, there are eight bits to a byte.

To store a value, the computer sets each bit of a selected memory cell to 0 or 1, thereby destroying what was previously in that bit. Each value is represented by a particular pattern of zeros and ones. To retrieve a value from a memory cell, the computer copies the pattern of zeros and ones stored in that cell to another storage area, the *memory buffer register*, where the bit pattern can be processed. The retrieval copy operation does not destroy the bit pattern currently in the memory cell. This process is the same regardless of the kind of information—character, number, or program instruction—stored in a memory cell.

Central Processor Unit

The CPU performs the actual processing or manipulation of information stored in memory; it also retrieves information from memory. This information can be data or instructions for manipulating data. The CPU can also store the results of those manipulations in memory for later use.

The *control unit* within the CPU coordinates all activities of the computer by determining which operations to perform and in what order to carry them out. The control unit then transmits coordinating control signals to the computer components.

Also found within the CPU are the *arithmetic-logic unit* (ALU) and special storage locations called *registers*. The ALU consists of electronic circuitry to perform arithmetic operations (addition, subtraction, multiplication, and division) and to make comparisons. The control unit copies the next program instruction from memory into the *instruction register* in the CPU. The ALU then performs the operation specified by this instruction on data that are copied from memory into registers, and the computational results are copied to memory. The ALU can perform each arithmetic operation in less than a millionth of a second. The ALU can also compare data stored in its registers (for example, Which value is larger? Are the values equal?); the operations that are performed next depend on the results of the comparison.

Modern computers use *integrated circuits* for both the memory and the CPU. An integrated circuit (IC) is a silicon chip containing a large number (sometimes millions) of miniature circuits. A *microprocessor* (see Fig. 1.6) is a single chip that contains the full circuitry of a central processor unit.

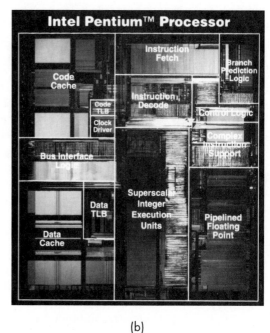

(a)   (b)

Figure 1.6   Microprocessor Chip. The Intel Pentium™ Processor chip (a) is an integrated circuit containing the full circuitry of a central processor unit (b). The Pentium™ executes 112 million instructions per second. (Courtesy Intel Corporation.)

Input and Output Devices

Input/output (I/O) devices enable us to communicate with the computer. Specifically, I/O devices provide us with the means to enter data for a computation and to observe the results of that computation.

A common I/O device used with large computers is the *computer terminal,* which is both an input and an output device. A terminal consists of a *keyboard* (used for entering information) and a *monitor* (used for displaying information). Frequently, microcomputers are connected to larger computers and are used as terminals.

A computer keyboard is similar to a typewriter keyboard except that it has some extra keys for performing special functions. On the IBM keyboard shown in Fig. 1.7, the 12 keys labeled F1 through F12 in the top row are *function keys.* The function performed by pressing one of these keys depends on the program that is executing.

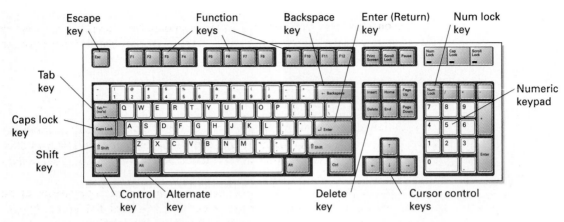

Figure 1.7   IBM Keyboard

Most PCs are equipped with *graphics capability* that enables the output to be displayed as a two-dimensional graph or picture (see Fig. 1.8). With some graphics systems, the user can communicate with the computer by using a *mouse,* an input device that moves an electronic pointer.

Figure 1.8   Sun SPARCstation LX with Color Monitor, Keyboard, Mouse, and Floppy Disk Drive (Photo courtesy of Sun Microsystems.)

The only problem with using a monitor as an output device is that it leaves no written record of the computation. If you want *hard-copy output,* you have to send your computational results to an output device such as a *printer.*

Secondary Storage

Because computers have only a limited amount of main memory, *secondary storage* provides additional data-storage capability on most computer systems. For example, a *disk drive,* which stores data on a disk, is a common secondary storage device for today's PCs.

There are two common kinds of disks, *hard disks* and *floppy disks,* and a computer may have one or more drives of each kind. A hard disk normally cannot be removed from its drive, so the storage area on a hard disk is often shared by all the users of a computer. However, each computer user may have his or her own floppy disks that can be inserted into a disk drive as needed. Hard disks can store much more data and can operate much more quickly than floppy disks, but they are also much more expensive.

Information stored on disk is organized into collections called *files.* The data for a program can be stored in a *data file* in advance rather than being entered at the keyboard while the program is executing. Results generated by the computer can be saved as *output files* on disk. Most of the programs that you write will be saved as *program files* on disk.

The names of all the files stored on a disk are listed in the disk's *directory.* This directory may be broken into one or more levels of *subdirectories.* The details of how files are named and grouped in directories vary from one computer system to another. The names of your files must follow the conventions that apply on your system.

Main Memory Versus Secondary Storage

Main memory is much faster and more expensive than the secondary memory provided by secondary storage devices. You must transfer data from secondary storage to main memory before it can be processed. Data in main memory is *volatile;* it disappears when you switch off the computer. Data in secondary storage is *permanent;* it does not disappear when the computer is switched off.

Computer Networks

Often several microcomputers in a laboratory are interconnected in what is called a *local area network* (LAN), so that they can share the use of a large hard disk and high-quality printers. The microcomputers in the network can also access common programs and data stored on the disk. Sharing computer resources is also a worldwide possibility: Millions of computer users around the world now share access to electronic mail systems and to a vast array of information services via the *wide area network* called Internet.

**EXERCISES FOR
SECTION 1.2**

Self-Check

1. What are the contents of memory cells 0 and 999 in Fig. 1.5? Which memory cells contain the letter X and the fraction 0.005?
2. Explain the purpose of memory, the central processor unit, and the disk drives. What input and output devices do you use with your computer?

1.3 PROBLEM SOLVING AND SOFTWARE DEVELOPMENT

To get a computer to do any useful work, we must provide it with a *program*—that is, a list of instructions. Programming a computer is a lot more involved than simply writing a list of instructions. Problem solving is a crucial component of programming. Before we can write a program to solve a particular problem, we must consider carefully all aspects of the problem and then develop and organize its solution.

Plan and Check Your Programs Carefully

Like most programming students, initially you will probably spend a great deal of time in the computer laboratory entering your programs. Later you will spend more time removing the errors that inevitably will be present in your programs.

You may be tempted to rush to the computer laboratory and start entering your program as soon as you have some idea of how to write it. Resist this temptation. Instead, think carefully about the problem and its solution before you write any program instructions. When you have a potential solution in mind, plan it out, using either paper and pencil or a word processor, and modify the solution if necessary before you write the program.

Once you have written out the program, *desk check* your solution by carefully performing each instruction much as the computer would. To desk check a program, simulate the result of each program instruction using sample data that are easy to manipulate (for example, small whole numbers). Compare these results with the expected results, and make any necessary corrections to your program. Only then should you go to the computer laboratory and enter your program. A few extra minutes spent evaluating the proposed solution using the process summarized in Fig. 1.9 often saves hours of frustration later.

In this text, we stress a methodology for problem solving that has proved useful in helping students to learn to program. We will describe this technique next.

**Figure 1.9
A Problem-
Solving and
Programming
Strategy**

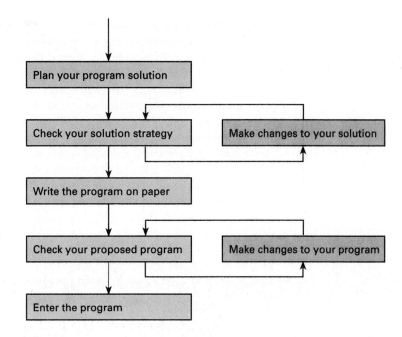

A Problem-Solving Method for Software Development

Students in many subject areas receive instruction in specific problem-solving methods. For example, engineering and science students are encouraged to follow the *engineering and scientific method.* Problem-solving methods for different fields of study have evolved over time. These methods vary greatly from field to field, but their essential ingredients, especially for analyzing complex system problems, are quite similar. We will outline one such method and explore it in more detail in subsequent chapters.

A *software engineer* is someone involved in the design and implementation of reliable software systems. As this title implies, programmers, like engineers, are concerned with developing practical, reliable solutions to problems. However, the product produced by a programmer is a software system rather than a physical system. Software engineers and software developers use the *software development method* for solving programming problems.

Software Development Method

1. *Requirements Specification.* State the problem and gain a clear understanding of what is required for its solution. Although this step sounds easy, it can be the most critical part of problem solving. You must study the problem carefully, eliminating aspects that are unimportant and zeroing in on the root

problem. If the problem is not totally defined, you should request more information from the person posing the problem.

2. *Analysis.* Identify the problem's inputs, desired outputs, and any additional requirements or constraints on the solution. Identify what information is to be supplied as the problem's data and what results should be computed and displayed. Determine the required form and units in which the results should be displayed (for example, as a table with specific column headings).

3. *Design.* Develop a list of steps called an *algorithm* to solve the problem, and verify that the algorithm solves the problem as intended. Writing the algorithm is often the most difficult part of the problem-solving process. Once you have an algorithm, you should verify that it is correct before proceeding further.

4. *Implementation.* Implement the algorithm as a program. A knowledge of a particular programming language is required because each algorithm step must be converted into a statement in that programming language.

5. *Verification and Testing.* Test the completed program and verify that it meets the original requirements specified for the program. Don't rely on just one test case; run the program using several different sets of data.

1.4 PROGRAMMING LANGUAGES

Programming languages fall into three broad categories: machine, assembly, and high-level languages. *High-level languages* are more popular with programmers than the other two programming language categories because they are much easier to use than machine and assembly languages. In addition, a high-level language program is *portable*—it can be used with little or no modification on many different types of computers. An *assembly language* or *machine language program,* on the other hand, can be used on only one type of computer.

Some common high-level languages are Fortran, BASIC, COBOL, C, Ada, Pascal, and Lisp. Each language was designed with a specific purpose in mind. Fortran is an acronym for **FOR**mula **TRAN**slation; its principal users are engineers and scientists. BASIC (**B**eginners **A**ll-purpose **S**ymbolic **I**nstructional **C**ode) and Pascal were designed to be easily learned and used by students. COBOL (**CO**mmon **B**usiness **O**riented **L**anguage) is used primarily for business data-processing operations. C combines the power of an assembly language with the ease of use and portability of a high-level language. Ada is a language designed by the Department of Defense for real-time distributed systems. Lisp is a language used primarily in artificial intelligence applications.

Each of these high-level languages has a *language standard* that describes the *syntax,* the grammatical form, of the language. Every high-level language instruction must conform to the syntax rules specified in the language standard. These rules are very precise—no allowances are made for instructions that are *almost* correct.

An important feature of high-level languages is that they allow us to write program instructions called *statements* that resemble English. We can reference data stored in memory using descriptive names like `height` and `width` rather than the numeric memory-cell addresses discussed in Section 1.2. We can also use familiar symbols to describe operations that we want performed. For example, in several high-level languages, the statement

```
value = value + delta;
```

means add `value` to `delta` and store the result back in `value`. `value` and `delta` are called *variables*. An example of numbers stored in `value` and `delta` before and after the execution of this instruction follows.

Before		After	
value	delta	value	delta
5	2	7	2

In *assembly language,* we can also use descriptive names to reference data; however, we must specify the operations to be performed on the data more explicitly. The high-level language instruction just shown might be written as

```
LOAD value
ADD delta
STORE value
```

in an assembly language.

Machine language is the native tongue of a particular kind of computer. Each instruction in machine language is a *binary string* (a string of zeros and ones). Some of you may be familiar with the use of binary numbers to represent decimal integers (for example, binary 11011 corresponds to decimal 27). In an analogous way, a binary string can be used to indicate an operation to be performed and the memory cell or cells that are involved. The assembly language instructions just given could be written in a machine language as

```
0010 0000 0000 0100
0100 0000 0000 0101
0011 0000 0000 0110
```

Obviously, what is easiest for a computer to understand is most difficult for a person to understand and vice versa.

A computer can understand only programs that are written in its own language. Consequently, each instruction in an assembly language program or a high-level language program must first be translated into machine language. Section 1.5 discusses the steps required to process a high-level language program.

Self-Check

1. What do you think the following high-level language statements mean?

```
x = a + b + c;
x = y / z;
d = c - b + a;
x = x + 1;
kelvin = celsius + 273.15;
```

1.5 PROCESSING A HIGH-LEVEL LANGUAGE PROGRAM

Before the computer can process a high-level language program, the programmer must enter it at the terminal. The program is stored on a disk as a file called the *program file* or *source file* (see Fig. 1.10). The programmer uses an *editor* or *word-processor* program to enter the program and to save it as a source file.

Once the source file is saved, it can be translated into machine language. A *compiler* program processes the source file and attempts to translate each statement. One or more statements in the source file may contain *syntax errors,* meaning that the statement does not correspond exactly to the syntax of the high-level language. In this case, the compiler causes an error message to be displayed on the monitor screen and does not attempt to create a machine-language version of the program.

At this point, you can make changes to your source file and have the compiler process the files again. If there are no more errors, the compiler creates an *object file,* which is your program translated into the target computer's machine language. The object file and any additional object files—for example, programs for input and output operations—that may be needed are combined by the *linker* program into a *load file.* Finally, the *loader* program places the load file into memory, ready for execution. The editor, compiler, linker, and loader programs are part of your computer system. The entire process of preparing a program for execution is shown in Fig. 1.10.

Executing a Program

To execute a program, the CPU must examine each program instruction in memory and send out the command signals required to carry out the instruction. Normally, the instructions are executed in sequence; however, as we will discuss later, it is possible to have the CPU skip over some instructions or to have it execute some instructions more than once.

**Figure 1.10
Preparing a
Program for
Execution**

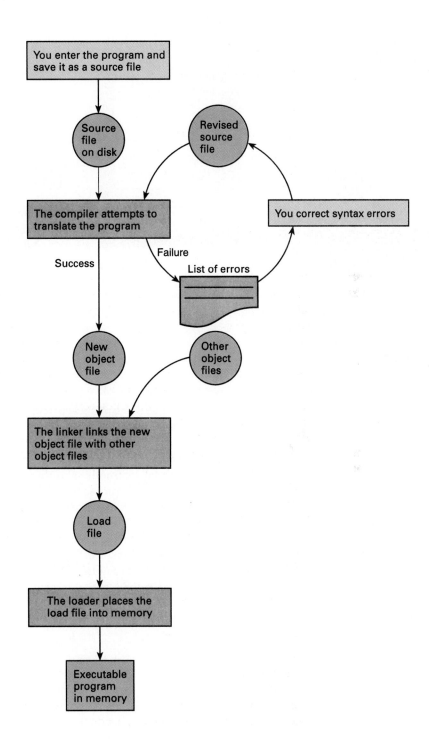

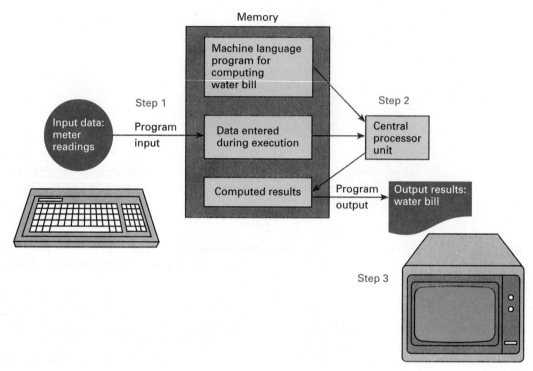

Figure 1.11   Flow of Information During Program Execution

During execution, data can be entered into memory and manipulated in some specified way. Program instructions are used to copy a program's data (called *input data*) into memory. Processing of the input data causes additional values to be stored in memory. Then instructions for displaying or printing values from memory can be executed to display the program results. The lines displayed by a program are called the *program output*.

Let's use the situation illustrated in Fig. 1.11—executing a water bill program stored in memory—as an example. In the first step, the program copies into memory data that describe the amount of water used. In Step 2, the program manipulates the data and stores the results of the computations in memory. In the final step, the computational results are displayed as a water bill.

**EXERCISES FOR
SECTION 1.5**

Self-Check

1. What is a source file? An object file? A load file? Which do you create, and which does the compiler create? Which does the linker create, and which is processed by the loader? What do the compiler, linker, and loader programs do?

2. What is a syntax error? In which file (source, object, or load) would a syntax error be found?

1.6 USING THE COMPUTER

The mechanics of entering a program as a source file and translating and executing a program differ from system to system. Although we cannot give specific details for a particular computer system, we will describe the general process in this section.

Operating Systems

Some of you will be using a *timeshared computer.* Universities often use timeshared computers for instructional purposes. In a timeshare environment, many users are connected by terminals to one central computer, and all users share the central facilities.

Many of you will be using a personal computer, which is a small desktop computer used by one individual at a time. Regardless of what type of computer you use, you will need to interact with a supervisory program called the *operating system* within the computer. In timeshared computers, the operating system allocates the central resources among many users. Operating system activities include the following tasks:

- Validating user identification and account number (system shared by several users)
- Making the editor, compiler, linker, and loader programs available to users
- Allocating memory and processor time
- Providing input and output facilities
- Retrieving needed files
- Saving new files

The operating system for a PC performs all but the first task.

Each computer has its own special *control language* for communicating with its operating system. Although space does not allow us to provide the details here, we will discuss the general process. Your instructor will provide the specific commands for your system.

Creating a Program or File

Before you can use a PC, you must first boot the computer. *Booting* a PC involves switching on the computer and may also require inserting an operating system disk into a disk drive. You will need to wait while the operating system program is loaded from secondary storage into main memory. Once the operating system begins executing, either the computer displays a *prompt* (for example, C>) to indicate that it is ready to accept typed commands or it displays a group of *icons* (small pictures) that allow the user to select commands with a mouse (see upper right corner of monitor in Fig. 1.8).

Before you can use a timeshared computer, you must *log on,* or *connect,* to the computer. To log on, enter your account name and password (given to you by your instructor). For security reasons, your password is not displayed. Figure 1.12 demonstrates this process for the Digital Equipment Corporation VAX™ computer. The computer user enters the characters that are in color; the other characters are those that the operating system displays. The timeshared operating system shown, ULTRIX Version 4.3, displays the symbol > as a prompt.

Once you have booted your PC or logged on to a timeshared computer, you can begin to create your program. In most cases, you will use a special program called a *word processor* or *editor* to enter your C program. After accessing the editor or word processor, you can start to enter a new C program. If you want a record of the program once it is entered, you must save it as a permanent file on disk; otherwise, your program disappears when your session with the word processor or editor is over. Follow these steps to create and save a program file:

1. Log on to a timeshared computer or boot up a PC.
2. Access the word processor or editor program.
3. Enter each line of the program file.
4. Name your program file (if not named in Step 2), and save it as a permanent file in secondary storage.
5. Exit from the editor or word processor.

When you have created your program and are satisfied that each line is entered correctly, you can attempt to compile, link, and execute the program. On some systems you must give three separate commands; on other systems one

Figure 1.12   Logging on to a Timeshared Computer

```
ULTRIX V4.3 (Rev. 44) (jubilee.uwyo.edu)
login: hanly
Password: madaket

Last login: Mon Jan 17 09:57:55 from outlaw

ULTRIX V4.3 (Rev. 44) System #4: Mon May 10
14:28:36 MDT 1993

Tue Jan 18 20:39:13 MST 1994
>
```

command, such as RUN or the name of the load file, initiates this sequence of operations.

If your program will not compile because it contains syntax errors, you must edit, or correct, the program. Follow these steps to correct and re-execute a program file:

1. Reaccess the editor or word processor program, and access your program file.
2. Correct the statements containing syntax errors.
3. Save your edited program file.
4. Compile, link, and execute the new program file.

Interactive and Batch Input

When a correctly compiled program is executing, it must receive input data to process. The program can receive these data in two basic modes: interactive and batch.

If the program is running in *interactive mode,* the user can interact with the program by using the keyboard or another input device to enter data while the program is executing. A program that is designed to run in interactive mode will display messages called *prompts* to advise the program user as to what type of information to enter. For example, the ULTRIX system program shown in Fig. 1.12 is running in interactive mode. The words login: and Password: are examples of prompts that this program displays to notify the user of the type of information needed as input.

When a program runs in *batch mode,* all data must be supplied in advance; that is, the program user cannot interact with the program while it is executing. To use batch mode, you must prepare a batch data file before you execute your program. You will create and save this data file using the same steps listed for creation of a program or source file.

CHAPTER REVIEW

This chapter described the basic components of a computer: main memory and secondary storage, the CPU, and I/O devices. Remember these important facts about computers:

1. A memory cell is never empty, although its initial contents may be meaningless to your program.
2. The current contents of a memory cell are destroyed whenever new information is placed in that cell.
3. Programs must first be placed in the computer's memory before they can be executed.

4. Data cannot be manipulated by the computer without first being copied into memory.
5. To instruct a computer to perform a task, you must use a programming language in a precise and unambiguous manner.
6. Programming a computer can be fun—if you are patient, organized, and careful.

We reviewed the history of computing and discussed the four generations of computers. We also described the different categories of computers: microcomputers, minicomputers, and mainframes, noting that a computer's size and performance capability determine its category.

We discussed problem solving and its importance in programming. We provided a method for software development that stresses a careful, organized approach to solving programming problems. The five phases of the software development method are requirements specification, analysis, design, implementation, and verification and testing.

We described the three different categories of programming languages—machine, assembly, and high-level—and showed the differences between these categories. We investigated how a high-level language source program is translated into a machine-language object file by a compiler, is linked with other object files by a linker, and finally is loaded into memory by a loader. We discussed how to use a computer and its operating system to accomplish the tasks of entering a new program and running it on a computer.

QUICK-CHECK EXERCISES

1. The ____ translates a ____ language program into ____ .
2. A ____ is a single-chip CPU.
3. Specify the correct order for these four operations: execution, linking, translation, loading.
4. A high-level language program is saved on disk as a(n) ____ file or a(n) ____ file.
5. The ____ finds syntax errors in the ____ file.
6. A machine language program is saved on disk as a(n) ____ file.
7. A(n) ____ program is used to create and save the source file.
8. The ____ creates the load file.
9. The ____ program is used to place the ____ file into memory.
10. Computers are becoming (more/less) expensive and (bigger/smaller) in physical size.
11. The first large-scale, general-purpose electronic computer was called the ____ . It (was/was not) a stored-program computer.
12. A list of the names of all the files stored on a disk is found in the ____ .

ANSWERS TO QUICK-CHECK EXERCISES

1. compiler, high-level, machine language
2. microprocessor
3. translation, linking, loading, execution
4. source, program
5. compiler, source
6. object
7. word processor or editor
8. linker
9. loader, load
10. less, smaller
11. ENIAC, was not
12. directory

REVIEW QUESTIONS

1. List at least three kinds of information stored in a computer.
2. List two functions of the CPU.
3. List two input/output devices and two secondary storage devices.
4. Today's computers can think. True or false?
5. List the three categories of programming languages.
6. Give three advantages of programming in a high-level language such as C.
7. What processes are needed to transform a C program into a machine language program that is ready for execution?
8. What is an integrated circuit?
9. What is the difference between the requirements specification and analysis phases of the software development method?
10. In which phase of the software development method is the algorithm for a solution developed?

PROBLEM SOLVING AND C

Programming is a problem-solving activity; if you are a good problem solver, you are likely to become a good programmer. Therefore one important goal of this book is to help you improve your problem-solving ability. We believe that it is beneficial to approach each programming problem in a systematic and consistent way. This chapter shows how to apply the software development method to solve programming problems.

This chapter also introduces the programming language C, a high-level, general-purpose programming language developed in 1972 at AT&T Bell Laboratories. (A *general-purpose programming language* is one that can be used in writing many different applications.) Because C was designed by Dennis Ritchie as a language in which to write the UNIX® operating system, it was originally used primarily for systems programming. Over the years, however, the power and flexibility of C, together with the availability of high-quality C compilers for computers of all sizes, have made it a popular language in industry for a wide variety of applications.

A *language standard,* which describes all C language constructs and specifies their syntax, ensures that a C program written on one computer will also execute on another. The C language standard, usually called "ANSI C," was adopted by the American National Standards Institute (ANSI) in 1989. The examples we use in this text conform to the ANSI C standard.

It is now accepted practice in industry to design systems using principles of structure and style that produce programs that are easy to read, understand, and keep in good working order. In this text, we strongly emphasize the use of C structures and style standards that contribute to the clarity of the program code.

This chapter describes C statements for performing computations and for getting input data and displaying results. Besides introducing problem solving and C, the chapter describes how to run C programs in interactive mode as well as in batch mode.

2.1 THE ART AND SCIENCE OF PROBLEM SOLVING

Problem-solving ability is a combination of art and science. The art of problem solving is the transformation of a problem given in word form to another form permitting a mechanical solution. An example of this process is the transformation of an algebra word problem to a set of algebraic equations that can then be solved for one or more unknowns.

In the real world, this process is more difficult because problem descriptions are often incomplete, imprecise, or ambiguous. The successful problem solver must be able to ask the right questions in order to clarify the problem and obtain any information that is missing from the problem statement. Next, the problem solver must analyze the problem and attempt to extract its essential features, identifying what is provided (the problem inputs) and what is required (the problem outputs). The problem solver must also be able to determine whether any constraints or simplifying assumptions can be applied to facilitate the problem solution. Often, we cannot solve the most general case of a problem; we must make some realistic assumptions that limit or constrain the problem so that it can be solved.

The science part of problem solving involves knowledge of the problem environment, knowledge of the formulas or equations that characterize the environment, and the ability to apply and manipulate those formulas. The problem solver can use this knowledge to develop a series of steps, the successful completion of which will lead to the solution of the problem. Once the solution is reached, the problem solver must verify its accuracy by comparing the computed results with observed results.

The Engineering and Scientific Method

Engineers and scientists are problem solvers. As part of the problem-solving process, they must follow these problem analysis steps:[†]

1. *Recognize and understand the problem.* Perhaps the most difficult part of problem solving is developing the ability to recognize and define the problem precisely. You must study the problem carefully, eliminating aspects that are unimportant and zeroing in on the root problem.
2. *Accumulate facts.* Ascertain all pertinent physical facts, such as sizes, temperatures, voltages, weights, and costs. Some problems require that Steps 1 and 2 be done simultaneously.
3. *Select the appropriate theory or principle.* Select appropriate theories or scientific principles that apply to the problem solution. Understand and identify limits or constraints that apply.
4. *Make necessary assumptions.* Perfect solutions to many real problems do not exist. Simplifications need to be made if problems are to be solved. Make sure your simplifications do not significantly affect the accuracy of the solution.
5. *Solve the problem.* If Steps 3 and 4 result in a set of mathematical equations (a model), you can solve the problem by applying mathematical theory, a trial-and-error solution, or some form of graphical solution.
6. *Verify and check results.* In engineering practice, the work is not finished merely because a solution has been reached. The solution must be checked to

----

[†] Adapted with permission from Arvid Eide et al., *Engineering Fundamentals and Problem Solving,* 2d ed. (New York: McGraw-Hill, 1986).

ensure that it is mathematically correct and that units have been properly specified.

Systems designers in the computer industry have found that the engineering and scientific method of problem solving can be adapted to the development of reliable software systems as well. In recent years, the term *software engineering* has been used to identify such a systematic approach to programming. In Chapter 1, we noted five phases in solving programming problems. Let's see how each aspect of the engineering and scientific method fits into these phases.

1. *Requirements Specification.* This phase includes elements of several steps of the engineering and scientific method. To determine completely what a program is required to do, we must fully understand the whole problem, accumulate facts about the problem environment, and make any necessary assumptions that pin down which part of the whole problem we are to solve. This phase may require further clarification from the person posing the problem, clarification obtained by asking the person detailed questions.
2. *Analysis.* During the analysis phase, we study the completed problem specification and attempt to identify the problem inputs and the desired outputs. We also look for appropriate theories or scientific principles that apply to the problem solution, and we list any formulas or relationships that might be relevant.
3. *Design.* Step 5 of the engineering method, "solve the problem," breaks down into two phases of software development: design and implementation (coding). These phases take into account that two entities—the human problem solver and the computer—must ultimately be able to solve the problem. During the design phase, the human figures out a way to solve the problem and writes an algorithm that lists major subproblems. Using a process called "divide and conquer," the problem solver solves these subproblems separately. For each subproblem, *refinements* are added to the initial algorithm until there is a clear, complete solution.

    We should note here that only for *very* simple problems is there likely to be a unique solution. When you solve a problem for which an answer is given in the back of this book, do not assume your solution is *wrong* if it differs from the answer shown. Simply use the answer key as a guide to improving your solutions, but be ready to recognize where your algorithm is better than the given "answer."
4. *Implementation.* During the implementation phase, we take the algorithm that is our refined solution and represent it as a C program, permitting a computer to solve the problem too. For this coding of the solution, the data requirements that are identified in the analysis phase form the basis of the constant definitions and declaration part of the program; the refined algorithm forms the basis for the executable statements of the program body.

5. *Verification and Testing.* The purpose of this fifth phase is the same as the last step of the engineering and scientific method—to verify that our solution is correct. Although we list this step last, verification really applies to all four previous steps. Verification of our requirements and analysis may call for us to interact with the person posing the problem and with other experts in the field. It is essential that we try out by hand the algorithm that is the product of Step 3 (Design) before we start to code it so we won't waste time implementing a faulty solution. Running the program that we produce in Step 4 is the final part of the whole verification process. As we test and debug this program, we first remove all obvious errors. Then, we run the program several times with a variety of test data to ensure that the program works properly. Finally, we check the program results against computations done by hand or by using a calculator.

Caution: Failure Is Part of the Process

Although having a step-by-step approach to problem solving is helpful, we must avoid jumping to the conclusion that if we follow these steps, we are *guaranteed* a correct solution the first time, every time. The fact that verification is so important implies an essential truth of problem solving: The first (also the second, the third, or the twentieth) attempt at a solution *may be wrong.* Probably the most important distinction between outstanding problem solvers and less proficient ones is that outstanding problem solvers are not discouraged by initial failures. Rather, they see the faulty and near-correct early solutions as a means of gaining a better understanding of the problem. One of the most inventive problem solvers of all time, Thomas Edison, is noted for his positive interpretation of the thousands of failed experiments that contributed to his incredible record of inventions. His friends report that he always saw those failures in terms of the helpful data they yielded about what did *not* work.

Understanding the Problem

In this section, we will apply our problem-solving method to a programming problem. The first step is to recognize and understand the problem. The ability to listen carefully is an important skill in human communication. Often we are too busy thinking of what our response will be to really hear what another person is saying. This can lead to a lack of understanding between speaker and listener.

Many of us suffer from a similar difficulty when we attempt to solve problems that are presented in either verbal or written form. We do not pay close enough attention to the problem statement to determine what really is being asked; consequently, either we are unable to solve the stated problem or we reach an incorrect solution because we solve the wrong problem.

You should analyze a problem statement carefully before attempting to solve it. Read each problem statement two or three times if necessary. The first time you read a problem, you should get a general idea of what is being asked; the second time you read it, you should try to answer these questions:

- What information should the solution provide?
- What data do I have to work with?

The answer to the first question will tell you the desired results, or the *problem outputs*. The answer to the second question will tell you what data are provided, or the *problem inputs*. You may find it helpful to underline in the problem statement the phrases that identify the inputs and the outputs. In the problem statement that follows, the input is in italics and outputs are in boldface.

Case Study: Finding the Area and Circumference of a Circle

 **PROBLEM**

Take the *radius* of a circle and compute and print its **area** and **circumference.**

ANALYSIS

Clearly, the problem input is the circle radius. There are two outputs requested: the area of the circle and its circumference. From our knowledge of geometry, we know the relationship between the radius of a circle and its area and circumference; we list these formulas along with the data requirements.

Data Requirements

Problem Constant
```
PI 3.14159
```

Problem Input
```
radius    /* radius of a circle         */
```

Problem Outputs
```
area      /* area of a circle           */
circum    /* circumference of a circle  */
```

Relevant Formulas
area of a circle = πr^2
circumference of a circle = $2\pi r$

◀ DESIGN ▶

Once you know the problem inputs and outputs, you should list the steps necessary to solve the problem. It is very important that you pay close attention to the order of the steps. The initial algorithm follows.

Initial Algorithm

1. Get circle radius.
2. Calculate area.
3. Calculate circumference.
4. Display area and circumference.

Algorithm Refinements

We must now decide whether any steps of the algorithm need further refinement or whether they are perfectly clear as stated. Step 1 (getting the data) and Step 4 (displaying two values) are basic steps and so require no further refinement. Steps 2 and 3 are fairly straightforward, but it might help to add some detail that explicitly states the formulas to be used. The refinements of Steps 2 and 3 follow.

Step 2 Refinement
2.1 Assign the product of `PI` and `radius` squared to `area`.

Step 3 Refinement
3.1 Assign the product of two times `PI` and `radius` to `circum`.

The complete algorithm with refinements resembles the outline for a paper. Each refinement is indented under the step to which it adds detail. We list the complete algorithm with refinements to show you how it all fits together.

Completed Algorithm

1. Get circle radius.
2. Calculate area.
   2.1 Assign the product of `PI` and `radius` squared to `area`.
3. Find circumference.
   3.1 Assign the product of two times `PI` and `radius` to `circum`.
4. Display area and circumference.

◀ IMPLEMENTATION ▶

To implement the solution, we must write the algorithm as a C program that contains all the information needed for a complete machine-language translation. Figure 2.1 shows the C program along with a sample execution (the last three lines of the figure). For easy identification, the program statements representing algorithm steps are in color, as is the input data value typed in by the program user in the sample execution. Don't worry about understanding the details of this program yet. We will give an overview of the main points of the program here and go into more detail later in the chapter.

Figure 2.1   Finding the Area and Circumference of a Circle

```
/*
 * Calculates and displays the area and circumference of a circle
 */

#include <stdio.h>
#define PI 3.14159

int
main(void)
{
      double radius,  /* input - radius of a circle        */
             area,    /* output - area of a circle         */
             circum;  /* output - circumference of a circle */

      /* Get the circle radius                              */
      printf("Enter radius> ");
      scanf("%lf", &radius);

      /* Calculate the area                                 */
      area = PI * radius * radius;

      /* Calculate the circumference                        */
      circum = 2 * PI * radius;

      /* Display the area and circumference                 */
      printf("The area is %f\n", area);
      printf("The circumference is %f\n", circum);

      return (0);
}

Enter radius> 5.0
The area is 78.539750
The circumference is 31.415900
```

In Fig. 2.1, you might notice a number of lines containing text with the characters /* at the beginning and */ at the end such as

```
/* Calculate the circumference */
```

In C, the slash-star and star-slash surround a program comment. A program *comment* is like a parenthetical remark in a sentence; its purpose is to provide supplementary information to the person reading the program. Program comments are ignored by the C compiler and are not translated into machine language. We will study various forms of comments in Section 2.5.

For the C language there are two steps in the translation process: First the C *preprocessor* revises and completes the text of the source code; then the C compiler generates the machine-language equivalent of the revised source file. The first part of our C program contains directives that are used by the preprocessor, directives that begin with a number sign (#). In the next section of the program, we tell the C compiler about the problem data requirements—that is, what memory cell names we are using and what kind of data will be stored in each memory cell. In the final section of the program, we write one or more C statements for each algorithm step. If an algorithm step has been refined, we convert its refinements into C statements.

The program in Fig. 2.1 consists of two parts: the preprocessor directives and the main function. The preprocessor directives specify the meanings of some names and tell the preprocessor where to find the meanings of others. For example, the #define directive in Fig. 2.1 informs the preprocessor that the name PI means 3.14159. The #include directive notifies the preprocessor that additional names that will be needed are defined in the C standard input/output library. (A *library* is a collection of named operations called *functions*.) For the program in Fig. 2.1, the definitions of printf (for printing) and scanf (for scanning input data) are found in <stdio.h>. Because you will always need to use these input/output functions, your programs will begin with this same

```
#include <stdio.h>
```

The two-line heading

```
int
main(void)
```

marks the beginning of the *main function*. The remaining lines of the program form the *body* of the function. The two major sections of the function body are the *declaration part* and the *executable statements*.

The declaration part tells the compiler what memory cells are needed in the program and is based on the problem data requirements identified previously during the problem analysis. Memory cells are needed for storing the variables `radius`, `area`, and `circum`. The word `double` in the declaration indicates that each variable can hold a number with a fractional part.

The executable statements following the declaration part are translated into machine language and later executed. Each statement that begins with the word `printf` causes some program output to be displayed. The first such line

```
printf("Enter radius> ");
```

displays the first output line in the sample execution, which asks the user to type in a value for `radius`. The next line

```
scanf("%lf", &radius);
```

copies the data value typed by the program user (`5.0`) into the memory cell named `radius`. The `&` operator allows `scanf` to change the value of the variable `radius`. The program statement

```
area = PI * radius * radius;
```

computes the area of the circle by multiplying the square of the circle's radius by `3.14159`. The product is stored in memory cell `area`. The statement

```
circum = 2 * PI * radius;
```

computes and stores the circumference of the circle. The program statements

```
printf("The area is %f\n", area);
printf("The circumference is %f\n", circum);
```

display a message composed of two lines of characters including the value of `area` and the value of `circum`. The last program line,

```
return (0);
```

ends execution of the function.

Some punctuation symbols appear in Fig. 2.1. For example, commas separate items in a list, a semicolon appears at the end of several lines, and braces (`{}`) mark the beginning and end of the body of function `main`. We will give guidelines for the use of these symbols later.

The last three lines of Fig. 2.1 show one sample run of this program, but how do we know that the program result is correct? We should always examine program results carefully to make sure that they make sense. The sample output shown provides a good test of the solution because it is relatively easy to compute the area and circumference by hand for a radius value of 5.0. The radius squared is 25.0, so the value of the area appears correct. The circumference should be ten times PI, also an easy number to compute by hand. To verify that the program works properly, we should enter a few more test values of radius. We really don't need to try more than a few test cases to verify that a simple program like this is correct.

EXERCISES FOR SECTION 2.1

Self-Check

1. List the five steps of the software development method.
2. What would be the data requirements and formulas for a computer program that converts a mass in slugs to a mass in kilograms?
3. Describe the problem inputs, outputs, and algorithm for this problem: Predict the population of an insect colony at the end of a week, given the current population and the weekly growth rate (a percentage).

2.2 OVERVIEW OF C

The rest of this chapter provides a description of some basic features of the C programming language. We will base our discussion on the programs in Fig. 2.1 and in Example 2.1.

EXAMPLE 2.1

Figure 2.2 contains a C program and a sample execution of that program (see the last three lines of the figure). The program asks for a nickname and the current year and then displays a personalized message to the program user.

The program line starting with char identifies the names of three memory cells (letter_1, letter_2, letter_3) that will be used to store each letter of the nickname. The program instruction

```
scanf("%c%c%c", &letter_1, &letter_2, &letter_3);
```

copies the three letters Bob (typed by the program user) into the three memory cells, one letter per cell. After prompting the user to enter a year and storing this

Figure 2.2   Printing a Welcoming Message

```
/*
 * Displays the user's nickname and the current year
 * in a welcoming message.
 */

#include <stdio.h> /* printf, scanf definitions */

int
main(void)
{
      char letter_1, letter_2, letter_3;   /* three letters */
      int  year;                           /* current year  */

      printf("Enter a 3-letter nickname and press return> ");
      scanf("%c%c%c", &letter_1, &letter_2, &letter_3);
      printf("Enter the current year and press return> ");
      scanf("%d", &year);
      printf("Welcome, %c%c%c. %d is a great year to study C!\n",
             letter_1, letter_2, letter_3, year);

      return (0);
}

Enter a 3-letter nickname and press return> Bob
Enter the current year and press return> 1994
Welcome, Bob. 1994 is a great year to study C!
```

value in the memory cell **year**, the program displays the welcoming message shown as the last line of the sample execution. The final program line

```
return (0);
```

is a statement that completes the execution of function **main** by returning a value that indicates that the function ran normally.

One of the nicest things about C is that it lets us write programs that resemble English. At this point, you probably can read and understand the two sample programs, even though you do not know how to write your own programs. In the following sections, you'll learn more details about the two C programs we've looked at so far.

Figure 2.3   Outline of a Simple C Program

preprocessor directives
main function prototype
{
     declarations
     statements
}

C Program Outline

When you review the sample programs in Figs. 2.1 and 2.2, you will note that they both follow the simple program outline shown in Fig. 2.3.

All *preprocessor directives* use commands that have a number-sign symbol (#) as the first nonblank character on the line. These directives give instructions to the C preprocessor, whose job it is to modify the text of a C program before it is compiled. The two most commonly used directives are the ones seen in Figs. 2.1 and 2.2: #include and #define.

The C language explicitly defines only a small number of operations: Many actions that are necessary in a computer program are not defined directly by C. Instead, every C implementation contains collections of useful functions and symbols called *libraries*. The ANSI standard for C requires that certain *standard libraries* be provided in every ANSI C implementation. A C system may expand the number of operations available by supplying additional libraries; an individual programmer can also create libraries of functions.

It is the #include directive that gives a program access to one of these libraries. This directive causes the preprocessor to insert definitions from a library file into a program before compilation. The sample programs we have seen must include definitions from the standard I/O library <stdio.h> so the compiler will know the meanings of printf and scanf.

The other preprocessor directive that we saw in Fig. 2.1 was #define, which was used to create the constant macro[†] PI with the meaning 3.14159. This directive instructs the preprocessor to replace the name defined by its meaning every time the name appears in your program. For example, the pre-processor would respond to

#define PI 3.14159

....

[†] What we refer to as a "constant macro" in this text is officially termed a "manifest" in C standard vocabulary.

by replacing the symbol `PI` by the value `3.14159` throughout the text of the program. As a result, the line

```
area = PI * radius * radius;
```

would read

```
area = 3.14159 * radius * radius;
```

by the time it was sent to the C compiler. Only data values that never change or change very rarely should be given names using a `#define`, because an executing C program cannot change the value of a name defined as a constant macro.

Main Function Prototype

One valid *prototype*[†] (header) for the main function of a simple C program is

```
int
main(void)
```

This prototype marks the function where program execution begins.

Main Function Body

The remaining parts of the simple C program outline form the body of the main function. The curly braces mark the beginning and end of this function body. The declarations identify the memory cells used by the function, and the statements list instructions to manipulate data according to the program's purpose.

Now that we have an idea of the overall structure of a simple C program, let's look in detail at the components of the body of the main function.

Reserved Words and Identifiers

Each line of the programs in Figs. 2.1 and 2.2 satisfies the syntax rules for the C language. Each line contains a number of different elements, such as reserved words, identifiers from standard libraries, special symbols, and names for memory cells. Let's look at the first two elements. All the *reserved words* appear in lowercase; they have special meaning in C and cannot be used for other pur-

----

[†] What we refer to as a "prototype" is officially termed a "function header in ANSI C prototype form."

poses. A complete list of ANSI C reserved words is found in Appendix G. The reserved words appearing in Figs. 2.1 and 2.2 are

```
int, void, double, char, return
```

Two identifiers in these programs are defined by the standard libraries that we access by using the #include directive. Although these names can be used by the programmer for other purposes, we don't recommend this practice. The standard identifiers appearing in Figs. 2.1 and 2.2 are

```
printf, scanf
```

What is the difference between reserved words and standard identifiers? Although you must not choose a reserved word as the name of a memory cell used by your program, you may choose a standard identifier. However, once you use a standard identifier to name a memory cell, the C compiler no longer associates the standard library definition with that identifier. For example, you could decide to use printf as the name of a memory cell, but then you would not be able to use printf to display program output, its usual purpose. Because standard identifiers already serve a valuable purpose, we don't recommend using them to name memory cells. (Other identifiers appearing in the programs in Figs. 2.1 and 2.2 are described in more detail in the next section.)

The preprocessor directives and the main function prototype introduced in this section are summarized in the following displays. Each display describes the syntax of the statement and provides examples and an interpretation of the statement.

#include Directive for Defining Identifiers from Standard Libraries

SYNTAX: #include <*standard header file*>

EXAMPLES: #include <stdio.h>
          #include <math.h>

INTERPRETATION: #include directives tell the preprocessor where to find the meanings of standard identifiers used in the program. These meanings are collected in files called *standard header files*. The header file stdio.h contains information about standard input and output functions such as scanf and printf. Descriptions of common mathematical functions are found in the header file math.h. We will investigate header files associated with other standard libraries in later chapters.

(continued)

#define Directive for Creating Constant Macros

SYNTAX: #define *NAME value*

EXAMPLES: #define MILES_PER_KM 0.62137
          #define PI 3.141593
          #define MAX_LENGTH 100

INTERPRETATION: The C preprocessor is notified that it is to replace each use of the identifier *NAME* by *value*. C program statements cannot change the value associated with *NAME*.

main Function Prototype

SYNTAX: int
        main(void)

INTERPRETATION: The main prototype marks the function where program execution begins.

EXERCISES FOR SECTION 2.2

Self-Check

1. What part of a C implementation changes the text of a C program just before the program is compiled? Name two directives that give instructions about these changes.
2. Why shouldn't we use identifiers from standard libraries as names of memory cells in a program? Can we use reserved words instead?
3. Why should E (2.71828) be defined as a constant macro?

2.3 VARIABLE DECLARATIONS IN C PROGRAMS

We have seen that we can associate names with constant values by using the C preprocessor directive #define. How do we tell C what names will be used to identify other data in a program?

The memory cells used for storing a program's input data and its computational results are called *variables* because the values stored in variables may change (and usually do) as the program executes. The *variable declaration*

```
double radius,    /* input - radius of a circle        */
       area,      /* output - area of a circle         */
       circum;    /* output - circumference of a circle */
```

in Fig. 2.1 gives the names of three memory cells used to store real numbers (for example, 5.0, 78.53975, 31.4159).

In Fig. 2.2, the declarations

```
char letter_1, letter_2, letter_3; /* three   letters  */
int  year;                         /* current year     */
```

provide names for three memory cells used to store single characters and for one memory cell used to store an integer (for example, 1994). These variable names are also identifiers.

In a variable declaration, the identifier (for example, `double`, `char`, `int`) that begins the statement tells the C compiler the *data type* (for example, a real number, a character, or an integer) of the information that is stored in a particular variable. A variable that is used for storing an integer value—that is, a number without a decimal point—has data type `int`.

You have quite a bit of freedom in selecting the identifiers that you use in a program. The rules for forming user-defined ANSI C identifiers are as follows:

1. An identifier cannot begin with a digit.
2. An identifier must consist only of letters, digits, or underscores.
3. A C reserved word cannot be used as an identifier.
4. An identifier defined in a C standard library should not be redefined.[†]

Valid Identifiers for a User Program

```
letter_1, UserName, NUM_STUDENTS, c3po
```

Invalid Identifiers for a User Program

```
1letter, int, Two-by-Four, scanf[†]
```

Although the syntax rules for identifiers do not place a limit on length, some ANSI C compilers do not consider two names to be different unless there is a variation within the first 31 characters. The two identifiers

```
per_capita_meat_consumption_in_1980
per_capita_meat_consumption_in_1990
```

would be viewed as identical by a C compiler that considered only the first 31 characters to be significant.

....

[†] Rule 4 is actually advice from the authors rather than ANSI C syntax.

Uppercase and Lowercase Letters

The C programmer must take great care in the use of uppercase and lowercase letters because the C compiler considers such usage significant. The names `Rate`, `rate`, and `RATE` are viewed by the compiler as *different* identifiers. Adopting a consistent pattern in the way you use uppercase and lowercase letters is helpful to the readers of your programs. You will see that all reserved words in C and the names of all standard library functions use only lowercase letters. One style that has been widely adopted in industry uses all uppercase letters in the names of constant macros. We follow this convention in this text; for variables we use all lowercase letters.

Program Style   *Choosing Names of Variables and Constant Macros*

Throughout the text, issues of good programming style are discussed in displays such as this one. These displays provide guidelines for improving the appearance and readability of programs. Because most programs will be examined or studied by someone other than the writer, programs that follow some consistent style conventions will be easier to read and understand than those that are sloppy or inconsistent. Although these conventions simplify how we understand programs, they have no effect whatsoever on the computer.

Pick meaningful names for variables and constant macros so that your program is easy to read. For example, `weight` would be a good name for a variable used to store the weight of an object; the identifiers w and `bagel` would be poor choices. If an identifier consists of two or more words, placing the underscore character (_) between words will improve the readability of the name (`newtons_per_sq_mm` rather than `newtonspersqmm`).

Choose identifiers long enough to convey your meaning, but avoid excessively long names because you are more likely to make a typing error in a longer name. For example, the shorter `newtons_per_sq_mm` is preferable to the longer `newtons_per_sq_millimeter` since both names are meaningful.

If you mistype a name so that the identifier looks like the name of another variable, often the compiler cannot help you detect your error. For this reason and to avoid confusion, do not choose names that are similar to each other. Especially avoid selecting two names that are different only in their use of uppercase and lowercase letters, such as `LARGE` and `large`. Also try not to use two names that differ only in the presence or absence of an underscore (`xcoord` and `x_coord`).

C requires that the user supply a declaration or definition for every identifier used in a program unless that identifier is defined in a standard library file mentioned in a `#include` preprocessor directive. The reserved words and identifiers used in Figs. 2.1 and 2.2 are shown in Table 2.1.

Table 2.1   Reserved Words and Identifiers in Figs. 2.1 and 2.2

Reserved Words	Identifiers from Standard Libraries	User-Defined Identifiers
int, void, double, char, return	printf, scanf	PI, main, radius, area, letter_1, letter_2, letter_3, circum, year

This section introduced the variable declaration; the syntax of this statement is summarized in the display that follows.

Syntax Display for Declarations

SYNTAX:
```
int variable_list;
double variable_list;
char variable_list;
```

EXAMPLES:
```
int    count,
       large;
double x, y, z;
char   first_initial;
char   ans;
```

INTERPRETATION: A memory cell is allocated for each name in the *variable_list*. The type of data (double, int, char) to be stored in each variable is specified at the beginning of the statement. One statement may extend over multiple lines. A single data type can appear in more than one variable declaration, so the following two declaration sections are equally acceptable ways of declaring the variables rate, time, and age.

```
double rate, time;        double rate;
int    age;               int    age;
                          double time;
```

Self-Check

1. Indicate which of the following words are C reserved words, which are identifiers conventionally used as names of constant macros, which are other valid identifiers, and which are invalid identifiers:

```
int   MAX_ENTRIES   double   time   G   Sue's
this_is_a_long_one   xyz123   part#2   "char"
```

2. Write an outline of a C program that has variables of type `double` representing the radius, height, and volume of a cylinder and a constant macro for p. The program should have access to the I/O functions `printf` and `scanf`. Include in your outline the entire program except for the executable statements of the main function.

2.4 EXECUTABLE STATEMENTS

One of the main purposes of a computer is to perform arithmetic computations and to display the results of the computations. These operations are specified by the *executable statements* that appear in the program body, following the variable declarations. Each executable statement is translated by the C compiler into one or more machine language instructions that are copied to the object file and later executed. The declarations, on the other hand, describe to the C compiler the meaning of each user-defined identifier; these declarations are not translated into machine language instructions and do not appear in the object file.

Programs in Memory

Before examining each kind of executable statement in detail, let's see what computer memory looks like after a program is first loaded into memory and again after that program executes. Figure 2.4(a) shows the circle characteristics program loaded into memory along with the program memory area before execution of the program body. The question marks in memory cells `radius`, `area`, and `circum` indicate that these variables are undefined—that is, the values are unknown—before program execution begins. During program execution, the data value `5.0` is copied from the input device into the variable `radius` by the execution of the statement

```
scanf("%lf", &radius);
```

After the assignment statements

```
area = PI * radius * radius;
circum = 2 * PI * radius;
```

execute, the variables are defined as shown in Fig. 2.4(b). We will study these statements next.

Figure 2.4
(a) Memory
Before Execution
of a Program;
(b) Memory
After Execution
of a Program

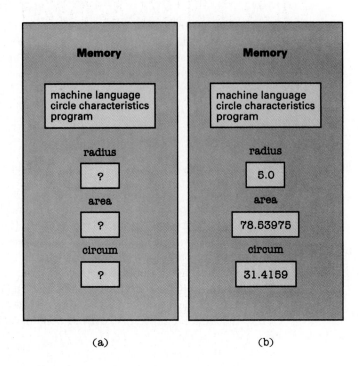

(a)   (b)

Assignment Statements

In C, one use of the *assignment statement* is to store in a variable the result of a computation. The assignment statement

```
area = PI * radius * radius;
```

in Fig. 2.1 assigns a value to the variable **area**. In this case, **area** is being assigned the result of multiplying (* means multiply) the value of the constant macro **PI** by the square of the value of the variable **radius**. Valid information must be stored in **radius** before the assignment statement is executed. As shown in Fig. 2.5, only the value of **area** is affected by the assignment statement; the definition of the constant macro **PI** and the value of the variable **radius** remain unchanged.

The symbol = is the *assignment operator* in C and should be read "becomes" or "gets" or "takes the value of" rather than "equals" because it is *not* equivalent to the "equal sign" of mathematics. In mathematics, this symbol states a relationship between two values, but in C it represents an action to be carried out by the computer. The general form of the assignment statement is shown in the next display.

Figure 2.5
Effect of `area =`
`PI * radius`
`* radius;`

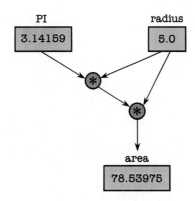

Syntax Display for Assignment Statements

SYNTAX: *result = expression;*

EXAMPLE: `x = x + z + 2.0;`

INTERPRETATION: The variable specified by *result* is assigned the value of *expression*. The previous value of *result* is destroyed. The *expression* can be a single variable or a single constant, or it may involve variables, constants, and the arithmetic operators listed in Table 2.2.

The division operator can yield surprising and even unpredictable results when it is used to find the quotient of two integers. We will explore assignment statements and expressions in greater detail in Chapter 3.

Table 2.2 Some Arithmetic Operators

Arithmetic Operator	Meaning
+	addition
–	subtraction or negation
*	multiplication
/	division

EXAMPLE 2.2 ▶ In C, you can write assignment statements of the form

```
sum = sum + item;
```

where the variable `sum` is used on both sides of the assignment operator. This is obviously not an algebraic equation, but it illustrates a common programming practice. The statement instructs the computer to add the current value of the variable `sum` to the value of `item`; the result is saved temporarily and then stored back into `sum`. The previous value of `sum` is destroyed in the process; however, the value of `item` is unchanged (see Fig. 2.6).   ◀

Figure 2.6
Effect of `sum =`
`sum + item;`

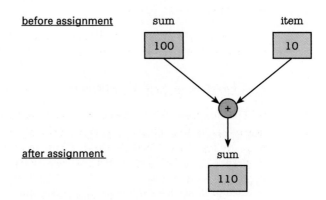

EXAMPLE 2.3 ▶ In C, you can also write assignment statements with an expression part that consists of a single variable or constant. The statement

```
new_x = x;
```

instructs the computer to copy the value of `x` into `new_x`. The statement

```
new_x = -x;
```

instructs the computer to get the value of `x`, negate this value, and store the result in `new_x` (for example, if `x` is `3.5`, `new_x` is `-3.5`). Neither of the assignment statements involving `new_x` changes the value of `x`.   ◀

Input/Output Operations

Data can be stored in variables in two ways: either through an assignment operation or through the use of a function like `scanf`. We have already introduced the assignment operator. The second method, copying data from an input device into a variable, is necessary if you want the program to manipulate different data each time the program executes. This data transfer from the outside world into memory is called an *input operation*.

As a program executes, it performs computations and assigns new values to variables. These program results can be displayed to the program user by an *output operation*.

All input/output operations in C are performed by executing special program units called *input/output functions*. The most common input/output functions are supplied in the C standard input/output library to which we gain access through use of the preprocessor directive

```
#include <stdio.h>
```

In this section, we will discuss how to use the input function named scanf and the output function named printf.

Using the scanf Function

In C, a *function call* is used to invoke or activate a function. Calling a function is analogous to asking a friend to perform an urgent task. You tell your friend what to do, but not how to do it. Then you wait for your friend to report back that the task is finished. After you hear from your friend, you can proceed with doing something else.

In Fig. 2.1, the function call statement

```
scanf("%lf", &radius);
```

causes the function scanf (pronounced "scan-eff") to copy input data into the variable radius. What is the source of the data that scanf stores in the variable radius? The source is the *standard input device*—in most cases, the keyboard. Consequently, the computer attempts to store in radius whatever information is typed at the keyboard by the program user. Because radius is declared as type double, the input operation will proceed without error only if the program user types in a number. The program user should press the key labeled <return> or <enter> after typing the number. The effect of the scanf operation is shown in Fig. 2.7.

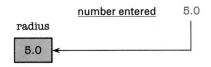

Figure 2.7
Effect of
scanf("%lf",
&radius);

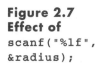

Figure 2.2 contains a similar example of the use of the `scanf` function for copying into a variable a number input by the user. The statement

```
scanf("%d", &year);
```

copies a whole number from the standard input device into the variable `year`. Let's compare the following two function calls that copy numbers from the input device:

```
scanf("%lf", &radius);
scanf("%d", &year);
```

What is the meaning of the quoted strings of characters `"%lf"` and `"%d"`? Each percent sign followed by one or two letters is a *placeholder* or *conversion specification* that tells `scanf` what type of data to copy into one variable. The `%lf` is a placeholder for a real number to be copied into a variable of type `double`.[†] The `%d` is a placeholder for a *d*ecimal integer. As we will see in Fig. 2.8, `%c` is a placeholder for a single *c*haracter. Because a string of placeholders gives the `scanf` function information about the format of the input data it is to process, we refer to such a string as a *format*.

The program in Fig. 2.2 also gets a person's nickname as input data. Each person using the program may have a different nickname, so the function call statement

```
scanf("%c%c%c", &letter_1, &letter_2, &letter_3);
```

causes the `scanf` function to copy data into each of the three variables, and the format includes one `%c` placeholder for each variable. Since these variables are declared as type `char`, one character will be stored in each variable. The next

....

[†] Before the standardization of C, the type `double` was also called `long float`, hence `lf`.

Figure 2.8
Effect of
`scanf("%c%c%c",`
`&letter_1,`
`&letter_2,`
`&letter_3);`

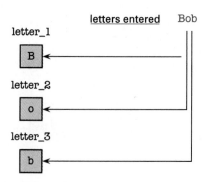

three characters that are entered at the keyboard are stored in these variables. Note that case is important for character data, so the letters B and b have different representations in memory. Again, the program user should press the <return> or <enter> key after typing in three characters. Figure 2.8 shows the effect of this statement when the letters Bob are entered.

The number of input characters consumed by the scanf function depends on the current format placeholder, which should reflect the type of the variable in which the data will be stored. Only one input character is used for a %c (type char variable); for a %lf or %d (type double or int variable), the program first skips any spaces and then scans characters until it reaches a character that cannot be part of the number. Usually the program user—that is, the person entering the data—indicates the end of a number by typing the blank character or by pressing the <return> or <enter> key.

Notice that in a call to scanf, the name of each variable that is to be given a value is preceded by the ampersand character (&). The & is the C *address-of* operator. In the context of this input operation, the & operator tells the scanf function *where* to find each variable into which it is to store a new value. If the ampersand were omitted, scanf would know only a variable's current value, not its location in memory, so scanf would be unable to store a new value in the variable.

How do we know when to enter the input data and what data to enter? Your program should print a prompting message that informs you of what data to enter and when. (Prompting messages are discussed in more detail in the next section.) Each character entered by the program user is *echoed* on the screen and is also processed by the scanf function.

Syntax Display for scanf Function call

SYNTAX: scanf(*format, input list*);

EXAMPLE: scanf("%d%c", &age, &first_initial);

INTERPRETATION: The scanf function copies into memory data typed at the keyboard by the program user during program execution. The *format* is a quoted string of placeholders, one placeholder for each variable in the *input list*. Placeholders for char, double, and int variables are

variable type	scanf placeholder
char	%c
double	%lf
int	%d

(continued)

> Each int, double, or char variable in the *input list* is preceded by an ampersand (&). Commas are used to separate variable names. The order of the placeholders must correspond to the order of the variables in the *input list*.
>
> The data must be entered in the same order as the variables in the *input list*. The data entered should insert one or more blank characters or carriage returns between numeric items. No blanks should be inserted between consecutive character data items unless the blank character is one of the data items to be stored.

Using the printf Function

To see the results of a program's execution, we must have some way of specifying what variable values should be displayed. In Fig. 2.1, the function call statement

```
printf("The area is %f\n", area);
```

causes the function `printf` (pronounced "print-eff") to display a line of program output. This line is the result of printing the format string `"The area is %f\n"` after substituting the values of the variables in the *print list* for their placeholders in the format string and replacing special combinations of characters called *escape sequences* by their meanings.

The format string we are considering contains one placeholder, `%f`, which must be replaced by the value of the variable in the print list, `area`. It also contains the *newline* escape sequence `\n`. Like all C escape sequences, `\n` begins with the backslash character. Including this sequence at the end of the format string terminates the current output line. The complete line that is displayed when the value of `area` is `78.53975` is

```
The area is 78.539750
```

This sentence completes a line of output. Notice that the quotation marks surrounding the `printf` format were not printed. The format used in a call to the `scanf` or `printf` function is an example of a *string literal,* a sequence of characters enclosed in quotation marks. The quotation marks are the indicators of the beginning and end of the string literal and are not part of its value. The placeholders used in `printf` formats are like those in `scanf` formats except for variables of type `double`. These use a `%f` placeholder in a `printf` format and a `%lf` placeholder in a `scanf` format.

In Fig. 2.2, the function call statement

```
printf
  ("Welcome, %c%c%c. %d is a great year to study C!\n",
  letter_1, letter_2, letter_3, year);
```

displays the line

```
Welcome, Bob. 1994 is a great year to study C!
```

In Fig. 2.9, we see the values of the four variables of the print list of the `printf` function call substituted for the placeholders of the format string.

In addition to observing the use of the `printf` function to print program results, we have also seen it called to display prompts or prompting messages in Figs. 2.1 and 2.2:

```
printf("Enter radius> ");
printf("Enter a 3-letter nickname and press return> ");
printf("Enter the current year and press return> ");
```

Notice that because the format strings of these calls to `printf` contain no placeholders, no print list of variables is needed. In an interactive program, you should always display a prompting message just before a call to the function `scanf` to remind the program user to enter data. The prompt may also describe the format of the data expected. It is very important to precede each `scanf` operation with a `printf` that prints a prompt; otherwise, the program user may have no idea that the program is waiting for data or what data to enter.

More About \n

We often end a `printf` format string with a \n so that the call to `printf` produces a completed line of output. If no characters are printed on the next line

**Figure 2.9
Substitution of
Print List Values
for Placeholders**

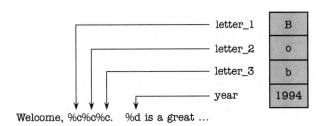

before another newline character is printed, a blank line will appear in the output. For example, the following calls produce two lines of text with a blank line in between:

```
printf("Here is the first line\n");
printf("\nand this is the second.\n");
```

```
Here is the first line

and this is the second.
```

If a `printf` format string contains a \n in the middle of the string, the characters after the \n appear on a new output line, as we see in this example:

```
printf("This sentence appears \non two lines.\n");
```

```
This sentence appears
on two lines.
```

The *cursor* is a moving place marker that indicates on the screen the next position where information will be displayed. When executing a `printf` function call, the cursor is advanced to the start of the next line on the screen if the \n escape sequence is encountered in the format string. Most of our `printf` calls include format strings ending in \n, so the cursor moves to the next line. However, the newline escape sequence is frequently omitted from the format strings of `printf` calls that display prompting messages. This omission allows the user to enter data on the same line with the prompt. The cursor is advanced to the next line when the user presses the <return> or <enter> key.

Syntax Display for printf Function Call

SYNTAX: printf(*format, print list*);
                    or
                printf(*format*);

EXAMPLES: printf("I am %d years old, and my gpa is %f\n",
                        age, gpa);
                printf("Enter the object mass in grams> ");

INTERPRETATION: The `printf` function displays the value of its *format* string after substituting in order the values of the expressions in the *print list* for their placeholders in the *format* and after replacing escape sequences such as \n by their meanings. Placeholders for

(continued)

char, double, and int variables are

Variable Type	printf Placeholder
char	%c
double	%f
int	%d

EXERCISES FOR SECTION 2.4

Self-Check

1. Show the output displayed by the following program lines when the data entered are 5 and 7:

```
printf("Enter two integers> ");
scanf("%d%d", &m, &n);
m = m + 5;
n = 3 * n;
printf("m = %d\nn = %d\n", m, n);
```

2. Show the contents of memory before and after the execution of the program lines shown in Exercise 1.
3. Show the output displayed by the following lines if the value of **exp** is **11**:

```
printf("My name is ");
printf("Jane Doe.");
printf("\n");
printf("I live in ");
printf("Ann Arbor, MI\n");
printf("and I have %d years ", exp);
printf("of programming experience.\n");
```

4. How could you modify the code in Exercise 3 so that a blank line would be displayed between the two sentences?

Programming

1. Write a statement that asks the user to type three integers and another statement that stores the three user responses into **first**, **second**, and **third**.
2. Write a statement that displays the value of the type **double** number **x** as indicated in the following line:

```
The value of x is _____
```

2.5 GENERAL FORM OF C PROGRAMS

The programs shown so far in this text have the general form described in Fig. 2.3. Each program begins with preprocessor directives that serve to provide definitions of functions from standard libraries and definitions of necessary program constants. Examples of such directives are #include and #define. Unlike the declarations and executable statements of the main function body, the preprocessor directives we have seen do not end in semicolons. A simple C program places the prototype of the main function after the preprocessor directives. Then, an open curly brace ({) signals the beginning of the main function body. Within this body, we first see the declarations of all the variables to be used by the main function. These variables are followed by the statements that are translated into machine language and are eventually executed. The statements we have looked at so far perform computations or input/output operations. The end of the main function body is marked by a closing curly brace (}).

As shown in Figs. 2.1 and 2.2, a C statement can extend over more than one line. For example, in the statement that follows from Fig. 2.1, the declaration of the variables radius, area, and circum extends over three lines so that comments describing the meanings of the variables can be inserted:

```
double radius,    /* input - radius of a circle           */
       area,      /* output - area of a circle            */
       circum;    /* output - circumference of a circle   */
```

In this statement from Fig. 2.2, a call to the function printf extends over two lines:

```
printf("Welcome, %c%c%c. %d is a great year to study C!\n",
       letter_1, letter_2, letter_3, year);
```

Notice that in both of these examples, the statement is split at a point where there is a natural break, and the indentation of the second part of the statement helps the reader see the structure of the statement. Although ANSI C provides a means of splitting a statement even in the middle of an identifier, a reserved word, a number, or a string, we recommend against this practice because dividing a statement in mid-word makes the statement more difficult to read.

It is also possible to write more than one statement on a line. For example, the line

```
printf("Enter a letter> "); scanf("%c", &let_1);
```

contains a statement that displays a prompt and a statement that gets the data requested. We recommend that you place only one statement on a line.

Program Style   *Use of Blank Space*

The consistent and careful use of blank spaces can significantly enhance the style of a program. Blanks are needed to separate many parts of a C statement in much the same way that blanks are used to separate words in an English sentence. For example, a blank space is required to separate the data type name from the first variable name in a variable declaration. If this space were omitted—if we wrote `doubleradius` in Fig. 2.1 instead of `double radius`—the statement would appear to begin with the identifier `doubleradius`.

The compiler ignores extra blanks between words and symbols. You may insert space to improve the style and appearance of a program. In the examples in this book, we have adopted a style that calls for leaving a blank space after a comma and before and after operators such as `*`, `−`, and `=`. We indent the body of the main function and use blank lines between sections of the program.

We take all of these measures for the sole purpose of improving the style—hence the clarity—of our programs. Stylistic issues have no effect whatever on the meaning of the program as far as the computer is concerned; however, they can simplify our reading and understanding of the program.

Be careful not to insert blank spaces where they do not belong. For example, a space is not allowed between the `/` and `*` characters when they form the sequence marking the opening (`/*`) or closing (`*/`) of a comment. Also, the identifier `MAXLEN` cannot be written as `MAX LEN`.

Comments in Programs

The programs in Figs. 2.1 and 2.2 contain some English phrases enclosed in slash-star and star-slash brackets; these phrases are *program comments*. Refer to these figures to see how programmers use comments to make the program easier to understand. Comments describe the purpose of the program (the first comment line), the use of identifiers (the comments in the variable declarations), and the purpose of each major program step (the comments in the program body). Comments are an important part of the *documentation* of a program because they help others read and understand the program. The compiler, however, ignores comments; they are not translated into machine language.

As shown in Fig. 2.1, a comment can appear by itself on a program line, can be at the end of a line after a statement, or can be embedded in a statement. In the following variable declarations, the first and second comments are embedded in the declaration, and the third comment follows the declaration statement:

```
double radius,    /* input - radius of a circle          */
       area,      /* output - area of a circle           */
       circum;    /* output - circumference of a circle  */
```

We will document the use of most variables in this way. The next displays describe the syntax and use of comments.

Syntax Display for a Program Comment

SYNTAX: */* comment text */*

EXAMPLES: `/* This is a one-line or partial-line comment */`
```
/*
 * This is a multiple-line comment in which the stars
 * not immediately preceded or followed by slashes have
 * no special syntactic significance, but simply help
 * the comment to stand out as a block. This style is
 * often used to document the purpose of a program.
 */
```

INTERPRETATION: A slash-star indicates the start of a *comment*; a star-slash indicates the end of a comment. Comments are listed with the program, but they are otherwise ignored by the C compiler. A comment may be put in a C program anywhere a blank space would be valid.

NOTE: ANSI C does not permit the placement of one comment inside another.

Program Style   *Using Comments*

Comments make a program more readable by describing the purpose of the program and the use of each identifier. For example, the comment shown in the declaration

```
double radius,  /* input - radius of a circle */
```

describes the use of variable `radius`.

You should also place comments within the program body to describe the purpose of each section of the program. Generally, you will include one comment in the program body for each major algorithm step. A comment within the program body should describe what the step does rather than simply restate the step in English. For example, the comment

```
/* Calculate the area */
area = PI * radius * radius;
```

is more descriptive and hence is preferable to

```
/* Multiply PI by radius times radius and save
   the result in area */
area = PI * radius * radius;
```

Before you implement each step in the initial algorithm, you should write a comment that summarizes the purpose of the algorithm step.

Each program should begin with a documentation section that consists of a series of comments specifying

- the programmer's name
- the date of the current version
- a brief description of what the program does.

If you write the program for a class assignment, you should also list the class identification and your instructor's name, as shown here:

```
/*
 * Programmer: William Bell    Date completed: May 9, 1994
 * Instructor: Janet Smith     Class: CIS61
 *
 * Calculates and displays the area and circumference of a
 * circle
 */
```

EXERCISES FOR SECTION 2.5

Self-Check

1. Explain what is wrong with the following comments:

```
/* This is a comment? *)
/* How about this one /* it seems like a comment
*/ doesn't it */
```

2. What is the purpose of including comments in a computer program?
3. Correct the syntax errors in the following program, and rewrite the program so that it follows our style conventions. What does each statement of your corrected program do? What output does it display?

```
/*
 * Calculate and display the difference of two input values
 *)
```

```
#include <stdio.h>

int
main(void) {int X, /* first input value */ x, /* second
    input value */
sum; /* sum of inputs */
scanf("%i%i"; X; x); X + x = sum;
printf("%d + %d = %d\n"; X; x; sum); return (0);}
```

2.6 FORMATTING NUMBERS IN PROGRAM OUTPUT

In the sample program output shown so far, all numbers were printed in C's default notation. Consequently, we had limited control over the appearance or format of each output line. In this section, we will learn how to specify the format of an output item.

Formatting Values of Type int

Specifying the format of an integer value displayed by a C program is fairly easy. All that we need to do is add a number between the % and the d of the %d placeholder for the integer in the printf format string. This number specifies how many columns are to be used for the display of digits, the *field width*. For example, the statement

```
printf("Results: %3d meters = %4d ft. %2d in.\n",
        meters, feet, inches);
```

indicates that 3 columns will be used to display the value of the first variable in the print list (meters), 4 columns will be used for the second variable (feet), and 2 columns will be used for the third (inches), a variable that in this context will always have a value between 0 and 11. If meters is 21, feet is 68, and inches is 11, the program output will be

```
Results:  21 meters =   68 ft. 11 in.
```

Note that in this line, there is one extra space before the value of meters (21), and there are two extra spaces before the value of feet (68). The reason is that the placeholder for meters (%3d) allows space for three digits to be printed. Because the value of meters is between 10 and 99, its two digits are displayed *right-justified,* preceded by one blank space. Because the placeholder

Table 2.3   Printing 234 and –234 Using Different Placeholders

Value	Placeholder	Printed Output
234	%4d	#234
234	%5d	##234
234	%6d	###234
–234	%4d	–234
–234	%5d	#–234
–234	%6d	##–234
234	%2d	234
234	%1d	234
–234	%2d	–234

for `feet` (%4d) allows room for 4 digits, printing its two-digit value right-justified leaves two extra blank spaces. We can use the placeholder %2d to display any integer output value between –9 and 99. The placeholder %4d works for values in the range –999 to 9999. For negative numbers, the minus sign is included in the count of digits displayed.

Table 2.3 shows how two integer values are printed using different format string placeholders. The character # represents a blank character. The last three lines show that when a field width that is too small is used, the number is printed with no blanks preceding it, and the number of print columns used varies with the size of the number (i.e., the display field expands as needed).

Formatting Values of Type double

To describe the format specification for a value of type `double`, we must indicate both the total field width needed and the number of decimal places desired. The total field width should be large enough to accommodate all digits, both those before and those after the decimal point. There will be at least one digit before the decimal point, since a zero is printed as the whole-number part of fractions that are less than 1.0 and greater than –1.0. We should also leave a display column for the decimal point and, for negative numbers, a column for the minus sign. The form of the necessary format string placeholder is %*n.m*f where *n* is a number representing the total field width and *m* is the desired number of decimal places.

If x is a type `double` variable whose value will be between –99.99 and 999.99, we could use the placeholder %6.2f to display the value of x accurate to two decimal places. Table 2.4 shows different values of x displayed using this format specification. The values shown in Table 2.4 are displayed right-justified in

Table 2.4 Displaying x Using Format String Placeholder %6.2f

x	Output Displayed
−99.42	−99.42
0.123	##0.12
−9.536	#−9.54
−25.554	−25.55
99.999	100.00
999.4	999.40

six columns, and all values are rounded to two decimal places. When you round to two decimal places, if the third digit of the value's fractional part is 5 or greater, the second digit is incremented by 1 (−9.536 becomes −9.54). Otherwise, the digits after the second digit in the fraction are simply dropped (−25.554 becomes −25.55).

Table 2.5 shows some values that were displayed using other placeholders. As shown in the table, it is legal to omit the total field width in the format string placeholder, specifying only the number of decimal places. Such a place-holder has the form %.*m*f, and it causes the value to be displayed with no leading blanks.

Table 2.5 Formatting Values of Type double

Value	Placeholder	Output
3.14159	%5.2f	#3.14
3.14159	%4.2f	3.14
3.14159	%3.2f	3.14
3.14159	%5.1f	##3.1
3.14159	%5.3f	3.142
3.14159	%8.5f	#3.14159
3.14159	%.4f	3.1416
0.1234	%4.2f	0.12
−0.006	%4.2f	−0.01
−0.006	%.4f	−0.0060
−0.006	%8.5f	−0.00600
−0.006	%8.3f	##−0.006

Program Style   *Eliminating Leading Blanks*

As shown in Tables 2.3–2.5, a value whose whole-number part requires fewer display columns than are specified by the format field width is displayed with leading blanks. To eliminate extra leading blanks, omit the field width from the format string placeholder. The simple placeholder %d will cause an integer value to be displayed with no leading blanks. A placeholder of the form %.*m*f has the same effect for values of type double, and this placeholder still allows you to choose the number of decimal places to be displayed.

EXERCISES FOR SECTION 2.6

Self-Check

1. Correct the statement

   ```
   printf("Length is %2.10f cm\n", length);
   ```

2. Show how the value −15.564 would be printed using the formats %8.4f, %8.3f, %8.2f, %8.1f, %8.0f, %.2f.
3. Assuming x (type double) is 12.335 and i (type int) is 100, show the output lines for the following statements. For clarity, use the symbol # to denote a blank space.

   ```
   printf("x is %6.2f  i is %4d\n", x, i);
   printf("i is %d\n", i);
   printf("x is %.1f\n", x);
   ```

Programming

1. If the variables a, b, and c are 504, 302.558, and −12.31, respectively, write a statement that will display the following line (for clarity, a # denotes a blank space):

   ```
   ##504#####302.56####-12.3
   ```

2.7 INTERACTIVE MODE, BATCH MODE, AND DATA FILES

In Section 1.6, we discussed the two basic modes of computer operation: batch and interactive. The programs that we have written so far are intended to be run in *interactive mode*. Our programs have included prompting messages so the program user can interact with the program and can enter data while the program is executing.

Input Redirection

Figure 2.10 shows the circle characteristics conversion program rewritten as a batch program. In Fig. 2.10, we assume that the standard input device is associ-

Figure 2.10   Batch Version of Circle Characteristics Program

```
/*
 * Calculates and displays the area and circumference of a
 * circle
 */

#include <stdio.h>
#define PI 3.14159

int
main(void)
{
      double radius, /* input - radius of a circle         */
             area,    /* output - area of a circle          */
             circum; /* output - circumference of a circle */

      /* Get circle radius                      */
      scanf("%lf", &radius);
      printf("The radius is %.2f\n", radius);

      /* Calculate the area                     */
      area = PI * radius * radius;

      /* Calculate the circumference            */
      circum = 2 * PI * radius;

      /* Display the area and circumference     */
      printf("The area is %.2f\n", area);
      printf("The circumference is %.2f\n", circum);

      return (0);
}

The radius is 5.00
The area is 78.54
The circumference is 31.42
```

ated with a batch data file instead of with the keyboard. In most systems, this association can be accomplished relatively easily through *input-output redirection* using operating system commands. For example, in the UNIX® and MS-DOS® operating systems, you can instruct your program to take its input from file `mydata` instead of from the keyboard by placing the symbols `<mydata` at the end of the command line that causes your compiled and linked program to execute. If you normally used the command line

```
metric
```

to execute this program, your new command line would be

```
metric <mydata
```

Program Style   *Echo Prints Versus Prompts*

In Fig. 2.10, the statement

```
scanf("%lf", &radius);
```

gets a value for `radius` from the first (and only) line of the data file. Because the program input comes from a data file, there is no need to precede this statement with a prompting message. Instead, we follow the call to `scanf` with the statement

```
printf("The radius is %.2f\n", radius);
```

This statement *echo prints* or displays the value just stored in `radius` and provides a record of the data manipulated by the program. Without it, we would have no easy way of knowing what value `scanf` obtained for `radius`. Whenever you convert an interactive program to a batch program, make sure you replace each prompt with an echo print that follows the call to `scanf`.

Output Redirection

You can also redirect program output to a disk file instead of to the screen. Then you can send the output file to the printer (using an operating system command) to obtain a hard copy of the program output. In UNIX® or MS-DOS®, use the symbols `>myoutput` to redirect output from the screen to file `myoutput`. These symbols should also be placed on the command line that causes your program to execute. The command line

```
metric >myoutput
```

executes the compiled and linked code for program `metric`, taking program input from the keyboard and writing program output to file `myoutput`. However, interacting with the running program will be difficult because all program output, including any prompting messages, will be sent to the output file. It would be better to use the command line

```
metric <mydata >myoutput
```

which takes program input from data file `mydata` and sends program output to output file `myoutput`.

Program-Controlled Input and Output Files

As an alternative to input/output redirection, C allows a program to explicitly name a file from which the program will take input and a file to which the program will send output. Figure 2.11 shows a version of the circle characteristics program that takes input data from a file named `b:circle.dat` and sends results to a file named `b:circle.out`.

Figure 2.11 Program-Controlled Files Example

```c
/* Calculates the area and circumference of a circle given a
 *      radius value from file b:circle.dat.
 * Stores results in b:circle.out
 */

#include <stdio.h>
#define PI 3.14159

int
main(void)
{
      double radius, /* input  - radius of a circle         */
             area,   /* output - area of a circle           */
             circum; /* output - circumference of a circle  */
      FILE  *inp,    /* pointer to input file               */
            *outp;   /* pointer to output file              */

      /* Open the input and output files                    */
      inp = fopen("b:circle.dat", "r");
      outp = fopen("b:circle.out", "w");
```

(continued)

Figure 2.11 (continued)

```
        /* Get and echo the circle radius                */
        fscanf(inp, "%lf", &radius);
        fprintf(outp, "The radius is %.2f\n", radius);

        /* Calculate the area                            */
        area = PI * radius * radius;

        /* Calculate the circumference                    */
        circum = 2 * PI * radius;

        /* Store the area and circumference in output file  */
        fprintf(outp, "The area is %.2f\n", area);
        fprintf(outp, "The circumference is %.2f\n", circum);

        /* Close files                                    */
        fclose(inp);
        fclose(outp);

        return (0);
}

Contents of input file circle.dat
5.0

Contents of output file circle.out
The radius is 5.00
The area is 78.54
The circumference is 31.42
```

A program that manipulates a specific file must first declare a *file pointer* variable in which to store the information necessary to permit access to a file. File pointer variables are of type `FILE *`. In Fig. 2.11, the statement

```
FILE *inp,     /* pointer to input file  */
     *outp;    /* pointer to output file */
```

declares that file pointer variables `inp` and `outp` will hold information allowing access to the program's input and output files, respectively. The operating system must prepare a file for input or output before permitting access. This preparation is the purpose of the calls to function `fopen` in the statements that follow:

```
inp = fopen("b:circle.dat", "r");
outp = fopen("b:circle.out", "w");
```

The first assignment statement *opens* (prepares for access) file `b:circle.dat` as a source of program input and stores the necessary access value in the file pointer variable `inp`. The "r" in the first call to `fopen` indicates that we wish to read (scan) data from the file opened. Because the second assignment statement includes a "w", indicating our desire to write to `b:circle.out`, `outp` is initialized as an output file pointer.

The next two statements demonstrate the use of the functions `fscanf` and `fprintf`, file equivalents of functions `scanf` and `printf`.

```
fscanf(inp, "%lf", &radius);
fprintf(outp, "The radius is %.2f\n", radius);
```

Function `fscanf` must first be given an input file pointer like `inp`. The remainder of a call to `fscanf` is identical to a call to `scanf`: It includes a format string and an input list. Similarly, function `fprintf` differs from function `printf` only in its requirement of an output file pointer like the value of `outp`.

When a program has no further use for its input and output files, it *closes* them by calling function `fclose` with the file pointers:

```
fclose(inp);
fclose(outp);
```

**EXERCISES FOR
SECTION 2.7**

Self-Check

1. Explain the difference in placement of calls to `printf` used to display prompts and calls to `printf` used to echo data. Which calls are used in interactive programs, and which are used in batch programs?
2. How is input data provided to an interactive program? How is input data provided to a batch program?

Programming

1. Rewrite the program in Fig. 2.2 as two batch programs. In the first version, assume that the data file will be made accessible through input redirection. In

the second version, use a program-controlled input file and a program-controlled output file.

2.8 COMMON PROGRAMMING ERRORS

One of the first things you will discover in writing programs is that a program very rarely runs correctly the first time it is submitted. Murphy's Law—"If something can go wrong, it will"—seems to be written with the computer programmer or programming student in mind. In fact, errors are so common that they have their own special name (*bugs*), and the process of correcting them is called *debugging a program.* To alert you to potential problems, we will provide at the end of each chapter a section on common errors.

When the compiler detects an error, the computer will display an *error message,* which indicates that you have made a mistake and what the cause of the error might be. Unfortunately, error messages are often difficult to interpret and are sometimes misleading. However, as you gain some experience, you will become more proficient at understanding them.

Two basic categories of error messages will occur: syntax error messages and run-time error messages. *Syntax errors,* or *compilation errors,* are detected and displayed by the compiler as it attempts to translate your program. If a statement has a syntax error, it cannot be translated and your program will not be executed.

Run-time errors are detected by the computer and are displayed during execution of a program. A run-time error occurs when the program directs the computer to perform an illegal operation, such as dividing a number by zero. When a run-time error occurs, the computer will stop executing your program and will print a diagnostic message that indicates the line where the error was detected.

Syntax Errors

Figure 2.12 shows a *compiler listing* of the circle characteristics program that is a listing produced by the compiler during program translation. The listing shows each line of the source program (preceded by a line number) and displays any syntax errors detected by the compiler. The errors are indicated by lines in the program listing that begin with five asterisks. The program contains the following syntax errors:

- Missing semicolon at the end of the variable declaration (in line 273)
- Undeclared variable `radius` (detected in lines 277, 280, and 283)
- Last comment not closed because of blank in `*/` close-comment sequence (in line 285)

The actual format of the listing and the error messages produced by your compiler may differ from the format in Fig. 2.12. Indeed, many C compilers do not produce a listing at all, but merely display error messages. In this listing, whenever an error is detected, the compiler prints a line starting with five asterisks in which the error message is displayed. You probably have already noticed that the line in which an error is detected is not always the line in which the programmer's mistake occurred. Also, you see that the compiler attempts to correct errors wherever it can. Look at line 273 in the listing. You probably noticed immediately the semicolon missing at the end of the declaration. However, the compiler cannot be sure that this semicolon is missing until it processes the `printf` symbol on line 276. Because the `printf` is not a comma or a semicolon, the compiler then knows that the variable declaration statement begun on line 273 is not being continued to another line.

Figure 2.12   Compiler Listing of a Program with Syntax Errors

```
  1    /*
  2     * Calculates and displays the area and circumference of a circle
  3     */
  4
  5    #include <stdio.h>
268    #define PI 3.14159
269
270    int
271    main(void)
272    {
273          double area, circum
274
275          /* Get circle radius */
276          printf("Enter radius> ");
***** Semicolon added at the end of the previous source line

277          scanf("%lf", &radius);
***** Identifier "radius" is not declared within this scope
***** Invalid operand of address-of operator

278
279          /* Calculate the area */
280          area = PI * radius * radius;
***** Identifier "radius" is not declared within this scope
***** Identifier "radius" is not declared within this scope
```

(continued)

Figure 2.12 (continued)

```
281
282          /* Calculate the circumference */
283          circum = 2 * PI * radius;
***** Identifier "radius" is not declared within this scope

284
285          /* Display the area and circumference * /
286          printf("The area is %f\n", area);
287          printf("The circumference is %f\n", circum);
288
289          return (0);
290   }
***** Unexpected end-of-file encountered in a comment
***** "}" inserted before end-of-file
```

We see several cases in this listing of one programmer mistake leading to the generation of multiple error messages. For example, our not declaring the variable radius causes an error message to be printed each time radius is used in the program. This message would also occur if we remembered to declare radius but mistyped it (perhaps as raddius) in the declaration statement. The fact that radius is not declared as a variable is also the cause of the second error message pertaining to line 277. Because the address-of operator must have a variable as its operand, the fact that radius is not declared as a variable makes it an invalid operand.

Another case of one error causing multiple messages is seen in the messages caused by the mistyped close-comment character sequence. Because any text is valid inside a comment, the compiler is unaware that there is a problem until it comes to the end of the source file without having encountered a } to end the program! After complaining about this unexpected turn of events (see line following line 290), it does what it can to correct the situation by closing the comment at the end of the source file text and adding a } to end the program properly. Mistyping a close-comment sequence can cause errors that are very difficult to find. If the comment that is not correctly closed is in the middle of a program, the compiler will simply continue to view source lines as comment text until it comes to the * / that closes the *next* comment. When you begin getting error messages that make you think your compiler isn't seeing part of your program, recheck your comments carefully. In the worst case, the executable statements that the compiler is viewing as comments may not affect the syntax of your program at all—and the program will simply run incorrectly. Mistyping the open-comment sequence /* will make the compiler attempt to process the comment as a C statement, causing a syntax error.

Your strategy for correcting syntax errors should take into account the fact that one error can lead to many error messages. It is often a good idea to concentrate on correcting the errors in the declaration part of a program first. Then recompile the program before you attempt to fix other errors. Many of the other error messages will disappear once the declarations are correct.

Syntax errors are often caused by the improper use of quotation marks with format strings. Make sure that you always use a quotation mark (") to begin and end a string. Another common syntax error results from the inclusion of a semicolon at the end of a #define preprocessor directive. This error will not be flagged on the #define line, but it will often lead to syntax errors on every line in which the defined name is used.

Run-Time Errors

Figure 2.13 shows an example of a run-time error. The program compiles successfully but cannot run to completion if the first integer entered is the additive inverse of the second. In this case, the value assigned to temp in line 271 will be zero. Using temp as a divisor in line 272 causes the **divide by zero** error shown.

Figure 2.13   A Program with a Run-Time Error

```
   1  #include <stdio.h>
 262
 263  int
 264  main(void)
 265  {
 266        int     first, second;
 267        double temp, ans;
 268
 269        printf("Enter two integers> ");
 270        scanf("%d%d", &first, &second);
 271        temp = second + first;
 272        ans = first / temp;
 273        printf("The result is %.3f\n", ans);
 274
```

(continued)

Figure 2.13   (continued)

```
275          return (0);
276  }
```

```
Enter two integers> -3 3
Arithmetic fault, divide by zero at line 272 of routine
     main
```

Undetected Errors

Many execution errors may not prevent a C program from running to completion, but they simply may lead to incorrect results. It is essential therefore that you predict the results your program should produce and verify that the actual output is correct. A very common source of incorrect results in C programs is the input of a mixture of character and numeric data. Errors can be avoided if the programmer always keeps in mind scanf's different treatment of the %c placeholder on the one hand, and of the %d and %lf placeholders on the other. We noted that scanf first skips any blanks and carriage returns in the input when a numeric value is scanned. In contrast, scanf skips nothing when it scans a character. Figure 2.14 shows what appears to be a minor revision of our welcoming message program from Fig. 2.2. We have merely reversed the order in which we ask for the nickname and year. However, the program in Fig. 2.14 prints a garbled welcoming message.

Figure 2.15 shows the status of memory at the time of the final call to printf. The value of year is correct, but the three characters stored are not 'B', 'o', 'b', but '\n', 'B', and 'o'. The '\n' in letter_1 is the character that results from the user's pressing the <return> key after entering the number 1994. The scan of 1994 stopped at this character, so it was the first character processed by the statement

```
scanf("%c%c%c", &letter_1, &letter_2, &letter_3);
```

The character 'b' was never scanned.

One way to repair the welcome message program would be to declare an additional character variable and to explicitly scan the extra character:

```
scanf("%c%c%c%c", &extra, &letter_1, &letter_2,
      &letter_3);
```

Figure 2.14   Program with Incorrect Results Due to Character and Numeric Scanning Problem

```
/*
 * Incorrect revision of welcoming message program
 */
#include <stdio.h> /* printf, scanf definitions */

int
main(void)
{
      char letter_1, letter_2, letter_3; /* three letters */
      int  year; /* current year */

      printf("Enter the current year and press return> ");
      scanf("%d", &year);
      printf("Enter a 3-letter nickname and press return> ");
      scanf("%c%c%c", &letter_1, &letter_2, &letter_3);
      printf("Welcome, %c%c%c. %d is a great year to study C!\n",
             letter_1, letter_2, letter_3, year);

      return (0);
}
Enter the current year and press return> 1994
Enter a 3 letter nickname and press return> Bob
Welcome,
Bo. 1994 is a great year to study C!
```

Figure 2.16 shows another error that does not cause the program to abort with a run-time error message. The programmer has left out the & (address-of) operators on the variables in the call to scanf. Because scanf does not know where to find first and second, it is unable to store in them the values entered by the user. In this instance, the program runs to completion using whatever "garbage" values were originally in the memory locations named first and second.

Figure 2.15
Memory Contents
During Execution
of Faulty Welcome
Message Program

letter_1	\n
letter_2	B
letter_3	o
year	1994

Figure 2.16   A Program That Produces Incorrect Results Due to & Omission

```
#include <stdio.h>

int
main(void)
{
      int     first, second, sum;

      printf("Enter two integers> ");
      scanf("%d%d", first, second); /* ERROR!! should be &first, &second */
      sum = first + second;
      printf("%d + %d = %d\n", first, second, sum);

      return (0);
}
```
```
Enter two integers> 14   3
5971289 + 5971297 = 11942586
```

As we indicated earlier, debugging a program can be very time-consuming. The best approach is to plan your programs carefully and to desk check them to eliminate bugs before running the program. If you are not sure of the syntax for a particular statement, look it up in the text or in the reference guide provided on the inside covers. If you follow this approach, you will save yourself much time and trouble.

CHAPTER REVIEW

In this chapter, you saw how to use the C programming language to perform some very fundamental operations. You learned how to instruct the computer to copy information into memory from the keyboard or a data file, to perform some simple computations, and to display the results of the computations. All of this was done using symbols (punctuation marks, variable names, and special operators such as *, −, and +) that are familiar, easy to remember, and easy to use. You do not need to know very much about your computer to understand and use the basics of C.

The remainder of this text introduces more features of the C language and provides rules for using these features. You must remember throughout that, unlike the rules of English, the rules of C are precise and allow no exceptions. The compiler will be unable to translate C instructions that violate these rules.

Remember to declare every identifier used as a variable and to end program statements with semicolons.

New C Constructs

Table 2.6 describes the new C constructs introduced in this chapter.

Table 2.6   Summary of New C Constructs

Construct	Effect
#include Directive	
`#include <stdio.h>`	Tells the preprocessor to give the program access to definitions from the standard I/O library. These include definitions of the `printf` and `scanf` functions.
#define Directive for Naming Constant Macros	
`#define PI 3.14159` `#define STAR '*'`	Tells the preprocessor to use `3.14159` as the definition of the name `PI` and `'*'` as the meaning of the identifier `STAR`.
main Function Prototype	
`int` `main(void)`	Marks the start of the function where program execution begins.
Variable Declaration	

`double pct, wt;`
`int    high, mid, low;`
`FILE   *inp, *outp;`
	Allocates memory cells named `pct` and `wt` for storage of double-precision real numbers, cells named `high`, `mid`, and `low` for storage of integers, and cells named `inp` and `outp` for storage of file pointers.

Assignment Statement	
`distance = speed * time;`	Stores the product of `speed` and `time` as the value of the variable `distance`.
File Open	
`inp = fopen("num.dat", "r");` `outp = fopen("num.out", "w");`	Opens `num.dat` as an input file, storing file pointer in `inp`. Opens `num.out` as an output file, storing file pointer in `outp`.
Calls to Input Functions	
`scanf("%lf%d", &pct, &high);`	Copies input data from the keyboard into the type `double` variable `pct` and the type `int` variable `high`.
`fscanf(inp, "%d%d", &mid,` `      &low);`	Copies input data from file `num.dat` into the type `int` variables `mid` and `low`.

(continued)

Table 2.6 (continued)

Construct	Effect
Calls to Output Functions	
`printf("Percentage is %.3f\n", pct);`	Displays a line with the string `"Percentage is"` followed by the value of `pct` rounded to three decimal places.
`fprintf(outp, "%5d%5d%5d",` `        high, mid, low;`	Stores in the file `num.out` a line containing the values of `high`, `mid`, and `low`.
File Close	
`fclose(inp);` `fclose(outp);`	Closes input file `num.dat` and newly created file `num.out`.
Return Statement	
`return (0);`	Final statement of function `main`.

QUICK-CHECK EXERCISES

1. What value is assigned to the type **double** variable x by the statement

   `x = 25.0 * 2.5;`

2. What value is assigned to x by the following statement, assuming x is 10.0?

   `x = x - 20.0;`

3. Show the exact form of the output line displayed when x is 3.456.

   ```
   printf("Three values of x are %4.1f*%5.2f*%.3f\n",
           x, x, x);
   ```

4. Show the exact form of the output line when n is 345.

   ```
   printf("Three values of n are %4d*%5d*%d\n",
           n, n, n);
   ```

5. What data types would you use to represent the following items: number of hydrogen atoms in a molecule, a letter grade on an exam, the average lead concentration in water samples?

6. In which step of the software development method are the problem inputs and outputs identified?
7. If function `scanf` is getting two numbers from the same line of input, what characters should be used to separate them?
8. How does the computer determine how many data values to get from the input source when a `scanf` or `fscanf` operation is performed?
9. In an interactive program, how does the program user know how many data values to enter when the `scanf` function is called?
10. The compiler listing shows which kind of errors (syntax or run-time)?

ANSWERS TO QUICK-CHECK EXERCISES

1. `62.5`
2. `-10.0`
3. `Three values of x are #3.5*#3.46*3.456` (# = 1 blank)
4. `Three values of n are #345*##345*345`
5. `int, char, double`
6. Analysis
7. Blank(s)
8. It depends on the number of placeholders in the format string.
9. From reading the prompt
10. Syntax errors

REVIEW QUESTIONS

1. What type of information should be specified in the block comment at the very beginning of the program?
2. Put a check mark next to the variables that are syntactically correct.

   ____ `income`   ____ `two fold`
   ____ `1time`   ____ `c3po`
   ____ `int`   ____ `income#1`
   ____ `Tom's`   ____ `item`

3. What is illegal about the following program fragment?

```
#include <stdio.h>
#define PI 3.14159

int
main(void)
```

```
    {
        double c, r;

        scanf("%lf%lf", c, r);
        PI = c / (2 * r);
        . . .
    }
```

4. Stylistically, which of the following identifiers would be good choices for names of constant macros?

   ```
   gravity   G   MAX_SPEED   Sphere_Size
   ```

5. Write the data requirements, necessary formulas, and algorithm for Programming Project 6 in the next section.
6. The average pH of citrus fruits is 2.2, and this value has been stored in the variable `avg_citrus_pH`. Provide a statement to display this information in a readable way.
7. List three standard data types of C.
8. Convert the following program statements to take input data and echo it in batch mode. Assume the data are provided through input redirection.

   ```
   printf("Enter two characters> ");
   scanf("%c%c", &c1, &c2);
   printf("Enter three integers separated by spaces> ");
   scanf("%d%d%d", &n, &m, &p);
   ```

9. Write an algorithm that allows for the input of an integer value, doubles it, subtracts 10, and displays the result.

PROGRAMMING PROJECTS

1. Write a program to convert a volume in milliliters to fluid ounces.

   Data Requirements

   Problem Input
   ```
   int ml        /* volume in milliliters  */
   ```

   Problem Output
   ```
   double fl_oz /* volume in fluid ounces */
   ```

Relevant Formula
fluid_ounces = 0.034 *(milliliters)*

2. Write a program to take a depth (in kilometers) inside the Earth as input data; compute and print the temperature at this depth in degrees Celsius and degrees Fahrenheit.

Data Requirements

Problem Input
```
double depth          /* depth in km */
```

Problem Outputs
```
double celsius        /* temperature in degrees
                         Celsius    */
double fahr           /* temperature in degrees
                         Fahrenheit */
```

Relevant Formulas
celsius = 10 *(depth)* + 20   /* Celsius temperature at depth in km */

fahrenheit = 1.8 *(celsius)* + 32

3. Write a program to take as input the speed (km/h) of an airplane in still air, a distance traveled (km), and the total time (hours) required for the plane to fly the given distance against the wind and then to return with the wind. Your program should calculate and display the wind speed.
4. Write a program that displays your first initial as a block letter. (Hint: Use a 6 × 6 grid for the letter and display six strings. Each string should consist of asterisks [*] interspersed with blanks.)
5. If a human heart beats on the average of once a second, how many times does the heart beat in a lifetime of 78 years? (Use 365.25 for days in a year.) Rerun your program for a heart rate of 75 beats per minute.
6. Write a program that takes the length and width of a rectangular yard and the length and width of a rectangular house situated in the yard. Your program should calculate and display the time required to cut the grass at the rate of two square feet a second.
7. Write a program that takes as input the numerators and denominators of two fractions. Your program should display the numerator and denominator of the fraction that represents the product of the two fractions. Also, display the percent equivalent of the resulting product.
8. Redo Project 7; this time compute the sum of the two fractions.

9. The Pythagorean theorem states that the sum of the squares of the sides of a right triangle is equal to the square of the hypotenuse. For example, if two sides of a right triangle have lengths of 3 and 4, then the hypotenuse must have a length of 5. Together the integers 3, 4, and 5 form a *Pythagorean triple*. There are an infinite number of such triples. Given two positive integers, *m* and *n*, where $m > n$, a Pythagorean triple can be generated by the following formulas:

$$side1 = m^2 - n^2$$
$$side2 = 2mn$$
$$hypotenuse = m^2 + n^2$$

The triple (3, 4, 5) is generated by this formula when $m = 2$ and $n = 1$. Write a program that takes values for *m* and *n* as input and displays the values of the Pythagorean triple generated by the preceding formulas.

10. Write a program to compute the rate of growth, expressed as a percentage, of an insect population. Take as input the initial size of the population and its size one week later. Then predict the size of the population in yet another week, assuming that growth continues at the same rate. (See Self-Check Exercise 3 in Section 2.1.)

DATA TYPES, OPERATORS, AND SIMPLE FUNCTIONS

In this chapter, we take a closer look at the data types `double`, `int`, and `char`. We study how to form arithmetic expressions using numeric values and the operators introduced in Chapter 2. We also present additional operations that C provides as standard functions, and we look at simple examples of functions that the C programmer can define.

3.1 DATA TYPES

An *abstraction* is a model or simplification of a physical object. We frequently use abstractions in problem solving and programming. For example, in problem solving we sometimes make simplifying assumptions that enable us to solve a limited version of a more general problem. In programming, *abstraction* is the process of focusing on what we need to know, ignoring irrelevant details.

Data Type double

A *data type* is a set of values and a set of operations on those values. A *standard data type* in C is a data type that is predefined, such as `char`, `double`, `int`. In C, we use the standard data type `double` as an abstraction for the real numbers (in the mathematical sense). The data type `double` is an abstraction because it does not include all the real numbers. Some real numbers are too large or too small, and some real numbers cannot be represented precisely because of the finite size of a memory cell. However, we can certainly represent enough of the real numbers in C to carry out most of the computations we wish to perform with sufficient accuracy.

The normal arithmetic operators for real numbers (+, −, *, /) can be performed on type `double` objects in C where * means multiply. The assignment operator (=) is another operator that can be used with type `double` objects, and we can also use the standard I/O functions `scanf` and `printf` with type `double` objects.

Objects of a data type may be variables or constants. A type `double` constant is a number that contains a decimal point, an exponent, or both. The exponent is an uppercase or lowercase E followed by a positive or negative integer. To pronounce a constant containing an exponent, simply read the letter E as "times 10 to the power." Thus `456.0E−2` means "456.0 times 10 to the power −2," that is, 456.0×10^{-2}, or 4.56. Examples of some constants of type `double` are shown in Table 3.1.

As shown by the last number in Table 3.1, `1.15E−3` means the same as 1.15×10^{-3} where the exponent −3 causes the decimal point to be moved left

Table 3.1   Constants of Type double (Real Numbers)

3.14159	
0.005	
12345.	
15.0e-6	(value of 15.0×10^{-6} or 0.000015)
2.345E2	(value of 2.345×10^2 or 234.5)
.12e+6	(value of $.12 \times 10^6$ or 120000.)
1.15E-3	(value of 1.15×10^{-3} or 0.00115)

three digits. A positive exponent causes the decimal point to be moved to the right; the + sign may be omitted when the exponent is positive. Numbers written with explicit exponents are said to be in *scientific notation.* You can display type double values in scientific notation by using the printf placeholder %e. Input values in scientific notation can be scanned using either %lf or %le.

Numeric constants in C are nonnegative numbers. Although it is perfectly legitimate to use a number like −273.15 in a program, C views the minus sign as the negation operator rather than as a part of the constant.

Data Type int

Another standard data type, or data abstraction, in C is type int, which is used to represent the integer numbers (for example, −77, 0, 999, +999). The data types double and int differ in one basic way: Type double objects represent numbers with a decimal point and a fractional part; type int objects represent only whole numbers. For this reason, type int objects are more restricted in their use. We often use them to represent a count of items (for example, the number of electrons in an atom) because a count must always be a whole number.

The data type of the object stored in a particular memory cell determines how the *bit pattern,* or *binary string,* in that cell is interpreted. For example, a bit pattern that represents a type double object is interpreted differently from a bit pattern that represents a type int object. However, we do not need to be concerned with this detail in order to use these data types in C. We can use arithmetic operators and the assignment operator with type int operands. When applied to integer operands, these operators, including the division operator (/), always give an integer result. An additional operator, the remainder operator (%), can be used with integer operands to find the remainder of longhand division. We will discuss the division and remainder operators in Section 3.2.

Differences Between Numeric Types

You may wonder why having more than one numeric type is necessary. Can the data type `double` be used for all numbers? Yes, but on many computers, operations involving integers are faster than those involving numbers of type `double`. Less storage space is needed to store type `int` values. Also, operations with integers are always precise, whereas some loss of accuracy, or *round-off error,* may occur when dealing with type `double` numbers.

These differences result from the way the numeric data types are represented internally in your computer's memory. All data are represented in memory as *binary strings,* strings of 0s and 1s. However, the binary string stored for the type `int` value 13 is not the same as the binary string stored for the type `double` number 13.0. The actual internal representation is computer dependent, and type `double` numbers usually require more bytes of computer memory than type `int`. Compare the sample `int` and `double` formats shown in Fig. 3.1.

Positive integers are represented by standard binary numbers. If you are familiar with the binary number system, you know that the integer 13 is represented as the binary number 01101.

The format of type `double` values is analogous to scientific notation. The storage area occupied by the number is divided into two sections: the *mantissa* and the *exponent.* The mantissa is a binary fraction between 0.5 and 1.0 for positive numbers and between −0.5 and −1.0 for negative numbers. The exponent is an integer. The mantissa and exponent are chosen so that the following formula is correct:

$$real\ number = mantissa \times 2^{exponent}$$

Because of the finite size of a memory cell, not all real numbers in the range allowed can be represented precisely as type `double` values. We will discuss this concept later.

We have seen that type `double` values may include a fractional part, whereas type `int` values cannot. An additional advantage of the type `double` format is that a much larger range of numbers can be represented as compared to type `int`. Actual ranges vary from one implementation to another, but the

Figure 3.1
Internal Formats
of Type int and
Type double

type int format

binary number

type double format

mantissa	exponent

Figure 3.2   Program to Print Implementation-Specific Ranges for Positive Numeric Data

```
/*
 * Find implementation's ranges for positive numeric data
 */

#include <stdio.h>
#include <limits.h> /* definition of INT_MAX                          */
#include <float.h>  /* definitions of DBL_MIN, DBL_MAX                */

int
main(void)
{
      printf("Range of positive values of type int: 1 . . %d\n",
             INT_MAX);
      printf("Range of positive values of type double: %e . . %e\n",
             DBL_MIN, DBL_MAX);

      return (0);
}
```

ANSI standard for C specifies that the minimum range of positive values of type int is from 1 to 32,767 (approximately 3.3×10^4). The minimum range specified for positive values of type double is from 10^{-37} to 10^{37}. To understand how small 10^{-37} is, consider the fact that the mass of one electron is approximately 10^{-27} grams, and 10^{-37} is one ten-billionth of 10^{-27}. The enormity of 10^{37} may be clearer when you realize that if you multiply the diameter of the Milky Way galaxy in kilometers by a trillion, your numeric result is just one ten-thousandth of 10^{37}.

You can determine the exact ranges of the (ANSI-conforming) C implementation you are using by running the program in Fig. 3.2.

Numerical Inaccuracies

One of the problems in processing data of type double is that sometimes an error occurs in representing real numbers. Just as certain fractions cannot be represented exactly in the decimal number system (e.g., the fraction 1/3 is 0.333333. . .), so some fractions cannot be represented exactly as binary numbers in the mantissa of the type double format. The *representational error* (sometimes called *round-off error*) will depend on the number of binary digits (bits) used in the mantissa: the more bits, the smaller the error. Because of this kind of error, an equality comparison of two type double values can lead to surprising results.

The number 0.1 is an example of a number that has a representational error as a type double value. The effect of a small error is often magnified through repeated computations. For example, the value of the expression

```
0.1 + 0.1 + 0.1 + 0.1 + 0.1
```

is not exactly equal to 0.5.

Other problems occur when manipulating very large and very small real numbers. When you add a large number and a small number, the larger number may "cancel out" the smaller number, resulting in a *cancellation error*. If x is much larger than y, then $x + y$ may have the same value as x (for example, 1000.0 + 0.0000001234 is equal to 1000.0 on some computers).

If two very small numbers are multiplied, the result may be too small to be represented accurately, so it will be represented as zero. This phenomenon is called *arithmetic underflow*. Similarly, if two very large numbers are multiplied, the result may be too large to be represented. This phenomenon, called *arithmetic overflow,* is handled in different ways by different C compilers. Arithmetic overflow can occur when processing very large integer values as well. Arithmetic overflow of type int variables is of special concern if you use a PC-based C implementation that offers only the minimum range of integers (−32,767 to 32,767). If you require integers of a larger magnitude, you can use either type double or another integer type. Most C implementations provide an integer type named long (or long int) that allows storage of a wider range of integers than is possible in type int.

Data Type char

Another standard data type in C is type char. We have already seen that type char variables can be used to store any single character value. A type char literal must be enclosed in single quotes (for example, 'A'); however, you don't use quotes when you enter character data at a terminal. When the scanf function is called to get an input value for a type char variable, the next character you enter at the terminal is stored in that variable. You enter the blank character by pressing the space bar; in a program the blank character is written as the literal ' '.

EXAMPLE 3.1

First, the program in Fig. 3.3 gets and echoes three characters entered at the keyboard. Next, it displays them in reverse order enclosed in asterisks. Each char-

Figure 3.3   Program for Example 3.1

```
/*
 * Gets three input characters and displays them in
 * reverse order
 */

#include <stdio.h>
#define BORDER '*'

int
main(void)
{
        char first, second, third; /* 3 characters */

        printf("Enter 3 characters> ");
        scanf("%c%c%c", &first, &second, &third);
        printf("%c%c%c%c%c\n", BORDER, third, second,
               first, BORDER);

        return (0);
}

Enter 3 characters> J H
*H J*
```

acter is stored in a variable of type char; the character value '*' is associated with the constant macro BORDER.

The line

```
printf("%c%c%c%c%c\n", BORDER, third, second,
       first, BORDER);
```

displays an asterisk, the three characters in reverse order, and another asterisk. As shown in the program output, each character value is displayed in a single print position. The second character entered in the sample run of Fig. 3.3 is a blank.

In Fig. 3.3, the string literal "Enter 3 characters> " is displayed as a prompt. In Example 3.1 and in earlier examples, we use strings as prompts and to clarify program output.

Only single characters, not strings, can be stored in type char variables. Internally within your computer, each character has its own unique numeric code; the binary form of this code is stored in a memory cell that has a character value. Three common character codes are shown in Appendix A. The digit characters are an increasing sequence of consecutive characters in all three codes. For example, in ASCII (American Standard Code for Information Interchange), the digit characters '0' through '9' have code values of 48 through 57 (decimal).

The uppercase letters are also an increasing sequence of characters, but they are not necessarily consecutive. In ASCII, uppercase letters do have consecutive codes, namely, the decimal code values 65 through 90. The lowercase letters are also an increasing, but not necessarily consecutive, sequence of characters. In ASCII, lowercase letters have the consecutive decimal code values 97 through 122. In our examples and programs, we will assume that the letters are consecutive characters.

In ASCII, the *printable characters* have codes from 32 (code for a blank or space) to 126 (code for the symbol ~). The other codes represent nonprintable *control characters*. Sending a control character to an output device causes the device to perform a special operation such as returning the cursor to column one, advancing the cursor to the next line, or ringing a bell.

Since characters are represented by integer codes, C permits conversion of type char to type int and vice versa. For example, if qmark_code were a type int variable, you could use the following to find out the code your implementation uses for a question mark:

```
qmark_code = '?';
printf("Code for ? = %d\n", qmark_code);
```

EXERCISES FOR SECTION 3.1

Self-Check

1. Indicate which of the following values are legal constants in C and which are not. Identify the data type of each valid constant value.

15	'XYZ'	'*'	$	25.123	15.
-999	.123	'x'	'9'	'-5'	32e-4

2. How does cancellation error differ from representational error?
3. If squaring 10^{-20} gives a result of zero, the type of error that has occurred is called _____ .

Programming

1. Run the program from Fig. 3.2 to determine the largest type int value and the largest type double value that can be used on your computer system's implementation of C.

3.2 ARITHMETIC EXPRESSIONS

In Section 2.4, we met the basic arithmetic operators available in C: + (addition), − (subtraction), * (multiplication), / (division), and % (remainder). In this section, we will study the behavior of / and %, and we will learn rules for writing expressions that use several operators.

Operators / and %

When applied to two positive integers, the division operator (/) computes the integral part of the result of dividing its first operand by its second. For example, the value of 7.0 / 2.0 is 3.5, but the value of 7 / 2 is the integral part of this result, 3. Similarly, the value of 299.0 / 100.0 is 2.99, but the value of 299 / 100 is the integral part of this result, 2. If the / operator is used with a negative and a positive integer, the result may vary from one C implementation to another. For this reason, you should avoid using division with negative integers. The / operation is undefined when the divisor (the second operand) is 0. Table 3.2 shows some examples of integer division.

Table 3.2 Results of Integer Division

```
3 / 15 = 0      18 / 3 = 6
15 / 3 = 5      16 / −3 varies
16 / 3 = 5      0 / 4 = 0
17 / 3 = 5      4 / 0 is undefined
```

Compare the values of the expressions 6.0 / 2.0 and 6 / 2. The value of 6.0 / 2.0 is the real number 3.0; the value of 6 / 2 is the integer 3. Although these two results are equivalent in a mathematical sense, they are not the same in C and are stored in memory as different binary strings.

The remainder operator (%) returns the *integer remainder* of the result of dividing its first operand by its second. For example, the value of 7 % 2 is 1 because the integer remainder is 1.

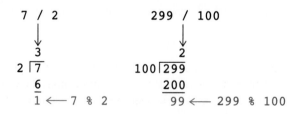

In the preceding longhand division problems, the diagram on the left shows the effect of dividing 7 by 2; that is, we get a quotient of 3 (7 / 2) and a remainder of 1 (7 % 2). The diagram on the right shows that 299 % 100 is 99 because we get a remainder of 99 when we divide 299 by 100.

   The magnitude of *m* % *n* must always be less than the divisor *n*, so if *m* is positive, the value of *m* % 100 must be between 0 and 99. The % operation is undefined when *n* is zero and varies from one implementation to another if *n* is negative. Table 3.3 shows some examples of the % operator.

Table 3.3   The % Operator

```
3 % 5 = 3      5 % 3 = 2
4 % 5 = 4      5 % 4 = 1
5 % 5 = 0     15 % 5 = 0
6 % 5 = 1     15 % 6 = 3
7 % 5 = 2     15 % -7 varies
8 % 5 = 3     15 % 0 is undefined
```

   The formula

$$m \text{ equals } (m / n) * n + (m \% n)$$

defines the relationship between the operators / and % for an integer dividend of *m* and an integer divisor of *n*. We can see that this formula holds for the two problems discussed earlier by plugging in values for *m*, *n*, *m* / *n*, and *m* % *n*. In the first example that follows, *m* is 7 and *n* is 2; in the second, *m* is 299 and *n* is 100:

```
7     equals (7 / 2) * 2 + (7 % 2)
      equals   3    * 2 +   1

299   equals (299 / 100) * 100 + (299 % 100)
      equals     2       * 100 +    99
```

Type of an Expression

The data type of each variable must be specified in its declaration, but how does C determine the data type of an expression? The data type of an expression depends on the type of its operands. Let's consider the types of expressions involving operands that are integers of type `int` or reals of type `double`.[†] For example, the expression

```
ace + bandage
```

is type `int` if both `ace` and `bandage` are type `int`; otherwise, it is type `double`. In general, an expression of the form

```
ace arithmetic_operator bandage
```

is of type `int` if *both* `ace` and `bandage` are of type `int`; otherwise, it is of type `double`.

An expression that has operands of both type `int` and type `double` is called a *mixed-type expression*. The data type of such a mixed-type expression will be `double`.

Mixed-Type Assignment Statement

When an assignment statement is executed, the expression is first evaluated; then the result is assigned to the variable listed to the left of the assignment operator (=). Either a type `double` or a type `int` expression may be assigned to a type `double` variable, so if m and n are type `int` and p, x, and y are type `double`, all assignment statements in the examples that follow are valid:

```
m = 3;
n = 2;
p = 2.0;
x = m / p;
y = m / n;
```

m	n	p	x	y
3	2	2.0	1.5	1.0

In a mixed-type assignment such as

```
y = m / n;
```

a common error is to assume that the type of y (the variable being assigned) causes the expression to be evaluated as if its operands were that type too.

[†] C defines additional integer and real data types besides `int` and `double`, but these two types are adequate for representing numbers in the great majority of programming applications.

Remember, the expression is evaluated before the assignment is made, and the type of the variable being assigned has no effect whatsoever on the expression value. For m = 3 and n = 2, the expression m / n evaluates to the integer 1. This value is converted to type double (1.0) before it is stored in y.

Assignment of a type double expression to a type int variable causes the fractional part of the expression to be lost because it cannot be represented in the integer variable. The expression in the assignment statements

```
x = 9 * 0.5;
n = 9 * 0.5;
```

evaluates to the real number 4.5. If x is of type double, the number 4.5 is stored in x, as expected. If n is of type int, only the integral part of the expression value is stored in n, as shown here:

Expressions with Multiple Operators

In our programs so far, most expressions have involved a single arithmetic operator; however, expressions with multiple operators are common in C. Expressions can include both unary and binary operators. *Unary operators* take only one operand. In these expressions, we see the unary negation (–) and plus (+) operators:

```
x = -y;
p = +x * y;
```

Binary operators require two operands. When + and – are used to represent addition and subtraction, they are binary operators:

```
x = y + z;
z = y - x;
```

For readability, do not use a space between a unary operator and its operand; do use spaces before and after binary operators.

To understand and write expressions with multiple operators, we must know the C rules for evaluating expressions. For example, in the expression x + y / z, is + performed before / or is + performed after /? Is the expression x / y * z evaluated as (x / y) * z or as x / (y * z)? Verify for yourself that the order of evaluation does make a difference by substituting some simple values for **x**, **y**, and **z**. In both of these expressions, the **/** operator is evaluated first; the reasons are explained in the C rules for evaluation of arithmetic expressions that follow. These rules are based on standard algebraic rules.

Rules for Evaluation of Arithmetic Expressions

a. All parenthesized subexpressions must be evaluated separately. Nested parenthesized subexpressions must be evaluated inside out, with the innermost subexpression evaluated first.

b. *The operator precedence rule.* Operators in the same subexpression are evaluated in the following order:

unary **+, −**	first
*, /, %	next
binary **+, −**	last

c. *The associativity rule.* Unary operators in the same subexpression and at the same precedence level (such as + and −) are evaluated right to left (*right associativity*). Binary operators in the same subexpression and at the same precedence level (such as + and −) are evaluated left to right (*left associativity*).

Knowledge of these rules will help you understand how C evaluates expressions. Use parentheses as needed to specify the order of evaluation. Often, it is a good idea to use extra parentheses to document clearly the order of operator evaluation in complicated expressions. For example, the expression

```
x * y * z + a / b - c * d
```

can be written using parentheses in the more readable form

```
(x * y * z) + (a / b) - (c * d)
```

EXAMPLE 3.2   We have seen that the formula for the area of a circle may be written in C as

```
area = PI * radius * radius
```

where the meaning of the constant macro **PI** is 3.14159. Figure 3.4 shows the *evaluation tree* for this formula. In this tree, the arrows connect each operand with

**Figure 3.4
Evaluation Tree
for** `area = PI *
radius * radius`

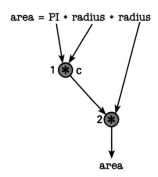

its operator. The order of operator evaluation is shown by the number to the left of each operator; the rules that apply are shown by the letters to the right. ◀

   In Fig. 3.5, we see a step-by-step evaluation of the same expression for a `radius` value of 2.0. You may want to use a similar notation when computing by hand the value of an expression with multiple operators.

**Figure 3.5
Step-by-Step
Expression
Evaluation**

```
area   =   PI    *    radius    *    radius
           3.14159     2.0             2.0
                6.28318
                             12.56636
```

EXAMPLE 3.3 ▶ The formula for the average velocity, v, of a particle traveling on a line between points p_1 and p_2 in time t_1 to t_2 is

$$v = \frac{p_2 - p_1}{t_2 - t_1}$$

This formula can be written and evaluated in C as shown in Fig. 3.6. ◀

**Figure 3.6
Evaluation Tree
and Step-by-
Step Evaluation
for** `v = (p2 -
p1) / (t2 - t1)`

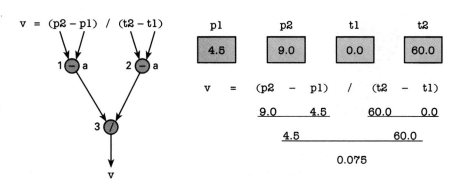

 **EXAMPLE 3.4** Consider the expression

        z - (a + b / 2) + w * -y

containing integer variables only. The parenthesized subexpression

        (a + b / 2)

is evaluated first (see Rules for Evaluation of Arithmetic Expressions, rule a) beginning with b / 2 (rule b). Once the value of b / 2 is determined, it can be added to a to obtain the value of (a + b / 2). Next, y is negated (rule b). The multiplication operation can now be performed (rule b) and the value for w * -y is determined. Then, the value of (a + b / 2) is subtracted from z (rule c). Finally, this result is added to w * -y. The evaluation tree and step-by-step evaluation for this expression are shown in Fig. 3.7.

Figure 3.7 Evaluation Tree and Step-by-Step Evaluation for z - (a + b / 2) + w * -y

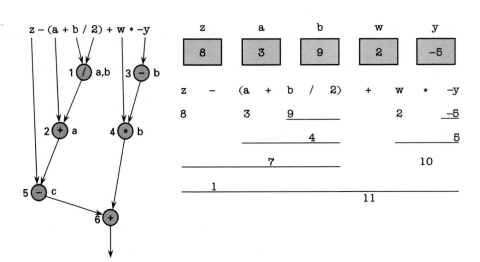

Writing Mathematical Formulas in C

The two problem areas in writing a mathematical formula in C concern multiplication and division. Multiplication can often be implied in a mathematical formula by writing the two items to be multiplied next to each other; for example, $a = bc$. In C, however, you must always use the * operator to indicate multiplication, as in

```
a = b * c
```

Another difficulty arises in formulas involving division. We normally write the numerator and denominator on separate lines, as in

$$m = \frac{y - b}{x - a}$$

In C, however, all assignment statements must be written in a linear form. Consequently, parentheses are often needed to mark the numerator and the denominator so as to clearly indicate the correct order of evaluation of the operators in the expression. The formula just shown would be written in C as

```
m = (y - b) / (x - a)
```

EXAMPLE 3.5   This example illustrates how several mathematical formulas can be written in C.

Mathematical Formula	C Expression
1. $b^2 - 4ac$	b * b - 4 * a * c
2. $a + b - c$	a + b - c
3. $\dfrac{a + b}{c + d}$	(a + b) / (c + d)
4. $\dfrac{1}{1 + x^2}$	1 / (1 + x * x)
5. $a \times -(b + c)$	a * -(b + c)

The points illustrated are summarized as follows:

- Always specify multiplication explicitly by using the operator * where needed (formula 1).
- Use parentheses when required to control the order of operator evaluation (formulas 3, 4).
- Two arithmetic operators can be written in succession if the second is a unary operator (formula 5).

Automatic and Explicit Conversion of Data Types

We have encountered several cases in which data of one numeric type are automatically converted to another numeric type. Table 3.4 summarizes the automatic

Table 3.4   Automatic Conversion of Numeric Data

Context of Conversion	Example	Explanation
Expression with binary operator and operands of different numeric types	`k + x` value is `6.5`	Value of `int` variable k is converted to type `double` format before operation is performed.
Assignment statement with type `double` target variable and type `int` expression	`z = k / m;` expression value is `1`; value assigned to z is `1.0`	Expression is evaluated *first*. Then, the result is converted to type `double` format for assignment.
Assignment statement with type `int` target variable and type `double` expression	`n = x * y;` expression value is `3.15`; value assigned to n is `3`	Expression is evaluated *first*. Then, the result is converted to type `int` format for assignment, and fractional part is lost.

conversions we have seen. The variables in the table are declared and initialized as follows:

```
int     k = 5, m = 4, n;
double  x = 1.5, y = 2.1, z;
```

In addition to automatic conversions, C also provides an explicit type conversion operation called a *cast*. The program in Fig. 3.8 uses cast operations to prevent integer division. Because both `total_score` and `num_students` are of type `int`, evaluation of the expression

```
total_score / num_students
```

would result in a loss of the fractional part of the average. Placing the name of the desired type in parentheses immediately before the value to be converted causes the value to be changed to the desired data format before it is used in computation. Because this explicit conversion is a very high-precedence operation, it is performed before the division.

Although we show explicit casts of both operands of the division operator in the expression in Fig. 3.8, explicitly converting only one would be suffi-

Figure 3.8   Using Casts to Prevent Integer Division

```
/*
 * Computes a test average
 */

#include <stdio.h>

int
main(void)
{
      int    total_score, num_students;
      double average;

      printf("Enter sum of students' scores> ");
      scanf("%d", &total_score);
      printf("Enter number of students> ");
      scanf("%d", &num_students);

      average = (double)total_score / (double)num_students;
      printf("Average score is %.2f\n", average);

      return (0);
}

Enter sum of students' scores> 1822
Enter number of students> 25
Average score is 72.88
```

cient because the rules for evaluation of mixed-type expressions would then cause the other to be converted as well. However, we could *not* achieve our goal by writing the expression as

```
average = (double)(total_score / num_students);
```

In this case, the quotient `total_score / num_students` is computed first, resulting in the loss of the fractional part. The cast to `double` simply converts this whole number quotient to type `double` format.

When a cast operation is applied to a variable, the conversion carried out determines the value of the expression, but the conversion does not change what is stored in the variable. For example, if **x** is a type **int** variable whose value is 5, the following statements will first display 5.00 and then display 5. The value of the expression

```
(double)x
```

is 5.0, but the value stored in **x** is still the integer 5.

Statements	Output
`printf("%.2f", (double)x);`	
`printf("%4d\n", x);`	5.00 5

**EXERCISES FOR
SECTION 3.2**

Self-Check

1. a. Evaluate the following expressions with 7 and 22 as operands:

   22 / 7   7 / 22   22 % 7   7 % 22

   Repeat this exercise for the following pairs of integers:

   b. 15, 16   c. 3, 23   d. −3, 16

2. Do a step-by-step evaluation of the expressions that follow if the value of **celsius** is 3 and **salary** is 12400.00:

   ```
   1.8 * celsius + 32.0
   (salary − 5000.00) * 0.20 + 1425.00
   ```

3. Given the constants and variable declarations

   ```
   #define PI 3.14159
   #define MAX_I 1000
   . . .
   double x, y;
   int a, b, i;
   ```

   indicate which of the following statements are valid, and find the value stored by each valid statement. Also indicate which are invalid and why. Assume that **a** is 3, **b** is 4, and **y** is −1.0.

```
a. i = a % b;          j. i = (MAX_I - 990) / a;
b. i = (989 - MAX_I) / a;   k. x = a / y;
c. i = b % a;          l. i = PI * a;
d. x = PI * y;         m. x = PI / y;
e. i = a / -b;         n. x = b / a;
f. x = a / b;          o. i = (MAX_I - 990) % a;
g. x = a % (a / b);    p. i = a % 0;
h. i = b / 0;          q. i = a % (MAX_I - 990);
i. i = a % (990 - MAX_I);
```

4. What values are assigned by the legal statements in Exercise 3, assuming a is 5, b is 2, and y is 2.0?

5. Assume that you have the following variable declarations:

```
int    color, lime, straw, yellow, red, orange;
double black, white, green, blue, purple, crayon;
```

Evaluate each of the following statements using these values: color is 2, black is 2.5, crayon is −1.3, straw is 1, red is 3, purple is 0.3E+1.

```
a. white = color * 2.5 / purple;
b. green = color / purple;
c. orange = color / red;
d. blue = (color + straw) / (crayon + 0.3);
e. lime = red / color + red % color;
f. purple = straw / red * color;
```

6. Let a, b, c, and x be the names of four type double variables; and let i, j, and k be the names of three type int variables. Each of the following statements contains one or more violations of the rules for forming arithmetic expressions. Rewrite each statement so that it is consistent with these rules.

```
a. x = 4.0 a * c;      d. k = 3(i + j);
b. a = ac;             e. x = 5a + bc;
c. i = 5j3;
```

7. Evaluate the following expressions if x is 10.5, y is 7.2, m is 5, and n is 2.

```
a. x / (double)m       d. (double)(n / m) + y
b. x / m               e. (double)n / m
c. (double)(n * m)
```

Programming

1. Write an assignment statement that might be used to implement the following heat transfer formula in C:

$$q = \frac{kA(T_1 - T_2)}{L}$$

2. Write a program that stores the values `'X'`, `'0'`, `1.345E10`, and `35` in separate memory cells. Your program should get the first three values as input data, but use an assignment statement to store the last value.

3.3 EXTENDING A PROBLEM SOLUTION

Quite often the solution of one problem turns out to be the basis for the solution to another problem. For example, we can easily solve the next problem by building on the solution to the circle characteristics problem in Section 2.1.

Case Study: Quality Control in Manufacturing Flat Washers

PROBLEM

High Plains Hardware is gradually automating its manufacturing plant. The company recently installed both a camera to photograph metal parts as they pass on a conveyor belt and image processing software to compute the area of each part as it appears in the photographs. You have been asked to establish an initial quality control check for 1/2-in. flat washers (a washer is identified by the diameter of its hole). The program will compute the difference between the expected and observed areas and will print the difference as a percentage of the expected area.

ANALYSIS

How would we find the percentage difference between the expected area of the rim of a 1/2-in. washer and the actual area of the rim of a washer photographed on a conveyor belt? Let's consider an example. In Fig. 3.9(a), we see a digitized photograph of a 1/2-in. washer. Figure 3.9(b) is an image in which the part of the photograph that is one washer is marked in color. The area of the marked washer, as computed by the image processing program, is 0.6942 sq. in.

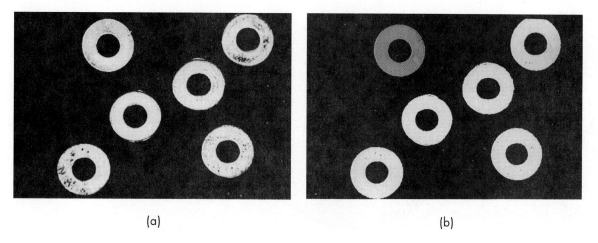

(a)   (b)

Figure 3.9   (a) Photograph of Flat Washers; (b) Image with One Washer Marked

How does the expected rim area of a 1/2-in. flat washer differ from the observed rim area of the washer (0.6942 sq. in.)? Clearly, we need to compute the area between the circle that represents the washer's outer edge and the circle that represents the hole. If we can calculate the area of the two circles, we can find the area of the rim by subtracting the area of the smaller circle from the area of the larger one. At this point, we realize that our requirements specification does not contain all the facts we need to solve the problem. We must ask the High Plains Hardware representative the size of the entire washer, including the rim. Eventually, we learn that the diameter of the outer circle is 17/16 in. We can now compute the expected size of the washer rim by subtracting the area of the inner circle (the hole) from the area of the outer circle (see Fig. 3.10).

Next, we must see how the expected area (0.6903 sq. in.) differs from the observed area (0.6942 sq. in.). We can apply the formula for computing the *relative error* in an approximation:

$$\frac{actual\ value - approximate\ value}{actual\ value}$$

Using our expected area as the *actual value* and our observed area as the *approximate value,* we have

$$\frac{-0.0039}{0.6903} \ = \ -0.00565 \ = \ -0.565\%$$

In the Data Requirements listed next, we see that problem constants come from two major sources. Some of the constants needed in a program's compu-

**Figure 3.10
Computing the
Expected Rim
Area of a 1/2-
in. Washer**

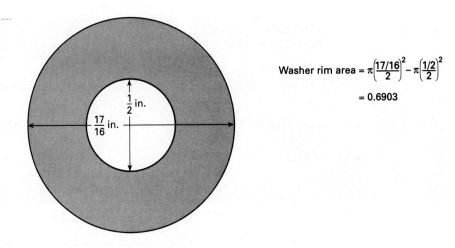

Washer rim area $= \pi \left(\frac{17/16}{2} \right)^2 - \pi \left(\frac{1/2}{2} \right)^2$

$= 0.6903$

tation are numerical constants from mathematics—for example, π. Other constants appear in the requirements specification: "quality control check for 1/2-in. flat washers." The radius of the washer (the hole) and the radius of the outer rim circle are listed as *program variables* because we need these values to compute the expected area of the washer. However, they are neither problem inputs nor explicitly stated problem constants. The expected area, another value that we need to compute, is not a problem output.

Data Requirements

Problem Constants

PI   3.14159

WASHER_DIAMETER   (1.0/2.0) /* diameter in inches
                                    of the hole of a
                                    flat washer*/

OUTER_DIAMETER   (17.0/16.0) /* diameter in inch-
                                     es of the circu-
                                     lar outer edge*/

Problem Input

double observed_area   /* observed area (in square
                               inches) of a washer rim */

Problem Output

double pct_differ   /* how much difference there is
                               between expected area and
                               observed area (as a per-
                               centage of expected area)*/

Program Variables

```
double washer_radius     /* expected radius of washer
                            hole     */

double outer_radius      /* expected radius of circular
                            outer edge     */

double rim_area          /* expected area of washer rim */
```

Relevant Formulas

$$area\ of\ a\ circle = \pi \times radius^2$$

$$radius\ of\ a\ circle = \frac{1}{2}\ diameter$$

$$percentage\ difference\ of\ 2\ areas = \frac{expected - observed}{expected} \times 100$$

DESIGN

Initial Algorithm

1. Get observed area of washer rim.
2. Compute expected area of rim.
3. Compute percentage difference between expected and observed areas.
4. Display percentage difference.

The algorithm refinements follow. The refinement of Step 2 shows that we must compute the radii of the washer and its outer edge before we can compute the washer's rim area. Algorithm steps 2.3 and 3.1 are expressed in *pseudocode,* which is a mixture of English and C used to describe algorithm steps.

Step 2   Refinement
2.1 Assign 1/2 WASHER_DIAMETER to washer_radius.
2.2 Assign 1/2 OUTER_DIAMETER to outer_radius.
2.3 rim_area is PI * outer_radius * outer_radius - PI * washer_radius * washer_radius.

Step 3   Refinement
3.1 pct_differ is
    (rim_area - observed_area) / rim_area * 100

IMPLEMENTATION

Figure 3.11 shows the C program. We will base this program on our analysis and design by using the data requirements to develop the declaration part and by tak-

Figure 3.11   Quality Control Program for 1/2-in. Washers

```
/*
 * Compute the percentage difference between the expected area of the rim
 * of a WASHER_DIAMETER-inch washer (with an outer rim diameter of
 * OUTER_DIAMETER inches) and the observed area of such a washer's rim
 */

#include <stdio.h>
#define WASHER_DIAMETER (1.0/2.0)    /* diameter in inches of a flat washer
                                         (diameter of the hole)            */
#define OUTER_DIAMETER  (17.0/16.0) /* diameter of edge of outer rim of a
                                         WASHER_DIAMETER-inch flat washer   */
#define PI              3.14159

int
main(void)
{
        double observed_area;  /* input - observed area (in square inches)
                                   of a washer rim                         */
        double pct_differ;     /* output - amount of difference between
                                   observed and expected rim size, as a per-
                                   centage of expected size                */
        double washer_radius;  /* expected washer radius (radius of hole)  */
        double outer_radius;   /* expected radius of washer rim's outer edge*/
        double rim_area;       /* expected area of washer rim              */

        /* Get observed area of washer rim                                 */
        scanf("%lf", &observed_area);
        printf("Observed area = %.4f sq. in.\n", observed_area);

        /* Compute expected area of rim                                    */
        washer_radius = 0.5 * WASHER_DIAMETER;
        outer_radius = 0.5 * OUTER_DIAMETER;
        rim_area = PI * outer_radius * outer_radius
                  - PI * washer_radius * washer_radius;

        /* Compute percentage difference between expected and observed
           rim area                                                        */
        pct_differ = (rim_area - observed_area) / rim_area * 100;

        /* Display percentage difference                                   */
        printf("Expected area differs from observed area by %.2f percent.\n",
                pct_differ);

        return (0);
}
Observed area = 0.6942 sq. in.
Expected area differs from observed area by -0.57 percent.
```

ing the initial algorithm with refinements as the starting point for the executable statements of the program body. This example is the first we have seen in which a constant macro's meaning is an expression, and it is perfectly legitimate provided that the expression is enclosed in parentheses and all of the expression's operands are constants. In this program, we use the expressions (1 . 0 / 2 . 0) and (17 . 0 / 16 . 0) rather than the decimal equivalents 0 . 5 and 1 . 0625 in order to maintain an obvious correspondence between the implementation and the specification of the problem.

You will notice that we have used the names of our constant macros wherever we need to refer to the washer's dimensions, even in our comments. We do this so that a revision of the program to handle a different size of washer will require only a change of the constant macro definitions. Pay careful attention to the fact that we *do not* use WASHER_DIAMETER everywhere we need the constant 1/2, but only where the 1/2 needed is actually the diameter of the washer.

TESTING

To test this program, run it with data files containing a few different observed sizes, some of which are larger and some of which are smaller than the expected size. As you test the program, you will find that not quite enough information is displayed to make it easy for you to prove the answers correct. How can you prove any relationship between the expected and observed areas when the output does not show the expected area? We could quickly modify the program to provide more information by changing the final printf to

```
printf("Expected area (%.4f sq. in) differs from ",
       rim_area);
printf("observed area by %.2f percent.\n", pct_differ);
```

EXERCISE FOR SECTION 3.3

Self-Check

1. What changes are required to revise the program in Fig. 3.11 to handle a 5/16-in. flat washer when the diameter of the washer rim's outer edge is 5/8 in.?

3.4 FUNCTIONS IMPLEMENTING ADDITIONAL OPERATORS

We have studied how to form simple arithmetic expressions in C using the operations +, −, *, /, and %. However, we do not yet have the ability to write in

C the full range of expressions to which we are accustomed in mathematics. For example, we cannot yet translate these expressions:

$$\sqrt{x} \qquad |q+z| \qquad \left(\frac{h}{12.3}\right)^3$$

C has no operator symbols meaning "square root," "absolute value," or "exponentiation." Instead, C provides program units called *functions* to carry out these and other mathematical operations. Each mathematical function produces a single value that is the result of applying an operator to its operand(s). Figure 3.12 is a diagram of a function that produces a single result.

**Figure 3.12
Function with
Multiple Inputs
and a Single
Output**

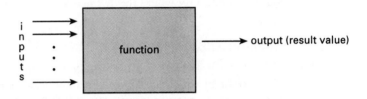

As an example, let's see how we might use a function named `sqrt` that performs the square root computation. This function is available in C's standard math library. If `x` is `16.0`, the assignment statement

```
y = sqrt(x);
```

is evaluated as follows:

1. Because `x` is `16.0`, function `sqrt` computes the $\sqrt{16.0}$ or `4.0`.
2. The function result, `4.0`, is assigned to `y`.

The expression part of the assignment statement is a function call consisting of the function name, `sqrt`, followed by the function *argument*, `x`, enclosed in parentheses. Because the result produced by `sqrt` is considered the value of the function call, the call is not a separate statement but appears wherever its result value would be appropriate.

A function can be thought of as a "black box" that is passed one or more input values (*input arguments*) and then automatically returns a single output value. Figure 3.13 illustrates this sequence for the call to function `sqrt`. The value of `x` (`16.0`) is the function input, and the function result or output is the square root of `16.0` (the result is `4.0`).

**Figure 3.13
Function sqrt as
a "Black Box"**

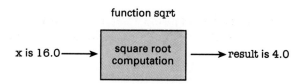

function sqrt

x is 16.0 ——→ square root computation ——→ result is 4.0

Functions are called into execution by writing a function call in an expression. After the function executes, its result is substituted for the function call. If w is 9.0, the assignment statement

```
z = 5.7 + sqrt(w);
```

is evaluated as follows:

1. Because w is 9.0, function sqrt computes the $\sqrt{9.0}$ or 3.0.
2. The values 5.7 and 3.0 are added together.
3. The sum, 8.7, is stored in z.

The two calls to function sqrt discussed so far have different arguments (x and w). We will illustrate this capability of functions again in the next example.

EXAMPLE 3.6 The program in Fig. 3.14 displays the square root of two numbers that are provided as input data (**first** and **second**) and also displays the square root of their sum. To accomplish this, the program must call the math library function sqrt three times:

```
first_sqrt = sqrt(first);
second_sqrt = sqrt(second);
sum_sqrt = sqrt(first + second);
```

Figure 3.14   Square Roots Program

```
/*
 * Performs three square root computations
 */

#include <stdio.h> /* definitions of printf, scanf */
#include <math.h>  /* definition of sqrt */
```

(continued)

Figure 3.14   (continued)

```
int
main(void)
{
        double first, second,     /* input - two data values                 */
               first_sqrt,        /* output - square root of first input value */
               second_sqrt,       /* output - square root of second input     */
               sum_sqrt;          /* output - square root of sum              */

        /* Get first number and display its square root.                      */
        printf("Enter a number> ");
        scanf("%lf", &first);
        first_sqrt = sqrt(first);
        printf("The square root of the number is %.2f\n",
               first_sqrt);

        /* Get second number and display its square root.                     */
        printf("Enter a second number> ");
        scanf("%lf", &second);
        second_sqrt = sqrt(second);
        printf("The square root of the second number is %.2f\n",
               second_sqrt);

        /* Display the square root of the sum of the two numbers.             */
        sum_sqrt = sqrt(first + second);
        printf("The square root of the sum of the two numbers is %.2f\n",
               sum_sqrt);

        return (0);
}
```

```
Enter a number> 9.0
The square root of the number is 3.00
Enter a second number> 16.0
The square root of the second number is 4.00
The square root of the sum of the two numbers is 5.00
```

For the first two calls, the function arguments are variables (`first` and `second`). The third call shows that a function argument may also be an expression (`first + second`). For each of the three calls, the result returned by function `sqrt` is assigned to a variable. Since the definition of the standard sqrt function is found in the standard math library, you will note that the program has an additional #include directive.   ←

Predefined Functions and Code Reuse

A primary goal of software engineering is to write error-free code. *Code reuse—* reusing, whenever possible, program fragments that have already been written and tested—is one way to accomplish this goal. Stated more simply, "Why reinvent the wheel?"

C promotes reuse by providing numerous library functions like sqrt that can be called to perform complicated mathematical computations. Table 3.5 lists the names and descriptions of some of the most commonly used functions along with the name of the file to #include in order to have access to each function. A more extensive list of standard library functions appears in Appendix B.

If one of the functions in Table 3.5 is called with a numeric argument that is not of the argument type listed, this value is converted to the required type before it is used. Conversions of type int to type double cause no problems, but a conversion of type double to type int leads to the loss of any fractional part, just as in a mixed-type assignment. For example, if we call the abs function with the type double value −3.47, the result returned is the type int value 3. This result is the reason the library has a separate absolute value function (fabs) for type double arguments.

Table 3.5 Some Mathematical Library Functions

Function	Library File	Purpose: Example	Argument(s)	Result
abs(x)	<stdlib.h>	Returns the absolute value of its integer argument: if x is −5, abs(x) is 5	int	int
ceil(x)	<math.h>	Returns the smallest whole number that is not less than x: if x is 45.23, ceil(x) is 46.0	double	double
cos(x)	<math.h>	Returns the cosine of angle x: if x is 0.0, cos(x) is 1.0 (radians)	double	double
exp(x)	<math.h>	Returns e^x where $e = 2.71828\ldots$: if x is 1.0, exp(x) is 2.71828	double	double
fabs(x)	<math.h>	Returns the absolute value of its type double argument: if x is −8.432, fabs(x) is 8.432	double	double

(continued)

Table 3.5   (continued)

Function	Library File	Purpose: Example	Argument(s)	Result
floor(x)	<math.h>	Returns the largest whole number that is not greater than x: if x is 45.23, floor(x) is 45.0	double	double
log(x)	<math.h>	Returns the natural logarithm of x for x > 0.0: if x is 2.71828, log(x) is 1.0	double	double
log10(x)	<math.h>	Returns the base-10 logarithm of x for x > 0.0: if x is 100.0, log10(x) is 2.0	double	double
pow(x, y)	<math.h>	Returns x^y. If x is negative, y must be a whole number: if x is 0.16 and y is 0.5, pow(x, y) is 0.4	double, double	double
rand()	<stdlib.h>	Returns a randomly chosen integer between 0 and the value associated with RAND_MAX, a constant macro defined in <stdlib.h>	no arguments	int
sin(x)	<math.h>	Returns the sine of angle x: if x is 1.5708, sin(x) is 1.0	double (radians)	double
sqrt(x)	<math.h>	Returns the nonnegative square root of x ($\sqrt{x}$) for x ≥ 0.0: if x is 2.25, sqrt(x) is 1.5	double	double
tan(x)	<math.h>	Returns the tangent of angle x: if x is 0.0, tan(x) is 0.0	double (radians)	double

Most of the functions in Table 3.5 perform common mathematical computations. The arguments for log and log10 must be positive; the argument for sqrt cannot be negative. The arguments for sin, cos, and tan must be expressed in radians, not in degrees.

EXAMPLE 3.7    We can use the C functions pow (power) and sqrt to compute the roots of a quadratic equation in x of the form

$$ax^2 + bx + c = 0$$

The two roots are defined as

$$root_1 = \frac{-b + \sqrt{b^2 - 4ac}}{2a} \qquad root_2 = \frac{-b - \sqrt{b^2 - 4ac}}{2a}$$

when the *discriminant* ($b^2 - 4ac$) is greater than zero. If we assume that this is the case, we can use these assignment statements to assign values to `root_1` and `root_2`:

```
/* Compute two roots, root_1 and root_2, for disc > 0.0 */
disc = pow(b,2) - 4 * a * c;
root_1 = (-b + sqrt(disc)) / (2 * a);
root_2 = (-b - sqrt(disc)) / (2 * a);
```

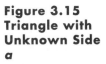 **EXAMPLE 3.8** If we know the lengths of two sides (*b* and *c*) of a triangle and the angle between them in degrees (α), we can compute the length of the third side (*a*) using the following formula (see Fig. 3.15):

$$a^2 = b^2 + c^2 - 2bc \cos \alpha$$

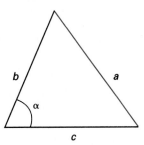

**Figure 3.15
Triangle with
Unknown Side
*a***

To use the math library cosine function (`cos`), we must express its argument angle in radians instead of degrees. To convert an angle from degrees to radians, we multiply the angle by π/180. If we assume `PI` represents the constant π, the C assignment statement that follows computes the unknown side length:

```
a = sqrt(pow(b,2) + pow(c,2)
       - 2 * b * c * cos(alpha * PI / 180.0));
```

**EXERCISES FOR
SECTION 3.4**

Self-Check

1. Rewrite the following mathematical expressions using C functions. Assume all variables should be of type `double`.
   a. $\sqrt{u + v} \times w^2$
   b. $\log_{10}(x^y)$

c. $\sqrt{(x-y)^2}$

d. $\left| xy - \frac{w}{z} \right|$

2. Evaluate the following:
   a. `floor(15.8)`
   b. `floor(15.8 + 0.5)`
   c. `ceil(-7.2) * pow(4.0,2.0)`
   d. `sqrt(floor(fabs(-16.8)))`
   e. `log10(1000.0)`

Programming

1. Write statements that compute and display the absolute difference of two type `double` variables, x and y ($|x - y|$).
2. Write a complete C program that prompts the user for the Cartesian coordinates of two points (x_1, y_1) and (x_2, y_2) and displays the distance between them computed using the following formula:

$$distance = \sqrt{(x_1 - x_2)^2 + (y_1 - y_2)^2}$$

3.5 SIMPLE USER-DEFINED FUNCTIONS

One advantage of using predefined functions such as `scanf` or `sqrt` is that the programmer needs to be concerned only with *what* the function does, not *how* it accomplishes its purpose. To the reader of a program, a simple call to `sqrt` is far easier to follow than the many lines of code needed to implement a square-root-finding algorithm.

In a complex software system, this principle of separating *what* is being done from the tedious details of *how* it is accomplished is an important aspect of managing the complexity of programs. C provides a mechanism for the programmer to define special-purpose functions with the same advantages as C's library functions. In this section, we will study the simplest type of user-defined functions, those that display one or more lines of output. These functions are useful for tasks such as providing instructions to the program user or for displaying copyright information or a title page.

A C function is a grouping of program statements into a single program unit. Just like `scanf` and `sqrt`, each function that we write can be activated through the execution of a function call. Figure 3.16 shows a revision of our square roots program that defines and calls function `instruct` to give instructions to the program user.

Just like other identifiers in C, a function must be declared before it can be referenced in a program body. C provides more than one way to include function declarations in a program. Here we take the simple approach of placing the function definition between the preprocessor directives and the definition of the main function. We will study another method in Chapter 11.

Figure 3.16 Program with a User-Defined Function

```c
/*
 * Performs three square root computations
 */

#include <stdio.h> /* definitions of printf, scanf */
#include <math.h>  /* definition of sqrt */

/*
 * Displays user instructions
 */
void
instruct(void)
{
      printf("This program demonstrates the use of the \n");
      printf("math library function sqrt (square root).\n");
      printf("You will be asked to enter two numbers --\n");
      printf("the program will display the square root of \n");
      printf("each number and the square root of their sum.\n\n");
}

int
main(void)
{
      double first, second,    /* input - two data values              */
             first_sqrt,       /* output - square root of first input value */
             second_sqrt,      /* output - square root of second input  */
             sum_sqrt;         /* output - square root of sum           */

      /* Display instructions.                                          */
      instruct();

      /* Get a number and display its square root.                      */
      printf("Enter a number> ");
```

(continued)

Figure 3.16 (continued)

```
        scanf("%lf", &first);
        first_sqrt = sqrt(first);
        printf("The square root of the number is %.2f\n", first_sqrt);

        /* Get second number and display its square root.              */
        printf("Enter a second number> ");
        scanf("%lf", &second);
        second_sqrt = sqrt(second);
        printf("The square root of the second number is %.2f\n",
               second_sqrt);

        /* Display the square root of the sum of the two numbers.       */
        sum_sqrt = sqrt(first + second);
        printf("The square root of the sum of the two numbers is %.2f\n",
               sum_sqrt);

        return (0);
}

This program demonstrates the use of the
math library function sqrt (square root).
You will be asked to enter two numbers --
the program will display the square root of
each number and the square root of their sum.

Enter a number> 9.0
The square root of the number is 3.00
Enter a second number> 16.0
The square root of the second number is 4.00
The square root of the sum of the two numbers is 5.00
```

The definition of a simple function such as `instruct` is similar to the definition of a main function: It consists of a prototype followed by the function body. We recommend that you place a block comment explaining the purpose of the function immediately before the function's *prototype*. The prototype of `instruct` consists of the keyword `void`, the function name `instruct`, and then the keyword `void` again in parentheses. The function body always starts with { and ends with }. In Fig. 3.16, the function body contains five calls to the function `printf` that display user instructions. The function call

```
instruct();
```

causes the `instruct` function's `printf` statements to execute.

Function Definition

SYNTAX: void
    fname(void)
    {
        executable statements
    }

EXAMPLE: /*
       * Print a block-letter H
      */
     void
     print_h(void)
     {
        printf("** **\n");
        printf("** **\n");
        printf("*****\n");
        printf("** **\n");
        printf("** **\n");
     }

INTERPRETATION: The function *fname* is defined. The *executable statements* of the function body describe the data manipulation to be performed by the function.

Relative Order of Execution of Function Subprograms and Function main

In Fig. 3.16, we placed the definition of the function subprogram `instruct` before the main function so that the C compiler would know about the function subprogram declaration before it translates the main function where the function subprogram is called. As it translates each function subprogram, when the com-

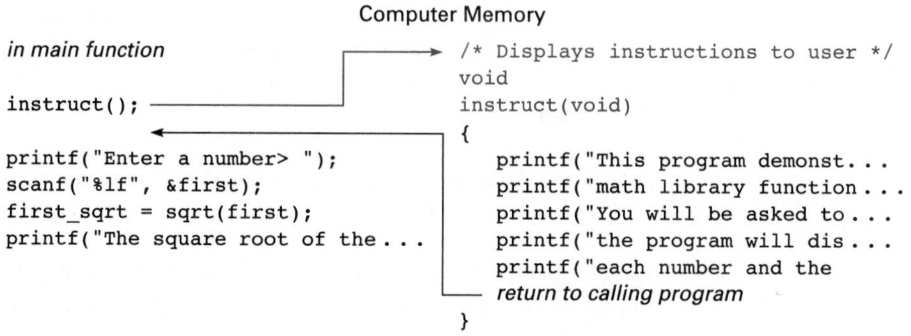

Computer Memory

**Figure 3.17
Flow of Control
Between
Function main
and Function
Subprogram**

```
in main function                    /* Displays instructions to user */
                                    void
instruct();                         instruct(void)
                                    {
printf("Enter a number> ");             printf("This program demonst...
scanf("%lf", &first);                   printf("math library function...
first_sqrt = sqrt(first);               printf("You will be asked to...
printf("The square root of the...       printf("the program will dis...
                                        printf("each number and the
                                        return to calling program

                                    }
```

piler reaches the end of the function body, it inserts a machine language statement that causes a *transfer of control* back from the function to the calling statement. In the main function body, the compiler translates a function call statement
as a transfer of control to the function.

Figure 3.17 shows the main function body and the function `instruct` of
the square roots program in separate areas of memory. Although, for simplicity,
the original C statements are shown in Fig. 3.17, the object code (the machine
language translation) corresponding to each statement is what is actually stored
in memory.

When we run the program, the first statement in the main function body
(the call to `instruct` in Fig. 3.17) is the first statement executed. When the
computer executes a function call statement, it transfers control to the function
that is referenced (the colored arrow). The computer performs the statements in
the function body. After the last statement in the function body is executed, control returns to the main program (the black arrow) and the next statement of
`main` will be executed (the call to `printf`).

EXERCISES FOR SECTION 3.5

Self-Check

1. Assume that you have functions `print_h`, `print_i`, `print_m`, and
   `print_o`, each of which draws a large block letter (for example, `print_o`
   draws a block-letter O). What is the effect of executing the following main
   function?

```
int
main(void)
{
        print_h();
        print_i();
```

```
        printf("\n\n\n");
        print_m();
        print_o();
        print_m();

        return(0);
    }
```

2. Why is it better to place the user instructions in a function rather than to insert the calls to `printf` in the program body itself?

Programming

1. Write a function similar to `instruct` for the flat washer program shown in Fig. 3.11.

3.6 COMMON PROGRAMMING ERRORS

Remember to use a `#include` preprocessor directive for every standard library from which you are using functions. For the time being, place the definitions of your own functions in the source file preceding any calls to these functions and use such functions only to display messages.

Syntax or run-time errors may occur when you use C standard library functions. Make sure that each function argument is the correct type or that conversion to the correct type will lose no information. Also be careful in using functions that are undefined on some range of values. For example, if the argument for function `sqrt`, `log`, or `log10` is negative, a run-time error will occur and the function will return meaningless results.

CHAPTER REVIEW

The first part of this chapter discussed the representation and conversion of the C standard data types `int`, `double`, and `char`. We studied how to form complex arithmetic expressions using the operators +, -, *, /, and %. We also examined how C uses standard library functions to provide additional arithmetic operations.

This chapter presented the use of pseudocode, a structured combination of C and English, for describing the steps of an algorithm. We showed how to use our solution to one problem as part of the solution for another problem. We also studied how to define and call our own functions for displaying messages. The new C constructs introduced in this chapter are described in Table 3.6.

Table 3.6   Summary of New C Constructs

Function Definition

```
void
display(void)
{
      printf("*\n*\n*\n*\n*\n");
}
```

Function `display` is defined and may be called to print a vertical line of five asterisks.

Function Call Statement (No Arguments)

```
display();
```

Calls function `display` and causes it to begin execution.

Function Call (with Arguments)

```
sqrt(x + y)
```

Calls function `sqrt` to compute the square root of expression `x + y` ($\sqrt{x + y}$).

QUICK-CHECK EXERCISES

1. If a is 4, b is 3.8, and c is 2, what is the value of this expression?

   `(int)b + a * c`

2. How would you write this expression in C? Assume all variables are of type double and are named with single letters.

$$\frac{\sqrt{a} + 5}{cd - |e|}$$

3. Assume that n and d represent positive integers. Write a more concise expression that is equivalent to

   `n - n / d * d`

4. How is a function executed in a program?
5. What is the purpose of a function's input arguments?
6. Write this equation as a C statement:

$$y = (e^{\,a \ln b})^2$$

7. What does the following function do?

```
void
nonsense(void)
{
        printf("*****\n");
        printf("*    *\n");
        printf("*****\n");
}
```

8. What does the following main function do?

```
int
main(void)
{
        nonsense();
        nonsense();
        nonsense();

        return (0);
}
```

ANSWERS TO QUICK-CHECK EXERCISES

1. 11
2. (sqrt(a) + 5) / (c * d - fabs(e))
3. n % d
4. It is called into execution by a function call, that is, the function name followed by its arguments in parentheses.
5. A function's input arguments take information into a function.
6. y = pow(exp(a * log(b)),2);
7. It displays a rectangle of asterisks.
8. It displays three rectangles of asterisks on top of one another.

REVIEW QUESTIONS

1. An explicit conversion from one data type to another is called a(n) _____ .
2. What are three advantages of using functions?
3. When is a function executed, and where should a user-defined function appear in the program source file?
4. Write a program that prompts the user for the lengths of two legs of a right triangle and makes use of the `pow` and `sqrt` functions to compute the length of the hypotenuse using the Pythagorean theorem. Include a function that gives instructions to the user.
5. Write a program that draws a rectangle made of a double border of asterisks. Use two functions: `draw_sides` and `draw_line`.
6. What are the advantages of data type `int` over data type `double`? What are the advantages of type `double` over type `int`?
7. List and explain three computational errors that may occur in type `double` expressions.

PROGRAMMING PROJECTS

1. Write functions that display each of your initials in block-letter form. Use these functions to display your initials.
2. Write a computer program that computes the duration of a projectile's flight and its height above ground when it reaches the target. As part of your solution, write and call a function that displays instructions to the program user.

   Problem Constant
   ```
   G 32.17 /* gravitational constant              */
   ```

   Problem Inputs
   ```
   double theta /* input - angle (radians) of elevation  */
   double distance /* input - distance (ft) to target */
   double velocity /* input - projectile velocity
                              (ft/sec)                    */
   ```

   Problem Outputs
   ```
   double time    /* output - time (sec) of flight    */
   double height  /* output - height at impact        */
   ```

Relevant Formulas

$$time = \frac{distance}{velocity \times cos\,(theta)}$$

$$height = velocity \times sin(theta) \times time - \frac{g \times time^2}{2}$$

Try your program on these data sets.

Inputs	Data Set 1	Data Set 2
Angle of elevation	0.3 radian	0.71 radian
Velocity	800 ft/sec	1,600 ft/sec
Distance to target	11,000 ft	78,670 ft

3. Write a program that computes the speed of sound (a) in air of a given temperature T (°F). Use the formula

$$a = 1086\ ft/s \sqrt{\frac{5T + 2297}{2457}}$$

Caution: Be sure your program does not lose the fractional part of the quotient in the formula shown. Write and call a function that displays instructions to the user.

4. Write a program that takes a positive number with a fractional part and rounds it to two decimal places. For example, 32.4851 would round to 32.49, and 32.4431 would round to 32.44. (Hint: See Problem 2b in the Self-Check Exercises for Section 3.4.)

5. Four track stars entered the mile race at the Penn Relays. Write a program that will take the race time in minutes and seconds for a runner, and compute and print the speed in feet per second (fps) and in meters per second (mps). (Hint: One mile equals 5280 feet and one kilometer equals 3282 feet.) Test your program on each of the following times:

Minutes	Seconds
3	52.83
3	59.83
4	00.03
4	16.22

Write and call a function that displays instructions to the program user.

6. A cyclist coasting on a level road slows from a speed of 10 mi/hr to 2.5 mi/hr in one minute. Write a computer program that calculates the cyclist's constant rate of acceleration and determines how long the cyclist will take to come to rest, given an initial speed of 10 mi/hr. (Hint: Use the equation

$$a = \frac{v_f - v_i}{t}$$

where a is acceleration, t is time interval, v_i is initial velocity, and v_f is the final velocity.) Write and call a function that displays instructions to the program user.

7. An electron moving freely in a magnetic field emits electromagnetic radiation. Physicists and engineers can measure this radiation and can then infer information about the electron. From physics, we know that

$$frequency = \frac{speed\ of\ light}{wavelength}$$

where the speed of light is 3.0E8 meters/second. It is also true that

$$energy = h \times frequency$$

where h is Planck's constant, equal to 6.63E-34 joule-seconds. Write a program that takes wavelength observed in meters as input and displays the frequency of the radiation generated by the electron, in hertz, and the energy of a photon emitted by the electron, in joules. Use variables of type `double` for all data, and try out your program for wavelengths in the range 10E-10 . . . 10E-3. Use `%e` `printf` placeholders to display your results in scientific notation. Define and call a function that describes the program's purpose to the user.

8. A manufacturer wishes to determine the cost of producing an open-top-cylindrical container. The surface area of the container is the sum of the area of the circular base plus the area of the outside (the circumference of the base times the height of the container). Write a program to take the radius of the base, the height of the container, the cost per square centimeter of the material (cost), and the number of containers to be produced (quantity). Calculate the cost of each container and the total cost of producing all the containers. Write and call a function that displays instructions to the user.

CHAPTER 4

SELECTION STRUCTURES: if AND switch STATEMENTS

This chapter shows how to represent decisions in algorithms by writing steps with two or more alternative courses of action. You will see how to implement conditional execution in C by using logical expressions and the C if and switch statements. We continue our study of problem solving and we show how to hand-trace or desk-check the execution of an algorithm or program to ensure that it does what we expect.

4.1 LOGICAL EXPRESSIONS AND THE if STATEMENT

In all the algorithms illustrated in previous chapters, we executed each algorithm step exactly once in the order in which it appeared. Often, we are faced with situations in which we must provide alternative steps that may or may not be executed, depending on the input data. For example, one indicator of the health of a person's heart is the resting heart rate. If this rate is 56 beats per minute or less, the heart is in excellent health. A resting heart rate between 57 and 65 beats per minute is evidence of good health, and a resting rate between 66 and 75 is average. Higher resting heart rates are a warning that the heart's condition is probably below average. A program that evaluates a person's health must be able to draw the correct conclusion from an input of the resting heart rate.

To accomplish this goal, a program must be able to determine whether the right answer to the question "Is resting heart rate more than 56 beats per minute?" is yes or no. In C, this goal is accomplished by evaluating a logical expression. Assume that the resting heart rate is stored in the type int variable rst_hrt_rate; then the logical expression corresponding to this question is

```
rst_hrt_rate > 56
```

There are only two possible values for a C expression that uses a relational or equality operator: 0 stands for false; 1 means true. If rst_hrt_rate is greater than 56, the preceding expression evaluates to 1 (true); if rst_hrt_rate is not greater than 56, the expression evaluates to 0 (false).

Most logical expressions or *conditions* that we use will have one of the following forms:

variable	*relational operator*	*variable*
variable	*relational operator*	*constant*
variable	*equality operator*	*variable*
variable	*equality operator*	*constant*

Relational operators are the familiar symbols < (less than), <= (less than or equal to), > (greater than), and >= (greater than or equal to). The *equality operators* are == (equal to) and ! = (not equal to). Take careful note of the difference between the "equal to" symbol == and the assignment operator =. These symbols are easy to confuse because we are accustomed to using = to mean "equal to" in mathematics. Unfortunately, the syntax rules of C permit the use of the assignment operator in most contexts where the "equal to" operator is legal, so the compiler often cannot recognize the substitution of an assignment operator for an equality operator as an error. Therefore a program containing such a mistake will frequently run to completion, but it will produce incorrect results.

**EXAMPLE 4.1**

Table 4.1 shows the relational and equality operators and some sample conditions. Each condition is evaluated assuming these variable values and constant macro meanings.

x	power	MAX_POW	y	item	MIN_ITEM	mom_or_dad	num	SENTINEL
−5	1024	1024	7	1.5	−999.0	'M'	999	999

Table 4.1   C Relational and Equality Operators and Sample Conditions

Operator	Condition	English Meaning	Value
<=	x <= 0	x less than or equal to 0	1 (true)
<	power < MAX_POW	power less than MAX_POW	0 (false)
>=	x >= y	x greater than or equal to y	0 (false)
>	item > MIN_ITEM	item greater than MIN_ITEM	1 (true)
==	mom_or_dad == 'M'	mom_or_dad equal to 'M'	1 (true)
!=	num != SENTINEL	num not equal to SENTINEL	0 (false)

The if Statement

We now know how to write in C an expression that is the equivalent of a question such as "Is resting heart rate more than 56 beats per minute?" Next, we need to investigate a way to use the value of the expression to select a course of action. The if statement

```
if (rst_hrt_rate > 56)
      printf("Keep up your exercise program!\n");
else
      printf("Your heart is in excellent health!\n");
```

selects one of the two calls to `printf`. It selects the statement following the parenthesized condition if the condition evaluates to 1 representing true (i.e., `rst_hrt_rate` is greater than 56), and it selects the statement following the keyword `else` if the condition evaluates to 0 representing false.

The condition in this particular `if` statement always evaluates to 1 or 0 because of the way the relational operators are defined. However, C does not require the logical value true to be represented by the integer 1; instead, C always uses the integer 0 to represent the value false and accepts *any nonzero value* as a representation of true. For now, we will always use the integer 1 when we need the value true, but knowing how C really views conditions will help you understand why some common mistakes that you may make will not be seen by the C compiler as syntax errors.

Figure 4.1 is a graphical description, called a *flowchart,* of the `if` statement just given. This figure shows that the condition enclosed in the diamond-shaped box (`rst_hrt_rate > 56`) is evaluated first. If the condition is true (that is, has a nonzero value), the arrow labeled *true* is followed, and the output on the right is executed. If the condition is false, the arrow labeled *false* is followed, and the output on the left is executed.

More if Statement Examples

The `if` statement shown in Fig. 4.1 has two alternatives, but only one alternative will be executed for a given value of `rst_hrt_rate`. Example 4.2 illustrates that an `if` statement can also have a single alternative executed only when the condition is true.

**Figure 4.1
Flowchart of
if Statement
with Two
Alternatives**

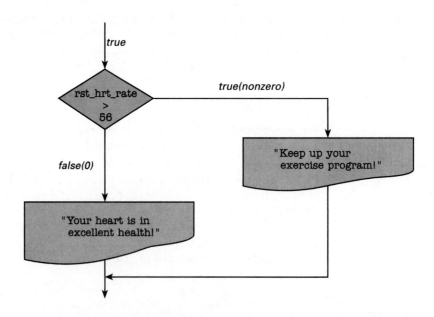

**Figure 4.2
Flowchart of if
Statement with
One Alternative**

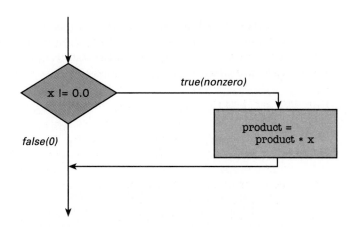

EXAMPLE 4.2 The following if statement has a single alternative that is executed only when x is not equal to zero. This alternative causes product to be multiplied by x; the new value is saved in product, replacing the old value. If x is equal to zero, the multiplication is not performed. Figure 4.2 is a flowchart of this if statement.

```
/* Multiply product by a nonzero x only */
if (x != 0.0)
        product = product * x;
```

The assignment statement in the rectangle on the right is carried out only if x is not zero.   ◄

EXAMPLE 4.3 The if statement below has two alternatives. It displays either Cruiser or Frigate, depending on the character stored in the type char variable crsr_or_frgt.

```
if (crsr_or_frgt == 'C')
        printf("Cruiser\n");
else
        printf("Frigate\n");
```
◄

EXAMPLE 4.4 The following if statement has one alternative; it displays the message Cruiser only when crsr_or_frgt has the value 'C'. Regardless of whether Cruiser is displayed, the message Combatant ship is always displayed.

```
if (crsr_or_frgt == 'C')
        printf("Cruiser\n");
printf("Combatant ship\n");
```

The program fragments that follow contain incorrect versions of this single-alternative `if` statement. The error in the first fragment, missing parentheses around the condition, violates C syntax rules and will be detected and possibly corrected by the compiler.

```
if crsr_or_frgt == 'C' /* error - missing
                               parentheses */
      printf("Cruiser\n");
printf("Combatant ship\n");
```

The extra semicolon in the fragment below does not cause a violation of C syntax rules because the compiler translates the first line as a single-alternative `if` statement in which there is no action to perform on the true branch (i.e., an *empty statement* follows the condition). The first `printf` loses its dependency on the value of the condition; so both calls to `printf` are executed unconditionally.

```
if (crsr_or_frgt == 'C'); /* mistake - improper
                                placement of ; */
      printf("Cruiser\n");
printf("Combatant ship\n");
```

Syntax Displays for if Statement

The following display summarizes the forms of the `if` statement we have used so far. Section 4.3 considers the use of `if` statements when multiple tasks are to be performed on either the true branch or the false branch.

---

if Statement (One Alternative)

SYNTAX: if (*condition*)
                  statement$_T$

EXAMPLE: if (x > 0.0)
                  pos_prod = pos_prod * x;

INTERPRETATION: If the *condition* evaluates to true, then *statement*$_T$ is executed; otherwise, it is skipped.

(continued)

---

if Statement (Two Alternatives)

SYNTAX: if *(condition)*
               statement$_T$
         else
               statement$_F$

EXAMPLE: if (x >= 0.0)
               printf("Positive");
         else
               printf("Negative");

INTERPRETATION: If the *condition* evaluates to true, then *statement*$_T$ is executed and *statement*$_F$ is skipped; otherwise, *statement*$_T$ is skipped and *statement*$_F$ is executed.

EXERCISES FOR SECTION 4.1

Self-Check

1. What do the following statements display?
   a. if (12 < 12)
            printf("Never\n");
      else
            printf("Always\n");
   b. var1 = 15.0;
      var2 = 25.12;
      if (var2 <= 2 * var1)
            printf("O.K.\n");
      else
            printf("Not O.K.\n");
2. What value is assigned to x for each of the following segments when y is 15.0?
   a. x = 25.0;
      if (y != (x - 10.0))
            x = x - 10.0;
      else
            x = x / 2.0;
   b. if (y < 15.0)
            if (y >= 0.0)
                  x = 5 * y;
            else
                  x = 2 * y;
      else
            x = 3 * y;

3. What value is assigned to the type int variable ans in this statement if the value of p is 100 and q is 50?

```
ans = (p > 95) + (q < 95);
```

This statement is not shown as an example of a reasonable assignment statement; rather, it is a sample of a statement that makes little sense to the reader. The statement is still legal and executable in C, however, because of the language's use of integers to represent the logical values true and false.

Programming

1. Write C statements to carry out the following steps:
   a. If item is nonzero, then multiply product by item and save the result in product; otherwise, skip the multiplication. In either case, display the value of product.
   b. Store the absolute difference of x and y in z, where the absolute difference is (x − y) or (y − x), whichever is positive. Do not use the abs or fabs functions in your solution.
   c. If x is zero, add 1 to zero_count. If x is negative, add x to minus_sum. If x is greater than zero, add x to plus_sum.

4.2 MORE LOGICAL EXPRESSIONS AND THE OPERATORS &&, ||, AND !

We have just studied logical expressions that use relational and equality operators (<, <=, >, >=, ==, !=). Actually, the simplest form of logical expression is a single type int value or variable intended to represent the value true or false. In the following code fragment, such a variable is used to represent the concept of whether or not a person's age places him or her in the category of senior citizen:

```
int senior_citizen;
. . .
senior_citizen = age >= 65;
```

A variable such as senior_citizen is a perfectly legitimate condition to use in a decision. Consider this example:

```
if (senior_citizen)
        printf("Send senior discount brochure.\n");
```

If we assume that the identifier TRUE has been defined to mean 1, then any one of the following assignment statements results in the variable senior_citizen having the value 1, meaning true.

```
senior_citizen = 1;
senior_citizen = TRUE;
senior_citizen = 66 >= 65;
```

The fact that C relational and equality operators give a result of 1 for true and 0 for false means that C interprets some common mathematical expressions in a way that seems surprising at first. The casual reader of the following statement would probably not anticipate the fact that Condition is true will be printed for all nonnegative values of x:

```
if (0 <= x <= 4)
      printf("Condition is true\n");
```

For example, let's consider the case when x is 5. The value of 0 <= 5 is 1, and 1 is certainly less than or equal to 4! To check whether x is in the range 0 to 4, we need to be able to combine the expressions 0 <= x and x <= 4 in a single logical expression whose value is true only when both subexpressions are true. To combine the results of logical expressions, we use C's logical operators && (read "and"), || (read "or"), and ! (read "not"). Some logical expressions formed using these operators are

```
0 <= x && x <= 4
salary < min_sal || num_depend > 5
temp > 90.0 && humidity > 0.90
winning_record && !probation
0 <= n && n <= 100
```

The first logical expression is a valid way of checking whether x is in the range 0 to 4. The second logical expression determines whether an employee is eligible for special scholarship funds. The expression evaluates to true if *either* the expression

```
salary < min_sal
```

or the expression

```
num_depend > 5
```

is true. The third logical expression describes an unbearable summer day with both temperature and humidity in the nineties. The expression evaluates to true only when *both* conditions are true. The fourth expression manipulates two type int variables that represent logical concepts (winning_record, probation). A college team for which this expression is true may be eligible for a postseason tournament. The final expression is true if n is between 0 and 100 inclusive.

The logical operators that are used to form complex logical expressions are described in Tables 4.2, 4.3, and 4.4. Table 4.2 shows that the && operator yields a true result of 1 only when both its operands are true (nonzero); Table 4.3 shows that the || operator yields a false result of zero only when both its operands are false (zero). The && operator requires that *both* operands evaluate to true in order to produce a result of 1; therefore if the first operand is zero, evaluating the second operand is not really necessary in order to know the result. In this case, C evaluates only the first (leftmost) operand. Similarly, since the || operator requires both operands to be zero to produce a result of

Table 4.2   && Operator

operand1	operand2	operand1 && operand2 (read *operand1* and *operand2*)
nonzero	nonzero	1
nonzero	0	0
0	nonzero	0
0	0	0

Table 4.3 || Operator

operand1	operand2	operand1 || operand2 (read *operand1* or *operand2*)
nonzero	nonzero	1
nonzero	0	1
0	nonzero	1
0	0	0

Table 4.4   ! Operator

operand1	!operand1 (read not *operand1*)
nonzero	0
0	1

Table 4.5 Precedence of Operations

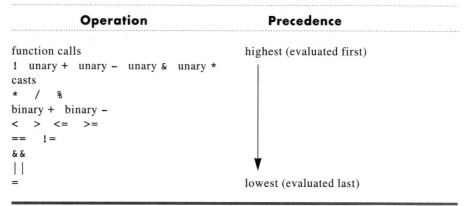

Operation	Precedence
function calls	highest (evaluated first)
! unary + unary − unary & unary *	
casts	
* / %	
binary + binary −	
< > <= >=	
== !=	
&&	
| |	
=	lowest (evaluated last)

zero, the value of the second operand is not needed and is not computed if the value of the first operand is nonzero. This evaluation of only as much of the logical expression as is needed to determine its value is called *short-circuit evaluation*.

The ! operator has a single operand. Table 4.4 shows that the ! operator yields the *logical complement,* or *negation,* of its operand—that is, if `shift` is true, `!shift` is false and vice versa.

The precedence of an operator determines its order of evaluation. Table 4.5 shows the precedence of all the C operations we have seen to this point.

As you can see, function calls have the highest precedence. They are followed by the unary arithmetic and logical operators, along with the address-of and indirection operators. Next are the cast operations for explicit type conversions; casts are also unary operations. The binary arithmetic operations follow with the multiplicative operators *, /, and %, one level higher in precedence than the additive operators + and −. After the binary arithmetic operations are the comparison operators, with relational operators applied before equality operators. The binary logical operators && (and) and | | (or) have quite low precedence, with && having the higher precedence of the two. The lowest precedence operator we have studied is the assignment operator. The precedence shown can always be overridden by use of parentheses, which can often make a complex expression more readable even when they do not change the order of evaluation.

Figure 4.3 shows a step-by-step evaluation for an expression that illustrates the application of several aspects of the precedence rules. Operations at six different precedence levels are shown. At the highest level, we see a call to the library function `ceil`. At level 2, we apply the conversion to type `int` due to a cast. At level 3, we evaluate the expression with the integer remainder operator %, and at 4, the addition operation. At level 5, the relational operator > is applied; the last operation is the assignment to `ans`.

Figure 4.3   Step-by-Step Evaluation of Expression with Operations of Many Precedence Levels

```
ans = 2 + (int)ceil(80.2) % 9 > 10          level
                  81.0                         1
             81                                2
                                 0             3
         2                                     4
                             0                 5
     0                                         6
```

Testing for a Range of Values

Expressions similar to the following are common in programming:

```
min_x <= x && x <= max_x
```

If `min_x` represents the lower bound of a range of values, and `max_x` represents the upper bound (`min_x` is less than `max_x`), this expression tests whether `x` lies within the range `min_x` through `max_x` inclusive. In Fig. 4.4, this range of values is shaded. The expression is true if `x` lies within this range and false if `x` is outside this range.

Figure 4.4 Range of True Values for `min_x <= x && x <= max_x`

min_x   max_x   x

More Logical Expressions

EXAMPLE 4.5

If `x`, `y`, and `z` are type `double` and `flag` is type `int`, all the following expressions are legal. The value of each expression, shown in brackets, assumes that `x` is `3.0`, `y` is `4.0`, `z` is `2.0`, and `flag` is `0`.

Expression	Value
1. x > z && y > z	[1]
2. x + y / z <= 3.5	[0]
3. z > x || z > y	[0]
4. !flag	[1]
5. x == 1.0 || x == 3.0	[1]
6. z < x && x < y	[1]
7. x <= z || x >= y	[0]
8. !flag || y + z >= x - z	[1]
9. !(flag || y + z >= x - z)	[0]

Expression 1 gives the C form of the relationship "x and y are greater than z." It is often tempting to write this expression as

x && y > z

However, if we apply the operator precedence rules to this expression, we quickly see that it does not have the intended meaning. Moreover, the type double variable x is an invalid operand for the logical operator &&. Expression 5 shows the correct way to express the relationship "x is equal to 1.0 or to 3.0."

Expression 6 is the C form of the relationship z < x < y (that is, "x is in the range 2.0 to 4.0"). The boundary values, 2.0 and 4.0, are excluded from the range of x values that yield a true result. Expression 7 is true if the value of x lies outside the range bounded by z and y.

In Fig. 4.5, the shaded areas represent the values of x that yield a true result. Both y and z are included in the set that yields a true result.

To verify the results, you may want to do step-by-step evaluations of Expressions 8 and 9 in a way similar to that shown in Fig. 4.3.

**Figure 4.5
Range of True
Values for** x <=
z || x >= y

Logical Assignment

At the beginning of this section, we saw how type int variables can be assigned the results of expressions representing logical concepts. Let's consider some additional examples of this type of assignment statement.

EXAMPLE 4.6

The assignment statements that follow assign values to two type int variables representing logical ideas, in_range and is_letter. Variable in_range gets the value 1 (for true) if n satisfies both of the conditions listed (n is greater than –10 and less than 10); otherwise, the expression's value is 0 for false. The expression in the second assignment statement uses the logical operators && and ||. The subexpression before the || is true if the value of ch is an uppercase letter; the subexpression after the || is true if ch is a lowercase letter. Consequently, the value assigned to is_letter represents true if ch is a letter (assuming consecutive character codes); otherwise, the value assigned represents false. The parentheses in this expression do not affect the order of evaluation; they are included for clarity.

```
in_range = n > -10 && n < 10;
is_letter = ('A' <= ch && ch <= 'Z') ||
            ('a' <= ch && ch <= 'z');
```

EXAMPLE 4.7

Either of the following assignment statements assigns a value meaning true to variable even if n is an even number.

```
even = n % 2 == 0;    even = !(n % 2 == 1);
```

The statement on the left assigns a value of 1 to even when the remainder of n divided by 2 is zero. (All even numbers are divisible by 2.) In the statement on the right, the expression in parentheses (n % 2 == 1) evaluates to true if n is an odd number—that is, if the remainder of n divided by 2 is 1. Applying the ! (not) operator to this expression yields the negation of "n is odd"—that is, n is even.

EXERCISES FOR SECTION 4.2

Self-Check

1. Assuming x is 15.0 and y is 25.0, what are the values of the following conditions?

```
x != y
x < x
x >= y - x
x == y + x - y
```

2. Evaluate each of the following expressions if a is 5, b is 10, c is 15, and flag is 1. Which parts of these expressions are not computed at all due to short-circuit evaluation?
   a. c == a + b || !flag
   b. a != 7 && flag || c >= 6
   c. !(b <= 12) && a % 2 == 0
   d. !(a > 5 || c < a + b)
3. Show step-by-step evaluations of Expressions 8 and 9 in Example 4.5.

4.3 if STATEMENTS WITH COMPOUND TASKS

In the if statements we have seen so far, the *statement* following the condition or the keyword else has always been a single executable statement such as an assignment statement or a function call statement. If multiple tasks are to be performed dependent on a condition, they can be grouped together within braces to form a single compound statement. Another if statement, whether a single- or double-alternative if, is also considered a single statement. The next three examples use if with compound statements following the condition or the else.

EXAMPLE 4.8 ▶ Suppose you are a biologist writing a program to report statistics about the growth rate of a fruit fly population. You could use the if statement that follows to compute the percentage of population increase over a one-day period, if there was, in fact, some growth. The statement first determines the amount of growth by subtracting today's population (pop_today) from yesterday's population (pop_ystday). It then computes what percentage of the original (yesterday's) population this growth represents. The compound statement is not executed when today's population is no larger than yesterday's.

```
if (pop_today > pop_ystday) {
    growth = pop_today - pop_ystday;
    gth_pct = 100.0 * growth / pop_ystday;
}
```

EXAMPLE 4.9 ▶ In later chapters, we will see that it is useful to be able to order a pair of data values in memory so that the smaller value is stored in one variable (for example, x) and the larger value in another (for example, y). The if statement in Fig. 4.6 rearranges any two values stored in x and y so that the smaller number will

Figure 4.6   if Statement to Order x and y

```
if (x > y) {
      temp = x;          /* Store old x in temp     */
      x = y;             /* Store old y in x        */
      y = temp;          /* Store old x in y        */
}
```

always be in x and the larger number will always be in y. If the two numbers are already in the proper order, the compound statement will not be executed.

The variables x, y, and temp should all be the same data type. Although the values of x and y are being switched, an additional variable, temp, is needed for storage of a copy of one of these values.

Table 4.6 is a step-by-step simulation of the execution of the if statement when x is 12.5 and y is 5.0. The table shows that temp is initially undefined (indicated by ?). Each line of the table shows the part of the if statement that is being executed, followed by its effect. If any variable gets a new value, the new value is shown on that line. The last value stored in x is 5.0, and the last value stored in y is 12.5 as desired.

Table 4.6   Step-by-Step Simulation of if Statement

Statement Part	x	y	temp	Effect
	12.5	5.0	?	
if (x > y){				12.5 > 5.0 — true
temp = x;			12.5	Store old x in temp
x = y;	5.0			Store old y in x
y = temp;		12.5		Store old x in y
}				

EXAMPLE 4.10   As manager of a company's automobile fleet, you may want to keep records of the safety ratings of the fleet cars. In the if statement that follows, the true task makes a record of an automobile (auto_id) whose crash test rating index (ctri) is at least as low (good) as the cutoff you have established for acceptably safe cars (MAX_SAFE_CTRI). The false task records an auto whose ctri does not meet your standard. In either case, an appropriate message is printed, and one is added to the count of safe or unsafe cars. Both the true and false statements are compound statements.

```
if (ctri <= MAX_SAFE_CTRI) {
      printf("Car #%d: safe\n", auto_id);
      safe = safe + 1;
} else {
      printf("Car #%d: unsafe\n", auto_id);
      unsafe = unsafe + 1;
}
```

If the braces enclosing the compound statements were omitted, the first `printf` call would end the `if` statement. The increment of **safe** would be translated as an unconditionally executed statement, and the compiler would mark the keyword **else** as an error, since a statement cannot begin with **else**. ◄

Program Style   *Format of the if Statement*

In all our **if** statement examples, the true and false tasks are indented. For double-alternative **if** statements, we place the **else** keyword (not indented) on a separate line. The purpose of the indentation is to increase *our* ability to read and understand an **if** statement; the C compiler ignores indentation.

When the true or false task of an **if** is a compound statement, the placement of the braces is a matter of personal preference. The style we use in our examples is one that is prevalent in major segments of the computer industry. We recommend using braces on both the true and the false tasks if *either* is a compound statement. Some C programmers prefer to always use the braces in **if** statements, even when only single-statement tasks are involved. This way, all of the **if** statements in the program have a consistent style. The most important aspect of style standards is the adoption of the *same* set of standards by all programmers working together so that they can easily read one another's code.

EXERCISES FOR SECTION 4.3

Self-Check

1. Insert braces where they are needed so the meaning matches the indentation.

```
if (x > y)
      x = x + 10.0;
      printf("x Bigger\n");
else
      printf("x Smaller\n");
      printf("y is %.2f\n", y);
```

2. Correct the following `if` statement; assume the indentation is correct:

```
if (num1 < 0);
      product = num1 * num2 * num3;
      printf("Product is %d\n", product);
else;
      sum = num1 + num2 + num3;
      printf("Sum is %d\n", sum);
printf("Data: %d, %d, %d\n", num1, num2, num3);
```

3. Revise the style of the following `if` statement to improve its readability:

```
if (engine_type == 'J') {printf("Jet engine");
speed_category = 1;}
else{printf("Propellers"); speed_category
= 2;}
```

Programming

1. Write an `if` statement that might be used to compute and print the average of a set of *n* numbers whose sum is stored in variable `total`. This average should be found only if *n* is greater than 0; otherwise, an error message should be displayed.
2. Write an interactive program that contains a compound `if` statement and that may be used to compute the area of a square (*area = side^2*) or a triangle (*area = 1/2 × base × height*) after prompting the user to type the first character of the figure name (S or T).

4.4 NESTED if STATEMENTS AND MULTIPLE-ALTERNATIVE DECISIONS

Until now, we used `if` statements to implement decisions involving up to two alternatives. In this section, we will see how the `if` statement can be used to implement decisions involving more than two alternatives.

A nested `if` statement occurs when the true or false statement of an `if` statement is itself an `if` statement. A nested `if` statement can be used to implement decisions with several alternatives, as shown in the next examples.

EXAMPLE 4.11 The nested `if` statement that follows has three alternatives. The statement causes one of three variables (`num_pos`, `num_neg`, or `num_zero`) to be increased by one depending on whether **x** is greater than zero, less than zero, or equal to zero, respectively.

```
/* increment num_pos, num_neg, or num_zero depending on x */
if (x > 0)
      num_pos = num_pos + 1;
else
      if (x < 0)
            num_neg = num_neg + 1;
      else /* x equals 0 */
            num_zero = num_zero + 1;
```

The execution of this **if** statement proceeds as follows: The first condition **(x > 0)** is tested; if it is true, **num_pos** is incremented and the rest of the **if** statement is skipped. If the first condition is false, the second condition **(x < 0)** is tested; if it is true, **num_neg** is incremented; otherwise, **num_zero** is incremented. It is important to realize that the second condition is tested only when the first condition is false.

Figure 4.7 is a flowchart of the execution of this **if** statement. This diagram shows that one (and only one) of the statements in rectangular boxes will be executed. Table 4.7 traces the execution of this statement when **x** is −7.

**Figure 4.7
Flowchart of
Nested if
Statement in
Example 4.11**

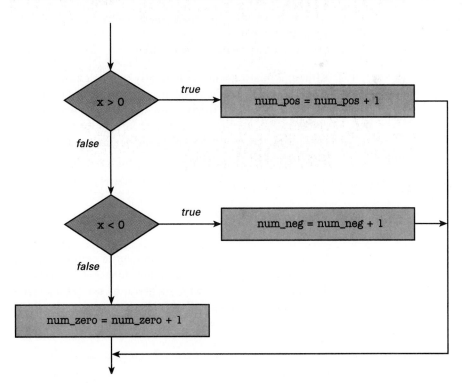

Table 4.7   Trace of if Statement in Example 4.11 for x = –7

Statement Part	Effect
`if (x > 0)`	–7 > 0: false
`else if (x < 0)`	–7 < 0: true
`    num_neg = num_neg + 1;`	Add 1 to num_neg

Program Style   *Nested if Statements Versus a Sequence of if Statements*

Beginning programmers sometimes prefer to use a sequence of `if` statements rather than a single nested `if` statement. For example, the nested `if` statement in Example 4.11 can be rewritten as a sequence of `if` statements:

```
if (x > 0)
    num_pos = num_pos + 1;
if (x < 0)
    num_neg = num_neg + 1;
if (x == 0)
    num_zero = num_zero + 1;
```

Although this sequence is logically equivalent to the original, it is not nearly as readable or as efficient as the original. Unlike the nested `if` statement, the sequence does not clearly show that exactly one of the three assignment statements is executed for a particular **x**. It is less efficient because all three of the conditions are always tested. In the nested `if` statement, only the first condition is tested when **x** is positive.

Writing a Nested if as a Multiple-Alternative Decision

Nested `if` statements may become quite complex. If there are more than three alternatives and indentation is not done consistently, one may have difficulty determining the `if` to which a given `else` belongs (in C, typically the closest `if` without an `else`). We find it easier to write the nested `if` statement in Example 4.11 as the *multiple-alternative decision* described in the next syntax display.

Multiple-Alternative Decision

SYNTAX:
```
if (condition₁)
        statement₁
else if (condition₂)
        statement₂
        •
        •
        •
else if (conditionₙ)
        statementₙ
else
        statementₑ
```

EXAMPLE:
```
/* increment num_pos, num_neg, or num_zero depending
   on x */
if (x > 0)
        num_pos = num_pos + 1;
else if (x < 0)
        num_neg = num_neg + 1;
else /* x equals 0 */
        num_zero = num_zero + 1;
```

INTERPRETATION: The conditions in a multiple-alternative decision are evaluated in sequence until a true condition is reached. If a condition is true, the statement following it is executed, and the rest of the multiple-alternative decision is skipped. If a condition is false, the statement following it is skipped, and the next condition is tested. If all conditions are false, then *statement*ₑ following the final **else** is executed.

NOTES: In a multiple-alternative decision, the word **else** and the next condition appear on the same line. All the words **else** align, and each dependent *statement* is indented under the condition that controls its execution.

Order of Conditions

Very often the conditions in a multiple-alternative decision are not *mutually exclusive*; in other words, more than one condition may be true for a given data value. If this is the case, then the order of the conditions becomes very important because only the statement sequence following the first true condition is executed.

EXAMPLE 4.12   Suppose you want to associate noise loudness measured in decibels with the effect of the noise. The following table shows the relationship between noise levels and human perceptions of noises.

Loudness in Decibels (db)	Perception
50 or lower	quiet
51–70	intrusive
71–90	annoying
91–110	very annoying
above 110	uncomfortable

The multiple-alternative decision below displays the perception of noise according to this table. If the noise were measured at 62 decibels, the last three conditions would be true if evaluated; however, the perception 62-decibel noise is intrusive. would be displayed because the first true condition is noise_db <= 70.

```
/* Display perception of noise loudness */

if (noise_db <= 50)
    printf("%d-decibel noise is quiet.\n", noise_db);
else if (noise_db <= 70)
    printf("%d-decibel noise is intrusive.\n",
            noise_db);
else if (noise_db <= 90)
    printf("%d-decibel noise is annoying.\n",
            noise_db);
else if (noise_db <= 110)
    printf("%d-decibel noise is very annoying.\n",
            noise_db);
else
    printf("%d-decibel noise is uncomfortable.\n",
            noise_db);
```

The order of conditions can also have an effect on program efficiency. If we know that loud noises are much more likely than soft ones, it would be more efficient to test first for noise levels above 110 db, next for levels between 91 and 110 db, and so on.

Writing the decision as follows would be incorrect. All but the loudest sounds (those 110 db or less) would be incorrectly categorized as "very annoying" because the first condition would be true and the rest would be skipped.

```
/* Incorrect perception of noise loudness */

if (noise_db <= 110)
```

```
        printf("%d-decibel noise is very annoying.\n",
                noise_db);
else if (noise_db <= 90)
        printf("%d-decibel noise is annoying.\n",
                noise_db);
else if (noise_db <= 70)
        printf("%d-decibel noise is intrusive.\n",
                noise_db);
else if (noise_db <= 50)
        printf(%d-decibel noise is quiet.\n", noise_db);
else
        printf("%d-decibel noise is uncomfortable.\n",
                noise_db);
```

Nested if Statements with More Than One Variable

All the nested if statements seen so far have involved testing different ranges of the value of a single variable; consequently, we were able to write each nested if statement as a multiple-alternative decision. In other situations, we will be able to use a multiple-alternative decision statement only if a flowchart of the decision process shows that each intermediate decision step is on the false branch of the previous decision. The next example requires decisions on true branches. Here we use a nested if statement as a "filter" to select out data that satisfy several different criteria.

EXAMPLE 4.13 The Department of Defense would like a program that identifies single males between the ages of 18 and 26 inclusive. One way to select such individuals is to use a nested if statement. In the nested if that follows, we assume that all variables already have values:

```
/* Print a message if all criteria are met. */
if (marital_status == 'S')
    if (gender == 'M')
        if (age >= 18)
            if (age <= 26)
                printf("All criteria are met.\n");
```

The call to printf at the end of the if statement executes only when all of the conditions listed above it are true. An equivalent statement that uses a single if with a compound condition is this statement:

```
if (marital_status == 'S' && gender == 'M'
    && age >= 18 && age <= 26)
    printf("All criteria are met.\n");
```

EXAMPLE 4.14 You are developing a program to control the warning signs at the exits of major tunnels. If roads are slick (`road_status` is `'S'`), you want to advise drivers that stopping times are doubled or quadrupled, depending on whether the roads are wet or icy. Your program will also have access to the current temperature in degrees Celsius (`temp`), so a check as to whether the temperature is above or below freezing would allow you to choose the correct message. The following nested `if` statement summarizes the decision process you should follow; the flowchart in Fig. 4.8 diagrams the process.

```
if (road_status == 'S')
    if (temp > 0) {
        printf("Wet roads ahead\n");
        printf("Stopping time doubled\n");
    } else {
        printf("Icy roads ahead\n");
        printf("Stopping time quadrupled\n");
    }
else
    printf("Drive carefully!\n");
```

To verify that the nested `if` statement in this example is correct, we trace its execution for all possible combinations of road status values and temperatures. The flowchart's rightmost output is executed only when both conditions are true. The leftmost output is always executed when the condition involving

**Figure 4.8
Flowchart of
Road Sign
Decision
Process**

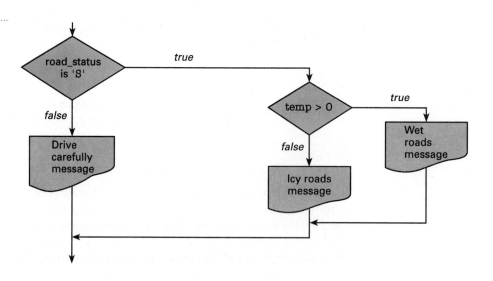

road_status is false. The output in the middle occurs when the condition involving road_status is true, but the condition involving temp is false.

When you are writing a nested if statement, it is important to be aware that C associates an else with the most recent incomplete if. For example, if the first else of the road sign decision were omitted, the following would be left:

```
if (road_status == 'S')
      if (temp > 0) {
            printf("Wet roads ahead\n");
            printf("Stopping time doubled\n");
      }
else
      printf("Drive carefully!\n");
```

Although the indentation would lead you to believe that the else remains the false branch of the first if, the C compiler actually sees it as the false branch of the second if. Indentation like this would match the actual meaning of the statement:

```
if (road_status == 'S')
      if (temp > 0) {
            printf("Wet roads ahead\n");
            printf("Stopping time doubled\n");
      } else
            printf("Drive carefully!\n");
```

To force the else to be the false branch of the first if, we use braces around the true task of this first decision:

```
if (road_status == 'S') {
      if (temp > 0) {
            printf("Wet roads ahead\n");
            printf("Stopping time doubled\n");
      }
} else {
      printf("Drive carefully!\n");
}
```

Note that we could not use a multiple-alternative decision statement to implement the flowchart in Fig. 4.8 because the intermediate decision (temp > 0) falls on the true branch of the initial decision. However, if we were to change the initial condition so the branches were switched, a multiple-alternative structure would work. We could do this simply by checking whether the road is dry:

```
if (road_status == 'D') {
    printf("Drive carefully!\n");
} else if (temp > 0) {
    printf("Wet roads ahead\n");
    printf("Stopping time doubled\n");
} else {
    printf("Icy roads ahead\n");
    printf("Stopping time quadrupled\n");
}
```

The first condition is true only if the road is dry. The second condition is tested only when the first condition fails, so its dependent statement executes only when the road is not dry and the temperature is above freezing. Finally, the `else` clause executes only when the two conditions fail; then we know that the roads are not dry and the temperature is not above freezing.   ⬅

EXERCISES FOR SECTION 4.4

Self-Check

1. Show the output of the correct nested `if` statement in Example 4.12 for a `noise_db` value of 95.
2. Write a nested `if` statement for the decision diagrammed in the accompanying flowchart. Use a multiple-alternative `if` for intermediate decisions where possible.

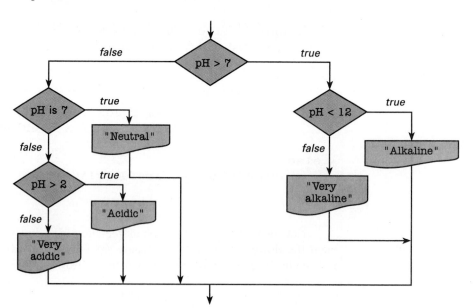

Programming

1. Rewrite the `if` statement for Example 4.12 using only the relational operator `>` in all conditions.
2. The Air Force has asked you to write a program to label supersonic aircraft as military or civilian. Your program is to be given the plane's observed speed in km/h and its estimated length in meters. For planes traveling in excess of 1100 km/h, you will label those longer than 52 meters "civilian" and shorter aircraft as "military." For planes traveling at slower speeds, you will issue an "aircraft type unknown" message.
3. Implement the following decision table using a multiple-alternative `if` statement. Assume that the wind speed is given as an integer.

Wind Speed (mph)	Category
below 25	not a strong wind
25–38	strong wind
39–54	gale
55–72	whole gale
above 72	hurricane

4.5 PROBLEM SOLVING WITH DECISIONS

In our next case study, we will use a multiple-alternative decision structure to convert compass headings to compass bearings. This decision structure also allows us to validate the value of the input variable so we can avoid performing the conversion on invalid data. Our program displays an error message if the input data value is outside the acceptable range.

The compass heading conversion program also demonstrates the use of expressions as values to be displayed. Such usage is advisable only if the value of an expression will not be needed later in the program and if the expression's presence in a call to `printf` does not harm the program's readability.

Case Study: Computing Compass Bearings

PROBLEM

While spending the summer as a surveyor's assistant, you decide to write a program that automates the table you use to transform compass headings in degrees (0 to 360 degrees) to compass bearings. The program should require entry of a compass heading, such as 110 degrees, and should display the corresponding bearing (south 70 degrees east).

**Figure 4.9
Compass
Headings**

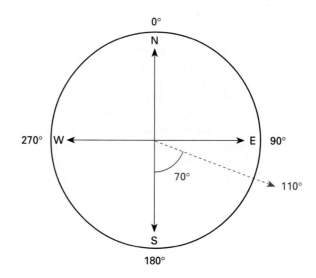

ANALYSIS

The compass bearing indicates a direction of travel corresponding to a compass heading. In this example, if you have a compass heading of 110 degrees, you should first face due south and then turn 70 degrees toward the east (see Fig. 4.9). Each compass bearing consists of three parts: the direction you face (north or south), an angle between 0 and 90 degrees, and the direction you turn before walking (east or west). Table 4.8 indicates how to transform compass headings into compass bearings. From the second line of this table, we see that a heading of 110 degrees corresponds to a bearing of south (180.0 − 110.0) east, or south 70 degrees east.

Table 4.8   Computing Compass Bearings

Heading in Degrees	Bearing Computation
0–89.999...	north (heading) east
90–179.999...	south (180.0 − heading) east
180–269.999...	south (heading − 180.0) west
270–360	north (360.0 − heading) west

Data Requirements

Problem Input
```
double heading /* the compass heading in degrees    */
```

Problem Output
equivalent bearing message

DESIGN

Initial Algorithm

1. Display instructions.
2. Get the compass heading.
3. Display the equivalent compass bearing.

Algorithm Refinements

To refine Step 3, we must specify Table 4.8 as a multiple-alternative decision step.

Step 3 Refinement
3.1 if heading is less than zero
      3.2 bearing is undefined
   else if heading is less than 90.0
      3.3 display the bearing north (heading) east
   else if heading is less than 180.0
      3.4 display the bearing south (180.0 − heading) east
   else if heading is less than 270.0
      3.5 display the bearing south (heading − 180.0) west
   else if heading is less than or equal to 360.0
      3.6 display the bearing north (360.0 − heading) west
   else
      3.7 bearing is undefined

IMPLEMENTATION

We could introduce an output variable, `bearing`, to hold the results of the bearing computation. However, this is not essential, because the value is never used again after it is displayed. When we consider the impact that the introduction of such a variable would have on readability, we see that the code we write will actually more closely resemble the table we are implementing if the table's original expressions appear in the calls to `printf`.

<hr>

TESTING

To test the program in Fig. 4.10, try compass headings in each of the four quadrants. Also, try compass headings at the quadrant boundaries: 0, 90, 180, 270, and 360 degrees. Finally, see what happens when the heading value is out of range.

Figure 4.10   Program to Compute Compass Bearings

```
/*
 * Transforms a compass heading to a compass bearing using this table:
 *
 *      HEADING
 *      IN DEGREES              BEARING COMPUTATION
 *
 *      0   - 89.999...     north (heading) east
 *      90  - 179.999...    south (180.0 - heading) east
 *      180 - 269.999...    south (heading - 180.0) west
 *      270 - 360           north (360.0 - heading) west
 */

#include <stdio.h>

/*
 * Display program purpose and user instructions
 */
void
instruct(void)
{
      printf("To convert a compass heading to a ");
      printf("compass bearing,\nenter a value ");
      printf("between 0.0 and 360.0 at the prompt.\n");
}

int
main(void)
{
        double heading; /* Input - compass heading in degrees         */

        instruct();

        /* Get compass heading.                                        */
        printf("Enter a compass heading> ");
```

(continued)

Figure 4.10   (continued)

```
        scanf("%lf", &heading);

        /* Display equivalent compass bearing.    */
        if (heading < 0.0)
                printf("Error--negative heading (%.1f)\n",
                        heading);
        else if (heading < 90.0)
                printf("The bearing is north %.1f degrees east\n",
                        heading);
        else if (heading < 180.0)
                printf("The bearing is south %.1f degrees east\n",
                        180.0 - heading);
        else if (heading < 270.0)
                printf("The bearing is south %.1f degrees west\n",
                        heading - 180.0);
        else if (heading <= 360.0)
                printf("The bearing is north %.1f degrees west\n",
                        360.0 - heading);
        else
                printf("Error--heading > 360 (%.1f)\n", heading);

        return (0);
}
```

```
To convert a compass heading to a compass bearing,
enter a value between 0.0 and 360.0 at the prompt.
Enter a compass heading> 110.0
The bearing is south 70.0 degrees east
```

EXERCISES FOR SECTION 4.5

Self-Check

1. Rewrite the multiple-alternative if of Fig. 4.10 so that the program would execute more efficiently if the most commonly entered headings were headings in the range 270 to 360 degrees.

Programming

1. Write a program that allows the user to convert either miles to kilometers or kilometers to miles.

4.6 THE switch STATEMENT FOR MULTIPLE ALTERNATIVES

The switch statement may also be used in C to select one of several alternatives. The switch statement is especially useful when the selection is based on the value of a single variable or of a simple expression (called the *controlling expression*). The value of this expression may be of type int or char, but not of type double.

EXAMPLE 4.15 ▶

The switch statement in Fig. 4.11 is one way of implementing the following decision table.

Class ID	Ship Class
B or b	Battleship
C or c	Cruiser
D or d	Destroyer
F or f	Frigate

The message displayed by the switch statement depends on the value of the controlling expression, that is, the value of the variable class (type char). First, this expression is evaluated; then, the list of case labels (case 'B':, case 'b':, case 'C':, etc.) is searched until one label that matches the value of the controlling expression is found. Statements following the matching case label are executed until a break statement is encountered. The break causes an exit from the switch statement, and execution continues with the statement that follows the closing brace of the switch statement body. If no case label matches the value of the switch statement's controlling expres-

Figure 4.11   Example of a switch Statement with Type char Case Labels

```
switch (class) {
case 'B':
case 'b':
      printf("Battleship\n");
      break;

case 'C':
case 'c':
      printf("Cruiser\n");
      break;
```

(continued)

Figure 4.11   (continued)

```
case 'D':
case 'd':
      printf("Destroyer\n");
      break;

case 'F':
case 'f':
      printf("Frigate\n");
      break;

default:
      printf("Unknown ship class %c\n", class);
}
```

sion, the statements following the default label are executed if there is a default label. If not, the entire switch statement body is skipped.   ←

Using a string such as "Cruiser" or "Frigate" as a case label is a common error. It is important to remember that type int and char values may be used as case labels, but strings and type double values cannot be used. Another common error is the omission of the break statement at the end of one alternative. In such a situation, execution "falls through" into the next alternative. We use a blank line after each break statement to emphasize the fact that there is no "fall-through."

Forgetting the closing brace of the switch statement body is also easy to do. If the brace is missing and the switch has a default label, the statements following the switch statement become part of the default case.

The following syntax display shows the form of the switch statement as a multiple-alternative decision structure.

Multiple-Alternative Decisions Using the switch Statement

SYNTAX: switch (*controlling expression*) {
       label set$_1$
         statements$_1$
       break;

(continued)

```
        label set₂
            statements₂
            break;

                •
                •
                •

        label setₙ
            statementsₙ
            break;

        default:
            statementsᵈ
        }
```

EXAMPLE:
```
/* Determine average life expectancy of a
       standard light bulb */
switch (watts) {
case 25:
        life = 2500;
        break;

case 40:
case 60:
        life = 1000;
        break;

case 75:
case 100:
        life = 750;
        break;

default:
        life = 0;
}
```

INTERPRETATION: The *controlling expression,* an expression with a value of type int or type char, is evaluated and compared to each of the case labels in the *label sets* until a match is found. A *label set* is made of one or more labels of the form case keyword followed by a constant value and a colon. When a match between the value of the controlling expression and a case label value is found, the statements following the case label are executed until a break statement is encountered. Then the rest of the switch statement is skipped. The *statements* may be *one or more* C statements, so it is not necessary to make multiple statements into a single compound statement as you must in an if statement. If no case label value matches the *controlling expression,* the entire switch statement body is skipped unless it contains a default label. If so, the statements following the default label are executed when no other case label value matches the *controlling expression.*

Comparison of Nested if Statements and the switch Statement

You can use a nested `if` statement, which is more general than the `switch` statement, to implement any multiple-alternative decision. The `switch` as described in the syntax display is more readable in many contexts and should be used whenever practical. Case labels that contain type `double` values or strings are not permitted.

You should use the `switch` statement when each label set contains a reasonable number of `case` labels (a maximum of ten). However, if the number of values is large, use a nested `if` statement. You should include a `default` label in `switch` statements wherever possible. The discipline of trying to define a default will help you to always consider what will happen if the value of your `switch` statement's controlling expression falls outside your set of `case` label values.

EXERCISES FOR SECTION 4.6

Self-Check

1. What will be displayed by this carelessly constructed `switch` statement if the value of `color` is `'R'`?

```
switch (color) { /* break statements missing */
case 'R':
      printf("red\n");
case 'B':
      printf("blue\n");
case 'Y':
      printf("yellow\n");
}
```

2. Why can't we rewrite our multiple-alternative `if` statement code from Example 4.12 using `switch` statements?

Programming

1. Write a `switch` statement that assigns to the variable `lumens` the expected brightness of a standard light bulb whose wattage has been stored in `watts`. Use this table:

Watts	Brightness (in Lumens)
15	125
25	215
40	500
60	880
75	1000
100	1675

Assign −1 to `lumens` if the value of `watts` is not in the table.

2. Write a multiple-alternative `if` statement equivalent to the `switch` statement described in the first programming exercise.

4.7 COMMON PROGRAMMING ERRORS

Remember that the C equality operator is `==`. It is easy to slip and use `=`, the mathematical equal sign. The compiler can detect this error only if the first operand is not a variable. Otherwise, your code will simply produce incorrect results. For example, the code fragment that follows always prints `x is 10`, regardless of the value of `x` when the statement is encountered.

```
if (x = 10)
      printf("x is 10");
```

The assignment operator stores the value 10 in `x`. The value of an assignment expression is the value assigned, so in this case the value of the `if` condition of the statement is 10. Since 10 is nonzero, C views it as meaning true and executes the true task.

Be careful when constructing complicated logical expressions using the operators `&&` and `||`. Remember that both operands must be complete logical expressions. For example, when verifying that `x` and `y` are both positive, we write

```
x > 0 && y > 0
```

not

```
x && y > 0
```

Don't forget to parenthesize the condition of an `if` statement and to enclose in braces a single-alternative `if` used as a true task within a double-alternative `if`. The braces will force the `else` to be associated with the correct `if`. Also enclose in braces a compound statement used as a true task or false task. If the braces are missing, only the first statement will be considered part of the task. This can lead to a syntax error if the braces are omitted from the true task of a double-alternative `if`. Leaving out the braces on the false task of a double-alternative `if` or on the true task of a single-alternative `if` will not usually generate a syntax error; the omission will simply lead to incorrect results. In the example that follows, the braces around the true task are missing.

The compiler assumes that the semicolon at the end of the assignment statement terminates the `if` statement.

```
if (x > 0)
      sum = sum + x;
      printf("Greater than zero\n");
else
      printf("Less than zero\n");
```

An `unexpected symbol` syntax error may be generated when the keyword `else` is encountered.

When you write a nested `if` statement, try to select the conditions so that the multiple-alternative format shown in Section 4.4 can be used. When possible, the logic should be constructed so each intermediate condition falls on the false branch of the previous decision. If the conditions are not mutually exclusive (i.e., more than one condition may be true), the most restrictive condition should come first.

When using a `switch` statement, make sure the controlling expression and `case` labels are of the same permitted type (`int` or `char` but not `double`). Remember that if the controlling expression evaluates to a value not listed in any of the `case` labels, the entire body of the `switch` statement will be skipped unless it contains a `default` label. It is wise to include such a `default` case whenever practical. Don't forget that the body of the `switch` statement is a single compound statement, enclosed in one set of braces. However, the statements of each alternative within the `switch` are not enclosed in braces; instead, each alternative is ended by a `break` statement.

CHAPTER REVIEW

In this chapter, we discussed how to represent decision steps in an algorithm using pseudocode and how to implement them in C using `if` and `switch` statements. We showed how to use traces to verify that an algorithm or a program is correct. Carefully tracing an algorithm or a program before entering the program in the computer will uncover errors in logic and will save you time in the long run.

A second selection structure, the `switch` statement, was introduced in this chapter as a convenient means of implementing decisions with several alternatives. We showed how to use the `switch` statement to implement decisions that are based on the value of a variable or simple expression (the controlling expression). This expression can be of type `int` or `char`, but not type `double`.

The new C constructs introduced in this chapter are described in Table 4.9.

Table 4.9   Summary of New C Constructs

Construct	Effect
if Statement	
Single-alternative	
| ```
if (x != 0.0)
     product = product * x;
``` | Multiplies product by x only if x is nonzero. |
| *Double-alternative* | |
| ```
if (tmp > 32.0)
     printf("%.1f: above freezing", tmp);
else
     printf("%.1f: freezing", tmp);
``` | If tmp is greater than 32.0, it is labeled as above freezing; otherwise, it is labeled freezing |
| *Multiple-alternative* | |
| ```
if (x < 0) {
     printf("negative");
     abs_x = -x;
} else if (x == 0) {
     printf("zero");
     abs_x = 0;
} else {
     printf("positive");
     abs_x = x;
}
``` | One of three messages is displayed, depending on whether x is negative, positive, or zero. abs_x is set to represent the absolute value or magnitude of x. |
| **switch Statement** | |
| ```
switch (next_ch) {
case 'A':
case 'a':
     printf("Excellent");
     break;

case 'B':
case 'b':
     printf("Good");
     break;
``` | Displays one of five messages based on the value of next_ch (type char). If next_ch is 'D', 'd', 'F', or 'f', the student is put on probation. Gives an error message if the value of next_ch is an invalid letter grade. |

(continued)

Table 4.9   (continued)

Construct	Effect

```
case 'C':
case 'c':
      printf("O.K.");
      break;

case 'D':
case 'd':
case 'F':
case 'f':
      printf("Poor, student is ");
      printf("on probation");
      break;

default:
      printf("Invalid letter grade");
}
```

QUICK-CHECK EXERCISES

1. An if statement implements _____ execution.
2. What is a compound statement?
3. A switch statement is often used instead of _____ .
4. What can be the values of an expression with a relational operator?
5. The relational operator <= means _____ .
6. Write an expression whose value will be true if the value of x is between 35 and 45 inclusive.
7. A(n) _____ checks whether a program is grammatically correct.
8. Correct the syntax errors.

```
if x > 25.0 {
      y = x
else
      y = z;
}
```

9. What value is assigned to fee by the if statement when speed is 75?

```
if (speed > 35)
        fee = 20.0;
```

```
else if (speed > 50)
      fee = 40.00;
else if (speed > 75)
      fee = 60.00;
```

10. Answer Exercise 9 for the if statement that follows. Which if statement seems reasonable?

```
if (speed > 75)
      fee = 60.0;
else if (speed > 50)
      fee = 40.00;
else if (speed > 35)
      fee = 20.00;
```

11. What output line(s) are displayed by the statements that follow when grade is 'I'? When grade is 'B'? When grade is 'b'?

```
switch (grade) {
case 'A':
      points = 4;
      break;

case 'B':
      points = 3;
      break;

case 'C':
      points = 2;
      break;

case 'D':
      points = 1;
      break;

case 'E':
case 'I':
case 'W':
      points = 0;
}

if (points > 0)
      printf("Passed, points earned = %d\n", points);
else
      printf("Failed, no points earned\n");
```

12. Explain the difference between the statements on the left and the statements on the right. For each group of statements, give the final value of x if the initial value of x is 1.

```
if (x >= 0)                if (x >= 0)
    x = x + 1;                 x = x + 1;
else if (x >= 1)           if (x >= 1)
    x = x + 2;                 x = x + 2;
```

ANSWERS TO QUICK-CHECK EXERCISES

1. conditional
2. One or more statements surrounded by braces
3. nested `if` statements or a multiple-alternative `if` statement
4. 0 and 1
5. less than or equal to
6. `x >= 35 && x <= 45`
7. compiler
8. Parenthesize condition, remove braces (or add them around `else`: `} else {`), and add a semicolon to the first assignment statement.
9. `20.00`, first condition is met
10. `40.00`, the one in 10
11. when `grade` is `'I'`:
        `Failed, no points earned`
    when `grade` is `'B'`:
        `Passed, points earned = 3`
    when `grade` is `'b'`:
        The `switch` statement is skipped so the output printed depends on the previous value of `points` (which may be garbage).
12. A nested `if` statement is on the left; a sequence of `if` statements is on the right. On the left, x becomes 2; on the right, x becomes 4.

REVIEW QUESTIONS

1. Making a decision between two alternative courses of action is usually implemented with a(n) _____ statement in C.
2. Trace the following program fragment; indicate which function will be called if a data value of `27.34` is entered.

```
printf("\Enter a temperature> ");
scanf("%lf", &temp);
```

```
if (temp > 32.0)
      not_freezing();
else
      ice_forming();
```

3. Write a multiple-alternative if statement to display a message based on the level of force, in newtons, being applied by a robot hand attempting to turn a large threaded part into a machine. Force levels and associated messages are: 0, Part not found; 1–44, Insecure grip; 45–88, Nominal grip; 89–100, Part may be misaligned, and above 100, DANGER-- Part may be stuck. Print a message to indicate bad data as well.

4. Write a switch statement to select an operation based on the color of a sample observed by an automated chemical-flow control system that is checking to see whether material flowing into a processing vat is acidic or basic. If the color is indicated as 'B' (for blue), add to the total_bases variable the value of the variable base_strength. If the color is indicated as 'R' (for red), increase the value of the variable total_acids by the value of acid_strength. If the color is 'P' (for purple), add to the variable neutrals the value of sample_size. Do nothing if the color is 'Y' (for yellow). Display an error message if the value of color is not one of these four values.

5. Implement the following flow diagram using a nested if structure.

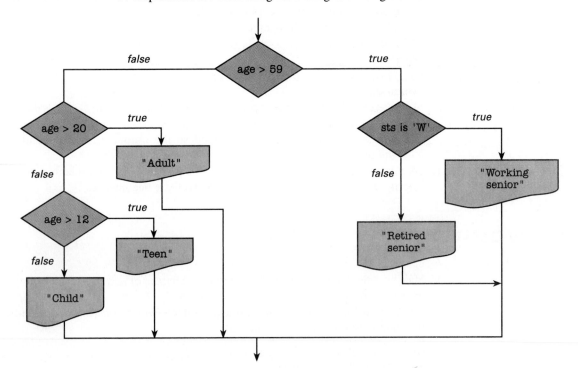

PROGRAMMING PROJECTS

1. A pharmaceutical engineer is testing out new types of synthetic antibiotics that should kill either one or both of the common classes of bacteria, *gram-negative* and *gram-positive* bacteria. Depending on the type of bacteria killed in a sample, the engineer wants to leave different lists of instructions for a technician who will perform follow-up tests. Write a program that takes as input a character indicating whether an antibiotic sample is effective against only gram-negative bacteria ('N'), only gram-positive bacteria ('P'), both classes ('B'), or neither class ('Z'). The program displays different lists of instructions to a technician based on effectiveness against gram-positive and gram-negative bacteria:

   ```
   Gram-positive: Perform standard tests 1 and 5.
                  Record results in notebook #2.
   Gram-negative: Perform standard tests 2, 3, and 4.
                  Record results in notebook #3.
   ```

   For samples effective on both classes, the program displays both sets of instructions. For samples effective on neither, the program displays `Throw away sample`.

   Your program should define and call two functions—one to display the gram-positive instructions and one for the gram-negative instructions.

2. Write a program to simulate a state police radar gun. The program should take an automobile speed and display the message `speeding` if the speed exceeds 65 mph.

3. The National Earthquake Information Center has asked you to write a program implementing the following decision table to characterize an earthquake based on its Richter scale number.

Richter Scale Number (n)	Characterization
$n < 5.0$	Little or no damage
$5.0 \leq n < 5.5$	Some damage
$5.5 \leq n < 6.5$	Serious damage: walls may crack or fall
$6.5 \leq n < 7.5$	Disaster: houses and buildings may collapse
higher	Catastrophe: most buildings destroyed

   Could you handle this problem with a `switch` statement? If so, use a `switch` statement; if not, explain why.

4. Write a program that takes a classroom number, its capacity, and the size of the class enrolled so far and displays an output line showing the classroom

number, the capacity, both the number of seats filled and the number available, and a message indicating whether the class is filled. Call a function to display the following heading before the requested output line.

Room   Capacity   Enrollment   Empty seats   Filled/Not Filled

Display each part of the output line under the appropriate column heading. Test your program four times using the following classroom data:

Room	Capacity	Enrollment
426	25	25
327	18	14
420	20	15
317	100	90

5. Write a program that takes the *x–y* coordinates of a point in the Cartesian plane and displays a message telling either an axis on which the point lies or the quadrant in which it is found.

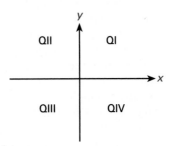

Sample lines of output:

```
(-1.0, -2.5) is in quadrant III
(0.0, 4.8) is on the y axis
```

6. Write a program that calculates and displays the reciprocal of an integer, both as a common fraction and as a decimal fraction. A typical output line would be

```
The reciprocal of 2 is 1/2 or 0.500.
```

The program should display a `Reciprocal undefined` message for an input of zero.

7. Los Angeles sometimes has very smoggy conditions. These conditions are largely due to L.A.'s location between mountain ranges, coupled with prevailing winds off the ocean that tend to blow pollutants from the city's many automobiles up against the mountains. Three components of smog—ozone, nitrogen dioxide, and carbon monoxide—are a particular health concern. A pollutant hazard index has been developed for each of the three primary irritants. If any index rises above 100, the air is listed as "unhealthful" in forecasts to Los Angeles residents. If the index for any one of the three rises above 200, a "first-stage smog alert" is issued and certain activities are restricted in the affected part of the Los Angeles basin. If an index goes over 275, a "second-stage alert" is called and more severe restrictions apply. Write a program that takes as input the daily hazard index for each of the three pollutants and that identifies unhealthful or first- or second-stage alert situations.

8. Engineers frequently must provide solutions based on imperfect or incomplete information. This is particularly true when dealing with somewhat subjective quantities, as one does when calculating risk–benefit trade-offs of a new technology. Assume that you are designing a study to decide which of several types of power plants is preferable to build in an area. You are to consider the following factors:

pollution_production   the pollutants generated by the plant
damage_risk   the risk of damage to neighboring
                           property if the plant explodes
cost_per_kwh   the cost per kilowatt hour for
                           electricity generated by the plant

To perform your study, you are going to develop a *cost function:*

$$cost = \frac{w1 \times pollution\_production}{MAX\_POLLUTION} + \frac{w2 \times damage\_risk}{MAX\_DAMAGE} + \frac{w3 \times cost\_per\_kwh}{MAX\_COST}$$

Write a program that allows a user to input values for *pollution_production, damage_risk,* and *cost_per_kwh* along with the three weighting values, *w1, w2,* and *w3*. Your program should display the *cost* for that user of the plant based on the inputs. Assume that the maximum units of pollutants that could be produced per kwh (*MAX_POLLUTION*) is 10, that the maximum number of households that could be displaced or damaged in an accident (*MAX_DAMAGE*) is 30,000, and that the maximum cost per kilowatt hour (*MAX_COST*) is $0.25. If the user weights one factor significantly higher (e.g., double or more) than both of the other values, the program should output a message following the cost display, suggesting that the user might like to run the program again using a lower value for that variable to obtain a comparison cost.

CHAPTER 5

REPETITION AND LOOP STATEMENTS

Chapters 3 and 4 introduced you to C control statements that allow programs to call functions and to make decisions as to which of several courses of action to take, based on current data values. The control statements of a programming language enable a programmer to control the sequence and frequency of execution of program segments. Control statements cause functions to carry out their tasks when needed and also implement decisions and repetition in programs. In this chapter, you will see how to specify the repetition of a group of program statements called a *loop* using the `while` and `for` statements. This ability to rapidly repeat groups of actions on vast quantities of information gives computers the awesome data processing power that has revolutionized both scientific research and many industries. This chapter describes how to design loops in C programs as well as how to place one control structure inside another. Numerous examples and a case study will be presented.

5.1 REPETITION IN PROGRAMS: USING LOOPS TO SOLVE PROBLEMS

Just as the ability to make decisions is an important programming tool, so is the ability to specify repetition of a group of operations. For example, the Mars Observer spacecraft's mission plan (see Fig. 5.1) called for seven orbit adjustment maneuvers in order to move from the craft's initial elliptical orbit to the desired orbit for mapping Mars. The spacecraft would have needed to execute similar sets of instructions seven times, one set for each maneuver. The *loop body* contains the steps to be repeated.

Writing out a solution to a specific case of a problem can be helpful in preparing you to define an algorithm to solve the same problem in general. After you solve the sample case, ask yourself some of the following questions to determine whether loops will be required in the general algorithm:

1. Were there any steps I repeated as I solved the problem? If so, which ones?
2. If the answer to question 1 is yes, did I know in advance how many times to repeat the steps?
3. If the answer to question 2 is no, how did I know how long to keep repeating the steps?

Your answer to the first question indicates whether your algorithm needs a loop and what steps to include in the loop body if it does need one. Your answers to the other questions will help you determine which loop structure to choose for your solution. Keep these questions in mind as we explore the kinds of loops available in C. Later in the chapter, we will summarize the relationship

(a)

Incoming path

1-Day drift orbit

3-Day capture orbit

Mars orbit insertion maneuver

2-Hour mapping orbit

4.2-Hour orbit

(b)

between your answers to these questions and the design of a correct loop for your algorithm.

The program segment shown in Fig. 5.2 computes and displays the time a flight controller for a spacecraft orbiting a planet must allow between each of seven planned spacecraft maneuvers. Each maneuver may change the amount of time required to orbit the planet once, the orbit period. The loop body (the steps that are repeated) is the compound statement that starts with the bracket at the end of the second line. The loop body requests two inputs from the user—the number of times the spacecraft will orbit the planet before the next maneuver and the orbit period (in minutes) after the current maneuver. The loop body concludes by computing and displaying the time between maneuvers. After seven maneuvers are processed, the last statement in Fig. 5.2 calls function printf to display the message All maneuvers complete.

The three lines in color in Fig. 5.2 control the looping process. The first statement

```
count_mvr = 0;  /* no maneuvers done yet */
```

stores an initial value of 0 in the variable count_mvr, which represents the number of maneuvers that have occurred so far. The next line evaluates the logical expression count_mvr < 7. If the expression is true, the compound statement representing the loop body is executed, calling for a new pair of data

....

Figure 5.1   (a) *Mars Observer* Spacecraft; (b) Diagram of Orbit Adjustment Plan.   The Jet Propulsion Laboratory *Mars Observer* spacecraft was to have arrived at the planet Mars on August 24, 1993, for a Mars-mapping mission scheduled to last at least one Mars year—about two Earth years. Researchers planned to place the spacecraft into an initial "capture orbit" around the planet at the end of its interplanetary cruise from Earth to Mars. A series of maneuvers would then have been performed to move the spacecraft progressively from its 3-day capture orbit, to a 1-day orbit, to a 4.2-hour orbit, and thence into its desired approximately 2-hour orbit.

Unfortunately, the *Mars Observer* spacecraft malfunctioned just a few days before starting the pictured sets of maneuvers. No engineer ever wants a technological creation to fail. However, one of the reasons for exploring space is to learn about the environment and to discover what devices will and will not work correctly in that environment. All we may ever know for sure of *Mars Observer*'s fate is that it disappeared; we hope that as we continue to explore space, we may someday learn what happened to it to help us expand our knowledge of the universe around us. (Courtesy of the Jet Propulsion Laboratory, California Institute of Technology)

Figure 5.2   Loop to Process Seven Spacecraft Maneuvers

```
count_mvr = 0;                      /* no maneuvers done yet    */
while (count_mvr < 7)  {            /* test value of count_mvr */
    printf("Number of orbits to next maneuver> ");
    scanf("%d", &orbits);
    printf("Orbit period, in hours and fraction of hours> ");
    scanf("%lf", &period);
    time_to_mvr = orbits * period;
    printf("Time to next maneuver is %6.1f hours\n", time_to_mvr);
    count_mvr = count_mvr + 1; /* increment count_mvr      */
}
printf("All maneuvers complete\n");
```

values to be input and a new duration to be computed and displayed. The last statement in the loop body

```
count_mvr = count_mvr + 1; /* increment count_mvr */
```

adds 1 to the current value of count_mvr. After executing the last step in the loop body, control returns to the line beginning with while and the condition is reevaluated for the next value of count_mvr. The loop body is executed once

**Figure 5.3
Flowchart of a
while Loop**

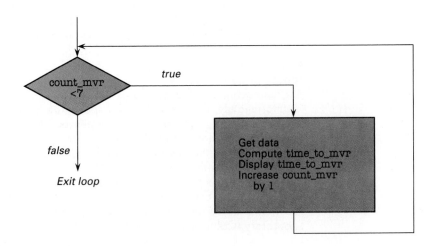

for each value of `count_mvr` from 0 to 6. Eventually, `count_mvr` becomes 7, and the logical expression evaluates to false (0). When this happens, the loop body is not executed and control passes to the display statement that follows the loop body. The logical expression following the reserved word `while` is called the *loop repetition condition*. The loop is repeated when this condition is true, that is, when its value is not 0. We say that the *loop is exited* when this condition is false (see Fig. 5.3).

The flowchart in Fig. 5.3 summarizes what we have explained so far about `while` loops. In the flowchart, the logical expression in the diamond-shaped box is evaluated first. If that expression is true, the loop body is executed, and the process is repeated. The `while` loop is exited when the expression becomes false. If the loop repetition condition is false when it is first tested, then the loop body is not executed at all.

Make sure you understand the difference between the `while` statement in Fig. 5.2 and the following `if` statement:

```
if (count_mvr < 7) {
      . . .
}
```

In an `if` statement, the compound statement after the parenthesized condition executes at most only once. In a `while` statement, the compound statement can execute more than once.

Syntax of the while Statement

In Fig. 5.2, the variable `count_mvr` is called the *loop control variable* because its value determines whether the loop body is repeated. Three critical steps involve the loop control variable `count_mvr`:

1. `count_mvr` is set to an initial value of 0 (initialized to 0) before the `while` statement is reached.
2. `count_mvr` is tested before the start of each loop repetition (called an *iteration* or a *pass*).
3. `count_mvr` is updated (its value increases by 1) during each iteration.

Steps similar to these three steps (initialization, test, and update) must be performed for every `while` loop. If the first step is missing, the initial test of `count_mvr` will be meaningless. The last step ensures that we progress toward the final goal (`count_mvr >= 7`) during each repetition of the loop. If the last step is missing, the value of `count_mvr` cannot change, so the loop will execute "forever" (an *infinite loop*). The syntax for the `while` statement is described in the next display.

---

while Statement

SYNTAX: while (*loop repetition condition*)
                   statement

EXAMPLE: /* Display N asterisks. */
          count_star = 0;
          while (count_star < N) {
                printf("*");
                count_star = count_star + 1;
          }

INTERPRETATION: The *loop repetition condition* (a condition to control the loop process) is tested; if it is true, the *statement* is executed, and the *loop repetition condition* is retested. The *statement* is repeated as long as (`while`) the *loop repetition condition* is true. When this condition is tested and found to be false, the `while` loop is exited and the next program statement after the `while` statement is executed.

EXERCISES FOR SECTION 5.1

Self-Check

1. Predict the output of this program fragment:

```
i = 0;
while (i <= 5) {
   printf("%3d %3d\n", i, 10 - i);
   i = i + 1;
}
```

2. What is displayed by this program fragment for an input of 10?

```
scanf("%d", &n);
ev = 0;
while (ev < n) {
   printf("%3d", ev);
   ev = ev + 2;
}
printf("\n");
```

Programming

1. Write a program fragment that produces this output:

```
0    1
1    2
2    4
3    8
4   16
5   32
6   64
```

5.2 COMPUTING A SUM OR A PRODUCT IN A LOOP

Often we use loops to compute a sum or a product by repeating an addition or multiplication operation. The next example uses a loop to accumulate a sum.

EXAMPLE 5.1  The program in Fig. 5.4 has a `while` loop similar to the loop in Fig. 5.2. Besides displaying the time between successive maneuvers, the program accumulates the total time spent in a series of maneuvers. The assignment statement

```
total_time = total_time + time_to_mvr;
```

adds the current value of `time_to_mvr` to the sum being accumulated in `total_time`. Figure 5.5 traces the effect of repeating this statement for the three values of `time_to_mvr` shown in the sample run. Prior to loop execution, the statement

```
total_time = 0.0;
```

initializes the value of `total_time` to zero. This step is critical; if it is omitted, the final sum will be off by whatever value happens to be stored in `total_time` when the program begins execution.

Figure 5.4   **Program to Compute Total Time to Complete Maneuvers**

```
/* Compute the total time for all initial orbit-correcting maneuvers. */

#include <stdio.h>

int
main(void)
{
      double period;      /* time to do one orbit around the planet,
                             in hours                                   */
      int    count_mvr;   /* current maneuver                           */
      int    orbits;      /* number of orbits until next maneuver       */
      double time_to_mvr; /* time to next maneuver                      */
      double total_time;  /* total time spacecraft has spent in orbit
                             so far, in hours                           */
      int    num_mvrs;    /* number of maneuvers to be performed        */

      /* Get number of maneuvers.  */
      printf("Enter number of maneuvers> ");
      scanf("%d", &num_mvrs);

      /* Compute the time for each set of orbits between maneuvers and
         add to the total. */
      total_time = 0.0;
      count_mvr = 0;
      while (count_mvr < num_mvrs)  {
          printf("Number of orbits to next maneuver> ");
          scanf("%d", &orbits);
          printf("Orbit period, in hours and fraction of hours> ");
          scanf("%lf", &period);
          time_to_mvr = orbits * period;
          printf("Time to next maneuver is %6.1f hours\n\n",
                  time_to_mvr);
          count_mvr  =  count_mvr + 1;
          total_time = total_time + time_to_mvr;
      }
```

(continued)

Figure 5.4   (continued)

```
        printf("All maneuvers complete\n");
        printf("Total time spent in maneuver phase is %6.1f hours\n",
               total_time);

        return (0);
}
Enter number of maneuvers> 3
Number of orbits to next maneuver> 1
Orbit period, in hours and fraction of hours> 24
Time to next maneuver is    24.0 hours

Number of orbits to next maneuver> 5
Orbit period, in hours and fraction of hours> 4.1
Time to next maneuver is    20.5 hours

Number of orbits to next maneuver> 10
Orbit period, in hours and fraction of hours> 2.0
Time to next maneuver is    20.0 hours

All maneuvers complete
Total time spent in maneuver phase is    64.5 hours
```

Generalizing a Loop

The first loop shown in Fig. 5.2 has a serious deficiency: It can be used only when the number of maneuvers is exactly seven. The loop in Fig. 5.4 is better because it can be used for any number of maneuvers. This program begins by copying from the input device the total number of maneuvers and storing this value in the variable num_mvrs. Before each execution of the loop body, the loop repetition condition compares the number of maneuvers processed so far (count_mvr) to the total number of maneuvers (num_mvrs).   ⬅

Multiplying a List of Numbers

In a similar way, we can use a loop to compute the product of a list of numbers as shown in the next example.

Figure 5.5
Accumulating
a Sum

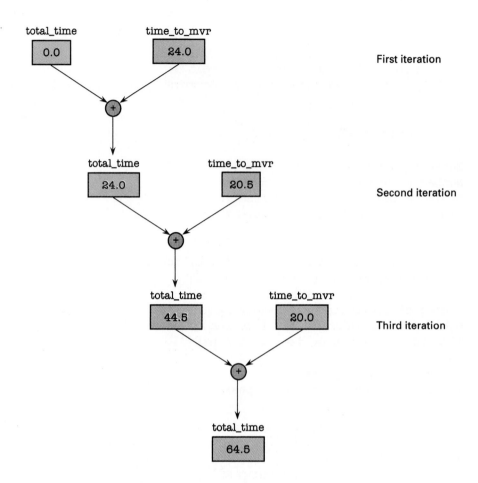

Second iteration

Third iteration

EXAMPLE 5.2 The loop that follows multiplies data items together as long as the product remains less than 10,000. It displays the product calculated up to this point just before asking for the next data value. The product of the data seen so far is updated on each iteration by executing the statement

```
product = product * item; /* Update product. */
```

Figure 5.6 traces the change in the value of `product` with each execution of the statement just shown. If the data items are 10, 500, and 3, the products 1 (initial value of `product`), 10, and 5000 are displayed.

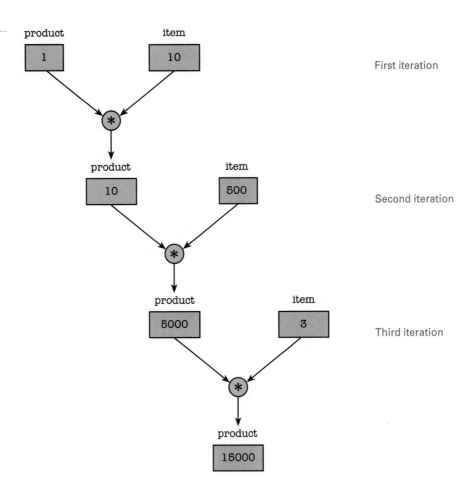

**Figure 5.6
Computing a
Product in
a Loop**

First iteration

Second iteration

Third iteration

```
/* Multiply data while product remains less than 10000 */
product = 1;
while (product < 10000) {
    printf("%d\n", product); /* Display product so far */
    printf("Enter next item> ");
    scanf("%d", &item);
    product = product * item; /* Update product */
}
```

Loop exit occurs when the value of **product** is greater than or equal to 10,000.
Consequently, the last value assigned to **product** (in Fig. 5.6, 15,000) is not
displayed.

The loop in this example differs from other loops in this section. Its repetition condition involves a test of the variable `product`. Besides controlling loop repetition, the variable `product` also holds the result of the computation that is performed in the loop. The other loops involve a test of `count_mvr`, a variable that represents the count of loop repetitions. The computation being performed in the loop does not directly involve `count_mvr`. We will discuss these differences further in Section 5.4.

Compound Assignment Operators

We have seen several instances of assignment statements of the form

$$variable = variable \ op \ expression;$$

These include increments and decrements of loop counters

```
ct = ct + 1;
time = time - 1;
```

as well as statements accumulating a sum or computing a product in a loop, such as

```
total_time = total_time + time_to_mvr;
product = product * data;
```

C provides special assignment operators that make possible a more concise notation of statements of this type. For the operations +, -, *, /, and %, C defines the compound *op=* assignment operators +=, -=, *=, /=, and %=. A statement of the form

$$variable \ op= \ expression;$$

is an alternative way of writing the statement

$$variable = variable \ op \ (expression);$$

Table 5.1 lists the assignment statements just noted along with their equivalents using compound assignment operators. In addition, the table shows one assignment that demonstrates the relevance of the parentheses around *expression* in the definition of an assignment statement with a compound operator.

Compound assignment operators are especially useful when the target of the assignment is a single component of one of the composite data structures that we will study in Chapters 7, 8, and 9. In these cases, the use of a compound assignment operator is not only more concise but also more efficient.

Table 5.1   Using Compound Assignment Operators

Statement with Simple Assignment Operator	Equivalent Statement with Compound Assignment Operator
`ct = ct + 1;`	`ct += 1;`
`time = time - 1;`	`time -= 1;`
`total_time = total_time + time_to_mvr;`	`total_time += time_to_mvr;`
`product = product * data;`	`product *= data;`
`n = n * (x + 1);`	`n *= x + 1;`

EXERCISES FOR SECTION 5.2

Self-Check

1. What output values are displayed by the following `while` loop for a data value of 5? Of 6? Of 7?

```
printf("Enter an integer> ");
scanf("%d", &x);
product = x;
count = 0;
while (count < 4) {
    printf("%d\n", product);
    product = product * x;
    count = count + 1;
}
```

   In general, for a data value of any number *n*, what does this loop display?
2. What values are displayed if the call to `printf` comes at the end of the loop instead of at the beginning?
3. The following segment needs some revision. Insert braces where they are needed and correct the errors. The corrected code should take five integers and display their sum.

```
count = 0;
while (count <= 5)
count = count + 1;
printf("Next number> ");
scanf("%d", &next_num);
next_num = sum + next_num;
printf("%d numbers were added; \n", count);
printf("their sum is %d.\n", sum);
```

4. Where possible, write equivalents for the following statements using compound assignment operators.

```
r = r / 10;
z = z * x + 1;
q = q + r * m;
m = m - (n + p);
```

Programming

1. Write a program segment that computes $1 + 2 + 3 + \cdots + (n - 1) + n$, where n is a data value. Follow the loop body with an `if` statement that compares this value to $(n * (n + 1)) / 2$ and displays a message that indicates whether the values are the same or different. What message do you think will be displayed?

5.3 COUNTING LOOPS

The `while` loop shown in Fig. 5.4 is called a *counter-controlled loop* (or *counting loop*) because its repetition is managed by a *loop control variable* whose value represents a count. A counter-controlled loop follows this general format described in pseudocode:

> Set *loop control variable* to an initial value of 0.
> while *loop control variable* < *final value*
> ...
> Increase *loop control variable* by 1.

We use a counter-controlled loop when we can determine prior to loop execution exactly how many loop repetitions will be needed to solve the problem. This number should appear as the *final value* in the `while` condition.

The for Statement

C provides the `for` statement as another form for implementing loops. The loops we have seen so far are typical of most repetition structures in that they have three major components in addition to the loop body:

1. initialization of the *loop control variable*,
2. test of the *loop repetition condition*, and
3. change (update) of the *loop control variable*.

An important feature of the `for` statement in C is that it supplies a designated place for each of these three components. A `for` statement implementation of the loop from Fig. 5.4 is shown in Fig. 5.7.

Figure 5.7 **Using a for Statement in a Counting Loop**

```
/* Compute the total time for all initial orbit-correcting maneuvers. */

#include <stdio.h>

int
main(void)
{
      double period;              /* time to do one orbit around the planet,
                                     in hours                             */
      int    count_mvr;           /* current maneuver                     */
      int    orbits;              /* number of orbits until next maneuver */
      double time_to_mvr;         /* time to next maneuver                */
      double total_time;          /* total time spacecraft has spent in
                                     orbit so far, in hours               */
      int    num_mvrs;            /* number of maneuvers to be performed  */

      /* Get number of maneuvers.  */
      printf("Enter number of maneuvers> ");
      scanf("%d", &num_mvrs);

      /* Compute the time for each set of orbits between maneuvers and
         add to the total. */
      total_time = 0.0;
      for  (count_mvr = 0;                    /* initialization         */
            count_mvr < num_mvrs;             /* loop repetition condition */
            count_mvr += 1) {                 /* update                 */
         printf("Number of orbits to next maneuver> ");
         scanf("%d", &orbits);
         printf("Orbit period, in hours and fraction of hours> ");
         scanf("%lf", &period);
         time_to_mvr = orbits * period;
         printf("Time to next maneuver is %6.1f hours\n\n",
                time_to_mvr);
         total_time += time_to_mvr;
      }
```

(continued)

Figure 5.7   (continued)

```
printf("All maneuvers complete\n");
printf("Total time spent in maneuver phase is %6.1f hours\n",
        total_time);

    return (0);
}
```

The effect of this `for` statement is exactly equivalent to the execution of the comparable `while` loop section of the program in Fig. 5.4. Because the `for` statement's heading

```
for  (count_mvr = 0;         /* initialization           */
        count_mvr < num_mvrs; /* loop repetition condition */
        count_mvr += 1) {     /* update                    */
```

combines the three loop control steps of initialization, testing, and update in one place, separate steps to initialize and update `count_mvr` must not appear elsewhere. The `for` statement can be used to count up or down by any interval. The program in Fig. 5.8 "counts down" from a specified starting value (an input variable) to "blast-off." Since the `for` statement update expression subtracts one from the variable `time`, the value of the loop control variable decreases by one each time the loop is repeated. Because the loop body is a single statement, we could omit the braces surrounding it. However, we would then need to be very careful if a later modification of the program called for the addition of another statement to the loop body. At that point, braces forming a compound statement would be essential.

for Statement

SYNTAX: for (*initialization expression*;
                  loop repetition condition;
                  update expression)
                statement

EXAMPLE: /* Display N asterisks. */
        for (count_star = 0;
              count_star < N;
              count_star += 1)
            printf("*");

(continued)

INTERPRETATION: First, the *initialization expression* is executed. Then, the *loop repetition condition* is tested. If it is true, the *statement* is executed, and the *update expression* is evaluated. Then the *loop repetition condition* is retested. The *statement* is repeated as long as the *loop repetition condition* is true. When this condition is tested and found to be false, the `for` loop is exited, and the next program statement after the `for` statement is executed.

Caution: Although C permits the use of fractional values for counting loop control variables of type `double`, we strongly discourage this practice. Counting loops with type `double` control variables will not always execute the same number of times on different computers.

Figure 5.8   A Countdown Program

```
/* Counting down to blast-off */

#include <stdio.h>

int
main(void)
{
    int time, start;

    printf("Enter starting time (an integer) in seconds> ");
    scanf("%d", &start);
    printf("\nBegin countdown\n");
    for  (time = start;
          time > 0;
          time -= 1) {
        printf("T - %d\n", time);
    }
    printf("Blast-off!\n");

    return (0);
}

Enter starting time (an integer) in seconds> 5

Begin countdown
T - 5
T - 4
T - 3
T - 2
T - 1
Blast-off!
```

Program Style   *Formatting the for Statement*

For clarity, we usually place each expression of the `for` heading on a separate line. If all three expressions are very short, we may place them together on one line. Here is an example:

```
/* Display nonnegative numbers < max */
for  (i = 0;  i < max;  i += 1)
    printf("%d\n", i);
```

The body of the `for` loop is indented. If the loop body is a compound statement or if we are using a style in which we bracket all loop bodies, we place the opening brace at the end of the `for` heading and terminate the statement by placing the closing brace on a separate line. This closing brace should be aligned with the "f" of the `for` that it is ending.

We have seen `for` statement counting loops that count up by one and down by one. Now we will use a loop that counts down by five to display a Celsius-to-Fahrenheit conversion table. Because of the values of the constant macros named CBEGIN and CLIMIT, the table displayed by the program in Fig. 5.9 runs from 10 degrees Celsius to −5 degrees Celsius. Since the loop update step subtracts CSTEP (5) from `celsius`, the value of the counter `celsius` decreases by five after each repetition. Loop exit occurs when `celsius` becomes less than CLIMIT, that is, when `celsius` is −10. Table 5.2 uses the small circled numbers to trace the execution of this counting `for` loop.

Figure 5.9   Displaying a Celsius-to-Fahrenheit Conversion Table

```
/* Conversion of Celsius to Fahrenheit temperatures */

#include <stdio.h>

/* Constant macros */
#define CBEGIN 10
#define CLIMIT -5
#define CSTEP 5

int
main(void)
{
      /* Variable declarations */
      int     celsius;
      double fahrenheit;
```

(continued)

Figure 5.9 (continued)

```
      /* Display the table heading */
      printf(" Celsius    Fahrenheit\n");

      /* Display the table */
①    for  (celsius = CBEGIN;
②          celsius >= CLIMIT;
③          celsius -= CSTEP) {
④       fahrenheit = 1.8 * celsius + 32.0;
⑤       printf("    %3d      %9.2f\n",   celsius, fahrenheit);
      }

      return (0);
}
```

```
   Celsius     Fahrenheit
      10         50.00
       5         41.00
       0         32.00
      -5         23.00
```

The trace in Table 5.2 shows that the loop control variable `celsius` is initialized to `CBEGIN (10)` when the `for` loop is reached. Since 10 is greater than or equal to `CLIMIT (-5)`, the loop body is executed. After each loop repetition, `CSTEP (5)` is subtracted from `celsius`, and `celsius` is tested in the loop repetition condition to see whether its value is still greater than or equal to `CLIMIT`. If the condition is true, the loop body is executed again and the next value of `fahrenheit` is computed and displayed. If the condition is false, the loop is exited.

Table 5.2   Trace of Program Loop in Fig. 5.9

	Statement	celsius	fahrenheit	Effect
①	for (celsius = CBEGIN;	10	?	Initialize `celsius` to 10
②	celsius >= CLIMIT;			10 >= −5 is true
	. . .			
④	fahrenheit = 1.8 *			
	celsius + 32.0;		50.0	Assign 50.0 to fahrenheit

(continued)

Table 5.2 (continued)

	Statement	celsius	fahrenheit	Effect
⑤	printf . . .			Display 10 and 50.0
	Update and test celsius			
③	. . . celsius -= CSTEP	5		Subtract 5 from celsius, giving 5
②	celsius >= CLIMIT;			5 >= -5 is true
④	fahrenheit = 1.8 * celsius + 32.0;		41.0	Assign 41.0 to fahrenheit
⑤	printf . . .			Display 5 and 41.0
	Update and test celsius			
③	. . . celsius -= CSTEP	0		Subtract 5 from celsius, giving 0
②	celsius >= CLIMIT;			0 >= -5 is true
④	fahrenheit = 1.8 * celsius + 32.0;		32.0	Assign 32.0 to fahrenheit
⑤	printf . . .			Display 0 and 32.0
	Update and test celsius			
③	. . . celsius -= CSTEP	-5		Subtract 5 from celsius, giving -5
②	celsius >= CLIMIT;			-5 >= -5 is true
④	fahrenheit = 1.8 * celsius + 32.0;		23.0	Assign 23.0 to fahrenheit
⑤	printf . . .			Display -5 and 23.0
	Update and test celsius			
③	. . . celsius -= CSTEP	-10		Subtract 5 from celsius, giving -10
②	celsius >= CLIMIT;			-10 >= -5 is false, so exit loop

Because the structure of the for statement makes it easy for the reader of a program to identify the major loop control elements, we will use it in the remainder of our study of repetition whenever a loop requires simple initialization, testing, and updating of a loop control variable.

Increment and Decrement Operators

The counting loops that you have seen have all included assignment expressions of the form

```
counter = counter + 1
```

or

```
counter += 1
```

The increment operator ++ takes a single variable of type int or type char as its operand. The *side effect* of applying the ++ operator is that the value of its operand is incremented by one. Frequently, ++ is used just for this side effect as in the following loop in which the counter ct is to run from 0 up to limit:

```
for (ct = 0;  ct < limit;  ++ct)
    . . .
```

The *value* of the expression in which the ++ operator is used depends on the position of the operator. When the ++ is placed immediately in front of its operand (*prefix increment*), the value of the expression is the variable's value *after* incrementing. When the ++ comes immediately after the operand (*postfix increment*), the expression's value is the value of the variable *before* it is incremented. Compare the action of the two code segments in Fig. 5.10, given an initial value of 2 in i.

Figure 5.10 Comparison of Prefix and Postfix Increments

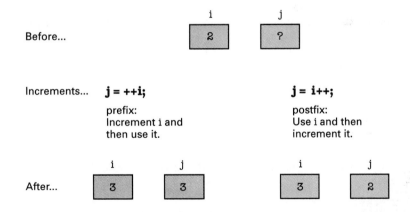

C also provides a decrement operator that can be used in either the prefix or postfix position. For example, if the initial value of n is 4, the code fragment on the left prints

3   3

and the one on the right prints

    4   3

```
printf("%3d", --n);              printf("%3d", n--);
printf("%3d", n);                printf("%3d", n);
```

You should avoid using the increment and decrement operators in complex expressions in which the variables to which they are applied appear more than once. C compilers are expected to exploit the commutativity and associativity of various operators in order to produce efficient code. For example, this code fragment may assign **y** the value 13 (2 * 5 + 3) in one implementation and the value 18 (3 * 5 + 3) in another.

```
x = 5;
i = 2;
y = i * x + ++i;
```

A programmer must not depend on side effects that will vary from one compiler to another.

**EXERCISES FOR
SECTION 5.3**

Self-Check

1. Trace the execution of the loop that follows for n = 8. Show values of odd and sum after the update of the loop counter for each iteration.

```
sum = 0;
for   (odd = 1;
           odd < n;
           odd += 2)
      sum = sum + odd;

printf("Sum of positive odd numbers less than %d is %d.\n",
           n, sum);
```

2. Given the constant macro definitions of Fig. 5.9 (repeated here)

```
#define CBEGIN 10
#define CLIMIT -5
#define CSTEP  5
```

indicate what values of celsius would appear in the conversion table displayed if the for loop header of Fig. 5.9 were rewritten as shown:

```
a. for  (celsius = CLIMIT;
             celsius >= CBEGIN;
             celsius += CSTEP)
b. for  (celsius = CLIMIT;
             celsius <= CBEGIN;
             celsius += CSTEP)
c. for  (celsius = CLIMIT;
             celsius <= CSTEP;
             celsius += CBEGIN)
d. for  (celsius = CSTEP;
             celsius >= CBEGIN;
             celsius += CLIMIT)
```

3. What is the smallest number of times that the body of a while loop can be executed? The body of a for loop?

4. What values are assigned to n, m, and p, given these initial values?

i	j	```n = ++i* --j;```
		```m = i +j--;```
		```p = i +j;```

3	9	

5. Rewrite the code shown in Exercise 4 so the effect is equivalent but no increment/decrement operator appears in an expression with another arithmetic operator.

6. What errors do you see in the following segment? Correct the code so it displays all multiples of 5 from 0 through 100.

```
for mult5 = 0;
mult5 < 100;
mult5 += 5;
printf("%d\n", mult5);
```

7. a. Trace the following program segment:

```
j = 10;
for  (i = 1;  i <= 5;  ++i) {
    printf("%d  %d\n", i, j);
    j -= 2;
}
```

b. Rewrite the previous program segment so that it produces the same output but uses 0 as the initial value of i.

Programming

1. Write a loop that displays a table of angle measures along with their sine and cosine values. Assume that the initial and final angle measures (in degrees) are available in `init_degree` and `final_degree` (type `int` variables), and that the change in angle measure between table entries is given by `step_degree` (also a type `int` variable). Remember that the math library's `sin` and `cos` functions take arguments that are in radians.
2. Write a program to display an inches-to-centimeters conversion table. The smallest and largest number of inches in the table are input values. Your table should give conversions in 6-inch intervals. One inch equals 2.54 cm.

5.4 CONDITIONAL LOOPS

In many programming situations, you will not be able to determine the exact number of loop repetitions before loop execution begins. When we multiplied a list of numbers in Example 5.2, the number of repetitions depended on the data entered. Although we did not know in advance how many times the loop would execute, we were still able to write a condition to control the loop. Here is another case of this type of repetition. You want to continue prompting the user for a data value as long as the response is unreasonable.

> Print an initial prompting message.
> Get the number of observed values.
> while the number of values is negative
> > Print a warning and another prompting message.
> > Get the number of observed values.

Like the counting loops we considered earlier, such a conditional loop typically has three parts that control repetition: initialization, testing of a loop repetition condition, and an update. Let's analyze the algorithm for ensuring valid input. Clearly, the loop repetition condition is

number of values < 0

Because it makes no sense to test this condition unless *number of values* has a meaning, getting this value must be the initialization step. The update action—the statement that, if left out, would cause the loop to repeat infinitely—remains to be identified. Getting a new number of observed values within the loop body is just such a step. Since we have found these three essential loop parts, we can write this validating input loop in C by using a `for` statement:

```
printf("Enter number of observed values> ");
for  (scanf("%d", &num_obs);            /* initialization      */
        num_obs < 0;            /* loop repetition condition   */
        scanf("%d", &num_obs))            /* update            */
      printf("Negative number invalid; try again> ");
```

At first, it may seem odd that the initialization and update steps are identical. In fact, this is very often the case for loops performing input operations in situations where the number of input values is not known in advance.

EXAMPLE 5.3  The program in Fig. 5.11 is designed to assist in monitoring the gasoline supply in a storage tank at the Super Oil Company refinery. The program is to alert the supervisor when the supply of gasoline in the tank falls below 10% of the tank's 80,000-barrel storage capacity. Although the supervisor always deals with the contents of the tank in terms of a number of *barrels,* the pump that is used to fill tanker trucks gives its measurements in *gallons.* The barrel used in the petroleum industry equals 42 U.S. gallons.

Figure 5.11   Program to Monitor Gasoline Storage Tank

```
/*
 * Monitor gasoline supply in storage tank. Issue warning when supply falls
 * below MIN_PCT % of tank capacity.
 */

#include <stdio.h>

/* constant macros */
#define CAPACITY      80000.0 /* number of barrels tank can hold           */
#define MIN_PCT       10       /* warn when supply falls below this percent
                                   of capacity                             */
#define GALS_PER_BRL 42.0     /* number of U.S. gallons in one barrel      */

int
main(void)
{
        double start_supply, /* initial supply in barrels                  */
```

(continued)

Figure 5.11 (continued)

```
                min_supply,    /* minimum number of barrels left without
                                   warning                                 */
                current,       /* current supply in barrels                */
                remov_gals,    /* amount of current delivery in            */
                remov_brls;    /*    barrels and gallons                    */

      /* Compute minimum supply without warning                            */
      min_supply = MIN_PCT / 100.0 * CAPACITY;

      /* Get initial supply and subtract amounts removed as long as
         minimum supply remains                                            */
      printf("Number of barrels currently in tank> ");
      scanf("%lf", &start_supply);
      for  (current = start_supply;
            current >= min_supply;
            current -= remov_brls) {
         printf("%.2f barrels are available.\n\n", current);
         printf("Enter number of gallons removed> ");
         scanf("%lf", &remov_gals);
         remov_brls = remov_gals / GALS_PER_BRL;

         printf("After removal of %.2f gallons (%.2f barrels),\n",
                remov_gals, remov_brls);
      }

      /* Issue warning                                                     */
      printf("only %.2f barrels are left.\n\n", current);
      printf("*** WARNING ***\n");
      printf("Available supply is less than %d percent of tank's ",
             MIN_PCT);
      printf("%.2f-barrel capacity.\n", CAPACITY);

      return (0);
}

Number of barrels currently in tank> 8500.5
8500.50 barrels are available.

Enter number of gallons removed> 5859.0
After removal of 5859.00 gallons (139.50 barrels),
8361.00 barrels are available.
```

(continued)

Figure 5.11   (continued)

```
Enter number of gallons removed> 7568.4
After removal of 7568.40 gallons (180.20 barrels),
8180.80 barrels are available.

Enter number of gallons removed> 8400.0
After removal of 8400.00 gallons (200.00 barrels),
only 7980.80 barrels are left.

*** WARNING ***
Available supply is less than 10 percent of tank's 80000.00-barrel capacity.
```

The program first requests that the operator enter the amount of gasoline currently stored in the tank. Then, after gasoline is pumped into each tanker, the operator enters the number of gallons removed and the program updates the number of barrels still available. When the supply drops below the 10% limit, the program issues a warning.

A counting loop would not be appropriate in this program because we do not know in advance how many tanker deliveries will need to be processed before the warning is issued. However, the `for` statement is still a good choice because we do have initialization, testing, and update steps.

Let's take a close look at the loop in the program of Fig. 5.11. Logically, we want to continue to record amounts of gasoline removed as long as the supply in the tank does not fall below the minimum. The loop repetition condition, the second expression in the `for` loop heading, states that we stay in the loop as long as

```
current >= min_supply;
```

Since `min_supply` does not change, `current` is the variable that controls the loop. Therefore the first and third expressions of the `for` statement's heading handle the initialization and update of this variable's value.

Walking through this program with the data shown, we come first to the assignment statement that computes a value for `min_supply` of `8000.0`, based on the tank capacity and minimum percentage. The call to `printf` just before the call to `scanf` generates the prompting message for entering the tank's initial supply. Next, the starting supply entered by the program operator is scanned into variable `start_supply`. The initialization expression of the `for` statement copies the starting supply into `current`, the loop control variable, giving `current` the value `8500.5`. When the loop repetition condition

```
current >= min_supply;
```

is first tested, it evaluates to true, causing the loop body (the compound statement in braces) to execute. The current supply is displayed followed by a prompting message. A value is obtained for gallons removed (5859.0), the value is converted to barrels, and this amount is displayed. When execution of the loop body is complete, the update expression of the for statement

```
current -= remov_brls;
```

is executed, subtracting from the current supply the amount removed. The loop repetition condition is retested with the new value of current (8361.00). Since 8361.00 > 8000.0 is true, the loop body once again displays the current supply and processes a delivery of 7568.4 gallons, or 180.20 barrels. The value of current is then updated to 8180.80 barrels, which is still not below the minimum, so the loop body executes a third time, processing removal of 200.00 barrels. This time execution of the for statement update expression brings the value of current to 7980.80. The loop repetition condition is tested again: Since 7980.8 >= 8000.0 is false, loop exit occurs, and the statements following the closing brace of the loop body are executed.

Just as in the counting loop shown in Fig. 5.7, there are three critical steps in Fig. 5.11 that involve the loop control variable current.

1. current is *initialized* to the starting supply in the for statement initialization expression.
2. current is *tested* before each execution of the loop body.
3. current is *updated* (by subtraction of the amount removed) during each iteration. ⬅

Remember that steps similar to these appear in virtually every loop you write. The C for statement heading provides you with a designated place for each of the three steps.

EXERCISES FOR SECTION 5.4

Self-Check

1. Give an example of data the user could enter for the storage tank monitoring program that would cause the body of the for loop to be completely skipped.
2. Correct the syntax and logic of the code that follows so that it prints all multiples of 5 from 0 through 100:

```
for sum = 0;
    sum < 100;
    sum += 5;
printf("%d\n", sum);
```

3. What output is displayed if this list of data is used for the program in Fig. 5.11?

   8350.8
   7581.0
   7984.2

4. How would you modify the program in Fig. 5.11 so that it also determines the number of deliveries (`count_deliv`) made before the gasoline supply drops below the minimum? Which is the loop control variable, `current` or `count_deliv`?

Programming

1. There are 9870 people in a town whose population increases by 10 percent each year. Write a loop that displays the annual population and determines how many years (`count_years`) it will take for the population to surpass 30,000.

5.5 LOOP DESIGN

Being able to analyze the operation of a loop is one thing; designing your own loops is another. In this section, we will consider the latter. The comment that begins the program in Fig. 5.11 is a good summary of the purpose of the loop in this program.

```
/*
 * Monitor gasoline supply in storage tank. Issue
 * warning when supply falls below MIN_PCT% of tank
 * capacity.
 */
```

Let's see how the problem-solving questions suggested in Sections 2.1 and 5.1 can help us formulate a valid loop structure. As always, the columns labeled "Answer" and "Implications . . ." in Table 5.3 represent an individual problem solver's thought processes and are not offered as the "one and only true path" to a solution.

Table 5.3 Problem-Solving Questions for Loop Design

Question	Answer	Implications for the Algorithm
What are the inputs?	Current supply of gasoline (barrels). Amounts removed (gallons).	Input variables needed: `current` `remov_gals` Value of `current` must be input once, but amounts removed are entered many times.
What are the outputs?	Amounts removed in gallons and barrels, the current supply of gasoline, and warning when current supply drops too low.	Values of `current` and `remov_gals` are echoed in the output. Output variable needed: `remov_brls`
Is there any repetition?	Yes. One repeatedly 1. gets amount removed 2. converts the amount to barrels 3. subtracts the amount removed from the current supply 4. checks to see whether the supply has fallen below the minimum.	Program variable needed: `min_supply`
Do I know in advance how many times steps will be repeated?	No.	Loop will not be controlled by a counter.
How do I know how long to keep repeating the steps?	As long as the current supply is not below the minimum.	The loop repetition condition is `current >= min_supply`

Sentinel-Controlled Loops

Frequently, you will not be able to determine exactly how many data items a program will process until after the program begins execution. There may be too many data items to count beforehand, or the number of data items provided may depend on how the computation proceeds. One way to handle this situation is to require the user to enter a unique data value to mark the end of the data. The program can compare each value to the *sentinel value* and terminate after this special value is input.

The typical form of a loop that is processing data until the sentinel value is entered is

1. Get a line of data.
2. while the sentinel value has not been encountered
    3. Process the data line.
    4. Get another line of data.

Note that this loop, like other loops we have studied, has an *initialization* (Step 1), a *loop repetition condition* (Step 2), and an *update* (Step 4). Step 1 gets the first line of data; Step 4 gets all the other data lines and then tries to obtain one more line. This attempted extra input permits entry of the sentinel value. The sentinel must be a value that would not be entered as a normal data item. For program readability, we usually name the sentinel by defining a constant macro.

EXAMPLE 5.4

This example shows a sentinel-controlled loop that accumulates the sum of a collection of exam scores, where each score is copied from the input device into the variable `score`. The outline for this solution is as follows:

Sentinel Loop

1. Initialize `sum` to zero.
2. Get first `score`.
3. while `score` is not the `sentinel`
    4. Add `score` to `sum`.
    5. Get next `score`.

One is tempted to try the following algorithm that reverses the order of Steps 4 and 5 so as to be able to omit the duplication of Step 5 in Step 2.

Incorrect Sentinel Loop

1. Initialize `sum` to zero.
2. while `score` is not the `sentinel`
    3. Get `score`.
    4. Add `score` to `sum`.

There are two problems associated with this strategy. First, with no initializing input statement, you will have no value for `score` on which to judge the loop repetition condition when it is first tested. Second, consider the last two iterations of the loop. On the next-to-last iteration, the last data value is copied into `score` and added to the accumulating `sum`; on the last iteration, the attempt to get another score obtains the sentinel value. However, this fact will not cause the loop to exit until the loop repetition condition is tested again. Before exit occurs, the sentinel is added to sum. For these reasons, it is important to set up sentinel-controlled loops using the recommended structure: one input to get the loop going (the *initialization* input), and a second to keep it going (the *update* input). The following program uses a for structure to implement the sentinel-controlled loop (Fig. 5.12). It also shows that the declaration of a variable may include an initialization.

The following sample dialogue would be used to enter the scores 55, 33, and 77:

```
Enter first score (or -99 to quit)> 55
Enter next score (-99 to quit)> 33
Enter next score (-99 to quit)> 77
Enter next score (-99 to quit)> -99

Sum of exam scores is 165
```

It is usually instructive (and often necessary) to question what happens when there are no data items to process. In this case, the sentinel value would be

Figure 5.12   Program Showing a Sentinel-Controlled Loop

```
/* Compute the sum of a list of exam scores. */

#include <stdio.h>

#define SENTINEL -99

int
main(void)
{
      int sum = 0,    /* sum of scores input so far            */
          score;      /* current score                         */
      printf("Enter first score (or %d to quit)> ", SENTINEL);
      for   (scanf("%d", &score);
             score != SENTINEL;
             scanf("%d", &score)) {
          sum += score;
          printf("Enter next score (%d to quit)> ", SENTINEL);
      }
```

(continued)

Figure 5.12 Program Showing a Sentinel-Controlled Loop

```
        printf("\nSum of exam scores is %d\n", sum);

        return (0);
}
```

entered at the first prompt. Loop exit would occur right after the first and only test of the loop repetition condition, so the loop body would not be executed—that is, it is a loop with zero iterations. The variable sum would correctly retain its initial value of zero. ←

Endfile-Controlled Loops

In Section 2.7, we discussed writing programs to run in batch mode using data files accessed either through file pointers or by input redirection. A data file is always terminated by an endfile character that can be detected by the scanf and fscanf functions. Therefore it is possible to write a batch program that processes a list of data of any length without requiring a special sentinel value at the end of the data.

To write such a program, you must set up your input loop so it notices when scanf or its file equivalent encounters the endfile character. So far we have discussed only the effect scanf has on the variables passed to it as arguments. However, scanf also returns a result value just like the functions we studied in Section 3.5. When scanf is successfully able to fill its argument variables with values from the standard input device, the result value that it returns is the number of data items it actually obtained. For example, successful execution of the scanf in this statement returns a 3, which is assigned to input_status:

```
input_status = scanf("%d%d%lf", &part_id, &num_avail, &cost);
```

However, if scanf runs into difficulty with invalid or insufficient data (for instance, if it comes across the letter 'o' instead of a zero when trying to get a decimal integer), the function returns as its value the number of data items scanned before encountering the error or running out of data. This means that for the example shown, a nonnegative value less than 3 returned by scanf indicates an error. The third situation scanf can encounter is detecting the endfile character before getting input data for any of its arguments. In this case, `scanf` returns as its result the value of the standard constant EOF (a negative integer).

It is possible to design a repetition statement very similar to the sentinel-controlled loop that uses the status value returned by the scanning function to control repetition rather than using the values scanned. An example of such a loop is shown in Fig. 5.13, which is a batch version of the exam scores program in Fig. 5.12.

Figure 5.13　Batch Version of Sum of Exam Scores Program

```
/*
 *  Compute the sum of the list of exam scores stored in the
 *  file scores.dat
 */

#include <stdio.h>        /* defines fopen, fclose, fscanf,
                              fprintf, and EOF                 */

int
main(void)
{
      FILE *inp;           /* input file pointer              */
      int   sum = 0,       /* sum of scores input so far      */
            score,         /* current score                   */
            input_status; /* status value returned by fscanf */

      inp = fopen("scores.dat", "r");

      printf("Scores\n");

      for  (input_status = fscanf(inp, "%d", &score);
            input_status != EOF;
            input_status = fscanf(inp, "%d", &score)) {
         printf("%5d\n", score);
         sum += score;
      }

      printf("\nSum of exam scores is %d\n", sum);
      fclose(inp);

      return (0);
}
```

(continued)

Figure 5.13 (continued)

```
Scores
   55
   33
   77

Sum of exam scores is 165
```

Infinite Loops on Faulty Data

The behavior of the `scanf` and `fscanf` functions when they encounter faulty data can quickly make infinite loops of the `for` statements in Figs. 5.12 and 5.13. For example, let's assume the user responds to the prompt

```
Enter next score (-99 to quit)>
```

in Fig. 5.12 with the faulty data 7o (the second character is the letter `'o'` rather than a zero). The function `scanf` would stop at the letter `'o'`, storing just the value 7 in `score` and leaving the letter `'o'` unprocessed. On the next loop iteration, there would be no wait for the user to respond to the prompt, for `scanf` would find the letter `'o'` awaiting processing. However, since this letter is not part of a valid integer, the `scanf` function would then leave the variable `score` unchanged and the letter `'o'` unprocessed, returning a status value of zero as the result of the function call. Because the sentinel-controlled loop of Fig. 5.12 does not use the value returned by `scanf`, the printing of the prompt and the unsuccessful attempt to process the letter `'o'` would repeat over and over.

Even though the loop of the batch program in Fig. 5.13 does use the status value returned by `fscanf`, it too would go into an infinite loop on faulty data. The only status value that causes this loop to exit is the negative integer meaning EOF. However, the endfile-controlled loop could be easily modified to exit when encountering end of file or faulty data. Changing the loop repetition condition to

```
input_status == 1
```

would cause the loop to exit on either end of file (`input_status` negative) or faulty data (`input_status` zero). We would also need to add an `if` statement after the loop to decide whether to simply print the results or to warn of bad input.

```
if (input_status == EOF) {
    printf("Sum of exam scores is %d\n", sum);
} else {
    fscanf(inp, "%c", &bad_char);
    printf("*** Error in input: %c ***\n", bad_char);
}
```

EXERCISES FOR SECTION 5.5

Self-Check

1. Identify these three steps in the pseudocode that follows: the initialization of the loop control variable, the loop repetition condition, and the update of the loop control variable.
   a. Get a value for n.
   b. Give p the value 1.
   c. while n is positive
         d. Multiply p by n.
         e. Subtract 1 from n.
   f. Print p with a label.
2. What would be the behavior of the loop in Fig. 5.13 if the braces around the loop body were omitted?

Programming

1. Translate the pseudocode from Exercise 1 using a `for` loop. Which of these three labels would it make sense to print along with the value of p?

   `n*i =`   `n! =`   `n to the ith power =`

2. Modify the loop in Fig. 5.4 so that it is a sentinel-controlled loop. Get an input value for `orbits` as both the initialization and update steps of the loop. Use the value −99 as the sentinel.
3. Rewrite the program in Fig. 5.4 to run in batch mode with an endfile-controlled loop.
4. Write a program segment that allows the user to enter values and prints out the number of positive and the number of negative values entered. Design this segment as a sentinel-controlled loop using zero as the sentinel value.

5.6 NESTED CONTROL STRUCTURES

In many programming situations, it is necessary to nest one control structure inside another. We discussed the nested `if` structure in Section 4.4 and considered several examples. It is also possible to nest if statements within loops and to nest loops within other control structures. The program in Fig. 5.14 contains an if statement nested within a loop that calculates the product of all nonzero data items. Each data item is tested, the nonzero values are included in the product being computed, and the loop is exited after the sentinel is encountered.

Figure 5.14   Program to Find the Product of Nonzero Data Items

```
/* Finds the product of nonzero data. */

#include <stdio.h>

#define SENT -9999.0

int
main(void)
{
      double product = 1.0; /* product so far of nonzero data        */
      int    status;        /* status of input operation             */
      double data_item;     /* current data value                    */

      printf("Enter a data item (%.1f to quit)> ", SENT);
      for  (scanf("%lf", &data_item);
            data_item != SENT;
            scanf("%lf", &data_item)) {
         if (data_item != 0)
             product *= data_item;

         printf("Enter next data item (%.1f to quit)> ", SENT);
      }

      printf("The product of nonzero data is %8.3f.\n", product);

      return (0);
}
```
```
Enter a data item (-9999.0 to quit)> 3.0
Enter next data item (-9999.0 to quit)> 0.0
Enter next data item (-9999.0 to quit)> -1.0
Enter next data item (-9999.0 to quit)> -9999.0
The product of nonzero data is   -3.000.
```

Nested Loops

The last category of nested structures that we will consider is nested loops, the most difficult of all nested structures to deal with. For each iteration of the outer loop, the control structure that is the inner loop is entered and repeated until done.

EXAMPLE 5.5   The program in Fig. 5.15 contains a sentinel loop nested within a counting loop. This structure is being used to tally by month the local Audubon Club members' sightings of bald eagles for the past year. The data for this program consists of a group of positive integers followed by a zero, then a second group of positive integers followed by a zero, then a third group, and so on, for twelve groups of numbers. The first group of numbers represents sightings in January, the second represents sightings in February, and so on, for all twelve months.

Figure 5.15   Program to Process Bald Eagle Sightings for a Year

```
/*
 * Tally by month the bald eagle sightings for the year. Each month's
 * sightings are terminated by the sentinel zero.
 */

#include <stdio.h>

#define SENTINEL    0
#define NUM_MONTHS 12

int
main(void)
{
        int month,      /* number of month being processed            */
            mem_sight, /* one member's sightings for this month      */
            sightings; /* total sightings so far for this month      */

        printf("BALD EAGLE SIGHTINGS\n");
        for (month = 1;
             month <= NUM_MONTHS;
             ++month) {
             sightings = 0;
```

(continued)

Figure 5.15 (continued)

```
for (scanf("%d", &mem_sight);
     mem_sight != SENTINEL;
     scanf("%d", &mem_sight)) {
   sightings += mem_sight;
}
      printf("  month %2d: %2d\n", month, sightings);
   }

   return (0);
}
```

Input data
2 1 4 3 0
1 2 0
0
5 4 1 0
. . .

Results
BALD EAGLE SIGHTINGS
  month 1: 10
  month 2: 3
  month 3: 0
  month 4: 10
  . . .

EXAMPLE 5.6 In Fig. 5.16, we see a sample run of a program with two nested counting loops. The outer loop is repeated three times (for i = 1, 2, and 3). Each time the outer loop is repeated, the statement

```
printf("Outer %6d\n", i);
```

displays the string "Outer" and the value of i (the outer loop control variable). Next, the inner loop is entered, and its loop control variable j is reset to 0. The number of times the inner loop is repeated depends on the current value of i. Each time the inner loop is repeated, the statement

```
printf("  Inner %9d\n", j);
```

displays the string "Inner" and the value of j.

Figure 5.16   Nested Counting Loop Program

```
/*
 * Illustrates a pair of nested counting loops
 */

#include <stdio.h>

int
main(void)
{
        int i, j;    /* loop control variables */

        printf("           I    J\n");            /* prints column labels */

        for  (i = 1;  i < 4;  ++i)   { /* heading of outer for loop */
            printf("Outer %6d\n", i);

            for  (j = 0;  j < i;  ++j)       { /* heading of inner loop */
                printf("  Inner%9d\n", j);
            }    /* end of inner loop */

        }    /*  end of outer loop */

        return (0);

}
```

```
          I   J
Outer     1
   Inner      0
Outer     2
   Inner      0
   Inner      1
Outer     3
   Inner      0
   Inner      1
   Inner      2
```

A compound statement executes each time the outer `for` loop is repeated. This statement displays the value of the outer loop control variable and then executes the inner `for` loop. The body of the inner `for` loop is a single statement

displaying the value of the inner loop control variable. This statement executes
i times where i is the outer loop control variable.

The outer loop control variable i appears in the condition that determines
the number of repetitions of the inner loop. Although this usage is perfectly
valid, it is not legitimate to use the same variable as the loop control variable of
both an outer and an inner for loop in the same nest.   ←

**EXERCISES FOR
SECTION 5.6**

Self-Check

1. What is displayed by the following program segments, assuming m is 3 and n
   is 5?

   a. ```
      for (i = 1;   i <= n;   ++i) {
          for (j = 0;   j < i;   ++j) {
              printf("*");
          }
          printf("\n");
      }
      ```
   b. ```
      for  (i = n;   i > 0;   --i) {
          for  (j = m;   j > 0;   --j) {
              printf("*");
          }
          printf("\n");
      }
      ```

2. Show the output displayed by these nested loops:

   ```
   for  (i = 0;   i < 2;   ++i) {
       printf("Outer %4d\n", i);
       for  (j = 0;   j < 3;   ++j) {
           printf("   Inner%3d%3d\n", i, j);
       }
       for  (k = 2;   k > 0;   --k) {
           printf("   Inner%3d%3d\n", i, k);
       }
   }
   ```

Programming

1. Write a program that displays the multiplication table for numbers 0 to 9.
2. Write nests of loops that cause the following output to be displayed:

```
0
0 1
0 1 2
0 1 2 3
0 1 2 3 4
0 1 2 3
0 1 2
0 1
0
```

5.7 FLAG-CONTROLLED LOOPS

In all the loops we have seen up to this point, we have viewed the loop initialization and update steps as two distinct entities. In many situations where repetition is used, this procedure is essential because not all the repeated steps are to
be executed the same number of times. For example, when we first list the
steps to be performed in a sentinel loop that is processing a list of numbers, we
have

1. Get a number.
2. Process the number.

However, when we begin to use these steps as the basis of a loop body repeated
as long as the number is not the sentinel, we soon realize that some revision is
necessary. In fact, it is not true that all numbers in our list are to receive identical processing. The number that is the sentinel must *not* be processed like the
other numbers. We saw that an efficient way to accomplish this was to designate
Step 1 as both the initialization and update steps of a `for` loop, leaving only
Step 2 as the loop body.

  In some circumstances, however, *all* elements of a list should actually be
processed identically. In such cases, C's `do-while` statement is an excellent
loop structure to choose. In Fig. 5.17, we see a program that repeatedly prompts
the user for a value falling in the range from n_min to n_max inclusive. The
outer `do-while` structure implements the stated purpose of the program; the
inner `do-while` skips the rest of a line of input by repeatedly scanning a
character and checking the input value to see whether it is the newline character
`'\n'`.

Figure 5.17   Validating Input Using do-while Statement

```
/*
 * Gets an integer input value in the range from n_min to n_max inclusive.
 * Gives an error message on input of an invalid data type, and clears
 * character causing error.
 */
int
main(void)
{
      int   n_min, n_max,     /* minimum and maximum valid values      */
            inval,            /* data value which user enters          */
            status;           /* status value returned by scanf        */
      char  skip_ch;          /* character to skip                     */
      int   error;            /* error flag for bad input              */

      printf("Enter minimum and maximum valid values> ");
      scanf("%d%d", &n_min, &n_max);
      do {
          printf("Enter an integer in the range from %d to %d inclusive> ",
                  n_min, n_max);
          status = scanf("%d", &inval);
          if (status == 1) {
                error = 0;
          } else {
                error = 1;
                scanf("%c", &skip_ch);
                printf("\nInvalid character>>%c>> Skipping rest of line.\n",
                        skip_ch);

                do {
                    scanf("%c", &skip_ch);
                } while (skip_ch != '\n');

          }
      } while (error || inval < n_min || inval > n_max);

      /* Rest of Processing */
}
```

Execution of the program in Fig. 5.17 would proceed as shown next, assuming that the user responds to the first prompt by mistyping the number 10 as a 1 followed by the letter o. Notice that when the program first encounters the o, it does not flag the character as an error. The program simply scans up to the o, stops scanning, and then stores the 1. Because the number 1 is outside the acceptable range of values, the `do-while` does not exit. Instead, it prompts again for input, but then `scanf` tries to convert the o to an integer. At this point, the error message is printed.

```
Enter an integer in the range from 10 to 20 inclusive> 1o
Enter an integer in the range from 10 to 20 inclusive>
Invalid character >>o>> Skipping rest of line.
Enter an integer in the range from 10 to 20 inclusive> 10
```

Getting a prompt with no opportunity to respond to it is annoying, but at least the prompts do not keep appearing indefinitely. Table 5.4 traces the execution of the program in Fig. 5.17.

Figure 5.18 shows a flowchart of an input validation loop like the `do-while` loop of Fig. 5.17. Notice that the first iteration of the loop body occurs unconditionally and that all input values receive the same processing.

Checking for valid input is one situation in which the `do-while` is often the structure to choose. The `do-while` used in Fig. 5.17 also shows one way to avoid the infinite input loops one can easily get into when using `scanf` if the user types an invalid character. As soon as the input loop of Fig. 5.17

**Figure 5.18
Flowchart of
Input Validation
Loop**

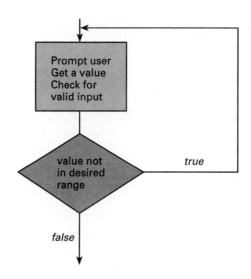

Table 5.4 Trace of Input-Validation Program

Statement	n_min	n_max	inval	status	skip_ch	error	Effect
`printf("Enter min...`	?	?	?	?	?	?	Initial prompting message
`scanf("%d%d", &n_min...`	10	20					n_min and n_max initialized to values entered: 10 and 20.
`printf("Enter...`							Prompting message displayed.
`status = scanf("%d", &inval);`			1	1			Assuming the characters 1 and o are typed, the 1 is stored in inval and the scanf function returns a 1. Scanning stops at the letter o.
`if (status == 1)`							Condition is true.
`error = 0;`						0	Error flag is set to false.
`while (error || inval < n_min || inval > nmax)`							1 < 10, so loop repetition condition is true.
`printf("Enter...`							Prompting message is displayed again.
`status = scanf("%d", &inval);`				0			scanf encounters the unprocessed letter o and returns an error code of 0.
`if (status == 1)`							Condition is false.
`error = 1;`						1	Error flag is set to true.

(continued)

Table 5.4 (continued)

Statement	n_min	n_max	inval	status	skip_ch	error	Effect
`scanf("%c", &skip_ch);` `printf(` `"Invalid...`					o		Letter causing a problem is copied into skip_ch and printed.
`do {` `    scanf(...` `} while (...`					\n		Remainder of input line is scanned.
`while (error ||` `inval < n_min` `|| inval >` `nmax)`							error is true, so loop repetition condition is true.
`printf("Enter...`							Prompting message is displayed again.
`status =` `scanf("%d",` `    &inval);`			10	1			This time user types 10 correctly, so 10 is stored in inval and scanf returns 1, which is stored in status.
`if (status == 1)`							Condition is true.
`error = 0;`						0	Error flag is set to false.
`while (error ||` `inval < n_min` `|| inval >` `nmax)`							error is false, 10 is not less than 10, and 10 is not greater than 20, so loop exits.
`...`							Processing continues using 10 for inval.

receives a status code from `scanf` indicating an error, the loop body explicitly scans and echoes the bad character, skips the rest of the input line, and sets the error flag so the loop will execute again, permitting fresh (and hopefully valid) input.

The syntax of the `do-while` follows.

---

do-while Statement

SYNTAX: do
           statement
       while (*loop repetition condition*);

EXAMPLE: /* Find first even number input */
       do
            status = scanf("%d", &num);
       while (status > 0 && num % 2 != 0);

INTERPRETATION: First, the *statement* is executed. Then, the *loop repetition condition* is tested, and if it is true, the *statement* is re-executed and the *condition* retested. The *statement* is executed repeatedly as long as the *loop repetition condition* is true. When this condition is tested and found to be false, the loop is exited and the next statement after the `do-while` is executed.

NOTE: If the loop body contains more than one statement, the group of statements must be surrounded by braces.

Flag-Controlled Loops for Input Validation

Sometimes a loop repetition condition becomes so complex that placing the full expression in its usual spot is awkward. In many cases, the condition may be simplified by using a *flag*. A *flag* is a type `int` variable used to represent whether or not a certain event has occurred. The program of Fig. 5.17 uses the variable `error` as a flag to record whether or not a bad character has been encountered in the input.

Frequently, a flag is initialized to 0 (false) at the beginning of processing and is changed to 1 (true) when the anticipated event occurs. Figure 5.19 uses another flag named `error` to represent whether or not any type of error in the form of the current input has been detected. The expected input is a common fraction or ratio entered as an integer numerator, the slash character, and a positive integer denominator.

Figure 5.19   Flag-Controlled Validation Loop for Input of a Common Fraction

```
/*
 * Gets a valid fraction
 * A valid fraction is of this form: integer/positive integer
 */

int
main(void)
{
      int  num, den;          /* numerator, denominator of fraction      */
      char slash;             /* character between numerator and
                                 denominator                             */
      int  status;            /* status code returned by scanf indicating
                                 number of valid values obtained         */
      int  error;             /* flag indicating whether or not an error has
                                 been detected in current input          */
      char discard;           /* unprocessed character from input line   */

      do {
         /* No errors detected yet                                       */
         error = 0;

         /* Get a fraction from the user                                 */
         printf("Enter a common fraction as two integers separated by ");
         printf("a slash\nand press <enter> or <return>\n ");
         status = scanf("%d%c%d", &num, &slash, &den);

         /* Validate the fraction                                        */
         if (status < 3) {
               error = 1;
               printf("Input invalid--please read directions carefully\n");
         } else if (slash != '/') {
               error = 1;
               printf("Input invalid--separate numerator and denominator");
               printf(" by a slash (/)\n");
         } else if (den <= 0) {
               error = 1;
               printf("Input invalid--denominator must be positive\n");
         }
```

(continued)

Figure 5.19   (continued)

```
            /* Discard extra input characters                      */
            do {
                scanf("%c", &discard);
            } while (discard != '\n');
        } while (error);

        /* Finish processing of fraction - code omitted            */
}
```

Let's see why the validation process shown in Fig. 5.19 needs a step to clear a line of invalid input. If the input provided were

85.0/3<return>

the format specifiers of the statement

status = scanf("%d%c%d", &num, &slash, &den);

would process the line as follows. The first %d would be used to scan the 85. Then, the decimal point would be processed using %c, and the 0 would be used by the second %d. If the remaining characters (/3<return>) are not discarded, they will be processed on the next iteration of the input loop. The input-discarding loop takes one character at a time until the newline character '\n' is recognized. This character results from the user's typing the <enter> or <return> key. On valid input, this character should be the very next one after the valid fraction's denominator.

EXERCISES FOR SECTION 5.7

Self-Check

1. Which of the following code segments is a better way to implement a sentinel-controlled loop? Why?

```
for  (scanf("%d", &num);         do {
      num != SENT;                     scanf("%d", &num);
      scanf("%d", &num)) {             if (num != SENT) {
     /* process num */                      /* process num */}
}                                } while (num != SENT);
```

2. Rewrite the following code using a `do_while` statement with no decisions in the loop body:

```
sum = 0;
for  (odd = 1;  odd < n;  odd = odd + 2)
     sum = sum + odd;
printf("Sum of the positive odd numbers less than %d is %d\n",
        n, sum);
```

In what situations will the rewritten code print an incorrect sum?

Programming

1. Design an interactive input loop that scans pairs of integers until it reaches a pair in which the first integer evenly divides the second.

5.8 PROBLEM SOLVING ILLUSTRATED

In this section, we will examine a programming problem that illustrates many of the concepts discussed in this chapter. The *top-down design* process will be demonstrated in solving this programming problem. The program will be implemented in a stepwise manner, starting with a list of major algorithm steps and continuing to add detail through refinement until the program can be written.

Case Study: Computing Radiation Levels

PROBLEM

In a certain building at a top secret research lab, some yttrium-90 has leaked into the computer analysts' coffee room. The leak would currently expose personnel to 150 millirems of radiation a day. The half-life of the substance is about three days; that is, the radiation level is only half of what it was three days ago. The analysts want to know how long it will be before the radiation is down to a safe level of 0.466 millirem a day. They would like a chart that displays the radiation level for every three days with the message `Unsafe` or `Safe` after every line. The chart should stop just before the radiation level is one-tenth of the safe level, because the more cautious analysts will require a safety factor of 10.

ANALYSIS

Displaying the chart will require the use of a loop that displays a line with a day number and a radiation level for each iteration. The loop should continue to repeat as long as the radiation level is above one-tenth of the safe level. The data requirements and algorithm follow.

Data Requirements

Problem Constants

```
SAFE_RAD          0.466 /* the safe radiation level in
                                 millirems                    */
SAFETY_FACT       10.0  /* the safety factor               */
```

Problem Input

```
int init_radiation     /* the initial radiation level */
```

Problem Outputs

```
int day              /* the day number                      */
int radiation_lev /* the radiation level in millirems */
```


DESIGN

Initial Algorithm

1. Initialize **day** to zero.
2. Compute the stopping level of radiation, that is, the safe level divided by the safety factor.
3. Prompt the user to enter the initial radiation level.
4. Compute and display the day number and the radiation level every three days that the radiation level exceeds the stopping radiation level. Also, indicate whether each level is safe or unsafe.

Algorithm Refinements

We will introduce a new variable (`min_radiation`) to hold the stopping level of radiation referred to in Step 1 of our initial algorithm. Since it is clear that some steps of our solution will be repeated, we will first use a `while` loop in our pseudocode for Step 4 and then look for the initialization and update steps that would permit us to use a `for` loop in our final implementation.

Additional Program Variable

```
double min_radiation  /* the stopping level of radiation  */
```

Step 4 Refinement

4.1 Initialize `radiation_lev` to `init_radiation`
4.2 while `radiation_lev` exceeds `min_radiation`

> 4.3 Display the value of `day`, `radiation_lev`, and the string "`Unsafe`" or "`Safe`".
> 4.4 Add 3 to the value of `day`.
> 4.5 Compute `radiation_lev` for the next period.

Let's see if our new refinements make it possible to identify initialization and update steps for our loop. We note that our loop repetition condition is a comparison between the variables `radiation_lev` and `min_radiation`. Since `min_radiation` does not change after it is first initialized, it must be `radiation_lev` that is our loop control variable; therefore Steps 4.1 and 4.5 are the initialization and update steps we need in order to use a `for` statement in our implementation. Now we can further refine Step 4.3 as shown next.

Step 4.3 Refinement

4.3.1 if `radiation_lev` exceeds `SAFE_RAD`

> Display `day`, `radiation_lev`, and "`Unsafe`".

else

> Display `day`, `radiation_lev`, and "`Safe`".

IMPLEMENTATION

The program appears in Fig. 5.20.

Figure 5.20   Program to Compute Radiation Levels

```
/*
 * Calculates and displays a chart showing the safety level of
 * a coffee room.
 */

#include <stdio.h>

#define SAFE_RAD     0.466  /* safe level of radiation               */
#define SAFETY_FACT  10.0   /* safety factor                         */
```

(continued)

Figure 5.20   (continued)

```
int
main(void)
{
      int    day;            /* days elapsed since substance leak    */
      double init_radiation, /* radiation level right after leak     */
             radiation_lev,  /* current radiation level              */
             min_radiation;  /* safe level divided by safety factor  */

      /* Initializes day and min_radiation          */
      day = 0;
      min_radiation = SAFE_RAD / SAFETY_FACT;

      /* Prompts user to enter initial radiation level   */
      printf("Enter the radiation level (in millirems)> ");
      scanf("%lf", &init_radiation);

      /* Displays table                                  */
      printf("\n   Day    Radiation   Status\n       (millirems)\n");
      for  (radiation_lev = init_radiation;
            radiation_lev > min_radiation;
            radiation_lev /= 2.0) {

         if  (radiation_lev > SAFE_RAD)
               printf("  %3d     %9.4f   Unsafe\n", day, radiation_lev);
         else
               printf("  %3d     %9.4f   Safe\n", day, radiation_lev);

         day += 3;
      }
      return (0);

}

Enter the radiation level (in millirems)> 150.0

   Day    Radiation   Status
         (millirems)
    0     150.0000   Unsafe
    3      75.0000   Unsafe
    6      37.5000   Unsafe
```

(continued)

Figure 5.20   (continued)

9	18.7500	Unsafe
12	9.3750	Unsafe
15	4.6875	Unsafe
18	2.3438	Unsafe
21	1.1719	Unsafe
24	0.5859	Unsafe
27	0.2930	Safe
30	0.1465	Safe
33	0.0732	Safe

◀ TESTING ▶

The only data item for this program is the initial radiation level. One run with a data value of 150.0 (millirems) will give you output that you can use to show correctness on valid, middle-of-the-road data. Check that each radiation value in the table displayed is one-half the previous value and that the number of days always increases by three. Also check that the first safe value is less than 0.466 millirem. Verify that your loop exited correctly by dividing the last radiation value displayed by 2.0. You must get a value that is less than or equal to 0.0466 (0.466/10.0 is 0.0466).

EXERCISES FOR SECTION 5.8

Self-Check

1. Replace the `for` statement in Fig. 5.20 with a `while` loop.
2. How would you get the program in Fig. 5.20 to stop the table display *after,* instead of before, the radiation level becomes less than or equal to the safe level divided by the safety factor?

5.9 HOW TO DEBUG AND TEST PROGRAMS

In Section 2.8, we described the general categories of error messages that you are likely to see: syntax errors and run-time errors. We also noted that it is possible for a program to execute without generating any error messages but still produce incorrect results. Sometimes the cause of a run-time error or the origin of incorrect results is apparent and the error can easily be fixed. However, very often the error is not obvious and may require considerable effort to locate.

The first step in attempting to find a hidden error is to examine the program output to determine which part of the program is generating incorrect results. Then you can focus on the statements in that section to determine which one(s) are at fault. To help you locate problem areas, you may need to insert extra debugging statements that display intermediate results at different points in your program. You may also want to insert extra calls to printf to trace the values of certain critical variables during program execution. For example, if the loop in Fig. 5.12 is not computing the correct sum, you might want to insert an extra diagnostic call to printf as shown by the line in color in the following loop.

```
for  (scanf("%d", &score);
       score != SENTINEL;
       scanf("%d", &score)) {
    sum += score;
    printf("***** score is %d, sum is %d\n", score, sum);
    printf("Enter next score (%d to quit)> ",
           SENTINEL);
}
```

The diagnostic call to printf will display each partial sum that is accumulated along with the current value of score. This call displays a string of asterisks at the beginning of its output line, making it easier to identify diagnostic output in the debugging runs. The string of asterisks also simplifies locating the diagnostic printf calls in the source program. We usually include a \n at the end of every printf format string. It is especially critical that you do this in diagnostic print statements so your output will be printed immediately; otherwise, if a run-time error occurs before a \n is encountered in another format string, you may never see the diagnostic message.

Take care when inserting extra diagnostic printf calls. Sometimes it will be necessary to add a set of braces if a single statement inside an if statement or a loop becomes a compound statement because of the additional call.

Once it appears that you have located an error, you will want to take out the extra diagnostic statements. As a temporary measure, it is sometimes advisable to make these diagnostic statements into comments by enclosing them in /* */. If these errors crop up again in later testing, it is easier to remove the comment symbols than to retype the diagnostic statements.

Off by One Loop Errors

A fairly common error in programs with loops is a loop that executes one time more, or one time less, than it should. If a sentinel-controlled loop performs an extra iteration, it may erroneously process the sentinel value as if it were a data value.

If a loop performs a counting operation, make sure that the initial and final values of the loop control variable are correct and that the loop repetition condition is right. For example, the following loop body executes n + 1 times instead of n times. If your intention is to execute the loop body n times, change the loop repetition condition to count < n.

```
for (count = 0;  count <= n;  ++count) {
    sum += count;
}
```

You can get a good idea whether a loop is correct by checking what happens at the *loop boundaries,* that is, at the initial and final values of the loop control variable. For a counting for loop, you should carefully evaluate the expression in the initialization step, substitute this value everywhere the counter variable appears in the loop body, and verify that it makes sense as a beginning value. Then choose a value for the counter that still causes the loop repetition condition to be true but that will make this condition false after one more evaluation of the update expression. Check the validity of this boundary value wherever the counter variable appears. As an example, in the for loop,

```
sum = 0;
k = 1;
for (i = -n;  i < n - k;  ++i)
    sum += i * i;
```

check that the first value of the counter variable i is supposed to be -n and that the last value should be n - 2. Next, check that the assignment statement

```
sum += i * i;
```

is correct at these boundaries. When i is -n, sum gets the value of n^2. When i is n - 2, the value of $(n - 2)^2$ is added to the previous sum. As a final check, pick some small value of n (for example, 2) and trace the loop execution to see that it computes sum correctly for this case.

Using Debugger Programs

Many computer systems have *debugger programs* available to help you debug a C program. The debugger program lets you execute your program one statement at a time (*single-step execution*) so that you can see the effect of each statement.

You can select several variables whose values will be automatically displayed after each statement executes. This feature allows you to trace the program's execution. Besides printing a diagnostic when a run-time error occurs, the debugger indicates the statement that caused the error and displays the values of the variables you selected.

You can also separate your program into segments by setting *breakpoints* at selected statements. A breakpoint is like a fence between two segments of a program. You can ask the debugger to execute all statements from the last breakpoint up to the next breakpoint. When the program stops at a breakpoint, you can select variables to examine, in this way determining whether the program segment executed correctly. If a program segment executes correctly, you will want to execute through to the next breakpoint. If it does not, you may want to set more breakpoints in that segment or perhaps perform single-step execution through that segment.

Testing

After all errors have been corrected and the program appears to execute as expected, the program should be tested thoroughly to make sure that it works. For a simple program, make enough test runs to verify that the program works properly for representative samples of all possible data combinations.

EXERCISES FOR SECTION 5.9

Self-Check

1. For the first counting loop in the subsection "Off by One Loop Errors," add debugging statements to show the value of the loop control variable at the start of each repetition. Also add debugging statements to show the value of sum at the end of each loop repetition.
2. Repeat Exercise 1 for the second loop in the same subsection.

5.10 COMMON PROGRAMMING ERRORS

Students sometimes confuse decision steps with while loops because the header for both structures contains a parenthesized condition. If the statements depending on the condition value are to be executed at most one time, you are dealing with a decision step and should use an if statement. You should use a while loop only if the statements depending on the condition may need to be executed more than once. The syntax of the `for` statement header is repeated.

`for`   (*initialization expression*;
         loop repetition condition;
         update expression)

Remember to end the initialization expression and the loop repetition condition with semicolons. Be careful not to put a semicolon before or after the closing parenthesis of the `for` statement header. A semicolon after this parenthesis would have the effect of ending the `for` statement without making execution of the loop body dependent on its condition.

Another common mistake in using `while` and `for` statements is to forget that the structure assumes that the loop body is a single statement. Remember to use braces around a loop body consisting of multiple statements. Some C programmers always use braces around a loop body, whether it contains one or many statements. Keep in mind that your compiler ignores indentation, so a loop defined as shown (with braces around the loop body left out)

```
while (x > xbig)
      x -= 2;
      ++xbig;
/* end while */
```

really executes as

```
while (x > xbig)
      x -= 2; /* only this statement is repeated */

++xbig;
```

The C compiler can easily detect that there is something wrong with code in which a closing brace has been omitted on a compound statement. However, the error message noting the symbol's absence may be far from the spot where the brace belongs, and other error messages often appear as a side effect of the omission. When compound statements are nested, the compiler will associate the first closing brace encountered with the innermost structure. Even if it is the terminator for this inner structure that is left out, the compiler may complain about the outer structure. In the example that follows, the body of the `for` statement is missing a brace. However, the compiler will associate the closing brace before the keyword `else` with the body of the `for` loop and then proceed to mark the `else` as improper.

```
printf("Experiment successful?(Y/N)> ");
scanf("%c", &ans);
```

```
if (ans == 'Y') {
    printf("Enter data one value per line (%d to quit)\n> ",
            SENT);
    for  (scanf("%d", &data);
          data != SENT;
          scanf("%d", &data)) {
        sum += data;
        printf("> ");
                    /* <- missing } */
} else {
    printf("Try it again tomorrow.\n");
    printf("Now follow correct shutdown procedure.\n");
}
```

Be very careful when using tests for inequality to control the repetition of a loop. The following loop is intended to process all transactions for a bank account while the balance is positive:

```
for  (scanf("%d%lf", &code, &amount);
      balance != 0.0;
      scanf("%d%lf", &code, &amount) {
  . . .
}
```

If the bank balance goes from a positive to a negative amount without ever being exactly 0.0, the loop will not terminate as planned. The loop that follows would be much safer:

```
for  (scanf("%d%lf", &code, &amount);
      balance > 0.0;
      scanf("%d%lf", &code, &amount) {
  . . .
}
```

You should verify that a loop's repetition condition will eventually become false (0); otherwise, an infinite loop may result. If a sentinel value is used to control loop repetition in an interactive program, make sure that the program's prompting messages tell what value to enter to stop loop repetition. One common cause of a nonterminating loop is the use of a loop repetition condition in which an equality test is mistyped as an assignment operation. Consider the following loop that expects the user to type the number 0 (actually any integer other than 1) to exit:

```
for  (again = 1; /* initialization        */
      again = 1; /* should be: again == 1  */
      scanf("%d", &again)) {
   . . .
   printf("One more time? (1 to continue/ 0 to quit)> ");
}
```

The value of the second assignment statement will always be 1, never 0 (false), so this loop will not exit on an entry of zero or of any other number.

With three looping constructs from which to choose, selecting one not best suited to the needs of your algorithm is easy to do. Before selecting the do-while statement, be sure that there is no possible situation in which you would want to skip execution of the loop body completely. If you ever find yourself adding an if statement to patch your code with a result like this,

```
if (condition₁)
      do {
         . . .
      } while (condition₁);
```

be ready to replace the segment with a while or for statement. Both of these statements automatically test the loop repetition condition *before* executing the loop body. Another misuse of the do_while has this general outline:

```
do  {
      first statement
      if (condition₁) {
            rest of loop body
      }
} while (condition₁);
```

This segment is essentially a sentinel loop that is better implemented using a for statement with *first statement* as both the initialization and update expressions. The for loop version tests *condition₁* only once per iteration of the loop.

Do not use increment, decrement, or compound assignment operators as subexpressions in complex expressions. At best, such usage leads to expressions that are difficult to read; at worst, to expressions that produce varying results in different implementations of C.

Remember the parentheses that are assumed to be around any expression that is the second operand of a compound assignment operator. Since the statement

```
a *= b + c;   is equivalent to   a = a * (b + c);
```

there is no shorter way to write

```
a = a * b + c;
```

Be sure that the operand of an increment or decrement operator is a variable and that this variable is referenced after executing the increment or decrement operation. Without a subsequent reference, the operator's side effect of changing the value of the variable is pointless. Do not use a variable twice in an expression in which it is incremented/decremented. Applying the increment/decrement operators to constants or expressions is illegal.

CHAPTER REVIEW

This chapter described how to repeat steps in a C program. You learned three repetition constructs: the `while` statement, which repeats its loop body as long as the condition in its header is true; the `for` statement, whose header provides places for the three aspects of loop control—initialization, testing, and update of the loop control variable; and the `do-while` statement, which executes its loop body once unconditionally and then repeats the loop body as long as the condition at the end of the statement remains true. You also studied how to write counting loops that allow you to repeat program segments a predetermined number of times, and you saw that the counters in these loops can count up or down in steps of any size. This chapter introduced how to use a `for` statement to implement a loop whose exact number of repetitions is not known before the loop begins executing. Two techniques were presented for input and processing of lists of data of varying lengths. In both approaches, `for` statements are used with calls to `scanf` for initialization and update of the loop control variable. If the list of data is terminated by a special sentinel value, the `for` statement's loop repetition condition is a comparison of the input variable and the sentinel value. If the end of the list coincides with the end of the input file, the value returned by the `scanf` or `fscanf` function is assigned to a status variable in the initialization and update sections of the `for` statement header, and the loop repetition condition is a comparison of the status variable and the expected status.

In this chapter, we also studied two groups of C operators that affect variable values: the unary increment/decrement operators and the binary compound assignment operators. We noted reasons why all of these operators should be used with care, and we also cited cases where they should not be used at all.

Examples of the loops introduced in this chapter are described in Table 5.5.

Table 5.5   Summary of New Constructs from Chapter 5

Construct	Effect
| **Counting for Loop**<br>```c
for (num = 0;
     num < 26;
     ++num) {
   square = num * num;
   printf("%5d %5d\n", num,
          square);
}
``` | Displays 26 lines, each containing an integer from 0 to 25 and its square. |
| **Counting for Loop with a Negative Step**<br>```c
for (volts = 20;
     volts >= -20;
     volts -= 10) {
   current = volts / resistance;
   printf("%5d %8.3f\n", volts,
          current);
}
``` | For values of `volts` equal to 20, 10, 0, −10, −20, computes value of `current` and displays `volts` and `current`. |
| **Sentinel-Controlled for Loop**<br>```c
product = 1;
printf("Enter %d to quit\n",
       SENVAL);
printf("Enter first number> ");
for  (scanf("%d", &dat);
      dat != SENVAL;
      scanf("%d", &dat)) {
   product *= dat;
   printf("Next number> ");
}
``` | Computes the product of a list of numbers. The product is complete when the user enters the sentinel value (SENVAL). |
| **Endfile-Controlled for Loop**<br>```c
sum = 0;
for  (status = scanf("%d", &num);
      status == 1;
      status = scanf("%d", &num)) {
   sum += num;

}
``` | Accumulates the sum of a list of numbers. The sum is complete when `scanf` detects the endfile character or encounters erroneous data. |

(continued)

Table 5.5   (continued)

Construct	Effect
Conditional Loop Using while Statement	

```
printf("Balloon's diameter> ");
scanf("%d", &diameter);
while (diameter < RIGHT_SIZE) {
    printf("Keep blowing!\n");
    printf("New diameter> ");
    scanf("%d", &diameter);
}
printf("Stop blowing!\n");
```

Instructs user to continue blowing as long as a balloon's diameter is below the desired size (RIGHT_SIZE).

do-while Loop

```
do {
    printf("Positive number < 10> ");
    scanf("d%, &num);
} while (num < 1 || num >= 10);
```

Repeatedly displays prompt and stores a number in num until user enters a number that is in range.

Increment / Decrement

```
z = ++j * k--;
```

Stores in z the product of the incremented value of j and the current value of k. Then k is decremented.

Compound Assignment

```
ans *= a - b;
```

Assigns to ans the value of ans * (a - b).

QUICK-CHECK EXERCISES

1. A loop that continues to process input data until a special value is entered is called a _____-controlled loop.
2. Some for loops cannot be rewritten as code using a while loop. True or false?
3. It is an error if the body of a for loop never executes. True or false?
4. In an endfile-controlled for loop, the initialization and update expressions typically include calls to the function _____ if the data file is made accessible through input redirection.

5. In a typical counter-controlled loop, the number of loop repetitions may not be known until the loop is executing. True or false?

6. During execution of the following program segment, how many lines of asterisks are displayed?

```
for (i = 0;  i < 10;  ++i)
    for (j = 0;  j < 5;  ++j)
        printf("**********\n");
```

7. During execution of the following program segment,
   a. How many times does the first call to `printf` execute?
   b. How many times does the second call to `printf` execute?
   c. What is the last value displayed?

```
for (i = 0;  i < 7;  ++i) {
    for (j = 0;  j < i;  ++j)
        printf("%4d", i * j);
    printf("\n");
}
```

8. If the value of n is 4 and m is 5, is the value of the following expression 21?

```
++(n * m)
```

Explain your answer.

9. What are the values of n, m, and p after execution of this three-statement fragment?

```
n = j - ++k;
m = j-- + k--;
p = k + j;
```

10. What are the values of x, y, and z after execution of this three-statement fragment?

```
x *= y + z;
y /= 2 * z + 1;
z += x;
```

11. What does the following code segment display? Try each of these inputs: 345, 82, 6. Then, describe the action of the code.

```
printf("\nEnter a positive integer> ");
scanf("%d", &num);
```

```
do {
    printf("%d  ", num % 10);
    num /= 10;
} while (num > 0);
printf("\n");
```

ANSWERS TO QUICK-CHECK EXERCISES

1. sentinel
2. False
3. False
4. scanf
5. False
6. 50
7. a. 0 + 1 + 2 + 3 + 4 + 5 + 6 = 21
   b. 7
   c. 30
8. No. The expression is illegal. The increment operator cannot be applied to an expression such as (n * m).
9. n=2, m=8, p=6
10. x=21, y=1, z=23
11. Enter a positive integer> 345
    5 4 3
    Enter a positive integer> 82
    2 8
    Enter a positive integer> 6
    6

The code displays the digits of an integer in reverse order and separated by spaces.

REVIEW QUESTIONS

1. In what ways are the for loop headings alike in a sentinel-controlled loop and an endfile-controlled loop? How are they different?
2. Write a program to compute and display the sum of a collection of Celsius temperatures entered at the terminal until a sentinel value of −275 is entered.
3. Hand-trace the program that follows given the following data:

   4 2 8 4   1 4 2 1   9 3 3 1   −22 10 8 2   3 3 4 5

```
#include <stdio.h>
#define SPECIAL_SLOPE   0.0
int
main(void)
{
      double slope, y2, y1, x2, x1;

      printf("Enter four numbers separated by spaces.");
      printf("\nThe last two numbers cannot be the ");
      printf("same, but\nthe program terminates if ");
      printf("the first two are.\n");

      printf("\nEnter four numbers> ");
      scanf("%lf%lf%lf%lf", &y2, &y1, &x2, &x1);

      for (slope = (y2 - y1) / (x2 - x1);
           slope != SPECIAL_SLOPE;
           slope = (y2 - y1) / (x2 - x1)) {
         printf("Slope is %5.2f.\n", slope);
         printf("\nEnter four more numbers> ");
         scanf("%lf%lf%lf%lf", &y2, &y1, &x2, &x1);
      }

      return (0);
}
```

4. Rewrite the program in Review Question 3 so it uses a `while` loop.
5. Rewrite the program segment that follows, using a `for` loop:

```
count = 0;
i = 0;
while (i < n) {
    scanf("%d", &x);
    if (x == i)
            ++count;
    ++i;
}
```

6. Rewrite this `for` loop heading, omitting any invalid semicolons.

```
for (i = n;
     i < max;
     ++i;);
```

7. Write a `do-while` loop that repeatedly prompts for and takes input until a value in the range 0 through 1.5 inclusive is input. Include code that prevents the loop from cycling indefinitely on input of a wrong data type.

PROGRAMMING PROJECTS

1. The rate of decay of a radioactive isotope is given in terms of its half-life H, the time lapse required for the isotope to decay to one-half of its original mass. The isotope strontium 90 (Sr^{90}) has a half-life of 28 years. Compute and display in table form the amount of this isotope that remains after each year for n years, given the initial presence of an amount in grams. The values of n and *amount* should be provided interactively. The amount of Sr^{90} remaining can be computed by using the following formula:

$$r = amount \times C^{(y/H)}$$

where *amount* is the initial amount in grams, C is expressed as $e^{-0.693}$ (e = 2.71828), y is the number of years elapsed, and H is the half-life of the isotope in years.

2. The value for π can be determined by the series equation

$$\pi = 4 \times \left(1 - \frac{1}{3} + \frac{1}{5} + \frac{1}{7} + \frac{1}{9} - \frac{1}{11} + \frac{1}{13} - \cdots\right)$$

Write a program to calculate the value of π using the formula given including terms up through 1/99.

3. Write a program that finds the equivalent series and parallel resistance for a collection of resistor values. Your program should scan first the number of resistors and then the resistor values. Then compute the equivalent series resistance for all resistors in the collection and also the equivalent parallel resistance. For example, if there are three resistors of 100, 200, and 300 ohms, respectively, their equivalent series resistance is 100 + 200 + 300 and their equivalent parallel resistance is

$$\frac{1}{\frac{1}{100} + \frac{1}{200} + \frac{1}{300}}$$

After your program works for a single collection of resistors, modify it so it can process several collections of resistors in a single run. Use a sentinel value of 0 (zero resistors in the collection) to signal the end of the program data.

4. a. The Fibonacci sequence is a sequence of numbers beginning

$$1, 1, 2, 3, 5, 8, 13, 21, \ldots$$

The first two elements are defined to be 1. Each of the other elements is the sum of its two predecessors. Write a program that takes a value for n in the range 1 to 30 and displays the first n elements of the Fibonacci sequence.

b. Modify your program to display the elements eight per line.

5. When an object radiating light or other energy moves toward or away from an observer, the radiation will seem to shift in frequency. This phenomenon, called the *Doppler shift,* is frequently used in measuring indirectly the velocity or changes in velocity of an object or weather pattern relative to an observer. For example, a weather radar that attempts to find dangerous wind shear near airports relies on this phenomenon.

For a radar transmitting at frequency f_t, the difference in transmitting and received frequencies due to a target moving at speed v (m/s) relative to the radar—that is, directly toward or away from the radar—is given by

$$\frac{f_r - f_t}{f_t} = \frac{2v}{c}$$

A thunderstorm approaches in the Wyoming high country. (Courtesy of Professor Robert D. Kelly, University of Wyoming, Department of Atmospheric Science.)

where f_r is the received frequency and c is the speed of light (3×10^8 m/s). A weather service station at a major municipal airport is using a new C-band Doppler radar ($f_t = 5.5$ GHz). During a severe thunderstorm, the following received frequencies are observed:

Time (s)	Frequency (GHz)
0	5.500000040
100	5.500000095
200	5.500000230
300	5.500001800
400	5.500000870
500	5.500000065
600	5.500000370

Write a program that scans this data and displays a table showing the data along with a third column displaying the Doppler velocities of the winds relative to the radar. What would happen if all the winds in the storm were moving perpendicular to the radar beam?

6. Let n be a positive integer consisting of up to ten digits, $d_{10}, d_9, \ldots, d_1$. Write a program to list in one column each of the digits in the number n. The rightmost digit, d_1, should be listed at the top of the column. Hint: If n is 3704, what is the value of the digit as computed according to the formula

```
digit = n % 10;
```

Test your program for values of n equal to 6, 3704, and 170498.

7. An integer n is divisible by 9 if the sum of its digits is divisible by 9. Use the algorithm developed for Project 6, and write a program to determine whether or not the following numbers are divisible by 9.

154368   621594   123456

8. The pressure of a gas changes as the volume and temperature of the gas vary. Write a program that uses the Van der Waals equation of state for a gas,

$$\left(P + \frac{an^2}{V^2}\right)(V - bn) = nRT$$

to display in tabular form the relationship between the pressure and the volume of n moles of carbon dioxide at a constant absolute temperature (T). P is the pressure in atmospheres and V is the volume in liters. The Van der Waals constants for carbon dioxide are $a = 3.592$ $L^2 \cdot$ atm/mol^2 and $b = 0.0427$ L/mol. Use 0.08206 L $\cdot$ atm/mol $\cdot$ K for the gas constant R. Inputs to the program include n, the Kelvin temperature, the initial and final volumes in milliliters, and the volume increment between lines of the table. Your program will display a table that varies the volume of the gas from the initial to the final volume in steps prescribed by the volume increment. Here is a sample run:

```
Please enter at the prompts the number of moles of carbon
dioxide, the absolute temperature, the initial volume in
milliliters, the final volume, and the increment volume
between lines of the table.

Quantity of carbon dioxide (moles)> 0.02
Temperature (kelvin)> 300
Initial volume (milliliters)> 400
Final volume (milliliters)> 600
Volume increment (milliliters)> 50

0.0200 moles of carbon dioxide at 300 kelvin

Volume (ml)          Pressure (atm)

    400                 1.2246
    450                 1.0891
    500                 0.9807
    550                 0.8918
    600                 0.8178
```

9. A concrete channel to bring water to Crystal Lake is being designed. It will have vertical walls and be 15 feet wide. It will be 10 feet deep, have a slope of .0015 feet/foot, and a roughness coefficient of .014. How deep will the water be when 1000 cubic feet per second is flowing through the channel? To solve this problem, we can use Manning's equation

$$Q = \frac{1.486}{N} AR^{2/3}S^{1/2}$$

where Q is the flow of water (cubic feet per second), N is the roughness coefficient (unitless), A is the area (square feet), S is the slope (feet/foot), and R is the hydraulic radius (feet).

The hydraulic radius is the cross-sectional area divided by the wetted perimeter. For square channels like the one in this example,

Hydraulic radius = depth × width / (2.0 × depth + width)

To solve this problem, design a program that allows the user to guess a depth and then calculates the corresponding flow. If the flow is too little, the user should guess a depth a little higher; if the flow is too high, the user should guess a depth a little lower. The guessing is repeated until the computed flow is within 0.1 percent of the flow desired.

To help the user make an initial guess, the program should display the flow for half the channel depth. Note the example run:

```
At a depth of 5.0000 feet, the flow is 641.3255 cubic
feet per second.

Enter your initial guess for the channel depth
when the flow is 1000.0000 cubic feet per second
Enter guess> 6.0

Depth: 6.0000  Flow: 825.5906 cfs  Target: 1000.0000 cfs
Difference: 174.4094  Error: 17.4409 percent

Enter guess> 7.0

Depth: 7.0000  Flow: 1017.7784 cfs  Target: 1000.0000 cfs
Difference: -17.7784  Error: -1.7778 percent

Enter guess> 6.8
. . .
```

10. Bunyan Lumber Co. needs to create a table of the engineering properties of its rectangular cross-section lumber. The dimensions of the wood are given as base and height in inches. The table is to include the following information:

cross-sectional area: $base \times height$

moment of inertia: $\dfrac{base \times height^3}{12}$

section modulus: $\dfrac{base \times height^2}{6}$

The owner, Paul, makes lumber with base sizes of 2, 4, 6, 8, and 10 inches. The height sizes are 2, 4, 6, 8, 10, and 12 inches. Produce a table with appropriate headings to show these values and the computed engineering properties. The first part of the table's outline is shown.

Lumber Size	Cross-sectional Area	Moment of Inertia	Section Modulus
2 x 2			
2 x 4			
2 x 6			
2 x 8			
2 x 10			
2 x 12			
4 x 2			
4 x 4			
4 x 6			
4 x 8			
4 x 10			
4 x 12			
.			
.			
.			

CHAPTER 6

MODULAR PROGRAMMING

Chapter 3 introduced functions, separate program modules corresponding to the individual steps in a problem solution. We have not yet used functions extensively, because we have not discussed how to pass information between our own function subprograms or between our own function subprograms and the main function.

Chapter 3 also introduced the idea that a function can be a module that returns a single result. You saw how to write expressions that call C library functions, and you did pass information into these functions through arguments. In addition, Chapter 3 discussed how functions could be used to facilitate structured design.

The use of arguments is a very important concept in programming. Arguments make function subprograms more versatile because they enable a module to manipulate different data each time the module is called. For example,

```
printf("%d", m);
```

displays the value of its argument m; whereas

```
printf("%d", n);
```

displays the value of its argument n.

Our goal throughout this course will be to use functions as building blocks of larger program systems. As you progress through the course, your programming skills and your own personal *library* of functions will grow. You should be able to reuse functions written for earlier applications in new programs.

We can make an analogy between a carefully designed program that uses functions and a stereo system. Each stereo component is an independent device that performs a specific operation. The stereo receiver and compact disc (CD) player are "black boxes" that we connect together. We know the purpose of each component, but we need not know what electronic parts are used inside each box or how they function in order to use the stereo system.

Information in the form of electronic signals is sent back and forth between these components over wires. If you look at the back of a stereo receiver, you will find that some connection points or plugs are marked as inputs and others are marked as outputs. The wires attached to the plugs marked inputs carry electronic signals into the receiver, where they are processed. (These signals may come from a cassette deck, tuner, or CD player.) New electronic signals, generated by the receiver, come out of the receiver from the plugs marked outputs and go to the speakers or back to the cassette deck for recording.

Currently, we know how to design the separate components (functions) of a programming system, but we don't know how to pass data between the main function and a function subprogram that we write. In this chapter, we will learn how to use arguments to provide communication paths between the main function and the other modules we write or between two function subprograms, just as we used arguments with library functions.

6.1 FUNCTIONS THAT RETURN A SINGLE RESULT

The mathematical library functions we have seen are convenient in that they permit us to perform a particular computation as often as we wish simply by referencing a function name in an expression. Each time we perform this computation, different arguments can be passed to the function. In the following example, we write our own function to compute the factorial of *n*, *n*!. The ANSI C math library includes no function that computes factorial, but we can have all the same conveniences if we write our own function.

EXAMPLE 6.1

The function `factorial` in Fig. 6.1 computes the factorial of an integer. The number whose factorial will be computed is represented by the variable n; its value is passed as an argument when the function is called.

The factorial function in Fig. 6.1 resembles the **void** functions we discussed in Chapter 3. The differences are these:

- The function prototype begins with the data type of the result value that the function computes. In parentheses, after the function name, is a list of type declarations for the *formal parameters* that are the inputs to the function. The prototype has the form

  > *ftype*
  > *fname(type$_1$ param$_1$, type$_2$ param$_2$, . . . , type$_n$ param$_n$)*

  Function `factorial` has a single formal parameter, n.
- The function does not print its result; instead, it executes a **return** statement to communicate its result back to the module that called it.

The variables i and **product** are called *local variables* because they are declared in the function and can be manipulated only within the function body. The local variables and formal parameters of a function cannot be referenced by name in any other function. For example, function `factorial` could not reference a variable declared in function **main**. However, all functions are allowed to use any names defined as constant macros in the same file, provided that the `#define` directive precedes the function definition.

Figure 6.1   Function to Compute Factorial

```
/*
 * Computes n! for n greater than or equal to zero
 */
int
factorial(int n)
{
      int i,              /* local variables */
          product = 1;

      /* Computes the product n x (n-1) x (n-2) x ... x 2 x 1 */
      for  (i = n;  i > 1;  --i) {
          product *= i;
      }

      /* Returns function result */
      return (product);
}
```

The syntax display that follows describes the form of a function definition.

Definition of a Function That Computes a Single Result

SYNTAX: *function interface comment*
           ftype
           fname (*formal parameter declaration list*)
           {
                   local variable declarations
                   executable statements
           }

EXAMPLE: `/*`
           ` * Finds the larger of two numbers`
           ` */`
           `double`
           `bigger(double n1, double n2)`

(continued)

```
    {
        double larger;

        if (n1 > n2)
                larger = n1;
        else
                larger = n2;

        return (larger);
    }
```

INTERPRETATION: The *function interface comment* is described in the next Program Style display. The next two lines are the function *prototype,* which specifies the function name, *fname,* and the type of the result returned, *ftype.* It also indicates the names and types of the *formal parameters* in the *formal parameter declaration list.* Note that the lines of the prototype do not end in semicolons. The braces enclose a block that forms the body of the function. The type of any additional variable needed should be declared in the *local variable declarations.* The *executable statements* describe the data manipulation that the function performs on the parameters and local variables in order to compute the result value. Execution of a `return` statement causes the value of the expression following the keyword `return` to be returned as the function's result value. The parentheses around this expression in the preceding example are optional.

NOTE: If the function does not have any formal parameters, the keyword `void` is used as the *formal parameter declaration list* in the function prototype.

Program Style   *Function Interface Comment*

The block comment and prototype that begin function `factorial` in Fig. 6.1 contain all the information that anyone needs to know in order to use this function. The function interface block comment is a statement of what the function does. If there are any restrictions on the values of the input arguments of the function, these restrictions should be listed in the function interface comment. For example, the initial comment of function `factorial` states that the value of its argument must be nonnegative. We recommend that you begin all function definitions in this way. The function interface comment combined with the prototype provide valuable documentation to other programmers who might want to reuse your functions in a new program without having to read the function code.

Figure 6.2 shows a complete program file that includes the function sub-program `factorial` and a main function that takes an integer input value, calls the `factorial` function, and prints the result returned by `factorial`. This program calls function `factorial` only with arguments that are no larger than 10. Even 10! is such a large number (3,628,800) that it cannot be represented as an `int` on many computer systems.

Figure 6.2   Complete Program Using Function factorial

```
/*
 * Computes and displays the factorial of a number to demonstrate a user-
 * defined function that has an input parameter and returns a result.
 */

#include <stdio.h>

/*
 * Computes n! for n greater than or equal to zero
 */
int
factorial(int n)
{
      int i,                   /* local variables */
          product = 1;

      /* Computes the product n x (n-1) x (n-2) x ... x 2 x 1 */
      for  (i = n;   i > 1;   --i) {
          product *= i;
      }

      /* Returns function result */
      return (product);
}

/*
 * Demonstrates a call from the main function that passes an argument to a
 * user-defined function.
 */
```

(continued)

Figure 6.2 (continued)

```
int
main(void)
{
      int num, fact;

      printf("Enter an integer between 0 and 10> ");
      scanf("%d", &num);
      if (num < 0) {
            printf("The factorial of a negative number (%d) is undefined\n",
                  num);
      } else if (num <= 10) {
            fact = factorial(num);
            printf("The factorial of %d is %d\n", num, fact);
      } else {
            printf("Number out of range: %d\n", num);
      }

      return (0);
}
```

If the input value stored in the variable `num` of function `main` is between 0 and 10, the statement

```
fact = factorial(num);
```

is executed. The expression references function `factorial`; therefore, function `factorial` is called into execution, and the assignment statement in the main function waits for the function result. Figure 6.3 illustrates how the value of `num`, the *actual argument* in the function call, is used as the actual value of the *formal parameter* `n` when the body of function `factorial` is executed. The result of the execution of `factorial` is returned to the main function, assigned to the variable `fact`, and displayed.

EXAMPLE 6.2 ▶ Engineers are often asked to discuss how many different ways something they are building might fail. For a critical system such as a spacecraft, an aircraft, or a nuclear power plant, oversight agencies and review boards may request a report on the number of possible ways that the system could fail. Frequently, a very critical system, like the main computer on an aircraft, will have one or sev-

Figure 6.3
Effect of
Execution of
factorial When
num Is 6

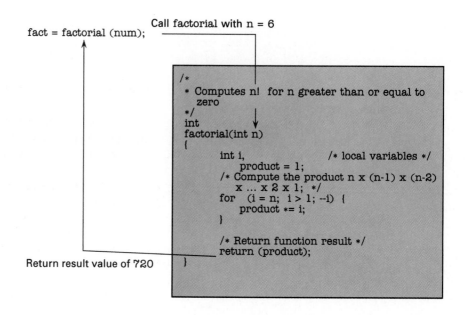

Call factorial with n = 6

fact = factorial (num);

```
/*
 * Computes n!  for n greater than or equal to
   zero
 */
int
factorial(int n)
{
    int i,                    /* local variables */
        product = 1;
        /* Compute the product n x (n-1) x (n-2)
           x ... x 2 x 1; */
        for   (i = n;  i > 1; --i) {
            product *= i;
        }

        /* Return function result */
        return (product);
}
```

Return result value of 720

eral backups to minimize the effect of the loss of any one component. However, as more and more backups are added to the system, the total number of components rises. In addition, the number of wiring or mechanical interconnects to allow different combinations to work together if a component fails usually rises even more quickly than the number of devices.

In developing contingency plans to deal with critical failures, you can use a formula from probability theory that computes the number of different ways in which r items can be selected from a collection of n items without regard to order. The formula is written as

$$C(n, r) = \frac{n!}{r!(n - r)!}$$

This formula represents the number of different combinations of n items taken r at a time. For example, let's assume that you are preparing a presentation on contingency plans and backups required for a mechanical relay system made up of five components, all of which are connected to each other. How many possible sets of two failures at once are there? To answer this question, you would perform the computation

$$C(5, 2) = \frac{5!}{2!(5 - 2)!} = \frac{5!}{2!3!} = \frac{120}{2 \times 6} = 10$$

The answer is ten different pairs of component failures.

The program in Fig. 6.4 uses function `factorial` to perform this computation. The user is first asked to enter n and r. If r is not greater than n, the statement

```
c = factorial(n) / (factorial(r) * factorial(n-r));
```

calls function `factorial` with three different actual arguments: the variable n, the variable r, and the expression n−r. The results of these calls are manipulated as previously described, and the number of different combinations of n items taken r at a time is saved in variable c.

In the main program of Fig. 6.4, a different actual argument is passed in each call to function `factorial`; consequently, a different result is computed

Figure 6.4   Program to Find Combinations of *n* Items Taken *r* at a Time

```
/*
 * Computes the number of combinations of n items taken r at a time
 */

#include <stdio.h>

/*
 * Computes n! for n greater than or equal to zero
 */
int
factorial(int n)
{
      int  i,              /* local variables */
           product = 1;

      /* Computes the product n x (n-1) x (n-2) x ... x 2 x 1 */
      for (i = n;  i > 1;  --i) {
          product *= i;
      }

      /* Returns function result */
      return (product);
}
```

(continued)

Figure 6.4   (continued)

```
/*
 * Demonstrates multiple calls from the main function passing different
 * actual arguments to a user-defined function.
 */
int
main(void)
{
      int n, r, c;

      printf("Enter total number of components> ");
      scanf("%d", &n);
      printf("Enter number of components selected> ");
      scanf("%d", &r);

      if (r <= n) {
            c = factorial(n) / (factorial(r) * factorial(n-r));
            printf("The number of combinations is %d\n", c);
      } else {
            printf("Components selected cannot exceed total number\n");
      }

      return (0);
}
```

each time. The effect of each call to function `factorial` is summarized in Table 6.1.

Table 6.1 illustrates one of the most important reasons for using functions. A function may be called several times in a program, each time with a different actual argument. Each call to the function causes the program statements associated with the function definition to be executed. Without using functions,

Table 6.1   **Effect of Each Call to factorial**

Call	Actual Argument	Formal Parameter Value	Function Result
1	n	5	120
2	r	2	2
3	n−r	3	6

these program statements would have to be listed several times in the main function. It is certainly easier to insert a function reference in a program than to insert the entire function body.

The Function Data Area

Each time a function call statement is executed, an area of memory is allocated to store that function's data. Included in the data area are storage cells for the formal parameters and any local variables that may be declared in the function. The function data area is erased when the function terminates; it is recreated when the function is called again. When a function's data area is created, each local variable is undefined unless its declaration includes an initialization. Each formal parameter is assigned the value of the corresponding actual argument. Figure 6.5 shows the data storage areas for functions `main` and `factorial` just after `factorial` is called with actual argument `n-r` and before it executes. There is a memory cell in `main` allocated for variable `n` (value 5) and a memory cell in `factorial`'s data area for the formal parameter `n`, whose value 3 is the result of evaluating the actual argument `n-r`. Even though they have the same names, the formal parameter `n` of `factorial` and the local variable `n` of `main` are unrelated. In fact, at the time the `scanf` function stores the value 5 in `main`'s `n`, `factorial`'s `n` has not yet been created. Only when a call to `factorial` is being executed is a cell allocated for the formal parameter `n`. Each call to `factorial` recreates and redefines its parameter `n`.

By the same reasoning, local variables `i` and `product` in `factorial` are unrelated to any other use of these names either in function `main` or in any other function subprogram. Moreover, variables `c` and `r` declared in function `main` may be manipulated *only* in function `main`. It would be illegal for function `factorial` to attempt to reference either `c` or `r`.

**Figure 6.5
Data Areas for
Functions main
and factorial**

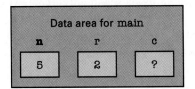
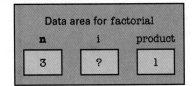

Source File Structure

For now, always organize your program source files according to the pattern shown in our examples. Begin with a block comment identifying the program's purpose; then include any preprocessor directives. Next place the definitions of your function subprograms ordered so a function's definition precedes any call to it from another function. Include your main function last. Notice that we have defined `main` as a function that returns a single type `int` result. Function `main` is called by the computer's operating system. The zero value returned by main indicates to the operating system that the program executed normally. Most C compilers also allow `main` to be declared as a `void` function.

Functions with Multiple Input Parameters and a Single Result Value

Our next example is similar to `factorial` in that it returns a single result value, but it has more than one input parameter. Figure 6.6 is a diagram of such a function.

When designing a function of your own, you may wish to draw a diagram like this as part of your analysis of the problem. For every input arrow of your diagram, you will need a formal parameter in your function prototype. A question you can ask yourself to help identify the input parameters of your function is this: What information do I need to know before I can start to carry out this function's purpose?

**Figure 6.6
Function with
Multiple Inputs
and a Single
Result**

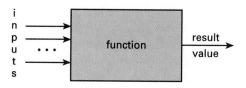

EXAMPLE 6.3  Function `round` in Fig. 6.7 is used to round its first input argument to the number of places indicated by its second argument. This means that the function reference

```
round(2.51863, 3)
```

returns the value 2.519. To compute the rounded value, the function first isolates the sign of x. It represents the sign by -1 for negative values of x and by 1 for nonnegative values. Then `round` works on rounding $|x|$, recognizing that multiplying the result by the value of variable `sign` will restore the sign of the number.

Rounding the number 2.51863 to three decimal places is equivalent to rounding 2518.63 (2.51863×10^3) to the nearest integer and then moving the decimal point three places to the left. The standard C math library does not include a "nearest integer" function. However, we can compute the integer near-

Figure 6.7   Function That Rounds Its Argument

....

```c
#include <stdio.h>
#include <math.h>

/*
 * Rounds the value of x to designated number of decimal places.
 * Argument places is greater than or equal to zero.
 */
double
round(double x, int places)
{
      int     sign;           /* -1 if x negative, 1 otherwise         */
      double power,           /* 10 raised to the places power         */
             temp_x,          /* copy of |x| with decimal point moved places
                                 places to the right.                  */
             x_rounded;       /* function result                       */

      /* Saves sign of x  */
      if (x < 0)
            sign = -1;
      else
            sign = 1;

      /* Computes rounded value */
      if (places >= 0) {
            power = pow(10.0, places);
            temp_x = fabs(x) * power;
            x_rounded = floor(temp_x + 0.5) / power * sign;
      } else {
            printf("\nError: second argument to round cannot be negative.\n");
            printf("No rounding done.\n");
            x_rounded = x;
      }
      return (x_rounded);
}
```

....

est to a positive value by adding 0.5 and then finding the largest whole number not greater than this sum:

$$
\begin{array}{r}
2518.63 \\
+\ 0.50 \\
\hline
2519.13
\end{array}
$$

The `floor` function that we studied in Chapter 3 finds exactly the whole number we need. Moving the decimal point is accomplished by dividing the number by 10^3.

Table 6.2 traces the execution of the preceding function call. The function result is `2519/1000.0`, or 2.519, as desired.

Function `round` illustrates that a user-defined function can call a C standard library function. Since the functions `pow` and `floor` are both from the math library, the source file in which the definition of `round` appears must have a `#include` directive for `<math.h>`. It is also possible for one user-defined function to call another or even to call itself.

When using multiple-argument functions, you must be careful to include the correct number of arguments in the function call. Also, the order of the actual arguments used in the function reference must correspond to the order of the formal parameters listed in the prototype of the function definition.

Finally, if the function is to return meaningful results, assignment of each actual argument to the corresponding formal parameter must not cause any loss of information. Usually, you should use an actual argument of the same data type as the corresponding formal parameter, although this is not always essential. For example, the `<math.h>` library description indicates that both parameters of the function `pow` are of type `double`. In our function `round` in Fig. 6.7, we call `pow` with a second actual argument that is of type `int` (`places`). This call does not cause a problem, because there is no loss of information when an `int` is

Table 6.2   Trace of round(2.51863, 3)

Statement	x	places	power	temp_x	x_rounded	Effect
	2.51863	3	?	?	?	
`if (places >= 0)`						True: does true task
`power =` `   pow(10.0, places);`			1000.0			Assigns 10^3 to power
`temp_x = x * power;`				2518.63		Copies x with decimal point moved 3 places to the right

`x_rounded =`
`   floor(temp_x+0.5)`
`   / power;`
					2.519	Assigns `floor(2519.13)` `/ 1000.0` to `x_rounded`

`return (x_rounded);`						Returns `2.519` as function result

assigned to a type `double` variable. If we were to try to pass an actual argument of type `double` to a formal parameter of type `int`, loss of the fractional part of our actual argument would likely lead to an unexpected function result. The rules for argument list correspondence are summarized next. ⬅

Argument List Correspondence

- The number of actual arguments used in a call to a function must be the same as the number of formal parameters listed in the function prototype.
- Each actual argument must be of a data type that can be assigned to the corresponding formal parameter with no unexpected loss of information. The first actual argument corresponds to the first formal parameter, the second actual argument corresponds to the second formal parameter, and so on.

Program Style   *Validating Function Arguments*

The `if` structure in Fig. 6.7 validates the value of the second formal parameter, `places`. The function cannot be executed in accordance with its purpose if `places` is negative. Rather than computing an answer that makes no sense, the function prints an error message and returns its first argument as the result. In this way, the program user is warned that the computation did not take place; however, the program is able to continue execution because a reasonable value is returned as the function result.

Testing Functions

A function is an independent program module and, as such, it can be tested separately from the program that uses it. To run such a test, you should write a short *driver* program that defines the function arguments, calls the function, and displays the value returned. For example, the function `main` in Fig. 6.8 could act as a driver program to test function `round`.

Figure 6.8   Driver Program to Test Function round

```
/*
 * Tests function round
 */

#include <stdio.h>
#include <math.h>
```

(continued)

Figure 6.8 (continued)

```
/*
 * Rounds the value of x to designated number of decimal places
 * Argument places is greater than or equal to zero.
 */
double
round(double x, int places)
{
      int    sign;        /* -1 if x negative, 1 otherwise              */
      double power,       /* 10 raised to the places power              */
             temp_x,      /* copy of |x| with decimal point moved places
                             places to the right.                       */
             x_rounded;   /* function result                           */

      /* Saves sign of x */
      if (x < 0)
            sign = -1;
      else
            sign = 1;

      /* Computes rounded value */
      if (places >= 0) {
            power = pow(10.0, places);
            temp_x = fabs(x) * power;
            x_rounded = floor(temp_x + 0.5) / power * sign;
      } else {
            printf("\nError: second argument to round cannot be negative.\n");
            printf("No rounding done.\n");
            x_rounded = x;
      }
      return (x_rounded);
}

int
main(void)
{
      double num;        /* number to round                            */
      int    dec_places; /* number of decimal places to round to       */
```

(continued)

Figure 6.8   (continued)

```
        printf("Enter a number to round or zero to quit> ");
        for  (scanf("%lf", &num);
             num != 0;
             scanf("%lf", &num)) {
            printf("Round to how many decimal places?> ");
            scanf("%d", &dec_places);
            printf("%.6f rounded to %d decimal places is %.6f\n", num,
                    dec_places, round(num, dec_places));
            printf("\nEnter another number to round or zero to quit> ");
        }

        return (0);
}
```

```
Enter a number to round or zero to quit> 38.56
Round to how many decimal places?> 1
38.560000 rounded to 1 decimal places is 38.600000

Enter another number to round or zero to quit> -5.98476
Round to how many decimal places?> 3
-5.984760 rounded to 3 decimal places is -5.985000

Enter another number to round or zero to quit> 84.9
Round to how many decimal places?> -2
Error: second argument to round cannot be negative
No rounding done
84.900000 rounded to -2 decimal places is 84.900000

Enter another number to round or zero to quit> 84.9
Round to how many decimal places?> 0
84.900000 rounded to 0 decimal places is 85.000000

Enter another number to round or zero to quit> 38.71
Round to how many decimal places?> 2
38.710000 rounded to 2 decimal places is 38.710000

Enter another number to round or zero to quit> 0
```

You should build a source file containing any necessary preprocessor directives, the function(s) to be tested, and the driver. Execute the driver program on a variety of data until you are satisfied that each function tested is working correctly.

Logical Functions

In Chapter 4, we saw that C uses integers to represent the logical concepts true and false. This means that a type int result returned by a function can be interpreted as a logical value. Such functions are often used to make conditions more readable.

EXAMPLE 6.4   Function even in Fig. 6.9 returns the integer 1 meaning true if its integer argument is an even number; otherwise, it returns 0 for false.

Function even is called in the following if statement, which could be used inside a loop to count even and odd numbers:

```
if (even(x))
        ++even_nums;
else
        ++odd_nums;
```

Figure 6.9   Function That Checks Whether a Value Is Even

```
/*
 * Indicates whether or not num is even (divisible by 2):
 *     returns 1 if it is, 0 if not
 */
int
even(int num)
{
      int ans;

      ans = ((num % 2) == 0);
      return (ans);
}
```

Case Study: Finding Prime Numbers

◄ PROBLEM ►

Prime numbers have been studied by mathematicians for many years. A prime number is an integer that has no divisors other than 1 and itself (for example, the integers 2, 3, 5, 7, and 11). Write a program that finds the smallest divisor of a number or determines that the number is a prime number.

◄ ANALYSIS ►

To determine whether an integer *n* is a prime number, our program will test integers smaller than *n* until it finds an integer that is a divisor. We will limit the number we test to 1000 or less. The data requirements are as follows:

Data Requirements

Problem Constant
```
1000 (NMAX)     /* largest number that can be tested   */
```

Problem Input
```
int n           /* number to be tested                 */
```

Problem Output
```
int min_div     /* smallest divisor greater than 1     */
```

◄ DESIGN ►

Initial Algorithm

1. Get the number to be checked to see whether it is prime.
2. Find the smallest divisor other than 1, or determine that the number is prime.
3. Display the smallest divisor or a message that the number is prime.

Algorithm Refinements

Because n must be an integer greater than 1, we will check the value entered to see whether it is in the valid range for the problem. The refinement of Step 1 follows.

Step 1 Refinement

1.1 Get a value for n.

1.2 if n < 2

Display an error message.

else if n <= NMAX

Do Steps 2 and 3.

else

Display an error message.

We will write a new function, find_div, to implement Step 2. This function will return the smallest divisor of n that is greater than 1—that is, if n is prime, find_div will return n. Our decision to write a function for Step 2 establishes this step as a subproblem to be solved separately. For now, we will assume we have a function that accomplishes the purpose of find_div. The value returned by this function will be stored in min_div and tested in Step 3. The refinement for Step 3 is

Step 3 Refinement

3.1 if the smallest divisor is n

Display a message that n is prime.

else

Display the smallest divisor of n.

◄ IMPLEMENTATION ►

We can now write the main function (see Fig. 6.10). The statement

```
min_div = find_div(n);
```

calls the function find_div to perform Step 2 of the algorithm. The outer if statement implements Step 1, and the inner if implements Step 3. We can now turn our attention to function find_div.

Figure 6.10 Function main of Prime Numbers Program

```
/*
 * Finds and displays the smallest divisor (other than 1) of the integer n.
 * Displays that n is a prime number if no divisor smaller than n is found.
 */

#include <stdio.h>
#define NMAX 1000
...
```

(continued)

Figure 6.10   (continued)

```
int
main(void)
{
      int n,          /* number to check to see if it is prime      */
          min_div; /* minimum divisor (greater than 1) of n         */

      /* Gets a number to test.                                      */
      printf("Enter a number that you think is a prime number> ");
      scanf("%d", &n);

      /* Checks that the number is in the range 2...NMAX             */
      if (n < 2) {
            printf("Error: number too small. The smallest prime is 2.\n");
      } else if (n <= NMAX) {

            /* Finds the smallest divisor (> 1) of n */
            min_div = find_div(n);

            /* Displays the smallest divisor or a message that n is prime. */
            if (min_div == n)
                  printf("%d is a prime number.\n", n);
            else
                  printf("%d is the smallest divisor of %d.\n", min_div, n);
      } else {
            printf("Error: largest number accepted is %d.\n", NMAX);

      }

      return (0);
}
```

Subproblem: Function find_div

Function find_div finds the smallest divisor of *n* that is greater than 1.

ANALYSIS

Function find_div finds a divisor of *n* by testing each integer that is a possible divisor, starting with 2. If 2 does not divide *n,* then no other even integer divides *n;* consequently, only 2 and the odd integers need to be tested. The data requirements for find_div follow.

Data Requirements

Problem Input (formal parameter)
```
int n          /* number to check to see if it is prime */
```

Problem Output (result to return)
```
int divisor  /* smallest divisor found;
                 0 means no value found yet        */
```
Program Variables (other local variables)
```
int trial     /* each trial divisor beginning
                  with 2                            */
```

DESIGN

Algorithm

1. if n is even

    Set divisor to 2.

  else

    Set divisor to 0 (meaning no divisor found).

    Set trial to 3.

2. As long as divisor is 0, keep trying odd integers (trial). If a divisor is found, store it in divisor. If trial exceeds $\sqrt{n}$, store n in divisor.
3. Return divisor.

First, we find out whether 2 divides n. If n is even, the 2 is stored in divisor, causing Step 2 to be skipped. Because we have already defined a function even, we can call it in our implementation of Step 1. If n is odd, divisor is set to 0, trial is set to the smallest odd integer greater than 1 (3), and the loop in Step 2 is executed. Step 2 is used to test each odd integer less than or equal to $\sqrt{n}$ as a possible divisor. The refinement of Step 2 follows.

Step 2 Refinement
2.1 Repeat as long as a divisor has not been found

    if trial > $\sqrt{n}$

        Set divisor to n.

    else if trial is a divisor of n

        Set divisor to trial.

    else

        Store the next odd integer in trial.

It is necessary to test as possible divisors only integers less than or equal to $\sqrt{n}$.

<hr>IMPLEMENTATION<hr>

In our code for `find_div`, we check to see whether `trial` is a divisor of n by determining whether the remainder of n divided by `trial` is zero (see Fig. 6.11). We use a `while` statement rather than a `for` statement to implement this loop because the initialization and update steps are not simple, unconditional statements.

Functions `even` and `find_div` should be inserted in the prime number program right after the preprocessor directives. In Fig. 6.10, an ellipsis (. . .) at this point notes the omission of part of the program. Function `even` should precede function `find_div` so the compiler will see its definition before meeting `find_div`'s call to it.

Figure 6.11   Function to Find the Smallest Divisor Greater Than 1 of an Integer

```
#include <math.h>

/*
 * Finds the smallest divisor of n between 2 and n (n is greater than 1)
 */
int
find_div(int n)
{
      int trial,    /* current candidate for smallest divisor of n         */
          divisor; /* smallest divisor of n; zero means divisor not yet
                       found                                                */

      /* Chooses initialization of divisor and trial depending on whether
         n is even or odd.                                                 */
      if (even(n)) {
           divisor = 2;
      } else {
           divisor = 0;
           trial = 3;
      }

      /* Tests each odd integer as a divisor of n until a divisor is found
         this way or until trial is so large that it is clear that n is the
         smallest divisor other than 1.
       */
```

(continued)

Figure 6.11   (continued)

```
    while (divisor == 0) {
          if (trial > sqrt(n))
                divisor = n;
          else if ((n % trial) == 0)
                divisor = trial;
          else
                trial += 2;
    }

    /* Returns problem output to calling module. */
    return (divisor);
}
```

TESTING

The complete program should be tested for both small and large integers that are prime numbers. You should be able to find a table of primes to help you select sample cases. Make sure you test odd numbers that are nonprimes, even numbers, and data values that are out of range.

Several sample runs of the prime number program are shown in Fig. 6.12. The test values used for n were selected to exercise all parts of the program and to verify that the program works for numbers that are prime as well as numbers

Figure 6.12   Six Sample Runs of Prime Number Program

```
Enter a number that you think is a prime number> 1000
2 is the smallest divisor of 1000.

Enter a number that you think is a prime number> 997
997 is a prime number.

Enter a number that you think is a prime number> 35
5 is the smallest divisor of 35.

Enter a number that you think is a prime number> 0
Error: number too small. The smallest prime is 2.
```

(continued)

Figure 6.12   (continued)

```
Enter a number that you think is a prime number> 1001
Error: largest number accepted is 1000.

Enter a number that you think is a prime number> 2
2 is a prime number.
```

that are not prime. The operation of the program at the boundaries (2 and 1000) was also checked, as was the operation of the program for invalid data values (0 and 1001). A very large prime number (997) was used as a test case as well as odd and even numbers that were not prime. Although a very large percentage of the valid data values were *not* tested, the sample selected is representative and provides a fair indication that the program is correct.

You should use a similar strategy when selecting test data to try out your programs. Avoid choosing sample test data that are very much alike; be sure to include select test data that are at or near any boundary values.

EXERCISES FOR SECTION 6.1

Self-Check

1. What value would be returned by function one_more for this reference?

        one_more(85.76)

```
int
one_more(int num)
{
        return (num + 1);
}
```

Programming

1. Write a function named prime that checks a positive integer to see whether it is prime. Your function should return a 1 for true if its argument is prime, and a 0 for false if it is not. You may call the function find_div in prime.
2. Write a function that computes the speed (km/h) one must average to reach a certain destination by a designated time. You need to deal only with arrivals occurring later on the same day as the departure. Function inputs include departure and arrival times as integers on a 24-hour clock (8:30 P.M. = 2030) and the distance to the destination in kilometers. Also write a driver program to test your function.

6.2 void FUNCTIONS WITH INPUT PARAMETERS

In Chapter 3, we wrote several void functions that did not return a result but simply produced some output. Such void functions are much more useful when they have input parameters. In the next example, we will reuse our function find_div to simplify the problem of factoring a number.

EXAMPLE 6.5

Function factor in Fig. 6.13 has a return type of void because its purpose is not to compute a value to return to the calling module. Rather, its intent is to print a message showing the prime factors of the argument passed to its formal parameter n. For example, in response to the call

    factor(84);

the function would print

    84 = 2 x 2 x 3 x 7

In keeping with our plan to reuse proven modules whenever possible, we call function find_div to find each factor. It is possible to use find_div here because the first factor printed, 2, is the smallest divisor of 84; the second

Figure 6.13   void Function That Factors an Integer

```
/*
 * Displays a message showing the prime factors of n (n > 1).
 * Example:  factor(12) would print  12 = 2 x 2 x 3
 */
void
factor(int n)
{
      int to_factor,   /* product of undisplayed factors of n      */
          cur_factor; /* current factor of n                       */

      /* Displays initial part of message including the smallest prime
         factor.                                                    */
      cur_factor = find_div(n);
      printf("%d = %d", n, cur_factor);
```

(continued)

Figure 6.13   (continued)

```
    /* Finds and displays remaining factors preceded by x signs.    */
    for  (to_factor = n / cur_factor;
            to_factor > 1;
            to_factor /= cur_factor) {
        cur_factor = find_div(to_factor);
        printf(" x %d", cur_factor);
    }
    printf("\n");
}
```

Table 6.3   Trace of factor(84) That Displays 84 = 2 × 2 × 3 × 7

Statement	n	to_factor	cur_factor	Effect
	84	?	?	
cur_factor = find_div(n);			2	find_div finds 84's smallest divisor > 1, and result is stored in cur_factor
printf("%d = %d", n, cur_factor);				Displays 84 = 2
for (to_factor = n / cur_factor;		42		Stores 84/2 = 42 in to_factor
to_factor > 1				True: loop continues
cur_factor = find_div(to_factor);			2	Smallest divisor of 42 (> 1) stored in cur_factor
printf(" x %d", cur_factor);				Displays x 2
to_factor /= cur_factor		21		Stores 42/2 = 21 in to_factor
to_factor > 1				True: loop continues
cur_factor = find_div(to_factor);			3	Smallest divisor of 21 (> 1) stored in cur_factor

(continued)

Table 6.3   (continued)

Statement	n	to_factor	cur_factor	Effect
	84	21	3	
printf(" x %d", cur_factor);				Displays x 3
to_factor /= cur_factor		7		Stores 21/3 = 7 in to_factor
to_factor > 1				True: loop continues
cur_factor = find_div(to_factor);			7	Smallest divisor of 7 (> 1) stored in cur_factor
printf(" x %d", cur_factor);				Displays x 7
to_factor /= cur_factor		1		Stores 7/7 = 1 in to_factor
to_factor > 1				False: loop exits
printf("\n");				Completes output line

factor, 2, is the smallest divisor of 42 (84/2); the third factor, 3, is the smallest divisor of 21 (42/2); and 7 is the smallest divisor of 7 (21/3). Our function will deal only with numbers greater than 1. Table 6.3 traces the call

factor(84);

In the next case study, we use one function that returns a result and also a void function with an input parameter.

Case Study: Computing Maximum Tensile Loads

Superb Steel Company produces steel reinforcing bars called rebars. The size of a rebar is designated by a number that, when divided by 8, gives the diameter of the cylindrical bar in inches (e.g., a number 5 rebar is 5/8 of an inch in diameter). The company needs to produce a chart showing the maximum tensile load of the bars when they are made from certain grades of steel. Superb makes number 2 to number 11 rebars. Each chart should have the following form:

```
****************************************************************
                    SUPERB STEEL COMPANY
                      Rebar Load Chart
          For bars with a steel strength of 8000.00 psi
     Bar                  Cross-Sectional              Max. Load
    Number                 Area (sq. in.)                (lbs.)
    ------                ---------------             ----------
      2                        0.05                       393.
      3                        0.11                       884.
      4                        0.20                      1571.
      5                        0.31                      2454.
      6                        0.44                      3534.
      7                        0.60                      4811.
      8                        0.79                      6283.
      9                        0.99                      7952.
     10                        1.23                      9817.
     11                        1.48                     11879.
****************************************************************
```

ANALYSIS

The maximum tensile load on a bar is the amount of force the bar can hold in tension. It is calculated by multiplying the cross-sectional area of the bar by the tensile strength of the steel. For a given tensile strength, we can display each line of the preceding chart by first determining the cross-sectional area corresponding to that number rebar. We can then use the formula given to compute the maximum load.

Data Requirements

Problem Constants
```
MIN_REBAR 2          /* smallest rebar Superb makes     */
MAX_REBAR 11         /* largest rebar Superb makes      */
```

Problem Input
```
double strength      /* tensile strength of the steel   */
```

Problem Outputs
```
int bar_num          /* the rebar number                */
```

```
double area      /* the cross-sectional area        */
double load      /* the maximum tensile load        */
```

Relevant Formula
load = area × steel strength

DESIGN

Algorithm

1. Get the steel strength.
2. Display the table heading.
3. Repeat for each rebar from number 2 (`MIN_REBAR`) to 11 (`MAX_REBAR`).
    4. Compute cross-sectional area.
    5. `load = area * strength`
    6. Display rebar number, area, and load.

IMPLEMENTATION

We will implement Steps 2 and 4 using function subprograms and write the rest of the algorithm as part of the main function. We will implement Step 2 as function `table_head` whose type is `void` because its purpose is not to compute and return a result value. Since the table heading includes the strength of the steel, our `void` function will have one input parameter. We will implement Step 4 as function `rebar_area` that returns a value of type `double` (the cross-sectional area). Again, there will be a single input parameter, since the rebar area is determined by the bar number. We will write the remaining steps in line (in the main function), since they are relatively straightforward and involve one or two lines of code.

Because the details of the table heading output and the cross-sectional area computation are handled in functions, the function `main` shown in Fig. 6.14 is very concise and readable. The statement

```
table_head(strength);
```

calls function `table_head` to display the table heading. Within the `for` loop, the statement

```
area = rebar_area(bar_num);
```

Figure 6.14   Function main for Maximum Tensile Load Program

```
/*
 * Displays a table of maximum tensile loads for rebars.
 */
#include <stdio.h>

/* Insert functions table_head and rebar_area along with associated
   constant macros here.                                                */

#define MIN_REBAR 2   /* smallest rebar Superb makes                    */
#define MAX_REBAR 11 /* largest rebar Superb makes                      */

int
main(void)
{
      double strength; /* tensile steel strength                        */
      int    bar_num;  /* size number of rebar                          */
      double area,     /* cross-sectional area of rebar                 */
             load;     /* maximum tensile load of rebar                 */

      /* Gets steel strength                                            */
      printf("Enter steel tensile strength in psi> ");
      scanf("%lf", &strength);

      /* Displays table heading                                         */
      table_head(strength);

      /* Displays table of cross-sectional areas and tensile loads      */
      for  (bar_num = MIN_REBAR;
            bar_num <= MAX_REBAR;
            ++bar_num) {
        area = rebar_area(bar_num);
        load = area * strength;
        printf("  %2d                        %4.2f", bar_num, area);
        printf("                        %6.0f\n",  load);
      }
      printf("*****************************");
      printf("*****************************\n");

      return (0);
}
```

calls function `rebar_area`, passing the current value of `bar_num` as the actual argument. The function result is returned to the main function and is stored in the variable `area`.

Solving the Subproblems

Now we can turn our attention to solving the problems that are the purposes of functions `table_head` and `rebar_area`. The first function is a simple collection of calls to `printf` as shown in Fig. 6.15. Function `rebar_area` computes the cross-sectional area (`csarea`) for a cylindrical bar whose rebar number is the value of the input parameter. This function uses the formulas

$$radius = \frac{rebar\ number}{16.0}$$

$$area = \pi \times radius^2$$

Figure 6.15 also shows function `rebar_area`. Notice that the variables `radius` and `csarea` are declared locally in function `rebar_area`, not in the main function, because `radius` and `csarea` are used only in the cross-sectional area computation and are not needed in `main`. Functions `table_head` and `rebar_area` can be inserted in Fig. 6.14 at the indicated spot to form a complete program source file.

Figure 6.15   Functions table_head and rebar_area

```
/*
 * Displays a heading for a table showing the maximum tensile loads of
 * rebars of different sizes made from steel whose tensile strength is
 * indicated by the value of the input parameter.
 */
void
table_head(double strength)
{
      printf("*****************************");
      printf("*****************************\n");
      printf("                    SUPERB STEEL COMPANY\n");
      printf("                      Rebar Load Chart\n");
      printf("           For bars with a steel strength of %.2f psi\n\n",
             strength);
```

(continued)

Figure 6.15   (continued)

```
        printf(" Bar              Cross-Sectional           Max. Load\n");
        printf("Number             Area (sq. in.)              (lbs.)\n");
        printf("------            ----------------          ---------\n");
}

#define PI 3.14159

/*
 * Calculates the cross-sectional area of a circular rebar identified by
 * number bar_num (bar_num > 0)
 */
double
rebar_area(int bar_num)
{
        double radius,   /* radius of rebar cross-section */
               csarea;   /* cross-sectional area          */

        /* Computes radius                                */
        radius = bar_num / 16.0;

        /* Computes and returns cross-sectional area      */
        csarea = PI * radius * radius;

        return (csarea);
}
```

EXERCISES FOR SECTION 6.2

Self-Check

1. What value would be computed by this call to function `rebar_area` (see Fig. 6.15)?

   ```
   rebar_area(32)
   ```

2. Write a **void** function `blast_off` to be called by function `main` in order to accomplish the same purpose as the countdown program in Fig. 5.8.

   ```
   int
   main(void)
   {
       int start;
   ```

```
        printf("Enter starting time (an integer) in seconds> ");
        scanf("%d", &start);
        blast_off(start);

        return (0);
}
```

6.3 FUNCTIONS WITH SIMPLE OUTPUT PARAMETERS

So far, we know how to pass inputs into a function and how to use the `return` statement to send back, at most, one result value from a function. In this section, we will learn how to return multiple results from a function. The `return` statement cannot accomplish the return of more than one value.

We have seen how, when a function call executes, the computer allocates memory space in the function data area for each formal parameter. The value of each actual parameter is stored in the memory cell allocated to its corresponding formal parameter. The function body can manipulate this value. We will next discuss how a function sends back multiple outputs to the function that calls it.

EXAMPLE 6.6

Function `separate` in Fig. 6.17 finds the sign, whole number magnitude, and fractional parts of its first parameter. In our previous examples, all the formal parameters of a function represent inputs to the function from the calling module. In function `separate`, however, only the first formal parameter, num, is an input; the other three formal parameters — `signp`, `wholep`, and `fracp` — are output parameters, used to carry multiple results from function `separate` back to the module calling it. Figure 6.16 gives a diagram of the function as a box with an input and several outputs.

The actual argument value passed to the formal parameter num is used to determine the values to be sent back through `signp`, `wholep`, and `fracp`. Notice that in Fig. 6.17 the declarations of these output parameters in the function prototype have asterisks before the parameter names. In the assignment

Figure 6.16 Diagram of Function separate That Computes Multiple Results

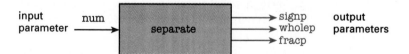

Figure 6.17   Function separate Which Has Input and Output Parameters

```
/*
 * Separates a number into three parts: a sign (+, -, or blank),
 * a whole number magnitude, and a fractional part.
 */
void
separate(double  num,        /* input - value to be split          */
         char    *signp,     /* output - sign of num               */
         int     *wholep,    /* output - whole number magnitude of num  */
         double  *fracp)     /* output - fractional part of num    */
{
      double magnitude; /* local variable - magnitude of num      */

      /* Determines sign of num */
      if (num < 0)
            *signp = '-';
      else if (num == 0)
            *signp = ' ';
      else
            *signp = '+';

        /* Finds magnitude of num (its absolute value) and
           separates it into whole and fractional parts */
        magnitude = fabs(num);
        *wholep = floor(magnitude);
        *fracp = magnitude - *wholep;
}
```

statements that use these parameters to send back the function results, there are also asterisks in front of the parameter names. The function type is `void`, as it is for functions returning no result, and the function body does not include a `return` statement to send back a single value as we saw in functions `factorial`, `round`, `even`, and `find_div`.

Let's focus for a moment on the prototype of the function in Fig. 6.17.

```
void
separate(double  num,     /* input - value to be split   */
```

```
char    *signp,  /* output - sign of num         */
int     *wholep, /* output - whole number
                               magnitude of num   */
double *fracp)   /* output - fractional part
                               of num             */
```

A declaration of a simple output parameter such as char *signp tells the compiler that signp will contain the *address* of a type char variable. Another way to express the idea that signp is the address of a type char variable is to say that the parameter signp is a *pointer* to a type char variable. Similarly, the output parameters wholep and fracp are pointers to variables of types int and double. We have chosen names for these output parameters that end in the letter 'p' because they are all pointers.

Figure 6.18 shows a complete program including a brief function main that calls function separate. Function separate is defined as it was in Fig. 6.17. It is the responsibility of the calling function to provide variables in which function separate can store the multiple results it computes. Function main in our example declares three variables to receive these results — a type char variable sn, a type int variable whl, and a type double variable fr. Notice that no values are placed in these variables prior to the call to function separate, for it is the job of separate to define their values. This change of the values of memory cells in the data area of the calling function is considered a *side effect* of the call to function separate.

Figure 6.18 Program That Calls a Function with Output Arguments

```
/*
 * Demonstrates the use of a function with input and output parameters.
 */

#include <stdio.h>
#include <math.h>

/*
 * Separates a number into three parts: a sign (+, -, or blank),
 * a whole number magnitude, and a fractional part.
 * Output parameters signp, wholep, and fracp must contain addresses
 *       of memory cells where results are to be stored
 */
```

(continued)

Figure 6.18   (continued)

```
void
separate(double   num,       /* input - value to be split               */
         char    *signp,     /* output - sign of num                    */
         int     *wholep,    /* output - whole number magnitude of num  */
         double *fracp)      /* output - fractional part of num         */
{
      double magnitude;  /* local variable - magnitude of num           */

      /* Determines sign of num */
      if (num < 0)
            *signp = '-';
      else if (num == 0)
            *signp = ' ';
      else
            *signp = '+';

      /* Finds magnitude of num (its absolute value) and separates
         it into whole and fractional parts                            */
      magnitude = fabs(num);
      *wholep = floor(magnitude);
      *fracp = magnitude - *wholep;
}

int
main(void)
{
      double value; /* input - number to analyze                        */
      char    sn;    /* output - sign of value                          */
      int     whl;   /* output - whole number magnitude of value        */
      double fr;    /* output - fractional part of value               */

      /* Gets data                                                      */
      printf("Enter a value to analyze> ");
      scanf("%lf", &value);

      /* Separates data value into three parts                          */
      separate(value, &sn, &whl, &fr);
```

(continued)

Figure 6.18 (continued)

```
      /* Displays results                                 */
      printf("Parts of %.4f\n  sign: %c\n", value, sn);
      printf("  whole number magnitude: %d\n", whl);
      printf("  fractional part:  %.4f\n", fr);
      return (0);
}
Enter a value to analyze> 35.817
Parts of 35.8170
  sign: +
  whole number magnitude: 35
  fractional part: 0.8170
```

Figure 6.19 shows the data areas of main and separate as they are set up by the function call statement

```
separate(value, &sn, &whl, &fr);
```

This statement causes the number stored in the actual argument value to be copied into the input parameter num and the addresses of the arguments sn,

**Figure 6.19
Correspondence
of Input and
Output
Parameters for**
separate(value,
&sn, &whl,
&fr);

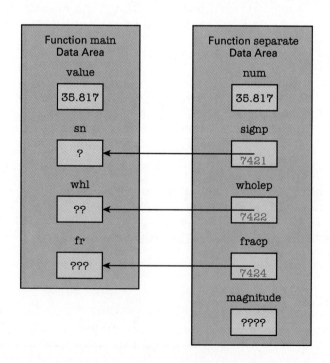

wh1, and fr to be stored in the corresponding output parameters signp, wholep, and fracp. The small numbers in color represent possible actual addresses in memory. Because it makes no difference to our program which specific cells are used, we normally diagram an address stored in a memory cell simply as a pointer like the arrow from signp to sn. Note that the use of the address-of operator & on the actual arguments sn, wh1, and fr is essential. If the operator were omitted, we would be passing to separate the *values* of sn, wh1, and fr, information that is worthless from the perspective of separate. The only way separate can store values in sn, wh1, and fr is if it knows where to find them in memory. The purpose of separate with regard to its second, third, and fourth arguments is comparable to the purpose of the library function scanf with regard to all of its arguments except the first (the format string).

In addition to the fact that the *values* of the actual output arguments in the call to separate are useless, these values are also of data types that do not match the types of the corresponding formal parameters. Table 6.4 shows the effect of the address-of operator & on the data type of a reference. You see that in general if a reference x is of type "whatever-type", the reference &x is of type "pointer to whatever-type", that is, "whatever-type *".

So far, we have examined how to declare simple output parameters in a function prototype and how to use the address-of operator & in a function call statement to pass pointers of appropriate types. Now we need to study how the function manipulates these pointers in order to send back multiple results. The statements in function separate that cause the return of results follow:

```
*signp = '-';
*signp = ' ';
*signp = '+';
*wholep = floor(magnitude);
*fracp = magnitude - *wholep;
```

In each case, the name of the formal parameter is preceded by the *indirection operator,* unary *. When the unary * operator is applied to a reference that is of

Table 6.4 Effect of & Operator on the Data Type of a Reference

Declaration	Data Type of x	Data Type of &x
char x	char	char * (pointer to char)
int x	int	int * (pointer to int)
double x	double	double * (pointer to double)

Figure 6.20
Comparison of
Direct Reference
and Indirect
Reference

Reference	Cell meant	Value
nump	gray cell	pointer (address of cell in color)
*nump	cell in color	84

some pointer type, it has the effect of following the pointer referenced by its operand. Figure 6.20 shows the difference between a *direct* reference to a variable of type "pointer to int" and an *indirect* or "pointer-following" reference to the same variable using the indirection operator.

For the data in Fig. 6.19, the statement

```
*signp = '+';
```

follows the pointer in signp to the cell that function main calls sn and stores in it the character '+'. The statement

```
*wholep = floor(magnitude);
```

follows the pointer in wholep to the cell called whl by main and stores the integer 35 there. Similarly, the statement

```
*fracp = magnitude - *wholep;
```

uses two indirect references: One accesses the value in main's local variable whl through the pointer in wholep, and another accesses fr of main through the pointer fracp to give the final output argument the value 0.817.

In this chapter, we have seen several kinds of functions, and we have studied how formal parameters are used in all of them. We have used input parameters to bring information into a function and output parameters to take results back to the calling function. It is also possible to use a single parameter as a two-way communication path to a function. Such an *input/output parameter* is implemented with a pointer just like an output parameter. Table 6.5 compares the various kinds of functions and indicates the circumstances in which each kind should be used.

Table 6.5   Kinds of Function Subprograms Seen So Far and Where to Use Them

Purpose	Function Type	Parameters	To Return Result
To compute or obtain as input a single numeric or character value.	Same as type of value to be computed or obtained.	Input parameters hold copies of data provided by calling function.	Function code includes a `return` statement with an expression whose value is the result.
To display output containing values of numeric or character arguments.	`void`	Input parameters hold copies of data provided by calling function.	No result is returned.
To compute multiple numeric or character results.	`void`	Input parameters hold copies of data provided by calling function. Output parameters are pointers to actual arguments.	Results are stored in the calling function's data area by indirect assignment through output parameters. No `return` statement is required.
To modify argument values.	`void`	Input/output parameters are pointers to actual arguments. Input data is accessed by indirect reference through parameters.	Results are stored in the calling function's data area by indirect assignment through output parameters. No `return` statement is required.

Program Style   *Preferred Kinds of Functions*

Although all the kinds of functions we consider in this chapter are useful in developing computer systems, we recommend that you use the first kind shown in Table 6.5 whenever possible. Functions that return a single value are the easiest functions for a program reader to deal with. You will note that all the mathematical functions we discussed in Section 3.4 are of this variety. Since such functions take only input arguments, the programmer is not concerned with using such complexities as indirect referencing in the function definition or applying the address-of operator in the function call. If the value returned by the function is to be stored in a variable, the reader sees an assignment statement in the code of the calling function. If a function subprogram has a meaningful name, the reader can often get a good idea of what is happening in the calling function without feeling obliged to read the function subprogram's code.

EXERCISES FOR SECTION 6.3

Self-Check

1. Write a prototype for a function `sum_n_avg` that has three type `double` input parameters and two output parameters.

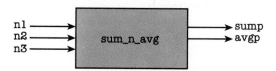

The function computes the sum and the average of its three input arguments and relays its results through two output parameters.

2. The following code fragment is from a function preparing to call `sum_n_avg` (see Exercise 1). Complete the function call statement.

```
{
      double one, two, three, sum_of_3, avg_of_3;
      printf("Enter three numbers> ");
      scanf("%lf%lf%lf", &one, &two, &three);
      sum_n_avg(_____);
   . . .
```

3. Given the memory setup shown, fill in the chart by indicating the data type and value of each reference as well as the name of the function in which the reference would be legal. Give pointer values by referring to cell attributes. For example, the value of `valp` would be "pointer to color shaded cell," and the value of `&many` would be "pointer to gray shaded cell."

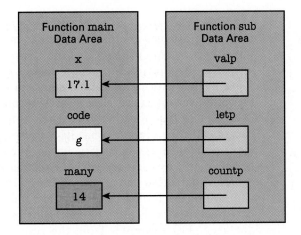

Reference	Where Legal	Data Type	Value
`valp`	sub	`double *`	pointer to color shaded cell
`&many`			
`code`			
`&code`			
`countp`			
`*countp`			
`*valp`			
`letp`			
`&x`			

Programming

1. Define the function `sum_n_avg` whose prototype you wrote in Self-Check Exercise 1. The function should compute both the sum and the average of its three input parameters and relay these results through its output parameters.

6.4 INTRODUCTION TO SCOPE OF NAMES

The *scope* of a name refers to the region of a program in which the name has a particular meaning. Let's consider the names in the program outline shown in

Fig. 6.21. The scope of the constant macro names MAX and LIMIT begins at their definition and continues to the end of the source file. This means that all three functions can use MAX, but only fun_two and main can use LIMIT.

The scope of each function name with the associated formal parameter types begins with its prototype and continues to the end of the source file, except for functions that have a local meaning for the same name. For example, even though function one is defined before function fun_two, fun_two cannot call one because it has its own meaning for the identifier one. Notice that one is the name of its first formal parameter. Therefore function one can be called only by itself and main. Function fun_two with one integer and one character parameter can also be called by itself and main.

All of the formal parameters and local variables in Fig. 6.21 are visible only from their declaration to the closing brace of the function in which they are declared. For example, from the line that is marked with the comment

Figure 6.21 Outline of Program for Studying Scope of Names

```
#define MAX   950

void
one(int anarg, double second)      /* prototype 1     */
{
        int onelocal;              /* local 1         */
        . . .
} /* end one */

#define LIMIT 200

int
fun_two(int one, char anarg)       /* prototype 2     */
{
        int localvar;              /* local 2         */
        . . .
} /* end fun_two */

int
main(void)                         /* prototype 3     */
{
        int localvar;
        . . .
} /* end main */
```

Table 6.6   Scope of Names in Fig. 6.21

Name	Visible in one	Visible in fun_two	Visible in main
MAX	yes	yes	yes
one (the function)	yes	no	yes
anarg (int)	yes	no	no
second	yes	no	no
onelocal	yes	no	no
LIMIT	no	yes	yes
fun_two	no	yes	yes
one (the formal parameter)	no	yes	no
anarg (char)	no	yes	no
localvar (inside fun_two)	no	yes	no
main	no	no	yes
localvar (inside main)	no	no	yes

/* prototype 1 */ to the line marked /* end one */, the identifier anarg means an integer variable in the data area of function one. From the line with the comment /* prototype 2 */ through the line marked /* end fun_two */, anarg refers to a character variable in the data area of fun_two. In the rest of the file, the identifier anarg is not visible.

Table 6.6 shows which identifiers are visible within each of the three functions.

EXERCISE FOR SECTION 6.4

Self-Check

1. Consider the following program outline. Create a table similar to Table 6.6 showing the visibility of names within each function.

```
int
one(double var1, char var2)
{
        char alocal, one;
        . . .
}
```

```
int
two(double one, int var1)
{
     . . .
}
#define LARGE 100
int
main(void)
{
     char var1;
     . . .
}
```

6.5 FORMAL OUTPUT PARAMETERS AS ACTUAL ARGUMENTS

So far, all of our actual arguments in calls to functions have been either local variables or input parameters of the calling function. However, sometimes we need to pass our output parameters as arguments. In Fig. 6.22, which we have left incomplete, we write a function based on the fraction-scanning program of Fig. 5.19. Function scan_fraction has two output parameters through which it stores the numerator and denominator of the fraction scanned. Function scan_fraction needs to pass its output parameters to library function scanf in order to scan the needed numerator and denominator. In all our previous calls to function scanf, we have always applied the address-of operator & to each variable to be filled. However, the situation in scan_fraction is different from our previous calls to scanf. Consider the diagram of part of scan_fraction's data area that is shown in Fig. 6.23. The three arguments that scan_fraction needs to pass to scanf are nump, denomp, and slash. In the case of local variable slash, scan_fraction wants scanf to store a single character in slash. Therefore scanf must be passed the address of slash. In contrast, scan_fraction does not want scanf to store values in parameters nump and denomp. Rather, scan_fraction needs scanf to store values in the variables pointed to by nump and denomp. Given the situation pictured in Fig. 6.23, it is the addresses of numerator and denominator that must be passed to scanf. These addresses are the current *values* of output parameters nump and denomp. Thus the correct call to scanf to complete Fig. 6.22 is

```
scanf("%d%c%d", nump, &slash, denomp);
```

Passing a formal output parameter to another function requires careful consideration of the purpose of the function being called. It is often advisable to

Figure 6.22   Function to Scan a Common Fraction

```
/*
 * Get a valid fraction
 * A valid fraction is of this form:  integer/positive integer
 */
void
scan_fraction(int *nump,     /* output - numerator    */
              int *denomp)   /* output - denominator */
{
      char slash;   /* local - character between numerator & denominator */
      int  status;  /* status code returned by scanf indicating number
                         of valid values obtained                       */
      int  error;   /* flag indicating whether or not an error has been
                         detected in current input                      */
      char discard; /* unprocessed character from input line            */

      do {
          /* No errors detected yet                                     */
          error = 0;

          /*  Get a fraction from the user                              */
          printf("Enter a common fraction as two integers separated by ");
          printf("a slash\nand press <enter> or <return>\n> ");
          status = scanf("%d%c%d", _____, _____, _____);

          /* Validate the fraction                                      */
          if (status < 3) {
                error = 1;
                printf("Input invalid--please read directions carefully\n");
          } else if (slash != '/') {
                error = 1;
                printf("Input invalid--separate numerator and denominator");
                printf(" by a slash (/)\n");
          } else if (*denomp <= 0) {
                error = 1;
                printf("Input invalid--denominator must be positive\n");
          }

          /* Discard carriage return and extra input characters         */
          do {
              scanf("%c", &discard);
          } while (discard != '\n');

      } while (error);
}
```

**Figure 6.23
Partial Data
Areas for
scan_fraction
and the
Function That
Called
scan_fraction**

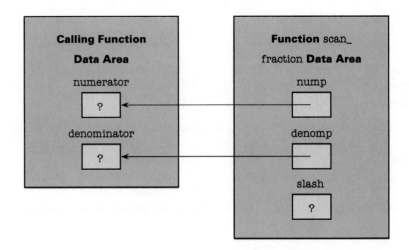

sketch the data areas of the affected functions before determining the correct references to use in the function calls. When the arguments involved are simple variables of types int, double, and char, the usage pattern described in Table 6.7 works well. Unfortunately, these rules do not generalize to cover all arguments of the composite types we will study in later chapters. In the interest of completeness, Table 6.7 includes some cases for which we have not yet seen any examples.

**Table 6.7   Passing to Function some_fun an Argument x
of Simple Base Type int, double, or char**

Actual Argument Type	Use in Calling Function	Purpose in Called Function (some_fun)	Formal Parameter Type	Call to some_fun	Example
int char double	local variable or input parameter	input parameter	int char double	some_fun(x)	Fig. 6.2, main: factorial(num)
int char double	local variable	output or input/ output parameter	int * char * double *	some_fun(&x)	Fig. 6.18, main: separate(value, &sn, &whl, &fr); (2nd–4th arguments)
int * char * double *	output or input/ output parameter	output or input/ output parameter	int * char * double *	some_fun(x)	Fig. 6.22 completed, scanf(..., nump, ..., denomp);

(continued)

Table 6.7   (continued)

Actual Argument Type	Use in Calling Function	Purpose in Called Function (some_fun)	Formal Parameter Type	Call to some_fun	Example
int * char * double *	output or input/ output parameter	input parameter	int char double	some_fun(*x)	Self-Check Ex. 2 in 6.5, trouble: double_trouble (y, *x); (2nd argument)

EXERCISES FOR SECTION 6.5

Self-Check

1. Box models of functions `onef` and `twof` follow. Do not try to define the complete functions; write only the portions described.

Assume that these functions are concerned only with integers, and write *prototypes* for `onef` and `twof`. Begin the body of function `onef` with a declaration of an integer local variable `tmp`. Show a call from `onef` to `twof` in which the input argument is `dat`, and `tmp` and `out2p` are the output arguments. Function `onef` intends for `twof` to store one integer result in `tmp` and one in the variable pointed to by `out2p`.

2. a. Classify each formal parameter of `double_trouble` and `trouble` as input, output, or input/output.

   b. What values of `x` and `y` are displayed by this program? Hint: Sketch the data areas of `main`, `trouble`, and `double_trouble` as the program executes.

```
void
double_trouble(int *p, int y)
{
        int x;
        x = 14;
        *p = 2 * x - y;
}

void
trouble(int *x, int *y)
```

```
{
      double_trouble(x, 5);
      double_trouble(y, *x);
}

int
main(void)
{
      int x, y;
      trouble(&x, &y);
      printf("x = %d, y = %d\n", x, y);
      return (0);
}
```

What naming convention introduced in Section 6.3 is violated in the prototype of `trouble`?

6.6 RECURSIVE FUNCTIONS

A function that calls itself is said to be *recursive*. A function `f1` is also recursive if it calls a function `f2`, which under some circumstances calls `f1`, creating a cycle in the sequence of calls. The ability to invoke itself enables a recursive function to be repeated with different parameter values. Generally, a recursive solution is less efficient than an iterative solution in terms of computer time due to the overhead for the extra function calls; however, in many instances, the use of recursion enables us to specify a very natural, simple solution to a problem that would otherwise be very difficult to solve. For this reason, recursion is an important and powerful tool in problem solving and programming.

Problems that lend themselves to a recursive solution have the following characteristics:

- One or more *simple cases* of the problem have a straightforward, nonrecursive solution.
- The other cases can be redefined in terms of problems that are closer to the simple cases.
- By applying this redefinition process every time the recursive function is called, eventually the problem is reduced entirely to simple cases, which are relatively easy to solve.

The recursive algorithms that we write will generally consist of an `if` statement with the following form:

if this is a simple case
    solve it
else
        redefine the problem using recursion

Figure 6.24 illustrates this approach. Let's assume that for a particular problem of size n, we can split the problem into a problem of size 1, which we can solve (a simple case), and a problem of size $n - 1$. We can split the problem of size $n - 1$ into another problem of size 1 and a problem of size $n - 2$, which we can split further. If we split the problem $n - 1$ times, we will end up with n problems of size 1, all of which we can solve.

Figure 6.24   Splitting a Problem into Smaller Problems

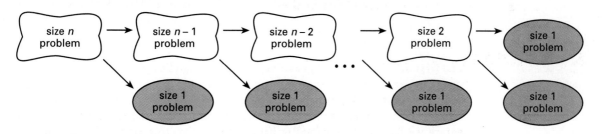

EXAMPLE 6.7   As a simple example of this approach, let's consider how we might solve the problem of multiplying 6 by 3, assuming we know our addition tables but not our multiplication tables. We do know, however, that any number multiplied by 1 gives us the original number, so if we ever come across this simple case, we'll just solve it. The problem of multiplying 6 by 3 can be split into the two problems:

1. Multiply 6 by 2.
2. Add 6 to the result of problem 1.

Because we know our addition tables, we can solve problem 2 but not problem 1. However, problem 1 is closer to the simple case than the original problem was. We can split problem 1 into the following two problems, 1.1 and 1.2, leaving us three problems to solve, two of which are additions:

1. Multiply 6 by 2.
    1.1   Multiply 6 by 1.
    1.2   Add 6 to the result.
2. Add 6 to the result of problem 1.

Problem 1.1 is one of the simple cases we were looking for. By solving problem 1.1 (the answer is 6) and problem 1.2, we get the solution to problem 1 (the answer is 12). Solving problem 2 gives us the final answer (18).

Figure 6.25 implements this approach to doing multiplication as the recursive C function multiply that returns the product m × n of its two arguments. The body of function multiply implements the general form of a recursive algorithm shown earlier. The simplest case is reached when the condition n == 1 is true. In this case, the statement

```
ans = m;    /* simple case  */
```

executes, so the answer is m. If n is greater than 1, the statement

```
ans = m + multiply(m, n - 1);   /* recursive step */
```

executes, splitting the original problem into the two simpler problems:

- multiply m by n-1
- add m to the result

The first of these problems is solved by calling multiply again with n-1 as its second argument. If the new second argument is greater than 1, there will be additional calls to function multiply.

At first, it may seem odd that we must rely on the function multiply before we have even finished writing it! However, this approach is the key to developing recursive algorithms. To solve a problem recursively, first we must

Figure 6.25 **Recursive Function multiply**

```
/*
 *  Performs integer multiplication using + operator.
 *  Assumes n > 0
 */
int
multiply(int m, int n)
{
     int ans;

     if (n == 1)
          ans = m;       /* simple case */
     else
          ans = m + multiply(m, n - 1);  /* recursive step */

     return (ans);
}
```

trust our function to solve a simpler version of the problem. Then we build the solution to the whole problem on the result from the simpler version. ⬅

Tracing a Recursive Function

Hand-tracing an algorithm's execution provides us with valuable insight into how that algorithm works. We can trace the execution of the function call

```
multiply(6, 3)
```

by drawing an *activation frame* corresponding to each call of the function. An activation frame shows the parameter values for each call and summarizes the execution of the call.

The three activation frames generated to solve the problem of multiplying 6 by 3 are shown in Fig. 6.26. The part of each activation frame that executes before the next recursive call is in color; the part that executes after the return from the next call is in gray. The darker the color of an activation frame, the greater the depth of recursion.

The value returned from each call is shown alongside a black arrow. The return arrow from each call points to the operator + because the addition is performed just after the return.

**Figure 6.26
Trace of
Function
multiply**

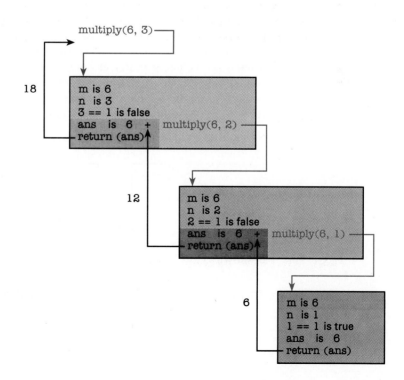

Figure 6.26 shows three calls to function `multiply`. Parameter m has the value 6 for all three calls; parameter n has the values 3, 2, and, finally, 1. Since n is 1 in the third call, the value of m (6) is assigned to `ans` and is returned as the result of the third and last call. After returning to the second activation frame, the value of m is added to this result, and the sum (12) is returned as the result of the second call. After returning to the first activation frame, the value of m is added to this result, and the sum (18) is returned as the result of the original call to function `multiply`. Notice that the function returns occur in the reverse order of the function calls—that is, we return from the last call first, then we return from the next-to-last call, and so on.

Parameter and Local Variable Stacks

You may be wondering how C keeps track of the values of m and n at any given point. C uses a special data structure called a *stack* that is analogous to a stack of dishes or trays. Think of the countless times you have stood in line in a cafeteria. Recall that clean dishes are always placed on top of a stack of dishes. When we need a dish, we always remove the one most recently placed on the stack and the next to last dish placed on the stack becomes the top dish of the stack.

Similarly, whenever a new call to `multiply` occurs, the argument values associated with that call are placed on top of the parameter stacks for m and n. A new cell whose value is initially undefined is also placed on top of the stack that is maintained for the local variable `ans`. Whenever m, n, or `ans` is referenced, the value at the top of the corresponding stack is always used. When a function return occurs, the value currently at the top of each stack is removed, causing the value just below it to become the top value.

As an example, let's look at the three stacks as they appear right after the first call to `multiply`. One cell is on each stack, as shown.

After first call to multiply

m	n	ans
6	3	?

After the second call to `multiply`, the numbers 6 and 2 are placed on top of the stacks for m and n, and the new top cell of the stack for `ans` is undefined, as shown next. The value in color is at the top of each stack.

After second call to multiply

m	n	ans
6	2	?
6	3	?

Similarly, the third call to `multiply` places the values 6 and 1 on the parameter stacks and an undefined cell on the local variable stack as shown.

After third call to multiply

m	n	ans
6	1	?
6	2	?
6	3	?

Execution of the third call to `multiply` places the value 6 in the local variable `ans`.

m	n	ans
6	1	6
6	2	?
6	3	?

The function return causes the values at the top of the stacks to be removed after the 6 in `ans` is returned as the result of the third call to `multiply`.

After first return

m	n	ans
6	2	?
6	3	?

Completing execution of the second call to `multiply` places the value 12 (the sum of the 6 returned from the third call and the 6 that is the current value of m) in the local variable `ans`.

m	n	ans
6	2	12
6	3	?

The function return removes the values at the top of the stacks and sends back the 12 in `ans` as the result of the second call to `multiply`.

After second return

m	n	ans
6	3	?

Completing execution of the first call to multiply places the value 18 (the sum of the 12 returned from the second call and the 6 that is the current value of m) in the local variable ans.

m	n	ans
6	3	18

The third and final return exits the original function call sending back the value 18 as the function result. There is no longer any memory allocated for m, n, and ans.

You can implement and manipulate a stack yourself using the data structure that we will study in Chapter 7. However, C automatically handles all the stack manipulation associated with function calls, so we can write recursive functions without needing to worry about the stacks.

Implementation of Parameter Stacks in C

For illustrative purposes, we have used separate stacks for each parameter in our discussion; however, the compiler actually maintains a single stack. Each time a call to a function occurs, all its parameters and local variables are pushed onto the stack along with the memory address of the calling statement. This address gives the computer the return point after execution of the function. Although multiple copies of a function's parameters may be saved on the stack, only one copy of the function body is in memory.

When and How to Trace Recursive Functions

Doing a trace by hand of multiple calls to a recursive function is helpful in understanding how recursion works but less useful when trying to develop a recursive algorithm. During algorithm development, it is best to trace a specific case simply by trusting any recursive call to return a correct value based on the function purpose. Then the hand trace can check whether this value is manipulated properly to produce a correct function result for the case under consideration.

However, if a recursive function's implementation is flawed, tracing its execution is an essential part of identifying the error. The function can be made to trace itself by inserting debugging print statements showing entry to and exit from the function. Figure 6.27 shows a self-tracing version of function multiply as well as output generated by the call

```
multiply(8, 3)
```

Figure 6.27   Recursive Function multiply with Print Statements to Create Trace and Output from multiply(8, 3)

```c
/*
 *   ***  Includes calls to printf to trace execution ***
 *   Performs integer multiplication using + operator.
 *   Assumes n > 0
 */
int
multiply(int m, int n)
{
        int ans;

    printf("Entering multiply with m = %d, n = %d\n", m, n);

        if (n == 1)
                ans = m;      /* simple case */
        else
                ans = m + multiply(m, n - 1); /* recursive step          */
    printf("multiply(%d, %d) returning %d\n", m, n, ans);

        return (ans);
}
```

```
Entering multiply with m = 8, n = 3
Entering multiply with m = 8, n = 2
Entering multiply with m = 8, n = 1
multiply(8, 1) returning 8
multiply(8, 2) returning 16
multiply(8, 3) returning 24
```

Roots of Equations

Many real-world problems can be solved by finding roots of equations. A value k is a *root* of an equation, $f(x) = 0$, if $f(k)$ equals zero. If we graph the function $f(x)$, as shown in Fig. 6.28, the roots of the equation are those points where the x-axis and the graph of the function intersect. The roots of the equation $f(x) = 0$ are also called the *zeros* of the function $f(x)$.

Consider this problem whose solution requires finding a function root. When firing a projectile at a target, one must determine the angle of elevation (θ) at which to fire the projectile. If we know the projectile's velocity (v) and

**Figure 6.28
Six Roots for
the Equation
f(x) = 0**

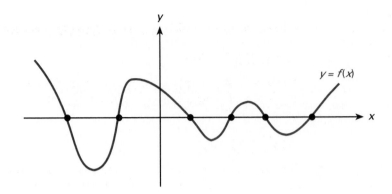

both the distance (s) to the base of the target and the height (h) of the desired impact point on the target, we can write a function of θ that will evaluate to zero when θ is the desired angle of elevation. Using g as the acceleration of gravity, we know that

$$h = v \sin\theta\, t - \frac{1}{2} g t^2$$

and

$$t = \frac{s}{v \cos\theta}$$

Substituting and simplifying, we have

$$h = s \tan\theta - \frac{1}{2} g \left(\frac{s^2}{v^2 \cos^2\theta} \right)$$

so a zero of the function

$$f(\theta) = s \tan\theta - \frac{1}{2} g \left(\frac{s^2}{v^2 \cos^2\theta} \right) - h$$

will give us the correct angle of elevation. The bisection method is one way of approximating a root of the equation $f(\theta) = 0$.

The bisection method repeatedly generates approximate roots until a true root is discovered or until an approximation is found that differs from a true root by less than *epsilon*, where *epsilon* is a very small constant (for example, 0.0001). The bisection method is well suited to a recursive implementation. In our next case study, we develop a recursive function to implement this method. Programming Project 11 at the end of this chapter calls for you to complete the solution of the projectile-firing problem for specific target data.

Case Study: Bisection Method for Finding Roots

> **PROBLEM**

Develop a function `bisect` that approximates a root of a function f on an interval that contains an odd number of roots.

> **ANALYSIS**

A program that is to call function `bisect` must first tabulate function values to find an appropriate interval in which to search for a root. If a change of sign occurs on an interval, that interval must contain an odd number of roots. Figure 6.29 shows two such intervals.

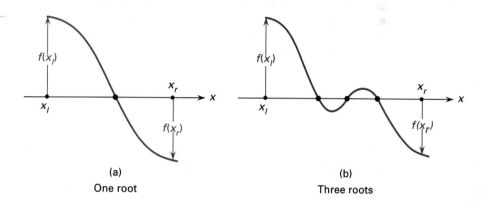

(a)
One root

(b)
Three roots

Let us assume that $[x_l, x_r]$ (`x_left` to `x_right`) is an interval on which a change of sign does occur and in which there is exactly one root. Furthermore, assume that the function $f(x)$ is continuous on this interval. If we bisect this interval by computing its midpoint x_{mid}, using the formula

$$x_{mid} = \frac{x_l + x_r}{2.0}$$

there are three possible outcomes: the root is in the lower half of the interval, $[x_l, x_{mid}]$; the root is in the upper half of the interval, $[x_{mid}, x_r]$; or $f(x_{mid})$ is zero. Figure 6.30 shows these three possibilities graphically.

A fourth possibility is that the length of the initial interval is less than *epsilon*. In this case, any point in the interval is an acceptable root approximation.

**Figure 6.30
Three
Possibilities
That Arise
When the
Interval $[x_l, x_r]$
Is Bisected**

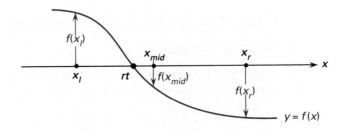

The root *rt* is in the half interval $[x_l, x_{mid}]$.

(a)

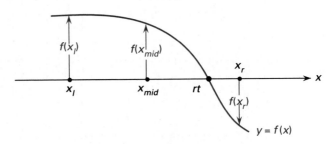

The root *rt* is in the half interval $[x_{mid}, x_r]$.

(b)

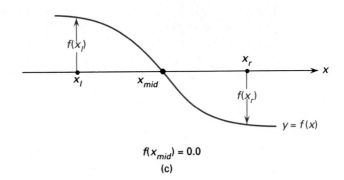

$f(x_{mid}) = 0.0$

(c)

Data Requirements

Problem Inputs

```
double x_l          /* left endpoint of interval  */
double x_r          /* right endpoint of interval */
double epsilon      /* error tolerance            */
```

Problem Output

```
double root        /* approximate root of f      */
```

Program Variable

```
double x_mid       /* interval midpoint           */
```

▬▬ **DESIGN** ▬▬

Writing a recursive bisection algorithm is merely a matter of dividing the four possibilities into simple and complex cases. Using our generic recursion format, we have

Initial Algorithm

1. *if this is a simple case, solve it*
   - 1.1 Simple Case 1   If the interval is shorter than epsilon, return the midpoint.
   - 1.2 Simple Case 2   If the function value at the midpoint is zero, return the midpoint.

   else redefine the problem using recursion
   - 1.3 Bisect the interval and execute a recursive call on the half interval that contains the root.

Algorithm Refinements

Our refinement of Step 1.3 looks for a change of sign of the function values on a half interval in order to find the half interval that contains the root.

1.3.1 if $f(x\_l) * f(x\_mid) < 0$
   - 1.3.2 Find the root by bisecting [x_l, x_mid].

   else
   - 1.3.3 Find the root by bisecting [x_mid, x_r].

▬▬ **IMPLEMENTATION** ▬▬

Figure 6.31 shows an implementation of our recursive algorithm.

▬▬ **TESTING** ▬▬

To test the `bisect` function, we would place it in a file after a definition of the function f for which we want to find roots. The last module in the file would be a main function that calls `bisect` with a variety of intervals and *epsilon* values. In Section 6.8 we examine in detail the design of such main functions that test single functions.

Figure 6.31   Bisection Method Implemented Recursively

```
/*
 * Implements the bisection method for approximating a root of a function f
 * in the interval [x_l, x_r].  Assumes signs of f(x_l) and f(x_r) are
 * different.  Approximation is within epsilon of a root.
 */
double
bisect(double x_l,      /* input - endpoints of interval in which  */
       double x_r,      /*                  to look for a root      */
       double epsilon)  /* input - error tolerance                 */
{
      double root,      /* approximate root  */
             x_mid;     /* interval midpoint */

      /* Compute midpoint of interval                              */
      x_mid = (x_l + x_r) / 2.0;

      if (x_r - x_l < epsilon)             /* simple case 1 */
            root = x_mid;
      else if (f(x_mid) == 0.0)            /* simple case 2 */
            root = x_mid;
      else if (f(x_l) * f(x_mid) < 0.0)    /* root in [x_l, x_mid] */
            root = bisect(x_l, x_mid, epsilon);
      else                                 /* root in [x_mid, x_r] */
            root = bisect(x_mid, x_r, epsilon);

      return (root);
}
```

EXERCISES FOR SECTION 6.6

Self-Check

1. Using diagrams similar to those in Fig. 6.24, show the specific problems that are generated by the following call:

    multiply(5, 4)

2. Trace the contents of stack representations of m, n, and ans for the evaluation of multiply(5, 4).

Programming

1. Add statements to function bisect to make it self-tracing like the version of multiply in Fig. 6.27.

6.7 TOP-DOWN DESIGN ILLUSTRATED

In our next case study, we manipulate numeric data of a type not provided as one of C's base types. To do this, we must write our own functions to perform many operations that we take for granted when using types `int` and `double`.

Case Study: Performing Arithmetic Operations on Common Fractions

PROBLEM

You are working problems in which you must display your results as integer ratios; therefore you need to be able to compute using common fractions and get results that are common fractions in reduced form. You want to write a program that will allow you to add, subtract, multiply, and divide common fractions. The program will prompt you for a fraction, an operator, and another fraction and then display the problem and the result. The process will be repeated until you enter an n to answer the question, `Continue? (y/n)`.

ANALYSIS

Because the problem specifies that results are to be in reduced form, we will need to include a fraction-reducing function in addition to the computational functions. If we break the problem into small enough chunks, there should be an opportunity to reuse code by calling the same function multiple times. The in-depth analysis of the problem is actually distributed through the development of these modules.

Data Requirements

Problem Inputs
```
int n1, d1 /* numerator, denominator of first fraction */
int n2, d2 /* numerator, denominator of second fraction */
char op    /* arithmetic operator + - * or /          */
char again /* y or n depending on user's desire to
              continue                                 */
```

Problem Outputs
```
int n_ans  /* numerator of answer                      */
int d_ans  /* denominator of answer                    */
```

As we develop an algorithm through stepwise refinement, we will look for instances in which a definition of a new function would simplify the design.

Initial Algorithm

1. Initialize `again` to `y`.
2. As long as user wants to continue,
   3. Get a fraction problem.
   4. Compute the result.
   5. Display problem and result.
   6. Check if user wants to continue.

Step 3 Refinement
3.1 Get first fraction.
3.2 Get operator.
3.3 Get second fraction.

Step 4 Refinement
4.1 Select a task based on operator:
    '+': 4.1.2 Add the fractions.
    '−': 4.1.3 Add the first fraction and the negation of the second.
    '*': 4.1.4 Multiply the fractions.
    '/': 4.1.5 Multiply the first fraction and the reciprocal of the second.
4.2 Put the result fraction in reduced form.

Step 4.2 Refinement
4.2.1 Find the greatest common divisor (gcd) of the numerator and denominator.
4.2.2 Divide the numerator and denominator by the gcd.

For Steps 3.1 and 3.3 we will use function `scan_fraction` from Fig. 6.22. We also plan to implement `get_operator` (Step 3.2), `add_fractions` (Steps 4.1.2 and 4.1.3), `multiply_fractions` (Steps 4.1.4 and 4.1.5), `reduce_fraction` (Step 4.2), `find_gcd` (Step 4.2.1), and `print_fraction` (refinement of Step 5) as function subprograms. As a result, coding function `main` is quite straightforward. Figure 6.32 shows most of the program; however, the functions `multiply_fractions` and `find_gcd` have been left as exercises. In their places, we have inserted *stubs*, skeleton functions that

Figure 6.32 **Program to Perform Arithmetic Operations on Common Fractions**

```c
/*
 * Adds, subtracts, multiplies and divides common fractions, displaying
 * results in reduced form.
 */

#include <stdio.h>
#include <stdlib.h>    /* provides function abs */

/* Function scan_fraction from Fig. 6.22    */

/*
 * Gets and returns a valid arithmetic operator.  Skips over newline
 * characters and permits re-entry of operator in case of error.
 */
char
get_operator(void)
{
      char op;

      printf("Enter an arithmetic operator (+,-,*, or /)\n> ");
      for  (scanf("%c", &op);
            op != '+'  &&  op != '-'  &&
            op != '*'  &&  op != '/';
            scanf("%c", &op)) {
         if (op != '\n')
               printf("%c invalid, reenter operator (+,-,*,/)\n> ",
                      op);
      }
      return (op);
}

/*
 * Adds fractions represented by pairs of integers.
 * Sum of n1/d1 and n2/d2 is stored in variables pointed
 * to by n_ansp and d_ansp.  Result is not reduced.
 */
void
add_fractions(int   n1,     int   d1,     /* input - first fraction    */
              int   n2,     int   d2,     /* input - second fraction   */
              int   *n_ansp, int  *d_ansp) /* output - sum of two fractions*/
```

(continued)

Figure 6.32 (continued)

```
{
      int denom,        /* common denominator used for sum
                           (may not be least)                */
          numer,        /* numerator of sum                  */
          sign_factor; /* -1 for a negative, 1 otherwise    */

      /* Finds a common denominator                                    */
      denom = d1 * d2;

      /* Computes numerator                                            */
      numer = n1 * d2 + n2 * d1;

      /* Adjusts sign (at most, numerator should be negative)          */
      if (numer * denom >= 0)
            sign_factor = 1;
      else
            sign_factor = -1;

      numer = sign_factor * abs(numer);
      denom = abs(denom);

      /* Returns result                                                */
      *n_ansp = numer;
      *d_ansp = denom;
}

/*
 ***** STUB *****
 * Multiplies fractions represented by pairs of integers.
 * Product of n1/d1 and n2/d2 is stored in variables pointed
 * to by n_ansp and d_ansp.  Result is not reduced.
 */
void
multiply_fractions(int    n1,     int  d1, /* input - first fraction    */
                   int    n2,     int  d2, /* input - second fraction   */
                   int    *n_ansp,          /* output -                  */
                   int    *d_ansp)          /* product of two fractions  */
{

      /* Displays trace message                                        */
      printf("\nEntering multiply_fractions with\n");
      printf("n1 = %d, d1 = %d, n2 = %d, d2 = %d\n", n1, d1, n2, d2);
```

(continued)

Figure 6.32 (continued)

```
        /* Defines output arguments                                       */
        *n_ansp = 1;
        *d_ansp = 1;
}

/*
 ***** STUB *****
 * Finds greatest common divisor of two integers
 */
int
find_gcd (int n1, int n2) /* input - two integers                         */
{
        int gcd;

        /* Displays trace message                                         */
        printf("\nEntering find_gcd with n1 = %d, n2 = %d\n", n1, n2);

        /* Asks user for gcd                                              */
        printf("gcd of %d and %d?> ", n1, n2);
        scanf("%d", &gcd);

        /* Displays exit trace message                                    */
        printf("find_gcd returning %d\n", gcd);
        return (gcd);
}

/*
 * Reduces a fraction by dividing its numerator and denominator by their
 * greatest common divisor.
 */
void
reduce_fraction(int  *nump,     /* input/output -                         */
                int  *denomp)   /*      numerator and denominator of
                                        fraction                          */
{
        int gcd;    /* greatest common divisor of numerator and
                       denominator                                        */
```

(continued)

Figure 6.32 (continued)

```
        gcd = find_gcd(*nump, *denomp);

        *nump /= gcd;
        *denomp /= gcd;
}

/*
 * Displays pair of integers as a fraction.
 */
void
print_fraction(int num, int denom) /* input - numerator and
                                             denominator                */
{
        printf("%d/%d", num, denom);
}

int
main(void)
{
        int  n1, d1;        /* numerator, denominator of first fraction   */
        int  n2, d2;        /* numerator, denominator of second fraction  */
        char op;            /* arithmetic operator + - * or /             */
        char again;         /* y or n depending on user's desire to
                               continue                                   */
        char endline;       /* endline character to ignore                */
        int  n_ans, d_ans;  /* numerator, denominator of answer           */

        /* As long as user wants to continue, takes and solves arithmetic
           problems with common fractions                                 */
        for  (again = 'y';
              again != 'n';
              scanf("%c%c", &endline, &again)) {

           /* Gets a fraction problem                                     */
           scan_fraction(&n1, &d1);
           op = get_operator();
           scan_fraction(&n2, &d2);
```

(continued)

Figure 6.32   (continued)

```
/* Computes the result                                        */
switch (op) {
case '+':
      add_fractions(n1, d1, n2, d2, &n_ans, &d_ans);
      break;

case '-':
      add_fractions(n1, d1, -n2, d2, &n_ans, &d_ans);
      break;

case '*':
      multiply_fractions(n1, d1, n2, d2, &n_ans, &d_ans);
      break;

case '/':
      multiply_fractions(n1, d1, d2, n2, &n_ans, &d_ans);
}
reduce_fraction(&n_ans, &d_ans);

/* Displays problem and result                                */
printf("\n");
print_fraction(n1, d1);
printf(" %c ", op);
print_fraction(n2, d2);
printf(" = ");
print_fraction(n_ans, d_ans);

/* Asks user about doing another problem                      */
printf("\nDo another problem? (y/n)> ");
}

return (0);
}
```

have complete comments and prototypes but merely assign values to their output parameters to allow testing of the partial system. Debugging and testing the system will be explained in Section 6.8.

⬤━━ **TESTING** ━━⬤

We have chosen to leave portions of our fraction system for you to write, but we would still like to test the functions that are complete. We have inserted a stub for each function not yet completed. Each stub displays an identification message and assigns values to its output parameters. We have made the `find_gcd` stub interactive so we can enter a correct greatest common divisor and see if this leads to correct results.

Figure 6.33 shows a run of the program in its present form. Notice that when the operator + is chosen and a correct greatest common divisor is entered interactively, the fraction problem's result is correct. However, when operator * is chosen, although the program continues execution by calling the stubs, the answer displayed is incorrect.

Figure 6.33   Sample Run of a Partially Complete Program Containing Stubs

```
Enter a common fraction as two integers separated by a slash
and press <enter> or <return>
> 3 4
Input invalid--separate numerator and denominator by a slash (/)
Enter a common fraction as two integers separated by a slash
and press <enter> or <return>
> 3/4
Enter an arithmetic operator (+,-,*, or /)
> +
Enter a common fraction as two integers separated by a slash
and press <enter> or <return>
> 5/8
Entering find_gcd with n1 = 44, n2 = 32
gcd of 44 and 32?> 4
find_gcd returning 4

3/4 + 5/8 = 11/8
Do another problem? (y/n)> y
Enter a common fraction as two integers separated by a slash
and press <enter> or <return>
> 1/2
```

(continued)

Figure 6.33   (continued)

```
Enter an arithmetic operator (+,-,*, or /)
> 5
5 invalid, reenter operator (+,-,*,/)
> *
Enter a common fraction as two integers separated by a slash
and press <enter> or <return>
> 5/7
Entering multiply_fractions with
n1 = 1, d1 = 2, n2 = 5, d2 = 7

Entering find_gcd with n1 = 1, n2 = 1
gcd of 1 and 1?> 1
find_gcd returning 1

1/2 * 5/7 = 1/1
Do another problem? (y/n)> n
```

EXERCISES FOR SECTION 6.7

Self-Check

1. Why are pointer types used for the parameters of `reduce_fraction`?
2. Why was it not necessary to include a default case in the `switch` statement that calls `add_fractions` and `multiply_fractions`?

Programming

1. Implement the following algorithm as the `find_gcd` function needed in the common fraction system of Fig. 6.32. Your function will find the greatest common divisor (that is, the product of all common factors) of integers n1 and n2.

   1. Put the absolute value of n1 in q and of n2 in p.
   2. Store the remainder of q divided by p in r.
   3. As long as r is not zero
      4. Copy p into q and r into p.
      5. Store the remainder of q divided by p in r.
   6. p is the gcd.

2. Write the function `multiply_fractions`. If your result has a zero denominator, display an error message and change the denominator to 1.

6.8 DEBUGGING AND TESTING A PROGRAM SYSTEM

As the number of statements in a program system grows, the possibility of error also increases. If we keep each module to a manageable size, the likelihood of error will increase much more slowly. It will also be easier to read and test each module.

In the last case study, we inserted stubs in the program for functions that were not yet written. When a team of programmers is working on a problem, using stubs is a common practice. Obviously, not all modules will be ready at the same time, and the use of stubs enables us to test and debug the main program flow and those modules that are available.

Each stub displays an identification message and assigns values to its output parameters to prevent execution errors caused by undefined values. We show the stub for function `multiply_fractions` again in Fig. 6.34. If a program contains one or more stubs, the message displayed by each stub when it is called provides a trace of the call sequence and allows the programmer to

Figure 6.34   Stub for Function multiply_fractions

```
/*
 ***** STUB *****
 * Multiplies fractions represented by pairs of integers.
 * Product of n1/d1 and n2/d2 is stored in variables pointed
 * to by n_ansp and d_ansp. Result is not reduced.
 */
void
multiply_fractions(int   n1,     int   d1, /* input - first fraction        */
                   int   n2,     int   d2, /* input - second fraction       */
                   int *n_ansp,            /* output -                       */
                   int *d_ansp)            /*    product of two fractions    */
{
    /* Displays trace message                                               */
    printf("\nEntering multiply_fractions with\n");
    printf("n1 = %d, d1 = %d, n2 = %d, d2 = %d\n", n1, d1, n2, d2);

    /* Defines output arguments                                             */
    *n_ansp = 1;
    *d_ansp = 1;
}
```

determine whether the flow of control within the program is correct. The process of testing a program in this way is called *top-down testing*.

When a module is completed, it can be substituted for its stub in the program. However, we often perform a preliminary test of a new module before substitution because it is easier to locate and correct errors when dealing with a single module rather than with a complete program system. We can perform such a *unit test* by writing a short driver program to call the module.

Don't spend a lot of time creating an elegant driver program, because you will discard it as soon as the new module is tested. A driver program should contain only the declarations and executable statements necessary to perform a test of a single module. A driver program should begin by giving values to all input and input/output parameters. Next comes the call to the function being tested. After calling the module, the driver program should display the module results. A driver program for function `scan_fraction` is shown in Fig. 6.35.

Once we are confident that a module works properly, it can then be substituted for its stub in the program system. The process of separately testing individual modules before inserting them in a program system is called *bottom-up testing*. Tests of individual functions are called *unit* tests, and tests of the entire system are *system integration* tests.

By following a combination of top-down and bottom-up testing, a programming team can be fairly confident that the complete program system will be relatively free of errors when it is finally put together. Consequently, the final debugging sessions should proceed quickly and smoothly.

Figure 6.35   Driver for Function scan_fraction

```
/* Driver for scan_fraction */

int
main(void)
{
      int num, denom;
      printf("To quit, enter a fraction with a zero numerator\n");
      for   (scan_fraction(&num, &denom);
             num != 0;
             scan_fraction(&num, &denom))
         printf("Fraction is %d/%d\n", num, denom);

      return (0);
}
```

Debugging Tips for Program Systems

A list of suggestions for debugging a program system follows.

1. Carefully document each module parameter and local variable using comments as you write the code. Also describe the module operation using comments.
2. Create a trace of execution by displaying the module name as you enter it.
3. Display the values of all input and input/output parameters upon entry to a module. Check that these values make sense.
4. Display the values of all module outputs after returning from a module. Verify that these values are correct by hand computation. Make sure that all input/output and output parameters are declared as pointer types.
5. Make sure that a module stub assigns a value to the variable pointed to by each output parameter.

It is a good idea to plan for debugging as you write each module rather than to wait for the whole program to be complete. Unless you plan to use a debugger program, include the output statements mentioned in Debugging Tips 2 through 4 in the original C code for the module. When you are satisfied that the module works as you want it to work, you can remove the debugging statements. One way to remove them is to change them to comments by enclosing them within the symbols /*, */. If you have a problem later, you can remove these symbols and change the comments to executable statements.

6.9 COMMON PROGRAMMING ERRORS

Many opportunities for error arise when you use functions with parameter lists, so be extremely careful. The proper use of parameters is difficult for beginning programmers to master, but it is an essential skill. One obvious pitfall occurs in ensuring that the actual argument list has the same number of items as the formal parameter list. Each actual input argument must be of a type that can be assigned to its corresponding formal parameter. An actual output argument must be of the same pointer data type as the corresponding formal parameter.

If a function produces a single result, the function name should be declared in its prototype to be the type of the result, and the value should be returned using a `return` statement. It is easy to introduce errors in a function that produces multiple results. If the output parameters are not of pointer types or if the calling module neglects to send correct variable addresses, the program results will be incorrect.

The most common problem with a recursive function is that it may not terminate properly. For example, if the terminating condition that checks for a simple case is not correct or is incomplete, the function may call itself indefinitely or until all available memory is used up. Frequently, a run-time error message noting stack overflow or an access violation is an indicator that a recursive function is not terminating. Make sure that you identify all simple cases and provide a terminating condition for each one. Also be sure that each recursive step redefines the problem in terms of arguments that are closer to simple cases so that repeated recursive calls will eventually lead to simple cases only.

In our examples of recursive functions, we have always used a local variable into which the function result is placed by the function's decision structure. Then we have ended the function's code with a `return` statement. Since C permits the use of the `return` statement anywhere in the function code, a function like multiply from Fig. 6.25 could also have been written as follows:

```
int
multiply(int m, int n)
{
      if (n == 1)
            return (m);
      else
            return (m + multiply(m, n - 1));
}
```

You should be aware that it is critical that every path through a `nonvoid` function lead to a `return` statement. In particular, the `return` statement to return the value of the expression containing the recursive call to `multiply` is just as important as the other `return` statement. However, when a multiple-`return` style is adopted, omitting one of these necessary `return` statements is easy to do.

The C scope rules determine where a name is visible and can therefore be referenced. If an identifier is referenced outside its scope, an `undeclared symbol` syntax error will result.

CHAPTER REVIEW

We discussed the use of parameters for passing data to and from functions. The parameter list provides a highly visible communication path between a module and its calling program. By using parameters, we can cause different data to be manipulated by a module each time we call it, making it easier to reuse the module in another program system.

Parameters may be used for input to a function, for output or sending back results, and for both input and output. An input parameter is used only for passing data into a module. The parameter's declared type is the same as the type of the data. Output and input/output parameters must be able to access variables in the calling module's data area so they are declared as pointers to the result data types. The actual argument corresponding to an input parameter may be an expression or a constant; the actual argument corresponding to an output or input/output parameter must be the address of a variable.

We also discussed the scope of identifiers. A parameter or local variable is visible and can be referenced anywhere within the function that declares it. Names of functions and of constant macros are visible from their definitions to the end of the source file except within functions that have local variables of the same names.

Table 6.8 summarizes the definition and calling of the various kinds of functions with parameters that were described in this chapter.

Table 6.8   Summary of Functions in Chapter 6

Function Example	Effect and Sample Call

Function That Returns a Single Result

```
char
sign(double x)
{
     char sign_symbol;

     if (x > 0)
          sign_symbol = '+';
     else if (x == 0)
          sign_symbol = ' ';
     else
          sign_symbol = '-';

     return (sign_symbol);
}
```

Returns a character value indicating the sign of its type `double` input argument.

```
double day;
char day_sign;
     . . .
day_sign = sign(day);
```

Function That Returns No Result

```
void
print_boxed(int num)
{
     printf("********\n");
     printf("*        *\n");
     printf("* %3d  *\n", num);
     printf("*        *\n");
     printf("********\n");
}
```

Displays its type `int` input argument inside a rectangle.

```
int score;
     . . .
print_boxed(score + 3);
```

(continued)

Table 6.8   (continued)

Function Example	Effect and Sample Call

Function That Returns Multiple Results

```
void
make_change(double   change,      /* input  */
            double  token_val,    /* input  */
            int    *num_tokenp,   /* output */
            double *leftp)        /* output */
{
     *num_tokenp = floor(change /
                         token_val);
     *leftp = change - *num_tokenp *
                       token_val;
}
```

Determines how many of a certain bill or coin (`token_val`) should be included in change amount. This number is sent back through the output parameter `num_tokenp`. The amount of change remaining to be made is sent back through the output parameter `leftp`. The following call assigns a 3 to `num_twenties` and 11.50 to `remaining_change`:

```
int    num_twenties;
double remaining_change;
      . . .
make_change(71.50, 20.00,
    &num_twenties,
    &remaining_change);
```

Function with Input/Output Parameters

```
void
correct_fraction(int *nump,     /* input/ */
                 int *denomp)   /* output */
{
     if ((*nump * *denomp) > 0)
          *nump = abs(*nump);
     else
          *nump = -abs(*nump);
     *denomp = abs(*denomp);
}
```

Corrects the form of a common fraction so the denominator is always positive (e.g., $-5/3$ rather than $5/-3$).

```
int num, denom;

num = 5;
denom = -3;
correct_fraction(&num, &denom);
```

QUICK-CHECK EXERCISES

1. The items passed in a function call are the _____ _____. The corresponding _____ _____ appear in the function prototype.
2. Constants and expressions can be actual arguments corresponding to formal parameters that are _____ parameters.

3. Formal parameters that are output parameters must have actual arguments that are _____.

4. If an actual argument of −35.7 is passed to a type `int` formal parameter, what will happen?

5. If an actual argument of 17 is passed to a type `double` formal parameter, what will happen?

6. Which of the following is used to test a function: a driver or a stub?

7. Which of the following is used to test program flow in a partially complete system: a driver or a stub?

8. What are the values of main function variables **x** and **y** at the point marked `/* values here */` in the following program?

```
/* nonsense */
void
silly(int x)
{
        int y;

        y = x + 2;
        x *= 2;
}

int
main(void)
{
        int x, y;

        x = 10; y = 11;
        silly(x);
        silly(y);    /* values here */
        . . .
}
```

9. Let's make some changes in our nonsense program. What are main's x and y at `/* values here */` in this version?

```
/* nonsense */
void
silly(int *x)
{
        int y;
```

```
        y = *x + 2;
        *x *= 2;
}

int
main(void)
{
        int x, y;

        x = 10;    y = 11;
        silly(&x);
        silly(&y);    /* values here */
          . . .
}
```

10. What problem do you notice in the following recursive function? Show two possible ways to correct the problem.

```
int
silly(int n)
{
        if (n <= 0)
                return (1);
        else if (n % 2 == 0)
                return (n);
        else
                silly(n - 3);
}
```

11. What is a common cause of a stack overflow error?
12. What can you say about a recursive algorithm that has the following form?

> *if condition*
> > *Perform recursive step.*

ANSWERS TO QUICK-CHECK EXERCISES

1. actual arguments; formal parameters
2. input
3. addresses of variables/ pointers
4. The formal parameter's value will be −35.

5. The formal parameter's value will be `17.0`.
6. Driver
7. Stub
8. `x is 10, y is 11`
9. `x is 20, y is 22`
10. One path through the function does not encounter a `return` statement. Either place a `return` statement in the final `else`

```
return (silly(n - 3));
```

or assign 1, n, `silly(n-3)` to a local variable, and place that variable in a `return` statement at the end of the function.
11. Too many recursive calls
12. Nothing is done when the simplest case is reached.

REVIEW QUESTIONS

1. Write the prototype for a function called `script` that has three input parameters. The first parameter will be the number of spaces to display at the beginning of a line. The second parameter will be the character to display after the spaces, and the third parameter will be the number of times to display the second parameter on the same line.
2. Write a function called `letter_grade` that has a type `int` parameter called `points` and returns the appropriate letter grade using a straight scale (90 – 100 is an A, 80 – 89 is a B, and so on).
3. Why would you choose to write a function that computes a single numeric or character value as a `nonvoid` function that returns a result through a `return` statement rather than to write a `void` function with an output parameter?
4. Explain the allocation of memory cells when a function is called.
5. Which of the functions in the following program outline *can* call the function `grumpy`? All prototypes and declarations are shown; only executable statements are omitted.

```
int
grumpy(int dopey)
{
      double silly;
      . . .
}
```

```
char
silly(double grumpy)
{
      double happy;
      . . .
}

double
happy(int goofy, char greedy)
{
      char grumpy;
      . . .
}

int
main(void)
{
      double p,q,r;
      . . .
}
```

6. Sketch the data areas of functions `main` and `silly` as they appear immediately before the return from the first call to `silly` in Quick-Check Exercise 9.
7. Present arguments against these statements:
   a. It is foolish to use function subprograms because a program written with functions has many more lines than the same program written without functions.
   b. The use of function subprograms leads to more errors because of mistakes in using argument lists.

PROGRAMMING PROJECTS

1. Two positive integers *i* and *j* are considered to be *relatively prime* if there exists no integer greater than 1 that divides them both. Write a function `relprm` that has two input parameters, *i* and *j*, and returns a value of 1 for true if and only if *i* and *j* are relatively prime. Otherwise, `relprm` should return a value of 0 for false.
2. Given the lengths *a, b, c* of the sides of a triangle, write a function to compute the area *A* of the triangle. The formula for computing *A* is given by

$$A = \sqrt{s(s-a)\ (s-b)\ (s-c)}$$

where s is the semiperimeter of the triangle

$$s = \frac{a + b + c}{2}$$

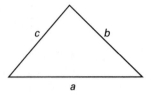

Write a driver program to get values for a, b, and c and call your function to compute A. The driver should display A, a, b, and c.

3. Determine the following information about each value in a list of positive integers.

   a. Is the value a multiple of 7, 11, or 13?

   b. Is the sum of the digits odd or even?

   c. What is the positive square root of the value?

   d. Is the value a prime number?

   You should have at least four function subprograms; label all output. Some sample input data might be `104    3773    13    121    77    30751`.

4. To design a square timber column in a structure, three formulas must be satisfied:

   a. Buckling load:

   $$maximum\ load = (0.30 \times E \times area)\ /\ (length/width)^2$$

   b. Compressive stress:

   $$maximum\ load = area \times maximum\ compressive\ strength$$

   c. Slenderness limits:

   $$length/width \leq 50$$

   where E is the modulus of elasticity (1,700,000 psi), the area is the cross-sectional area in square inches, and

   $$maximum\ compressive\ strength = 445\ psi\ (Douglas\ fir).$$

   Write a program that uses these three formulas to give an initial design to a structural engineer. Assume the columns to be used are square and are available in intervals of 2 inches (i.e., 2 by 2, 4 by 4, and so on). Have the output look like the following:

```
Please enter the expected load in pounds> 9000
Please enter the length of the column in inches> 120
```

```
. . .Testing a beam with width of 2.0 inches -- failed the
      tests
. . .Testing a beam with width of 4.0 inches -- failed the
      tests
. . .Testing a beam with width of 6.0 inches -- OK
For a load of 9000.0 pounds and a length of 120.0 inches,
recommended square beam has sides of 6.0 inches.
```

Write a function for each of the three tests. Each function should return a 1 if the test is passed, a 0 otherwise.

5. The square root of a number N can be approximated by repeated calculation using the formula

$$NG = 0.5(LG + N/LG)$$

where NG stands for next guess and LG stands for last guess. Write a function that calculates the square root of a number using this method.

   The initial guess will be the starting value of LG. The program will compute a value for NG using the formula given. The difference between NG and LG is checked to see whether these two guesses are almost identical. If they are, NG is accepted as the square root; otherwise, the new guess (NG) becomes the last guess (LG) and the process is repeated (another value is computed for NG, the difference is checked, and so on). The loop should be repeated until the difference is less than 0.005. Use an initial guess of 1.0.

   Write a driver function and test your square root function for the numbers 4, 120.5, 88, 36.01, 10000.

6. When an aircraft or an automobile is moving through the atmosphere, it must overcome a force called *drag* that works against the motion of the vehicle. The drag force can be expressed as

$$F = \tfrac{1}{2}CD \times A \times \rho \times V^2$$

where F is the force (in newtons), CD is the drag coefficient, A is the projected area of the vehicle perpendicular to the velocity vector (in m^2), ρ is the density of the gas or fluid through which the body is traveling (kg/m^3), and V is the body's velocity. The drag coefficient CD has a complex derivation and is frequently an empirical quantity. Sometimes the drag coefficient has its own dependencies on velocities: For an automobile, the range is from approximately 0.2 (for a very streamlined vehicle) through about 0.5. For simplicity, assume a streamlined passenger vehicle is moving through air at sea level (where $\rho = 1.23$ kg/m^3). Write a program that allows a user to input A and CD interactively and calls a function to compute the drag force. Your program should display a table showing the drag force for the input shape for a range of velocities from 0 m/s to 40 m/s.

7. Write a function `ln_approx` that computes an approximation of the natural logarithm of a number between 1 and 2 by summing a given number of terms of this series:

$$\ln(1 + x) = \sum_{n=1}^{\infty} \frac{(-1)^{n+1} x^n}{n}$$

Also, write a driver that calls `ln_approx` twice with the same value, requesting first the sum of four terms of the series and then requesting seven terms. The program should display a message comparing the results of the two calls to the value returned by the math library function `log`.

8. Write a function that computes the necessary score on a 100-point final exam to achieve the desired grade in a course. The function inputs are the final exam weight, the student's average in all other course work, and the desired letter grade. Use a grading scale of 90–100 is an A, 80–89 is a B, and so on. For example, if the test weight were 0.25, the student's average were 88.4, and the desired grade were an A, the necessary score would be

$$\text{ceil}\left(\frac{90 - .75(88.4)}{.25}\right) = 95 \text{ points}$$

9. Experiments that are impossible to perform under normal conditions are often simulated on a computer. A particularly computationally intensive type of simulation called the Monte Carlo method is used to simulate individual molecules in situations involving very rarefied gases. For example, experiments on the dispersing gas from a rocket fired in vacuum are very hard to perform on the ground because the pumps used to create the vacuum environment tend to alter the flow out of the rocket nozzles, and the vacuum chamber fills with rocket exhaust quickly.

Assume that you have 10 molecules in a box, with velocity vectors of random direction and magnitude. You are interested in any molecule that has a positive x-direction vector and a velocity magnitude greater than 0.5 in some units. These molecules might, for example, be impinging on a piece of metal that will become hot if a lot of hot molecules collide with it.

Actual Monte Carlo simulations are very sophisticated and require much analysis to set up. For our simple example, generate two random values for each of 10 molecules—a velocity vector direction between −1 and 1 and a velocity magnitude between 0 and 1. Count how many molecules out of ten fit the given criteria, and see how the answer changes for various runs. Your program should allow the user to set the number of 10-molecule experiments to run and should display the results of individual experiments and their average.

Hint: Use library function `rand` (see Table 3.5) in defining your own type `double` pseudorandom number generator functions that will return values in the range −1 to 1 for the direction of the molecules and 0 to 1 for their velocity magnitude.

10. A control system applies a force to an actuator proportional to the voltage of a signal coming into the control system. It is desired not to allow the actuator to quiver back and forth in the presence of small corrections near the zero-force point. More force is required for the actuator to move to the left (negative direction of motion) than is required for motion to the right (positive direction of motion.) Assume that the transfer function (the relationship between the voltage and the movement) of the actuator is

   - Voltage less than −0.2 volt: Actuator moves 1 cm/volt in the negative direction
   - Absolute value of voltage less than or equal to 0.2 volt: No motion
   - Voltage greater than 0.2 volt: Actuator moves 2 cm/volt in the positive direction.

   Write a function to compute the total motion for any single signal input. Write a main function that repeatedly calls the motion calculation function using an input signal stream such as this: −10.0 v, −8.0 v, −0.21 v, −0.20 v, −0.05 v, 1.5 v, 0.00 v, 4.5 v. The main function should also take as user input an initial position of the actuator and should output a final position resulting from applying the signals of the given control stream. For one test, simulate the effect of the given voltages for an initial position of 1.5 cm to find the final position of the actuator.

11. Use the recursive bisection function from Fig. 6.31 and a variant of function $f(\theta)$ from the "Roots of Equations" introduction in a program to approximate the necessary angle of elevation (radians) at which to launch a projectile traveling 250 m/s in order to impact a target 3300 m away at a height of 3 m. The approximation should be within 0.00001 of the actual angle. Use $g = 9.81$ m/s^2 as the gravitational acceleration. Your program should repeatedly prompt the user to enter endpoints of subintervals of the interval $[0, \pi/2]$ radians until an interval is entered that contains an odd number of roots of f. Then call `bisect` with this interval and display the root returned.

CHAPTER 7

ARRAYS

In all previous programs in this text, each variable was associated with memory for a single value; such variables are called *simple variables*. In this chapter, we will study a C *data structure*. A data structure is a grouping of related data items in memory. The items in a data structure can be processed individually, although some operations may be performed on the structure as a whole.

An *array* is a data structure used for storage of a collection of data items that are all the same type (for example, all the exam scores for a class). By using an array, we will be able to associate a single variable name (`scores`) with a group of related data items (exam scores). The individual data items in an array are stored in adjacent cells of main memory (one item per memory cell). Since each item is saved in a separate memory cell, we can process the individual items more than once and in any order we wish.

In earlier programs, we reused the same memory cell to store each exam score. Each time a new item was placed in the cell, its previous value was lost. Consequently, we could no longer access the third score after getting the fourth score. This inability to work with earlier data values after seeing the entire list severely limited the analysis we could do of the data. By using an array to store each data value in a separate memory cell, accessing earlier data will no longer be a problem.

7.1 DECLARING AND REFERENCING ARRAYS

An array is a collection of two or more adjacent memory cells, called *array elements*, that are associated with a particular symbolic name. To set up an array in memory, we must declare both the name of the array and the number of cells associated with it.

The declaration

```
double x[8];
```

instructs the compiler to associate eight memory cells with the name x; these memory cells will be adjacent to each other in memory. Each element of array x may contain a single type `double` value, so a total of eight such numbers may be stored and referenced using the array name x.

To process the data stored in an array, we reference each individual element by specifying the array name and identifying the element desired (for example, element 3 of array x). The *subscripted variable* x[0] (read as x sub zero) may be used to reference the initial or 0th element of the array x, x[1] the next element, and x[7] the last element. The integer enclosed in brackets is the *array subscript*, and its value must be in the range from zero to one less than the number of memory cells in the array.

Figure 7.1 The Eight Elements of Array x

```
double x[8];
```

Array x

x[0]	x[1]	x[2]	x[3]	x[4]	x[5]	x[6]	x[7]
16.0	12.0	6.0	8.0	2.5	12.0	14.0	−54.5

EXAMPLE 7.1

Let x be the array shown in Fig. 7.1. Notice that x[1] is the second array element and x[7], not x[8], is the last array element. A sequence of statements that manipulate this array is shown in Table 7.1. The contents of array x after execution of these statements are shown after Table 7.1. Only x[2] and x[3] are changed.

Table 7.1   Statements That Manipulate Array x

Statement	Explanation
`printf("%.1f", x[0]);`	Displays the value of x[0], which is 16.0.
`x[3] = 25.0;`	Stores the value 25.0 in x[3].
`sum = x[0] + x[1];`	Stores the sum of x[0] and x[1], which is 28.0 in the variable sum.
`sum += x[2];`	Adds x[2] to sum. The new sum is 34.0.
`x[3] += 1.0;`	Adds 1.0 to x[3]. The new x[3] is 26.0.
`x[2] = x[0] + x[1];`	Stores the sum of x[0] and x[1] in x[2]. The new x[2] is 28.0.

Array x

x[0]	x[1]	x[2]	x[3]	x[4]	x[5]	x[6]	x[7]
16.0	12.0	28.0	26.0	2.5	12.0	14.0	−54.5

EXAMPLE 7.2

Two arrays are declared as follows:

```
int    id[50];
double gpa[50];
```

The arrays id and gpa each have 50 elements. Each element of array id can be used to store an integer value; each element of array gpa can be used to store a value of type double. If these declarations are used in a problem to assess the range and distribution of grade point averages, the first student's id can be stored in id[0], and the same student's gpa can be stored in gpa[0]. Because the data stored in id[i] and gpa[i] relate to the ith student, the two arrays are called *parallel arrays*. Samples of these arrays are shown next.

id[0]	609465503		gpa[0]	2.71
id[1]	512984556		gpa[1]	3.09
id[2]	323415691		gpa[2]	2.98
	. . .			. . .
id[49]	512009146		gpa[49]	1.92

EXAMPLE 7.3 The statement

```
char answer[10];
```

declares an array answer with ten elements; each element can store a single character. This array could be used to store the ten answers for a true–false quiz (e.g., answer[0] is 'T', answer[1] is 'F'). A sample array is shown next.

answer[0]	T
answer[1]	F
answer[2]	F
	. . .
answer[9]	T

EXAMPLE 7.4 More than one array may be declared in a single type declaration. The statements

```
double cactus[5], needle, pins[6];
int    factor[12], n, index;
```

declare cactus and pins to be arrays with five and six type double elements, respectively. The variable factor is an array with 12 type int elements. In addition, individual memory cells will be allocated for storage of the simple variables needle, n, and index.

Naming the constant that specifies the number of array elements to allocate is advisable. By doing so, one can easily change the size of an array. ⬅

EXAMPLE 7.5 ▶ The statements

```
#define NUM_READINGS 20
. . .
double gauge[NUM_READINGS];
int    time[NUM_READINGS];
```

allocate storage for two arrays of numbers. The array `gauge` can hold 20 type `double` values, and array `time` can hold 20 integers. ⬅

Array Initialization

A simple variable can be initialized when it is declared, as we see in the statement

```
int sum = 0;
```

An array can also be initialized in its declaration. The size of an array that is being fully initialized can optionally be omitted from the declaration, since it can be deduced from the initialization list. For example, in the following statement, a 25-element array is initialized with the prime numbers less than 100:

```
int prime_lt_100[] = {2, 3, 5, 7, 11, 13, 17, 19, 23, 29, 31,
                      37, 41, 43, 47, 53, 59, 61, 67, 71,
                      73, 79, 83, 89, 97};
```

All the points illustrated so far are summarized in the next display.

Array Declaration

SYNTAX: *element-type aname*[*size*];   /* uninitialized */
         element-type aname[*size*] = {*initialization list*};/* initialized */

EXAMPLE: #define A_SIZE 5
         . . .
         double a[A_SIZE];
         char vowels[] = {'A', 'E', 'I', 'O', 'U'};

(continued)

INTERPRETATION: The general uninitialized array declaration just given allocates storage space for array *aname* consisting of *size* memory cells. Each memory cell can store one data item whose data type is specified by *element-type* (i.e., `double`, `int`, or `char`). The individual array elements are referenced by the subscripted variables *aname*[0], *aname*[1], ..., *aname*[*size*-1]. A constant expression of type `int` is used to specify an array's *size*.

In the initialized array declaration shown, the *size* shown in brackets is optional, since the array's size can also be indicated by the length of the *initialization list*. The *initialization list* consists of constant expressions of the appropriate *element-type* separated by commas. Element 0 of the array being initialized is set to the first entry in the *initialization list*, element 1 to the second, and so forth.

EXERCISES FOR SECTION 7.1

Self-Check

1. What is the difference in meaning between `x3` and `x[ 3 ]`?
2. For the declaration

   `char grades[5];`

   how many memory cells are allocated for data storage? What type of data can be stored there? How does one refer to the initial array element? To the final array element?
3. Declare one array for storing the square roots of the integers from 0 through 10 and a second array for storing the cubes of the same integers.

7.2 ARRAY SUBSCRIPTS

A subscript is used to differentiate between the individual array elements and to allow us to specify which array element is to be manipulated. Any expression of type `int` may be used as an array subscript. However, to create a valid reference, the value of this subscript must lie between 0 and one less than the declared size of the array.

Understanding the distinction between an array subscript value and an array element value is essential. The original array `x` from Fig. 7.1 follows. The subscripted variable `x[ i ]` references a particular element of this array. If `i` has the value 0, the subscript value is 0 and `x[ 0 ]` is referenced. The value of `x[ 0 ]` in this case is `16.0`. If `i` has the value 2, the subscript value is 2 and the value of x[i] is 6.0. If i has the value 8, the subscript value is 8, and we cannot predict the value of x[i] because the subscript value is out of the allowable range.

Array x

	x[0]	x[1]	x[2]	x[3]	x[4]	x[5]	x[6]	x[7]
	16.0	12.0	6.0	8.0	2.5	12.0	14.0	-54.5

EXAMPLE 7.6

Table 7.2 lists some sample statements involving the preceding array x. The variable i is assumed to be of type int with value 5. Make sure you understand each statement.

The two attempts to display element x[10], which is not in the array, may result in a run-time error, but they are more likely to print incorrect results. Consider the call to printf that uses (int)x[4] as a subscript expression. Since this expression evaluates to 2, the value of x[2] (*not* x[4]) is printed. If the value of (int)x[4] were outside the range 0 through 7, its use as a subscript expression would not reference a valid array element.

Table 7.2   Code Fragment That Manipulates Array x

Statement	Explanation
`i = 5;`	
`printf("%d  %.1f", 4, x[4]);`	Displays 4 and 2.5 (value of x[4])
`printf("%d  %.1f", i, x[i]);`	Displays 5 and 12.0 (value of x[5])
`printf("%.1f", x[i] + 1);`	Displays 13.0 (value of x[5] plus 1)
`printf("%.1f", x[i] + i);`	Displays 17.0 (value of x[5] plus 5)
`printf("%.1f", x[i + 1]);`	Displays 14.0 (value of x[6])
`printf("%.1f", x[i + i]);`	Invalid. Attempt to display x[10].
`printf("%.1f", x[2 * i]);`	Invalid. Attempt to display x[10].
`printf("%.1f", x[2 * i - 3]);`	Displays -54.5 (value of x[7])
`printf("%.1f", x[(int)x[4]]);`	Displays 6.0 (value of x[2])
`printf("%.1f", x[i++]);`	Displays 12.0 (value of x[5]); then assigns 6 to i
`printf("%.1f", x[--i]);`	Assigns 5 (6 - 1) to i and then displays 12.0 (value of x[5])
`x[i - 1] = x[i];`	Assigns 12.0 (value of x[5]) to x[4]
`x[i] = x[i + 1];`	Assigns 14.0 (value of x[6]) to x[5]
`x[i] - 1 = x[i];`	Illegal assignment statement

Array Subscripts

SYNTAX: *aname*[*subscript*]

EXAMPLE: b[i + 1]

INTERPRETATION: The *subscript* may be any expression of type int. Each time a subscripted variable is encountered in a program, the subscript is evaluated and its value determines which element of array *aname* is referenced.

NOTE: It is the programmer's responsibility to verify that the *subscript* is within the declared range. If the subscript is in error, an invalid reference will be made. Although occasionally a run-time error message will be printed, more often an invalid reference will cause a side effect whose origin is difficult for the programmer to pinpoint. The side effect can also lead to incorrect program results.

Using Indexed for Loops for Array Subscripting

Very often, we wish to process the elements of an array in sequence, starting with element zero. An example would be scanning data into the array or printing its contents. In C, we can accomplish this processing easily using an *indexed* for loop, a counting loop whose loop control variable runs from zero to one less than the array size. Using the loop counter as an array *index* (subscript) gives access to each array element in turn.

EXAMPLE 7.7

The following array square will be used to store the squares of the integers 0 through 10 (e.g., square[0] is 0, square[10] is 100). We assume that the name SIZE has been defined to be 11.

```
int square[SIZE], i;
```

The for loop

```
for  (i = 0;  i < SIZE;  ++i)
    square[i] = i * i;
```

initializes this array, as shown here:

Array square

[0]	[1]	[2]	[3]	[4]	[5]	[6]	[7]	[8]	[9]	[10]
0	1	4	9	16	25	36	49	64	81	100

Statistical Computations Using Arrays

One common use of arrays is for storage of a collection of related data values. Once the values are stored, some simple statistical computations may be performed. In Fig. 7.2, the array **x** is used for this purpose.

Figure 7.2 Program to Display a Table of Differences

```
/*
 * Computes the mean and standard deviation of an array of data and displays
 * the difference between each value and the mean.
 */

#include <stdio.h>
#include <math.h>

#define MAX_ITEM  8  /* maximum number of items in list of data        */

int
main(void)
{
      double x[MAX_ITEM], /* data list                                  */
             mean,        /* mean (average) of the data                 */
             st_dev,      /* standard deviation of the data             */
             sum,         /* sum of the data                            */
             sum_sqr;     /* sum of the squares of the data             */
      int    i;

      /* Gets the data                                                  */
      printf("Enter %d numbers separated by blanks or <return>s\n> ",
             MAX_ITEM);
      for  (i = 0;  i < MAX_ITEM;  ++i)
          scanf("%lf", &x[i]);

      /* Computes the sum and the sum of the squares of all data        */
      sum = 0;
      sum_sqr = 0;
      for  (i = 0;  i < MAX_ITEM;  ++i) {
          sum += x[i];
          sum_sqr += x[i] * x[i];
      }
```

(continued)

Figure 7.2 (continued)

```
      /* Computes and displays the mean and standard deviation          */
      mean = sum / MAX_ITEM;
      st_dev = sqrt(sum_sqr / MAX_ITEM - mean * mean);
      printf("The mean is %.2f.\n", mean);
      printf("The standard deviation is %.2f.\n", st_dev);

      /* Displays the difference between each item and the mean          */
      printf("\nTable of differences between data values and mean\n");
      printf("Index          Item        Difference\n");
      for  (i = 0;  i < MAX_ITEM;  ++i)
          printf("%3d      %9.2f      %9.2f\n", i, x[i], x[i] - mean);
      return (0);
}
```

```
Enter 8 numbers separated by blanks or <return>s
> 16   12   6   8   2.5   12   14   -54.5
The mean is 2.00.
The standard deviation is 21.75.

Table of differences between data values and mean
Index        Item        Difference
  0         16.00          14.00
  1         12.00          10.00
  2          6.00           4.00
  3          8.00           6.00
  4          2.50           0.50
  5         12.00          10.00
  6         14.00          12.00
  7        -54.50         -56.50
```

The program in Fig. 7.2 uses three for loops to process the array x. The constant macro MAX_ITEM determines the size of the array. The variable i is used as the loop control variable and array subscript in each loop.

The first for loop,

```
for  (i = 0;  i < MAX_ITEM;  ++i)
    scanf("%lf", &x[i]);
```

stores one input value into each element of array x (the first item is placed in x[0], the next in x[1], and so on). The call to scanf is repeated for each value of i from 0 to 7; each repetition gets a new data value and stores it in x[i]. The subscript i determines which array element receives the next data value.

The second for loop is used to accumulate (in sum) the sum of all values stored in the array. The loop also accumulates (in sum_sqr) the sum of the squares of all element values. The formulas implemented by this loop are

$$sum = x[0] + x[1] + \cdots + x[6] + x[7] = \sum_{i=0}^{MAX\_ITEM - 1} x[i]$$

$$sum\_sqr = x[0]^2 + x[1]^2 + \cdots + x[6]^2 + x[7]^2 = \sum_{i=0}^{MAX\_ITEM - 1} x[i]^2$$

This loop will be discussed in detail later.

The last for loop,

```
for (i = 0;  i < MAX_ITEM;  ++i)
    printf("%3d      %9.2f     %9.2f\n", i, x[i],
           x[i] - mean);
```

displays a table. Each line of the table displays an array subscript, an array element, and the difference between that element and the mean, x[i] − mean. Notice that the placeholders in the format string of the call to printf cause each column of values in the output table to be lined up under its respective column heading.

Now that we have seen the entire program, we will take a closer look at the computation for loop:

```
/* Computes the sum and the sum of the squares of all data */
sum = 0;
sum_sqr = 0;
for (i = 0;  i < MAX_ITEM;  ++i) {
    sum += x[i];
    sum_sqr += x[i] * x[i];
}
```

This loop accumulates the sum of all eight elements of array x in the variable sum. Each time the loop body is repeated, the next element of array x is added to sum. Then this array element value is squared, and its square is added to the sum being accumulated in sum_sqr. The execution of this program fragment is traced in Table 7.3 for the first three repetitions of the loop.

The *standard deviation* of a set of data is a measure of the spread of the data values around the mean. A small standard deviation indicates that the data

Table 7.3   Partial Trace of Computing for Loop

Statement	i	x[i]	sum	sum_sqr	Effect
sum = 0;			0.0		Initializes sum
sum_sqr = 0;				0.0	Initializes sum_sqr
for (i = 0;	0	16.0			Initializes i to 0,
i < MAX_ITEM;					which is less than 8
...					
sum += x[i];			16.0		Adds x[0] to sum
sum_sqr +=					
x[i] * x[i];				256.0	Adds 256.0 to sum_sqr
increment and test i	1	12.0			1 < 8 is true
sum += x[i];			28.0		Adds x[1] to sum
sum_sqr +=					
x[i] * x[i];				400.0	Adds 144.0 to sum_sqr
increment and test i	2	6.0			2 < 8 is true
sum += x[i];			34.0		Adds x[2] to sum
sum_sqr +=					
x[i] * x[i];				436.0	Adds 36.0 to sum_sqr

values are all relatively close to the average value. For MAX_ITEM data items, if we assume that x is an array whose lowest subscript is 0, the standard deviation is given by the formula

$$\text{standard deviation} = \sqrt{\frac{\displaystyle\sum_{i=0}^{MAX\_ITEM-1} x[i]^2}{MAX\_ITEM} - mean^2}$$

In Fig. 7.2, this formula is implemented by the statement

```
st_dev = sqrt(sum_sqr / MAX_ITEM - mean * mean);
```

Program Style   *Using Loop Control Variables as Array Subscripts*

In Fig. 7.2, the variable i, which is the counter of each indexed for loop, determines which array element is manipulated during each loop repetition. The use of the loop control variable as an array subscript is common, because it allows the programmer to specify easily the sequence in which the elements of an array are to be manipulated. Each time the value of the loop control variable is increased, the next array element is automatically selected. Note that the same loop control variable is used in all three loops. This reuse is not necessary but is permitted, since the loop control variable is always initialized at loop entry. Thus i is reset to 0 when each loop is entered.

**EXERCISES FOR
SECTION 7.2**

Self-Check

1. Show the contents of array x after executing the valid statements in Table 7.2.

2. For the new array derived in Exercise 1, describe what happens when the valid statements in Table 7.2 are executed for i = 3.

Programming

1. Write indexed for loops to fill the arrays described in Exercise 3 at the end of Section 7.1. Each array element should be assigned the value specified for it.

7.3 USING INDIVIDUAL ARRAY ELEMENTS AS INPUT ARGUMENTS

We have seen that we can use individual elements of numeric arrays in expressions for computation just as we would use simple numeric variables. We can also use array elements as actual arguments in function calls. However, array elements *cannot* be used as formal parameters in function prototypes. An array element used as an actual input argument should correspond to a formal parameter that is a simple variable of the same type as the array element. For example, the program in Fig. 7.3 assigns to array rounded_x the result of calling function round on each element of x. The definition of function round is taken from Fig. 6.7.

**Figure 7.3   Program to Compute Differences from Mean
with Original and Rounded Data**

```
/*
 * Rounds each element of data list leaving FRAC_PLACES digits to the
 * right of the decimal point. Investigates the effect of the rounding on
 * a table of differences from the mean.
 */
#include <stdio.h>
#include <math.h>
```

(continued)

Figure 7.3   (continued)

```
#define X_SIZE      8
#define FRAC_PLACES 2

/*
 * Rounds the value of x to designated number of decimal places
 * Assumes places is greater than or equal to zero.
 */
double
round(double x, int places)
{
      int    sign;       /* -1 if x negative, 1 otherwise              */
      double power,      /* 10 raised to the places power              */
             temp_x,     /* copy of |x| with decimal point moved places */
                         places to the right.                         */
             x_rounded;  /* function result                           */

      /* Saves sign of x  */
      if (x < 0)
            sign = -1;
      else
            sign = 1;

      /* Computes rounded value */
      if (places >= 0) {
           power = pow(10.0, places);
           temp_x = fabs(x) * power;
           x_rounded = floor(temp_x + 0.5) / power * sign;
      } else {
           printf("\nError:  second argument to round cannot be negative.\n");
           printf("No rounding done.\n");
           x_rounded = x;
      }
      return (x_rounded);
}

int
main(void)
{
      double x[X_SIZE],        /* data list                          */
             x_rounded[X_SIZE], /* rounded data list                 */
```

(continued)

Figure 7.3   (continued)

```
        sum, rd_sum,       /* sums of two lists      */
        mean, rd_mean;     /* means of the two lists */
   int    i;

   /* Gets data                                           */
   printf("Enter %d values> ", X_SIZE);
   for (i = 0;  i < X_SIZE;  ++i)
      scanf("%lf", &x[i]);

   /* Rounds the data and computes means                  */
   sum = 0;
   rd_sum = 0;
   for (i = 0;  i < X_SIZE;  ++i) {
      x_rounded[i] = round(x[i], FRAC_PLACES);
      sum += x[i];
      rd_sum += x_rounded[i];
   }
   mean = sum / X_SIZE;
   rd_mean = round(rd_sum / X_SIZE, FRAC_PLACES);

   /* Displays table of differences from the means        */
   printf
     ("\n Original    Difference       Rounded    Difference from\n");
   printf("    data        from mean        data      rounded mean\n");
   for (i = 0;  i < X_SIZE;  ++i)
      printf("%10.4f      %9.4f    %11.2f      %10.2f\n", x[i],
              x[i] - mean, x_rounded[i], x_rounded[i] - rd_mean);
   /* Compares means                                       */
   printf("\nmean of original data:        %.4f\n", mean);
   printf("rounded mean of rounded data: %.2f\n", rd_mean);
   printf("Original is %.4f ", fabs(mean - rd_mean));
   if (mean > rd_mean)
        printf("greater than rounded mean\n");
   else
        printf("less than rounded mean\n");

   return (0);
}
```

(continued)

Figure 7.3 (continued)

```
Enter 8 values> 1.111 2.222 3.333 4.444 5.555 6.666 7.777 8.888

  Original      Difference      Rounded      Difference from
    data        from mean        data        rounded mean
   1.1110        -3.8885          1.11           -3.89
   2.2220        -2.7775          2.22           -2.78
   3.3330        -1.6665          3.33           -1.67
   4.4440        -0.5555          4.44           -0.56
   5.5550         0.5555          5.56            0.56
   6.6660         1.6665          6.67            1.67
   7.7770         2.7775          7.78            2.78
   8.8880         3.8885          8.89            3.89

mean of original data:          4.9995
rounded mean of rounded data:   5.00
Original is 0.0005 less than rounded mean
```

The call to function round in Fig. 7.3

```
x_rounded[i] = round(x[i], FRAC_PLACES);
```

uses the array element x[i] as an actual input argument. This call is valid because each element of array x is of type double and the first formal parameter of function round is also of type double. The for loop in which we find this call to round,

```
for (i = 0;  i < X_SIZE;  ++i) {
    x_rounded[i] = round(x[i], FRAC_PLACES);
    sum += x[i];
    rd_sum += x_rounded[i];
}
```

causes the call to be executed once for each element of array x, since the loop control variable i takes on the values 0, 1, . . . , 6, 7, and this same variable is used as the subscript on x. The variable i is also the subscript used on array x_rounded, so on each iteration of the for loop, a rounded data value is stored in a different element of x_rounded.

Notice that the definition of the function `round` is exactly as it was in Fig. 6.7. No modification is necessary for `round` to process type `double` values taken one at a time from an array. It simply does not matter to function `round` whether the value of its first formal parameter comes from an actual argument that is a simple type `double` variable, from an argument that is a type `double` array element, or from an argument that is any other numeric expression.

EXERCISES FOR SECTION 7.3

Self-Check

1. Write a statement that assigns to `seg_len` the length of a line segment from $x_i y_i$ to $x_{i+1} y_{i+1}$ using the formula

$$\sqrt{(x_{i+1} - x_i)^2 + (y_{i+1} - y_i)^2}$$

Assume that x_i represents the ith element of array `x`, that y_i represents the ith element of array `y`, and that the minimum i is 0.

2. Write a `for` loop that sums the even values from the `LIST_SIZE`-element array `list`. For example, the sum for this list would be `104` (`30 + 12 + 62`).

Array list

list[0]	list[1]	list[2]	list[3]	list[4]	list[5]
30	12	51	17	45	62

Call function `even` from Fig. 6.9.

3. Write a `for` loop that sums the even-numbered elements (elements 0, 2, and 4) from array `list`. For the list shown in Exercise 2, the sum would be `126` (`30 + 51 + 45`).

Programming

1. Write a program to store an input list of ten integers in an array; then display a table similar to the following showing each data value and what percentage each value is of the total of all ten values:

```
n       % of total

8          4.00
12         6.00
18         9.00
25        12.50
```

```
n      % of total
.........................
24       12.00
30       15.00
28       14.00
22       11.00
23       11.50
10        5.00
```

7.4 USING INDIVIDUAL ARRAY ELEMENTS AS OUTPUT ARGUMENTS

An individual array element can be used in all the ways a simple variable of the same type can be used, including as an actual output argument. We saw an example of this usage in the program of Fig. 7.2. The very first `for` loop of the program calls the `scanf` function with the address of each element of array `x` in succession:

```
for (i = 0;  i < MAX_ITEM;  ++i)
    scanf("%lf", &x[i]);
```

Using array elements as output arguments in calls to user-defined functions is equally valid.

In Example 7.8 we discuss a function that converts a 24-hour-clock time to a different time zone and records any necessary day change.

 **EXAMPLE 7.8**

When spacecraft are launched on their missions, tracking stations around the globe must know when to send commands to each spacecraft. For spacecraft far from the earth, three stations—in Madrid, Spain, in Canberra, Australia (see Fig. 7.4), and at a site called Goldstone in the California Mojave Desert—share the tracking duty. Each tracking site operates 24 hours a day, seven days a week, and sends commands to many spacecraft in the course of a day. The mission controllers who plan the spacecraft activities, however, do not want to keep track of three different time zones. Therefore everything the tracking stations need to do is spelled out in "Universal Time (Coordinated)," or UTC, which happens to be local time in Greenwich, England. The tracking stations then must figure out at what local time to send a command based on this Universal Time. For example, a tracking station whose local time is 8 hours behind Universal Time would convert UTC Day 40, Time 248 (2:48 A.M. on February 9—Day 40 = 31 days of January + 9 of February) to local Day 39, Time 1848 (6:48 P.M. on February 8).

The program outlined in Fig. 7.5 is intended to convert a list of spacecraft contact times from Universal Time to local time. The figure includes the pro-

Figure 7.4   Tracking Station in Canberra, Australia (Courtesy of the Jet Propulsion Laboratory, California Institute of Technology.)

totype of a function that converts an integer time on a 24-hour clock to a time in a different time zone. The function takes the old time and the time change as input parameters and computes the new time as an output parameter, also modifying if necessary the day number that is an input/output parameter. Adding 1 to the day value indicates a change to the following day; subtracting 1 indicates a change to the previous day. We show only the program outline. You will be asked to complete the program in the exercises at the end of this section.

Figure 7.5   Outline of Program to Convert List of Times to New Time Zone

```
/*
 * Converts a list of universal times to a list of local times,
 * adjusting corresponding day numbers.
 */

#define T_SIZE 20

/*
 * Converts a 24-hour-clock time in one time zone to an equivalent time
 * in another zone where the time differs from the first zone by time_diff
 * hours.  The effect of the time change on the day is recorded in day_num:
 * no change => same day, 1 added => next day, 1 subtracted => previous day.
 */
void
time_change(int  time,       /* input - 24-hour-clock time            */
            int  time_diff, /* input - time difference in hours      */
            int *new_timep, /* output - converted time               */
            int *day_nump)  /* input/output - day number             */
{
      /* conversion code */
}

int
main(void)
{
      int utc[T_SIZE],     /* list of Universal times               */
          time_diff,       /* time difference in hours              */
          local[T_SIZE],   /* list of local times                   */
          day[T_SIZE],     /* list of corresponding day numbers     */
          i;

      /*  Code to fill utc, day, and time_diff with input data     */
      . . .

      /*  Conversion of Universal times to local times             */
      for  (i = 0;   i < T_SIZE;   ++i)
          time_change(utc[i], time_diff, &local[i], &day[i]);

      /*  Further processing                                       */
      . . .
}
```

In the `for` loop that converts the list of times, the argument list in the function call

```
time_change(utc[i], time_diff, &local[i], &day[i]);
```

supplies the value of an element of array `utc` and the value of variable `time_diff` as input arguments along with the addresses of corresponding elements of `local` (an output argument) and `day` (an input/output argument). Table 7.4 traces the first few calls to `time_change`, assuming these contents of `utc` and day.

Array utc

	utc[0]	utc[1]	utc[2]	utc[3]	utc[4]	
	605	720	915	1041	1255	· · ·

Array day

	day[0]	day[1]	day[2]	day[3]	day[4]	
	62	62	62	62	62	· · ·

Table 7.4 **Partial Trace of for Loop Calling time_change with Time Difference of -8**

Statement	i	utc[i]	local[i]	day[i]	Effect
`for (i=0; i<T_SIZE;...` `time_change`	0	605	?	62	0 < 20 is true.
`(utc[i], time_diff,` `&local[i], &day[i]);`			2205	61	605 is converted to 2205 the previous day, storing 2205 in the ith element of `local` and decrementing the ith element of day.

`Increment and test i`
`(... i<T_SIZE; ++i) {`
   `time_change`
	1	720	?	62	

`(utc[i], time_diff,` `&local[i], &day[i]);`			2320	61	720 is converted to 2320 the previous day, storing 2320 in the ith element of local and decrementing the ith element of day.

(continued)

Table 7.4 (continued)

Statement	i	utc[i]	local[i]	day[i]	Effect
Increment and test i (... i<T_SIZE; ++i) { time_change (utc[i], time_diff, &local[i], &day[i]);	2	915	? 115	62 62	915 is converted to 115 the same day, storing 115 in the ith element of local.
... See Fig. 7.6.					

The time 605 on day 62 represents 6:05 A.M. on March 3 in a nonleap
year (31 days in January + 28 in February + 3 in March). Figure 7.6 shows the
data areas of functions main and time_change as they appear just before the
return from the third call to time_change. Clearly, the conversion code needed to complete function time_change must contain assignment statements
beginning

```
*new_timep = . . .
*day_nump = . . .
```

These statements use indirection to follow the pointers in new_timep and
day_nump to send the function results back to the calling module. ◀

Self-Check

1. Complete function time_change from Fig. 7.5.

Programming

1. Complete the program in Fig. 7.5 so that it displays a table listing the universal times and the converted times, both with day numbers.

**Figure 7.6
Data Areas
of Functions
main and
time_change Just
Before Return
from Third Call**

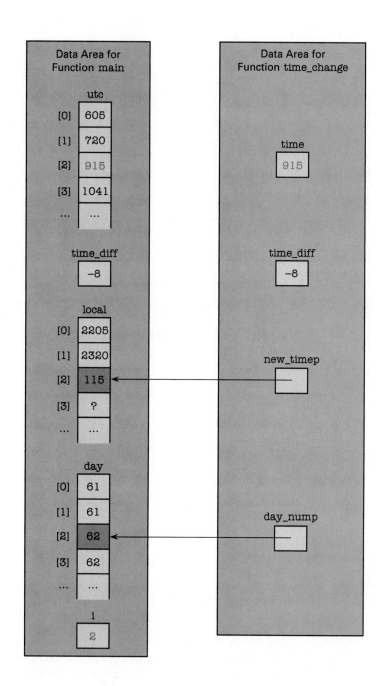

7.5 USING ARRAYS AS INPUT ARGUMENTS

Until now, all input arguments to a function that we have seen have been single values that were copied into formal parameters inside the function's data area. The function then worked with its own copy of each argument value. C provides no analogous automatic copying of whole arrays used as input arguments. Rather, when an array name with no subscript appears in the argument list of a function call, what is actually stored in the function's corresponding formal parameter is the address of the initial array element. Subscripting operations can then be applied to the formal parameter to access all of the array's elements. However, the function is manipulating the original array, not its own personal copy, so an assignment to one of the array elements by a statement in the function changes the contents of the original array. ANSI C does provide a qualifier that we can include in the declaration of the array formal parameter in order to notify the C compiler that the array is only an input to the function and that the function does not intend to modify the array. This qualifier allows the compiler to mark any attempt to change an array element within the function.

EXAMPLE 7.9  Function `get_max` in Fig. 7.7 can be called to find the largest value in an array. It uses the variable `list` as an array input parameter.

Figure 7.7   Function to Find the Largest Element in an Array

```
/*
 *  Returns the largest of the first n values in array list
 *  Assumes first n elements of array list are defined and n > 0
 */
int
get_max(const int list[], /* input - list of n integers                */
        int        n)      /* input - number of list elements to examine */
{
      int i,
          cur_large;       /* largest value so far                      */

      /*  Initial array element is largest so far.                      */
      cur_large = list[0];

      /*  Compare each remaining list element to the largest so far;
          save the larger                                               */
```

(continued)

Figure 7.7 (continued)

```
    for  (i = 1;  i < n;  ++i)
        if (list[i] > cur_large)
            cur_large = list[i];

    return (cur_large);
}
```

Let's focus on the declaration of the formal parameter `list` within the prototype of function `get_max`:

```
const int list[]
```

The type qualifier `const` alerts both the reader of the code and the compiler that `list` is an input argument only. Note that we have not stated in the argument declaration how many elements are in `list`. Because we are not allocating space in memory for copying the array, the compiler does not need to know the size of the array parameter. In fact, since we do not provide the size, we have the flexibility to pass to the function an array of any number of integers.

If `x` is a five-element array of type `int` values, the statement

```
x_large = get_max(x, 5);
```

causes function `get_max` to search array `x` for its largest element; this value is returned and stored in `x_large`. Figure 7.8 shows the argument correspondence for this call. Notice that what is stored in `list` is actually the address of the type `int` variable `x[0]`. Because `&` is the address-of operator, this call to `get_max` would execute exactly like the call pictured in Fig. 7.8:

```
x_large = get_max(&x[0], 5);
```

However, this call using `&x[0]` leads the reader of the code to expect that `get_max` may be using `x[0]` as an output argument. For readability, you should use the name of an array (with no subscript) when you call a function that processes the list the array represents.

In Section 7.4, when we passed individual array elements as output arguments as in

```
time_change(utc[i], time_diff, &local[i], &day[i]);
```

**Figure 7.8
Argument
Correspondence
for** x_large =
get_max(x, 5);

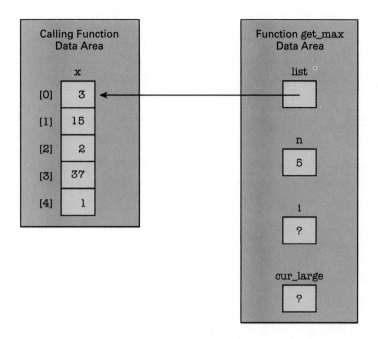

from Fig. 7.5, the formal parameters corresponding to actual arguments
&local[i] and &day[i] were declared to be of type int *. Yet in the
alternative form of the call to get_max, get_max(&x[0], 5), the address
of an array element is matched with a formal parameter declared as

```
const int list[]
```

Because we have already discussed the reason that the const qualifier is used,
let's just consider these possible parameter declarations:

```
int  list[]
int *list
```

The first tells us that the actual argument is an array. However, because C
passes an array argument by passing the address of its initial element, the second
declaration would be equally valid for an integer array parameter. In this text,
we will usually use the first form to declare a parameter representing an array,
saving the second form to represent simple output parameters. You should take
care, however, to remember that a formal parameter of the form

$type_1$ *param

is compatible with an actual argument that is an array of $type_1$ values.

EXAMPLE 7.10  In Fig. 7.9, we have rewritten the program from Fig. 7.2 that displays a table of differences between array elements and the average of the array values. We have omitted the standard deviation computation and defined a function to find the average of the array elements.

Figure 7.9   Program with Function to Average an Array of Numbers

```c
/*
 * Computes the average (mean) of a list of data and displays the
 * difference between each value and the average.
 */

#include <stdio.h>

/*
 * Computes the average of the first n elements of a list of numbers (n > 0)
 */
double
average(const double list[], /* input - list of numbers                    */
        int            n)     /* input - number of list elements to process */
{
      int    i;
      double sum = 0;

      for  (i = 0;  i < n;  ++i)
           sum += list[i];

      return (sum / n);
}

#define MAX_ITEM 8

int
main(void)
{
      int    i;
      double x[MAX_ITEM], mean;

      /*  Gets the data                                                     */
      printf("Enter %d numbers> ", MAX_ITEM);
      for  (i = 0;  i < MAX_ITEM;  ++i)
           scanf("%lf", &x[i]);
```

(continued)

Figure 7.9 (continued)

```
/*  Computes and displays the mean                              */
mean = average(x, MAX_ITEM);
printf("The mean is %.2f\n", mean);

/*  Displays the difference between each item and the mean      */
printf("\nTable of differences between data values and mean\n");
printf("Index      Item      Difference\n");
for  (i = 0;  i < MAX_ITEM;  ++i)
     printf("%3d     %9.2f      %9.2f\n", i, x[i], x[i] - mean);

return (0);
}
```

In the main function of Fig. 7.9, the statement

```
mean = average(x, MAX_ITEM);
```

calls function `average` to compute the mean of all `MAX_ITEM` elements of array `x`. The result returned is stored in `mean`. The fact that function `average` uses the value passed as its second argument to determine how many array elements to include in its computation means that we could use the same function to average just the first four array elements by executing the statement

```
mean = average(x, 4);
```

Later in this chapter, we will see that sometimes an array is only partially filled by a program, so a function's flexibility regarding the number of array elements it processes is very useful.

An Array Input Parameter

SYNTAX: const *element-type array-name*[ ]
          or
     const *element-type* *array-name*

EXAMPLE: double
        find_min(const double data[], /* input – array of numbers */
                int   data_size) /* input – number of
                                          elements   */

(continued)

```
{
    int    i;
    double small;  /* smallest value so far          */

    small = data[0];
    for (i = 1;   i < data_size;   ++i)
        if (data[i] < small)
            small = data[i];

    return (small);
}
```

INTERPRETATION: The syntax shown is valid within the parameter list of a function prototype. In this context, the reserved word `const` indicates that the variable declared is strictly an input parameter and will not be modified by the function. This fact is important because the value of the declared formal parameter will be the address of the actual argument array; if `const` were omitted, modification of the argument would be possible. The data type of an array element is indicated by *element-type*. The [ ] after *array_name* means that the corresponding actual argument will be an array. What is actually stored in the formal parameter when the function is called is the address of the initial element of the actual argument array. Since this value is a pointer to a location used to store a value of type *element-type*, the second syntax option is equivalent to the first.

Searching an Array

A common problem encountered in programming is the need to search an array in order to find the location of a desired value. For example, to find information about one piece of used milling machinery that we are considering purchasing, we might wish to search an array of serial numbers of machines that have failed before to see whether our particular machine is on the list. We call the serial number we are searching for the *target*. This search can be accomplished by examining in turn each array element using a loop and by testing whether the element matches the target. The search loop should be exited when the target value is found; this process is called a *linear search*. An algorithm for a linear search follows.

Algorithm

1. Assume the target has not been found.
2. Start with the initial array element.

3. Repeat while the target is not found and there are more array elements
    4. if the current element matches the target
        5. Set a flag to indicate that the target has been found.
    else
        6. Advance to the next array element.
7. if the target was found
    8. Return the target index as the search result.
  else
    9. Return −1 as the search result.

A function that implements this algorithm is shown in Fig. 7.10. This function returns the index of the target if it is present in the array; otherwise, it returns −1. The local variable i (initial value 0) selects the array element that is compared to the target value.

Figure 7.10   **Function That Searches for a Target Value in an Array**

```
#define NOT_FOUND -1    /* Value returned by search function
                           if target not found */

/*
 * Searches for target item in first n elements of array arr (n >= 0)
 * Returns index of target or NOT_FOUND
 */
int
search(const int arr[],  /* array to search                          */
       int        target, /* value searched for                       */
       int        n)      /* number of array elements to search       */
{
      int i,
          found = 0,      /* whether or not target has been found     */
          where;          /* index where target found or NOT_FOUND    */

      /* Compares each element to target                              */
      i = 0;
      while (!found && i < n) {
          if (arr[i] == target)
                found = 1;
          else
                ++i;
      }
```

(continued)

Figure 7.10 (continued)

```
/* Returns index of element matching target or NOT_FOUND          */
if (found)
      where = i;
else
      where = NOT_FOUND;

return (where);
}
```

The type int variable found is used to represent the logical concept of whether the target has been found yet and is tested in the loop repetition condition. The variable is initially set to 0 for false (the target is certainly not found before we begin searching for it) and is reset to 1 for true only if the target is found. After found becomes true or the entire array has been searched, the loop is exited and the decision statement following the loop defines the value returned. If array serial_nums is declared in the calling function, the assignment statement

```
index = search(serial_nums, 4902, NUM_MACH);
```

calls function search to search the first NUM_MACH elements of array serial_nums for the target 4902. The subscript of the first occurrence of 4902 is saved in index. If 4902 is not found, then index is set to −1.

EXERCISES FOR SECTION 7.5

Self-Check

1. What value is returned by function search if array elements 1, 3, and 5 all contain the target? Modify search so that it returns the number of times target is found in the array, instead of returning *where* target is first found.

Programming

1. Define a function multiply that computes and returns the product of the type int elements of its array input argument. The function should have a second input argument telling the number of array elements to use.

2. Define a function `abs_table` that takes an input array argument with type `double` values and displays a table of the data and their absolute values like the table shown here:

```
    x       |x|
   38.4     38.4
 -101.7    101.7
   -2.1      2.1
    .  .  .
```

7.6 USING ARRAYS AS OUTPUT OR INPUT/OUTPUT ARGUMENTS

In C, it is not legal for a function's return type to be an array; therefore, defining a function of the variety modeled in Fig. 7.11 requires use of an output argument to send the result array back to the calling module.

**Figure 7.11
Diagram of a
Function That
Computes an
Array Result**

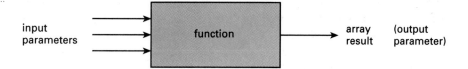

input parameters → function → array result (output parameter)

In Section 6.3, we saw that when we use simple output parameters, the calling function must declare variables into which the function subprogram will store its results. Similarly, a function computing an array result depends on its caller to provide an array variable into which the result can be stored.

EXAMPLE 7.11

As an example of the use of a function to manipulate several parallel arrays, consider the problem faced by someone designing a detection system to monitor a pipeline for leaks. Usually, it is a good idea to use several kinds of detectors that take very different measurements. Sounding an alarm only when all or nearly all of the detectors register problems in the same spot will eliminate most of the false alarms caused by one detector's reaction to some sort of interference.

As a first step in monitoring a pipe carrying a flow of mixed liquid and gas, we will place *N* equally spaced temperature sensors along the pipe and *N* corresponding microphones for detecting excessive turbulence. Our program will use an array `temp` to store temperature alarm flags and an array `turb` to store turbulence indicators. A value of zero in `temp[i]` means that the temperature

Figure 7.12   Function to Add Two Arrays

```
/*
 *  Adds corresponding elements of arrays ar1 and ar2, storing the result
 *  in arsum. Processes first n elements only (n >= 0)
 */
void
add_arrays(const int ar1[],    /* input -                                  */
           const int ar2[],    /*     arrays being added                   */
           int       arsum[],  /* output - sum of corresponding
                                           elements of ar1 and ar2          */
           int       n)        /* input - number of element pairs summed   */
{
      int i;

      /* Adds corresponding elements of ar1 and ar2                         */
      for  (i = 0;  i < n;  ++i)
          arsum[i] = ar1[i] + ar2[i];
}
```

registered by sensor i is in the normal range. A value of one indicates an abnormal temperature. Similarly, turb[i] is zero when microphone i records normal conditions, and is one under abnormal conditions. We use the function in Fig. 7.12 to add corresponding elements of the two sensor arrays, storing the results in a third array, alarm. The presence of the value 2 in alarm[i] implies that both sensors at position i are recording abnormal conditions, a situation calling for an alarm.

Function add_arrays is designed to add corresponding elements of any two type int arrays that have at least n elements. If our pipeline-monitoring program is using 5 of each type of sensor, and if the temp and turb arrays have already been filled with sensor data, the call

```
add_arrays(temp, turb, alarm, 5);
```

would lead to the memory setup pictured in Fig. 7.13.

After execution of the function, alarm[0] will contain the sum of temp[0] and turb[0], or 1; alarm[1] will contain the sum of temp[1] and turb[1], or 1; and so on. Input argument arrays temp and turb will be unchanged; output argument alarm will have these new contents:

alarm after call to add_arrays

1	1	0	2	0

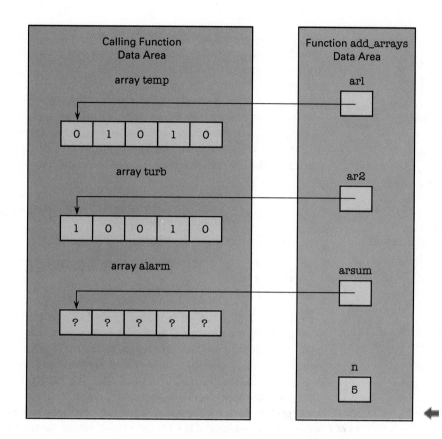

Figure 7.13
Function Data
Areas for
`add_arrays`
`(temp, turb,`
`alarm, 5);`

Address-of Operator Not Used

Note carefully that in the *call* to `add_arrays` there is no notational difference between the references to input argument arrays `temp` and `turb` and the reference to output argument array `alarm`. Specifically, the `&` (address-of) operator is *not* applied to the name of the output array argument. We discussed earlier the fact that C always passes whole arrays used as arguments by storing the *address* of the initial array element in the corresponding formal parameter. Since the output parameter `arsum` is declared with no `const` qualifier, function `add_arrays` automatically has access and authority to change the corresponding actual array argument.

Partially Filled Arrays

Frequently, a program will need to process many lists of similar data; these lists may not all be the same length. To reuse an array for processing more than one data set, the programmer often declares an array large enough to hold the largest data set anticipated. This array can be used for processing shorter lists as well, provided that the program keeps track of how many array elements are actually in use.

EXAMPLE 7.12

The purpose of function `fill_to_sentinel` is to fill a type `double` array with data until the designated sentinel value is encountered in the input data. Figure 7.14 shows both the input parameters that `fill_to_sentinel` requires and the results that are communicated through its output parameters.

**Figure 7.14
Diagram of
Function
fill_to_sentinel**

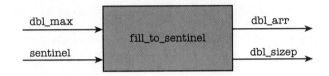

When we use an array that may be only partially filled (such as `dbl_arr` in Fig. 7.14), we must deal with *two* array sizes. One size is the array's declared size, represented by the input parameter `dbl_max`, shown in Fig. 7.14. The other is the size counting only the elements in use, represented in Fig. 7.14 by the output parameter `dbl_sizep`. The declared size is only of interest at the point in a program where the array is being filled, for it is important not to try to store values beyond the array's bounds. However, once this input step is complete, the array size relevant in the rest of the processing is the number of elements actually filled. Figure 7.15 shows an implementation of function `fill_to_sentinel`.

Figure 7.15   Function Using a Sentinel-Controlled Loop to Store Input Data in an Array

```
/*
 *  Gets data to place in dbl_arr until value of sentinel is encountered
 *  in the input. Returns number of values stored through dbl_sizep.
 *  Stops input prematurely if there are more than dbl_max data values
 *  before the sentinel or if an invalid data item is encountered.
 */
void
fill_to_sentinel(int      dbl_max,  /* input - declared size of dbl_arr  */
                 double   sentinel, /* input - end of data value in input
                                                list                     */
                 double   dbl_arr[],/* output - array of data            */
```

(continued)

Figure 7.15   (continued)

```
                   int     *dbl_sizep)/* output - number of data values
                                          stored in dbl_arr           */
{
    double data;
    int    i, status;

    /* Sentinel input loop                                            */
    i = 0;
    for  (status = scanf("%lf", &data);
          status == 1  &&  data != sentinel  &&  i < dbl_max;
          status = scanf("%lf", &data)) {
       dbl_arr[i] = data;
       ++i;
    }

    /* Issues error message on premature exit                         */
    if (status != 1) {
         printf("\n*** Error in data format ***\n");
         printf("*** Using first %d data values ***\n", i);
    } else if (data != sentinel) {
         printf("\n*** Error: too much data before sentinel ***\n");
         printf("*** Using first %d data values ***\n", i);
    }

    /* Sends back size of used portion of array                       */
    *dbl_sizep = i;
}
```

Figure 7.16 shows a main function that calls `fill_to_sentinel`. The main function is using batch mode; it issues no prompting message, but it does echo print its input data. Notice that after the call to `fill_to_sentinel`, the expression used as the upper bound on the subscripting variable in the loop that echo prints the data is not the array's declared size, `A_SIZE`. Rather, it is the variable `in_use` that designates how many elements of `arr` are currently filled.

In the call to `fill_to_sentinel` in Fig. 7.16, we see another example of the difference between the way an array output argument is passed to a function and the way a simple output argument is passed. Both `arr` and `in_use` are

Figure 7.16 **Driver for Testing fill_to_sentinel**

```
/* Driver to test fill_to_sentinel function */

#define A_SIZE  20
#define SENT    -1.0

int
main(void)
{
      double arr[A_SIZE];
      int    in_use,     /* number of elements of arr in use */
             i;

      fill_to_sentinel(A_SIZE, SENT, arr, &in_use);

      printf("List of data values\n");
      for  (i = 0;  i < in_use;  ++i)
          printf("%13.3f\n", arr[i]);

      return (0);
}
```

output arguments, but the address-of operator & is applied only to the simple variable in_use. Since arr is an array name with no subscript, it already represents an address, the address of the initial array element.

Sorting an Array

Many situations call for presenting a list of data in order. For example, if we collect temperature and atmospheric pressure measurements at various altitudes during a flight, we may want to display the data in ascending order by altitude—that is, in order beginning with the lowest altitude and ending with the highest altitude.

In this section, we present a fairly simple (but not very efficient) algorithm for sorting the elements of an array—the *bubble sort*. A bubble sort compares adjacent array elements and exchanges their values if they are out of order. In this way, the smaller values "bubble" to the top of the array (toward element 0), while the larger values sink to the bottom of the array. The data requirements and one algorithm for a bubble sort function follow.

Problem Inputs
the array being sorted
the number of array elements

Problem Output
the sorted array

An Algorithm for a Bubble Sort

1. Repeat
    2. Examine every pair of adjacent array elements and exchange
       values that are out of order
   as long as the array is not sorted.

As an example, we will trace through one execution of Step 2; that is, we will do one *pass* through an array being sorted. By scanning the diagrams in Fig. 7.17 from left to right, we see the effect of each comparison. The pair of array elements being compared is shown in a darker color in each diagram. The first pair of values (m[0] is 60, m[1] is 42) is out of order, so the values are exchanged. The next pair of values (m[1] is now 60, m[2] is 75) is compared in the second array; this pair is in order, as is the next pair (m[2] is 75, m[3] is 83). The last pair (m[3] is 83, m[4] is 27) is out of order, so the values are exchanged, as shown in the last diagram of Fig. 7.17.

**Figure 7.17
One Pass of a
Bubble Sort of
Array m**

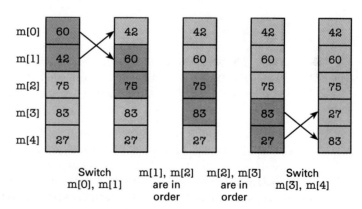

The last array shown in Fig. 7.17 is closer to being sorted than the original is. The only value that is out of order is the number 27 in m[3]. Unfortunately, the algorithm will need to complete three more passes through the entire array before this value bubbles to the top of the array. In each of these passes, only one pair of values will be out of order, so only one exchange will be made. The contents of array m after the completion of each pass are shown in Fig. 7.18.

We can tell by looking at the contents of the array at the end of pass 4 that the array is now sorted. However, the algorithm we have chosen calls for the

**Figure 7.18
Array m after
Completion of
Each Pass**

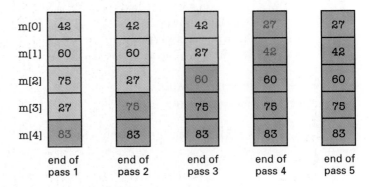

computer to recognize that the sorting is completed by making one additional pass in which no exchanges are necessary. If no exchanges are made, then all pairs must be in order. This is the reason for the extra pass shown in Fig. 7.18 and for the flag named `sorted` that is described here.

Program Variables
```
int sorted   /* flag to indicate whether any exchanges
                have been made in the current pass      */
int i        /* loop control variable and subscript     */
int pass     /* number of current pass starting with 1 */
```

Step 2 Refinement
2.1 Initialize `sorted` to 1 (for true).
2.2 Repeat for each pair of adjacent array elements
    2.3 if the values in a pair are out of order
        2.4 Exchange the values.
        2.5 Set `sorted` to 0 (false).

Step 2 will be implemented using a `for` loop. The loop control variable `i` will also be the subscript of the first element in each pair; consequently, `i + 1` will be the subscript of the second element in each pair. During each pass, the initial value of `i` is 0. The final value of `i` must be less than the highest valid array subscript so that `i + 1` will also be in range.

For an array of n elements, the number of pairs of elements compared in a particular pass is n − `pass`, where `pass` is the number of the current pass, starting with 1 for the first pass. The reason that the number of pairs to compare decreases with each pass is that we do not need to examine array elements that are already in place. At the end of pass 1, the last array element must be in its correct place and at the end of pass 2, the last two array elements must be in their correct places, and so on. The section of the array that is already certain to be sorted is shown in a darker color in Fig. 7.18.

Function `bubble` in Fig. 7.19 performs a bubble sort on the array represented by formal parameter `list`, which is an input/output parameter. You notice that its declaration is of the same form as the output parameter arrays discussed earlier in this section.

Figure 7.19   Bubble Sort Function for an Array of Integers

```
/*
 *  Sorts the data in the first n elements of array list (n >= 0)
 */
void
bubble(int list[], /* input/output - array being sorted          */
       int n)      /* input - number of elements to sort         */
{
     int i,
         pass,     /* number of current pass through array       */
         temp,     /* temporary variable used in exchange of
                       out-of-order pairs                         */
         sorted;   /* whether or not array is definitely sorted   */

     pass = 1;
     do {
         /*  Assumes array is sorted until an out-of-order pair
             is found                                             */
         sorted = 1;

         /*  Makes a pass through possibly unsorted elements      */
         for (i = 0;  i < n - pass;  ++i) {
             if (list[i] > list[i + 1]) {
                 /* Exchanges out-of-order pair  */
                 temp = list[i];
                 list[i] = list[i + 1];
                 list[i + 1] = temp;
                 sorted = 0;
             }
         }
         ++pass;
     } while(!sorted);
}
```

Our implementation uses the `do-while` statement for the outer loop because we can be sure the loop body must be executed at least once. There is no way to know that the array is sorted without making at least one pass through the data.

Self-Check

1. Modify function `fill_to_sentinel` from Fig. 7.15 so its return type is `int` rather than `void`. Have the function return the value 1 if no error conditions occur and 0 if there is an error. In all other respects, leave the function's purpose unchanged.
2. Can you think of a way to combine the following two statements that form the body of the `for` loop of function `fill_to_sentinel` into just one statement?

```
dbl_arr[i] = data;
++i;
```

3. Modify the prototype and declarations of function `bubble` so it would sort an array of type `double` values. Be careful—some variables should still be of type `int`!
4. Assume that a main function contains declarations for three type `int` arrays—c, d, and e, each with six elements. Also assume that values have been stored in all array elements. Explain the effect of each valid call to `add_arrays` (see Fig. 7.12). Explain why each invalid call is invalid.
   a. `add_arrays(ar1, ar2, c, 6);`
   b. `add_arrays(c[6], d[6], e[6], 6);`
   c. `add_arrays(c, d, e, 6);`
   d. `add_arrays(c, d, e, 7);`
   e. `add_arrays(c, d, e, 5);`
   f. `add_arrays(c, d, 6, 3);`
   g. `add_arrays(e, d, c, 6);`
   h. `add_arrays(c, c, c, 6);`
   i. `add_arrays(c, d, e, c[1]);` (if c[1] is 4? if c[1] is 9?)
   j. `add_arrays(&c[2], &d[2], &e[2], 4);`

Programming

1. Write a function that negates the type `double` values stored in an array. The first argument should be the array (an input/output parameter) and the second should be the number of elements to negate.
2. Write a function that takes two type `int` array input arguments and their effective size and produces a result array containing the absolute differences between corresponding elements. For example, for the three-element input arrays 5 -1 7 and 2 4 -2, the result would be an array containing 3 5 9.

7.7 USING CHARACTER ARRAYS AS STRINGS

So far, we have seen limited use of character data because most applications that process character data deal with a grouping of characters, a data structure called a *string*. Because C implements the string data structure using arrays of type `char`, we could not explore strings until we had a foundational understanding of arrays.

Strings are important in programming because many computer applications are concerned with the manipulation of textual data rather than numerical data. Strings play an important role in many scientific areas. The chemist works with elements and compounds whose names often combine alphabetic and numeric characters (e.g., $C_{12}H_{22}O_{11}$)—data easily represented by a string. Genetic engineers identify amino acids by name and map DNA with strings of amino acid abbreviations. Many mathematicians, physicists, and engineers spend more time modeling our world with equations (strings of character and numeric data) than they do crunching numbers.

String Basics

We have already used string constants extensively in our earlier work. Indeed, every one of our calls to `scanf` or `printf` used a string constant as the first argument. Consider this call:

```
printf("Average = %.2f", avg);
```

The first argument is the string constant `"Average = %.2f"`, a string of 14 characters. Notice that the blanks in the string are characters just as valid as those requiring ink! Like other constant values, a string constant can be associated with a symbolic name using the `#define` directive:

```
#define ERR_PREFIX   "*****Error - "
#define INSUFF_DATA  "Insufficient Data"
```

Declaring and Initializing String Variables

As we mentioned earlier, a string in C is implemented as an array, so declaring a string variable is the same as declaring an array of type `char`. In

```
char string_var[30];
```

the variable `string_var` will hold strings from 0 to 29 characters long. It is C's handling of this varying length characteristic that distinguishes the string data structure from other arrays. C permits initialization of string variables using either a brace-enclosed character list as shown in Section 7.1 or a string constant as shown in the following declaration of `str`:

```
char str[20] = "Initial value";
```

Let's look at `str` in memory after this declaration with initialization:

[0]				[4]					[9]					[14]					[19]
I	n	i	t	i	a	l		v	a	l	u	e	\0	?	?	?	?	?	?

Notice that `str[13]` contains the character `'\0'`, the *null* character that marks the end of a string. Using this marker allows the string's length within the character array to vary from 0 to one less than the array's declared size. All of C's string-handling functions simply ignore whatever is stored in the cells following the null character. The following diagram shows `str` holding a string that is the longest it can represent—19 characters plus the null character:

[0]				[4]					[9]					[14]					[19]
n	u	m	b	e	r	s		a	n	d		s	t	r	i	n	g	s	\0

Arrays of Strings

Because one string is an array of characters, an array of strings is a two-dimensional array of characters in which each row is one string. The following are statements to declare an array to store up to 30 names, each of which is less than 25 characters long:

```
#define NUM_NAMES 30
#define NAME_LEN  25
     . . .
char names[NUM_NAMES][NAME_LEN];
```

We can initialize an array of strings at declaration in the following manner:

```
char month[12][10] = {"January", "February", "March", "April",
                "May", "June", "July", "August",
                "September", "October", "November",
                "December"};
```

Input/Output with printf and scanf

Both `printf` and `scanf` can handle string arguments as long as the place-holder `%s` is used in the format string:

```
printf("Topic: %s\n", string_var);
```

The `printf` function, like other standard library functions that take string arguments, depends on finding a null character in the character array to mark the end of the string. If `printf` were passed a character array that contained no `'\0'`, the function would first interpret the contents of each array element as a character and display it. Then `printf` would continue to display as characters the contents of memory locations following the array argument until it encountered a null character or until it attempted to access a memory cell that was not assigned to the program, causing a run-time error. When we write our own string-building functions, we must be sure that a null character is inserted at the end of every string. This inclusion of the null character is automatic for constant strings.

The `%s` placeholder in a `printf` format string can be used with a minimum field width as shown here:

```
printf("***%8s***%3s***\n", "Short", "Strings");
```

The first string is displayed right-justified in a field of eight columns. The second string is longer than the specified field width, so the field is expanded to accommodate it exactly with no padding. We are more accustomed to seeing lists of strings displayed left-justified rather than right-justified. Consider the two lists in Fig. 7.20.

Placing a minus sign prefix on a placeholder's field width causes left justification of the value displayed. If `president` is a string variable, repeated execution of this call to `printf` will produce a left-justified list:

```
printf("%-20s\n", president);
```

Figure 7.20   Right and Left Justification of Strings

Right-Justified	Left-Justified
George Washington	George Washington
John Adams	John Adams
Thomas Jefferson	Thomas Jefferson
James Madison	James Madison

The scanf function can be used for input of a string. However, when we call scanf with a string variable as an argument, we must remember that array output arguments are *always* passed to functions by sending the address of the initial array element. Therefore we do not apply the address-of operator to a string argument passed to scanf or to any other function. In Fig. 7.21, we see a brief main function performing string I/O with scanf and printf. In this program, the user is expected to type in a string representing an academic department, an integer course code, a string abbreviation for the days of the week the course meets, and an integer that gives the meeting time of the class.

The approach scanf takes to string input is very similar to its processing of numeric input. As shown in Fig. 7.22, when it scans a string, scanf skips leading whitespace characters such as blanks, newlines, and tabs. Starting with the first nonwhitespace character, scanf copies the characters it encounters

Figure 7.21   String Input/Output with scanf and printf

```
#include <stdio.h>

#define STRING_LEN  10

int
main(void)
{
      char dept[STRING_LEN];
      int  course_num;
      char days[STRING_LEN];
      int  time;

      printf("Enter department code, course number, days and ");
      printf("time like this:\n> COSC 2060 MWF 1410\n> ");
      scanf("%s%d%s%d", dept, &course_num, days, &time);
      printf("%s %d meets %s at %d\n", dept, course_num, days, time);

      return (0);
}

Enter department code, course number, days and time like this:
> COSC 2060 MWF 1410
> MATH 1270 TR 800
MATH 1270 meets TR at 800
```

**Figure 7.22
Execution of**
`scanf`
    `("%s", dept);`

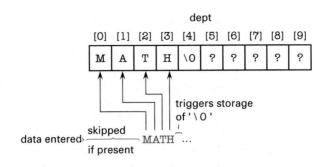

*note: gets (arrayname);
will read blanks in a
string of characters*

into successive memory cells of its character array argument. When it comes across a whitespace character, scanning stops, and `scanf` places the null character at the end of the string in its array argument.

Because of the way `scanf` treats whitespace, the values could be spaced on the data lines in many ways that would result in variables `dept`, `course_num`, `days`, and `time` receiving correct values upon execution of the `scanf` call in Fig. 7.21. For example, the data could have been entered one value per line with extra whitespace:

```
>        MATH
 1270
     TR
                  1800
```

or two values per line:

```
> MATH 1270
  TR 1800
```

Function `scanf` would have difficulty if some essential whitespace between values were omitted or if a nonwhitespace separator were substituted. For example, if the data were entered as

```
> MATH1270 TR 1800
```

`scanf` would store the 8-character string `"MATH1270"` in `dept` and would then be unable to convert `T` to an integer for storage using the next parameter. The situation would be worse if the data were entered as

```
> MATH,1270,TR,1800
```

Figure 7.23 **Execution of** `scanf("%s%d%s%d", dept, &course_num,` `days, &time);` **on Entry of Invalid Data**

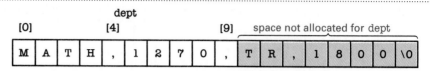

Then the `scanf` function would store the entire 17-character string plus `'\0'` in the `dept` array, causing characters to be stored in eight locations not allocated to `dept` as shown in Fig. 7.23. To help prevent this problem, an interactive program that requires user entry of strings must give very explicit instructions to the user. The string manipulation necessary to consistently prevent overflow of string variables regardless of the data entered is beyond the scope of this text.

EXAMPLE 7.13 Earlier in this chapter, we declared an array of strings suitable for holding 30 names (a two-dimensional array of type `char` values). Let's see how to use `scanf` and `printf` to fill this array and echo print it.

You will recall from our study of arrays that no address-of operator is needed when an array is passed as an output argument. Because each element `names[i]` of an array of strings represents a kind of array, it is passed as an output argument without using the `&` operator. The following code segment fills parallel arrays `names` and `ages` with data. In the call to `scanf`, note the contrasting application of the `&` operator to elements of the `ages` array, since these elements are simple output arguments of type `int`.

```
#define NUM_NAMES 30
#define NAME_LEN  25
    . . .
char names[NUM_NAMES][NAME_LEN];

for  (i = 0;  i < NUM_NAMES;  ++i) {
    scanf("%s%d", names[i], &ages[i]);
    printf("%-35s %d\n", names[i], ages[i]);
}
```

EXAMPLE 7.14 The program in Fig. 7.24 plots the values of the function $t^2 - 4t + 5$ for values of t between 0 and 10 by storing an asterisk in the element of the string `plot` corresponding to the function value, while all other elements are blank. The character array `plot` is first initialized to all blanks. This could be done with an

Figure 7.24 Plot of Function $t^2 - 4t + 5$

```
/*                               2
 *   Plots the function  f(t) = t  -   4t  +  5  for t between 0 and 10
 */

#include <stdio.h>

#define MAX_VAL 65   /*  maximum function value */

/*
 *            2
 *   f(t) = t  -   4t  +  5
 */
int
f (int t)
{
     return (t * t - 4 * t + 5);
}

int
main(void)
{
     char plot[MAX_VAL + 2];   /* one line of plot */
     int i, t, funval;

     /* Displays heading lines                                        */
     for  (i = 0;   i <= MAX_VAL;   i += 5)
          printf("%5d", i);
     printf("\n");

     for  (i = 0;   i <= MAX_VAL;   i += 5)
          printf("    |");
     printf("\n");

     /* Initializes plot to all blanks                                */
     for  (i = 0;   i <= MAX_VAL + 1;   ++i)
          plot[i] = ' ';

     /* Computes and plots f(t) for each value of t from 0 through 10  */
     for  (t = 0;   t <= 10;   ++t) {
          funval = f(t);
```

(continued)

Figure 7.24   (continued)

```
            plot[funval] = '*';
            plot[funval + 1] = '\0';
            printf("t=%2d%s\n", t, plot);
            plot[funval] = ' ';
            plot[funval + 1] = ' ';
        }

        return (0);
}
```

```
          0    5   10   15   20   25   30   35   40   45   50   55   60   65
          |    |    |    |    |    |    |    |    |    |    |    |    |    |
t= 0           *
t= 1      *
t= 2    *
t= 3      *
t= 4          *
t= 5              *
t= 6                  *
t= 7                       *
t= 8                            *
t= 9                                     *
t=10                                                    *
```

initialization in the declaration of plot. However, it is certainly easier for the computer to count 66 blanks accurately than for the programmer to do so. Within the computing for loop, the assignment statement

```
funval = f(t);
```

calls the function f and saves the value returned in funval. The first of the two assignment statements

```
plot[funval] = '*';
plot[funval + 1] = '\0';
```

places an asterisk in the string element that corresponds to the function value; the second statement ends the string immediately after this value. The call to printf

```
printf("t=%2d%s\n", t, plot);
```

displays a line that begins with the value of t followed by the string plot. The string contains a single asterisk; the position of the asterisk depends on the value of funval. After each line is displayed, the assignment statements

```
plot[funval] = ' ';
plot[funval + 1] = ' ';
```

reset the nonblank elements to blanks.

Three calls to printf in Fig. 7.24 are executed repeatedly. The first of these calls displays the heading line consisting of the integers 0, 5, 10, and so on, spaced five columns apart. The second call displays a line consisting of 14 occurrences of the symbol '|' spaced five columns apart directly beneath the first line. As mentioned, the last repeated call to printf displays the current value of t and the corresponding function value (denoted by the symbol *). The first output line shows that f[0] is 5.

String Assignment and String Length

We have become accustomed to using the assignment operator = to copy data into a variable. Although we do use the assignment symbol in a declaration of a string variable with initialization, this context is the *only* one in which the operator means to copy the string that is the right operand into the variable that is the left operand. We have seen that an array name with no subscript represents the address of the initial array element. This address is constant and cannot be changed through assignment, so the following code fragment will cause a compiler error message such as Invalid target of assignment:

```
char one_str[20];
one_str = "Test string";   /* Does not work */
```

In fact, C defines no string assignment operator. C handles this deficiency just as it handles the lack of square root and absolute value operators—by providing a library function. The C string library, accessed by use of the directive

```
#include <string.h>
```

includes a string assignment function, strcpy, that copies the value of its second argument (a string) into the character array provided as its first argument. Thus the string assignment attempted above would be correctly written as

```
strcpy(one_str, "Test string");
```

Like function `scanf` with the `%s` format specification, function `strcpy` assumes there is enough room in its character array output argument to store a full copy of the second argument. We saw in Fig. 7.23 the consequences when this assumption by `scanf` was false. Function `strcpy` is equally able to overflow its string output argument, so the programmer must take care to provide a large enough character array for a successful copy.

The C string library provides a function that checks the length of a string. Function `strlen` takes a single string argument and returns the number of characters in it, not counting the null character at the end. For example, if the value of string variable `machine` were `"industrial robot"`, the function call

```
strlen(machine)
```

would return the value `16`. Notice that the blank is counted in the string length.

String Comparison

In earlier chapters, we studied the fact that characters are represented by numeric codes, and we used equality operators to compare characters. Relational operators can also be used in comparisons of characters. For example, if `ch1` and `ch2` are both variables containing uppercase characters, we can use the comparison

```
ch1 < ch2
```

to see whether `ch1` precedes `ch2` alphabetically. This comparison is valid because all of the character sets use a numeric code for `'A'` that is less than the code for `'B'`, and a code for `'B'` that is less than the code for `'C'`, and so on. Unfortunately, the relational operators cannot be used for comparison of strings because of C's representation of strings as arrays.

Because an array name used with no subscript represents the address of the initial array element, if `str1` and `str2` are string variables, the condition

```
str1 < str2
```

is *not* checking whether `str1` precedes `str2` alphabetically. However, the comparison *is* legal, for it determines whether the place in memory where storage of `str1` begins precedes the place in memory where `str2` begins.

The standard string library provides the `int` function `strcmp` for comparison of two strings that we will refer to as `str1` and `str2`. Function `strcmp` separates its argument pairs into three categories as shown in Table 7.5.

Table 7.5   Possible Results of strcmp(str1, str2)

Relationship	Value Returned	Example
str1 is less than str2	negative integer	str1 is "marigold" str2 is "tulip"
str1 equals str2	zero	str1 and str2 are both "end"
str1 is greater than str2	positive integer	str1 is "shrimp" str2 is "crab"

In this table, we are using the expression "less than" as a string generalization of the "less than" comparison of characters. We have seen that for character variables ch1 and ch2, ch1 < ch2 is true if the numeric character code value of ch1 is less than the code in ch2. ANSI C extends this concept to strings by stating the following two conditions to define "less than":

1. If the first n characters of str1 and str2 match and str1[n], str2[n] are the first nonmatching corresponding characters, str1 is less than str2 if str1[n] < str2[n]:

```
str1    t h r i l l      str1    e n e r g y
str2    t h r o w         str2    f o r c e
                *                 *
First 3 letters match.    First 0 letters match.
str1[3] < str2[3]         str1[0] < str2[0]
    'i' < 'o'                 'e' < 'f'
```

2. If str1 is shorter than str2 and all the characters of str1 match the corresponding characters of str2, str1 is less than str2:

```
str1    j o y
str2    j o y o u s
```

EXAMPLE 7.15    When we process a list of string data interactively, we often do not know in advance how much data will be entered. In this situation, we can use a sentinel-controlled loop, prompting the user to type in the sentinel value when entry of the data is complete. Figure 7.25 outlines such a loop, using strcmp to check for entry of the sentinel.

Figure 7.25   Sentinel-Controlled Loop for String Input

```
printf("Enter list of words on as many lines as you like.\n");
printf("Separate words by at least one blank.\n");
printf("When done, enter %s to quit.\n", SENT);

for  (scanf("%s", word);
        strcmp(word, SENT) != 0;
        scanf("%s", word)) {
     /* process word */
}
```

EXERCISES FOR SECTION 7.7

Self-Check

1. When the `scanf` function is scanning a string, if there is more input data (with no blanks) than will fit in the array output argument, `scanf` _____ (choose one).

   a. copies in only the characters that will fit and ignores the rest.
   b. copies in the whole string overflowing the output argument, because `scanf` has no way of knowing the array's declared size.
   c. scans all the characters but stores only the ones that fit, discarding the rest.

2. When `printf` is given a string argument to display using a `%s` placeholder, how does it know how many characters to display?

3. Declare a 30-character array, and initialize it at declaration to a string of 29 blanks.

4. Write C code to accomplish each of the following goals.

   a. Write a message indicating whether `name1` and `name2` match.
   b. Store in the string variable `word` either the value of `w1` or of `w2`. Choose the value that comes first alphabetically.
   c. Store in `mtch` matching initial portions of `s1` and `s2`. For example, if `s1` is `"placozoa"` and `s2` is `"placement"`, `mtch` becomes `"plac"`. If `s1` is `"joy"` and `s2` is `"sorrow"`, `mtch` becomes the empty string.

Programming

1. Write a program that takes a word less than 25 characters long and displays a statement like this:

   `fractal starts with the letter f`

   Have the program process words until it encounters the sentinel `"999"`.

7.8 ARRAY PROCESSING ILLUSTRATED

Genetic engineers are on the forefront of our society's efforts to combat disease, to increase food production, and to fight pollution. Using gene-splicing, genetic engineers are producing new vaccines, creating disease-resistant strains of crops, and growing bacteria that can break down oil spills. Our next case study demonstrates how character arrays can be used to represent pieces of the genetic code.

Case Study: Finding Palindromes in Nucleotide Sequences

◄ PROBLEM ►

A genetic engineer is developing a program to identify palindromes of a certain length in strings representing the nucleotide sequences of a portion of a DNA molecule. Palindromic regions are of great interest to researchers studying the transmission of the genetic information encoded in DNA.

◄ ANALYSIS ►

Although we recall that a palindrome is a string that reads the same forward and backward, such as "Madam, I'm Adam" or "Able was I ere I saw Elba," we must first see how closely this definition applies to the palindromes of DNA molecules.

DNA is a double-stranded molecule composed of pairs of the nucleotides Adenine, Thymine, Cytosine, and Guanine. Adenine always pairs with Thymine, and Cytosine pairs with Guanine. Figure 7.26 shows a portion of a DNA molecule in which the complementary strands are ATCGCAT . . . and TAGCGTA. . . .

**Figure 7.26
Model of a
Portion of a
DNA Molecule**

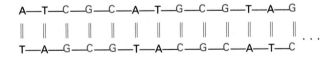

The molecule portion shown contains a palindromic sequence of eight nucleotide pairs, the sequence inside the added color rectangle of Fig. 7.27. This region is palindromic because the sequence of nucleotides along the top strand, CGCATGCG, is exactly the reverse of the sequence along the bottom strand, GCGTACGC.

. . . .

Figure 7.27
Palindromic
Region of
Length 8 in a
DNA Molecule

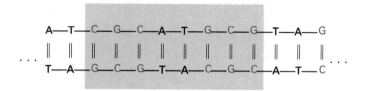

Given strings representing the complementary strands and a length value, we must identify all palindromic sequences of the specified length.

Data Requirements

Problem Constant
```
STRANDSIZ  100   /*  maximum space for a strand    */
```

Problem Inputs
```
char    strand1[STRANDSIZ], /* complementary strands */
        strand2[STRANDSIZ]  /* of DNA                */
int     palin_len           /* length of palindromic
                               sequences of interest */
```

Problem Outputs
index and value of each palindromic sequence of length `palin_len`

DESIGN

Algorithm

1. Get input data: complementary strands and palindrome length.
2. For each starting subscript of a substring of the desired length
   2.1 if the substring from `strand1` matches the reverse of the corresponding substring of `strand2`
      2.1.1 Print the position where palindrome found and the two substrings.

IMPLEMENTATION

The implementation in Fig. 7.28 uses nested `for` loops to carry out the substring comparisons. The outer loop generates the starting subscript of each candidate piece of the strands. The inner loop carries out the comparison of characters of `STRAND1` to characters of the reverse of `STRAND2`.

Figure 7.28   Program to Find Specified-Length Palindromic Sequences of Nucleotide Pairs

```
/*
 *   Finds specified-length palindromic sequences of nucleotide pairs in a
 *   portion of a DNA molecule whose complementary strands are represented
 *   as strings
 */

#include <stdio.h>
#include <string.h>

#define STRANDSIZ  100   /*  maximum space for storing a strand            */

int
main(void)
{
      char strand1[STRANDSIZ],    /* complementary strands               */
           strand2[STRANDSIZ];    /*     of DNA                          */
      int  palin_len;             /* length of palindromic sequences of
                                              interest                   */
      int  i, j, match;

      /* Gets input data and displays reference lines                    */
      printf("Enter one strand of DNA molecule segment\n> ");
      scanf("%s", strand1);
      printf("\nEnter complementary strand\n> ");
      scanf("%s", strand2);
      printf("\nEnter length of palindromic sequence\n> ");
      scanf("%d", &palin_len);
      printf("\n%s\n%s\n", strand1, strand2);
      for  (i = 0;  i < strlen(strand1);  ++i)
          printf("%d", i % 10);
      printf("\n\nPalindromes of length %d\n\n", palin_len);

      /* Displays palindromes of interest                                */
      for  (i = 0;  i <= strlen(strand1) - palin_len;  ++i) {
          match = 1;
          for  (j = 1;
                match && j <= palin_len;
                ++j)
              if (strand1[i + j - 1] != strand2[i + palin_len - j])
                  match = 0;
```

                                                                (continued)

Figure 7.28 (continued)

```
        if (match) {
                printf("Palindrome at position %d\n", i);
                for  (j = i;  j < i + palin_len;  ++j)
                    printf("%c", strand1[j]);
                printf("\n");
                for  (j = i;  j < i + palin_len;  ++j)
                    printf("%c", strand2[j]);
                printf("\n");
        }

    }

    return (0);

}
```

```
Enter one strand of DNA molecule segment
> ATCGCATGCGTAG

Enter complementary strand
> TAGCGTACGCATC

Enter length of palindromic sequence
> 8

ATCGCATGCGTAG
TAGCGTACGCATC
0123456789012

Palindromes of length 8

Palindrome at position 2
CGCATGCG
GCGTACGC
```

◄ TESTING ►

Try the program on sequence lengths ranging from two to the full strand length. For this particular application, only palindromic sequences of even lengths are of interest. Be sure to try the program on some strands containing two or more palindromic sequences of the desired length as well as on some strands containing no palindromes of interest.

Self-Check

1. Make changes to the input section of the palindromic nucleotide sequence program so that `strand2` is not an input, but rather is automatically created based on `strand1`.

7.9 COMMON PROGRAMMING ERRORS

The most common error in using arrays is a subscript-range error. An out-of-range reference occurs when the subscript value used is outside the range specified by the array declaration. For the array `celsius`,

```
int celsius[100];
```

a subscript-range error occurs when `celsius` is used with a subscript that has a value less than `0` or greater than `99`. If the value of `i` is `150`, a reference to the subscripted variable `celsius[i]` may cause an error message such as

```
access violation at line no. 28
```

In many situations, however, no run-time error message will be produced—the program will simply produce incorrect results. In ANSI C, the prevention of subscript-range errors is entirely the responsibility of the programmer. Subscript-range errors are not syntax errors; consequently, they will not be detected until program execution, and often not even then. They are most often caused by an incorrect subscript expression, a loop counter error, or a nonterminating loop. Before spending considerable time in debugging, you should check all suspect subscript calculations carefully for out-of-range errors. View the successive values of a subscripting variable in a debugger program, or insert diagnostic output statements that print subscript values that are of concern.

If a subscript-range error occurs inside an indexed loop, verify that the subscript is in range for both the initial and the final values of the loop control variable. If these values are in range, it is likely that all other subscript references in the loop are in range as well.

If a subscript-range error occurs in a loop controlled by a variable other than the array subscript, check that the loop control variable is being updated as required. If it is not, the loop may be repeated more often than expected, causing the subscript-range error. This error could happen if the control-variable update step was inside a condition or was inadvertently omitted.

When using arrays as arguments to functions, be careful not to apply the address-of operator to the array name even if the array is an output argument. However, do remember to use the **&** on an array *element* that is being passed as an output argument.

Be sure to use the correct forms for declaring array input and output parameters in function prototypes. Remember when reading C code that a parameter declared as

```
int *z
```

could represent a single integer output parameter or an integer array parameter. Comment your own prototypes carefully and use the alternate declaration form

```
int z[]
```

for array parameters to assist readers of your code.

Another error that creeps into C programs with array and string use is the misuse or neglect of the **&** operator. The fact that this operator is *not* applied to strings or to any other whole arrays used as output arguments often leads beginning users of C to forget that the address-of operator must still be used on simple output arguments such as variables of type **int**, **char**, or **double**, as well as on single array elements of these types when used as output arguments. You may want to review the use of the **&** on simple variables as shown in Table 6.4.

Another problem that is common with string use is the overflow of character arrays allocated for strings. Since library functions like **scanf** and **strcpy** just assume that the calling module has provided adequate space for whatever may need to be stored, calling these functions with inadequate storage causes errors that are really difficult to find. In Fig. 7.23, which is repeated here, we see such a situation.

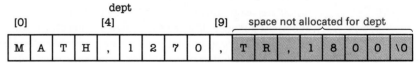

Execution of scanf("%s%d%s%d", dept, &course_num, days, &time);
on Entry of Invalid Data

Whatever was stored in the cells following array **dept** has just been overwritten. If that memory was being used for other program variables, their values will appear to change spontaneously.

A relatively minor error that can lead to difficult bugs is forgetting that all strings end with the null character. The programmer must remember the null character both when allocating space for a string and when building a string one character at a time.

It is easy to slip and use equality or relational operators when comparing strings or the assignment operator for copying them. Remember to use `strcmp` for comparisons and `strcpy` for copying strings.

If you are working on a computer system with very limited memory, you may find that some correct C programs generate run-time error messages indicating an access violation. The use of arrays can cause a program to require large amounts of memory for function data areas. The portion of memory set aside for function data areas is called the *stack*. You may need to tell your operating system that an increased stack size is necessary in order to be able to run programs using large arrays.

CHAPTER REVIEW

In this chapter, we introduced a data structure called an *array*, which is a convenient facility for naming and referencing a collection of like items. We discussed how to declare one-dimensional arrays as local variables where space is actually allocated for the structure and how to declare an array in a function prototype as an input or output parameter. We showed how to reference an individual array element by placing a square-bracketed subscript for each dimension immediately following the array name.

We also described character string manipulation. We saw C's representation of strings as arrays of characters ended by the null character `'\0'`. We studied how to declare, initialize, copy, and compare strings.

Table 7.6 summarizes the declaration and manipulation of arrays as covered in this chapter.

Table 7.6   Using Arrays in C Programs

Example	Effect
Array Declarations	
Local Variables	
`double data[30];`	Allocates storage for 30 type `double` items in array `data` (`data[0]`, `data[1]`, ... , `data[29]`).
`char    str[100];`	Allocates space for a string of up to 99 characters plus the null character.

(continued)

Table 7.6   (continued)

Example	Effect
`char str[11] = "          ";`	Allocates space for a string of up to 10 characters plus the null and initializes it to all blanks.

Input Parameter
`void`
`print_alpha(const char alpha[],`
`           const int   m[],`
`           int         m_size)`
`    or`
`... (const char *alpha, ...`
	States that function `print_alpha` uses arrays `alpha` and m as input parameters only— `print_alpha` will not change their contents.

Output or Input/Output Parameter
`void`
`fill(int nums[], int n)`
`      or`
`... (int *nums,...`
	States that function `fill` can both look at and modify the actual argument array passed to `nums`.

Array References `if (data[0] < 39.8)`	Compares value of initial element of array `data` to `39.8`.
`for  (i = 0;  i < 30;  ++i)` `   data[i] /= 2.0;`	Divides each element of array `data` by 2, changing the array contents.
Calls to String Library `strlen(a_string)`	Returns the number of characters in the string `a_string` up to but not including the null character.
`strcmp(str1, str2)`	Returns a negative integer if `str1` precedes `str2` alphabetically, a positive integer if `str2` precedes `str1`, and zero if `str1` and `str2` are equal.
`strcpy(str_result, str_src)`	Copies all the characters of `str_src` including the null character into `str_result`. Assumption is that `str_result` has enough room for all these characters.

QUICK-CHECK EXERCISES

1. What is a data structure?
2. Of what data type are array subscripting expressions?
3. Can two elements of the same array be of different data types?
4. If an array is declared to have ten elements, must the program use all ten?

5. Let `nums` be an array of 12 type `int` locations. Describe how the following loop works.

```
i = 0;
for  (status = scanf("%d", &n);
         status == 1 && i < 12;
         status = scanf("%d", &n))
      nums[i++] = n;
```

6. An _____ loop allows us to access easily the elements of an array in sequential order.

7. What is the difference in the use of array b that is implied by these two prototypes?

```
int                     int
fun_one(int b[], n)     fun_two(const int b[], n)
```

8. Look again at the prototypes in Exercise 7. Why does neither array declaration indicate a size?

9. Which of the following strings could represent space allocated for a local variable? Which could represent a formal parameter of any length?

```
char str1[50]     char str2[]
```

10. A program you have written is producing incorrect results on your second data set, although it runs fine on the first. You discover after adding extra print statements for debugging that the value of one of your strings is spontaneously changing from `"blue"` to `"al"` in the following code segment. What could be wrong?

```
. . .
printf("%s\n", s1);  /*  displays "blue" */
scanf("%s", s2);
printf("%s\n", s1);  /*  displays "al"   */
. . .
```

11. Declare a variable `str` with as little space as would be reasonable given that `str` will hold each of the following values in turn:

```
carbon    uranium    tungsten    bauxite
```

12. If `x` is an array declared

```
int x[10];
```

and you see a function call such as

```
some_fun(x, n);
```

how can you tell whether **x** is an input or an output argument?

ANSWERS TO QUICK-CHECK EXERCISES

1. A data structure is a grouping of related values in main memory.
2. Type `int`
3. No
4. No
5. As long as `scanf` continues to return a value of 1 meaning a valid integer has been obtained for n, unless the subscript `i` is ≥ 12, the loop body will store the input in the next element of `nums` and will increment the loop counter. The loop exits on EOF (`scanf` returns a negative value), on invalid data (`scanf` returns zero), or on `i` no longer being less than 12.
6. indexed
7. In `fun_one`, b can be used as an output parameter or as an input/output parameter. In `fun_two`, b is strictly an input parameter array.
8. The size of b is not needed because the function does not allocate storage for copying parameter arrays. Only the starting address of the actual argument array will be stored in the formal parameter.
9. local variable: `str1`   parameter: `str2`
10. The call to `scanf` may be getting a string too long to fit in `s2`, and the extra characters could be overwriting memory allocated to `s1`.
11. `char str[9]` The longest value (`"tungsten"`) has eight characters, and one more is needed for the null character.
12. You can't tell by looking at the function call, nor can you rely on the prototype of `some_fun` to tell you either unless the corresponding formal parameter declaration has a `const` qualifier. If it does, x must be an input argument.

REVIEW QUESTIONS

1. Identify an error in the following C statements:

```
int x[8], i;
for  (i = 0;   i <= 8;   ++i)
     x[i] = i;
```

Will the error be detected? If so, when?

2. Declare an array of type double values called **exper** that can be referenced by using any day of the week as a subscript where 0 represents Sunday, 1 represents Monday, and so on.

3. The statement marked /* this one */ in the following code is valid. True or false?

```
int counts[10], i;
double x[5];
printf("Enter an integer between 0 and 4> ");
i = 0;
scanf("%d", &counts[i]);
x[counts[i]] = 8.384;  /* this one */
```

4. Write a program segment that would make a copy of a string variable with the first occurrence of a specified letter deleted.

5. Write a C program segment to display the index of the smallest and the largest numbers in an array **x** of 20 integers. Assume array **x** already has values assigned to each element.

6. Write a C function called **reverse** that takes an array named **x** as an input parameter and an array named **y** as an output parameter. A third function parameter is n, the number of values in **x**. The function should copy the integers in x into y but in reverse order (i.e., $y[0]$ gets $x[n - 1]$, . . . $y[n - 1]$ gets $x[0]$).

PROGRAMMING PROJECTS

1. Write a program to take two numerical lists of the same length ended by a sentinel value and store the lists in arrays **x** and **y**, each of which has 20 elements. Let n be the actual number of data values in each list. Store the product of corresponding elements of x and y in a third array, z, also of size 20. Display the arrays **x**, **y**, and **z** in a three-column table. Then compute and display the square root of the sum of the items in **z**. Make up your own data, and be sure to test your program on at least one data set with number lists of exactly 20 items. One data set should have lists of 21 numbers, and one set should have significantly shorter lists.

2. Let **arr** be an array of 20 integers. Write a program that first fills the array with up to 20 input values and then finds and displays both the *subscript* of the largest item in **arr** and the value of the largest item.

3. Healthfair Pharmaceuticals runs a continual color and opacity quality check on its liquid-antibiotic production line. The test is performed by shining a

laser through each vial on the production line and recording how much light is detected on the far side of the vial. The following statistics are needed for each 30-vial batch of antibiotics: the average (mean) light absorptivity of the vials of antibiotics, the variance, and the standard deviation of the absorptivity data. The formula for standard deviation shown in Section 7.2 represents the standard deviation of a population. Since this quality-check problem does not call for computing the standard deviation of absorptivity data for the entire population of Healthfair antibiotics, but only the standard deviation of a 30-vial sample, use this slightly different formula for the standard deviation of a sample of size *n:*

$$\textit{Standard deviation} = \sqrt{\frac{\sum\limits_{i=0}^{n-1} (a[i] - mean)^2}{n-1}}$$

The absorptivity of the *i*th vial of antibiotics is $a[i]$. The variance is the square of the standard deviation. Write a program that computes the needed statistics for a stream of user-entered absorptivity data (values between 0 and 1).

4. Having spent a lot of time typing in C programs, you have resolved to invent a specialized new kind of keyboard to aid you. (There have been a variety of attempts to improve keyboards for standard typing applications, notably the "Dvorak keyboard.") In your product, you plan to place the most commonly used keys for C programming in the shortest finger-travel positions. You suspect that keys such as "*" and ";" are more commonly used in C programs than in English prose. However, before designing this keyboard, you need to get some hard data about the keys most commonly used in writing C source code.

Write a program that takes as input a C source code file, counts the number of occurrences of each keyboard character in the file, and writes the results to another file. Keep the count data in a one-dimensional array of integers, each element of which corresponds to the number of occurrences of one character. Recall that every character is represented by an integer character code. Assume that the possible character code range is 0–127. Write the characters found in the file and the number of times each character occurs, one entry per line. Hint: The character `'A'` can be converted to its integer character code by using the cast `(int)'A'`, and the ASCII character code 65 can be converted to its character equivalent (`'A'`) by using the cast `(char)65`.

5. Generate a table that indicates the rainfall for the city of Plainview and compares the current year's rainfall for the city with the rainfall from the previous year. Display summary statistics that will indicate both the annual rainfall for each year and the average monthly rainfall for each year. The input data will consist of twelve pairs of numbers. The first number in each

pair will be the current year's rainfall for a month, and the second number will be what fell during the same month the previous year. The first data pair will represent January, the second will be February, and so forth. If you assume the data begin

```
3.2    4      (for January)
2.2    1.6    (for February)
```

the output should resemble the following:

```
              Table of monthly rainfall

                    January      February      March . . .
This year            3.2          2.2
Last year            4.0          1.6

Total rainfall this year:  35.7
Total rainfall last year:  42.8
Average monthly rainfall for this year:  3.6
Average monthly rainfall for last year:  4.0
```

6. Write and test a function `hydroxide` that returns a 1 for true if its string argument ends in the substring `OH`.
   Try the function `hydroxide` on the following data:

```
KOH   H2O2   NaCl   NaOH   C9H8O4   MgOH
```

7. Write a function that will merge the contents of two sorted (ascending order) arrays of type `double` values, storing the result in an array output parameter (still in ascending order). The function should not assume that both its input parameter arrays are the same length but can assume that one array does not contain two copies of the same value. The result array should also contain no duplicate values.

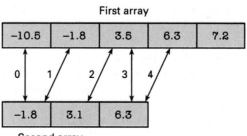

First array

Second array

Result array

−10.5	−1.8	3.1	3.5	6.3	7.2

Hint: When one of the input arrays has been exhausted, do not forget to copy the remaining data in the other array into the result array. Test your function with cases in which (1) the first array is exhausted first, (2) the second array is exhausted first, and (3) the two arrays are exhausted at the same time (i.e., they end with the same value). Remember that the arrays input to this function *must already be sorted.*

8. The binary search algorithm that follows may be used to search an array when the elements are in order. This algorithm is analogous to the following approach for finding a name in a telephone book.
   a. Open the book in the middle, and look at the middle name on the page.
   b. If the middle name isn't the one you're looking for, decide whether it comes before or after the name you want.
   c. Take the appropriate half of the section of the book you were looking in and repeat these steps until you land on the name.

Algorithm for Binary Search

1. Let `bottom` be the subscript of the initial array element.
2. Let `top` be the subscript of the last array element.
3. Let `found` be false.
4. Repeat as long as `bottom` isn't greater than `top` and the target has not been found
   5. Let `middle` be the subscript of the element halfway between `bottom` and `top`.
   6. if the element at `middle` is the target
      7. Set `found` to true and `index` to `middle`.
      else if the element at `middle` is larger than the target
         8. Let `top` be `middle − 1`.
      else
         9. Let `bottom` be `middle + 1`.

Write and test a function `binary_srch` that implements this algorithm for an array of integers. When there is a large number of array elements, which function do you think is faster: `binary_srch` or the linear search function of Fig. 7.10?

9. Statistical analysis of data makes heavy use of arrays. One such analysis, called cross-tabulation, is used to help decide whether a relationship exists between two or more variables. For example, the following data might represent opinions from a survey concerning an amendment to the U.S. Constitution making it illegal to destroy or damage the U.S. flag in any way.

Opinion	Male	Female	Total
In Favor	63	27	90
Opposed	19	42	61
No Opinion	6	39	45
Totals	88	108	196

Write a C program that will take pairs of male/female response totals (one pair per line)

```
63   27
19   42
 6   39
```

and display the cross-tabulation matrix including the row totals and the column totals.

MULTI-DIMENSIONAL ARRAYS

In this chapter, we study arrays of more than one dimension: These data structures are widely used in software to model tables of data, matrices, data plots, relationships among the variables of a system, maps, and images of all kinds—photographic, radar, X-ray, ultrasound, infrared, and magnetic resonance. The chapter presents the fundamentals of multidimensional array manipulation in C along with numerous applications using arrays of two or more dimensions.

8.1 DECLARING AND REFERENCING MULTIDIMENSIONAL ARRAYS

In this section, we show how to declare and reference *multidimensional arrays,* that is, arrays with two or more dimensions. Suppose that we are programming a robot to place nine Christmas tree ornaments in a box and to check that the task is correctly completed. The box has nine cushioned compartments, in a 3 × 3 grid. The array declaration

```
char box[3][3]
```

allocates storage for our program's model of the box, a two-dimensional array with three rows and three columns (see Fig. 8.1). The array has nine elements, each of which is referenced by specifying a row subscript (0, 1, or 2) and a column subscript (0, 1, or 2). Each array element contains a character value: A blank represents an empty location, an X a filled one. The array element box[1][2] marked in Fig. 8.1 is in row 1, column 2 of the array; the element contains the character X. All the elements of box are filled except box[2][1] and box[2][2].

A function that takes a box as a parameter will have a declaration similar to this in its prototype:

```
char box[][3]
```

**Figure 8.1
An Ornament
Box Modeled
as Array box**

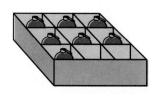
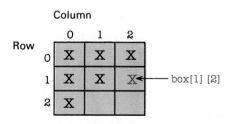

In the declaration of a multidimensional array parameter, only the first dimension, the number of rows, can be omitted. Including both dimensions is also permissible. If our ornament company buys just one standard-sized box, using the declaration that follows would make more sense:

```
char box[3][3]
```

Multidimensional Array Declaration

SYNTAX: *element-type aname* [*size₁*] [*size₂*] ... [*sizeₙ*] ;   /* storage
                                                                                   allocation   */

element-type aname [ ] [*size₂*] ... [*sizeₙ*]   /* parameter in
                                                                    prototype   */

EXAMPLES: ```double table[NROWS][NCOLS];```   /* storage allocation   */

```
void
process_matrix(int in[][4],   /* input parameter     */
               int out[][4],  /* output parameter    */
               int nrows)     /* input - number of
                                 rows                 */
```

INTERPRETATION: The first form shown allocates storage space for an array *aname* consisting of *size₁* × *size₂* × . . . × *sizeₙ* memory cells. Each memory cell can store one data item whose data type is specified by *element-type*. The individual array elements are referenced by the subscripted variables *aname* [0] [0] ... [0] through *aname* [*size₁*–1] [*size₂*–1] ... [*sizeₙ*–1]. An integer constant expression is used to specify each *sizeᵢ*.

The second declaration form shown is valid when declaring a multidimensional array parameter in a function prototype. The size of the first dimension (the number of rows) is the only size that can be omitted. As for one-dimensional arrays, the value actually stored in an array formal parameter is the address of the initial element of the actual argument.

NOTE: ANSI C requires that an implementation allow multidimensional arrays of at least six dimensions.

EXAMPLE 8.1

The array `table`

```
double table[7][5][6];
```

consists of three dimensions: The first subscript may take on values from 0 to 6; the second, from 0 to 4; and the third, from 0 to 5. A total of 7 × 5 × 6, or 210, type `double` values may be stored in the array `table`. All three subscripts must be specified in each reference to array `table` in order to access a single number (e.g., `table[2][3][4]`). ◀

EXAMPLE 8.2   Function `filled` (see Fig. 8.2) checks whether a robot has correctly put one Christmas tree ornament in each compartment of a box. The function's argument is an array like `box` in Fig. 8.1 into which the robot stores an X if its scan of a compartment detects an ornament, and a blank if the scan detects an empty compartment. If the box contains no cells with the value blank, the function returns 1 for true; otherwise it returns 0 for false.

Figure 8.2   Function to Check Whether Box Is Filled

```
/*
 * Checks whether a box is completely filled
 */
int
filled(char box[3][3])  /* input - box to check     */
{

    int   r,c,  /* row and column subscripts     */
          ans;  /* whether or not box is filled.  */

    /* Assumes box is filled until blank is found */
    ans = 1;

    /* Resets ans to zero if a blank is found     */
    for  (r = 0;  r < 3;  ++r)
       for  (c = 0;  c < 3;  ++c)
          if (box[r][c] == ' ')
                ans = 0;

    return (ans);
}
```

◀

Initialization of Multidimensional Arrays

Multidimensional arrays may be initialized in their declarations in a manner similar to the initialization of one-dimensional arrays. However, instead of listing all table values in one list, the values are usually grouped by rows. For example, the following statement would declare an ornament box and initialize its contents to blanks:

```
char box[3][3] = { {' ', ' ', ' '}, {' ', ' ', ' '},
                   {' ', ' ', ' '} };
```

Arrays with Several Dimensions

The array `soil_type` declared here,

```
int soil_type[4][7][MAXDEPTH];
```

north-south   *east-west*   *depth*

and pictured in Fig. 8.3 is a three-dimensional array that may be used to store data about the types of soil under a proposed housing tract in an area prone to earthquakes. We will assume that we have data on the soil below the tract on a grid down to a level of MAXDEPTH × 10 meters, at 10 meter resolution. We are interested in various statistics about the amount and distribution of silt under the housing tract. We will assume that we are interested in distribution down to 1 km (MAXDEPTH = 100) under a 4-by-7-km region. We would like to know how much silt there is in various cross-sections of this block of soil. This information is of interest to a builder, since the distribution of silt and rock can

Figure 8.3   Three-Dimensional Array soil_type

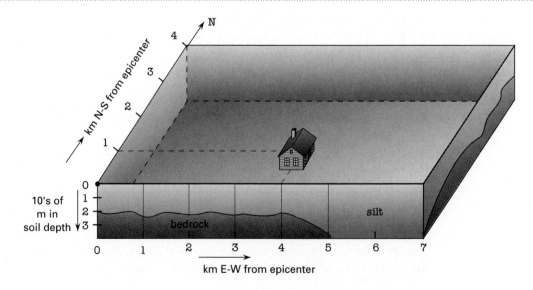

make a big difference for an individual house that may get reflections of earthquake pressure waves off the bedrock. If there is primarily silt in a box whose upper southeast corner coordinates are [2 km north of epicenter][3 km west of epicenter][30 m down from surface], the element `soil_type[2][3][3]` will contain a 1. Otherwise, if that box contains mostly bedrock, the element will contain a 0. Note that C's use of array subscripts that start at zero is convenient for distance measurements like the coordinates in this problem.

Array `soil_type` is composed of a total of 2800 ($4 \times 7 \times 100$) elements. A potential pitfall exists when you are dealing with multidimensional arrays: Memory space can be used up rapidly if several multidimensional arrays are declared in the same program. Therefore you should be aware of the amount of memory required by each large array in a program.

We can answer many different questions by processing the data in Fig. 8.3. We can determine the total amount of silt under one particular square kilometer; we can determine the percentages of silt and bedrock along a north–south line one kilometer wide at a certain distance east from a possible earthquake epicenter, and so on. The type of information desired determines the order in which we must reference the array elements.

EXAMPLE 8.3 The program fragment that follows finds and displays the total number of blocks of silt in each north–south strip:

```
/* Finds and displays how much silt is contained in each
   north-south strip */
for  (north_south = 0;  north_south < 4;  ++north_south)  {
    silt_amount = 0;

    for  (east_west = 0;  east_west < 7;  ++east_west)  {

        for  (depth = 0;  depth < MAXDEPTH;  ++depth)  {
            silt_amount += soil_type[north_south][east_west]
                [depth];
        }

    }

    printf("There are %d soil cells containing silt in ",
            silt_amount);
    printf("north-south segment %d.\n", north_south);
}
```

Since we are interested in looking at soil types in north–south segments, the loop control variable for the outermost indexed loop is the subscript that denotes north–south distance.

The program fragment that displays the number of blocks of silt in each east–west strip is

```
/* Finds and displays how much silt is contained in each
 * east-west strip. */
for  (east_west = 0;  east_west < 7;  ++east_west)  {
    silt_amount = 0;
    for  (north_south = 0;  north_south < 4;  ++north_south)  {
        for  (depth = 0;  depth < MAXDEPTH;  ++depth)  {
            silt_amount += soil_type[north_south][east_west]
                [depth];
        }
    }
    printf("There are %d soil cells containing silt in east-",
        silt_amount);
    printf("west segment %d.\n", east_west);
}
```

EXERCISES FOR SECTION 8.1

Self-check

1. Redefine MAXDEPTH as 5, and write program segments that perform the following operations:
   a. Initialize all the soil type values to bedrock, and then change some of the surface cells to silt. (Which index and what value range of that index correspond to "surface cells"?)
   b. Find the percentage of silt-containing cells from among all the cells at a depth of 20 meters. Recall that each increment of 1 in the depth corresponds to 10 meters.
   c. Find the surface cells, if any, that have more than 30 meters of silt below them. Display the surface coordinates (north_south and east_west) of any cells of this type.

Programming

1. Write a function that has three input parameters: the soil type array, a north–south coordinate, and a depth. The function is to display the soil types at the given depth and north–south coordinate for all east–west coordinates. Try using your function to find the soil types for 2 kilometers north of the epicenter at a depth of 20 meters.

8.2 MODELING WITH TWO-DIMENSIONAL ARRAYS

One significant consequence of the growing use of microprocessors has been the development of cellular telephone networks to provide telephone service to customers on the move. In our next case study, we use a two-dimensional array to model the grid of cells into which a metropolitan area has been divided in a cellular phone system design.

Case Study: Cellular Telephone System[†]

◀ **PROBLEM** ▶

You are the vice president of planning for JEJ Cellular Telephones, Inc. You have just obtained the frequency licenses to set up a cellular service in the city of Flat Spot and its suburbs, Burbville and Mosquito Lakes. Burbville and Mosquito Lakes have essentially no industry of their own, and there is a heavy flow of people into Flat Spot every day from these two communities. During the day, the businesspeople of metropolitan Flat Spot move around mostly within that city. In the evening, there is a heavy flow out of Flat Spot toward Burbville and Mosquito Lakes. Later in the evening and on weekends, there is a general flow among and within the three communities as people go about their daily business.

Your cellular telephone company plans to use microwave transmitters to carry calls. Many factors determine the best way to build a cellular network: The terrain, the traffic patterns, and radio noise sources are a few of these factors. Since the tri-city area you are serving is essentially flat and more or less devoid of interference sources, you will be able to concentrate on the traffic patterns. Your investors have given you the resources to build up to ten transmitters to serve the traffic. Each transmitter can handle 200 calls simultaneously and can cover a one-square-mile area reliably. You have some marketing data for the 5-by-5-mile tri-city area that predicts what the call demand will be at three times of interest (see Fig. 8.4):

- 8:30 A.M. on a weekday when the inbound rush hour to Flat Spot is at its peak
- 11 A.M. on a weekday when business calls are at their peak
- Noon on a Saturday when suburban traffic peaks

[†]More information on designing this type of system can be found in W.C.Y. Lee, *Mobile Communications Design Fundamentals,* 2nd Ed. Wiley Series in Telecommunications (New York: John Wiley and Sons, 1993); and J. M. Holtzman, and D. J. Goodman (eds.), *Wireless Communications: Future Directions* (Boston: Kluwer Academic Publishers, 1993).

**Figure 8.4
Predicted
Calling Patterns
for Three Time
Periods**

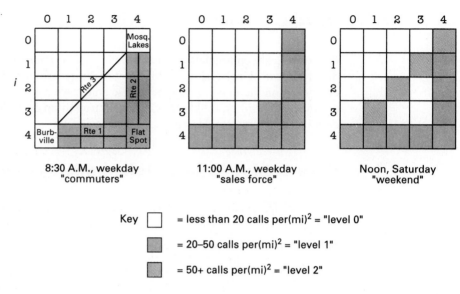

Key ☐ = less than 20 calls per(mi)^2 = "level 0"

☐ = 20–50 calls per(mi)^2 = "level 1"

☐ = 50+ calls per(mi)^2 = "level 2"

Note that with only ten transmitters, you cannot cover the whole area. You want to write a program to help you analyze the call demand data so that you can place your transmitters in a configuration that will serve the greatest number of potential customers.

ANALYSIS

In a "trade-off" problem like this one, the program must evaluate the available data in light of how important each data item is to the ultimate problem solution. For example, if the commuter calling pattern lasts only 15 minutes a day, how important is that 15 minutes to the customers' satisfaction? In our solution, we will reflect the relative importance of each of our data sets by "weighting" the three sets of data. Then we will investigate how our solution varies with different sets of weights.

We will input the data shown in Fig. 8.4 by declaring three 5 × 5 matrices, one for each data set. The input data file will give each cell of the three matrices one of three values—0, 1, or 2—signifying which of the three levels of traffic density is observed at that position at the time represented by the matrix. After scanning the data file, we will allow the user to associate a relative weight with each of the data sets. The program will then take the weighted data and call for a transmitter to be placed on each of the ten cells with the heaviest traffic.

Data Requirements

Problem Constants

```
GRID_SIZE          5   /* length and width in miles of area
                          studied   */
NUM_TRANSMITTERS  10   /* number of transmitters to be
                          placed   */
SELECTED          -1   /* negative value marking cells
                          already selected */
```

Problem Inputs

```
int commuters[GRID_SIZE][GRID_SIZE]   /* 8:30 A.M.
                                         predicted traffic
                                         data          */
int salesforce[GRID_SIZE][GRID_SIZE] /* 11 A.M. predicted
                                         traffic data    */
int weekend[GRID_SIZE][GRID_SIZE]    /* weekend predicted
                                         traffic data    */
int commuter_weight    /* weighting factors for commuter, */
int salesforce_weight /*          sales force,           */
int weekend_weight     /*          and weekend data       */
```

Problem Outputs

```
int summed_data[GRID_SIZE][GRID_SIZE] /* weighted output
                                         data          */
int location_i, location_j            /* coordinates
                                         of each
                                         transmitter   */
```

Program Variable

```
int current_max          /* heaviest traffic seen so far  */
```

DESIGN

The program first takes the commuter, sales force, and weekend data from the data file to fill the three matrices. Next, the user must supply integers to weight the data. The data in each of the matrices is multiplied by the relevant weight, the corresponding elements of the three weighted matrices are summed, and the matrix of sums is displayed. Finally, the coordinates of the NUM_TRANSMITTERS highest values in the matrix of sums are displayed as the locations of the transmitters.

Initial Algorithm

1. Get the traffic data for the three time periods from the data file.
2. Get the weights from the user.
3. Multiply each matrix entry by the relevant weight, and store the sum of the corresponding entries in `summed_data`.
4. Find the `NUM_TRANSMITTERS` highest-valued cells in the matrix `summed_data`, and store the subscripts of these in `location_i` and `location_j`, displaying each pair.

Refinement of Step 4

4.1 Repeat `NUM_TRANSMITTERS` times.
    4.2 Find the coordinates of the largest value in `summed_data` (`location_i`, `location_j`);
    4.3 Display the coordinates as the location of a transmitter.
    4.4 Set `summed_data[location_i][location_j]` to `SELECTED`.

◀ IMPLEMENTATION ▶

Figure 8.5 shows an implementation of our algorithm to place transmitters. We implement Step 1 as a function, `get_traffic_data`. The program in Fig. 8.5 is the first we have seen in which we take data from two input sources—a file and the keyboard. Note that we handle the file input using functions `fopen`, `fscanf`, and `fclose`, just as we did in the exam scores program of Fig. 5.13. Input from the keyboard is obtained by calling `scanf`.

Figure 8.5   **Program to Place Transmitters for a Cellular Phone System**

```c
/*
 *  Using traffic data for peak times and user-supplied weights,
 *  determines placement of NUM_TRANSMITTERS microwave transmitters
 *  for cellular telephone network
 */

#include <stdio.h>
#define GRID_SIZE         5
#define SELECTED          -1    /* value lower than all grid data values */
#define TRAFFIC_FILE      "traffic.dat"        /* file of traffic data */
#define NUM_TRANSMITTERS 10         /* number of transmitters available */
```

(continued)

Figure 8.5   (continued)

```c
/*
 * Fills 3 GRID_SIZE x GRID_SIZE arrays with traffic data from
 * TRAFFIC_FILE
 */
void
get_traffic_data(int commuters[GRID_SIZE][GRID_SIZE],  /* output */
                 int salesforce[GRID_SIZE][GRID_SIZE], /* output */
                 int weekend[GRID_SIZE][GRID_SIZE])    /* output */
{
      int   i, j;  /* loop counters */
      FILE *fp;    /* file pointer  */

      fp = fopen(TRAFFIC_FILE, "r");

      for (i = 0;  i < GRID_SIZE;  ++i)
         for (j = 0;  j < GRID_SIZE;  ++j)
            fscanf(fp, "%d", &commuters[i][j]);

      for (i = 0;  i < GRID_SIZE;  ++i)
         for (j = 0;  j < GRID_SIZE;  ++j)
            fscanf(fp, "%d", &salesforce[i][j]);

      for (i = 0;  i < GRID_SIZE;  ++i)
         for (j = 0;  j < GRID_SIZE;  ++j)
            fscanf(fp, "%d", &weekend[i][j]);

      fclose(fp);
}

/*
 * Displays contents of a GRID_SIZE x GRID_SIZE matrix of integers
 */
void
print_matrix(int matrix[GRID_SIZE][GRID_SIZE])
{
      int i, j;  /* loop counters */
      for (i = 0;  i < GRID_SIZE;  ++i) {
         for (j = 0;  j < GRID_SIZE;  ++j)
```

(continued)

Figure 8.5 (continued)

```
            printf("%3d  ", matrix[i][j]);
        printf("\n");
    }
}
int
main(void)
{
    int commuters[GRID_SIZE][GRID_SIZE];   /* 8:30 A.M.  traffic data */
    int salesforce[GRID_SIZE][GRID_SIZE];  /* 11 A.M. traffic data    */
    int weekend[GRID_SIZE][GRID_SIZE];      /* weekend traffic data    */

    int commuter_weight,    /* Weighting factor for commuter data    */
        salesforce_weight,  /* Weighting factor for salesforce data  */
        weekend_weight;     /* Weighting factor for weekend data     */

    int summed_data[GRID_SIZE][GRID_SIZE]; /* Weighted output data    */

    int location_i,             /* Location of each of the           */
        location_j;             /*    transmitters.                  */

    int current_max;         /* Largest value so far in summed data  */

    int i,j,                    /* Loop counters over grid            */
        tr;                     /* Loop counter over transmitters     */

    /*  Fills and displays traffic matrices       */
    get_traffic_data(commuters, salesforce, weekend);
    printf("8:30 A.M. WEEKDAY TRAFFIC DATA\n\n");
    print_matrix(commuters);
    printf("\n\n11 A.M. WEEKDAY TRAFFIC DATA\n\n");
    print_matrix(salesforce);
    printf("\n\nWEEKEND TRAFFIC DATA\n\n");
    print_matrix(weekend);

    /* Asks the user for the weighting factors     */
    printf("\n\nPlease input the following values: \n");
    printf("Weight (an integer >=0) for the 8:30 A.M. commuter data> ");
    scanf("%d", &commuter_weight);
    printf("Weight (an integer >=0) for the 11:00 A.M. sales force data> ");
    scanf("%d", &salesforce_weight);
```

(continued)

Figure 8.5 (continued)

```
        printf("Weight (an integer >=0) for the weekend data> ");
        scanf("%d", &weekend_weight);

        /* Computes and displays the weighted, summed data */
        for  (i = 0;  i < GRID_SIZE;  ++i)
            for  (j = 0;  j < GRID_SIZE; ++j)
                summed_data[i][j] = commuter_weight * commuters[i][j] +
                                    salesforce_weight * salesforce[i][j] +
                                    weekend_weight  * weekend[i][j];
        printf("\n\nThe weighted, summed data is:\n\n");
        print_matrix(summed_data);

        /* Finds the NUM_TRANSMITTERS highest values in the summed_data matrix.
           Temporarily stores the coordinates in location_i and location_j,
           and then displays the resulting locations */
        printf("\n\nLocations of the %d transmitters:\n\n", NUM_TRANSMITTERS);

        for  (tr = 1;  tr <= NUM_TRANSMITTERS;  ++tr) {
            current_max = SELECTED;  /* Starts off our search with a value
                                        that is known to be too low. */
            for  (i = 0;  i < GRID_SIZE;  ++i) {
                for  (j = 0;  j < GRID_SIZE;  ++j) {
                    if (current_max < summed_data[i][j]) {
                        current_max = summed_data[i][j];
                        location_i = i;
                        location_j = j;
                    }
                }
            }

            /* Sets the cell just chosen to a new low value so it
               will not be chosen next time and displays result   */
            summed_data[location_i][location_j] = SELECTED;
            printf(" Transmitter %3d: at location %3d %3d\n",
                   tr, location_i, location_j);
        }

        return (0);
}
```

◄ **TESTING** ►

For an initial test that will produce results that are easily verified by hand, run the program using weights of 1. The run in Fig. 8.6 uses weights of 1 and the traffic data illustrated in Fig. 8.4. Verify that the transmitters are indeed placed on the `NUM_TRANSMITTERS` highest-valued cells. For another test, set two of the weights to 0 and the third weight to 1 and check that the summed data matches the original data in the matrix to which the weight of 1 is applied.

Figure 8.6   Transmitter Selection for Traffic Data from Fig. 8.4

....

```
8:30 A.M. WEEKDAY TRAFFIC DATA
    0    0    0    0    0
    0    0    0    0    1
    0    0    0    0    2
    0    0    0    1    2
    0    1    2    2    2

11 A.M. WEEKDAY TRAFFIC DATA
    0    0    0    0    1
    0    0    0    0    1
    0    0    0    0    1
    0    0    0    1    2
    1    1    1    2    2

WEEKEND TRAFFIC DATA
    0    0    0    0    2
    0    0    0    2    1
    0    0    2    0    1
    0    2    0    0    1
    2    1    1    1    1

Please input the following values:
Weight (an integer >=0) for the 8:30 A.M. commuter data> 1
Weight (an integer >=0) for the 11:00 A.M. sales force data> 1
Weight (an integer >=0) for the weekend data> 1

The weighted, summed data is:
    0    0    0    0    3
    0    0    0    2    3
    0    0    2    0    4
    0    2    0    2    5
    3    3    4    5    5
```

(continued)

Figure 8.6   (continued)

```
Locations of the 10 transmitters:
  Transmitter   1: at location   3   4
  Transmitter   2: at location   4   3
  Transmitter   3: at location   4   4
  Transmitter   4: at location   2   4
  Transmitter   5: at location   4   2
  Transmitter   6: at location   0   4
  Transmitter   7: at location   1   4
  Transmitter   8: at location   4   0
  Transmitter   9: at location   4   1
  Transmitter  10: at location   1   3
```

EXERCISES FOR SECTION 8.2

Self-Check

1. Why do we set the value of a `summed_data` element to a negative value after it is chosen as the largest value, rather than setting it to zero, the smallest value that the program can produce?

2. If there were only three transmitters but each covered four square miles rather than one, how would the final transmitter placement algorithm change? Display of each transmitter placed should list all the blocks covered. For example:

```
Transmitter 2 covers locations (2,3), (2,4), (3,3), (3,4)
```

   Write down the code fragment that would replace the current transmitter selection loop, defining any additional variables you may need.

Programming

1. If an interference source were going to block all traffic in cell [3][3] during commuter time only, how would the cellular telephone system transmitter placement algorithm change? To the case study code in Fig. 8.5, add a definition of another 5×5 array, `interference`. Data stored in this array will use zero to represent cells with no interference source, nonzero values to represent the presence of an interference source. Revise the program so that cells containing interference sources cannot be chosen as locations of transmitters.

2. Write a version of the original cellular telephone program that does not ask the user to input the weights, but uses nested loops to automatically vary the values of the three weights from 0 to 2. The program should display transmitter placements for all 27 weight combinations.

8.3 PLOTTING A FUNCTION OF ONE VARIABLE

In this section, we will use a two-dimensional array to implement a simplified means of having the computer plot graphs of functions of one variable:

$$y = f(x)$$

We present this example to demonstrate some of the problems you encounter when developing graphics software. In practice, you would use a specialized graphics package to create a high-quality plot of a function.

Mapping a Function onto a Screen

The method we are about to describe is general and will work for any function that has no singularities in the range of x values that we are plotting. A *singularity* exists at x_0 if $|f(x_0)|$ is too large to be represented in the computer (see Numerical Inaccuracies in Section 3.1). Be careful, though, because this definition of singularity differs from the mathematical definition, according to which a singularity exists at x_0 if $|f(x_0)|$ is undefined at x_0.

To plot a function of one variable, we compute $f(x)$ on a sequence of equally spaced x values. Our goal is to develop a program that will allow the user to specify the first and the last of the x values:

1. x_init: the initial x value
2. x_final: the final x value

The program will then plot $f(x)$ on the interval [x_init, x_final]. The number of points plotted will depend on the characteristics of the output device. We will assume the computer screen has 24 rows and 80 columns.

Plotting a function of one variable involves mapping a rectangular region of the x-y plane onto our computer screen. Since the x-y plane is a two-dimensional continuum and our computer screen is a two-dimensional arrangement of discrete cells, a considerable amount of information will be lost. Figure 8.7 depicts the function plotting problem. The shaded region in the x-y plane is to be mapped onto the computer screen, causing the curve $y = f(x)$ to be represented as a finite sequence of characters.

The region of the x-y plane that will be mapped onto the computer screen is bounded by four lines:

1. The line $x = $ x_init on the left
2. The line $x = $ x_final on the right
3. The line $y = $ y_min, the minimum computed value for $f(x)$ on the interval [x_init, x_final]
4. The line $y = $ y_max, the maximum computed value for $f(x)$ on the interval [x_init, x_final]

**Figure 8.7
Mapping a
Graph onto
a Computer
Screen**

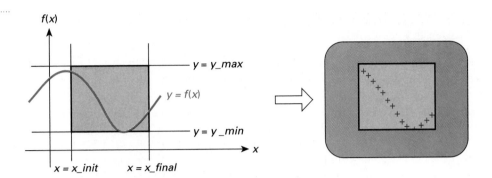

The maximum and minimum values of $f(x)$ will be relative to a finite number of tabulation points. We will discuss how these tabulation points are determined later in this section.

Plotting the continuous curve $y = f(x)$ requires imposing a grid structure upon the rectangular region of the x-y plane in Fig. 8.7. Suppose we plan to organize our computer screen so that 20 rows and 70 columns will be devoted to displaying the graph (see Fig. 8.8). The rest of the screen will be used to present labeling information. We can use `graph`, a two-dimensional array of 20 rows and 70 columns, to represent our graph; each element in array `graph` corresponds to a cell of our grid structure.

Figure 8.9 shows a portion of the screen in more detail. A 10×11 cell portion of our screen is superimposed on the corresponding portion of the x-y plane. The plotting program requires that the graph of the function, which is a continuous curve, be represented by a finite number of characters, one for each column. We will use the character `'*'` in plotting the function. Now how do we determine where each asterisk should be placed?

**Figure 8.8
Detail of
Computer
Screen Layout**

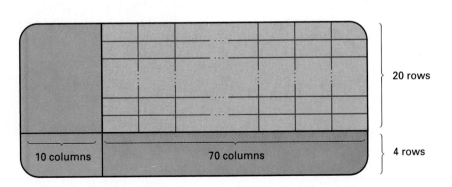

**Figure 8.9
Segment of
Graph and
Its Plot**

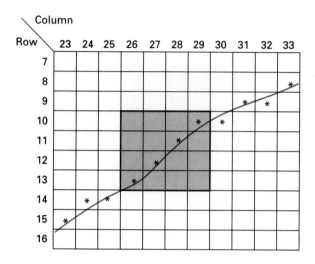

Figure 8.10 shows a part of Fig. 8.9 but with additional detail. Our plotting method progresses column by column. In each column, a row is marked with an asterisk. Figure 8.10 shows us at column 27; columns 1–26 have already been marked. An important observation is that each column corresponds to a particular interval of x values, for example, [xl, xr]. More significantly for our algorithm, these intervals have a midpoint xm. It is at this midpoint that we will evaluate the function f, yielding a number, yv = f(xm). This y value, yv, will then be converted to a row number, and the corresponding cell in array graph will be marked with an asterisk.

**Figure 8.10
Plotting the
Point (xm, yv)**

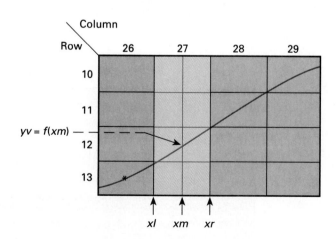

The Scaling Problem

The *scaling problem* is central to plotting functions with a computer. The scaling problem consists of deriving the mathematical relationships between columns and xm values on the one hand and rows and yv values on the other. In terms of Fig. 8.10, the scaling problem is to compute xm given a particular column number k, and to compute a row number r for a particular function value yv.

Let us first consider how the midpoint xm is determined by the column number k. Figure 8.11 illustrates the decision that x_init will correspond to the midpoint of the first column and that x_final will correspond to the midpoint of the last column of the graph. (We are referring to columns relative to the graph, not relative to the computer screen.) This decision completely determines the relationship between column number k and midpoint xm. There are 69 increments of size x_incr separating x_init and x_final. Therefore the increment size is

```
x_incr = (x_final - x_init) / 69.0;
```

and the midpoint for column k is

```
xm = x_init + k * x_incr;
```

This equation is the solution to the scaling problem along the *x* dimension of the graph. The divisor, in this case, 69.0, will change with the dimensions of the plot, but it will always be one less than the number of columns to be plotted.

We want to be able to compute a row number r along the *y* dimension, given the functional value yv = *f*(xm). This problem is a little tricky. Figure 8.12 shows a decision to make the midpoint of row 0 correspond to the maximum value for *f*(x), y_max, and to make the midpoint of row 19 correspond to the

**Figure 8.11
Scaling Problem
in the x
Dimension**

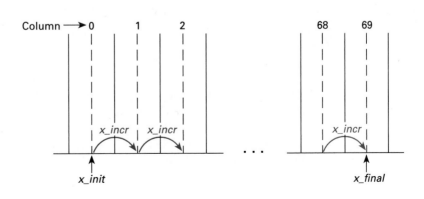

**Figure 8.12
Scaling Problem
in the *y*
Dimension**

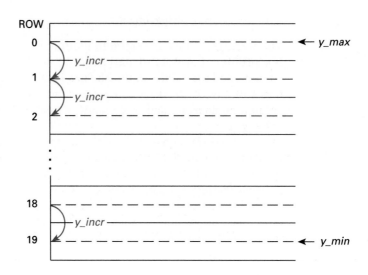

minimum value for *f*(*x*), `y_min`. This decision determines that the distance between successive midpoints is

`y_incr = (y_max - y_min) / 19.0;`

The row number `r` for a given *y* value `yv` depends on the distance between `yv` and `y_max` measured in terms of *y* increments, `y_incr`. This distance, `y_dist`, is computed as follows:

`y_dist = (y_max - yv) / y_incr;`

For example, `y_dist` is `1.0` means that `yv` is one *y* increment away from `y_max`, so `yv` belongs in row `1`. If `y_dist` is `19.0`, then `yv` is `y_min` and belongs in row `19`.

Adding `0.5` to round and using a cast to truncate the fractional part of the value, we can express the relationship between row `r` and `y_dist` as

`r = (int)(y_dist + 0.5);`

Table 8.1 shows the relationship between `y_dist` and `r` imposed by this formula. This table covers all possibilities, since `y_dist` cannot be less than `0.0` or greater than `19.0`.

Now that we have solved the scaling problem, we can write a program that plots mathematical functions.

Table 8.1   Relationship Between y_dist and r

y_dist	r
y_dist < 0.0	impossible
0.0 ≤ y_dist < 0.5	0
0.5 ≤ y_dist < 1.5	1
1.5 ≤ y_dist < 2.5	2
2.5 ≤ y_dist < 3.5	3
3.5 ≤ y_dist < 4.5	4
. . .	. . .
17.5 ≤ y_dist < 18.5	18
18.5 ≤ y_dist < 19.5	19
y_dist ≥ 19.5	impossible

A Function Plotting Program

In our program to plot a given function $f(x)$ on a specified interval [x_init, x_final], the user provides the values for x_init and x_final as input. The output consists of a discrete representation of the graph $y = f(x)$.

The main program variables include the two-dimensional array graph. The array graph is declared to be of element type char and is initialized to all blanks by nested for loops. The function get_data gets the initial and final x values: x_init and x_final. In addition, this function computes and returns the value for x_incr, which is needed by two of the other functions. Variable x_final is local to get_data, since none of the other functions need this value.

The function plot_points does the actual plotting of the function by initializing the graph array to all blanks and then marking the appropriate row of each column with an asterisk. This function is the heart of the plotting program. The function we are plotting is

$$f(x) = 4\left(x - \frac{1}{2}\right)^2$$

The function plotted must have no singularities on the interval [x_init, x_final].

There are two phases in the logic of plot_points. First, we must determine the maximum and minimum values for the function $f(x)$ at the 70 evaluation points xm given by

xm = x_init + k * x_incr for k = 0, 1, . . . , NCOL − 1

This phase involves 70 evaluations of the function $f(x)$. Because we will need these same 70 values during the second phase of our function, we store them in an array yv declared:

```
double yv[NCOL];
```

This storage of the 70 values is a matter of saving time by the expenditure of space (computer storage). Once the maximum and minimum values, y_max and y_min, are known, we can compute the increment value y_incr.

During the second phase of the function plot_points, we use the scaling formula derived earlier to convert each of the 70 functional values yv[k] to a unique row value r. The cell graph[r][k] is then marked with an asterisk.

The function print_graph displays the graph row by row along with appropriate labels. To get the x scale displayed at the bottom of the graph, the function uses array x_scale to store the x values that will be displayed. The complete program is shown in Fig. 8.13.

The output generated by the program shown in Fig. 8.13 is given in Fig. 8.14.

Figure 8.13   Plotting a Function f(x)

```
/*
 *  Plots the function
 *                             2
 *       f(x) = 4.0 * (x - 0.5)
 *  on an NROW row by NCOL column grid
 */
#include <stdio.h>
#include <math.h>

#define NROW  20           /* number of rows in grid    */
#define NCOL  70           /* number of columns in grid */

/*                            2
 * Function to plot 4(x - 0.5)
 */
double
f(double x)
{
     return (4.0 * pow(x - 0.5, 2.0));
}
```

(continued)

Figure 8.13   (continued)

```
/*
 *  Asks the user for the initial and final x values
 *  and computes the x increment
 */
void
get_data(double *x_initp,  /*  output - initial x value */
         double *x_incrp)  /*  output - x increment     */
{
    double x_final;

    /*  Gets initial and final x values from user    */
    printf("The function will be plotted between the values you enter.");
    printf("\nEnter initial X value> ");
    scanf("%lf", x_initp);
    printf("Enter final X value> ");
    scanf("%lf", &x_final);

    /*  Computes and returns x increment              */
    *x_incrp = (x_final - *x_initp) / (NCOL - 1);
}

/*
 *  Plots the function by marking appropriate cells of the array
 *  graph with asterisks.
 */
void
plot_points(char    graph[NROW][NCOL], /* output - grid representing plot */
            double  x_init,            /* input  - initial x value        */
            double  x_incr,            /* input  - x increment            */
            double *y_maxp,            /* output - largest y value        */
            double *y_incrp)           /* output - y increment            */
{
    double yv[NCOL], y_dist, ymin, ymax, xm;
    int    i, j, r, k;

    /*  Initializes graph grid to all blanks              */
    for  (i = 0;  i < NROW;  ++i)
        for  (j = 0;  j < NCOL;  ++j)
            graph[i][j] = ' ';
```

(continued)

Figure 8.13   (continued)

```
    /*  Phase ONE:  Determines maximum and minimum functional values    */
    ymax = f(x_init);
    ymin = ymax;
    yv[0] = ymax;

    for (k = 1;  k < NCOL; ++k) {
        xm = x_init + k * x_incr;
        yv[k] = f(xm);
        if (yv[k] > ymax)
            ymax = yv[k];
        if (yv[k] < ymin)
            ymin = yv[k];
    }

    /*  Returns y maximum and computes and returns y increment    */
    *y_maxp = ymax;
    *y_incrp = (ymax - ymin) / (NROW - 1);

    /*  Phase TWO:  Marks graph column by column using computed
                    function values                              */
    for (k = 0;  k < NCOL;  ++k) {
        y_dist = (ymax - yv[k]) / *y_incrp;
        r = (int)(y_dist + 0.5);
        graph[r][k] = '*';
    }
}

#define SCALE_INTERVAL 10  /* number of columns between x scale labels    */

/*
 *  Displays graph with labels
 */
void
print_graph(char graph[NROW][NCOL], /* input - grid of characters in plot    */
            double    x_init,       /* input - initial x value               */
            double    x_incr,       /* input - x increment                   */
            double    y_max,        /* input - largest y value               */
            double    y_incr)       /* input - y increment                   */
{
    int r, k, i;
    double x, y,
```

(continued)

Figure 8.13 (continued)

```
          x_scale[NCOL / SCALE_INTERVAL];/* labels for xscale at bottom
                                          of graph                    */

   /*  Displays graph row by row with labels to the left of the first row
       and every fifth row                                            */
   printf("\n    Y\n");
   printf("%6.1f    ", y_max);    /*  label and print initial row */
   for (k = 0;  k < NCOL; ++k)
       printf("%c", graph[0][k]);
   printf("\n");

   for  (r = 1;  r < NROW;  ++r) {  /* print rest of plot    */
       if ((r + 1) % 5 == 0) {        /* label every fifth row */
            y = y_max - r * y_incr;
            printf("%6.1f    ", y);
       } else {
            printf("          ");
       }
       for (k = 0;  k < NCOL; ++k)
           printf("%c", graph[r][k]);
       printf("\n");
   }

   /*  Computes the x scale values  */
   k = SCALE_INTERVAL;
   for  (i = 0;  i < NCOL / SCALE_INTERVAL;  ++i) {
       x = x_init + (k - 1) * x_incr;  /* x value for column k */
       x_scale[i] = x;
       k += SCALE_INTERVAL;
   }

   /*  Displays the x scale at the bottom of the graph  */
   printf("          |--------|");
   for  (i = 0; i < NCOL / SCALE_INTERVAL - 1;  ++i)
       printf("---------|");
   printf("\n    %6.1f", x_init);
   for  (i = 0;  i < NCOL / SCALE_INTERVAL;  ++i)
       printf("   %6.1f ", x_scale[i]);
   printf("\n                                    X-->\n");
}
```

(continued)

Figure 8.13 (continued)

```
int
main(void)
{
      double x_init, x_incr, y_max, y_incr;
      char graph[NROW][NCOL];

      /*  Gets interval starting point and increment,
          plots function, and displays results              */
      get_data(&x_init, &x_incr);
      plot_points(graph, x_init, x_incr, &y_max, &y_incr);
      print_graph(graph, x_init, x_incr, y_max, y_incr);

      return (0);
}
```

Figure 8.14 Sample Function Plot

```
The function will be plotted between the values you enter.
Enter initial X value> -10.0
Enter final X value> 10.0
   Y
 441.0    *
           *
            *
             *
             *
 348.2      *                                               *
             *                                               *
              *                                               *
             **                                              *
              *                                             *
 232.1         *                                          **
               *                                          *
              **                                         **
               **                                       *
                *                                      **
 116.1          **                                   **
                 **                                 **
                  ***                              **
                   ***                           ***
                    ****                       ****
   0.0               ***********
        |--------|---------|---------|---------|---------|---------|---------|
        -10.0    -7.4      -4.5      -1.6      1.3       4.2       7.1       10.0
                                     X-->
```

**EXERCISES FOR
SECTION 8.3**

Self-Check

1. What changes would you make in the function plotting program of Fig. 8.13 to cause it to plot the function

$$f(x) = x^2 - 4$$

on a 30×60 grid?

Programming

1. Convert function `plot_points` from Fig. 8.13 to a function that creates a 250×250 image where the character 1 represents a point on the graph of the function and all other points are represented by zeros.

8.4 VECTORS AND MATRICES

In many technical applications in science and engineering, arrays are used to represent mathematical objects called vectors and matrices. In this section, we will learn how vectors and matrices are represented in C and how to write C functions that perform basic operations on these objects.

Representing Vectors

A *vector* is a mathematical object consisting of a sequence of numbers (the components of the vector). A vector is said to be of dimension n if it consists of n components. Unfortunately, the use of the word "dimension" in C is not consistent with the standard mathematical terminology for vectors. The C array **x** in Fig. 8.15(a) is one-dimensional (in C terms), whereas the vector it represents, shown in Fig. 8.15(b), is three-dimensional (in mathematical terms). An n-

**Figure 8.15
C Representa-
tion of a Vector:
C array x;
Vector X**

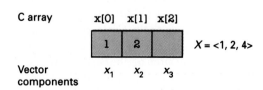

dimensional vector is represented in C as a one-dimensional array of size n. You will also notice some disparity between the standard notation for a vector component and the C notation. Vector X's third component (the 4) is represented in mathematics texts as x_3. In C, however, it will be called $x[2]$, since C array subscripts always start with 0.

The Scalar Product

Two vectors with the same number of components can be multiplied together, forming the scalar (dot or inner) product, by computing the sum of the products of corresponding components. Hence, if X = <1, 2, 4> and W = <2, 3, 1>, their scalar product is

$$X \bullet W = <1, 2, 4> \bullet <2, 3, 1> = 1 * 2 + 2 * 3 + 4 * 1 = 12$$

In general, if X = $<x_1, x_2, \ldots, x_n>$ and W = $<w_1, w_2, \ldots, w_n>$ are two vectors of dimension n, their scalar product is

$$\sum_{k=1}^{n} x_k * w_k$$

where x_k and w_k denote the kth components of the vectors X and W, respectively.

Coding the computation of the scalar product of two n-dimensional vectors X and W is straightforward. A counting `for` loop is required to traverse the vectors component by component. A variable `sum_prod` is required to accumulate the sum. The C code for this calculation is shown next:

```
sum_prod = 0;
for  (k = 0;  k < n;  ++k)
    sum_prod += x[k] * w[k];
```

Many of the functions we will develop in the rest of this chapter will require us to calculate a sum, as we did in computing the scalar product. Translating from summation notation to C is a fairly mechanical process. Figure 8.16 shows in some detail the correspondence between the mathematical expression of the scalar product and its implementation in C. When the summation expression involves vector components, some adjustment of the counter variable is required to accommodate C's use of arrays with an initial

**Figure 8.16
Summation
Notation and
for Loop
Parameters**

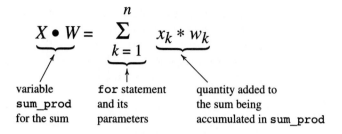

$$X \bullet W = \sum_{k=1}^{n} x_k * w_k$$

variable
sum_prod
for the sum

for statement
and its
parameters

quantity added to
the sum being
accumulated in **sum_prod**

subscript of 0. Although a literal translation of the summation symbol in Fig. 8.16 would be

```
for (k = 1; k <= n; ++k)
```

since vector components 1 through *n* are represented by array elements 0 through n−1, we must modify our **for** loop header slightly, giving us the new header

```
for (k = 0; k < n; ++k)
```

Representing Matrices

A *matrix* is a mathematical object that consists of a rectangular arrangement of numbers called the *elements* of the matrix. An $m \times n$ matrix consists of *m* rows and *n* columns. Each row is an *n*-dimensional vector, and each column is an *m*-dimensional vector. The element in the *i*th row and *j*th column is denoted by a_{ij}, which is **a[i][j]** in C (assuming use of zero as the starting point for **i** and **j** in C). Thus an $m \times n$ matrix can be implemented in C as a two-dimensional array with *m* rows and *n* columns.

Figure 8.17(a) shows an $m \times n$ (in this case 4×3) matrix, and Fig. 8.17(b) shows its implementation as a two-dimensional array.

Multiplying a Matrix by a Vector

If *A* is an $m \times n$ matrix and *X* is an *n*-dimensional vector, then we can form the product of *A* and *X*, denoted by $A * X$, yielding an *m*-dimensional vector *V*. A

**Figure 8.17
(a) Four × Three
Matrix and (b)
Its Implemen-
tation as a
Two-Dimen-
sional Array**

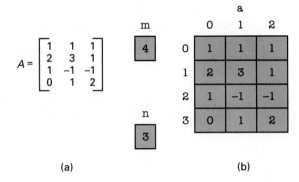

(a)   (b)

matter with m rows and n columns can be multiplied on the right only by a
vector of dimension n. If A is an $m \times n$ matrix and W is an m-dimensional vector,
then we can form the product W and A, denoted by $W * A$, yielding an n-dimen-
sional vector Z. A matrix with m rows and n columns can be multiplied on the
left only by a vector of dimension m. Figure 8.18(a) shows the multiplication of
A, a 4×3 matrix, on the right, and Fig. 8.18(b) shows the multiplication on the
left. We will restrict our detailed discussion to Fig. 8.18(a).

How were the components of the result vector in Fig. 8.18(a) computed?
The ith component of V, $v[i]$, is the scalar product of the ith row of the matrix
A and the vector X. Keep in mind that with regard to C, we begin counting
with zero. For example, $v[1]$ (the *second* component of vector V) is the scalar
product of row 1 (the *second* row) of A (considered as a vector) and the vector
X. These vectors are in color in Fig. 8.18(a). The relevant computation is

v[1] = <2, 3, 1> · <1, 2, 2> = 2 * 1 + 3 * 2 + 1 * 2 = 10

Figure 8.18   Multiplying a Matrix by a Vector

$$
\begin{array}{ccccc}
A & * & X & = & V \\
\begin{bmatrix} 1 & 1 & 1 \\ 2 & 3 & 1 \\ 1 & -1 & -1 \\ 0 & 1 & 2 \end{bmatrix} & * & \begin{bmatrix} 1 \\ 2 \\ 2 \end{bmatrix} & = & \begin{bmatrix} 5 \\ 10 \\ -3 \\ 6 \end{bmatrix}
\end{array}
\qquad
\begin{array}{ccccccc}
W & * & A & = & Z \\
\begin{bmatrix} 2 & 0 & 1 & -1 \end{bmatrix} & * & \begin{bmatrix} 1 & 1 & 1 \\ 2 & 3 & 1 \\ 1 & -1 & -1 \\ 0 & 1 & 2 \end{bmatrix} & = & \begin{bmatrix} 3 & 0 & -1 \end{bmatrix}
\end{array}
$$

(a) Multiplication on the right   (b) Multiplication on the left

The mathematical formula for computing v_i in the general case of the multiplication of an $m \times n$ matrix A and an n-dimensional vector X is

$$v_i = \sum_{k=1}^{n} a_{ik} * x_k$$

Translating mathematical summation notation into C with the appropriate adjustments for zero-based array subscripts, we get the code for computing v_i:

```
v[i] = 0;
for  (k = 0;  k < n;  ++k)
     v[i] += a[i][k] * x[k];
```

Once we have a description of how to compute a typical element of a vector, it is a simple matter to code the computation of the entire vector. All we need to do is embed the computation of the typical element v[i] in a counting for loop where i is the loop index. The C function mat_vec_prod in Fig. 8.19 uses this idea to compute the product of an $m \times n$ matrix A and an n-dimensional vector X. The result is an m-dimensional vector V. As is typical in C functions that compute an array result, mat_vec_prod expects the function that calls it to provide space in which to store this vector. As always, we are using capital letters for the row and column dimensions to imply that they are defined as constant macros. Although our function could allow dimension m (the number of rows) to vary, since the number of columns must be a constant, we have elected to use constants for both dimensions.

Figure 8.19   Function mat_vec_prod That Computes the Product of a Matrix and a Vector

```
/*
 *  Computes the product of M-by-N matrix a and the N-dimensional vector x.
 *  The result is stored in the output parameter v, an M-dimensional vector.
 */
void
mat_vec_prod(double v[],      /* output - M-dimensional product vector */
             double a[M][N],  /* input  - M-by-N matrix                */
             double x[])      /* input  - N-dimensional vector         */
{
     int i, k;
```

(continued)

Figure 8.19   (continued)

```
for  (i = 0;  i < M;  ++i) {
    v[i] = 0;

    for  (k = 0;  k < N;  ++k) {
        v[i] += a[i][k] * x[k];
    }

}
}
```

Matrix Multiplication

Multiplying a matrix by a vector is just a special case of multiplying a matrix by a matrix, since an n-dimensional vector can be viewed as either a matrix with n rows and 1 column or a matrix with 1 row and n columns. We will now develop a C function that will multiply two matrices, returning the product matrix.

Two matrices A and B can be multiplied together, yielding a new matrix, $C = A * B$, if the number of columns in A is equal to the number of rows in B. In this case, the matrices A and B are said to be "conformable" for multiplication. If A is an $m \times n$ matrix and B is $n \times p$, then the product matrix C will be $m \times p$. This result is consistent with our earlier discussion of multiplying a matrix ($m \times n$) by a vector ($n \times 1$) yielding a new vector ($m \times 1$).

In analyzing the computation of the product of two matrices, we first consider the computation of a typical element. For example, a typical element in the product matrix C is the element in the ith row and jth column. This element is denoted by c[i][j]. Once we know how to compute c[i][j], it is a trivial matter to compute the rest of the matrix C. All we have to do is embed the computation of c[i][j] in an appropriate looping mechanism, which allows i and j to take on all relevant values:

```
for  (i = 0;  i < m;  ++i) {
    for  (j = 0;  j < p;  ++j) {
        ... Compute c[i][j] ...
    }
}
```

Let us now describe the computation of that typical element, c[i][j], of the product matrix, $C = A * B$. Element c[i][j] is just the scalar product of the ith row of A and the jth column of B. Figure 8.20 shows the computation of C when the *square* matrices A and B are multiplied together. (A matrix is square if it has the same number of rows and columns.) For example, in computing the

	A			$*$		B		$=$		C	

$$\begin{bmatrix} 1 & 1 & 1 \\ 2 & 3 & 1 \\ 1 & -1 & -1 \end{bmatrix} \quad \begin{bmatrix} 2 & 0 & 1 \\ 1 & -1 & 0 \\ 3 & 1 & -1 \end{bmatrix} \quad \begin{bmatrix} 6 & 0 & 0 \\ 10 & -2 & 1 \\ -2 & 0 & 2 \end{bmatrix}$$

Figure 8.20
Multiplying
Matrix *A* by
Matrix *B*

brown element of *C* in Fig. 8.20, the brown row of *A* (considered as a vector) is multiplied by the brown column of B (considered as a vector).

The C code that follows accomplishes this vector multiplication of the *i*th row of *A* and the *j*th column of *B* to compute c[i][j]:

```
c[i][j] = 0;
for  (k = 0;  k < n;  ++k)
     c[i][j] += a[i][k] * b[k][j];
```

Embedding the computation just shown into the appropriate nested for loop structure yields the computation of the entire product matrix. This computation is done in the function mat_prod of Fig. 8.21.

Figure 8.21   Function mat_prod to Multiply Two Matrices

```
/*
 *  Multiplies matrices A and B yielding product matrix C
 */
void
mat_prod(double c[M][P],   /* output - M by P product matrix     */
         double a[M][N],   /* input  - M by N matrix             */
         double b[N][P])   /* input  - N by P matrix             */
{
     int i, j, k;

     for  (i = 0;  i < M;  ++i) {
          for  (j = 0;  j < P;  ++j) {
               c[i][j] = 0;

               for  (k = 0;  k < N;  ++k)
                    c[i][j] += a[i][k] * b[k][j];
          }

     }
}
```

The += operator is used in Fig. 8.21 not only because it is concise but also because it is efficient. An ANSI C implementation must ensure that in evaluating the statement

```
c[i][j] += a[i][k] * b[k][j];
```

the computation of `c[i][j]`'s memory address occurs only once. In contrast, the computation could occur twice for the statement

```
c[i][j] = c[i][j] + a[i][k] * b[k][j];
```

Self-Check

1. Could function `mat_vec_prod` in Fig. 8.19 accomplish its purpose if it used variable `i` as the loop counter for both of its loops?

Programming

1. Define a function `scalar_times_mat` that creates a new matrix by multiplying every element of its $M \times N$ matrix parameter by a scalar value.

8.5 SOLVING SYSTEMS OF LINEAR EQUATIONS

In Section 8.4, we saw that if we multiplied a matrix

$$A = \begin{bmatrix} 1 & 1 & 1 \\ 2 & 3 & 1 \\ 1 & -1 & -1 \end{bmatrix}$$

by a vector

$$X = \begin{bmatrix} 1 \\ 2 \\ 1 \end{bmatrix}$$

on the right, then the result is a vector

$$Y = \begin{bmatrix} 4 \\ 9 \\ -2 \end{bmatrix}$$

Now, let us consider another sort of problem. Suppose we know the matrix A and the vector Y, but we don't know the vector X. We want to know which vector X can be multiplied on the left by matrix A to produce the vector Y. The problem is to find the three unknowns, x_1, x_2, and x_3, in the equation:

$$
\begin{array}{ccc}
A & * & X & = & Y
\end{array}
$$

$$
\begin{bmatrix}
1 & 1 & 1 \\
2 & 3 & 1 \\
1 & -1 & -1
\end{bmatrix}
*
\begin{bmatrix}
x_1 \\
x_2 \\
x_3
\end{bmatrix}
=
\begin{bmatrix}
4 \\
9 \\
-2
\end{bmatrix}
$$

To find the values of x_1, x_2, and x_3, we must solve a system of three linear equations in three unknowns. We illustrate this problem by showing how each component of the vector Y is computed in terms of the matrix A and the vector of unknowns X. For example, y_1 is the scalar product of the first row of the matrix A and the vector X, as in

$$
y_1 = a_{1,1} * x_1 + a_{1,2} * x_2 + a_{1,3} * x_3 = 4
$$

Replacing the matrix elements a_{ij} with their numerical values, we get the entire system of three linear equations in three unknowns, x_1, x_2, and x_3:

$$
\begin{array}{rcrcrcr}
x_1 & + & x_2 & + & x_3 & = & 4 \\
2x_1 & + & 3x_2 & + & x_3 & = & 9 \\
x_1 & - & x_2 & - & x_3 & = & -2
\end{array}
$$

Such a system can be used to model many kinds of problems. For example, suppose we have a spacecraft with three thrusters pointing in different directions and we want to calibrate these thrusters. We can determine from tracking data the actual acceleration of the spacecraft, and we know that

force = mass × acceleration

Further, we know that if we have a three-dimensional system, the force equation holds true for each of three perpendicular components. Therefore we can determine the magnitude of the forces that have caused the spacecraft to accelerate and then derive the performance of each individual thruster.

Gaussian elimination can be used to solve problems like this one. We will now demonstrate the technique using a simple numerical example.

Gaussian Elimination

In Gaussian elimination, we attempt to reduce the original system of n linear equations to triangular form (also called upper triangular form). In *triangular form*, the coefficients below the diagonal in the matrix of coefficients are all 0. The most useful triangular form for Gaussian elimination is one in which the rows are scaled so that the diagonal elements are all 1. Figure 8.22 shows the

Figure 8.22
Original System of
Equations in Scaled
Triangular Form

$$\begin{bmatrix} 1 & 1 & 1 \\ 0 & 1 & -1 \\ 0 & 0 & 1 \end{bmatrix} * \begin{bmatrix} x_1 \\ x_2 \\ x_3 \end{bmatrix} = \begin{bmatrix} 4 \\ 1 \\ 1 \end{bmatrix}$$

original system of equations in scaled triangular form. The coefficients above the diagonal (in color) and the components of the constant vector Y no longer have their original values.

The three equations that correspond to Fig. 8.22 are shown here:

$$\begin{aligned} x_1 + x_2 + x_3 &= 4 \\ x_2 - x_3 &= 1 \\ x_3 &= 1 \end{aligned}$$

This system can easily be solved for x_1, x_2, and x_3 by solving the last equation for x_3 (i.e., x_3 is 1), substituting this value in the next to last equation and solving for x_2 (i.e., x_2 is 2), and substituting these values in the first equation and solving for x_1 (i.e., x_1 is 1). This process is called *back substitution*. The algorithm for Gaussian elimination follows.

Algorithm for Gaussian Elimination

1. Transform the original system into scaled triangular form.
2. Solve for the x_i by back substitution.

The Augmented Matrix

Before we can proceed, we must decide on appropriate data structures for representing a system of n linear equations in n unknowns. One widely used method of representation for such systems is the *augmented matrix*. This particular representation allows for concise coding of both triangularization and back substitution.

Figure 8.23 shows the form of an augmented matrix for a system of n linear equations in n unknowns. The augmented matrix will be represented by a two-dimensional array, *Aug*. Note that the augmented matrix has n rows and $n + 1$ columns. The last column of the augmented matrix (shown in color) contains the

Figure 8.23
Original
Augmented
Matrix *Aug*

$$\begin{bmatrix} a_{1,1} & a_{1,2} & a_{1,3} & y_1 \\ a_{2,1} & a_{2,2} & a_{2,3} & y_2 \\ a_{3,1} & a_{3,2} & a_{3,3} & y_3 \end{bmatrix} \qquad \begin{bmatrix} 1 & 1 & 1 & 4 \\ 2 & 3 & 1 & 9 \\ 1 & -1 & -1 & -2 \end{bmatrix}$$

(a) General form   (b) Our example

**Figure 8.24
Triangularized
and Scaled
Augmented
Matrix**

$$\begin{bmatrix} 1 & a_{1,2}' & a_{1,3}' & y_1' \\ 0 & 1 & a_{2,3}' & y_2' \\ 0 & 0 & 1 & y_3' \end{bmatrix} \qquad \begin{bmatrix} 1 & 1 & 1 & 4 \\ 0 & 1 & -1 & 1 \\ 0 & 0 & 1 & 1 \end{bmatrix}$$

(a) General form   (b) Our example

constant vector Y (e.g., $aug_{1,4}$ is y_1). The matrix of coefficients A is stored in the rest of the columns of the augmented matrix (e.g., $aug_{1,1}$ is $a_{1,1}$). Note that the vector of unknowns is nowhere to be seen. When a system of linear equations is represented as an augmented matrix, the unknowns are implicit.

Our first goal is to scale and triangularize the coefficients in the augmented matrix—that is, to reduce the matrix to a form in which $aug_{1,1}$, $aug_{2,2}$, and $aug_{3,3}$ are 1 and $aug_{2,1}$, $aug_{3,1}$, and $aug_{3,2}$ are zero, as shown in Fig. 8.24. All other values, shown in color in Fig. 8.24(a), are written as symbols such as a_{ij}' and y_i'. The primes are used to emphasize that these values are not the same as the ones in the original system of equations.

Triangularizing and Scaling the Augmented Matrix

Let us now turn our attention to the process of triangularization and scaling, which transforms the original system of equations into a new system in scaled upper triangular form. The rules of linear algebra guarantee that this new system will have the same solution as the original system if we confine ourselves to the following operations on the augmented matrix Aug:

1. Multiply any row of Aug by a nonzero number.
2. Add to any row of Aug a multiple of any other row.
3. Swap any two rows.

If the system has a unique solution, we can get the system into the desired form by using these three operations. (If our system does not have a unique solution, our algorithm will detect this.)

We triangularize the augmented matrix by systematically moving down the diagonal, starting at $aug_{1,1}$. When we are working with a particular diagonal element, we call that element the *pivot*. When $aug_{p,p}$ is the pivot, we have two goals:

• Scale the pivot row, so that the pivot will take the desired value 1.
• Set all coefficients in the column below the pivot to zero—that is, give the elements $aug_{p+1,p}$, $aug_{p+2,p}$, . . . , $aug_{n,p}$ the value 0.

The first goal is achieved by multiplying the pivot row (e.g., row p) by an appropriate constant (i.e., $1/aug_{p,p}$); this is an application of operation 1. The second goal is achieved by applying operation 2 to the rows beneath the pivot row.

Experts recommend that to minimize computational round-off errors during the triangularization process, you should always place the largest possible coefficient (in absolute value) in the pivoting position. When you work with the pth pivot, you should examine all the coefficients in the column beneath the pivot to find the coefficient that has the largest absolute value. The pivot row and the row containing that largest coefficient should be swapped. In no way is the solution of the system of equations changed, because swapping rows is one of the three permissible operations (operation 3). The process of switching the current row with the one containing the maximum pivot is called *pivoting*.

What if we encounter a maximum pivot element whose value is zero? This can happen only when all values beneath the pivot element are also zero. If a nonzero value cannot be found in the column beneath the pivot, the given system of equations does not have a unique solution.

The operations just discussed are summarized in the algorithm that follows. The local variable `ok` indicates whether the system of equations has a solution.

Local Variables
```
int p    /* the current row */
int ok   /* a flag indicating whether the system has a
            unique solution */
```

Algorithm for Function gauss

1. Initially assume the system has a unique solution.
2. Initialize p to the subscript of the initial row.
3. Repeat as long as there is a solution possible and p < subscript of final row
    4. Pivot using the maximum pivot strategy.
    5. if a solution is still possible
        6. Scale the pivot row.
        7. Eliminate the coefficients beneath the pivot.
    8. Go on to the next row (++p)
9. if last coefficient is zero
    10. No unique solution.
   else if there is a solution
    11. Scale last row.

Function `gauss` is shown in Fig. 8.25. In the statements that perform the scaling of the pivot row (Step 6), first the reciprocal of the pivot value is saved. Then, the pivot element is set to 1, and the elements to the right of the pivot (in columns p + 1 through N) are multiplied by the pivot's reciprocal. The row elements to the left of the pivot element require no change, because they are all zeros. The test in Step 9 detects the situation where scaling the last row will cause division by zero. In Step 11, only the elements in the last two columns need to be changed.

Figure 8.25   Function gauss

```
#define FALSE 0
#define TRUE  1
#define N     3

/*
 *  Triangularizes the augmented matrix aug.  If no unique solution exists,
 *  sends back FALSE through sol_existsp
 */
void
gauss(double aug[N][N+1], /* input/output - augmented matrix representing
                             system of N equations                         */
      int    *sol_existsp) /* output - flag indicating whether system has a
                              unique solution                              */
{
      int j, k, p;
      double piv_recip,  /*  reciprocal of pivot  */
             xmult;

      /*  System is assumed nonsingular;  moves down the diagonal          */
      *sol_existsp = TRUE;

      for  (p = 0;  *sol_existsp && p < (N - 1);  ++p) {

           /*  Pivots with respect to the pth row and the pth column  */
           pivot(aug, p, sol_existsp);
           if (*sol_existsp) {
                 /*  Scales pivot row  */
                 piv_recip = 1.0 / aug[p][p];
                 aug[p][p] = 1.0;
                 for  (k = p + 1;  k < N + 1;  ++k)
                     aug[p][k] *= piv_recip;

                 /*  Eliminates coefficients beneath pivot  */
                 for  (j = p + 1;  j < N;  ++j) {
                     xmult = -aug[j][p];
                     aug[j][p] = 0;
                     for  (k = p + 1;  k < N + 1;  ++k)
                         aug[j][k] += xmult * aug[p][k];
                 }
           }
      }
}
```

(continued)

Figure 8.25 (continued)

```
    /*  If last coefficient is zero, there is no unique solution */
    if (aug[N-1][N-1] == 0) {
          *sol_existsp = FALSE;
    } else if (*sol_existsp) {    /* Scales last row */
          piv_recip = 1.0 / aug[N-1][N-1];
          aug[N-1][N-1] = 1.0;
          aug[N-1][N] *= piv_recip;
    }
}
```

In Step 7, each row j beneath the pivot ($j = p+1, p+2, \ldots, N-1$) is modified so that the element in $aug[j][p]$ becomes zero. This modification is done by multiplying the pivot row (row p) by $-aug[j][p]$ (saved in $xmult$) and then adding the pivot row to row j.

Step 4 of $gauss$ (the pivot step) is performed by function $pivot$. The data requirements and algorithm for $pivot$ follow; the function shown in Fig. 8.26 assumes access to function $fabs$ from the math library.

Data Requirements

Input Parameters
```
int p                  /* the current row                */
```

Input/Output Parameter
```
double aug[N][N+1]   /* augmented matrix               */
```

Output Parameter
```
int    piv_foundp  /* flag indicating whether a
                      nonzero pivot was found      */
```

Local Variables
```
double xmax       /* largest absolute value in column p*/
int    max_row  /* row containing the maximum value   */
```

Algorithm for pivot

1. Starting at row p, find the row, max_row, whose element in column p has the largest absolute value.

2. if the largest absolute value is zero
   3. Set `piv_foundp` to false.
else if `max_row` is not row p
   4. Swap rows p and `max_row`.

Figure 8.26   **Function pivot**

```
/*
 *  Performs pivoting with respect to the pth row and the pth column
 *  If no nonzero pivot can be found, FALSE is sent back through piv_foundp
 */
void
pivot(double aug[N][N+1],  /* input/output - augmented matrix            */
      int     p,           /* input        - current row                */
      int     *piv_foundp) /* output       - whether or not nonzero pivot
                                             found                       */
{
      double xmax, xtemp;
      int j, k, max_row;

      /* Finds maximum pivot                                             */
      xmax = fabs(aug[p][p]);
      max_row = p;
      for  (j = p+1;  j < N;  ++j) {
          if (fabs(aug[j][p]) > xmax) {
                xmax = fabs(aug[j][p]);
                max_row = j;
          }
      }

      /* Swaps rows if nonzero pivot was found                          */
      if (xmax == 0) {
            *piv_foundp = FALSE;
      } else {
            *piv_foundp = TRUE;
            if (max_row != p) {   /* swap rows */
                  for  (k = p;  k < N+1;  ++k) {
                        xtemp = aug[p][k];
```

(continued)

Figure 8.26   (continued)

```
                        aug[p][k] = aug[max_row][k];
                        aug[max_row][k] = xtemp;
                  }
            }
      }
}
```

Back Substitution

We can now derive the C code for back substitution in terms of the augmented matrix `aug`. We will also need an array `x` to represent the vector of unknowns. The scaled and triangularized augmented matrix for our example system, shown in Fig. 8.24(b), is rewritten here on the left with the corresponding storage locations in array `aug` shown on the right (e.g., the contents of `aug[0][3]` is `4`).

$$\begin{bmatrix} 1 & 1 & 1 & 4 \\ 0 & 1 & -1 & 1 \\ 0 & 0 & 1 & 1 \end{bmatrix} \quad \begin{bmatrix} \text{aug}[0][0] & \text{aug}[0][1] & \text{aug}[0][2] & \text{aug}[0][3] \\ \text{aug}[1][0] & \text{aug}[1][1] & \text{aug}[1][2] & \text{aug}[1][3] \\ \text{aug}[2][0] & \text{aug}[2][1] & \text{aug}[2][2] & \text{aug}[2][3] \end{bmatrix}$$

The part of the matrix that is used in back substitution is shown in color. Applying the principle of back substitution to the diagram just shown, we can observe from the last row that

```
x[2] = aug[2][3] = 1
```

Next, we see from row number 1 that

```
x[1] = aug[1][3] - (aug[1][2] * x[2]))  = 1 - (-1 * 1) = 2
```

Finally, we see from row 0 that

```
x[0] = aug[0][3] - (aug[0][1] * x[1] + aug[0][2] * x[2])
       = 4 - (1 * 2 + 1 * 1) = 4 - (3) = 1
```

These observations lead to the following algorithm for back substitution.

Algorithm for Back Substitution Using the Revised Augmented Matrix (with Zero-Based Subscripts)

1. Set the last element of the vector of unknowns to be the last element of the augmented matrix.
2. For each $i = N-2, \ldots, 1, 0$ in turn, compute

$$x[i] = aug[i][N] - \sum_{j=i+1}^{N-1} aug[i][j] * x[j]$$

This algorithm is implemented as function **back_sub** shown in Fig. 8.27.

Figure 8.28 shows a main function that tests functions **gauss** and **back_sub** on one system of linear equations. The declaration of the augmented matrix **aug** initializes it to the matrix of Fig. 8.23; the sample run displays the solution vector **x**.

Figure 8.27   Function back_sub

```
/*
 *  Performs back substitution to compute a solution vector to a system of
 *  linear equations represented by the augmented matrix aug. Assumes that
 *  the coefficient portion of the augmented matrix has been triangularized,
 *  and its diagonal values are all 1.
 */
void
back_sub(double aug[N][N+1],    /* input -  scaled, triangularized
                                               augmented matrix            */
         double x[N])            /* output - solution vector                */
{
      double sum;
      int    i, j;

      x[N - 1] = aug[N - 1][N];
      for  (i = N - 2;  i >= 0;  --i) {
          sum = 0;
          for  (j = i + 1;  j < N;  ++j)
              sum += aug[i][j] * x[j];
          x[i] = aug[i][N] - sum;
      }
}
```

Figure 8.28   Function main for Gaussian Elimination Program

```
/*
 * Solves a system of linear equations using Gaussian elimination and back
 * substitution
 */
#define N 3   /*  size of coefficient matrix; augmented matrix is N by N+1   */

int
main(void)
{
      double aug[N][N+1] = {{ 1.0,   1.0,   1.0,   4.0},   /* augmented matrix */
                            { 2.0,   3.0,   1.0,   9.0},
                            { 1.0,  -1.0,  -1.0,  -2.0}},
             x[N];          /* solution vector */
      int    sol_exists; /* flag indicating whether or not a solution can be
                            found                                            */

      /* Calls gauss to scale and triangularize coefficient matrix within
         aug                                                                 */
      gauss(aug, &sol_exists);

      /* Finds and displays solution if one exists                          */
      if (sol_exists) {
            back_sub(aug, x);
            printf("The values of x are: %10.2f%10.2f%10.2f\n", x[0], x[1],
                   x[2]);
      } else {
            printf("No unique solution\n");
      }
      return (0);
}

The values of x are:      1.00      2.00      1.00
```

Ill-Conditioned Systems

Unfortunately, not every system of *n* equations in *n* unknowns has a unique solution. A system may have no solution or it may have an infinite number of solutions. The triangularization process will fail if the given system does not have a unique solution. A more serious danger is that our system of equations may be *ill conditioned*. In the two-dimensional case (*n* is 2), this occurs when the two lines whose intersection we are trying to find are nearly parallel.

Another problem that arises in practice is that computational round-off errors can be significant when *n* is large. The larger *n* is, the larger the number of multiplication operations required to triangularize the matrix. In large systems, these accumulating round-off errors may make the results obtained from Gaussian elimination useless.

**EXERCISES FOR
SECTION 8.5**

Self-Check

1. Give examples of augmented matrices representing

   a. a system that has no solution.
   b. a system that has many solutions.

   Identify how the Gaussian elimination program in Figs. 8.25–8.28 would detect the absence of a unique solution in each case.

Programming

1. Revise function `gauss` from Fig. 8.25 so that it eliminates nonzero coefficients *above* as well as below the pivot. This change would eliminate the need for function `back_sub`.

8.6 COMMON PROGRAMMING ERRORS

It is important to remember to use constants for each dimension's size when declaring multidimensional arrays. Although you can omit the first dimension when declaring an array parameter of a function, you must supply all other dimensions as constants. For a matrix argument m to have its elements correctly accessed using a reference such as m[i][j], its declared dimensions must match exactly those specified for the corresponding function parameter.

Avoiding subscript-range errors is just as important when manipulating multidimensional arrays as when using one-dimensional arrays. Since array access often involves nested counting loops, it is easy to make out-of-range references.

If you are working on a computer system with very limited memory, you may find that some correct C programs generate run-time error messages indicating an access violation. The use of multidimensional arrays as local variables can cause a program to require large amounts of memory for function data areas. To be able to run programs using large arrays, you may need to tell your operating system that an increased stack size is necessary.

CHAPTER REVIEW

In this chapter, we introduced the multidimensional array data structure. We discussed this data structure's declaration and use both as a local variable and as a function parameter. We studied numerous applications of multidimensional arrays including modeling land areas for earthquake studies and cellular telephone systems, plotting functions on a two-dimensional grid, performing matrix operations, and using Gaussian elimination to solve systems of linear equations.

Table 8.2 summarizes the declaration and manipulation of arrays as covered in this chapter.

Table 8.2   Using Multidimensional Arrays in C Programs

Example	Effect
Array Declarations	
Local Variables	
`int matrix[2][3];` `double cube[4][4][10];`	Allocates storage for six type `int` items (2 rows of 3 columns) in two-dimensional array `matrix` (`matrix[0][0]`, `matrix[0][1]`, `matrix[0][2]`, `matrix[1][0]`, `matrix[1][1]`, `matrix[1][2]`). Also allocates 160 ($4 \times 4 \times 10$) type `double` memory cells in three-dimensional array `cube`.
Initialization	
`int id[2][2] =` `   { {1, 0}, {0, 1} };`	Allocates four locations for the 2×2 matrix `id`, initializing the storage so `id[0][0]` = 1, `id[0][1]` = 0, `id[1][0]` = 0, `id[1][1]` = 1.
Function Parameter	

`void`
`mod_mat(double cb[][4][10],`
`        int     nrows)`
	States that function `mod_mat` uses `cb` to reference the three-dimension array passed as the function's first argument.

(continued)

Table 8.2   (continued)

Example	Effect
Array Reference	

```
for  (i = 0;  i < 2;  ++i) {
    for  (j = 0;  j < 3;  ++j)
        printf("%6d", matrix[i][j]);
    printf("\n");
}
```

Displays contents of `matrix` in 2 rows with 3 columns.

QUICK-CHECK EXERCISES

1. If m is a 5 × 5 integer matrix, what is displayed by this loop?

   ```
   for  (i = 0;  i < 5;  ++i)
       printf("%8d", m[2][i]);
   ```

   What is displayed by this loop?

   ```
   for  (i = 0;  i < 5;  ++i)
       printf("%8d", m[i][4]);
   ```

2. Which of the arrays shown would be valid actual arguments to pass to a function whose prototype was

   ```
   int
   fun(double arr[][3][10])    ?
   ```

   ```
   double m[6][3][10];
   int n[4][3][10];
   double z[8][2][11];
   double q[20][3][10];
   ```

3. How many elements are in each of the arrays declared in Exercise 2?
4. Declare and initialize C arrays to represent the vector <4, 12, 19> and the matrix

$$\begin{bmatrix} 4.1 & 8.3 \\ 7.9 & 6.2 \end{bmatrix}$$

5. A matrix composed of the coefficients of a system of linear equations and of the vector of constants representing the right-hand side of the system is called a(n) _____ _____ .

ANSWERS TO QUICK-CHECK EXERCISES

1. The middle row of m; the last column of m
2. Arrays m and q
3. m—180 elements; n—120 elements; z—176 elements; q—600 elements

4.
```
int vect[3] = {4, 12, 19};
double mat[2][2] = {{4.1, 8.3}, {7.9, 6.2}};
```

5. augmented matrix

REVIEW QUESTIONS

1. Identify an error in this C program fragment:

```
int    i, j;
double grid[5][3];

for (i = 0;  i < 5;  ++i)
    for (j = 0;  j < 3;  ++j)
        printf("%.3f\n", grid[j][i]);
```

How would you correct the error?

2. If sq is a C array representing the matrix

$$\begin{bmatrix} 4 & 5 & 18 \\ 2 & 4 & 9 \\ 8 & 4 & 12 \end{bmatrix}$$

what is displayed by this code fragment?

```
for (i = 0;  i < 3;  ++i)
    printf("%8d", sq[i][i]);
```

3. Explain the scaling problem.

4. Write the augmented matrix that corresponds to the following system of equations:

$$2x_1 + x_2 - 4x_3 = -4$$
$$x_1 - 4x_2 + x_3 = -5$$
$$-x_1 + 3x_2 - 2x_3 = 1$$

5. Scale and triangularize the augmented matrix in Question 4. Then use back substitution to solve the system.
6. Write a program segment to display the sum of the values in each row of a 5×3 type `double` array named `table`. How many row sums will be displayed?
7. Answer Question 6 for the column sums.

PROGRAMMING PROJECTS

1. You have been asked to write one part of a detector analysis software package for a telescope. Your program takes as input the brightness of each point in a two-dimensional array representing an image of the sky. Use a 10×10 integer array for this image. Find and display the x and y coordinates and the value of the brightest pixel. If more than one pixel has this highest value, information for all highest-valued pixels should be displayed.
2. A robot that can rotate on a pedestal has a sensor that measures Cartesian coordinates (x',y') relative to the robot itself. It is desired, however, to know object coordinates (x,y) relative to the fixed coordinate system in which the robot rotates. If the robot is rotated counterclockwise through the angle θ relative to the fixed system,

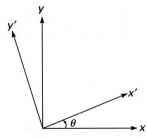

then coordinates in the fixed system are related to the robot's coordinate system by the following transformation:

$$\begin{bmatrix} x \\ y \end{bmatrix} = M \begin{bmatrix} x' \\ y' \end{bmatrix}$$

where *M* is the matrix

$$M = \begin{bmatrix} \cos\theta & -\sin\theta \\ \sin\theta & \cos\theta \end{bmatrix}$$

Write a program that takes positions in the (x',y') system (as measured by the sensor) and reports the equivalent coordinates in the fixed (x,y) coordinate system for user-input values of θ between 0 and π radians.

3. The *Game of Life,* invented by John H. Conway, is supposed to model the genetic laws for birth, survival, and death (see *Scientific American,* October 1970, p. 120). We will play the game on a board that consists of 25 squares in the horizontal and vertical directions (a total of 625 squares). Each square can be empty, or it can contain an X indicating the presence of an organism. Each square (except for the border squares) has eight neighbors. The color shading shown in the following segment of the board marks the neighbors of the organism named X*:

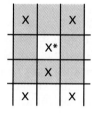

Generation 1

The next generation of organisms is determined according to the following criteria:

a. Birth—an organism will be born in each empty location that has exactly three neighbors.

b. Death—an organism with four or more organisms as neighbors will die from overcrowding. An organism with fewer than two neighbors will die from loneliness.

Survival—an organism with two or three neighbors will survive to the next generation. Possible generations 2 and 3 for the sample follow:

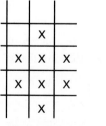

Generation 2   Generation 3

Take an initial configuration of organisms as input data. Display the original game array, calculate the next generation of organisms in a new array, copy the new array into the original game array, and repeat the cycle for as many generations as you wish. Hint: Assume that the borders of the game array are infertile regions where organisms can neither survive nor be born; you will not have to process the border squares.

4. Plot each of the following functions over a suitable interval:
   a. $x^4 - 6x^3 - 5x^2 - 70x - 9$
   b. $3\cos(x) - x$
   c. $\sqrt{|\sin(x)| + |\cos(x)|}$
   d. $e^{-\left(\frac{x^2}{2}\right)}$

5. Write a program that plots two functions on an interval [x_init,x_final], for example

$$y = f(x)$$
$$y = g(x)$$

Use different symbols for the plots of f and g. Wherever the two functions intersect, use a third plotting symbol. Try your program on

$$f(x) = \sqrt{4.0 - x^2}$$
$$g(x) = 1.0 + x^2$$

6. Modify the program you wrote for Project 5 so that the area between the two functions that are being plotted will appear shaded (i.e., filled with the symbol / as shown in Fig. 8.29). Try your program on the functions given in Project 5 and on any other functions you might want to try.

7. Write a program that will take a 4×4 *square matrix A* (same number of rows and columns) and a nonnegative integer p and will compute A^p, that is, *A raised to the power p*. A^p is defined as

$A^0 = $ the *identity matrix, I*   (all 0s except for 1s on the diagonal)
$A^p = A * A^{p-1}, p \geq 1$

Figure 8.29
Plot of Two
Functions with
Area Between
Curves Shaded

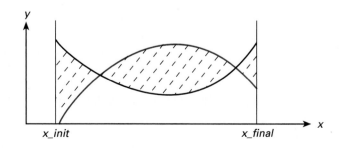

8. Write a program that uses Gaussian elimination to solve each of the following systems of equations:

   a. $x + 2y + z = 4$
       $2x + y - z = -1$
       $-x + y + z = 2$

   b. $x - y + 2z = 3$
       $2x + 3y - 6z = 1$
       $4x + y - 2z = 7$

   c. $3x - z = 7$
       $2x + y = 6$
       $3y - z = 7$

9. The *inverse of a square matrix A* is defined to be the matrix *A_inv* that satisfies

$$A * A\_inv = I \quad \text{(See the identity matrix in Project 7.)}$$

   If *A_inv* exists, then *A* is said to be invertible. (If *A* is invertible, then *A_inv* is also invertible, and *A* is the inverse of *A_inv*.) The inverse of a matrix *A* can be computed using Gaussian elimination. This technique will also tell us if *A* is not invertible.

   First let us describe with an example how to set up the data to find the inverse of a matrix *A*. Suppose we want to find the inverse of the following matrix:

$$A = \begin{bmatrix} 1 & 2 & 1 \\ 2 & 1 & -1 \\ -1 & 1 & 1 \end{bmatrix}$$

   The problem solution is derived by setting up a work matrix *W* that has the original matrix *A* as its first three columns and the identity matrix as its last three columns:

$$A = \left[\begin{array}{ccc|ccc} 1 & 2 & 1 & 1 & 0 & 0 \\ 2 & 1 & -1 & 0 & 1 & 0 \\ -1 & 1 & 1 & 0 & 0 & 1 \end{array} \right]$$

   We now apply Gaussian elimination to the three leftmost columns. However, we modify Gaussian elimination as presented in the text, so that the three leftmost columns become the identity matrix. In other words, it is not sufficient to get the three leftmost columns in scaled triangular form. Getting these columns in the correct form requires only a slight modification of the function `gauss`. When we eliminate coefficients in the pivot column, we do so both above and beneath the pivot.

The key to this method is that as we apply Gaussian elimination to the left half of W, we apply all row operations throughout the matrix W. When the left side of W is the identity matrix, the right side will contain the inverse of A. If Gaussian elimination fails because no nonzero pivot is found for a certain pivot element, then the original matrix A must be noninvertible.

Write a program that will take a square matrix and compute its inverse by this modification of Gaussian elimination.

STRUCTURE TYPES

In previous chapters, we have seen how to represent in C numbers, characters, words, other strings, and lists (arrays) of these objects. But surely there is more to the world we live in than words and lists of numbers! Every day the role of computers in this complex universe widens, and a programming language must be able to model not only numbers and names, but also protozoa, particles, and planets.

In this chapter, we will study how to broaden the modeling facilities of C by defining our own data types that represent structured collections of data pertaining to particular objects. Unlike an array, a structure can have individual components that contain data of different types. A single variable of a composite type designed for planets can store a planet's name, diameter, distance from the sun, the number of years to complete one solar orbit, and the number of hours to make one rotation on its axis. Each of these data items is stored in a separate component of the structure and can be referenced by using the component name.

9.1 USER-DEFINED STRUCTURE TYPES

A *database* is a collection of information stored in a computer's memory or in a disk file. A database is subdivided into records, which normally contain information regarding specific data objects. The structure of the record is determined by the structure of the object's data type.

Structure Type Definition

Before a structured data object can be created or saved, the format of its components must be defined. Although C provides several ways to define structures, we will explore just one approach—defining a new data type for each category of structured objects.

EXAMPLE 9.1  As part of a project for our local observatory, we are developing a database of the planets in our solar system. For each planet, we need to represent the following descriptive information:

Name: Jupiter
Diameter: 142,800 km
Distance from sun (average): 778.3 million km
Orbital period: 11.9 yr
Axial rotation period: 9.925 hr

We can define a *structure type* `planet_t` to use in declaring a variable in which to store this information. There must be five *components* in the structure type, one for each data item. We must specify the name of each component and the type of information stored in each component. We choose the names in the same way we choose all other identifiers: The names describe the nature of the information represented. The contents of each component determine the appropriate data type. For example, the planet's name should be stored in a component that is an array of characters.

The structure type `planet_t` has five distinct components. One is an array of characters; the other four are of type `double`. Although the value in kilometers for distance from the sun will be a whole number, its magnitude is likely to be too great to be stored as type `int` in many C implementations.

```
#define STRSIZ 10

typedef struct {
    char    name[STRSIZ];
    double  diameter,           /* equatorial diameter in
                                      km                  */
            dist_sun,           /* average distance from sun
                                      in km               */
            orbital_prd,        /* years to orbit sun once */
            axial_rot_prd;      /* hours to complete one
                                      revolution on axis  */
} planet_t;
```

This type definition is a template that describes the format of a planet structure and the name and type of each component. A name chosen for a component of one structure may be the same as the name of a component of another structure or the same as the name of a variable. We will see that the approach C takes to referencing these components will rule out confusion of matching names used in these different contexts. The `typedef` statement itself allocates no memory. A variable declaration is required to allocate storage space for a structured data object. The variables `current_planet` and `previous_planet` are declared next, and the variable `blank_planet` is declared and initialized:

```
{
    planet_t current_planet,
             previous_planet,
             blank_planet = {"", 0, 0, 0, 0};
    . . .
```

The structured variables `current_planet`, `previous_planet`, and `blank_planet` all have the format specified in the definition of type `planet_t`. Thus the memory allocated for each consists of storage space for five distinct values. The variable `blank_planet` is pictured as it appears after initialization:

Variable blank_planet, a structure of type planet_t

.name	\0 ? ? ? ? ? ? ? ? ?
.diameter	0.0
.dist_sun	0.0
.orbital_prd	0.0
.axial_rot_prd	0.0

A user-defined type like `planet_t` can be used to declare both simple and array variables and to declare components in other structure types. A structure containing components that are themselves structures is sometimes called a *hierarchical structure*. The following definition of a structure type includes a component that is an array of planets:

```
typedef struct {
      double   diameter;
      planet_t planets[9];
      char     galaxy[STRSIZ];
} solar_sys_t;
```

Structure Type Definition

SYNTAX:
```
typedef struct {
        type₁ id_list₁;
        type₂ id_list₂;
                .
                .
                .
        typeₙ id_listₙ;
} struct_type;
```

EXAMPLE:
```
typedef struct { /* complex number structure */
        double real_pt,
               imag_pt;
} complex_t;
```

(continued)

INTERPRETATION: The identifier *struct_type* is the name of the structure type being defined. Each *id_list*$_i$ is a list of one or more component names separated by commas; the data type of each component in *id_list*$_i$ is specified by *type*$_i$.

NOTE: *type*$_i$ can be any standard or previously specified user-defined data type.

Manipulating Individual Components of a Structured Data Object

We can reference a component of a structure by using the *direct component selection* operator, which is a period. The period is preceded by the name of a structure type variable and is followed by the name of a component.

EXAMPLE 9.2

Figure 9.1 shows as an example the manipulation of the components of the variable `current_planet` listed at the beginning of Example 9.1. The statements in the figure store in the variable the data pictured earlier.

Once data are stored in a record, they can be manipulated in the same way as other data in memory. For example, the statement

```
printf("%s's equatorial diameter is %.1f km.\n",
        current_planet.name, current_planet.diameter);
```

Figure 9.1
Assigning
Values to
Components
of Variable
current_planet

```
strcpy(current_planet.name, "Jupiter");
current_planet.diameter = 142800;
current_planet.dist_sun = .7783e+9;
current_planet.orbital_prd = 11.9;
current_planet.axial_rot_prd = 9.925;
```

Variable current_planet, a structure of type planet_t

.name	J u p i t e r \0 ? ?
.diameter	142800.0
.dist_sun	.7783e+9
.orbital_prd	11.9
.axial_rot_prd	9.925

displays the sentence

```
Jupiter's equatorial diameter is 142800.0 km.
```
←

Review of Operator Precedence

With the addition of the direct component selection operator to our repertory of operators, we will take a moment to see how this operator fits into our overall scheme of precedence rules. Table 9.1 not only shows operator precedence answering the question, In an expression with two operators, which is applied first? It also lists operator associativity answering the question, In an expression containing two of these operators in sequence, which is applied first?

In a generic expression containing two of the same operators in sequence,

$$operand_1 \quad op \quad operand_2 \quad op \quad operand_3$$

if *op* has left associativity, the expression is evaluated as

$$(operand_1 \quad op \quad operand_2) \quad op \quad operand_3$$

Table 9.1 **Precedence and Associativity of Operators Seen So Far**

Precedence	Symbols	Operator Names	Associativity
highest	`a[j] f(...) .`	subscripting, function calls, direct component selection	left
	`++ --`	postfix increment and decrement	left
	`++ -- !` `- + & *`	prefix increment and decrement, logical not, unary negation and plus, address of, indirection	right
	`( type name )`	casts	right
	`* / %`	multiplicative operators (multiplication, division, remainder)	left
	`+ -`	binary additive operators (addition and subtraction)	left
	`< > <= >=`	relational operators	left
	`== !=`	equality / inequality operators	left
	`&&`	logical and	left
	`||`	logical or	left
lowest	`= += -=` `*= /= %=`	assignment operators	right

whereas if *op* has right associativity, the implied order of evaluation is

$$operand_1 \;\; op \;\; (operand_2 \;\; op \;\; operand_3)$$

Manipulating Whole Structures

The name of a structure type variable used with no component selection operator refers to the entire structure. A new copy of a structure's value can be made by simply assigning one structure to another as in the following statement:

```
previous_planet = current_planet;
```

We will see other instances of the manipulation of whole structures in the next section when we study the use of structures as input and output parameters of functions and as function result types.

Program Style   *Naming Convention for Types*

When we write programs that define new types, it is easy to confuse type names and variable names. To help reduce confusion, in this text we choose user-defined type names that use lowercase letters and end in the suffix _t (a practice recommended in some industrial software design environments).

EXERCISES FOR SECTION 9.1

Self-Check

1. Define a type named `long_lat_t` that would be appropriate for storing longitude or latitude values. Include components named **degrees** (an integer), **minutes** (an integer), and **direction** (one of the characters `'N'`, `'S'`, `'E'`, or `'W'`).
2. The following are a type to represent a geographic location and a variable of this hierarchical structure type. We will assume that `STRSIZ` means `20`.

```
typedef struct {
      char        place[STRSIZ];
      long_lat_t  longitude,
                  latitude;
} location_t;

location_t resort;
```

Given that the values shown have been stored in `resort`, complete the following table to check your understanding of component selection.

Variable resort, a structure of type location_t

.place	F i j i \0 ? ? . . .		
.longitude	178	0	E
.latitude	17	50	S

Reference	Data Type of Reference	Value
resort.latitude	long_lat_t	17 50 'S'
resort.place	_____	_____
resort.longitude.direction	_____	_____
_____	char	'E'
resort.place[3]	_____	_____

3. A catalog listing for a textbook consists of the authors' names, the title, the publisher, and the year of publication. Declare a structure type `catalog_entry_t` and a variable `book`, and write statements that store the relevant data for this textbook in `book`.

9.2 STRUCTURE TYPE DATA AS INPUT AND OUTPUT PARAMETERS

When a structured variable is passed as an input argument to a function, all of its component *values* are copied into the components of the function's corresponding formal parameter. When such a variable is used as an output argument, the address-of operator must be applied in the same way that we would pass output arguments of the standard types `char`, `int`, and `double`.

EXAMPLE 9.3

Our observatory program from Examples 9.1 and 9.2 frequently needs to output as a unit all of the descriptive data about a planet. Figure 9.2 shows a function to do this.

To display the value of our structure `current_planet`, we would use the call statement

```
print_planet(current_planet);
```

Figure 9.2 **Function with a Structured Input Parameter**

```
/*
 * Displays with labels all components of a planet_t structure
 */
void
print_planet(planet_t pl) /* input - one planet structure */
{
      printf("%s\n", pl.name);
      printf("  Equatorial diameter: %.0f km\n", pl.diameter);
      printf("  Average distance from the sun: %.4e km\n", pl.dist_sun);
      printf("  Time to complete one orbit of the sun: %.2f years\n",
             pl.orbital_prd);
      printf("  Time to complete one rotation on axis: %.4f hours\n",
             pl.axial_rot_prd);
}
```

Having an output function like `print_planet` helps us to view the planet object as a concept at a higher level of abstraction rather than as an ad hoc collection of components.

Another function that would help us think of a planet as a data object is a function that would perform an equality comparison of two planets. Although C permits copying of a structure using the assignment operator, the equality and inequality operators cannot be applied to a structured type as a unit. Figure 9.3 shows a `planet_equal` function that takes two planets as input arguments and returns 1 or 0, depending on whether all components match. ◀

Figure 9.3 **Function Comparing Two Structured Values for Equality**

```
#include <string.h>

/*
 * Determines whether or not the components of planet_1 and planet_2 match
 */
int
planet_equal(planet_t planet_1, /* input - planets to        */
             planet_t planet_2) /*          compare          */
```

(continued)

Figure 9.3   (continued)

```
{
      return (strcmp(planet_1.name, planet_2.name) == 0      &&
              planet_1.diameter == planet_2.diameter         &&
              planet_1.dist_sun == planet_2.dist_sun         &&
              planet_1.orbital_prd == planet_2.orbital_prd   &&
              planet_1.axial_rot_prd == planet_2.axial_rot_prd);
}
```

A planet input function would also help us to process current_planet as planet_t data. Figure 9.4 shows the function scan_planet that resembles scanf in that it takes an output argument and returns the value 1 if its single output argument is successfully filled, returns the value 0 if there is an error, and returns the negative value EOF if the end of the file is encountered.

As you can see from this example, manipulating a structured output argument really requires you to keep C's operator precedence rules straight. To use

Figure 9.4   Function with a Structured Output Argument

```
/*
 * Fills a type planet_t structure with input data. Integer returned as
 * function result is success/failure/EOF indicator.
 *     1 => successful input of one planet
 *     0 => error encountered
 *     EOF => insufficient data before end of file
 * In case of error or EOF, value of type planet_t output argument is
 * undefined.
 */
int
scan_planet(planet_t *plnp) /* output - address of planet_t structure
                                         to fill                         */
{
      int result;

      result = scanf("%s%lf%lf%lf%lf", (*plnp).name,
                                       &(*plnp).diameter,
                                       &(*plnp).dist_sun,
                                       &(*plnp).orbital_prd,
                                       &(*plnp).axial_rot_prd);
```

(continued)

Figure 9.4 (continued)

```
    if (result == 5)
            result = 1;
    else if (result != EOF)
            result = 0;

    return (result);
}
```

scanf to store a value in one component of the structure whose address is in plnp, we must carry out the following steps (in order):

1. Follow the pointer in plnp to the structure.
2. Select the component of interest.
3. Unless this component is an array (e.g., component name in Fig. 9.4), get its address to pass to scanf.

When we check our precedence chart (see Table 9.1), we find that the reference

&*plnp.diameter

would attempt Step 2 before Step 1. For this reason, the program in Fig. 9.4 overrides the default operator precedence by parenthesizing the application of the indirect referencing (pointer-following) operator, the unary *. Figure 9.5 shows the data areas of functions main and scan_planet during execution of the following statement in main:

status = scan_planet(&current_planet);

We are assuming that the assignment statement of scan_planet calling scanf has just finished executing and that it has successfully obtained input values for all components of the output argument structure.

In Table 9.2, we analyze the reference &(*plnp).diameter from our function scan_planet. C also provides a single operator that combines the functions of the indirection and component selection operators. This *indirect component selection* operator is represented by the character sequence -> (a "minus" sign followed by a "greater than"). Thus these two expressions are equivalent.

(*structp).component   structp->component

We elect to use the (*structp).component notation in our examples in this chapter so that all nonarray output parameters will be referenced using the * operator.

Figure 9.5 Data Areas of main and scan_planet during Execution of
status = scan_planet(&current_planet);

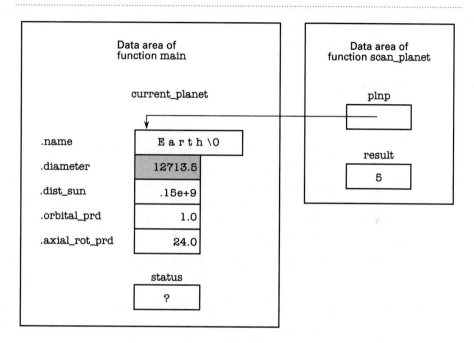

Table 9.2 Step-by-Step Analysis of Reference &(*plnp).diameter

Reference	Type	Value
plnp	planet_t *	address of structure that main refers to as current_planet
*plnp	planet_t	structure that main refers to as current_planet
(*plnp).diameter	double	12713.5
&(*plnp).diameter	double *	address of colored component of structure that main refers to as current_planet

In the next section, we will see how to write a function that fills up a `planet_t` structure with input data and returns this structure as the function value. This alternative way of approaching input of structures avoids the need for indirect referencing, but it cannot return a status indicator as the function value in the same way `scan_planet` does.

**EXERCISES FOR
SECTION 9.2**

Self-Check

1. Write functions `print_long_lat`, `long_lat_equal`, and `scan_long_lat` to perform output, equality comparison, and input of type `long_lat_t` data (see Self-Check Exercise 1 at the end of Section 9.1).

2. Assume that you have a function `verify_location` that manipulates a structured input/output argument of type `location_t` (see Self-Check Exercise 2 at the end of Section 9.1). The figure that follows shows the data areas of functions `main` and `verify_location` during execution of the call

   `code = verify_location(&resort);`

   Complete the table following the figure with references appropriate for use in `verify_location` (if such references were needed).

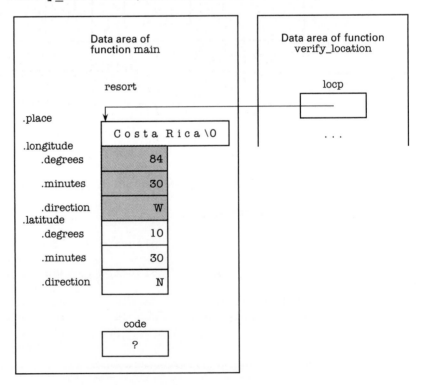

Reference in verify_location	Type of Reference	Value of Reference
locp	location_t *	address of the structure that main refers to as resort
_____	_____	the structure that main refers to as resort
_____	_____	"Costa Rica"
_____	_____	address of the colored component of the structure that main refers to as resort
_____	_____	84

9.3 FUNCTIONS WHOSE RESULT VALUES ARE STRUCTURED

In our study so far, we have seen many situations in which user-defined structured data types are treated just like C's own simple types, yet we have seen only one situation in which structures are handled differently, namely, in equality comparisons. In Chapters 7 and 8, we saw that C's processing of the array data structure differs significantly from its handling of simple data types. One of the many differences is the fact that the values of an entire array cannot be returned as a function result. Rather, functions computing array results typically require the calling module to provide an array output argument in which to store the result.

Since arrays and structure types are both data *structures*, one might expect that C would handle them in a similar fashion. In fact, learning C is greatly assisted by doing away with this expectation, because C's approach to processing structure types closely resembles its facilities for working with simple data types, but is very different from its handling of arrays.

A function that computes a structured result can be modeled on a function computing a simple result. A local variable of the structure type can be allocated, filled with the desired data, and returned as the function result.

EXAMPLE 9.4

In Fig. 9.6, we see a function that obtains from the input device values for all components of a planet_t structure and returns the structure as the function result. Our function get_planet requires no arguments. If we assume entry of correct data, the statement

```
current_planet = get_planet();
```

Figure 9.6   Function get_planet Returning a Structured Result Type

```c
/*
 * Gets and returns a planet_t structure
 */
planet_t
get_planet(void)
{
      planet_t planet;

      scanf("%s%lf%lf%lf%lf", planet.name,
                              &planet.diameter,
                              &planet.dist_sun,
                              &planet.orbital_prd,
                              &planet.axial_rot_prd);
      return (planet);
}
```

has the same effect as

```c
scan_planet(&current_planet);
```

However, the assumption of correct data entry format is frequently unjustified, so **scan_planet** with its ability to return an integer error code is the more generally useful function.

←

EXAMPLE 9.5

Before performing a potentially dangerous or costly experiment in the laboratory, we can often use a computer program to simulate the experiment. In computer simulations, we need to keep track of the time of day as the experiment progresses. Normally, the time of day is updated after a certain period has elapsed. Assuming a 24-hour clock, the structure type **time_t** is defined as follows:

```c
typedef struct {
      int hour, minute, second;
} time_t;
```

Function **new_time** in Fig. 9.7 returns as its value an updated time based on the original time of day and the number of seconds that have elapsed since the

Figure 9.7   Function to Compute an Updated Time Value

```
/*
 * Computes a new time represented as a time_t structure
 * and based on time of day and elapsed seconds.
 */
time_t
new_time(time_t time_of_day,    /* input - time to be
                                            updated            */
         int     elapsed_secs)  /* input - seconds since
                                            last update        */
{
     int new_hr, new_min, new_sec;

     new_sec = time_of_day.second + elapsed_secs;
     time_of_day.second = new_sec % 60;
     new_min = time_of_day.minute + new_sec / 60;
     time_of_day.minute = new_min % 60;
     new_hr = time_of_day.hour + new_min / 60;
     time_of_day.hour = new_hr % 24;

     return (time_of_day);
}
```

previous update. If `time_now` were 21:58:32 and `secs` had the value 97, the result returned by the call

```
new_time(time_now, secs)
```

would be 22:00:09. Because `new_time`'s variable `time_of_day` is strictly an input parameter, the value of `time_now` will not be affected by the call to `new_time`. If the intent is to update `time_now`, an assignment statement is used.

```
time_now = new_time(time_now, secs);
```

Figure 9.8 traces the assignment statement just mentioned showing the structured `time_t` value used as an input argument and the type `time_t` function value.

Figure 9.8
Structured
Values as a
Function Input
Argument and
as a Function
Result

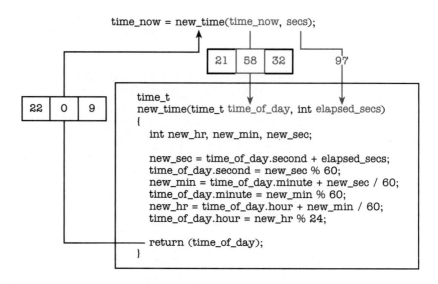

```
                    time_now = new_time(time_now, secs);


                              21   58   32            97

              time_t
              new_time(time_t time_of_day, int elapsed_secs)
     22  0  9 {
                  int new_hr, new_min, new_sec;

                  new_sec = time_of_day.second + elapsed_secs;
                  time_of_day.second = new_sec % 60;
                  new_min = time_of_day.minute + new_sec / 60;
                  time_of_day.minute = new_min % 60;
                  new_hr = time_of_day.hour + new_min / 60;
                  time_of_day.hour = new_hr % 24;

                  return (time_of_day);
              }
```

EXERCISES FOR
SECTION 9.3

Self-Check

1. Why does function `new_time`'s assignment of new values to the `second`, `minute`, and `hour` components of its formal parameter `time_of_day` have no effect on the components of actual argument `time_now` in the call `new_time(time_now, secs)`?
2. Could you modify function `get_planet` so that it would still have a type `planet_t` result but would also indicate input success or failure to the calling function?

Programming

1. Define a structure type to represent a common fraction. Write a program that gets a fraction and displays both the fraction and the fraction reduced to lowest terms using the following code fragment:

```
frac = get_fraction();
print_fraction(frac);
printf(" = ");
print_fraction(reduce_fraction(frac));
```

9.4 PROBLEM SOLVING WITH STRUCTURE TYPES

When we solve problems using C's standard data types, we take for granted the fact that C provides us with all the basic operations we need to manipulate our data. However, when we work with a problem whose data objects are more

**Figure 9.9
Data Type
planet_t
and Basic
Operations**

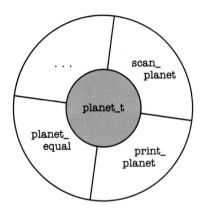

complex, we find that defining our own data types is just the first step in building a tool with which to attack the problem. To be able to think about the problem on the basis of our own data types, we must also provide basic operations for manipulating these types.

Combining a user-defined type with a set of basic operations that allow one truly to see the type as a unified concept creates what is called an *abstract data type* (ADT). Figure 9.9 shows one view of our data type `planet_t` combined with its operations.

If we take the time to define enough basic operations for a structure type, we then find it possible to think about a related problem at a higher level of abstraction; we are no longer bogged down in the details of manipulating the type's components.

In our next case study, we develop such a group of basic operations for processing complex numbers.

Case Study: A User-Defined Type for Complex Numbers

PROBLEM

We are working on an engineering project that uses complex numbers for modeling of electrical circuits. We need to develop a user-defined structure type and a set of operations that will make complex arithmetic virtually as straightforward as arithmetic on C's built-in numeric types.

ANALYSIS

A complex number is a number with a real part and an imaginary part. For example, the complex number $a + jb$ has a real part a and an imaginary part b, where the symbol j represents $\sqrt{-1}$. We will need to define functions for complex I/O as well as for the basic arithmetic operations (addition, subtraction, multiplication, and division) and for finding the absolute value of a complex number.

DESIGN

The two major aspects of our solution to this problem are defining the structure of the user-defined type and describing the function name, parameters, and purpose of each operation. Each function purpose then forms a subproblem to be solved separately. The details of these subproblems will be of interest to us as we develop our operations. However, once this group of functions is complete, we will be concerned only with *what* each function does, not with *how* it does it. In the same way, when we use C's built-in multiplication operator, we are interested only in the fact that * does multiplication, not caring in the least *how* it manages to accomplish this.

Specification of Type complex_t and Associated Operations

STRUCTURE: A complex number is an object of type complex_t that consists of a pair of type double values.

OPERATORS:

```
/*
 * Complex number input function returns standard scanning
 * error code
 */
int
scan_complex(complex_t *c)  /* output - address of complex
                                         variable to fill   */

/*
 * Complex output function displays value as a + jb or a - jb.
 * Displays only a if imaginary part is 0.
 * Displays only jb if real part is 0.
 */
void
print_complex(complex_t c)  /* input - complex number to
                                display                      */

/*
 * Returns sum of complex values c1 and c2
 */
complex_t
add_complex(complex_t c1, complex_t c2)          /* input */
```

(continued)

```
/*
 * Returns difference c1 - c2
 */
complex_t
subtract_complex(complex_t c1, complex_t c2)      /* input */

/*
 * Returns product of complex values c1 and c2
 */
complex_t
multiply_complex(complex_t c1, complex_t c2)      /* input */

/*
 * Returns quotient of complex values (c1 / c2)
 */
complex_t
divide_complex(complex_t c1, complex_t c2)        /* input */

/*
 * Returns absolute value of complex number c
 */
complex_t
abs_complex(complex_t c)                           /* input */
```

As soon as this specification is complete, our co-workers on the circuit modeling project can begin designing algorithms that assume the availability of these operations. Then, when our implementation is complete, our code can either be added to their programs or packaged for inclusion in a way we will describe in Chapter 11.

Figure 9.10 shows a partial implementation of our specification together with a driver function. Functions `multiply_complex` and `divide_complex` have been left as an exercise. Notice that the definition of type `complex_t` is placed immediately after our preprocessor directives so that it is visible throughout the entire program. Function `abs_complex` uses the following formula to compute the absolute value of a complex number:

$$\left| a + jb \right| = \sqrt{(a + jb)(a - jb)} = \sqrt{a^2 + b^2}$$

This result always has an imaginary part of zero, so `print_complex` will display the result as a real number.

Figure 9.10   Partial Implementation of Type and Operators for Complex Numbers

```
/*
 *  Operators to process complex numbers
 */
#include <stdio.h>
#include <math.h>

/*  User-defined complex number type */
typedef struct {
     double real, imag;
} complex_t;

/*
 *  Complex number input function returns standard scanning error code
 *    1 => valid scan, 0 => error, negative EOF value => end of file
 */
int
scan_complex(complex_t *c) /* output - address of complex variable to
                                          fill                        */
{
     int status;

     status = scanf("%lf%lf", &(*c).real, &(*c).imag);
     if (status == 2)
          status = 1;
     else if (status != EOF)
          status = 0;

     return (status);
}

/*
 *  Complex output function displays value as (a + jb) or (a - jb),
 *  dropping a or b if they round to 0 unless both round to 0
 */
void
print_complex(complex_t c) /* input - complex number to display     */
{
     double a, b;
     char   sign;

     a = c.real;
     b = c.imag;
```

(continued)

Figure 9.10 (continued)

```c
        printf("(");

        if (fabs(a) < .005 && fabs(b) < .005) {
                printf("%.2f", 0.0);
        } else if (fabs(b) < .005) {
                printf("%.2f", a);
        } else if (fabs(a) < .005) {
                printf("j%.2f", b);
        } else {
                if (b < 0)
                        sign = '-';
                else
                        sign = '+';
                printf("%.2f %c j%.2f", a, sign, fabs(b));
        }

        printf(")");
}

/*
 *  Returns sum of complex values c1 and c2
 */
complex_t
add_complex(complex_t c1, complex_t c2) /* input - values to add   */
{
        complex_t csum;

        csum.real = c1.real + c2.real;
        csum.imag = c1.imag + c2.imag;

        return (csum);
}

/*
 *  Returns difference c1 - c2
 */
complex_t
subtract_complex(complex_t c1, complex_t c2) /* input parameters    */
{
        complex_t cdiff;
```

(continued)

Figure 9.10 (continued)

```c
        cdiff.real = c1.real - c2.real;
        cdiff.imag = c1.imag - c2.imag;

        return (cdiff);
}

/*  ** Stub **
 *  Returns product of complex values c1 and c2
 */
complex_t
multiply_complex(complex_t c1, complex_t c2) /* input parameters    */
{
        printf("Function multiply_complex returning first argument\n");
        return (c1);
}

/*  ** Stub **
 *  Returns quotient of complex values (c1 / c2)
 */
complex_t
divide_complex(complex_t c1, complex_t c2) /* input parameters    */
{
        printf("Function divide_complex returning first argument\n");
        return (c1);
}

/*
 *  Returns absolute value of complex number c
 */
complex_t
abs_complex(complex_t c) /* input parameter                       */
{
        complex_t cabs;

        cabs.real = sqrt(c.real * c.real + c.imag * c.imag);
        cabs.imag = 0;

        return (cabs);
}
```

(continued)

Figure 9.10 (continued)

```
/*   Driver                                                        */
int
main(void)
{
      complex_t com1, com2;

      /*  Gets two complex numbers                                 */
      printf("Enter the real and imaginary parts of a complex number\n");
      printf("separated by a space> ");
      scan_complex(&com1);
      printf("Enter a second complex number> ");
      scan_complex(&com2);

      /*  Forms and displays the sum                               */
      printf("\n");
      print_complex(com1);
      printf("  +  ");
      print_complex(com2);
      printf("  =  ");
      print_complex(add_complex(com1, com2));

      /*  Forms and displays the difference                        */
      printf("\n\n");
      print_complex(com1);
      printf("  -  ");
      print_complex(com2);
      printf("  =  ");
      print_complex(subtract_complex(com1, com2));

      /*  Forms and displays the absolute value of the first number  */
      printf("\n\n|");
      print_complex(com1);
      printf("|  =  ");
      print_complex(abs_complex(com1));
      printf("\n");

      return (0);
}
Enter the real and imaginary parts of a complex number
separated by a space> 3.5 5.2
Enter a second complex number> 2.5 1.2

(3.50 + j5.20)  +  (2.50 + j1.20)  =  (6.00 + j6.40)

(3.50 + j5.20)  -  (2.50 + j1.20)  =  (1.00 + j4.00)

|(3.50 + j5.20)|  =  (6.27)
```

Self-Check

1. What does the following program segment display if the data entered are 6.5 5.0 3.0 −4.0?

```
complex_t a, b, c;

scan_complex(&a);
scan_complex(&b);

print_complex(a);
printf(" + ");
print_complex(b);
printf(" = ");
print_complex(add_complex(a, b));

c = subtract_complex(a, abs_complex(b));
printf("\n\nSecond result = ");
print_complex(c);
printf("\n");
```

Programming

1. Write functions `multiply_complex` and `divide_complex` to implement the operations of multiplication and division of complex numbers defined as follows:

$$(a + jb) \times (c + jd) = (ac - bd) + j(ad + bc)$$

$$\frac{(a + jb)}{(c + jd)} = \frac{ac + bd}{c^2 + d^2} + j\frac{bc - ad}{c^2 + d^2}$$

9.5 PARALLEL ARRAYS AND ARRAYS OF STRUCTURES

Often a data collection contains items of different types or items that, although of the same type, represent quite distinct concepts. For example, the data used to represent a list of students might consist of an integer identification number and a type `double` gpa for each student. The data representing a polygon might be a list of the (x, y) coordinates of the polygon's corners.

Parallel Arrays

In Chapter 7, we learned how to represent such data collections using *parallel arrays* such as the following:

```
int     id[50];      /* id numbers and                 */
double gpa[50];      /*   gpa's of up to 50 students   */
double x[NUM_PTS],   /* (x,y) coordinates of           */
       y[NUM_PTS];   /*   up to NUM_PTS points         */
```

Arrays id and gpa are called parallel arrays because the data items with the same subscript (for example, *i*) pertain to the same student (the *i*th student). Similarly, the *i*th elements of arrays x and y are the coordinates of one point. A better way to organize data collections like these is shown next.

Declaring an Array of Structures

A more natural and convenient organization of student data or polygon points is to group the information pertaining to one student or to one point in a structure whose type we define. Declarations of arrays whose elements are structures follow:

```
#define MAX_STU 50
#define NUM_PTS 10

typedef struct {
     int     id;
     double gpa;
} student_t;

typedef struct {
     double x, y;
} point_t;

. . .

{
     student_t stulist[MAX_STU];
     point_t   polygon[NUM_PTS];
```

A sample array stulist is shown in Fig. 9.11. The data for the first student are stored in the structure stulist[0]. The individual data items are stulist[0].id and stulist[0].gpa. As shown, stulist[0].gpa is 2.71.

If a function scan_student is available for scanning a student_t structure, the following for statement can be used to fill the entire array stulist with data:

```
for  (i = 0;  i < MAX_STU;  ++i)
     scan_student(&stulist[i]);
```

Figure 9.11
An Array of
Structures

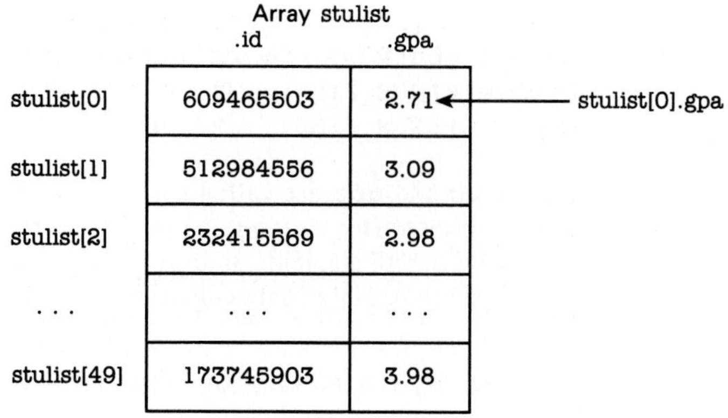

This `for` statement would display all the `id` numbers:

```
for  (i = 0; i < MAX_STU;  ++i)
    printf("%d\n", stulist[i].id);
```

In our next case study, we see how to use an array of descriptive information about units of measurement in order to make possible conversion of any measurement to any other unit of the same category.

Case Study: Universal Measurement Conversion

In a day when our computer software spell-checks text and looks up synonyms for words, it seems primitive to use printed tables for hand conversion of feet to meters, liters to quarts, and so on.

PROBLEM

We would like a program that takes a measurement in one unit (e.g., 4.5 yards) and converts it to another unit (e.g., meters). For example, this conversion request

```
450 km miles
```

would result in this program output

```
Attempting conversion of 4.5000e+02 km to miles . . .
4.5000e+02 km  =  2.7962e+02 miles
```

The program should produce an error message if a conversion between two units of different classes (e.g., mass to distance) is requested. The program should take a database of conversion information from an input file before accepting conversion problems entered interactively by the user. The user should be able to specify units either by name (e.g., kilograms) or by abbreviation (e.g., kg).

◀ ANALYSIS ▶

This program's basic data objects are units of measurement. We need to define a structure type that groups all relevant attributes about one unit. We can then store a database of these structures in an array and look up conversion factors as needed. To convert a measurement, the user will need to provide the measurement as a number and a string (e.g., 5 kg or 6.5 inches). The user must also enter the name or abbreviation of the desired units.

The attributes of a unit include its name and abbreviation, its class (mass, distance, and so on), and a representation of the unit in terms of the chosen standard unit for its class. If we allow the actual unit name, class names, and standard units to be determined by the contents of the input file, the program will be usable for any class of measurements and for units in any language based on our character set.

Data Requirements

Structured Data Type
```
unit_t
   components:
   name     /* character string such as "milligrams" */
   abbrev   /* shorter character string such as "mg"  */
   class    /* character string "pressure",
                  "distance", or "mass"                */
   standard /* number of standard units that are
                  equivalent to this unit              */
```

Problem Constants
```
NAME_LEN    30  /* storage allocated for a unit name   */
ABBREV_LEN  15  /* storage allocated for a unit
                       abbreviation                     */
CLASS_LEN   20  /* storage allocated for a
                       measurement class                */
MAX_UNITS   20  /* maximum number of different units
                       handled                          */
```

Problem Inputs
```
unit_t units[MAX_UNITS]    /* array representing unit
                               conversion factors
                               database                 */
```

```
      double quantity          /* value to convert          */
      char old_units[NAME_LEN]  /* name or abbreviation of
                                   units to be converted */
      char new_units[NAME_LEN]  /* name or abbreviation of
                                   units to convert to      */
```

Problem Output
message giving conversion

DESIGN

Algorithm

1. Load units of measurement database.
2. Get value to convert and old and new unit names.
3. Repeat until data format error encountered
    4. Search for old units in database.
    5. Search for new units in database.
    6. if conversion is impossible
        7. Issue appropriate error message.
      else
        8. Compute and display conversion.
    9. Get value to convert and old and new unit names.

The refinement of Step 1 follows.

1.1 Open database file.
1.2 Initialize subscripting variable i.
1.3 Scan a unit structure from the database file.
1.4 Repeat until EOF, data format error, or attempted overflow of units list
    1.4.1 Store unit structure in units array.
    1.4.2 Update i.
    1.4.3 Scan next unit structure from file.
1.5 Close database file.

We will develop separate functions for Step 1 (load_units), for Step 1.3 and Step 1.4.3 (fscan_unit), for the search used in Step 4 and Step 5, and for the conversion aspect of Step 8. We can base our search function on the linear search algorithm used in Fig. 7.10.

IMPLEMENTATION

Code that implements our universal conversion program is shown in Fig. 9.12. In the universal conversion program, it makes sense to use two sources of input, just as we did in the cellular telephone case study in Chapter 8. The database of units is taken from a file (`units.dat`) that can be created once and then used for many runs of the program. In contrast, the program expects that the conversion problems will be entered interactively.

Figure 9.12   Universal Measurement Conversion Program Using an Array of Structures

```
/*
 *  Converts measurements given in one unit to any other unit of the same
 *  category that is listed in the database file, units.dat.
 *  Handles both names and abbreviations of units.
 */
#include <stdio.h>
#include <string.h>

#define NAME_LEN    30      /* storage allocated for a unit name         */
#define ABBREV_LEN  15      /* storage allocated for a unit abbreviation */
#define CLASS_LEN   20      /* storage allocated for a measurement class */

typedef struct {            /* unit of measurement type                  */
      char    name[NAME_LEN];      /* character string such as "milligrams" */
      char    abbrev[ABBREV_LEN];/* shorter character string such as "mg" */
      char    class[CLASS_LEN];  /* character string such as "pressure",
                                     "distance", "mass"                  */
      double standard;          /* number of standard units equivalent
                                   to this unit                         */
} unit_t;

/*
 *  Gets data from a file to fill output argument
 *  Returns standard error code:  1 => successful input,  0 => error,
 *                                negative EOF value => end of file
 */
int
fscan_unit(FILE    *filep,  /*  input - input file pointer        */
           unit_t *unitp)   /*  output - unit_t structure to fill */
{
      int status;
```

(continued)

Figure 9.12   (continued)

```
        status = fscanf(filep, "%s%s%s%lf", (*unitp).name,
                                            (*unitp).abbrev,
                                            (*unitp).class,
                                            &(*unitp).standard);

        if (status == 4)
              status = 1;
        else if (status != EOF)
              status = 0;

        return (status);
}

/*
 * Opens database file units.dat and gets data to place in units until end
 * of file is encountered.  Stops input prematurely if there are more than
 * unit_max data values in the file or if invalid data is encountered.
 */
void
load_units(int          unit_max,   /* input - declared size of units      */
           unit_t       units[],    /* output - array of data              */
           int          *unit_sizep) /* output - number of data values
                                                 stored in units            */
{
      FILE  *inp;
      unit_t data;
      int    i, status;

      /*  Gets database of units from file                                  */
      inp = fopen("units.dat", "r");
      i = 0;

      for  (status = fscan_unit(inp, &data);
            status == 1  &&  i < unit_max;
            status = fscan_unit(inp, &data)) {
          units[i++] = data;
      }
      fclose(inp);
```

(continued)

Figure 9.12   (continued)

```
        /* Issue error message on premature exit                       */
        if (status == 0) {
              printf("\n*** Error in data format ***\n");
              printf("*** Using first %d data values ***\n", i);
        } else if (status != EOF) {
              printf("\n*** Error: too much data in file ***\n");
              printf("*** Using first %d data values ***\n", i);
        }

        /* Send back size of used portion of array                     */
        *unit_sizep = i;
}

#define NOT_FOUND -1    /*  Value returned by search function if target
                            not found                                  */
/*
 *  Searches for target key in name and abbrev components of first n
 *     elements of array units
 *  Returns index of structure containing target or NOT_FOUND
 */
int
search(const unit_t units[],   /*  array of unit_t structures to search  */
       const char   *target,   /*  key searched for in name and abbrev
                                    components                          */
       int          n)         /*  number of array elements to search   */
{
      int i,
          found = 0,     /*  whether or not target has been found       */
          where;         /*  index where target found or NOT_FOUND      */

      /*  Compare name and abbrev components of each element to target  */
      i = 0;
      while (!found && i < n) {
            if (strcmp(units[i].name,   target) == 0  ||
                strcmp(units[i].abbrev, target) == 0)
                  found = 1;
            else
                  ++i;
      }
```

(continued)

Figure 9.12 (continued)

```
        /* Return index of element containing target or NOT_FOUND      */
        if (found)
                where = i;
        else
                where = NOT_FOUND;
        return (where);
}


/*
 *  Converts one measurement to another given the representation of both
 *  in a standard unit.  For example, to convert 24 feet to yards given a
 *  standard unit of inches:  quantity = 24, old_stand = 12 (there are 12
 *  inches in a foot), new_stand = 36 (there are 36 inches in a yard),
 *  result is 24 * 12 / 36 which equals 8
 */
double
convert(double quantity,      /* value to convert                       */
        double old_stand,     /* number of standard units in one of     */
                              /*     quantity's original units          */
        double new_stand)     /* number of standard units in 1 new unit */
{
        return (quantity * old_stand / new_stand);
}


#define MAX_UNITS   20      /* maximum number of different units handled */


int
main(void)
{
        unit_t units[MAX_UNITS];     /* units classes and conversion factors*/
        int    num_units;            /* number of elements of units in use  */
        char   old_units[NAME_LEN],  /* units to convert (name or abbrev)   */
               new_units[NAME_LEN];  /* units to convert to (name or abbrev)*/
        int    status;               /* input status                        */
        double quantity;             /* value to convert                    */
        int    old_index,            /* index of units element where        */
                                     /*     old_units found                 */
               new_index;            /* index where new_units found         */

        /*  Load units of measurement database                         */
        load_units(MAX_UNITS, units, &num_units);
```

(continued)

Figure 9.12 (continued)

```
/*  Convert quantities to desired units until data format error
       (including error code returned when q is entered to quit)        */
printf("Enter a conversion problem or q to quit.\n");
printf("To convert 25 kilometers to miles, you would enter\n");
printf("> 25 kilometers miles\n");
printf("      or, alternatively,\n");
printf("> 25 km mi\n> ");
for  (status = scanf("%lf%s%s", &quantity, old_units, new_units);
         status == 3;
         status = scanf("%lf%s%s", &quantity, old_units, new_units)) {
    printf("Attempting conversion of %.4e %s to %s . . .\n",
             quantity, old_units, new_units);
    old_index = search(units, old_units, num_units);
    new_index = search(units, new_units, num_units);
    if (old_index == NOT_FOUND)
          printf("Unit %s not in database\n", old_units);
    else if (new_index == NOT_FOUND)
          printf("Unit %s not in database\n", new_units);
    else if (strcmp(units[old_index].class,
                    units[new_index].class) != 0)
          printf("Cannot convert %s (%s) to %s (%s)\n",
                   old_units, units[old_index].class,
                   new_units, units[new_index].class);
    else
          printf("%.4e %s  =  %.4e %s\n", quantity, old_units,
                   convert(quantity, units[old_index].standard,
                             units[new_index].standard),
                   new_units);
    printf("\nEnter a conversion problem or q to quit.\n> ");
}

return (0);
}
```

▶ TESTING ◀

In addition to testing the conversion of units of pressure, distance, and mass using values whose conversions are easy to verify, we should also select test cases that exercise each of the error message facilities of the program. Figure 9.13 shows a small data file and one run of the conversion program. The database in this file assumes standard units of meters, atmospheres, and kilograms. Note that all that is required by the program is that the database consistently use *some* standard units. It does not prescribe *what* units these must be.

Figure 9.13   Data File and Sample Run of Measurement Conversion Program

Data file units.dat:

miles	mi	distance	1609.3
kilometers	km	distance	1000
yards	yd	distance	0.9144
meters	m	distance	1
atmospheres	atm	pressure	1
pascals	Pa	pressure	9.8692e-6
pounds/square_inch	psi	pressure	6.8046e-2
kilograms	kg	mass	1
grams	g	mass	0.001
slugs	slugs	mass	0.14594

Sample run:

```
Enter a conversion problem or q to quit.
To convert 25 kilometers to miles, you would enter
> 25 kilometers miles
     or, alternatively,
> 25 km mi
> 450 km miles
Attempting conversion of 4.5000e+02 km to miles . . .
4.5000e+02 km  =  2.7962e+02 miles

Enter a conversion problem or q to quit.
> 55 psi atm
Attempting conversion of 5.5000e+01 psi to atm . . .
5.5000e+01 psi  =  3.7425e+00 atm

Enter a conversion problem or q to quit.
> 100 meters atmospheres
Attempting conversion of 1.0000e+02 meters to atmospheres . . .
Cannot convert meters (distance) to atmospheres (pressure)

Enter a conversion problem or q to quit.
> 1234 mg g
Attempting conversion of 1.2340e+03 mg to g . . .
Unit mg not in database
```

(continued)

Figure 9.13   (continued)

```
Enter a conversion problem or q to quit.
> q
```

Self-Check

1. In function `main` of our universal conversion program, we see the statement

    ```
    load_units(MAX_UNITS, units, &num_units);
    ```

    Inside `load_units` we see the function call

    ```
    fscan_unit(inp, &data);
    ```

    Variables `units`, `num_units`, and `data` are all being used as output arguments in these statements. Why is the `&` applied to `num_units` and `data`, but not to `units`?
2. Write a code fragment that would add `0.2` to all the `gpa`'s in `stulist` (see Fig. 9.11). If the addition of `0.2` would inflate a `gpa` past `4.0`, just set the `gpa` to `4.0`.

9.6 COMMON PROGRAMMING ERRORS

When programmers manipulate structure types, their most common error is incorrect use of a component selected for processing. When using the direct selection operator (`.`), always be aware of the type of the component selected, and use the value in a manner consistent with its type. For example, if the component selected is an array, passing it to a function as an output argument does not require application of the address-of operator.

If a structure type output parameter is used in a function, one can easily forget that the precedence of the direct selection operator (`.`) is higher than the precedence of the address-of and indirection operators (`&` and `*`). When attempting to write a reference using a combination of these operators, one should first describe the operations in the order desired and compare this sequence to the order imposed by the precedence rules. If the two do not match, parentheses must be included in the reference to override the default precedence.

C allows the use of structure type values in assignment statements, as function arguments, and as function results, so one can easily forget that expressions of these types cannot be operands of equality comparators nor arguments of `printf` and `scanf`. You can select simple components from a structure to use in these contexts, or you can write your own type-specific equality and I/O functions.

CHAPTER REVIEW

This chapter examined structure types and C's facilities for integrating such user-defined types into its overall system of data types. We discussed how to reference each individual component of a composite type through the use of the direct selection operator (.) placed between the structure variable name and the component name.

We saw that user-defined structure types can be used in most of the situations where built-in types are valid. Structured values can be function arguments and function results, and they can be copied using the assignment operator. Structure types are legitimate in declarations of variables, of structure components, and of array elements. However, structured values cannot be compared for equality using the == and != operators.

We saw that structure types play an important role in the process of data abstraction, and we studied how to implement operator functions that assist the programmer in thinking of the structure type as a unified concept.

The C constructs introduced in this chapter are described in Table 9.3.

Table 9.3   Summary of New C Constructs

Construct	Effect
Definition of a Structure Type	
| ```
typedef struct {
      char    name[20];
      int     quantity;
      double price;
} part_t;
``` | A structure type `part_t` is defined with components that can store a string and two numbers, one of type `int` and one of type `double`. |

(continued)
```

Table 9.3   (continued)

Construct	Effect
Declaration of Variables to Hold One Structure or an Array of Structures	

`part_t nuts, bolts, parts_list[40];`
`part_t mouse = {"serial mouse", 30,`
`                145.00};`
	nuts, bolts, and mouse are structured variables of type part_t; parts_list is an array of 40 such structures. The three components of mouse are initialized in its declaration.

Component Reference	
`cost = nuts.quantity * nuts.price;`	Multiplies two components of type part_t variable nuts.
`printf("Part: %s\n",` `       parts_list[i].name);`	Displays name component of ith element of parts_list.
Structure Copy	
`bolts = nuts;`	Stores in bolts a copy of each component of nuts.

QUICK-CHECK EXERCISES

1. What is the primary difference between a structure and an array? Which would you use to store the catalog description of a course? To store the names of students in the course?
2. How do you access a component of a structure type variable?

Exercises 3–8 refer to the following type `student_t` and to variables `stu1` and `stu2`:

```
typedef struct {
     char fst_name[20],
          last_name[20];
     int  score;
     char grade;
} student_t;
. . .
student_t stu1, stu2;
```

3. Identify the following statements as possibly valid or definitely invalid. If invalid, explain why.
   a. `student_t stulist[30];`
   b. `printf("%s", stu1);`
   c. `printf("%d %c", stu1.score, stu1.grade);`
   d. `stu2 = stu1;`
   e. `if (stu2.score == stu1.score)`
      `      printf("Equal");`
   f. `if (stu2 == stu1)`
      `      printf("Equal structures");`
   g. `scan_student(&stu1);`
   h. `stu2.last_name = "Martin";`
4. Write a statement that displays the initials of `stu1` (with periods).
5. How many components does variable `stu2` have?
6. Write functions `scan_student` and `print_student` for type `student_t` variables.
7. Declare an array of 40 `student_t` structures, and write a code segment that displays on separate lines the names (*last name, first name*) of all the students in the list.
8. Identify the type of each of the following references:
   a. `stu1`
   b. `stu2.score`
   c. `stu2.fst_name[3]`
   d. `stu1.grade`

ANSWERS TO QUICK-CHECK EXERCISES

1. A structure can have components of different types, but an array's elements must all be of the same type. Use a structure for the catalog item and an array of strings for the list of student names.
2. Components of structures are accessed using the direct selection operator followed by a component name.
3. a. Valid
   b. Invalid: `printf` does not accept structured arguments.
   c. Valid
   d. Valid
   e. Valid
   f. Invalid: Equality operators cannot be used with structure types.
   g. Valid (assuming parameter type is `student_t *`)
   h. Invalid: cannot copy strings with = except in declaration (this case needs `strcpy`)

```
4. printf("%c.%c.",  stu1.fst_name[0],
            stu1.last_name[0]);
5. Four
6. int
   scan_student(student_t *stup) /* output - student struc-
                                    ture to fill */
   {
        int  status,
        char temp[4]; /* temporary storage for grade */
        status = scanf("%s%s%d%s", (*stu).fst_name,
                                   (*stu).last_name,
                                   &(*stu).score,
                                   temp);
        if (status == 4) {
             status = 1;
             (*stu).grade = temp[0];
        } else if (status != EOF) {
             status = 0;
        }

        return (status);
   }

   void
   print_student(student_t stu) /* input - student structure
                                   to display */
   {
        printf("Student: %s, %s\n", stu.last_name,
             stu.fst_name);
        printf("   Score: %d      Grade: %c\n", stu.score,
             stu.grade);
   }

7. student_t students[40];

   for  (i = 0;  i < 40;  ++i)
       printf("%s, %s\n", students[i].last_name,
             students[i].fst_name);

8. a. student_t
   b. int
   c. char
   d. char
```

REVIEW QUESTIONS

1. Define a structure type called `subscriber_t` that contains the components `name`, `street_address`, and `monthly_bill` (i.e., how much the subscriber owes).

2. Write a C program that scans data to fill the variable `competition` declared here and then displays the contents of the structure with suitable labels:

```
#define STR_LENGTH 20

typedef struct {
      char event[STR_LENGTH],
            entrant[STR_LENGTH],
            country[STR_LENGTH];
      int  place;
} olympic_t;
. . .
olympic_t competition;
```

3. How would you call a function `scan_olympic` passing `competition` as an output argument?

4. Identify and correct the errors in the following program:

```
typedef struct
      char    name[15],
               start_date[15],
      double hrs_worked,
summer_help_t;

/* code for function scan_sum_hlp goes here */

int
main(void)
{
      summer_t operator;

      scan_sum_hlp(operator);
      printf("Name: %s\nStarting date: %s\nHours worked:
            %.2f\n", operator);

      return(0);
}
```

5. Define a data structure to store the following student data: gpa, major, address (consisting of street_address, city, state, zip), and class_schedule (consisting of up to six class records, each of which has description, time, and days components). Define whatever data types are needed.

PROGRAMMING PROJECTS

1. Define a structure type `auto_t` to represent an automobile. Include components for the make and model (strings), the odometer reading, the manufacture and purchase dates (use another user-defined type called `date_t`), and the gas tank (use a user-defined type `tank_t` with components for tank capacity and current fuel level, giving both in gallons). Write I/O functions `scan_date`, `scan_tank`, `scan_auto`, `print_date`, `print_tank`, and `print_auto`, and also write a driver function that repeatedly fills and displays an auto structure variable until EOF is encountered in the input file.

   Here is a small data set to try:

   ```
   Mercury Sable    49842 1 18 1989 5 30 1991 16    12.5
   Mazda    Navajo  14560 2 20 1993 6 15 1993 19.3 16.7
   ```

2. Define a structure type `element_t` to represent one element from the periodic table of elements. Components should include the atomic number (an integer); the name, chemical symbol, and class (strings); a numeric field for the atomic weight; and a 7-element array of integers for the number of electrons in each shell. The following are the components of an `element_t` structure for sodium.

   ```
   11  Sodium  Na  alkali_metal  22.9898  2 8 1 0 0 0 0
   ```

   Define and test I/O functions `scan_element` and `print_element`.

3. A number expressed in scientific notation is represented by its mantissa (a fraction) and its exponent (an integer). Define a type `sci_not_t` that has separate components for these two parts. Define a function `scan_sci` that takes from the input source a string representing a positive number in scientific notation and breaks it into components for storage in a `sci_not_t` structure. The mantissa of an input value (m) should satisfy this condition: $0.1 <= m < 1.0$. Also write functions to compute the sum, difference, product, and quotient of two `sci_not_t` values. All these functions should have a result type of `sci_not_t` and should ensure that the result's mantissa is in the prescribed range. Define a `print_sci` function as well.

Then, create a driver program to test your functions. Your output should be of this form:

```
Values input:   0.25000e3   0.20000e1
Sum:   0.25200e3
Difference:   0.24800e3
Product:   0.50000e3
Quotient:   0.12500e3
```

4. Researchers are studying new ways to model the earth's weather in order to try to understand the local, short-term effects of global phenomena such as the El Nino Southern Oscillation (ENSO). The ENSO is a three- to seven-year development of warm water in the South Pacific Ocean, the existence of which seems to be related to instances of flooding and drought throughout the world. It is valuable to tie the results of these weather models to actual observations. You are developing a database of measured meteorological data for use in weather and climate research. Define a structure type measured_data_t with components site_id_number (a four-digit integer), wind_speed, day_of_month, and temperature. Each site measures its data daily, at noon local time. Write a program that scans a table of input data and calculates the average wind speed measured at all sites for a given day. The program should also determine the site with the greatest variation in temperature (defined here as the biggest difference between extrema). Test the program on the following July daily data for three sites:

ID	Wind Speed (knots)	Day	Temperature (deg C)
1001	10	3	25
1001	12	4	27
1001	15	5	30
1001	8	6	27
1001	10	7	33
1002	0	3	15
1002	1	4	17
1002	1	5	20
1002	0	6	15
1002	2	7	18
2121	11	3	30
2121	12	4	20
2121	13	5	30
2121	14	6	27
2121	10	7	33

5. Numeric addresses for computers on the international network Internet are composed of four parts, separated by periods, of the form

   `xx.yy.zz.mm`

   where `xx`, `yy`, `zz`, and `mm` are positive integers. Locally, computers are usually known by a nickname as well. You are designing a program to process a list of Internet addresses, identifying all pairs of computers from the same locality. Create a structure type called `address_t` with components for the four integers of an Internet address and a fifth component to store an associated nickname of fewer than 20 characters. Your program should scan a list of up to 100 addresses and nicknames terminated by a sentinel address of all zeros and a sentinel nickname. Here is a sample data set:

   ```
   111.22.3.44      platte
   555.66.7.88      wabash
   111.22.5.66      green
   0.0.0.0          none
   ```

   The program should display a list of messages identifying each pair of computers from the same locality, that is, each pair of computers with matching values in the first two components of the address. In the messages, the computers should be identified by their nicknames. An example of a message follows:

   `Machines platte and green are on the same local network.`

   Follow the messages by a display of the full list of addresses and nicknames. Include in your program a `scan_address` function, a `print_address` function, and a `local_address` function. Function `local_address` should take two address structures as input parameters and return 1 (for true) if the addresses are on the same local network, and 0 (for false) otherwise.

6. Using type `complex_t` from Section 9.4, develop a Gaussian elimination program to solve systems of linear equations with complex coefficients. Hint: Review Section 8.5.

7. Rewrite the common fraction program from Chapter 6 using a structure type to represent a fraction.

8. In the Self-Check Exercises of Sections 9.1 and 9.2, you defined a data type `location_t` to represent a geographic location and some functions to process certain components of the type. Write functions `print_location`, `location_equal`, and `scan_location` for processing type `location_t` data, and develop a driver to use in testing this group of functions.

ADVANCED FILE PROCESSING

This chapter will explore in greater depth the use of standard input, standard output, and program-controlled text files. We also will introduce binary files and compare the advantages and disadvantages of text and binary files.

10.1 INPUT/OUTPUT FILES: REVIEW AND FURTHER STUDY

C can process two kinds of files: text files and binary files. We will study text files in this section and binary files later in this chapter. All the files you have created using an editor or word processor have been text files. A *text file* is a named collection of characters saved in secondary storage (e.g., on a disk). A text file has no fixed size. To mark the end of a text file, the computer places a special *end-of-file* character, which we will denote <eof>, after the last character in the file. As you create a text file using an editor program, pressing the <return> key causes the newline character (represented by C as '\n') to be placed in the file.

The following lines represent a text file consisting of two lines of letters, blank characters, and the punctuation characters . and ! .

```
This is a text file!<newline>
It has two lines.<newline><eof>
```

Each line ends with the newline character, and the eof character follows the last newline in the file. For convenience in examining the file's contents, we listed each line of the file (through <newline>) as a separate line, although this would not be the case in the actual disk file. The disk file consists of a sequence of characters occupying consecutive storage locations on a track of the disk, as shown here:

```
This is a text file!<newline>It has two lines.<newline><eof>
```

The first character of the second line (I) follows directly after the last character of the first line (the newline character). Because all textual input and output data are actually a continuous stream of character codes, we sometimes refer to a data source or destination as an *input stream* or an *output stream*. These general terms can be applied to files, to the terminal keyboard and screen, and to any other sources of input data or destinations of output data.

The Keyboard and Screen as Text Streams

In interactive programming, C associates system names with the terminal keyboard and screen. The name `stdin` represents the keyboard's input stream. Two system streams, the "normal" output stream `stdout` and the "error" output stream `stderr`, are associated with the screen. All three streams can be treated like text files because their individual components are characters.

Normally at the keyboard, we enter one line of data at a time, pressing <return> or <enter> to indicate the end of a data line. Pressing one of these keys inserts the newline character in system stream `stdin`. Normally in interactive programming, we use a sentinel value to indicate the end of data rather than attempting to place the eof character in system stream `stdin`. However, the eof character could be used. No single key represents the eof character, so most systems use the control key followed by a letter (for example, on computers running the UNIX operating system, the stroke <control-d> would be used).

Writing characters to the streams `stdout` and `stderr` causes a display on the screen in an interactive program. We have studied the use of the `printf` function to write characters to the screen. Using a `'\n'` in the `printf` format string causes output of a newline character that moves the cursor to the start of the next line of the screen.

Newline and EOF

We have seen that C handles the special newline character differently than the eof character, even though they have similar purposes. The <newline> marks the end of a line of text, and the <eof> marks the end of the entire file. The <newline> can be processed like any other character: It can be input using `scanf` with the `%c` specifier, it can be compared to `'\n'` for equality, and it can be output using `printf`.

However, input of the special eof character is regarded as a failed operation, and the input function responsible returns as its value the negative integer associated with the identifier `EOF`. Because this special return value gives the calling function an indication that no more data are in the input file, the C runtime support system is under no obligation to provide an error message if the program ignores the warning value and continues to attempt to get input from the stream in question. The following is another example of the input loops that we studied that base their exit condition on the appearance of the `EOF` return value:

```
for  (status = scanf("%d", &num);
      status != EOF;
      status = scanf("%d", &num))
    process(num);
```

File Pointer Variables

We saw in Chapter 2 that before using a nonstandard text file for input or output, we must declare a file pointer variable and give it a value, allowing us to access the desired file. The system must prepare the file for input or output before permitting access. This preparation is the purpose of the stdio library function `fopen`. The statements that follow declare and initialize the file pointer variables `infilep` and `outfilep`:

```
FILE *infilep;
FILE *outfilep;

infilep = fopen("b:data.txt", "r");
outfilep = fopen("b:results.txt", "w");
```

Notice that the data type of `infilep` and `outfilep` is `FILE *`. Remember that C is case sensitive, so you must use all capital letters when writing the type name `FILE`. It is possible to declare both `infilep` and `outfilep` in the same statement, but each must be immediately preceded by the asterisk denoting "pointer to," as shown here:

```
FILE *infilep, *outfilep;
```

We use the stdio library function `fopen` to open or create an additional text file. The `"r"` in the first call to `fopen` just shown indicates that we wish to use the text file opened as an input file from which we will read (scan) data. The `"w"` in the second call conveys that our intention is to write to the file, that is, to use it as an output destination. The first argument to `fopen` is a string that is the name of the text file to manipulate. The correct form of such a file name will vary from one operating system to another. The result returned by `fopen` is the file pointer to be used in all further operations on the file. This pointer is the address of a structure of type `FILE` that contains the information necessary to access the file opened by `fopen`. The pointer must be saved in a variable of type `FILE *`. In a program containing the lines just shown, the variable `infilep` will be used to access the input file named `"b:data.txt"`, and the variable `outfilep` will be used to access the newly created output file named `"b:results.txt"`. The identifiers `stdin`, `stdout`, and `stderr` also name variables of type `FILE *`, variables initialized by the system prior to the start of a C program.

If the `fopen` function is unable to accomplish the requested operation, the file pointer that it returns is equal to the value associated with the identifier `NULL` by the stdio library. For example, if execution of this call to `fopen`

```
infilep = fopen("b:data.txt", "r");
```

were unsuccessful due to the nonexistence of a file named `"b:data.txt"`, then execution of the following statement would display an appropriate error message:

```
if (infilep == NULL)
        printf("Cannot open b:data.txt for input\n");
```

A pointer whose value equals NULL is called a *null pointer*. Take care not to confuse this concept with the *null character*, whose value is the character `'\0'`. A null pointer is *not* equivalent to a null character.

Using `fopen` with mode `"w"` to open for output a file that already exists usually causes loss of the contents of the existing file. However, if the computer's operating system automatically numbers file versions and creates a new version when it opens an output file, the contents of the existing file will not be lost.

Functions That Take File Pointer Arguments

Table 10.1 compares calls to `printf` and `scanf` with calls to analogous functions for input from the file accessed by `infilep` and for output to the file accessed by `outfilep.` In this table, we assume that `infilep` and `out-filep` have been initialized as shown earlier.

Line 1 shows input of a single integer value to be stored in `num`. The call to `scanf` obtains this value from the standard input stream, typically the keyboard. The call to `fscanf` obtains the integer value from `"b:data.txt"`, the file accessed through the file pointer `infilep`. Like `scanf`, function `fscanf` returns as its result the number of input values it has successfully stored through its output arguments. Function `fscanf` also returns the negative EOF value when it encounters the end of the file accessed by its file pointer argument.

Table 10.1   Comparison of I/O with Standard Files and I/O with User-Defined File Pointers

Line	Functions That Access stdin and stdout	Functions That Can Access Any Text File
1	`scanf("%d", &num);`	`fscanf(infilep, "%d", &num);`

2	`printf`
	`("Number = %d\n",`
	`num);`
		`fprintf(outfilep,`
		`"Number = %d\n", num);`

Similarly, the behavior of `fprintf` is fully comparable to the behavior of its standard I/O equivalent—`printf`—except that `fprintf` takes a file pointer argument through which to access its input source or output destination.

Closing a File

When a program has no further use for a file, it should *close* the file by calling the library function `fclose` with the file pointer. The following statement closes the file accessed through `infilep`:

```
fclose(infilep);
```

Function `fclose` disposes of the structure that was created to store file access information and carries out other "cleanup" operations.

If necessary, a program can create an output file and can then rescan the file. The file is first opened in `"w"` mode, and data are stored using a function such as `fprintf`. The file is then closed using `fclose` and reopened in `"r"` mode, allowing the data to be rescanned with a function such as `fscanf`.

EXAMPLE 10.1

For security reasons, having a backup or duplicate copy of a file is a good idea, in case the original is lost. Even though operating systems typically provide a command that will copy a file, we will write our own C program to do this. The program in Fig. 10.1 copies each character in one file to a backup file and allows the user to enter interactively both the name of the file to copy and the name of the backup file.

Figure 10.1   Program to Make a Backup Copy of a Text File

```
/*
 *  Makes a backup file.  Repeatedly prompts for the name of a file to
 *  back up until a name is provided that corresponds to an available
 *  file.  Then it prompts for the name of the backup file and creates
 *  the file copy.
 */

#include <stdio.h>
#define  STRSIZ 80

int
main(void)
```

(continued)

Figure 10.1   (continued)

```
{
     char  in_name[STRSIZ],  /* strings giving names                  */
           out_name[STRSIZ]; /*    of input and backup files          */
     FILE *inp,              /* file pointers for input and           */
          *outp;             /*    backup files                       */
     char ch;               /* one character of input file           */
     int  status;           /* status of input operation             */

     /*  Get the name of the file to back up and open the file for
             input                                                    */
     printf("Enter name of file you want to back up> ");
     for  (scanf("%s", in_name);
           (inp = fopen(in_name, "r")) == NULL;
            scanf("%s", in_name)) {
        printf("Cannot open %s for input\n", in_name);
        printf("Re-enter file name> ");
     }

     /*  Get name to use for backup file and open file for output    */
     printf("Enter name for backup copy> ");
     for  (scanf("%s", out_name);
           (outp = fopen(out_name, "w")) == NULL;
            scanf("%s", out_name)) {
        printf("Cannot open %s for output\n", out_name);
        printf("Re-enter file name> ");
     }

     /*  Make backup copy one character at a time                    */
     for  (status = fscanf(inp, "%c", &ch);
           status != EOF;
           status = fscanf(inp, "%c", &ch))
        fprintf(outp, "%c", ch);

     /*  Close files and notify user of backup completion            */
     fclose(inp);
     fclose(outp);
     printf("Copied %s to %s.\n", in_name, out_name);

     return(0);
}
```

The program in Fig. 10.1 begins by displaying a prompting message on the screen using `printf`. Then `scanf` is executed to take the file name typed at the keyboard.

The repetition condition of the first `for` loop is

```
(inp = fopen(in_name, "r")) == NULL
```

The call to function `fopen` causes the system to try to open for input the file whose name is stored in `in_name`. If this attempt is successful, a file pointer is returned and assigned to `inp`. The value of this assignment will equal `NULL` only if the file could not be successfully opened; in this case, the user is asked to reenter the name of the file.

In the next program segment, a similar `for` loop is used to get the name of an output file and to open the file, storing the file pointer in `outp`.

The `for` loop that follows manipulates not the standard I/O streams but rather the input and output files accessed through the file pointers in `inp` and `outp`. Function `fscanf` is called repeatedly to take one character at a time from the input file, and `fprintf` echoes these characters to the output file. When the copy is complete, the calls to `fclose` release the two files after writing an <eof> on the output file.

Figure 10.2 shows the input and output streams used by the file backup program. ←

Figure 10.2   Input and Output Streams for File Backup Program

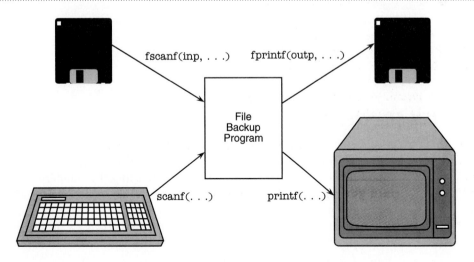

Self-Check

1. Assume these declarations for the problem that follows:

```
double x;
int    n;
char   ch, str[40];
```

Indicate the contents of these variables after each of the following input operations is performed. Assume that the file accessed by `indatap` consists of the data given and that each lettered group of operations occurs at the beginning of a program, immediately following a statement that opens the file.

123 3.145 xyz<newline>35 z<newline>

a. `fscanf(indatap, "%d%lf%s%c", &n, &x, str, &ch);`
b. `fscanf(indatap, "%d%lf", &n, &x);`
   `fscanf(indatap, "%s%c", str, &ch);`
c. `fscanf(indatap, "%lf%d%c%s", &x, &n, &ch, str);`
d. `fscanf(indatap, "%s%s%s%d%c%c", str, str, str, &n,`
   `     &ch, &ch);`
2. List the library functions we have studied that require a file pointer argument.

Programming

1. Rewrite the file backup program in Fig. 10.1 so it uses a function with file pointer parameters to do the actual file copy.

10.2 PROBLEM SOLVING ILLUSTRATED

In this section, we present a case study that demonstrates the use of files for input of data and for storage of results while using the standard I/O streams to obtain from the user the necessary file names at the time the program is running. The program also uses the screen to show the user the results and to provide messages when errors are detected. This case study reviews the use of array elements that are of a structured data type.

Case Study: Land Boundary Survey

PROBLEM

The surveying firm of Harris, Neilson, and Gallop has completed a land boundary survey. The result consists of the (x, y) coordinates of points defining the edges of a piece of property. These coordinates are stored in a data file, one pair per line. The firm needs to know the distance between adjacent points and the total length of the boundary. For error correction purposes, the firm would also like to know the percentage of the total length of each line and the cumulative percentage, starting with the first line. The output results will be written to an output file and also displayed on the screen in tabular form, as shown in Fig. 10.3.

ANALYSIS

First the program copies into an array of points the survey data from the input file named by the program user. Each point has an x component and a y component. The distance between adjacent points, whose (x, y) components are (x_i, y_i) and (x_j, y_j), is given by the formula

$$distance = \sqrt{(x_i - x_j)^2 + (y_i - y_j)^2}$$

The total length of the land boundary is the sum of the individual lengths. After we compute the total length, we can determine the percentage of the total boundary represented by each individual length, add it to the cumulative percentage, and write the required output file and table.

**Figure 10.3
Land Survey
Table**

Harris, Neilson, and Gallop, Surveyors

The number of points processed was 6.
Total boundary length is 1365.685 feet.

Line Number	Start Point x	y	Line length (in feet)	% of Boundary	Cumulative %
1	100.000	100.000	141.421	10.355	10.355
2	200.000	200.000	141.421	10.355	20.711
3	300.000	300.000	141.421	10.355	31.066
4	400.000	400.000	400.000	29.289	60.355
5	0.000	400.000	400.000	29.289	89.645
6	0.000	0.000	141.421	10.355	100.000

Data Requirements

Input File
file of coordinates

Output File
file of line lengths and percentages

Structured Data Type
```
point_t
    components: double x, y  /*  (x, y) coordinates    */
```

Problem Constant
```
MAX   100              /*  size of the arrays              */
```

Problem Inputs
```
point_t pts[MAX]   /*  edge points                          */
```

Problem Outputs
coordinates of edge points
```
double length[MAX]   /*  distance between adjacent
                             points                        */
double pct[MAX]      /*  percentage of total boundary
                             length                        */
double cum_pct[MAX]  /*  cumulative percentage so far */
int     n            /*  number of points on the
                             boundary                      */
double perim         /*  total boundary length           */
```

◀ DESIGN ▶

Initial Algorithm

1. Get all points from the data file and count them.
2. Calculate the length of each line segment and the total boundary length.
3. Compute percentages of total boundary represented by each line segment and cumulative percentages.
4. Write the output file and table.

◀ IMPLEMENTATION ▶

We use a separate function to implement each step of the algorithm. Figure 10.4 shows the main function. It contains declarations for all arrays and simple variables listed in the data requirements section and includes calls to the four functions.

Figure 10.4   Function main for Land Boundary Survey Program

```
/*
 * This program takes a collection of edge points around the boundary of
 * a plot of land and computes the distances between adjacent points. The
 * coordinates of the edge points, the lengths of the individual lines,
 * and their percentages of the total perimeter are written along with
 * the cumulative percentages to an output file. They are also displayed
 * in a table.
 */
#include <stdio.h>

typedef struct {
      double x, y;
} point_t;

/*  Include functions from Figs. 10.5-10.8 here                          */

#define MAX 100

int
main(void)
{
      int     n;              /*  number of edge points                  */
      point_t pts[MAX];       /*  edge points                            */
      double  length[MAX],    /*  boundary line lengths                  */
              pct[MAX],       /*  percentages of perimeter               */
              cum_pct[MAX],   /*  cumulative percentages of perimeter    */
              perim;          /*  perimeter length                       */
      /*  Get edge points                                                */
      get_points(MAX, pts, &n);

      /*  Calculate the length of each line and the total perimeter      */
      calc_lengths(pts, n, length, &perim);

      /*  Compute percentage each boundary line is of total perimeter    */
      compute_pct(length, n, perim, pct, cum_pct);

      /*  Write output file and table                                    */
      write_results(pts, length, pct, cum_pct, n, perim);

      return(0);
}
```

Function get_points

Function `get_points` begins by using the standard I/O stream to get from the user the name of the file containing the points (see Fig. 10.5). It then opens this file and uses `fscanf` in a loop with endfile/error-driven exit to fill the array of points. After loop exit, the output parameter accessed through `np` is defined.

Figure 10.5 Function get_points for Land Boundary Survey Program

```c
#define STR_SIZ 80

/*
 *  Prompts user for name of text file containing survey data, loads
 *  points from this file, and sends back number of points loaded through
 *  output parameter np.
 */
void
get_points(int     max,    /* input - declared size of pts          */
           point_t pts[],  /* output - array of data                */
           int     *np)    /* output - number of data values
                                        stored in pts               */
{
      int     i, status;
      point_t point;
      char    file_name[STR_SIZ];
      FILE    *filep;

      /*  Get name of data file and open it                         */
      printf("Enter name of file containing points> ");
      scanf("%s", file_name);
      filep = fopen(file_name, "r");

      if (filep == NULL) { /* if file cannot be opened, give error
                       message and send back zero as number of points */
          printf("Cannot open file %s\n", file_name);
          *np = 0;
      } else { /* input loop exits on EOF, error, or when array filled */
          i = 0;
          for  (status = fscanf(filep, "%lf%lf", &point.x, &point.y);
                status == 2  &&  i < max;
                status = fscanf(filep, "%lf%lf", &point.x, &point.y)) {
              pts[i++] = point;
          }
```

(continued)

Figure 10.5 (continued)

```
                    /* Issue error message on premature exit              */
                    if (status > EOF  &&  status < 2) {
                            printf("*** Error in data format ***\n");
                            printf("*** Using first %d points ***\n", i);
                    } else if (status == 2) {
                            printf("*** Error: more than %d points in file %s ",
                                    max, file_name);
                            printf("***\n*** Using first %d points only ***\n", i);
                    }

                    /* Send back size of used portion of array              */
                    *np = i;

            }
}
```

Function calc_lengths

Function `calc_lengths` computes the length of each line on the boundary. The first line connects the first two points, the second line connects the second and third points, and so on. The last line connects the last and first points. The function also tabulates the length of the perimeter. The algorithm follows.

Algorithm for calc_lengths

1. Initialize `perim` to zero.
2. For i from 0 through n – 2
   3. Set `length[i]` to the length of the line from `pts[i]` to `pts[i+1]`.
   4. Add new line length to `perim`.
5. Set `length[n-1]` to the length of the line from `pts[n-1]` to `pts[0]`.
6. Add the new line length to `perim`.

Figure 10.6 shows function `calc_lengths` along with function `distance`. Function `distance` calculates the length of the line whose end points are its input arguments.

Figure 10.6 Functions distance and calc_lengths for Land Boundary Survey Program

```
#include <math.h>

/*
 *  Computes the distance between points start and end.
 */
```

(continued)

Figure 10.6 (continued)

```
double
distance(point_t start, point_t end) /* input - end points of a line */
{
      double xdiff, ydiff;

      xdiff = end.x - start.x;
      ydiff = end.y - start.y;

      return (sqrt(xdiff * xdiff + ydiff * ydiff));
}

/*
 *  Calculates the length of each line and the total boundary.
 */
void
calc_lengths(const point_t pts[],     /*  input - list of points        */
             int           n,         /*  input - number of points      */
             double        length[],  /*  output - length of each line   */
             double        *perim)    /*  output - total boundary length */
{
      int i;

      /*  Defines each individual line length and adds it to the total  */
      *perim = 0;
      for  (i = 0;  i < n - 1;  ++i) {
          length[i] = distance(pts[i], pts[i + 1]);
          *perim += length[i];
      }

      length[n - 1] = distance(pts[n - 1], pts[0]);
      *perim += length[n - 1];
}
```

Function compute_pct

Function `compute_pct` performs the percentage calculations for each line, defining arrays `pct` and `cum_pct`. Figure 10.7 shows function `compute_pct`. In the `for` loop, the statements

```
pct[i] = length[i] / perim * 100.0;
tot_pct += pct[i];
cum_pct[i] = tot_pct;
```

Figure 10.7   Function compute_pct for Land Boundary Survey Program

```
/*
 *  Calculates each line's percentage of the full perimeter
 *  and the cumulative percentages.
 */
void
compute_pct(const double length[],   /*  input - length of each line       */
            int            n,         /*  input - number of points          */
            double         perim,     /*  input - length of full perimeter  */
            double         pct[],     /*  output - percentages corresponding
                                                   to lengths                */
            double         cum_pct[]) /*  output - cumulative percentages    */
{
        int    i;
        double tot_pct = 0;

        for  (i = 0;  i < n;  ++i) {
             pct[i] = length[i] / perim * 100.0;
             tot_pct += pct[i];
             cum_pct[i] = tot_pct;
        }
}
```

define the current line's percentage of the full perimeter pct[i] and the cumulative percentage cum_pct[i]. The latter is obtained by adding pct[i] to the previous cumulative percentage tot_pct.

Function write_results displays a table of results on the screen and saves the same table in the file named by the program user. The table contains one line for each segment of the land boundary. This line includes the coordinates of the segment's starting point, its length, the percentage of the total length, and the cumulative percentage so far. We display only the starting point of each line because of screen width limitations. In our heading, we need to display a percent sign (%), a character normally used in a format string to signal the beginning of a placeholder. To have *one* percent sign displayed, we must put *two* percent signs in the format string. Figure 10.8 shows function write_results.

TESTING

A sample run of the survey program will produce a table similar to the one shown in Fig. 10.3. Make sure that all values displayed are positive and that the final cumulative percentage is 100. To verify the correctness of the table, try some adjacent points with the same *x* coordinates but with different *y* coordinates (or the

Figure 10.8   Function write_results for Land Boundary Survey Program

```
/*
 * Displays survey results on the screen and also saves this table in a
 * text file.
 */
void
write_results(const point_t pts[],     /*  input - edge points on boundary      */
              const double  length[], /*  input - lengths of boundary lines    */
              const double pct[],      /*  input - each line's % of total       */
                                       /*                         boundary      */
              const double cum_pct[], /*  input - cumulative % of total        */
                                       /*                         so far        */
              int       n,             /*  input - number of edge points        */
              double    perim)         /*  input - total boundary length        */
{
      char  file_name[STR_SIZ];  /*  name of output file                 */
      FILE *outp;                 /*  file pointer for text output file   */
      int   i;

      /*  Determine and open output file                                  */
      printf("Enter name of file in which to place results\n> ");
      scanf("%s", file_name);
      outp = fopen(file_name, "w");

      /*  Display and save table heading                        */
      printf("\n           Harris, Neilson, and Gallop, Surveyors\n\n");
      fprintf(outp,
             "           Harris, Neilson, and Gallop, Surveyors\n\n");
      printf("Land boundary has %d edge points.\n", n);
      fprintf(outp, "Land boundary has %d edge points.\n", n);
      printf("Boundary length = %.3f feet.\n\n", perim);
      fprintf(outp, "Boundary length = %.3f feet.\n\n", perim);
      printf
        ("Line          Start Point      Line Length      %% of Cumulative\n");
      fprintf
        (outp,
         "Line          Start Point      Line Length      %% of Cumulative\n");
      printf
        ("Number      x          y      (in feet)      Boundary       %%\n\n");
      fprintf
        (outp,
         "Number      x          y      (in feet)      Boundary       %%\n\n");
```

(continued)

Figure 10.8 (continued)

```
/*  Display and save table of results                               */
for  (i = 0;  i < n;  ++i) {
    printf("%3d%12.3f%12.3f%12.3f%12.3f%12.3f\n", i + 1, pts[i].x,
            pts[i].y, length[i], pct[i], cum_pct[i]);
    fprintf(outp, "%3d%12.3f%12.3f%12.3f%12.3f%12.3f\n", i + 1, pts[i].x,
            pts[i].y, length[i], pct[i], cum_pct[i]);
}

/*  Close output file                                                */
fclose(outp);
}
```

same y coordinates but different x coordinates). In this case, the line length should be the absolute value of the difference between the y coordinates. See what happens to the display table when the first point is placed at the end of the data file instead of at the beginning. All the table lines should move up one position, and the last line displayed should be the same as the former first line.

Also exercise your statements on test cases that give error messages. Try an incorrect input file name. In addition, try an input file with a data format error and one with too much data.

EXERCISE FOR SECTION 10.2

Self-Check

1. The code for function `scan_complex` that we used in Chapter 9 to scan one complex number is shown with some blanks added. Fill in the blanks to create `fscan_complex`, a function that takes a file pointer argument in addition to the `complex_t` output argument. This function should scan a complex number from the file accessed by the file pointer.

```
/*
 * Complex number _____  input function returns standard
 * scanning error code
 *     1 => valid scan,  0 => error,  negative EOF value =>
 *     end of file
 */
```

```
int
fscan_complex(_____

              complex_t *c) /* output - address of complex
                                        variable to fill */
{
     int status;

     status = __scanf(_____,
                      "%lf%lf", &(*c).real, &(*c).imag);

     if (status == 2)
          status = 1;
     else if (status != EOF)
          status = 0;

     return (status);
}
```

10.3 BINARY FILES

When we use text files for storage of data, a program must expend a significant amount of effort to convert the stream of characters from an input file into the binary integers, type `double` mantissas and exponents, and character strings that are the representation in main memory of the same data. The program must again expend time in converting the internal data format back into a stream of characters for storage in an output file of text. In a C program, these conversions are carried out by functions such as `scanf` and `printf`.

Many programs produce output files that are used as input files for other programs. If there is no need for a human to read the file, it is a waste of computer time for the first program to convert its internal data format to a stream of characters, and then for the second program to have to apply an inverse conversion to extract the intended data from the stream of characters. We can avoid this unnecessary translation by using a binary file rather than a text file.

A *binary file* is a file created by executing a program that stores directly in the file the computer's internal representation of each file component. For example, the code fragment in Fig. 10.9 creates a binary file named `"nums.bin"`, which contains the even integers from 2 to 500.

You see in Fig. 10.9 that a binary file is declared in exactly the same way as a text file. The `fopen` and `fclose` functions are used just as they are for text files, except that the second argument to `fopen` is either `"wb"` (write binary) for output files or `"rb"` (read binary) for input files. However, a dif-

Figure 10.9   Creating a Binary File of Integers

```
FILE *binaryp;
int   i;

binaryp = fopen("nums.bin", "wb");

for  (i = 2;   i <= 500;  i += 2)
    fwrite(&i, sizeof (int), 1, binaryp);

fclose(binaryp);
```

ferent stdio library function is used for copying values into the file: function `fwrite`, which has four input parameters. The first parameter is the *address* of the first memory cell whose contents are to be copied to the file. In Fig. 10.9, we want the contents of the variable i copied to the file, so we provide `fwrite` with the address of i (`&i`) as the first argument.

The second parameter of function `fwrite` is the number of bytes to copy to the file for one component. In Chapter 1, we noted that a memory cell is a collection of smaller units called *bytes* and that a byte is the amount of storage needed to represent one character. A C operator `sizeof` can be applied to any data type name to find the number of bytes that the current implementation uses for storage of the data type. For example, these statements will print a sentence indicating how many bytes are being occupied by one integer:

```
printf("An integer requires %d bytes ", sizeof (int));
printf("in this implementation.\n");
```

The `sizeof` operator can be applied to both built-in and user-defined types.

The third parameter of `fwrite` is the number of values to write to the binary file. In our example, we are writing one integer at a time, so we provide the constant 1 as this argument. However, it is possible to save the contents of an entire array using just one call to `fwrite` by providing the array's size as the third argument. The final argument to `fwrite` is a file pointer to the file being created, a file previously opened in mode `"wb"` using function `fopen`. For example, if array `score` is an array of 10 integers, the statement

```
fwrite(score, sizeof (int), 10, binaryp);
```

writes the entire array to the output file.

Writing the value of an integer variable `i` to a binary file using `fwrite` is faster than writing `i` to a text file. For example, if the value of `i` is `244`, the statement from the `for` loop

```
fwrite(&i, sizeof (int), 1, binaryp);
```

copies the internal binary representation of `i` from memory to the file accessed by `binaryp`. If your computer uses two bytes to store an `int` value, the byte that stores the highest order bits would contain all zeros, and the byte that stores the lowest order bits would contain the binary string `11110100` (244 = 128 + 64 + 32 + 16 + 4). Both bytes would be written to disk as the next file component.

Assuming `textp` is a pointer to a text output file, the statement

```
fprintf(textp, "%d ", i);
```

writes the value of `i` to the file using four characters (four bytes). The computer must first convert the binary number in `i` to the character string `"244 "` and then write the binary codes for the characters 2, 4, 4, and blank to the file. Obviously, it takes more time to do the conversion and copy each character than it does to copy the internal binary representation to disk. Also, twice as much disk space is required to store four characters as to store the internal binary representation of the type `int` value (four bytes versus two).

Using a binary file has another advantage. Each time we write a type `double` value to a text file, the computer must convert this value to a character string whose precision is determined by the placeholder in the format string. A loss of precision may result.

There is a negative side to binary file usage, however. A binary file created on one computer is rarely readable on another type of computer. Since a binary file can be read only by a specialized computer program, a person cannot proofread the file by printing it out or by examining it in a word processor. Furthermore, a binary file cannot be created or modified in a word processor, so a program that expects binary file input cannot be tested until the program that produces the needed binary file is complete.

The stdio library includes an input function `fread` that is comparable to `fwrite`. Function `fread` also requires four arguments:

1. Address of first memory cell to fill.
2. Size of one value.
3. Maximum number of elements to copy from the file into memory.
4. File pointer to a binary file opened in mode `"rb"` using function `fopen`.

Function `fread` returns as its value an integer indicating how many elements it successfully copied from the file. This number will be less than the value of the third argument of `fread` if `EOF` is encountered prematurely.

It is very important not to mix file types. A binary file created (written) using `fwrite` must be read using `fread`. A text file created using `fprintf` must be read using a text file input function such as `fscanf`.

Table 10.2 compares the use of text and binary files for input and output of data of various types. The statements in both columns assume the following constant macros, type definition, and variable declarations.

```
#define STRSIZ   10
#define MAX      40

typedef struct {
     char name[STRSIZ];
     double diameter,         /* equatorial diameter in
                                 km                      */
               dist_sun,      /* average distance from sun
                                 in km                   */
               orbital_prd,   /* years to orbit sun once */
               axial_rot_prd; /* hours to complete one
                                 revolution on axis      */
} planet_t;
. . .
double    nums[MAX], data;
planet_t a_planet;
int i, n, status;
FILE *plan_bin_inp, *plan_bin_outp, *plan_txt_inp,
     *plan_txt_outp;
FILE *doub_bin_inp, *doub_bin_outp, *doub_txt_inp,
     *doub_txt_outp;
```

In Example 1 of Table 10.2, we use `fopen` to open our input files, and we store the file pointers returned by `fopen` in variables of type `FILE *`. Notice that the form of the call to `fopen` for opening a binary file differs from the call for opening a text file only in the value of the mode argument. In fact, even this difference is *optional*. Also notice that the type of the file pointer does not vary. We see a similar situation in the opening of output files in Example 2. One consequence of this similarity is that the ability of the C compiler and run-time support system to detect misuse of a file pointer is severely limited. It is the programmer's responsibility to keep track of which type of file each file pointer accesses and to use the right I/O function at the right time.

In Examples 3 and 4 of Table 10.2, we compare input/output of a user-defined structure type as it is done with text and binary files. In Examples 5 and 6, we see input/output of an array of type `double` values. In the text file code, array elements are scanned or written one at a time in an indexed loop. When we use a binary file, we can fill the array from or copy it to the file using just one call to

Table 10.2 Data I/O Using Text and Binary Files

Example	Text File I/O	Binary File I/O	Purpose

1	`plan_txt_inp =`
	`    fopen("planets.txt", "r");`
	
	`doub_txt_inp =`
	`    fopen("nums.txt", "r");`
		`plan_bin_inp =`
		`    fopen("planets.bin", "rb");`
		
		`doub_bin_inp =`
		`    fopen("nums.bin", "rb");`
			Open for input a file of planets and a file of numbers, saving file pointers for use in calls to input functions.

2	`plan_txt_outp =`
	`    fopen("pl_out.txt", "w");`
	
	`doub_txt_outp =`
	`    fopen("nm_out.txt", "w");`
		`plan_bin_outp =`
		`    fopen("pl_out.bin", "wb");`
		
		`doub_bin_outp =`
		`    fopen("nm_out.bin", "wb");`
			Open for output a file of planets and a file of numbers, saving file pointers for use in calls to output functions.

3	`fscanf(plan_txt_inp,`
	`    "%s%lf%lf%lf%lf",`
	`    a_planet.name,`
	`    &a_planet.diameter,`
	`    &a_planet.dist_sun,`
	`    &a_planet.orbital_prd,`
	`    &a_planet.axial_rot_prd);`
		`fread(&a_planet,`
		`    sizeof (planet_t),`
		`    1, plan_bin_inp);`
			Copy one planet structure into memory from the data file.

4	`fprintf(plan_txt_outp,`
	`    "%s%e%e%e%e",`
	`    a_planet.name,`
	`    a_planet.diameter,`
	`    a_planet.dist_sun,`
	`    a_planet.orbital_prd,`
	`    a_planet.axial_rot_prd);`
		`fwrite(&a_planet,`
		`    sizeof (planet_t),`
		`    1, plan_bin_outp);`
			Write one planet structure to the output file.

Example	Text File I/O	Binary File I/O	Purpose
| 5 | ```
for  (i = 0;  i < MAX;   ++i)
    fscanf(doub_txt_inp,
           "%lf", &nums[i]);
``` | ```
fread(nums, sizeof (double),
      MAX, doub_bin_inp);
``` | Fill array nums with type double values from input file. |
| 6 | ```
for  (i = 0;  i < MAX;   ++i)
    fprintf(doub_txt_outp,
            "%e\n", nums[i]);
``` | ```
fwrite(nums, sizeof (double),
       MAX, doub_bin_outp);
``` | Write contents of array nums to output file. |
| 7 | ```
n = 0;
for (status =
         fscanf(doub_txt_inp,
                "%lf", &data);
     status != EOF &&
     n < MAX;
     status =
         fscanf(doub_txt_inp,
                "%lf", &data))
    nums[n++] = data;
``` | ```
n = fread(nums,
          sizeof (double),
          MAX, doub_bin_inp);
``` | Fill nums with data until EOF encountered, setting n to the number of values stored. |
| 8 | ```
fclose(plan_txt_inp);
fclose(plan_txt_outp);
fclose(doub_txt_inp);
fclose(doub_txt_outp);
``` | ```
fclose(plan_bin_inp);
fclose(plan_bin_outp);
fclose(doub_bin_inp);
fclose(doub_bin_outp);
``` | Close all input and output files. |

`fread` or `fwrite`. We see that the calls used to read/write array `nums` provide the size of one array element as the second argument to `fread` or `fwrite` and the number of array elements to process as the third argument. Example 7 demonstrates partially filling array `nums` and setting n to the number of elements filled. Example 8 shows that all files—binary or text, input or output—are closed in the same way.

EXERCISES FOR SECTION 10.3

Self-Check

Assume the environment shown, and complete the statements that follow so that they are valid:

```c
#define NAME_LEN 50
#define SIZE      30

typedef struct {
      char    name[NAME_LEN];
      int     age;
      double income;
} person_t;
. . .
int      num_err[SIZE];
person_t exec;
FILE    *nums_inp, *psn_inp, *psn_outp, *nums_outp;
         /* binary files */
FILE    *nums_txt_inp, *psn_txt_inp, *psn_txt_outp;
         /* text files    */

nums_inp = fopen("nums.bin", "rb");
nums_txt_inp = fopen("nums.txt", "r");
psn_inp = fopen("persons.bin", "rb");
psn_txt_inp = fopen("persons.txt", "r");
psn_outp = fopen("persout.bin", "wb");
psn_txt_outp = fopen("persout.txt", "w");
nums_outp = fopen("numsout.bin", "wb");
```

1. `fread(_____, sizeof (person_t), 1,`
   `_____);`
2. `fscanf(psn_txt_____, "%s", _____);`
3. `fwrite(&exec, _____, 1, psn_____);`
4. `fwrite(num_err, _____, _____,`
   `      nums_outp);`

5. `fread(&num_err[3], _____, _____,`
   `      nums_inp);`
6. `fprintf(psn_txt_outp, "%s %d %f\n", _____,`
   `      _____, _____);`

Programming

1. Write a function `fread_units` that is similar to the `load_units` function from the Universal Measurement Conversion Program (see Fig. 9.12) except it assumes that the unit conversion data have been stored as a binary file. The function should ask the user for the name of a binary file, open the file, and get up to `unit_max` `unit_t` values to place in array `units`. Be sure to send back to the calling function the size of the used portion of the array.

10.4 SEARCHING A DATABASE

Computerized matching of data against a file of records is a common practice. Solutions of many engineering problems require searching for materials or manufactured components that satisfy a list of constraints. For example, you might need to find a metal for an engine part that must bear heavy stresses at high temperatures. You also need the metal to be as light as possible, and you have a limit on the number of days you can wait for delivery. Searching for candidate metals can be accomplished very quickly if you have computerized access to a large file of information about available components or materials.

Such a large file of data is called a *database*. In this section, we will write a program that searches a database to find all records that match a proposed set of requirements.

Case Study: Metals Database Inquiry

 **PROBLEM**

Metals 'n More is a mail-order metal supply company that maintains its inventory as a computer file in order to facilitate answering questions regarding that database. Questions of interest might include the following:

- What metals are available that can withstand pressures of 135 gigapascals (1 gigapascal [GPa] = 1 kilonewton/mm^2)?

- What are the characteristics (density, melting point, tensile modulus) of vanadium?
- What metals whose melting points are at least 1400°C can be delivered within 15 days of the order date?

These questions and others can be answered if we know the correct way to ask them.

ANALYSIS

A database inquiry program has two phases: setting the search parameters and searching for records that satisfy those parameters. In our program, we will assume that all the structure components can be involved in the search. The program user must enter low and high bounds for each field of interest. Let's illustrate how we might set the search parameters to answer the question, What metals whose melting points are at least 1400°C can be delivered within 15 days of the order date?

Given that all Metals 'n More materials can be delivered within 90 days, that no metal's density exceeds 20 g/cm^3, that all metals melt at temperatures below 4000°C, and that no metal can withstand pressures in excess of 350 GPa, we can use the following menu-driven dialogue to set the search parameters:

```
Select by letter a search parameter to set, or enter q to
accept parameters shown.

Search Parameter                                      Current Value
  [a]  Low bound for name                                  aaaa
  [b]  High bound for name                                 zzzz
  [c]  Low bound for density  (g/cm^3)                     0.00
  [d]  High bound for density (g/cm^3)                    20.00
  [e]  Low bound for melting point  (degrees C)             0
  [f]  High bound for melting point (degrees C)          4000
  [g]  Low bound for tensile modulus  (GPa)                 0
  [h]  High bound for tensile modulus (GPa)               350
  [i]  Low bound for days to delivery                       0
  [j]  High bound for days to delivery                     90

Selection> e
New low bound for melting point> 1400

Select by letter a search parameter to set, or enter q to
accept parameters shown.
```

```
Search Parameter                                    Current Value
 [a]  Low bound for name                                 aaaa
 [b]  High bound for name                                zzzz
 [c]  Low bound for density  (g/cm^3)                    0.00
 [d]  High bound for density (g/cm^3)                   20.00
 [e]  Low bound for melting point  (degrees C)          1400
 [f]  High bound for melting point (degrees C)          4000
 [g]  Low bound for tensile modulus  (GPa)                 0
 [h]  High bound for tensile modulus (GPa)              350
 [i]  Low bound for days to delivery                      0
 [j]  High bound for days to delivery                    90

Selection> j
New high bound for days to delivery> 15

Select by letter a search parameter to set, or enter q to
accept parameters shown.

Search Parameter                                    Current Value
 [a]  Low bound for name                                 aaaa
 [b]  High bound for name                                zzzz
 [c]  Low bound for density  (g/cm^3)                    0.00
 [d]  High bound for density (g/cm^3)                   20.00
 [e]  Low bound for melting point  (degrees C)          1400
 [f]  High bound for melting point (degrees C)          4000
 [g]  Low bound for tensile modulus  (GPa)                 0
 [h]  High bound for tensile modulus (GPa)              350
 [i]  Low bound for days to delivery                      0
 [j]  High bound for days to delivery                    15

Selection> q
```

Data Requirements

Problem Inputs
```
search_params_t params;      /* search parameter
                                 bounds                 */
char inv_filename[STR_SIZ]  /* name of inventory file */
```

Problem Outputs
all metals that satisfy the search

Initial Algorithm

1. Open inventory file.
2. Get search parameters.
3. Display all metals that satisfy the search parameters.

The refinement of this algorithm is distributed through the development of functions `get_params` and `display_match` for Step 2 and Step 3.

In Fig. 10.10, we see an outline of the database program's implementation including the full code of function `main`. Our design and implementation of the functions called by `main` and most of their helper functions follow this outline.

Figure 10.10   Outline and Function main for Metals Database Inquiry Program

```
/*
 *  Displays all metals in the database that satisfy the search
 *  parameters specified by the program user.
 */
#include <stdio.h>
#include <string.h>

#define MAX_DENSITY   20.0    /* maximum density (g/cm^3)           */
#define MAX_MELT_PT   4000    /* maximum melting point (degrees C)  */
#define MAX_TENS_MOD  350     /* maximum tensile modulus (GPa)      */
#define MAX_DAYS      90      /* maximum days to delivery           */
#define STR_SIZ       80      /* number of characters in a string   */

typedef struct {              /* metal structure type */
    char    name[STR_SIZ];
    double  density;                 /* g/cm^3                       */
    int     melt_pt,                 /* melting point in degrees C   */
            tens_mod,                /* tensile modulus in GPa       */
            days_to_deliv;           /* days from order to delivery  */
} metal_t;

typedef struct {              /* search parameter bounds type */
    char    low_name[STR_SIZ], high_name[STR_SIZ];
    double  low_density, high_density;
```

(continued)

Figure 10.10 (continued)

```
        int     low_melt_pt, high_melt_pt,
                low_tens_mod, high_tens_mod,
                low_days, high_days;
} search_params_t;

/*  Insert functions needed by get_params and display_match.              */

/*
 *  Prompts the user to enter the search parameters.
 */
search_params_t
get_params(void)
{
   /* body of get_params to be inserted */
}

/*
 *  Displays records of all metals in the inventory that satisfy search
 *  parameters.
 */
void
display_match(FILE              *databasep, /* input - file pointer to binary
                                               database file              */
              search_params_t params)    /* input - search parameter
                                               bounds                     */
{
   /* body of display_match to be inserted */
}

int
main(void)
{
     char            inv_filename[STR_SIZ];  /* name of inventory file     */
     FILE            *inventoryp;            /* inventory file pointer     */
     search_params_t params;                /* search parameter
                                               bounds                     */

     /*  Get name of inventory file and open it                           */
     printf("Enter name of inventory file> ");
     scanf("%s", inv_filename);
```

(continued)

Figure 10.10 (continued)

```
    inventoryp = fopen(inv_filename, "rb");

    /*  Get the search parameters                              */
    params = get_params();

    /*  Display all metals that satisfy the search parameters  */
    display_match(inventoryp, params);

    return(0);
}
```

Design of the Function Subprograms

Function get_params must first initialize the search parameters to allow the widest search possible and then let the user change some parameters to narrow the search. The local variables and algorithm for get_params follow. The implementation is Programming Exercise 1 at the end of this section.

Local Variables for get_params

```
search_params_t params;   /* structure whose components
                             must be defined           */
char choice;              /* user's response to menu  */
```

Algorithm for get_params

1. Initialize params to permit widest possible search.
2. Display menu and get response to store in choice.
3. Repeat while choice is not 'q'
    4. Select appropriate prompt and get new parameter value.
    5. Display menu and get response to store in choice.
6. Return search parameters.

Function display_match must examine each file record with a name between the low and high bounds for names. If a record satisfies the search parameters, it is displayed. Function display_match will also display a message if no matches are found. The local variables and algorithm for the function follow.

Local Variables for display_match

```
metal_t next_metal   /* the current metal           */
int no_matches       /* a flag indicating whether or
                        not there are any matches    */
```

Algorithm for display_match

1. Initialize no_matches to true(1).
2. Advance to the first record whose name is within range.
3. while the current name is still in range repeat
    4. if the search parameters match
        5. Display the metal and set no_matches to false(0).
    6. Get the next metal record.
7. if there are no matches
    8. Display a no metals available message.

◀▬ **IMPLEMENTATION** ▬▶ **of the function subprograms**

Figure 10.11 shows the code of functions display_match, menu_choose, and match, along with a stub for function show.

Figure 10.11   Functions display_match, menu_choose, and match
....

```
/*
 *  Displays a lettered menu with the current values of search parameters.
 *  Returns the letter the user enters.  A letter in the range a..j selects
 *  a parameter to change;  q quits, accepting search parameters shown.
 */
char
menu_choose(search_params_t params) /* input - current search parameter
                                                bounds                      */
{
      char choice;

      printf("Select by letter a search parameter to set, ");
      printf("or enter q to\naccept parameters shown.\n\n");
      printf("Search Parameter                       ");
      printf("Current Value\n");
      printf(" [a]  Low bound for name                        %s\n",
             params.low_name);
      printf(" [b]  High bound for name                       %s\n",
             params.high_name);
      printf(" [c]  Low bound for density  (g/cm^3)           %5.2f\n",
             params.low_density);
      printf(" [d]  High bound for density (g/cm^3)           %5.2f\n",
             params.high_density);
```

(continued)

Figure 10.11 (continued)

```
            printf(" [e]  Low bound for melting point  (degrees C)    %4d\n",
                    params.low_melt_pt);
            printf(" [f]  High bound for melting point (degrees C)    %4d\n",
                    params.high_melt_pt);
            printf(" [g]  Low bound for tensile modulus  (GPa)      %3d\n",
                    params.low_tens_mod);
            printf(" [h]  High bound for tensile modulus (GPa)      %3d\n",
                    params.high_tens_mod);
            printf(" [i]  Low bound for days to delivery           %3d\n",
                    params.low_days);
            printf(" [j]  High bound for days to delivery          %3d\n\n",
                    params.high_days);

            printf("Selection> ");
            for  (scanf("%c", &choice);
                  !(choice >= 'a' && choice <= 'j' || choice == 'q');
                  scanf("%c", &choice)) {}

            return (choice);
}

/*
 *  Determines whether metal satisfies all search parameters
 */
int
match(metal_t          metal,   /* input - metal record to check  */
      search_params_t params)  /* input - parameters to satisfy  */
{
        return (params.low_density <= metal.density      &&
                params.high_density >= metal.density     &&
                params.low_melt_pt <= metal.melt_pt      &&
                params.high_melt_pt >= metal.melt_pt      &&
                params.low_tens_mod <= metal.tens_mod    &&
                params.high_tens_mod >= metal.tens_mod   &&
                params.low_days <= metal.days_to_deliv   &&
                params.high_days >= metal.days_to_deliv);
}
```

(continued)

Figure 10.11   (continued)

```
/*
 *  *** STUB *** Displays each component of metal record.  Leaves a blank line
 *  after metal display.
 */
void
show(metal_t metal)
{
     printf("Function show entered with metal %s\n", metal.name);
}

/*
 *  Displays records of all metals in the inventory that satisfy search
 *  parameters.
 */
void
display_match(FILE            *databasep, /* file pointer to binary
                                            database file            */
              search_params_t params)    /* input - search parameter
                                             bounds                  */
{
     metal_t next_metal;      /* current metal from database         */
     int     no_matches = 1;  /* flag indicating if no matches have
                                 been found                          */
     int     status;          /* input file status                   */

     /* Advances to first record with a name the same as or that
        alphabetically follows the lower bound                       */
     for  (status = fread(&next_metal, sizeof (metal_t), 1, databasep);
           status == 1 && strcmp(params.low_name, next_metal.name) > 0;
           status = fread(&next_metal, sizeof (metal_t), 1, databasep)) {}

     /* Displays a list of the metals that satisfy the search
        parameters                                                   */
     printf("\nMetals satisfying the search parameters:\n");
     while (strcmp(next_metal.name, params.high_name) <= 0  &&
            status == 1) {
       if (match(next_metal, params)) {
             no_matches = 0;
             show(next_metal);
       }
       status = fread(&next_metal, sizeof (metal_t), 1, databasep);
     }
```

(continued)

Figure 10.11   (continued)

```
        /* Displays a message if no metals found              */
        if (no_matches)
                printf("Sorry, no metals available\n");
}
```

Self-Check

1. What values would you use as search parameter bounds to answer the questions listed at the beginning of this section?
2. Which function in our database search program determines whether a particular record matches the search parameters? Which one displays each matching record?
3. Why does function `match` not need to check a metal's `name` field?

Programming

1. Write the functions `get_params` and `show` described in the metals database inquiry problem. Since `get_params` calls function `menu_choose`, your implementation of algorithm Step 4 for `get_params` must be sure to account for the fact that `menu_choose` does not validate the value the user enters.
2. Write a `void` function `make_metals_file` that would convert a text file containing information on metals to a binary file of `metal_t` structures. The function's parameters are file pointers to the text input and binary output files.

10.5 COMMON PROGRAMMING ERRORS

File processing in any programming language has many pitfalls; C is no exception. Remember to declare a file pointer variable (type `FILE *`) for each file you want to process. Because C makes no type distinction between file pointers accessing text files and those accessing binary files, it is easy to use the wrong library function with a file pointer. In a program that manipulates both file types, choose names for your file pointers that remind you of the type of file accessed. For example, you could choose names containing "_txt_" for text file pointers and names containing "_bin_" for binary file pointers. It is also critical that you remember that library functions `fscanf` and `fprintf` must be used for text I/O only; functions `fread` and `fwrite` are applied exclusively to binary files.

If you are permitting the program user to enter the name of a file to process, you will have two variables identifying the file—one to hold its name (a character string) and one to hold the pointer for file access. It is essential to remember that the only file operation in which the file *name* is used is the call to `fopen`. Keep in mind that opening a file for output by calling `fopen` with a second argument of `"w"` or `"wb"` typically results in a loss of any existing file whose name matches the first argument.

It is easy to forget that binary files cannot be created, viewed, or modified using an editor or word processor program. Rather, they must be created and interpreted by a program that reads values into or writes values from variables of the same type as the binary file's elements.

CHAPTER REVIEW

In this chapter, we reviewed the use of C's standard input/output files and explored the manipulation of additional I/O streams. We created a backup of a text file, processed a land boundary survey, and searched a database represented as a binary file of records.

First we focused on text files, continuous streams of character codes that can be viewed as broken into lines by the newline character. We saw that processing text files requires the transfer of sequences of characters between main memory and disk storage. To be processed as numbers, character strings taken as input from a text file must be converted to a different format such as `int` or `double` for storage in memory. We studied how output of numeric values to a text file requires conversion of the internal formats back to a sequence of characters.

We also studied binary files that permit storage of information using the computer's internal data format. Such files cannot be created using a word processor and are not meaningful when printed. However, the fact that their representation of data matches the format used in main memory means that neither time nor accuracy is lost through conversion of values transferred between main and secondary storage.

Table 10.3 summarizes the file processing constructs and functions discussed in this chapter.

Table 10.3 **Statements Used in File Processing**

Statement	Effect
Declarations	
`char name_txt_in[50],` `    name_bin_out[50];`	Declares two string variables whose names imply that they may be used to hold names of a text file to be used for input and of a binary output file.
`FILE *text_inp, *text_outp,` `    *bin_inp, *bin_outp;`	Declares four file pointer variables.
Calls to stdio Library	

`text_inp = fopen(name_txt_in, "r");`
`text_outp = fopen("result.txt", "w");`
`bin_inp = fopen("data.bin", "rb");`
`bin_outp = fopen(name_bin_out, "wb");`
	Opens `"data.bin"` and the file whose name is the value of `name_txt_in` as input files; opens `"result.txt"` and the file whose name is the value of `name_bin_out` as output files. Pointers accessing the open files are stored in file pointer variables `text_inp`, `text_outp`, `bin_inp`, and `bin_outp`.

`fscanf(text_inp, "%s%d%lf", animal,` `    &age, &weight);`	Copies string, `int`, and `double` values from the *text* input file accessed by file pointer `text_inp`, storing the values in variables `animal`, `age`, and `weight`.
`fprintf(text_outp, "(%.2f, %.2f)",` `    x, y);`	Writes to the *text* output file accessed by file pointer `text_outp` a set of parentheses enclosing the values of x and y rounded to two decimal places.
`fread(&var, sizeof (double), 1,` `    bin_inp);`	Copies into type `double` variable `var` the next value from the *binary* input file accessed by file pointer `bin_inp`.
`fwrite(&insect, sizeof (insect_t), 1,` `    bin_outp);`	Copies the value of type `insect_t` variable `insect` into the *binary* output file accessed by file pointer `bin_outp`.
`fclose(text_outp);` `fclose(bin_inp);`	Closes text file accessed by file pointer `text_outp` after writing the eof character. Closes binary file accessed by `bin_inp` so it is no longer available as an input source.

QUICK-CHECK EXERCISES

1. A _____ file consists of a stream of character codes; a _____ file is a sequence of values of any type represented exactly as they would be in main memory.
2. For each of these library functions, indicate whether it is used in processing binary or text files:

   ```
   fread      fwrite
   fscanf     fprintf
   ```

3. What file pointer name(s) does a C program associate with the keyboard? With the screen?
4. A word processor can be used to create or view a _____ file but not a _____ file.
5. Write a prototype for a function `fprintf_blob` that writes to a text output file the value of a structure of type `blob_t`. The function does *not* open the output file; the function assumes the file is already open.
6. Write a prototype for a function `fwrite_blob` that writes to a binary output file the value of a structure of type `blob_t`. The function does *not* open the output file; the function assumes the file is already open.
7. The _____ character separates a _____ file into lines, and the _____ character appears at the end of a file.
8. Can a file be used for both input and output by the same program?
9. Comment on the correctness of this statement: It is more efficient to use a text file because the computer knows that each component is a single character that can be copied into a single byte of main memory; with a binary file, however, the size of the components may vary.
10. Consider the following code segment, and then choose the correct "next" statement from the two options given. Indicate how you know which is the right choice. If you can't determine which is right, explain what additional information you would need in order to decide.

```
FILE *inp;
int   n;

inp = fopen("data.in", "r");
```

"next" option 1
```
    fread(&n, sizeof (int), 1, inp);
```

"next" option 2
```
    fscanf(inp, "%d", &n);
```

ANSWERS TO QUICK-CHECK EXERCISES

1. text, binary
2. `fread`: binary; `fscanf`: text; `fwrite`: binary; `fprintf`: text
3. Keyboard: `stdin`; screen: `stdout`, `stderr`
4. text, binary
5. `void`
   `fprintf_blob(FILE *filep, blob_t blob)`
6. `void`
   `fwrite_blob(FILE *filep, blob_t blob)`
7. newline (or `'\n'`), text, eof
8. Yes, it can be opened in one mode, closed, and then reopened in another mode.
9. The statement is not correct. Because no data conversions are necessary when you use binary files, binary files are more efficient than text files.
10. The code segment shown could be followed by either statement. To choose one option, it would be necessary to know whether `data.in` was a text file or a binary file of integers. If one were certain that the code's author always used the mode `"rb"` when opening a binary file, then option 2 would be the expected next statement.

REVIEW QUESTIONS

1. Where are files stored?
2. How would you modify the program in Fig. 10.1 so the data would be sent to the screen as well as written to the backup file?
3. What are the characteristics of a binary file?
4. Explain what a file pointer is.
5. A sparse matrix is one in which a large number of the elements are zero. Write a `void` function `store_sparse` that writes to a binary file a compressed representation of a 50×50 sparse matrix of type `int`. The function's parameters are the file pointer and the matrix. The function will store only the nonzero matrix values, writing for each of these a record containing three components: row subscript, column subscript, and value.
6. How would the prototype of function `store_sparse` be different if its purpose were to write the sparse matrix representation to a text file (see Review Question 5)? Discuss the implications of your answer.

PROGRAMMING PROJECTS

1. Write a `void` function that will merge the contents of two text files containing chemical elements sorted by atomic number and will produce a sorted file of binary records. The function's parameters will be three file pointers. Each text file line will contain an integer atomic number followed by the element name, chemical symbol, and atomic weight. Here are two sample lines:

   ```
   11  Sodium    Na  22.99
   20  Calcium   Ca  40.08
   ```

   The function can assume that one file does not have two copies of the same element and that the binary output file should have this same property. Hint: When one of the input files is exhausted, do not forget to copy the remaining elements of the other input file to the result file.

2. Develop a database inquiry program to search a binary file of aircraft data sorted in descending order by maximum cruise speed. Each aircraft record should include the name (up to 25 characters), maximum cruise speed (in km/h), wing span and length (in m), the character M (for military) or C (for civilian), and a descriptive phrase (up to 80 characters). Your system should implement a menu-driven interface that allows the user to search on all components except the descriptive phrase. Here are data for three aircraft to start your database:

   ```
   SR-71_Blackbird                    (name)
   3500                               (max cruise speed)
   16.95  32.74  M                    (wing span, length, military/civilian)
   high-speed_strategic_reconnaissance

   EF-111A_Raven
   2280
   19.21  23.16  M
   electronic_warfare

   Concorde
   2140
   25.61  62.2  C
   supersonic_airliner
   ```

3. Each year the state legislature rates the productivity of the faculty of each of the state-supported colleges and universities. The rating is based on reports

submitted by the faculty members indicating the average number of hours worked per week during the school year. Each faculty member is rated, and the university receives an overall rating based on the average of the reports from its faculty.

The faculty productivity ratings are computed as follows:
a. "Highly productive" means reported hours per week are over 55.
b. "Satisfactory" means reported hours per week are between 35 and 55.
c. "Overpaid" means reported hours per week are less than 35.
Take the following data from a text file:

Name	Hours
Herm	63
Flo	37
Jake	20
Maureen	55
Saul	72
Tony	40
Al	12

Your program should include functions corresponding to the prototypes shown.

```
/*  Displays table heading  */
void
print_header(void)


/*  Displays name, hours, and productivity rating  */
void
print_productivity(faculty_t fac) /* input */


/*   Gets one faculty member's data from text file returns 1
 *   for successful input, 0 for error, EOF for end of file
 */
int
scan_faculty(FILE      *text_inp, /* input - file pointer
                                     to data file         */
             faculty_t *fac)      /* output - structure of
                                     faculty data         */
```

4. Neurobiologists are slowly starting to understand some of the mechanisms by which the brain stores and processes information. Computer designers are very interested in understanding these processes as well, since there is much

interest in mimicking the brain's ability to work with imperfect input while producing (more or less!) reliable output.

You are interested in building a model of a small part of the brain. The brain is made up of neurons interconnected in a network. Each neuron receives signals from the other neurons to which it is connected and then in turn passes information to these other neurons. Some researchers believe that information is stored in the brain by the connection patterns between networks and by the strength of those connections.

We will model a neuron by saying that depending upon the sum of the signals coming in from other neurons, weighted by their connections to each other, the neuron will or will not *fire* (send out a signal to other neurons). Mathematically, for the ith neuron of a total of k neurons,

$$input_i = \sum_{j=1}^{k} w_{ij}s_j$$

This signal input to neuron i is then processed as follows:

> if $input_i >$ a threshold value, then $s^*_i = 1$
> else $s^*_i = 0$.

where s_j is the state of neuron j at a previous time, s^*_i is the new state of neuron i, and w_{ji} is the strength of the connection between two neurons i and j. Many theories exist for how w_{ij} can be determined; for example, *see Parallel Distributed Processing* by David Rumelhart and James McClelland, MIT Press, 1986. For this problem, assume the weights are random numbers between 0 and 1.

Write a simulation program that starts off with an initial neuron state (either a zero or a one) for 20 neurons and tracks the states for 50 time steps. The initial state should be scanned from a text file (format follows). Random integers between zero and `RAND_MAX` can be obtained by using the ANSI standard random-number generator function `rand`. For this problem, assume that $w_{ij} = w_{ji}$. The weights should be fixed: They should be stored for the duration of the simulation rather than being generated at each time step. The threshold value at which the neuron fires should be a user input. The program is to create an output file containing one neuron state for each time step, beginning with the initial state. Be careful to distinguish between s_i and s^*_i for each neuron; you will need to store both values until you have computed s^*_i for all i.

At the end of the simulation, the file created should have the format

```
0 1 0 1 0 0 1 1 1 1 0 0 1 1 0 1 1 0 1 1
0 0 0 0 0 0 1 1 1 1 1 1 1 0 1 1 0 1 1 0
```

```
0 0 0 0 0 0 0 0 1 1 0 0 1 1 0 1 1 0 1 1
. . .
```

That is, for each time step, there will be one line of twenty values, each either zero or one for each neuron. Look at the output values for various neuron-firing thresholds between 0 and 10. How does the persistence of patterns and signals vary with thresholds even in the presence of a different set of weights each time?

5. A neurobiologist wishes to set up a program to compute special values of the neural-network interconnect weights discussed in Project 4. Write a program that generates a set of n random numbers between 0 and 1, where n is a user input. The program should write the numbers generated to a binary file. Run the program to produce a file of 210 random numbers (enough numbers to serve as weights for a 20×20 neural network with $w_{ij} = w_{ji}$ and taking the w_{ii} cases into account). Modify the program in Project 4 to take these weights as input, then run the program with this fixed set of weights for several thresholds.

6. You are designing an expert system that will alert air traffic controllers to potential aircraft collisions. You are writing an interface between this program and a program that creates a file with aircraft positions, in (x, y, z) format, where x, y, and z are the distances in kilometers (east-west, north-south, up-down) from your aircraft.

   First, write a program that generates a binary file consisting of `aircraft_position_t` structures containing four components: an aircraft ID—a five-character *alphanumeric* (mixture of letters and digits) string, for example, EA722—and three randomly generated numbers. Values for x and y should be between -100.0 and $+100.0$. Value for z should be between -3.0 and $+3.0$. Create ten structures to represent ten nearby aircraft.

   Then, write a second program that reads the binary file created by your first program and calculates the distance

   $$\sqrt{x^2 + y^2 + z^2}$$

   for each of these aircraft. Write to a text file the (x, y, z) positions of the nearest two aircraft. For any aircraft less than 55 km from another aircraft, write an alarm message to the screen (not the file).

7. College football teams need a service to keep track of records and vital statistics. Write a program that will maintain this information in a binary file. An update file will be posted weekly against the master file of all team statistics to date, and all the records will be updated. All the information in both files will be stored in order by ID number. Each master record will contain the team's ID number; the team's name; the number of games won, lost, and tied; total yards gained by the team's offense; total yards gained by the other

teams against this one; total points scored by this team; and total points scored by the other teams against this one.

For this program, use the master file `teams.bin` and update the master using file `weekly.bin`. Write the updated records to a new binary file called `newteams.bin`. In addition, each record of the weekly file should be echoed to the screen. At the completion of file processing, display a message indicating the number of weekly scores processed, the team that scored the most points, and the team with the most offensive yardage for this week.

8. Write a program that takes a master file of college football information (such as `teams.bin` from Project 7) and displays teams that match a specified set of search parameters. The bounds on the search parameters could be set using a menu like the one used in our metals database inquiry case study. Some information you might want to display includes all teams with a certain range of points scored or scored upon; all teams with a certain range of yardage gained or given up; all teams with a certain number of games won, tied, or lost.

9. Cooking recipes can be stored on a computer and, with the use of files, can be quickly referenced.

    a. Write a function that will create a text file of recipes from information entered at the terminal. The format of the data to be stored is
        1) recipe type (dessert, meat, etc.)
        2) subtype (for dessert, use cake, pie, or cookies)
        3) name (e.g., German chocolate)
        4) number of lines in the recipe to follow
        5) the actual recipe

       Item 3 should be on a separate line.

    b. Write a function that will accept as parameters a file and a structured record of search parameter bounds. The function should display all recipes satisfying the search parameters.

CHAPTER 11

PROGRAMMING IN THE LARGE

In this chapter, we examine the special difficulties associated with the development of large software systems. We explore how separating our expression of *what* we need to do from *how* we actually plan to accomplish it reduces the complexity of system development and maintenance (upkeep). This chapter introduces C's facilities for formalizing this separation of concerns.

We study how to define flexible macros that help to make a program more readable as well as easier to maintain. This chapter describes the storage classes of variables and functions we have been using along with some additional storage classes that may be useful in large program development. We also investigate how to build a library of reusable code from functions developed for specific contexts. We meet additional preprocessor directives that allow us to format libraries so they are easy to include in any combination.

11.1 USING ABSTRACTION TO MANAGE COMPLEXITY

Up to this point in your study of programming, you have been primarily concerned with writing relatively short programs that solve individual problems but otherwise have little general use. In this chapter, we focus on the design and maintenance of large-scale programs. We discuss how to modularize a large project so that individual pieces can be implemented by different programmers at different times. We also see how to write software modules in ways that simplify their reuse in other projects.

Procedural Abstraction

When a team of programmers is assigned the task of developing a large software system, they must have a rational approach to breaking down the overall problem into solvable chunks. Abstraction is a powerful technique that helps problem solvers deal with complex issues in a piecemeal fashion. The dictionary defines *abstraction* as the process of separating the inherent qualities or properties of something from the actual physical object to which they belong. One example of the use of abstraction is the representation of a program variable (for example, `velocity`) by a storage location in memory. We don't have to know anything about the physical structure of memory in order to use such a variable in programming.

In this text, we have applied aspects of two types of abstraction to program development. First, we practiced *procedural abstraction*, which is the philosophy that function development should separate the concern of *what* is to be achieved by a function from the details of *how* it is to be achieved. In other words, you can specify what you expect a function to do and then use that function in the design of a problem solution before you know how to implement the function.

For example, in Chapter 10, when we tackled our metals database inquiry problem, our initial algorithm was one that could lead directly to an outline of a program fragment that identifies three functions representing the major steps of a solution. The following outline defers the details of parameter lists and use of function values.

Initial Algorithm	Program Outline
1. Open inventory file.	`fopen(...)`
2. Get the search parameters.	`get_params(...)`
3. Display all metals that satisfy the search parameters.	`display_match(...)`

In this example of procedural abstraction, we see that *what* one of the functions must accomplish (i.e., open a file) corresponds to the purpose of a library function we have studied. Reuse of this existing function means that we *never* have to concern ourselves with the details of *how* this task is accomplished. Clearly, the availability of powerful libraries of functions is of significant benefit in reducing the complexity of large systems. As we have already seen, the use of such libraries is a fundamental feature of the C programming language.

In the example shown, the other two functions identified in this first level of procedural abstraction are excellent candidates for assignment to separate members of a program development team. Once the purpose and parameter lists of each function are spelled out, neither developer will have any need to be concerned about the details of *how* the other member carries out the assigned task.

Data Abstraction

Data abstraction is another powerful tool we have seen for breaking down a large problem into manageable chunks. When we apply data abstraction to a complex problem, we initially specify the data objects involved and the operations to be performed on these data objects without being overly concerned with how the data objects will be represented and stored in memory. We can describe *what* information is stored in the data object without being specific as to *how* the information is organized and represented. This is the *logical view* of the data object as opposed to its *physical view*, the actual internal representation in memory. Once we understand the logical view, we can use the data object and its operators in our programs; however, we (or someone else) will eventually need to implement the data object and its operators before we can run any program that uses them.

One simple example of data abstraction is our use of the C data type `double`, which is an abstraction for the set of real numbers. The computer hardware limits the range of real numbers that can be represented, and not all real numbers within the specified range can be represented. Different computers use a variety of representation schemes for type `double`. However, we can generally use the data type `double` and its associated operators (+, −, *, /, =, ==, <, and so on) without being concerned with these details of its implementation. Another example of data abstraction is the definition of a data type and associated operators for complex numbers given in Chapter 9.

Information Hiding

One advantage of procedural abstraction and data abstraction is that they enable the designer to make implementation decisions in a piecemeal fashion. The designer can postpone making decisions regarding the actual internal representation of the data objects and the implementation of its operators. At the top levels of the design, the designer focuses on how to use a data object and its operators; at the lower levels of design, the designer works out the implementation details. In this way, the designer can hierarchically break down a large problem, controlling and reducing its overall complexity.

If the details of a data object's implementation are not known when a higher-level module is implemented, the higher-level module can access the data object only through its operators. This limitation is actually an advantage: It allows the designer to change his or her mind at a later date and possibly to choose a more efficient method of internal representation or implementation. If the higher-level modules reference a data object only through its operators, a change in the data object's representation will require no change in a higher-level module. The process of protecting the implementation details of a lower-level module from direct access by a higher-level module is called *information hiding*.

Reusable Code

One of the keys to productivity in software development is the writing of *reusable code*, code that can be reused in many different applications, preferably without having to be modified or recompiled. One way to facilitate reuse in C is to *encapsulate* a data object together with its operators in a personal library. Then we can use the `#include` preprocessor directive to give functions in a file access to this library.

Encapsulation is a powerful concept in everyday life that can be applied very profitably to software design. For example, one encapsulated object that we are all familiar with is an aspirin. Our familiarity is based strictly on *what* the object does (relieves pain and reduces fever) when activated through the standard interface (swallowing). Only its producers and prescribers care *how* an aspirin does what it does (the effect of acetylsalicylic acid on inflammation and blood flow to the skin surface). By applying the principles of procedural and data abstraction, we can package the "bitter" details of a complex problem's solution in equally neat, easy-to-use capsules.

EXERCISE FOR SECTION 11.1

Self-Check

1. Describe how each of the following encapsulated objects allows the user to focus on *what* the object does with little or no concern for *how* it does it:

> microwave oven   television set   calculator

11.2 PERSONAL LIBRARIES: HEADER FILES

We have seen how the availability of C's standard libraries simplifies program development. However, the standard libraries are not extensive enough to handle every programming need. Often we write a function that would be useful in a context other than the one for which it was originally written. Copying the code of functions into other programs to allow reuse is possible but cumbersome, especially when compared to the way we get access to standard libraries. In fact, one can use the C preprocessor directive #include to make available personal libraries as well. Since C permits source code files to be compiled separately and then linked prior to loading and execution, we can provide our personal libraries as object files; programs using our personal libraries need not first compile the functions in them. If we take another look at a diagram first presented in Chapter 1 and now repeated in Fig. 11.1, we are in a better position to understand the bubble that is marked with a colored arrow. Until now, the "other object files" that have been linked to our code have been the standard C libraries. When we learn to make our own library files, these files can also be provided to the linker as part of preparing our program for execution.

Header Files

To create a personal library, we must first make a *header file*. A header file is a text file containing all the information about a library needed by the compiler when compiling a program that uses the facilities defined in the library.

**Figure 11.1
Preparing a
Program for
Execution**

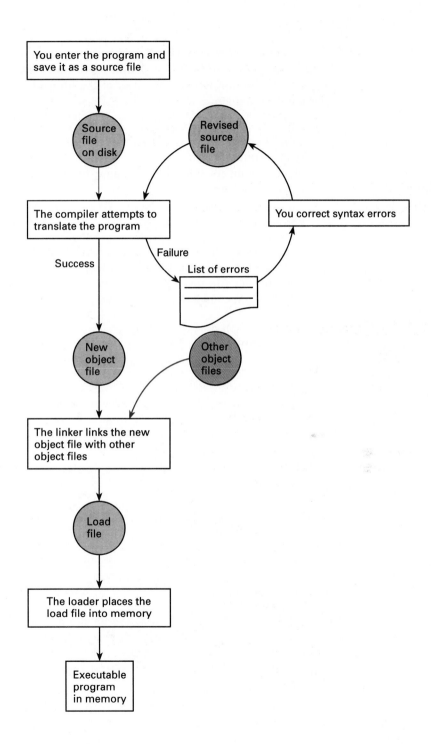

Precisely this type of data is found in system header files such as `stdio.h`, `math.h`, and `string.h`. The form we recommend for a header file also provides all the information that a user of the library needs. Typical contents of a header file include

1. a block comment summarizing the library's purpose
2. `#define` directives naming constant macros
3. type definitions
4. block comments stating the purpose of each library function and declarations of the form

> **extern** *prototype*;

The use of the keyword `extern` in a function declaration notifies the compiler that the function's definition will be provided to the linker. Figure 11.2 shows a header file for our planet data type and operators from Chapter 9. In Fig. 11.3, we see the beginning of a source file that has need of facilities from

Figure 11.2   Header File planet.h for Personal Library with Data Type and Associated Functions

```
/*  planet.h
 *
 *  abstract data type planet
 *
 *  Type planet_t has these components:
 *       name, diameter, dist_sun, orbital_prd, axial_rot_prd
 *
 *  Operators:
 *       print_planet, planet_equal, scan_planet
 */

#define PLANET_STRSIZ  10

typedef struct { /* planet structure */
      char name[PLANET_STRSIZ];
      double diameter,        /* equatorial diameter in km              */
             dist_sun,        /* average distance from sun in km        */
             orbital_prd,     /* years to orbit sun once                */
             axial_rot_prd;   /* hours to complete one revolution on
                                        axis                            */
} planet_t;
```

(continued)

Figure 11.2   (continued)

```
/*
 *  Displays with labels all components of a planet_t structure
 */
extern void
print_planet(planet_t pl);  /* input - one planet structure             */

/*
 *  Determines whether or not the components of planet_1 and planet_2
 *  match
 */
extern int
planet_equal(planet_t planet_1,  /* input - planets to               */
             planet_t planet_2); /*          compare                 */

/*
 *  Fills a type planet_t structure with input data.  Integer returned as
 *  function result is success/failure/EOF indicator.
 *       1 => successful input of planet
 *       0 => error encountered
 *       EOF => insufficient data before end of file
 *  In case of error or EOF, value of type planet_t output argument is
 *  undefined.
 */
extern int
scan_planet(planet_t *plnp); /* output - address of planet_t structure to
                                         fill                          */
```

this library. We are assuming here that the header file is named `planet.h`, and that it is located in the directory in which the preprocessor first looks for files whose names appear in quotation marks after a `#include`. This issue is system dependent, but, in many cases, the directory first searched would be the one in which the current source file resides.

In our programming so far, we have used angular brackets (<>), as in

```
#include <stdio.h>
```

to indicate to the preprocessor that a header file is to be found in a system

Figure 11.3   Portion of Program That Uses Functions from a Personal Library

```
/*
 * Beginning of source file in which a personal library and system I/O library
 * are used.
 */

#include <stdio.h>       /* system's standard I/O functions              */

#include "planet.h"      /* personal library with planet_t data type and
                                operators                                 */
. . .
```

directory. Quotes around the header file name, as in

```
#include "planet.h"
```

mark it as information about a library belonging to the programmer.

When revising a source file, the C preprocessor replaces each #include line by the contents of the header file it references.

In Chapters 3 and 6, when we first met user-defined functions, we emphasized the importance of the block comment placed at the beginning of the function and the importance of the function prototype and the comments on its parameters. When taken together, this prototype and its associated commentary provide the basic information needed by a programmer desiring to call the function: what the function does, what type of value it returns (if any), and what types of arguments it operates on. Notice that this is precisely the information placed in the header file.

An important aspect of dividing any problem into manageable chunks is defining the points at which the chunks of the solution come together to form the complete solution. The common boundary between two separate parts of a solution is called the *interface*. The header file's purpose is to define the interface between a library and any program that uses the library.

Cautionary Notes for Header File Design

You will notice that in our header file example, the constant macro defined (PLANET_STRSIZ) has a long name that begins with the library name. This naming strategy reduces the likelihood that the name associated with a constant in the header file will conflict with other constant macro names in the program.

In Section 11.3, we will see how to create an implementation file for a personal library. The header (interface) file and the implementation file are the two essential source files in a personal library.

Self-Check

1. How can the C preprocessor determine whether a header file name in an `#include` statement is the name of a system library or of a personal library?
2. A function's _____ and associated _____ are the collection of information that a programmer must know about the function in order to be able to use it.
3. A header (interface) file describes _____ the functions of a library do, not _____ they do it.

Programming

1. Look at the table of math library functions in Chapter 3 (Table 3.5). Define a header file `myops.h` that contains a full description of the interfaces of functions `fabs`, `sqrt`, and `pow`. Then add to this file information about the `factorial` function (see Chapter 6). Would anything about your interface information for `factorial` require your implementation of the function to be iterative? Would anything require the implementation to be recursive?

11.3 PERSONAL LIBRARIES: IMPLEMENTATION FILES

In Section 11.2, we saw how to create a library header file containing all the interface information needed by a program and programmer using the library. We created a header file for a planet library and studied a program that uses the `#include` directive in order to make this header a part of the program's code. In this section, we investigate how to create a library implementation file. The header file describes *what* the functions of the library do; the implementation file will show *how* the functions do it.

A library's implementation file is a C source file that contains both the code of all the library functions and any other information needed for compilation of these functions. The elements of an implementation file are the same as the elements of any program and have many similarities with the elements of the library's header file. These elements are

1. a block comment summarizing the library's purpose

2. #include directives for this library's header file and for other libraries used by the functions in this library
3. #define directives naming constant macros used only inside this library
4. type definitions used only inside this library
5. function definitions including the usual comments

It may seem odd that we #include the header file for the library we are implementing since the prototypes found in it are redundant. We do this to make maintenance and modification of the library more straightforward. Alternatively, we could simply restate the constant macro and type definitions from the header file in the implementation file. However, then a modification of one of these definitions would require changes in *two* files. Using the header file #include as shown, we would simply modify the header file; when the implementation file is recompiled, the change will be taken into account. Figure 11.4 shows an implementation file that might be associated with the header file planet.h.

Figure 11.4   Implementation File planet.c Containing Library with Planet Data Type and Operators

```
/*
 *
 *       planet.c
 */
#include <stdio.h>
#include <string.h>
#include "planet.h"
/*
 *  Displays with labels all components of a planet_t structure
 */
void
print_planet(planet_t pl)  /* input - one planet structure */
{
      printf("%s\n", pl.name);
      printf("  Equatorial diameter:  %.0f km\n", pl.diameter);
      printf("  Average distance from the sun:  %.4e km\n", pl.dist_sun);
      printf("  Time to complete one orbit of the sun:  %.2f years\n",
             pl.orbital_prd);
      printf("  Time to complete one rotation on axis:  %.4f hours\n",
             pl.axial_rot_prd);
}
```

(continued)

Figure 11.4 (continued)

```
/*
 *  Determines whether or not the components of planet_1 and planet_2 match
 */
int
planet_equal(planet_t planet_1,   /* input - planets to                      */
             planet_t planet_2)  /*            compare                       */
{
      return (strcmp(planet_1.name, planet_2.name) == 0     &&
              planet_1.diameter == planet_2.diameter        &&
              planet_1.dist_sun == planet_2.dist_sun        &&
              planet_1.orbital_prd == planet_2.orbital_prd  &&
              planet_1.axial_rot_prd == planet_2.axial_rot_prd);
}


/*
 *  Fills a type planet_t structure with input data.  Integer returned as
 *  function result is success/failure/EOF indicator.
 *      1 => successful input of planet
 *      0 => error encountered
 *      EOF => insufficient data before end of file
 *  In case of error or EOF, value of type planet_t output argument is
 *  undefined.
 */
int
scan_planet(planet_t *plnp) /* output - address of planet_t structure to
                                        fill                                 */
{
      int result;

      result = scanf("%s%lf%lf%lf%lf", (*plnp).name,
                                       &(*plnp).diameter,
                                       &(*plnp).dist_sun,
                                       &(*plnp).orbital_prd,
                                       &(*plnp).axial_rot_prd);
      if (result == 5)
            result = 1;
      else if (result != EOF)
            result = 0;

      return (result);
}
```

Using a Personal Library

To use a personal library, one must complete these steps:

Creation

C1 Create a header file containing the interface information for a program needing the library.

C2 Create an implementation file containing the code of the library functions and other details of the implementation that are hidden from the user program.

C3 Compile the implementation file. This step must be repeated any time either the header file or the implementation file is revised.

Use

U1 Include the library's header file in the user program through an `#include` directive.

U2 After compiling the user program, include both its object file and the object file created in C3 in the command that activates the linker.

Self-Check

1. Why do we openly define the constant macro `PLANET_STRSIZ` in the header file `"planet.h"` rather than protecting this name as one of the implementation details?

2. If you see the following `#include` directives in a program, what do you assume about libraries red and blue?

```
#include <red.h>
#include "blue.h"
```

Programming

1. Create a library named complex that defines the complex arithmetic operators from Section 9.4.

11.4 DEFINING MACROS WITH PARAMETERS

We have consistently used the `#define` preprocessor directive we met in Chapter 2 for associating symbolic names with constant values. In Chapter 2, we discussed the fact that C's preprocessor actually revises the text of the source code, replacing each occurrence of a defined name by its meaning before turning the code over to the compiler. In this section, we study how to define macros that have formal parameters. The form of such a macro definition is

#define *macro_name*(*parameter list*) *macro body*

Like functions, macros allow us to give a name to a commonly used statement or operation. Because macros are handled through textual substitution, however, macro calls execute without the overhead of space allocation and deallocation on the stack that is associated with functions. Of course, since the macro's meaning appears in the program at every call, the object file produced by the compiler typically requires more memory than the same program would require if it used a function rather than a macro.

Figure 11.5 shows a brief program that uses a macro named `LABEL_PRINT_INT` to display the value of an integer variable or expression with a label (a string). Notice that in the directive that defines `LABEL_PRINT_INT`, there is no space between the macro name and the left parenthesis of the parameter list. This detail is critical, for if there were a space, the preprocessor would misinterpret the macro definition and would replace every occurrence of `LABEL_PRINT_INT` by

```
(label, num) printf("%s = %d", (label), (num))
```

Figure 11.5   Program Using a Macro with Formal Parameters

```
/*  Shows the definition and use of a macro                          */

#include <stdio.h>

#define LABEL_PRINT_INT(label, num) printf("%s = %d", (label), (num))

int
main(void)
{
      int r = 5, t = 12;

      LABEL_PRINT_INT("rabbit", r);
      printf("      ");
      LABEL_PRINT_INT("tiger", t + 2);
      printf("\n");

      return(0);
}
rabbit = 5      tiger = 14
```

Figure 11.6 Macro Expansion of Second Macro Call of Program in Fig. 11.5

```
LABEL_PRINT_INT("tiger", t + 2)
                   ↓        ✓
LABEL_PRINT_INT(label, num)
```
parameter matching →

```
                              "tiger"   t + 2
                                 ↓         ↓
              printf("%s = %d", (label), (num))
```
parameter replacement in body →

```
                    printf("%s = %d", ("tiger"), (t + 2))
```
result of macro expansion

The process of replacing a macro call such as

```
LABEL_PRINT_INT("rabbit", r)
```

by its meaning,

```
printf("%s = %d", ("rabbit"), (r))
```

is called *macro expansion*. When doing this replacement, the C preprocessor matches each macro parameter name with the corresponding actual argument. Then, in a copy of the macro body, every occurrence of a formal parameter name is replaced by the actual argument. This modified macro body takes the place of the macro call in the text of the program. Figure 11.6 diagrams the process of macro expansion of the last macro call in our sample program. Notice that only the macro name and its argument list are involved in the macro expansion process. The semicolon at the end of the macro call line is unaffected. It would be a mistake to include a semicolon at the end of the `printf` call in the macro body. If a semicolon were placed there, the statements resulting from macro expansion of our two macro calls would both end in *two* semicolons.

Use of Parentheses in Macro Body

You will notice that in the body of **LABEL_PRINT_INT**, each occurrence of a formal parameter of the macro is enclosed in parentheses. The use of adequate parentheses in a macro's body is essential for correct evaluation. In Fig. 11.7, we see a program fragment that uses a macro to compute n^2. We show two versions of the macro definition and the different program outputs that result.

Figure 11.7   Macro Calls Showing Importance of Parentheses in Macro Body

Version 1	Version 2
`#define SQUARE(n)  n * n`	`#define SQUARE(n)  ((n) * (n))`

```
                . . .
                double x = 0.5, y = 2.0;
                int    n = 4, m = 12;

                printf("(%.2f + %.2f)squared = %.2f\n\n",
                        x, y, SQUARE(x + y));

                printf("%d squared divided by\n", m);
                printf("%d squared is %d\n", n,
                        SQUARE(m) / SQUARE(n));
```

`(0.5 + 2.0)squared = 3.5`	`(0.5 + 2.0)squared = 6.25`
`12 squared divided by` `4 squared is 144`	`12 squared divided by` `4 squared is 9`

Figure 11.8   Macro Expansions of Macro Calls from Fig. 11.7

Version 1	Version 2

`SQUARE(x + y)`
   becomes
`x + y * x + y`

*Problem: multiplication done
   before addition.*

`SQUARE(x + y)`
   becomes
`((x + y) * (x + y))`

`SQUARE(m) / SQUARE(n)`
   becomes
`m * m / n * n`

*Problem: multiplication and
   division are of equal precedence;
   they are performed left to right.*

`SQUARE(m) / SQUARE(n)`
   becomes
`((m) * (m)) / ((n) * (n))`

Let's look at the different macro expansions that occur in Version 1 and Version 2. Examination of Fig. 11.8 reveals that the incorrect results of Version 1 are a simple consequence of the operator precedence rules.

To avoid the problems illustrated in Figs. 11.7 and 11.8, use parentheses liberally in macro bodies. Specifically, parenthesize each occurrence of a parameter in the macro body, and enclose the entire body in parentheses if it produces a result value. For instance, here is a macro for finding one real root of a quadratic equation:

```
#define ROOT1(a,b,c) ((-(b)+sqrt((b)*(b)-4*(a)*(c)))/(2*(a)))
```

The black parentheses are those normally required for proper evaluation of the expression. The parentheses in color are added in accordance with our guidelines for parenthesizing a macro definition.

One should avoid using operators with side effects in expressions passed as arguments in a macro call, since these expressions may be evaluated multiple times. For example, the statement

```
r = ROOT1(++n1, n2, n3);  /* error:  applying ++ in a macro
                                      argument */
```

would be expanded as

```
r = ((-(n2)+sqrt((n2)*(n2)-4*(++n1)*(n3)))/(2*(++n1)));
```

resulting in a statement that violates the principle that the object of an operator with a side effect should not be reused in the expression.

We urge you to use parentheses routinely in macro bodies as described earlier, even if you cannot conceive of any circumstance when a given set of parentheses could matter. One needs only to work with macros a short time to realize how limited is this ability of a programmer to foresee *all* possible situations!

We also encourage you to use all capital letters in your macro names. Remembering that you are calling a macro rather than a function is critical in helping you avoid the use of operators with side effects in your actual arguments.

Extending a Macro Over Two or More Lines

The preprocessor assumes that a macro definition fits on a single line unless the program indicates otherwise. To extend a macro over multiple lines, all but the last line of the definition must end with the backslash character \. For example, here is a macro that implements the header of a `for` statement to count from the value of `st` up to, but not including, the value of `end`:

```
#define INDEXED_FOR(ct, st, end)  \
        for  ((ct) = (st);  (ct) < (end);  ++(ct))
```

The following code fragment uses INDEXED_FOR to display the first X_MAX elements of array x:

```
INDEXED_FOR(i, 0, X_MAX)
        printf("x[%2d] = %6.2f\n", i, x[i]);
```

After macro expansion, the statement will be

```
for  ((i) = (0);  (i) < (X_MAX);  ++(i))
        printf("x[%2d] = %6.2f\n", i, x[i]);
```

Self-Check

Given these macro definitions, write the macro expansion of each statement that follows. If the expansion seems not to be what the macro definer intended (you may assume the macro names are meaningful), indicate how you would correct the macro definition.

```
#define DOUBLE(x)  (x) + (x)
#define DISCRIMINANT (a,b,c)  ((b) * (b) - 4 * (a) * (c))
#define PRINT_PRODUCT(x, y)\
        printf("%.2f X %.2f = %.2f\n", (x), (y), (x) * (y));
```

1. `y = DOUBLE(a - b)*c;`
2. `y = y - DOUBLE(p);`
3. `if (DISCRIMINANT(a1, b1, c1) == 0)`
   `        r1 = -b1 / (2 * a1);`
4. `PRINT_PRODUCT(a + b, a - b);`

Programming

1. Define a macro named F_OF_X that would evaluate the following polynomial for the x value passed as its argument. You may assume that the math library has been included.

$$x^5 - 3x^3 + 4$$

2. Define a macro to display its argument preceded by a dollar sign and with two decimal places.

11.5 STORAGE CLASSES

C has five storage classes; so far we have seen three. Formal parameters and local variables of functions are variables that are *auto*matically allocated on the stack when a function is called and *auto*matically deallocated when the function returns; they are of storage class `auto`. In Chapter 6, we studied that the *scope* of these names, that is, the program region in which the name is visible, extends from the point of declaration to the end of the function in which the declaration appears.

The names of the functions themselves are of storage class `extern`, meaning that they will be available to the linker. These functions may be called by any other function in a program, provided that necessary precautions are taken. From a function's definition to the end of the source file in which the definition appears, the scope rules we studied in Chapter 6 make the function directly visible. If there is a need to reference a function from a spot in its source file that precedes the function's definition or from anywhere in a different source file, the compiler must be assured that the linker will know where to find the function. The compiler also needs to know the following vital information about the function in order to translate a call to it: its return type, how many arguments it takes, and the data types of the arguments. Providing this information is the purpose of the

`extern` *prototype*;

statement of which we have seen numerous examples in library header files. This statement *does not create* a function of storage class `extern`; it merely *notifies* the compiler that such a function exists and that the linker will know where to find it. Figure 11.9 shows the two storage classes, `auto` and `extern`. Names in color are of storage class `auto`; those in boldface black are of storage class `extern`.

Figure 11.9   Storage Classes auto and extern as Previously Seen

```
void
fun_one(int arg_one, int arg_two)
{
     int one_local;
     . . .
}
```

(continued)

Figure 11.9   (continued)

```
int
fun_two (int a2_one, int a2_two)
  {
      int local_var;
      . . .
  }

int
main (void)
  {
      int num;
      . . .
  }
```

The shaded area of Fig. 11.9 marks the program's *top level*. Class `extern` is the default storage class for all names declared at this level.

Global Variables

We have seen only declarations of functions at the top level of a program. However, it is also possible (though usually inadvisable) to declare variables at the top level. The scope of such a variable name, like the scope of a function name, extends from the point of declaration to the end of the source file, except in functions where the same name is declared as a formal parameter or local variable. If we need to reference a top-level variable in the region of its source file that precedes its declaration or in another source file, the compiler can be alerted to the variable's existence by placing a declaration of the variable that begins with the keyword `extern` in the file prior to the first reference. Such a variable can be made accessible to *all* functions in a program and is therefore sometimes called a *global* variable. Figure 11.10 shows the declaration at the top level of `int` variable `global_var_x` of storage class `extern` in file `eg1.c` and an `extern` statement in `eg2.c` that makes the global variable accessible throughout this file as well. Only the *defining declaration*, the one in `eg1.c`, allocates space for `global_var_x`. A declaration beginning with the keyword `extern` allocates no memory; it simply provides information for the compiler.

Although there are applications in which global variables are unavoidable, such unrestricted access to a variable is generally regarded as detrimental to a program's readability and maintainability. Global access conflicts with the

**Figure 11.10
Declaration of a
Global Variable**

```
/* eg1.c */

int global_var_x;

void
afun(int n)
. . .
```

```
/* eg2.c */

extern int global_var_x;

int
bfun(int p)
. . .
```

principle that functions should have access to data on a need-to-know basis only, and then strictly through the documented interface as represented by the function prototype. However, one context in which a global variable can be used without reducing program readability is when the global represents a constant. We have been using globally visible macro constants throughout this text, and they have been a help, not a hindrance, in clarifying the meaning of a program. In Fig. 11.11, we see two global names that represent constant data structures. Because we plan to initialize these memory blocks and never change

**Figure 11.11
Use of Variables
of Storage Class
extern**

```
/* fileone.c */

typedef struct{
            double real,
                   imag;
} complex_t;

/* Defining declarations of
    global structured constant
    complex_zero and of global
    constant array of month
    names */
const complex_t complex_zero
    = {0, 0};
const char months[12][10] =
        {"January", "February",
        "March", "April", "May",
        "June", "July", "August",
        "September", "October",
        "November", "December"};

int
f1_fun1(int n)
{ . . . }

double
f1_fun2(double x)
{ . . . }

char
f1_fun3(char c1, char c2)
{ double months; . . . }
```

```
/* filetwo.c */

/* #define's and typedefs
    including complex_t */

void
f2_fun1(int x)
{ . . . }

/* Compiler-notifying
    declarations -- no
    storage allocated */
extern const complex_t
    complex_zero;
extern const char
    months[12][10];

void
f2_fun2(void)
{ . . . }

int
f2_fun3(int n)
{ . . . }
```

Table 11.1   Functions in Fig. 11.11 with Global Variable Access and Reasons

Function(s)	Can Access Variables of Class extern	Reason
`f1_fun1` and `f1_fun2`	`complex_zero` and `months`	Their definitions follow in the same source file the top-level defining declarations of `complex_zero` and `months`. The functions have no parameters or local variables by these names.
`f1_fun3`	`complex_zero` only	Its definition follows in the same source file the top-level defining declaration of `complex_zero`, and it has no parameter or local variable by this name.
`f2_fun1`	none	Its definition precedes the declarations that notify the compiler of the existence of `complex_zero` and `months`.
`f2_fun2` and `f2_fun3`	`complex_zero` and `months`	Their definitions follow in the same source file the declarations containing keyword `extern` that notify the compiler of the existence of global names `complex_zero` and `months`. The functions have no parameters or local variables by these names.

their values, there is no harm in letting our whole program access them. We include the `const` type qualifier in our declarations that define the globals as well as in the `extern` declarations that give additional functions access to the globals. This qualifier notifies the compiler that the program can look at, but not modify, these locations.

Figure 11.11 also shows the third storage class that we have met before, namely, `typedef`. Including `typedef` in the set of storage classes is merely a notational convenience. As we saw in Chapter 9, a `typedef` statement does not allocate storage space!

Table 11.1 shows which functions are allowed to access globals `complex_zero` and `months` and why. We assume that any local variable declarations affecting access to the globals are shown.

Storage Classes static and register

C's remaining storage classes are `static` and `register`. Placing the `static` keyword at the beginning of a local variable declaration changes the way the variable is allocated. Let's compare variables `once` and `many` in the following function fragment:

```
int
fun_frag(int n)
{
       static int once = 0;
       int        many = 0;
       . . .
}
```

As a variable of storage class `auto`, `many` is allocated space on the stack each time `fun_frag` is called; for every call `many` is initialized to zero. Every time `fun_frag` returns, `many` is deallocated. In contrast, `static` variable `once` is allocated and initialized *one time*, prior to program execution. It remains allocated until the entire program terminates. If `fun_frag` changes the value of `once`, that value is retained between calls to `fun_frag`.

Using a `static` local variable to retain data from one call to a function to the next is usually a poor programming practice. If the function's behavior depends on these data, then the function is no longer performing a transformation based solely on its input arguments, and the complexity of its purpose from the program reader's perspective is vastly increased.

One situation in which the use of a `static` local variable does not degrade readability is in function `main`, since a return from this function terminates the program. On a system that allocates a relatively small run-time stack, one might wish to declare large arrays as `static` variables in function `main`. Then these arrays will not use up stack space.

The final storage class, `register`, is closely related to storage class `auto` and may be applied only to local variables and parameters. In fact, C implementations are not required to treat `register` variables differently from `auto` variables. Designating that a variable is of storage class `register` simply alerts the compiler to the fact that this memory cell will be referenced more often than most. By choosing storage class `register`, the programmer indicates an expectation that the program would run faster if a *register,* a special high-speed memory location *inside* the central processor, could be used for the variable. Variables serving as subscripts for large arrays are good candidates for this storage class. Here are declarations of variables in storage classes `static` and `register`:

```
static double matrix[50][40];
register int  i, j;
```

EXERCISES FOR SECTION 11.5

Self-Check

Reread the program in Fig. 9.12 that converts units of measure.

1. Identify the storage classes of the following names used in the program:

unit_max (first parameter of load_units)
found (in function search)
convert
quantity (in function main)

2. For which one of the variables in function search would it be a good idea to request storage class register?

11.6 MODIFYING FUNCTIONS FOR INCLUSION IN A LIBRARY

When building a personal library based on functions originally developed for use in a specific context, usually some modifications are advisable. A library function should be as general as possible, so all constants used should be examined to see whether they could be replaced by input parameters. Any restrictions on the library function's parameters should be carefully defined.

In previous work, our functions have dealt with an error either by returning an error code or by displaying an error message and returning a value that should permit continued execution. In some situations, however, it is better not to permit continued processing. For example, manipulation of a large two-dimensional array can be very time-consuming, and it might be pointless to expend this time on a matrix that contains erroneous data. Similarly, if our factorial function is called with a negative number, there is no way it can return a valid answer. Therefore, we might want to print a message and then terminate execution of a program in which this error occurs.

C's exit function from the standard library stdlib can be used in these types of situations to terminate execution prematurely. Calling exit with the argument 1 indicates that some failure led to the exit. Using the value 0 in an exit call implies no such failure, just as a 0 returned from function main indicates successful function completion. The exit function may also use one of the predefined constants EXIT_SUCCESS or EXIT_FAILURE as its return value. These constants are an option for use in the return statement as well, providing that the standard library stdlib is included. Figure 11.12 shows a library form of function factorial that terminates program execution prematurely on a negative input.

Figure 11.12   Function factorial with Premature Exit on Negative Data

```
/*
 * Computes n!
 * n is greater than or equal to zero -- premature exit on negative data
```

(continued)

Figure 11.12   (continued)

```
 */
int
factorial(int n)
{
    int i,              /* local variables */
        product = 1;

    if (n < 0) {
        printf("\n***Function factorial reports ");
        printf("ERROR:  %d! is undefined***\n", n);
        exit(1);
    } else {
        /* Compute the product n x (n-1) x (n-2) x ... x 2 x 1 */
        for  (i = n;  i > 1;  --i) {
            product = product * i;
        }

        /* Return function result */
        return (product);
    }
}
```

The following syntax display describes the `exit` function.

exit Function

SYNTAX: **exit**(*return_value*);

EXAMPLE: ```
            /*
             * Gets next positive number from input
             * stream. Returns EOF if end of file
             * is encountered. Exits program with error
             * message if erroneous input is encountered.
             */
            int
            get_positive(void)
            {
            ```

*(continued)*
            ```

```
             int n, status
             char ch;

             for  (status = scanf("%d", &n);
                   status == 1 && n <= 0;
                   status = scanf("%d", &n)) {}

             if (status == 0) {
                  scanf("%c", &ch);
                  printf("\n***Function get_positive ");
                  printf("reports ERROR in data at ");
                  printf(">>%c<<***\n", ch);
                  exit(1);
             } else if (status == EOF) {
                  return (status);
             } else {
                  return (n);
             }
        }
```

INTERPRETATION: Execution of a call to exit causes program termination from any point in a program. The *return_value* is used to indicate whether termination was brought on by some type of failure. A *return_value* of 0 means normal exit. In general, the use of

exit(0);

should be avoided in functions other than main since placing "normal" termination of a program in one of its function subprograms tends to diminish the readability of function main. The use of

exit(1);

should be reserved for terminating execution in cases where error recovery is not possible or not useful.

Case Study: Developing an Image Enhancement Library

Many of today's technologies deal with images. These images range from photographs of manufactured parts used for quality control to ultrasound, X-ray, and magnetic resonance images used in medical diagnosis to images collected by satellite for intelligence gathering. Images often require sophisticated processing to bring out features useful in the particular application area. In this case study, we make a start on a C library of image enhancement functions.

We make the assumption that the analysis and design of the enhancement algorithms to be included has already been carried out and that in each case we are working from a program that is an implementation of an algorithm for a particular environment. Our focus will be on the types of changes we need to make in these programs in order to create functions appropriate for inclusion in our library. We will seek to generalize our functions to permit their application in a wide spectrum of image systems. We should note that images of the size we process in this problem are too large for use on some personal computers.

◀ **PROBLEM** ▶

Our initial library is to include two functions that process black-and-white photographs. A black-and-white photograph is actually composed of many shades of gray. Digitizing the photograph produces a grid of integers ranging from zero to a maximum value based on the number of shades of gray that are distinguished by the imaging system. This type of digitized picture is called a *gray-scale image*. The purpose of one of our two library functions is to remove noise. The other function must sharpen an image by reducing the number of shades of gray. Figure 11.13 shows successive application of these two functions to a noisy image of four mushrooms.

Noise Reduction

The quality of a gray-scale image can be degraded by the introduction of noise when the image is transmitted long distances or collected under less than ideal conditions. A *pixel* (picture element) value that is very different from its neighboring pixels often represents noise. For example, in the image section

```
2 4 5 5 6
2 4 4 5 6
3 4 1 8 7
4 8 8 9 9
5 8 9 9 9
```

the pixel with the value 1 is likely to be noise because its value is so different from its neighbors. The program on which we will base our noise reduction library function assumes that if a pixel has a value that is different by 3 or more from its eight neighbors (the numbers in color in the section of pixels shown), it can be assumed to be noise. The program ignores the pixels on the edge of the pic-

Figure 11.13   Reducing Noise and Reducing Shades of Gray in an Image

(a) Noisy mushroom image

(b) Mushrooms with noise reduced

**(c) Mushrooms sharpened by use of just
three gray-scale shades**

ture and replaces a noisy value by the rounded average of all eight neighbors. In
the example, the 1 would be replaced by a 6, the integer nearest to 6.25:

$$\frac{(4 + 4 + 4 + 5 + 8 + 9 + 8 + 8)}{8.0} = 6.25$$

Figure 11.14 shows the function `clean` on which we are to base our library function.

Figure 11.14   Function clean, Candidate for Image Enhancement Library

```c
#include <stdlib.h>

#define NOISE_DIFF   3
#define MAXCOL    1024

/*
 * Finds each noisy pixel (a pixel whose value differs from all its neighbors
 * by NOISE_DIFF or more) and substitutes the average of its neighbors' values.
 * No change is made in boundary cells.
 */
void
clean(int image[][MAXCOL], /* input/output - numrow x MAXCOL gray-scale
                                              image to clean          */
      int numrow)          /* input - number of rows in image         */
{
      int pixel;   /* pixel currently being examined */
      int i, j;

      for (i = 1;  i < numrow - 1;  ++i) {
         for (j = 1;  j < MAXCOL - 1;  ++j) {
            pixel = image[i][j];
            if (abs(pixel - image[i - 1][j - 1]) >= NOISE_DIFF &&
                abs(pixel - image[i - 1][j]) >= NOISE_DIFF &&
                abs(pixel - image[i - 1][j + 1]) >= NOISE_DIFF &&
                abs(pixel - image[i][j - 1]) >= NOISE_DIFF &&
                abs(pixel - image[i][j + 1]) >= NOISE_DIFF &&
                abs(pixel - image[i + 1][j - 1]) >= NOISE_DIFF &&
                abs(pixel - image[i + 1][j]) >= NOISE_DIFF &&
                abs(pixel - image[i + 1][j + 1]) >= NOISE_DIFF)
                   image[i][j] = (int)((image[i - 1][j - 1] + image[i - 1][j]
                         + image[i - 1][j + 1] + image[i][j - 1]
                         + image[i][j + 1] + image[i + 1][j - 1]
                         + image[i + 1][j] + image[i + 1][j + 1])
                         / 8.0 + 0.5);
         }
      }
}
```

This function requires very little revision for inclusion in our library. We will make just three changes. First, because the function name is a bit vague, we will name our library function `reduce_noise`. Second, we must recognize that a difference of 3 between a pixel and all its neighbors is less likely to indicate noise in an image with 256 shades of gray than in an image with 16 shades. To accommodate this difference in imaging systems, we will make `noise_diff` an input parameter rather than a constant. Third, we will include the library name in the name of our constant macro, so `MAXCOL` becomes `IMAGE_MAXCOL`. Our revised function is shown in Fig. 11.15.

Figure 11.15   Image Enhancement Library Function reduce_noise

```c
#include <stdlib.h>

#define IMAGE_MAXCOL     1024

/*
 * Finds each noisy pixel (a pixel whose value differs from all its neighbors
 * by noise_diff or more) and substitutes the average of its neighbors' values.
 * No change is made in boundary cells.
 */
void
reduce_noise(int image[][IMAGE_MAXCOL], /* input/output - numrow x IMAGE_
                                    MAXCOL gray-scale image to clean */
            int numrow,             /* input - number of rows in image      */
            int noise_diff)         /* input - minimum pixel difference
                                             meaning noise                   */
{
    int pixel;    /* pixel currently being examined */
    int i, j;

    for  (i = 1;  i < numrow - 1;  ++i) {
        for  (j = 1;  j < IMAGE_MAXCOL - 1;  ++j) {
            pixel = image[i][j];
            if (abs(pixel - image[i - 1][j - 1]) >= noise_diff &&
                abs(pixel - image[i - 1][j]) >= noise_diff &&
                abs(pixel - image[i - 1][j + 1]) >= noise_diff &&
                abs(pixel - image[i][j - 1]) >= noise_diff &&
                abs(pixel - image[i][j + 1]) >= noise_diff &&
                abs(pixel - image[i + 1][j - 1]) >= noise_diff &&
```

(continued)

Figure 11.15   (continued)

```
        abs(pixel - image[i + 1][j]) >= noise_diff &&
        abs(pixel - image[i + 1][j + 1]) >= noise_diff)
      image[i][j] = (int)((image[i - 1][j - 1] + image[i - 1][j]
                    + image[i - 1][j + 1] + image[i][j - 1]
                    + image[i][j + 1] + image[i + 1][j - 1]
                    + image[i + 1][j] + image[i + 1][j + 1])
                    / 8.0 + 0.5);
    }
  }
}
```

Reducing Number of Shades of Gray

Our library function to reduce the number of shades of gray to just three shades will be based on a program that replaces all pixels with values 3 or less by a 0, pixels with values between 4 and 6 by a 1, and all others by a 4. This original program was designed to produce an image distinguishable when its pixel values (ranging from 0 to 9) were simply displayed rather than interpreted as gray-scale values (see Fig. 11.16). The function we will modify is shown in Fig. 11.17.

When we evaluate function sharpen for inclusion in our image library, its heavy reliance on constants (0, 1, 4, 3, and 6) is immediately a concern. Clearly, the cutoff values for dividing shades of gray into three groups would vary depending on the number of shades distinguished by the imaging system. The cutoff values should also be allowed to vary to accommodate very light or very dark images. Our library function will need the boundaries of the middle grouping to be input parameters. Similarly, the numeric values for white, medium gray, and black should not be rigidly prescribed but must also be allowed to vary. Thus the three standard values should also be input parameters.

Our revised sharpen function is shown in Fig. 11.18. For those who find seven function arguments burdensome, there is another option. We could include the library of image functions and then write our own MY_SHARPEN macro, which takes only the parameters that are expected to vary and whose body provides the others as constants in a call to sharpen. For example, macro MY_SHARPEN would simulate the original sharpen function if defined as

```
#define MY_SHARPEN(img, nrow)\
        sharpen(img, nrow, 3, 6, STAND1, STAND2, STAND3)
```

Figure 11.16   Digital Image Before (Top) and After (Bottom) Enhancement

```
211111122222121111122121222211212111211222111111133311111111112211212111211111
121100013233221110033130322201322212322221020002123320000101223200202000032011
128808870021322117778999219888779979799997898911128899958770113232177787888220
101464447221211284554549166655404546165656544920246546456591222213664564458333
114564545822300946460468024555455444651661540712366516554493120222641656558212
236140414582226460454258224464604146545455545800065646154471233213555646649032
126452565159186664546458326504445450566446464700254545654580092122652454569222
135514466464965645651548321222014445569321193331156614646470132131565455447323
126554745646651565146649032221125650568233333330156665465481226220464245549101
105504814646566652146569202021104664649232333331116551651547011236545645481233
104646700465454511165467323231104450659349333333134666645659119225656154471123
125404721255664020264149101822105544418222333332326651455149212126456565681122
116464800011222140145458133108024044657332333330006546554471233256616614691213
236645912211111112154048232810004545559211333339091454155155701356465544722232
216565702211111110165658121123815404553333333333266446464470314505254061022
226654710213333311144067203823126565533333333333331606514145711165446464712310
224555711113333311146459222121111440646722233333211255066454471545604447212213
124464200113333312146540122832814445662326333332213126664565645665566671019012
623200102111111120200002102022201100032333333333333333330033330232212311312
122002011111111110101101122800808080828161333331001323231100023232232210119210
222331121333132322201000113421101010121220333330002202121101101132232110011112
```

```
0000000000000000000000000000000000000000000000000000000000000000000000000000000
0000000000000000000000000000000000000000000000000000000000000000000000000000000
004404440000000004444444004444444444444444440000444414440000000044444444000
000111140000000411111140111111111114111111140000111111114000000111111114000
001111114000004111101140011111111111111111114000011111111140000000111111114000
001110111140004111110140011111111111111111114000011111111140000000111111114000
001110111114040111111101400110111111111111111114000011111111400000110111114000
001101111114111111111400000001111114000000000011111111114000000011111111148000
001111411111111110111400000001111114000000000001111111114000000011011114000
001111140111111110011140000000011111140000000001111111111400001111111140000
001111140011111110001114000000011111140100000000011111111114000001111111140000
001111400011110001114000000001111114000000000011111111114000001111111140000
001111400000000100111400000000111114000000000011111111114000001111111140000
001111400000000000111140000000011111400000000001111111114000111111111400000
001111400000000000001111400000000111110000000000011111111140001111101111100000
001111400000000000001114000000000111110000000000010110111140000111101111400000
0011114000000000000111140000000011111400000000000110111114011111111114000000
001111000000000000001110000000001111100000000000011111111111111111140000000
1000000000000000000000000000000000000000000000000000000000000000000000000000000
0000000000000000000000000000000000000000000000000000000000000000000000000000000
0000000000000000000000000000000000000000000000000000000000000000000000000000000
```

Figure 11.17   Function sharpen on Which Library Function Will Be Based

```
#define MAXCOL 1024
#define STAND1 0
#define STAND2 1
#define STAND3 4
```

(continued)

Figure 11.17   (continued)

```
/*
 *   Replaces each digit in numrow x MAXCOL image by one of three
 *   standard values
 *
 *       digit      standard value
 *       0-3           STAND1
 *       4-6           STAND2
 *       7-9           STAND3
 */
void
sharpen(int image[][MAXCOL], /* input/output - image to sharpen   */
        int numrow)          /* input - number of rows in image   */
{
     int i, j;

     for  (i = 0;  i < numrow;  ++i) {
         for  (j = 0;  j < MAXCOL;  ++j) {
             if (image[i][j] <= 3)
                     image[i][j] = STAND1;
             else if (image[i][j] <= 6)
                     image[i][j] = STAND2;
             else
                     image[i][j] = STAND3;
         }
     }
}
```

Figure 11.18   Library Function sharpen

```
#define IMAGE_MAXCOL 1024  /* (appears just once in header file) */

/*
 *   Reduces to three the number of gray-scale values in the image.
 *   Assigns value low_val to pixels in the range 0..low_bd, value mid_val
 *   to pixels in the range low_bd + 1..high_bd, value high_val to others.
 */
```

(continued)

Figure 11.18 (continued)

```
void
sharpen(int image[][IMAGE_MAXCOL], /* input/output - image to sharpen   */
        int numrow,                 /* input - number of rows in image   */
        int low_bd, int high_bd,    /* input - cutoffs for highest values
                                          in low and middle pixel groups */
        int low_val, int mid_val,   /* input - values to assign to pixels*/
        int high_val)               /*    in low, middle, and high
                                          groupings                      */
{     int i, j;

      for  (i = 0; i < numrow;  ++i) {
          for  (j = 0; j < IMAGE_MAXCOL;  ++j) {
              if (image[i][j] <= low_bd)
                    image[i][j] = low_val;
              else if (image[i][j] <= high_bd)
                    image[i][j] = mid_val;
              else
                    image[i][j] = high_val;
          }
      }
}
```

In Fig. 11.19, we show the header file for our image library along with an outline of the implementation file.

Figure 11.19   Image Library

```
/*
 *  image.h  -  header file
 *
 *  Library of image processing functions designed for images of width
 *  IMAGE_MAXCOL pixels;  length may vary.
 *             reduce_noise
 *             sharpen        - uses only 3 gray-scale values
 */

#define IMAGE_MAXCOL 1024
```

(continued)

Figure 11.19   (continued)

```
/*
 *  Finds each noisy pixel (a pixel whose value differs from all its neighbors
 *  by noise_diff or more) and substitutes the average of its neighbors'
 *  values. No change is made in boundary cells.
 */
extern void
reduce_noise(int image[][IMAGE_MAXCOL], /* input/output - numrow x
                                                IMAGE_MAXCOL gray-scale image
                                                to clean                    */
             int numrow,                /* input - number of rows in image */
             int noise_diff);           /* input - minimum pixel difference
                                                meaning noise               */
/*
 *  Reduces to three the number of gray-scale values in the image.  Assigns
 *  value low_val to pixels in the range 0..low_bd, value mid_val to pixels
 *  in the range low_bd + 1..high_bd, value high_val to others.
 */
extern void
sharpen(int image[][IMAGE_MAXCOL], /* input/output - image to sharpen       */
        int numrow,                /* input - number of rows in image       */
        int low_bd, int high_bd,   /* input - cutoffs for highest values
                                        in low and middle pixel groups      */
        int low_val, int mid_val,  /* input - values to assign to pixels    */
        int high_val);             /*    in low, middle, and high groupings */
/*------------------------------------------------------------------------- */
/*
 *  Outline of implementation file - image.c
 */

#include "image.h"

/*  Full definitions of reduce_noise and sharpen                            */
```

**EXERCISES FOR
SECTION 11.6**

Self-Check

1. Why should you #include the header file of a library in the library's own
   implementation file?
2. How could you revise function sharpen so it could handle any number of
   pixel groups?

Programming

1. Write a library function `threshold` that takes a gray-scale image and a threshold value as parameters and sets all pixels over the threshold to one particular value and all other pixels to a different value.

11.7 CONDITIONAL COMPILATION

C's preprocessor recognizes commands that allow the user to select parts of a program to be compiled and parts to be omitted. This ability can be helpful in a variety of situations. For example, one can build in debugging `printf` calls when writing a function and then include these statements in the compiled program only when they are needed. Inclusion of header files is another activity that may need to be done conditionally. For example, we might have two libraries, sp_one and sp_two, that both use a data type and operators of a third library, sp. The header files `sp_one.h` and `sp_two.h` would both have the directive `#include "sp.h"`. However, if we wanted a program to use the facilities of both sp_one and sp_two, including both of their header files would lead to inclusion of `sp.h` twice, resulting in duplicate declarations of the data type defined in `sp.h`. Because C prohibits such duplicate declarations, we must be able to prevent this situation. A third case in which conditional compilation is very helpful is the design of a system for use on a variety of computers. Conditional compilation allows one to compile only the code appropriate for the current computer.

Figure 11.20 shows a recursive function containing `printf` calls to create a trace of its execution. Compilation of these statements depends on the value of the condition

```
defined (TRACE)
```

The `defined` operator evaluates to 1 if the name that is its operand is defined in the preprocessor. Such definition is the result of using the name either in a `#define` directive or in a compiler option that simulates a `#define`. Otherwise, the `defined` operator evaluates to 0.

After creating functions like the one in Fig. 11.20, one need only include the directive

```
#define TRACE
```

somewhere in the source file prior to the function definition to "turn on" the

Figure 11.20   Conditional Compilation of Tracing printf Calls

```
/*
 *  Computes an integer quotient (m/n) using subtraction
 */
int
quotient(int m, int n)
{
        int ans;
#if defined (TRACE)
        printf("Entering quotient with m = %d, n = %d\n",
                m, n);
#endif

        if (n > m)
                ans = 0;
        else
                ans = 1 + quotient(m - n, n);

#if defined (TRACE)
        printf("Leaving quotient(%d, %d) with result = %d\n",
                m, n, ans);
#endif

        return (ans);
}
```

compilation of the tracing `printf` calls. It is not necessary to explicitly associate a value with **TRACE**. Remember that, as for all preprocessor directives, the # of the conditional compilation directives *must* be the first nonblank character on the line. The `defined` operator exists exclusively for application in `#if` and `#elif` directives. The `#elif` means "else if" and is used when selecting among multiple alternatives, as in Fig. 11.21.

One approach to the coordination of included files is illustrated in Fig. 11.22. Each header file is constructed so as to prevent duplicate compilation of its contents, regardless of the number of times the header file is included. The entire contents of a header file are enclosed in an `#if` that tests whether a name based on the header file name has been defined in a `#define` directive. Then the first time the header file is included, its entire contents are passed to

Figure 11.21 Conditional Compilation of Tracing printf Calls

```
/*
 * Computes an integer quotient (m/n) using subtraction
 */
int
quotient(int m, int n)
{
      int ans;

#if defined (TRACE_VERBOSE)
      printf("Entering quotient with m = %d, n = %d\n",
             m, n);
#elif defined (TRACE_BRIEF)
      printf(" => quotient(%d, %d)\n", m, n);
#endif

      if (n > m)
            ans = 0;
      else
            ans = 1 + quotient(m - n, n);

#if defined (TRACE_VERBOSE)
      printf("Leaving quotient(%d, %d) with result = %d\n",
             m, n, ans);
#elif defined (TRACE_BRIEF)
      printf("quotient(%d, %d) => %d\n", m, n, ans);
#endif

      return (ans);
}
```

Figure 11.22 Header File That Protects Itself from Effects of Duplicate Inclusion

```
/*  Header file planet.h
 *
 *  abstract data type planet
 *
 *  Type planet_t has these components:
 *       name, diameter, dist_sun, orbital_prd, axial_rot_prd
```

(continued)

Figure 11.22   (continued)

```
 *
 *  Operators:
 *        print_planet, planet_equal, scan_planet
 */

#if !defined (PLANET_H_INCL)
#define PLANET_H_INCL

#define PLANET_STRSIZ   10

typedef struct { /* planet structure */
      char name[PLANET_STRSIZ];
      double diameter,        /* equatorial diameter in km            */
             dist_sun,        /* average distance from sun in km      */
             orbital_prd,     /* years to orbit sun once              */
             axial_rot_prd;   /* hours to complete one revolution on
                                  axis                                */
} planet_t;

/*
 *  Prints with labels all components of a planet_t structure
 */
extern void
print_planet(planet_t pl);  /* input - one planet structure          */

/*
 *  Determines whether or not the components of planet_1 and planet_2
 *  match
 */
extern int
planet_equal(planet_t planet_1,  /* input - planets to               */
             planet_t planet_2); /*           compare                */

/*
 *  Fills a type planet_t structure with input data.  Integer returned as
 *  function result is success/failure/EOF indicator.
 *        1 => successful input of planet
 *        0 => error encountered
```

(continued)

Figure 11.22 (continued)

```
*      EOF => insufficient data before end of file
*   In case of error or EOF, value of type planet_t output argument is
*   undefined.
*/
extern int
scan_planet(planet_t *plnp); /* output- address of planet_t structure to
                                        fill                       */

#endif
```

the compiler. Since a #define of the critical name is in the file, additional #include directives for the same file will provide no code to the compiler.

C's #if and #elif directives are complemented by an #else directive to make possible a full range of selective compilation constructs. An #undef directive that cancels the preprocessor's definition of a particular name is also available.

EXERCISES FOR SECTION 11.7

Self-Check

1. Use conditional compilation to select an appropriate call to printf. Assume that on a UNIX operating system, the name UNIX will be defined in the C preprocessor; on the VMS operating system, the name VMS will be defined. The desired message on UNIX is

   Enter <ctrl-d> to quit.

   The desired message on VMS is

   Enter <ctrl-z> to quit.

2. Consider the header file shown in Fig. 11.22. Describe what happens (a) when the preprocessor first encounters a #include "planet.h" directive and (b) when the preprocessor encounters a second #include "planet.h" directive.

11.8 ARGUMENTS TO FUNCTION main

Up to this point, we have always defined function main with a void parameter list. However, as another possibility, we could use the following prototype that indicates that main has two formal parameters: an integer and an array of pointers to strings:

```
int
main(int    argc,    /* input - argument count (including
                                 program name)               */
        char *argv[]) /* input - argument vector             */
```

The way you cause your program to run varies from one operating system to another. However, most operating systems provide some way for you to specify values of options when you run a program. For example, on the ULTRIX operating system, one would specify options opt1, opt2, and opt3 when running a program named prog by typing the command line

```
prog opt1 opt2 opt3
```

The formal parameters argc and argv provide a mechanism for a C main function to access these *command line arguments*. If the program prog just mentioned were the machine code of a C program whose main function prototype had parameters argc and argv, then the command line

```
prog opt1 opt2 opt3
```

would result in these formal parameter values within main:

```
argc    4          argv[0]    "prog"
                       [1]     "opt1"
                       [2]     "opt2"
                       [3]     "opt3"
                       [4]     ""    (empty string)
```

Figure 11.23 shows a revised version of our program from Chapter 10 to make a backup copy of a text file. Rather than prompting the user for the names of the file to copy and the file to be the backup, the new version expects the user to enter this information on the command line. For example, if the program is named backup and the user activates it by typing

```
backup old.txt new.txt
```

the formal parameters of `main` will have these values:

```
argc   3       argv[0]   "backup"
                   [1]    "old.txt"
                   [2]    "new.txt"
                   [3]    ""
```

If the program encounters any difficulty in opening either of the files named by
the user, it exits with an appropriate error message. Otherwise, it proceeds with
the copy operation.

Figure 11.23   File Backup Using Arguments to Function main

```
/*
 *  Makes a backup of the file whose name is the first command line argument.
 *  The second command line argument is the name of the new file.
 */
#include <stdio.h>
#include <stdlib.h>

int
main(int    argc,   /* input - argument count (including program name) */
     char *argv[]) /* input - argument vector                          */
{
        FILE *inp,    /* file pointers for input     */
             *outp;   /*    and backup files         */
        char  ch;     /* one character of input file */
        int   status; /* status of input operation   */

        /* Open input and backup files if possible                     */
        inp = fopen(argv[1], "r");
        if (inp == NULL) {
               printf("\nCannot open file %s for input\n", argv[1]);
               exit(1);
        }

        outp = fopen(argv[2], "w");
        if (outp == NULL) {
               printf("\nCannot open file %s for output\n", argv[2]);
               exit(1);
        }
```

(continued)

Figure 11.23   (continued)

```
/* Make backup copy one character at a time                        */
for  (status = fscanf(inp, "%c", &ch);
        status != EOF;
        status = fscanf(inp, "%c", &ch))
    fprintf(outp, "%c", ch);

/*  Close files and notify user of backup completion               */
fclose(inp);
fclose(outp);
printf("\nCopied %s to %s\n", argv[1], argv[2]);

return(0);
}
```

EXERCISES FOR SECTION 11.8

Self-Check

1. How would you modify the program in Fig. 11.23 so that if a user typed a command line with fewer than two file names provided, an appropriate error message would be displayed?

Programming

1. Write a program that takes a single command line argument. The argument should be the name of a text file containing integers, and the program should sum the integers in the file. If any invalid data are encountered, the program should terminate with an error message that includes the file name and the invalid character.

11.9 COMMON PROGRAMMING ERRORS

The most common problem in the development of large systems by teams of programmers is a lack of agreement regarding the details of a system's design. If you apply the software development method presented in earlier chapters, you can achieve a rational, stepwise division of a large problem into smaller subproblems that correspond to individual functions. Then you can devise detailed descriptions of *what* each function is to do and *what type*(s) of data it is to manipulate. Only when representatives of all teams are in full agreement about this fundamental interface information is it wise to proceed with a system's implementation.

When developing personal libraries, it is easy to forget the long-range goal of having reusable functions in the rush of completing a current project. An unnecessarily restrictive assumption built into a library function can quickly negate the function's usefulness in another context.

Although macros provide a quick and often quite readable shorthand for the expressions they represent, they are also fertile ground for error growth. It is easy to slip and type a blank after the macro name in the definition of a macro with parameters, causing the preprocessor to misinterpret the definition. Operator precedence mistakes are sure to crop up unless the programmer is absolutely meticulous about parenthesizing every macro body that produces a result value as well as parenthesizing every occurrence of a macro parameter within the body. Following a consistent naming convention for macros can save hours of unnecessary debugging resulting from the programmer's erroneous assumption that a function, not a macro, is being called.

In the history of computing, the inappropriate use of global variables is notorious for corrupting a system's reliability. We cannot overemphasize the importance of maintaining visible interfaces among functions through their parameter lists. Only functions with visible interfaces are good candidates for reuse through inclusion in a library.

CHAPTER REVIEW

In this chapter, we ventured beyond the sheltered world of single problems solved by individual programs to grapple with the special difficulties associated with large systems. We have emphasized the importance of abstraction in dealing with complexity and have focused on C's provisions for personal libraries. We saw how dividing a library into a header file and an implementation file provides a natural separation of the description of *what* the library functions do from *how* they do it.

We met some additional features of C such as macros with parameters, the `exit` function, conditional compilation directives, and arguments to function `main`; and we studied how various declarations relate to the storage classes of the names declared. A library development case study gave us an opportunity to see specific ways in which library functions differ from typical special-purpose functions.

Table 11.2 summarizes the new constructs studied.

Table 11.2 **Summary of New C Constructs**

C Construct	Meaning
Header File (with #if...#endif directives)	

Header File (with #if...#endif directives)

```
/*  somelib.h  */
#if !defined (SOMELIB_H_INCL)
#define SOMELIB_H_INCL

#define SOMELIB_MAX 20
typedef struct {
  int   comp;
  char  s[SOMELIB_MAX];
} some_t;

/*  Purpose of function make_some
 */
extern some_t
make_some(int        n,
          const char str[]);

/* other extern prototypes */

#endif
```

somelib.h is a header file to be included (#include "somelib.h") in any program desiring to use its facilities. somelib.h uses conditional compilation (#if...#endif) to protect its contents from duplicate inclusion.

Implementation File

```
/* somelib.c */
#include "somelib.h"
#include <string.h>

/*  Purpose of function make_some
 */
some_t
make_some(int        n,
          const char str[])
{
    some_t result;

    result.comp = n;
    strcpy(result.s, str);

    return (result);
}

/*  other function definitions  */
```

somelib.c is the implementation file associated with somelib.h. Its object file must be linked to any other program that includes somelib.h.

(continued)

Table 11.2 (continued)

C Construct	Meaning

Macro Definition and Call

```
#define AVG(x,y) (((x) + (y)) / 2.0)
. . .

ans = AVG(2*a, b);
```

Preprocessor will replace each call to AVG by its macro expansion. Statement shown becomes
```
    ans = (((2*a) + (b)) / 2.0);
```

exit Function

```
/*  Compute decimal equivalent of a
 *  common fraction
 */
double
dec_equiv(int num, int denom)
{
    if (denom == 0) {
        printf("Zero-divide: %d/%d\n",
               num, denom);
        exit(1);
    } else {
        return ((double)num /
                (double)denom);
    }
}
```

Function causes premature program termination if called with an invalid argument.

Arguments to Function main

```
int
main(int argc, char *argv[])
{
    if (argc == 3)
        process(argv[1], argv[2]);
    else
        printf
          ("Wrong number of options");

    return (0);
}
```

Function main is expecting two command line arguments to pass to function process.

QUICK-CHECK EXERCISES

1. A system designer who is breaking down a complex problem using _____ _____ will focus first on *what* a function is to do, leaving the details of *how* this is accomplished for later.

2. To use a library function, one must know the function's _____ , _____ , and _____ .

3. Functions that can be used in a variety of applications are examples of _____ code.

4. In C, a(n) _____ file contains information about *what* a library's functions do. The _____ file contains the details of *how* these actions are accomplished.

5. The keyword `extern` in a declaration notifies the _____ that the name declared will be known by the _____ .

6. When defining an implementation file `lib1.c`, why is it advantageous to `#include "lib1.h"`?

7. Given this definition of macro `ABSDF`,

   ```
   #define ABSDF(x, y)  (fabs((x) - (y)))
   ```

   show what this statement will be after macro expansion:

   ```
   if (ABSDF(a + b, c) > ABSDF(b + c, a))
         lgdiff = ABSDF(a + b, c);
   ```

8. Where are variables of storage class `auto` allocated and when? When are they deallocated?

9. When are variables of storage class `static` allocated? When are they deallocated?

10. Which of the following prototypes would be followed immediately by the code of function `mangle`?

    ```
    double                        extern double
    mangle(double x, double y)    mangle(double x, double y);
    ```

11. When generalizing a function for inclusion in a library, named constants are often replaced by _____ .

12. What directives could we add to header file `mylib.h` so that no matter how many `#include "mylib.h"` directives were processed, the contents of `mylib.h` would be compiled just once?

ANSWERS TO QUICK-CHECK EXERCISES

1. procedural abstraction
2. name, purpose, parameter list
3. reusable
4. header, implementation
5. compiler, linker

6. Any necessary macros and data types are defined in just one file, the header file, so modification of a macro or of a data type does not require changes in more than one place.

7. ```
if ((fabs((a + b) - (c))) > (fabs((b + c) - (a))))
       lgdiff = (fabs((a + b) - (c)));
```

8. The variables are allocated on the stack at the time when a function is entered. They are deallocated when the function to which they belong returns.

9. The variables are allocated before program execution. They are deallocated at program termination.

10. The prototype on the left

11. function parameters

12. ```
#if !defined (MYLIB_H_INCL)
    #define MYLIB_H_INCL
          . . . rest of mylib.h . . .
    #endif
```

REVIEW QUESTIONS

1. Define *procedural abstraction* and *data abstraction*.
2. What feature of C encourages the encapsulation of data objects and their operators?
3. Compare the typical contents of a library header file to the contents of an implementation file. Which of these files defines the interface between a library and a program?
4. How does the C compiler know whether to look for an included file in the system directory or in the program's directory?
5. Compare the execution of the macro call

   ```
   MAC(a, b)
   ```

   to the execution of an analogous function call

   ```
   mac(a, b)
   ```

   Which of the following two calls is sure to be valid and why?

   ```
   mac(++a, b)    or    MAC(++a, b)
   ```

6. When you write the body of a macro definition, where should you use parentheses?

7. What are C's five storage classes? What are the default storage classes for variables declared in each of the following environments?

declared at the top level
declared as function parameters
declared as local variables of a function

8. What is the purpose of storage class `register`?

9. Discuss this statement: If a program has five functions that manipulate an array of data values, it makes more sense to declare this array at the program's top level so that each function does not need to have an array parameter.

10. Why is the argument value 1 used much more often than the argument value 0 in calls to the `exit` function?

11. Describe the purpose of the `defined` operator.

12. When function `main` of a C program has a `nonvoid` parameter list, why is the value of its first parameter never less than 1?

PROGRAMMING PROJECTS

1. Create a library that defines a data type to represent a common fraction and provides functions for I/O, comparison (less than, equal to), and arithmetic operations (+, −, *, /) on these fractions. Use the library in a program that processes a list of fractions, finding the sum, the mean, the median, and the greatest absolute difference between consecutive elements. All results should be expressed as common fractions in reduced form.

2. Twenty-one global positioning satellites (GPSs) are in orbit around the earth. They are distributed such that at least four satellites are visible from any point on earth at any time. Each satellite continuously broadcasts its identity, its status, its position, and the current value of its on-board clock. Since the clocks are very accurate and the speed of transmission of radio waves is very well known, a small hand-held receiver can get signals from the satellites visible to it and, by subtracting the times of origination and receipt of each signal, can deduce its own position relative to the position broadcast by each satellite.

There are many applications for this reliable positioning information. You are developing a library of functions to be used in conjunction with a GPS hand-held receiver to allow a user to perform his or her own special positioning applications. Define two data structures: type `user_t` structure `our_user` in which to store your user's own position and current time, and an array of type `user_t` structures `other_users` with the same data for each of several other users we need to be able to find. A position is represented by type `double` components `latitude`, `longitude`, and `altitude`. Component latitude represents the distance south of a given reference latitude, in meters. Component longitude represents the distance west of a reference longitude, in meters. For this problem, assume all users are south and west of these references, and assume that distances are relatively small to avoid some second-order effects that would occur if a significant part of the earth's surface were involved. Type double component time should represent elapsed nanoseconds since some reference time. String component name should hold the name of the user. Write the functions in (a)–(d).

a. Function scan_user that scans position and time data into one user_t structure.

b. A function that calls scan_user to fill the our_user structure and the other_users array.

c. A function that calculates the difference in position between our_user and each of the other users and stores these distances in an array of structures. This array of structures should consist of records each of which contains the name of another user and the distance relative to our user. Because we assume small distances, the distance can be calculated approximately as:

$$\sqrt{(lat_1 - lat_2)^2 + (long_1 - long_2)^2 + (alt_1 - alt_2)^2}$$

where lat_1, $long_1$, and alt_1 refer to the position of one user, and lat_2, $long_2$, and alt_2 indicate the position of another user.

d. A function that searches through this relative position array of structures and finds the closest other user to our user, returning the structure representing this closest user.

e. Write a main program that calls these library functions to scan position and time data and to find the name and position of the nearest user.

3. Many operational engineering systems require complex scheduling of people, machines, and supplies to provide a service or produce a product. To schedule a system, one needs to know three things: the resources available to the system, the resources required to provide the desired service, and any constraints on the resources. Many sophisticated algorithms are available to minimize the cost or time required to provide a service. Here we will build a small library of functions useful for solving constrained scheduling problems.

You are head of maintenance scheduling for Brown Bag Airlines. You have three crews, with different qualifications as follows:

Crew Number	Level	Cost of Crew Per Hour
0	1	$200.
1	2	$300.
2	3	$400.

Crew 2 is certified to do all levels of maintenance work, but costs more per hour than the other crews. Crew 1 can do maintenance work requiring skills 1 and 2, but not skill 3. Crew 0 can do maintenance work only at level 1. You need to schedule the following maintenance:

Aircraft ID	Level of Maintenance	Number of Hours
7899	1	8
3119	1	6
7668	1	4
2324	2	4
1123	2	8
7555	2	4
6789	3	2
7888	3	10

Write the following functions and create a scheduling library from them:

a. A function to scan and store crew data in an appropriate structure.
b. A function to scan and store in an appropriate structure the required maintenance data.
c. A function that checks maintenance level required against the crew abilities and returns the number of the lowest-cost crew that can perform the maintenance.
d. A function that checks the maintenance level required against the crew abilities and current schedule and returns the number of the qualified crew that will be free to perform the maintenance at the earliest time. If more than one crew satisfies the function's constraints, the number of the lowest-cost qualified crew is returned.
e. A function that accumulates hours required for each crew as each maintenance task is scheduled.

Write a main program that calls these functions and any others you feel are needed for scheduling crews to do the listed maintenance jobs. Assume that all three crews can work at the same time and that the crews are paid only when they work. Jobs must be done in their entirety by one crew. Develop one algorithm to find the quickest way to get the maintenance done and another to find the cheapest way to get the work done. How big is the difference between these two solutions in time required to complete the given list of maintenance jobs?

4. You are developing a personal library of functions to assist in solving heat transfer problems. Your first step is to develop functions to solve simple

conduction problems using various forms of the formula

$$H = \frac{kA\,(T_2 - T_1)}{X}$$

where H is the rate of heat transfer in watts, k is the coefficient of thermal conductivity for the particular substance, A is the cross-sectional area in m^2, T_2 and T_1 are the kelvin temperatures on the two sides of the conductor, and X is the thickness of the conductor in m.

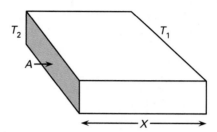

Your library will include not only a function to compute H given k, A, T_2, T_1, and X, but also functions to compute A given H, k, T_2, T_1, and X; T_2 given H, k, A, T_1, and X; and so on. Your library will define a data type `substance_t` with components `name` and `coef_cond` to be used in representing substance names and their coefficients of thermal conductivity. Your program should have available an array of common substances so the user can choose a substance by name rather than entering the actual constant.
Here are a few representative thermal conductivity values:

Substance	Thermal Conductivity (k) (W/m·K)
Oak	0.15
Glass	0.8
Lead	35.3
Copper	401
Steel	46

Using your library, develop a program that would interact with the user in the following way:

```
Respond to the prompts with the data known. For the
unknown quantity, enter a question mark (?)

Rate of heat transfer (watts)> 755.0
```

```
Substance:   (1) oak    (2) glass   (3) lead    (4) copper
             (5) steel (6) other
> 2
Cross-sectional area of conductor (m^2)> 0.12
Temperature on one side (kelvin)> 298
Temperature on the other side (kelvin)> ?
Thickness of conductor (m)> 0.003


      kA (T2 - T1)
H = ------------
          X

H = 755.0 W
k = 0.800 W/m-K
A = 0.120 m^2
T2 = 298 K
T1 = 274 K
X = 0.003 m

Temperature on the other side is 274 K.
```

If the user were to choose other for substance, the program would prompt for the substance's coefficient of thermal conductivity.

5. Write a program that takes a command line argument that is the name of a text file and creates a new text file with a heading line

```
**************** file name ********************
```

and the contents of the original file with line numbers added. If the file's name contains a period, use the part of the name before the period concatenated with .lis as the name of the new file. Otherwise, just concatenate .lis to the whole file name.

INTRODUCTION TO NUMERICAL METHODS

Numerical analysis is the field of study concerned with developing methods to use a computer to solve computational problems in mathematics. The approach to solving systems of linear equations that we presented in Section 8.5 is an example of a numerical method. In this chapter we will discuss several computational techniques that are widely used in solving problems in engineering, economics, statistics, business, natural science, and social science. These techniques include finding roots of equations, fitting a line to a data set, performing numerical differentiation and integration, and solving first-order differential equations. We will also discuss ANSI C's facility for passing a function as an argument, a feature that is quite useful in numerical computation.

The sections in this chapter are fairly independent and may be studied in any order. Due to space limitations, we have generally presented only one method for performing a particular numerical operation. Several different methods are available for each of the operations discussed in this chapter. A list of references is provided for those wishing to delve deeper into the topic of numerical methods. An extensive set of programming projects is also provided.

12.1 FINDING ROOTS OF EQUATIONS

In Section 6.6, we saw that the roots of an equation

$$f(x) = 0$$

are values for x that make this equation true. We also studied the bisection method, one approach to approximating the real roots of $f(x) = 0$. We noted that these roots are also called the zeros of the function $f(x)$.

In this section, we will discuss Newton's method, another numerical method for approximating the zeros of a function. When a numerical method is successful in finding a root, it is said to have *converged* to the root. When a numerical method fails, it is said to have *diverged*. In general, the bisection method converges relatively slowly as compared to Newton's method. The speed with which a method converges becomes an important issue when the function $f(x)$, whose roots we are computing, requires extensive computations; finding roots of equations involves repeated evaluations of this function.

Convergence Criteria

In general, root-finding methods generate a sequence of approximations to a root:

$$x_1, x_2, x_3, \ldots, x_j, \ldots$$

One problem is deciding when to terminate this generation process. In other words, when is a given x_j value "good enough" to be accepted as our answer?

There are three criteria for judging whether a given x_j is "good enough." Since the satisfaction of one of these criteria causes the root-finding method to terminate, or converge, these criteria, which follow, are called *convergence criteria*. The true root is denoted by *rt*; the *epsilon_i* are some predetermined small numbers (that may or may not be equal), x_j is the latest approximation, and x_{j-1} is the approximation before that.

Criteria for Convergence to the Root

1. $|f(x_j)| < epsilon_1$
2. $|x_j - rt| < epsilon_2$
3. $|x_j - x_{j-1}| < epsilon_3$

Criterion 1 states that x_j is considered a good enough approximation to the root if the value of $|f(x_j)|$ is very small. Criterion 2 states that x_j is considered a good enough approximation to the root if it is very close to the true root. Criterion 3 states that x_j is considered a good enough approximation to the root if it is very close to the previous approximation, x_{j-1}. In other words, we do not expect to gain required accuracy by generating additional approximations.

One might wonder how the second criterion can be applied in practice unless *rt* is already known. Actually, we do not need to know *rt* to claim that x_j is within *epsilon_2* of *rt*. It is sufficient to know that x_j and *rt* have been isolated to the same sufficiently small interval.

The convergence criteria are not equivalent even when

$$epsilon_1 = epsilon_2 = epsilon_3$$

For example, Fig. 12.1(a) shows a situation in which x_j is within a distance *epsilon* of *rt*, but $|f(x_j)|$ is greater than *epsilon*. Figure 12.1(b) also shows a situation where $|f(x_j)| < epsilon$, but here the distance of x_j from *rt* is greater than *epsilon*.

The bisection method that we studied in Chapter 6 applies the second convergence criterion. We repeatedly generate approximate roots x_j until we have an approximation that is certain to be within a distance of *epsilon* from the true root *rt*. This approximation is found by isolating the true root and the approximate root within the same interval whose length is less than *epsilon*.

Newton's Method

Newton's method for finding a root of an equation applies the third convergence criterion. In this method, we repeatedly generate approximate roots until two successive approximations differ by less than the small constant *epsilon*. Newton's

Figure 12.1
Showing
Nonequivalence
of Convergence
Criteria 1 and 2

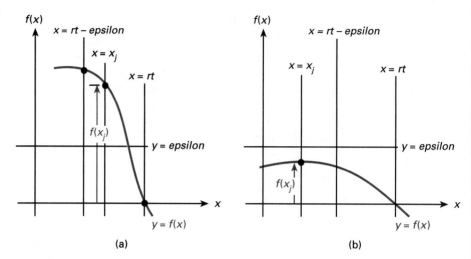

Figure 12.1 Showing Nonequivalence of Convergence Criteria 1 and 2

(a)   (b)

method starts with an initial guess for a root, x_0, and then generates successive approximate roots $x_1, x_2, \ldots, x_j, x_{j+1}, \ldots$, using the iterative formula

$$x_{j+1} = x_j - \frac{f(x_j)}{f'(x_j)}$$

where $f'(x_j)$ is the derivative of function f evaluated at $x = x_j$. The formula generates a new guess, x_{j+1}, from a previous one, x_j. Sometimes Newton's method will fail to converge to a root. In this case, the program should terminate after many trials, perhaps 100.

Figure 12.2 shows the geometric interpretation of Newton's method where x_0, x_1, and x_2 represent successive guesses for the root. At each point x_j, the derivative, $f'(x_j)$, is the slope of the tangent to the curve, $f(x)$. The next guess for the root, x_{j+1}, is the point at which the tangent crosses the x axis.

From geometry, we get the equation

$$\frac{y_{j+1} - y_j}{x_{j+1} - x_j} = m$$

where m is the slope of the line between points (x_{j+1}, y_{j+1}) and (x_j, y_j). In Fig. 12.2, we see that y_{j+1} is zero, y_j is $f(x_j)$, and m is $f'(x_j)$; therefore by substituting and rearranging terms, we get

$$-f(x_j) = f'(x_j) \times (x_{j+1} - x_j)$$

leading to the formula shown at the beginning of the presentation of Newton's method.

**Figure 12.2
Geometric
Interpretation
of Newton's
Method**

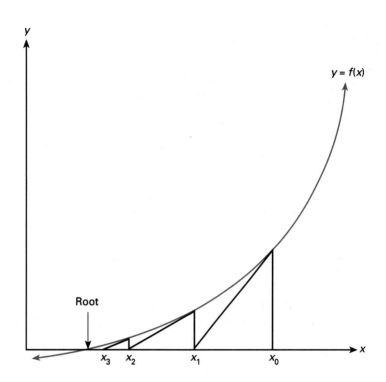

A Program Using Newton's Method

The C program in Fig. 12.3 attempts to approximate zeros for functions f and g
using Newton's method. The initial approximation of a zero is a guess obtained

Figure 12.3   Finding a Function Root Using Newton's Method

```
/*
 *  Finds roots of the equations
 *       f(x) = 0   and   g(x) = 0
 *  given a user-supplied guess and applying Newton's method
 *  from a personal numerical methods library.
 */

#include <stdio.h>
#include <math.h>
#include "methods.h"   /* Header file for personal numerical methods
                          library containing function newton         */
```

(continued)

Figure 12.3 (continued)

```
/*  Functions for which roots are sought and functions' derivatives     */

/*    3      2
 *  5x   - 2x   + 3
 */
double
f(double x)
{
      return (5 * pow(x, 3.0) - 2 * pow(x, 2.0) + 3);
}

/*      2
 *  15x   - 4x
 */
double
fprime(double x)
{
      return (15 * pow(x, 2.0) - 4 * x);
}

/*    3     2
 *  8x   - 6x   - 12x
 */
double
g(double x)
{
      return (8 * pow(x, 3.0) - 6 * pow(x, 2.0) - 12 * x);
}

/*      2
 *  24x   - 12x - 12
 */
double
gprime(double x)
{
      return (24 * pow(x, 2.0) - 12 * x - 12);
}
```

(continued)

Figure 12.3   (continued)

```
int
main(void)
{
      double guess,      /* user's guess for function root */
             epsilon,    /* error tolerance */
             root;
      int    error;

      /*  Get guess and error tolerance from user for f root
          approximation                                           */
      printf("\nEnter guess for root of f> ");
      scanf("%lf", &guess);
      printf("\nEnter tolerance> ");
      scanf("%lf", &epsilon);

      /*  Use function newton to look for root of f             */
      printf("\nFunction f\n");
      root = newton(f, fprime, guess, epsilon, &error);
      if (error)
           printf("   Root of f not found for guess of %.7f\n", guess);
      else
           printf("   f(%.7f) = %e\n", root, f(root));

      /*  Get guess and error tolerance from user for g root
          approximation                                           */
      printf("\nEnter guess for root of g> ");
      scanf("%lf", &guess);
      printf("\nEnter tolerance> ");
      scanf("%lf", &epsilon);

      /*  Use function newton to look for root of g             */
      printf("\nFunction g\n");
      root = newton(g, gprime, guess, epsilon, &error);
      if (error)
           printf("   Root of g not found for guess of %.7f\n", guess);
      else
           printf("   g(%.7f) = %e\n", root, g(root));

      return (0);
}
```

from the user. This guess is passed to function `newton` along with the names of the function whose zero is sought and of the first derivative of the function. Function `newton` repeatedly computes the next approximation of the root value, `approx`, from the last approximation, `previous`. The loop continues to execute until either the successive computations converge to an acceptable approximation or there is a reason to abandon the search. Then function `newton` either returns an approximate root or signals an error by setting its output parameter `errp` to TRUE. The error flag is set if a call to the derivative function returns a value of 0.0 or if the method does not converge to a solution in `MAX_APPROX` iterations.

The main function gets the initial approximation from the user, calls function `newton` (shown in Fig. 12.4), and displays the final results.

Figure 12.4   Personal Library Function newton

```c
#include <stdio.h>
#include <math.h>

#define TRACE
#define FALSE       0
#define TRUE        1
#define MAX_APPROX 100  /* iterations allowed before divergence assumed */

/*
 *   Implements Newton's method for finding a root of a function f.
 *   Finds a root (and sets output parameter error flag to FALSE) if two
 *   successive approximations are found that differ by less than epsilon.
 *   Sets output parameter error flag to TRUE if fderiv (the derivative
 *   of f) returns a value of zero or if method fails to converge in
 *   MAX_APPROX iterations
 */
double
newton(double  f(double farg),       /* input  - the function        */
       double  fderiv(double fdarg), /* input  - the function's first
                                                  derivative          */
       double  guess,        /* input  - user's guess for a root      */
       double  epsilon,      /* input  - error tolerance              */
       int     *errp)        /* output - error flag                   */
{
     double previous,        /* previous approximation       */
            approx,          /* new approximation            */
            deriv_val;       /* value of derivative          */
```

(continued)

Figure 12.4   (continued)

```
    int    num_approx = 0;   /* number of iterations so far    */

    *errp = FALSE;

    approx = guess;
    do {
        ++num_approx;
        previous = approx;
        deriv_val = fderiv(previous);
        if (num_approx > MAX_APPROX)
                *errp = TRUE;
        else if (deriv_val == 0)
                *errp = TRUE;
        else
                approx = previous - f(previous) / deriv_val;

        /* Numbers and displays new approximation if trace is on        */
        #if defined(TRACE)
                if (*errp)
                        printf("Approximation does not converge\n");
                else
                        printf("%3d. Function value at %.7f = %e\n",
                                num_approx, approx, f(approx));
        #endif
    } while (!(*errp)  &&  fabs(approx - previous) >= epsilon);

    return (approx);
}
```

A sample run of the program is shown in Fig. 12.5. Note that because TRACE is defined, the intermediate approximations are displayed by newton, showing the convergence to the final answer.

Figure 12.5   Sample Run of Newton's Method Program with Trace Code Included

```
Enter guess for root of f> 1
Enter tolerance> 0.0005
Function f
```

(continued)

Figure 12.5   (continued)

```
1. Function value at  0.4545455 =  3.056349e+00
2. Function value at -1.9313783 = -4.048279e+01
3. Function value at -1.2956445 = -1.123235e+01
4. Function value at -0.9257091 = -2.680249e+00
5. Function value at -0.7638280 = -3.950800e-01
6. Function value at -0.7303660 = -1.488104e-02
7. Function value at -0.7290036 = -2.403310e-05
8. Function value at -0.7290014 = -6.302531e-11
 f(-0.7290014) = -6.302531e-11


Enter guess for root of g> 1
Enter tolerance> 0.0005
Function g
Approximation does not converge
  Root of g not found for guess of 1.0000000
```

Functions as Arguments

Notice that each call to `newton` passes function names as the first and second arguments. This is the first time we have seen a function name used as an argument. Because Newton's method as implemented in Fig. 12.4 can be applied to any function and first derivative function that return type `double` values and take single type `double` arguments, using functions as input parameters gives `newton` great flexibility. Function `newton`'s parameters `f` and `fderiv` each represent addresses of code to carry out a function's purpose. ANSI C allows function parameters like `f` and `fderiv` to be used in a function call expression in the same way that a function name would be used. Thus, when `newton` is executing as a result of function `main`'s statement

```
root = newton(f, fprime, guess, epsilon, &error);
```

the statements

```
deriv_val = fderiv(previous);
approx = previous - f(previous) / deriv_val;
```

are equivalent to

```
deriv_val = fprime(previous);
approx = previous - f(previous) / deriv_val;
```

However, when `newton` executes as a result of the call

```
root = newton(g, gprime, guess, epsilon, &error);
```

the same statements mean

```
deriv_val = gprime(previous);
approx = previous - g(previous) / deriv_val;
```

Of course, if `newton` were to use functions `f`, `g`, `fprime`, and `gprime` directly, rather than calling them through its function parameters, the file in which `newton` is found would need to contain prototypes of `f`, `g`, `fprime`, and `gprime`. No such advance knowledge is required when function parameters are used.

**EXERCISES FOR
SECTION 12.1**

Self-Check

1. Determine the results displayed by these calls to function `newton` of Fig. 12.4.

```
printf("%7.3f\n",
       newton(f, fprime, 1.0, 0.0001, &error));
printf("%7.3f\n",
       newton(f, fprime, -1.0, 0.0001, &error));
printf("%7.3f\n",
       newton(f, fprime, 10.0, 0.0001, &error));
printf("%7.3f\n",
       newton(f, fprime, -10.0, 0.0001, &error));
```

if

$$f(x) = 2x^2 - 2x - 1.5$$
$$f'(x) = 4x - 2$$

Do the results make sense? Can you suggest a more direct way to compute these results?

Programming

1. Rewrite function `bisect` from Fig. 6.31 so it has a function parameter.

12.2 LINEAR REGRESSION AND CORRELATION

In this section, we will discuss how two important ideas from statistics—linear regression and correlation—are translated into C code. Our discussion will be rather sketchy because we do not have the space to develop the full rationale behind some of the formulas or to elaborate on certain issues. The interested reader is referred to the references at the end of the chapter.

The Concept of Regression

Regression is normally used for prediction. Suppose X and Y are two measurable quantities (or observables). The concept of regression is to determine a relationship

$$Y = f(X)$$

on the basis of a finite sample of X and Y scores. Regression is normally used for prediction of one variable with respect to another, or in testing that one measurable feature of something really has an expected dependency with respect to some known quantity. For example, X might be a day of the month during a week in July and Y might be the average highest temperature at a given location, or X might be some dimension of a bar of a complex shape and Y the bar's maximum loading along that dimension before failure. The latter dependency is an example of a nonlinear dependency.

Our discussion will be confined to linear regression, where the relationship $f(X)$ is linear. The linear relationship is then called the best fit line through the sample data. The line is of the form

$$Y = A + BX$$

To determine the best fit line through sample data, we must make assumptions about X and Y. Different assumptions will yield different solutions for the coefficients A and B. Because we assume that Y and not X is the dependent variable, we can measure X exactly; the Y values for a given X are assumed to be normally distributed about some mean.

Figure 12.6 shows three X values and the distributions of Y values for the populations they determine. The mean of the Y values for a given X value is denoted by $M_{Y|X}$. We will denote the standard deviation of the Y values for a given X by $S_{Y|X}$.

Figure 12.7 shows the distribution of Y values for the population associated with a given X value. The mean, $M_{Y|X}$, is a measure of central tendency for the Y values for this population, and the standard deviation, $S_{Y|X}$, is a measure of the dispersion (or spread) of the Y values for this population. For example, Fig. 12.7 might represent the distribution of intelligence quotients for professors with a given income. The shaded region indicates all professors whose intelligence quotient is within one standard deviation of the mean for this population.

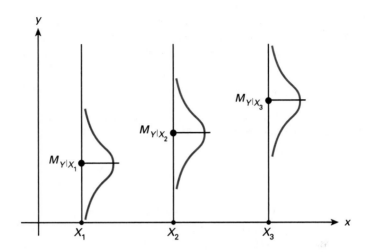

In linear regression, we assume that the means $M_{Y|X}$ lie on some line

$$M_{Y|X} = \alpha + \beta X$$

The problem is that we cannot determine this line exactly because we have only a finite amount of data relating to just some of the X values. On the basis of this finite sample, we must compute an estimate for the preceding linear relationship. That estimate is called the *best fit line* through the sample data. Its equation is

$$Y = A + BX$$

As you can see, A is a statistical estimate for α, and B is a statistical estimate for β. Depending on the statistical properties of our finite sample, the estimates A

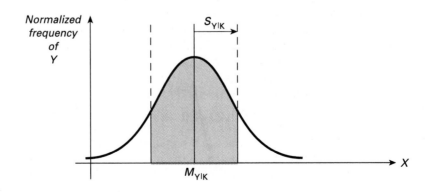

**Figure 12.8
Scatter Plot
Showing Best
Fit and Actual
Lines**

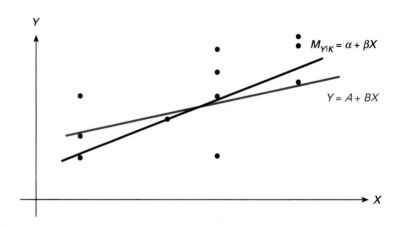

and B will be more or less reliable. (We will not discuss further the issue of how confident we can be in the predictions we make with the computed coefficients A and B. There are, however, formulas for determining this confidence.)

Figure 12.8 shows a *scatter plot* for some sample data. A scatter plot represents each observed pair of X–Y values in a sample as a point on a coordinate grid. Superimposed over the scatter plot are lines representing the actual linear relationship

$$M_{Y|X} = \alpha + \beta X$$

and the best fit line,

$$Y = A + BX$$

based on the data available (eleven data points). As shown in Fig. 12.8, the best fit line (in color) is a statistical estimate for the relationship based on a finite sample of data.

Computing the Linear Regression Coefficients, A and B

The values A and B are called *linear regression coefficients*. How are these coefficients computed on the basis of a finite sample? Suppose we have a collection of n data points. Let us denote the ith data point by the pair (X_i, Y_i). That is, Y_i was observed in conjunction with X_i. The best fit line is defined as the unique line that minimizes the sum of the squares of the distances d_i shown in Fig. 12.9. Each d_i is the distance, measured parallel to the Y axis, between the point (X_i, Y_i) and the best fit line. Thus

$$d_i = Y_i - (BX_i + A)$$

**Figure 12.9
Best Fit Line
Minimizes the
Sum of the
Squares of the
Distances d_i**

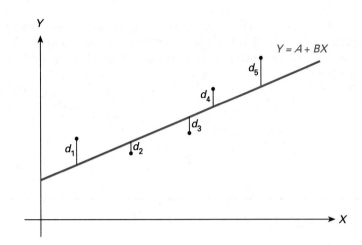

One of the marvels of calculus is that we can discuss the distance d_i to the best fit line when it is the best fit line that we are trying to determine. The sum that we are trying to minimize,

$$\sum_{i=1}^{n} d_i^2 = \sum_{i=1}^{n} (Y_i - (BX_i - A))^2 = F(A, B)$$

is a function of the linear regression coefficients. We have called this function $F(A, B)$. By computing the partial derivatives of $F(A, B)$ with respect to A and B and setting these partial derivatives equal to 0, we get two linear equations in two unknowns A and B:

$$\frac{\delta F(A, B)}{\delta A} = 0$$

$$\frac{\delta F(A, B)}{\delta B} = 0$$

When we solve the resulting system of equations, we get

$$B = \frac{\displaystyle\sum_{i=1}^{n} (X_i - \overline{X})(Y_i - \overline{Y})}{\displaystyle\sum_{i=1}^{n} (X_i - \overline{X})^2}$$

$$A = \overline{Y} - B\overline{X}$$

where $\overline{X}$ and $\overline{Y}$ denote the means of the observed X and Y values, respectively.

The C function in Fig. 12.10 returns the linear regression coefficients A and B for a given collection of data points, (X_i, Y_i). Variables x_mean and y_mean denote the means $\bar{X}$ and $\bar{Y}$, respectively. Variable sum_xy is

$$\sum_{i=1}^{n} (X_i - \bar{X})(Y_i - \bar{Y})$$

and sum_xds is

$$\sum_{i=1}^{n} (X_i - \bar{X})^2$$

Variable x_diff is introduced so that (x[i] - x_mean) need not be computed twice for every execution of the for loop.

Figure 12.10 Computing the Linear Regression Coefficients A and B

```
/*
 *  Computes the linear regression coefficients a and b for the n data points
 *  (x[i], y[i]), given x_mean and y_mean.
 */
void
linear_regress(const double x[],      /* input - arrays of (x,y) coordinates */
               const double y[],      /*             of n data points        */
               int          n,        /* input - number of data points       */
               double       x_mean,   /* input - mean of x values            */
               double       y_mean,   /* input - mean of y values            */
               double *ap,            /* output - the linear regression      */
               double *bp)            /*              coefficients           */
{
    double sum_xy, sum_xds, x_diff;
    int    i;
    sum_xy = 0;
    sum_xds = 0;
    for (i = 0;  i < n;  ++i) {
        x_diff = x[i] - x_mean;
        sum_xy += x_diff * (y[i] - y_mean);
        sum_xds += x_diff * x_diff;
    }
    *bp = sum_xy / sum_xds;
    *ap = y_mean - *bp * x_mean;
}
```

Correlation

Correlation differs from regression in that it measures the strength of a relationship rather than the actual parameters of that relationship. In computing the correlation between X and Y, we assume that both variables are random. In other words, we do not assume that the X values or Y values can be determined exactly.

Correlation is said to be high if there is a strong linear relationship between X and Y values. Otherwise, correlation is said to be low. Figure 12.11 shows four scatter plots along with a qualitative assessment of the correlation between X and Y. Although there is obviously a quadratic relationship between X and Y values in Fig. 12.11(d), the correlation is low because correlation is a measure of the strength of linear relationships. Correlation techniques are often used by engineers to discover the source of a problem in a complex system. That is, engineers will take a measured quantity (such as times of the occurrences of a certain kind of failure) and look for a relationship with some other measured quantity (such as ambient temperatures measured at approximately those times).

Figure 12.11 Scatter Plots with Correlations

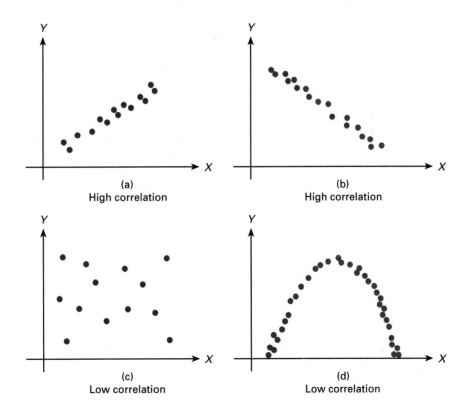

A formula for a statistic r, which is a measure of correlation, follows. This statistic is called the *correlation coefficient*. This statistic will be presented in terms of another statistic called *z-scores*. Z-scores are measured for the X and Y values independently. Again we assume a sample of n data points, (X_i, Y_i). The z-score for a given X_i is its distance from the sample mean $\overline{X}$, measured in terms of the standard deviation S_X:

$$Z_{X_i} = \frac{X_i - \overline{X}}{S_X}$$

An unbiased estimate of the standard deviation for our sample is

$$S_X = \sqrt{\frac{\sum_{i=1}^{n} (X_i - \overline{X})^2}{n-1}}$$

The z-score for a given Y_i value is

$$Z_{Y_i} = \frac{Y_i - \overline{Y}}{S_Y}$$

where $\overline{Y}$ is the mean and S_Y is the standard deviation for the observed Y values.

The correlation coefficient r is computed in terms of the z-scores as follows:

$$r = \sum_{i=1}^{n} \frac{Z_{X_i} Z_{Y_i}}{n-1}$$

The values for r range between -1 and 1. If $|r| = 1$, then the given data points all lie on a line. If $r = 0$, then the X and Y values are said to be uncorrelated, meaning that absolutely no linear relationship is observed between X and Y values.

A C function that computes the correlation coefficient r is given in Fig. 12.12. The arguments provided to the function are type **double** arrays x and y,

Figure 12.12   Function for Computing the Correlation Coefficient

```
/*
 *  Computes the correlation coefficient, r, using z-scores for the n data
 *  points (x[i], y[i])
 */
double
r(const double x[],     /* input - (x, y) coordinates of n       */
  const double y[],     /*             data points               */
  int          n,       /* input - number of data points         */
```

(continued)

Figure 12.12   (continued)

```
double       x_mean, /* input - means of x                    */
double       y_mean, /*           and y values                */
double       sx,     /* input - standard deviations of        */
double       sy)     /*           x and y values              */
{
    double ps, zxi, zyi;
    int i;

    ps = 0;
    for  (i = 0;  i < n;   ++i) {
        zxi = (x[i] - x_mean) / sx;
        zyi = (y[i] - y_mean) / sy;
        ps += zxi * zyi;
    }

    return (ps / (n - 1));
}
```

which store the data points, and the `int` variable n, which denotes the number of data points in the sample. The variables `x_mean` and `y_mean` represent the means, and the variables `sx` and `sy` represent the standard deviations. The z-score for X_i is denoted by `zxi`; `zyi` denotes the z-score for Y_i. The sum of the products of `zxi` and `zyi` is accumulated in `ps`.

EXERCISES FOR SECTION 12.2

Self-Check

1. What linear regression coefficients would be computed by function `linear_regress` in Fig. 12.10 for these data points?

   (0,0), (2,4), (4,6), (6,7)

2. Would very noisy data likely have a high or a low standard deviation?

Programming

1. As a practicing engineer, you will often deal with complex systems that do not work precisely as planned due to the unexpected impact of some outside factor. Assume that you have designed a small, lightweight engine that per-

forms perfectly on the floor of your lab. Everything checks out, and the engine is attached to a prototype of the new high-performance motorboat into which your company plans to invest all its capital for the next several years. For two days you test the engine system in the boat and everything works perfectly. However, when (with great fanfare) you demonstrate the system with the company president in the boat, the engine makes a horrible noise and fails.

What happened? You run many tests, and sometimes the engine fails and sometimes it runs perfectly. One engineer suggests that maybe the engine fails when the water is cold. Another suggests that it fails when the air is hot. A third engineer proposes (discreetly) that the failures may be related to the amount of mass in the boat. You collect the following data, where N is the number of failures per hour, T(air) is the average air temperature during the testing hour, T(water) is the average water temperature, and "Mass in boat" is the mass in the boat when the failures take place:

N (fails/hr)	*T*(air) (degrees C)	*T*(water) (degrees C)	Mass in boat (kg)
45	35	20	300
5	21	16	330
8	21	17	245
0	20	15	450
16	22	19	450

Write a program to determine which variables are linearly correlated with the number of failures per hour. Also check whether any of these variables are in turn linearly correlated with each other. Run your program once, looking for correlation coefficients satisfying

$$|r| \geq 0.95$$

In a second run, try a threshold of 0.7. What are the implications of your program's results?

12.3 NUMERICAL DIFFERENTIATION

Engineers frequently deal with functions for which they have no formulas. Rather, the function is represented as a collection of data points. For example, Table 12.1 represents the distance traveled by a vehicle as a function of time. If

Table 12.1   Distance Traveled by a Vehicle as a Function of Time

t (min)	0	1	2	3	4	5	6
$f(t)$ (km)	0	0.3	1.2	2.7	4.5	6.3	8.1

we would like to know the vehicle's velocity at any of the times t, we would need to estimate the rate of change of the distance function over time. This rate of change of f is called the *first derivative of f* , dy/dx or f'. If function f were represented by a formula, we could apply the techniques of elementary calculus to find the first derivative. In the absence of a formula for f, we can approximate the value of $f'(t)$ as the slope of the line through the points $(t - h, f(t - h))$ and $(t + h, f(t + h))$ where h is a constant representing the difference between successive t values. In Fig. 12.13, we see in color the line segment whose slope is used to approximate $f'(2)$.

**Figure 12.13
Approximating
$f'(2)$ Using
Central
Difference
Formula**

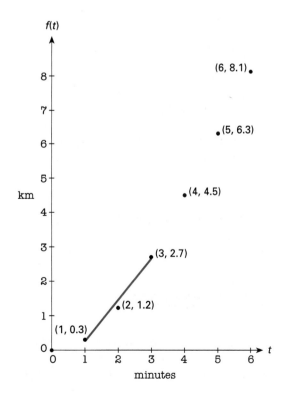

Thus we can approximate $f'(1), f'(2), f'(3), f'(4)$, and $f'(5)$ using the *central difference formula*

$$f'(t) \approx \frac{f(t+h) - f(t-h)}{2h} \qquad \text{(Eq. 12.1)}$$

However, the best approximation of $f'(0)$ that we can compute is the slope of the line through $(0, f(0))$ and $(1, f(1))$:

$$f'(t) \approx \frac{f(t+h) - f(t)}{h} \qquad \text{(Eq. 12.2)}$$

Equation (12.2) is called the *forward difference formula*. We can use the *backward difference formula* (Eq. 12.3) to approximate $f'(6)$. Table 12.2 shows the approximation of $f'(t)$ for the function of Table 12.1.

$$f'(t) \approx \frac{f(t) - f(t-h)}{h} \qquad \text{(Eq. 12.3)}$$

While the first derivative gives the rate of change of one variable with respect to another, the second derivative gives the rate of change of that rate. In physical terms, the second derivative can be thought of as an acceleration—the rate of change of the velocity in the previous example. A second derivative based on three values — $f(t-h)$, $f(t)$, and $f(t+h)$ — can be approximated using the formula

$$f''(t) \approx \frac{f(t+h) - 2f(t) + f(t-h)}{h^2} \qquad \text{(Eq. 12.4)}$$

To check the validity of this formula, we would first find the equation of a parabola through the three points $(t-h, f(t-h))$, $(t, f(t))$, and $(t+h, f(t+h))$. Equation (12.4) is the second derivative of the parabola. Since the parabola is close to f near the point $(t, f(t))$, the value of its second derivative at t is a rea-

Table 12.2 Approximation of First Derivative

t (min)	0	1	2	3	4	5	6
$f(t)$ (km)	0	0.3	1.2	2.7	4.5	6.3	8.1
$f'(t)$ (km/min)	0.3	0.6	1.2	1.65	1.8	1.8	1.8

sonable approximation of $f''(t)$. Notice that computation of each second derivative value requires knowledge of three data points.

EXAMPLE 12.1

To calculate the force a race car's brakes are exerting during a high-speed stop, we can apply the fact that acceleration is the second derivative of distance, rewriting the equation

$$force = mass \times acceleration$$

as

$$force = mass \times f''(t)$$

for a constant mass. In this problem, the easiest quantity to measure is the car's distance down the runway as a function of time beginning with the time when the brakes are applied. Given the distance data in Table 12.3, we can use our second derivative formula to approximate the car's acceleration. Of course, since the car is *decelerating,* these second derivative values will be negative.

Table 12.3   Distance Traveled Down a Test Straightaway

t (sec)	0	1	2	3	4	5	6	7	8
$f(t)$ (m)	0	44	82	115	143	166	181	186	190

Figure 12.14 shows a program that approximates both the acceleration and the force as a function of time, given a user-supplied set of distance points and the mass of the car. Our solution ignores the fact that the car is burning fuel and has atmospheric drag and other forces acting on it.

Figure 12.14   Program to Compute Forces After Approximating Acceleration

```
#include <stdio.h>

/*
 * Finds forces on a race car's brakes by approximating the
 * second derivative of distance traveled from point when
 * brakes are applied.
 */
```

(continued)

Figure 12.14   (continued)

```
int
main(void)
{
        int  t;         /* current time (seconds)              */
        int  h = 1;     /* time step (seconds)                 */
        int  steps;     /* number of time steps                */
        double f[20];   /* input - distance traveled (m)       */
        double mass;    /* input - mass of the car (kg)        */
        double accel;   /* output - acceleration (m/sec^2)     */
        double force;   /* output - force data(kg-m/sec^2)     */

        /* Prompt the user for input */

        printf("How many data points do you have?\n> ");
        scanf("%d", &steps);
        printf("What is the mass of the car (kg)?\n> ");
        scanf("%lf", &mass);

        for (t = 0;  t < steps;  ++t)  {
            printf("Input distance at %d seconds> ", h * t);
            scanf("%lf", &f[t]);
        }

        /* force = mass * acceleration
           acceleration = [f(t+h) - 2*f(t) + f(t-h)] / h^2

           Note that we can only approximate accelerations
           for a set of points of size steps-2 data points. */

        printf("\n\nRESULTS\n\nTime  Distance Acceleration    Force");
        printf("\n(sec)    (m)      (m/sec^2)   (kg-m/sec^2)\n\n");

        printf("%3d%10.3f\n", 0, f[0]);
        for  (t = 1;  t < (steps - 1);  ++t)  {
            accel = (f[t + 1] - 2 * f[t] + f[t - 1]) / (h * h);
            force = mass * accel;
            printf("%3d%10.3f%11.3f%13.3f\n", t * h, f[t], accel, force);
        }
        printf("%3d%10.3f\n", (steps - 1) * h, f[steps - 1]);
```

(continued)

Figure 12.14   (continued)

```
        return (0);
}
```

```
How many data points do you have?
> 9
What is the mass of the car (kg)?
> 200
Input distance at 0 seconds> 0
Input distance at 1 seconds> 44
Input distance at 2 seconds> 82
Input distance at 3 seconds> 115
Input distance at 4 seconds> 143
Input distance at 5 seconds> 166
Input distance at 6 seconds> 181
Input distance at 7 seconds> 186
Input distance at 8 seconds> 190

RESULTS
```

Time (sec)	Distance (m)	Acceleration (m/sec^2)	Force (kg-m/sec^2)
0	0.000		
1	44.000	-6.000	-1200.000
2	82.000	-5.000	-1000.000
3	115.000	-5.000	-1000.000
4	143.000	-5.000	-1000.000
5	166.000	-8.000	-1600.000
6	181.000	-10.000	-2000.000
7	186.000	-1.000	-200.000
8	190.000		

EXERCISES FOR SECTION 12.3

Self-Check

1. Assume that the vehicle that is the subject of Table 12.1 accelerated from rest at a constant rate of 0.6 km/min^2 until it achieved a cruising speed of 1.8 km/min and then maintained this speed. Remembering that

$$distance = \frac{1}{2} \times acceleration \times time^2$$

$$final\_velocity = acceleration \times time$$

the function f would be defined as

$$f(t) = \begin{cases} \dfrac{0.6}{2} t^2 & 0 \le t \le 3 \\[2mm] 2.7 + 1.8(t - 3) & t > 3 \end{cases}$$

Compute the error (*exact − approximation*) in the approximated derivative values shown in Table 12.2.

Programming

1. Write a function `first_deriv` that takes as input parameters an array of function values and the array size, and fills an output parameter array with approximations of the values of the function's first derivative. Assuming that h is 1 for some units, use the central difference formula for interior points to compute a forward difference for the left endpoint and a backward difference for the right endpoint.

12.4 NUMERICAL INTEGRATION

The definite integral

$$\int_a^b f(z) \, dz$$

denotes the area in the Euclidean plane bounded by the z axis, the line $z = a$, the line $z = b$, and the curve $y = f(z)$. In Fig. 12.15, this area is shown for two different functions. Note that if the curve $y = f(z)$ dips below the z axis, the part of the curve below the z axis makes a negative contribution to the integral.

There are two general classes of solutions to the problem of evaluating definite integrals by computer. Both classes involve evaluating the function $f(z)$, which we are integrating, at a collection of sample points. The *quadrature*

**Figure 12.15
Geometric
Meaning of the
Definite
Integral**

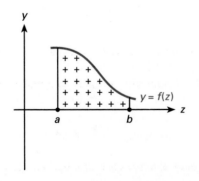
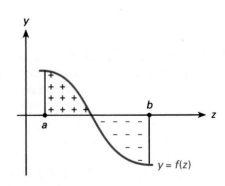

**Figure 12.16
Dividing the
Interval of
Integration into
Subintervals**

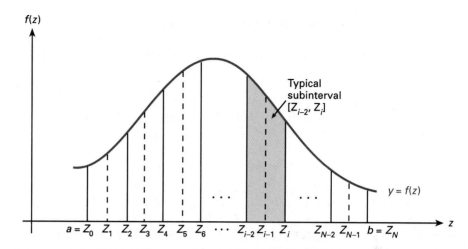

methods determine the sampling points by analysis of the function. *Simpson's rule* and members of its class choose the sampling points independently of the function being integrated. In practice, Simpson's rule is an effective and efficient method for doing numerical integration despite its simplicity.

Derivation of Simpson's Rule

Simpson's rule is derived from the following considerations. Suppose we want to integrate $f(z)$ over the interval $[a, b]$, as shown in Fig. 12.16. Clearly, if we divide the interval $[a, b]$ into an even number, n, of intervals as shown in Fig. 12.16, then

$$\int_a^b f(z)\, dz = \sum_{\substack{i=2 \\ \text{Step 2}}}^{n} \int_{z_{i-2}}^{z_i} f(z)\, dz \qquad \text{(Eq. 12.5)}$$

Our notation

$$\sum_{\substack{i=2 \\ \text{Step 2}}}^{n}$$

means that i takes on the values 2, 4, 6, . . . , $n-2$, n. (Don't forget that n is assumed to be even.)

Equation (12.5) shows that the original integral equals the sum of the $\frac{n}{2}$ integrals

$$\int_{z_{i-2}}^{z_i} f(z)\, dz$$

These $\frac{n}{2}$ integrals are computed over the subintervals $[z_{i-2}, z_i]$. Note that z_{i-1} is the midpoint of the subinterval $[z_{i-2}, z_i]$. Furthermore, the subscript $i-1$ of a midpoint is always odd. The subscripts $i-2$ and i at the endpoints are always even.

A typical subinterval $[z_{i-2}, z_i]$ and the integral we are computing on that subinterval are shown in Fig. 12.17. The three points

$$\text{Point 1} = (z_{i-2}, f(z_{i-2}))$$
$$\text{Point 2} = (z_{i-1}, f(z_{i-1}))$$
$$\text{Point 3} = (z_i, f(z_i))$$

determine a unique quadratic polynomial. That is, there is a unique polynomial,

$$P_i(z) = rz^2 + sz + t$$

that passes through the three given points. This polynomial is called an *interpolating polynomial*. In Fig. 12.17, the polynomial $P_i(z)$ is drawn as a black curve.

The fact that the polynomial $P_i(z)$ passes through three known points gives us enough information to solve for the coefficients r, s, and t. We know that $P_i(z) = f(z)$ when z is z_{i-2}, z_{i-1}, or z_i. This information yields three equations in the three unknowns, r, s, and t. This system can be solved for r, s, and t (the solution is not shown).

Simpson's rule approximates

$$\int_{z_{i-2}}^{z_i} f(z)\, dz$$

as

$$\int_{z_{i-2}}^{z_i} P_i(z)\, dz$$

Figure 12.17
Interpolating
Polynomial $P_i(z)$

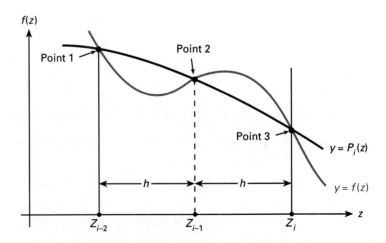

When we substitute the coefficients r, s, and t in $P_i(z)$ and integrate, we get

$$\int_{z_{i-2}}^{z_i} P_i(z)\,dz = \frac{h}{3}\left(f(z_{i-2}) + 4f(z_{i-1}) + f(z_i)\right) \qquad \text{(Eq. 12.6)}$$

where $h = \frac{b-a}{n}$ is the size of one of the n intervals. Equation (12.6) approximates the integral of the original function $f(z)$ over the interval $[z_{i-2},\,z_i]$ in terms of the values of $f(z)$ at the endpoints and the midpoint of the interval.
Substituting Eq. (12.6) into Eq. (12.5), we get Simpson's rule:

$$\int_a^b f(z)\,dz = \sum_{\substack{i=2\\ \text{Step } 2}}^{n} \int_{z_{i-2}}^{z_i} f(z)\,dz$$

$$\approx \sum_{\substack{i=2\\ \text{Step } 2}}^{n} \int_{z_{i-2}}^{z_i} P_i(z)\,dz$$

$$= \frac{h}{3} \sum_{\substack{i=2\\ \text{Step } 2}}^{n} \left(f(z_{i-2}) + 4f(z_{i-1}) + f(z_i)\right)$$

Recalling that $z_0 = a$ and $z_n = b$, we can rewrite the approximate integral as

$$\int_a^b f(z)\,dz \approx \frac{h}{3}\left(f(a) + 4f(z_1) + f(z_2) + f(z_2) + 4f(z_3) + f(z_4) + f(z_4)\right.$$

$$\left. + 4f(z_5) + \cdots + f(z_{n-2}) + 4f(z_{n-1}) + f(b)\right) \qquad \text{(Eq. 12.7)}$$

$$= \frac{h}{3}\left(f(a) + f(b) + 4\sum_{\substack{i=2\\ \text{Step } 2}}^{n} f(z_{i-1}) + 2\sum_{\substack{i=2\\ \text{Step } 2}}^{n-2} f(z_i)\right)$$

C Implementation of Simpson's Rule

Next we will write a C function to implement Simpson's rule as expressed in Eq. (12.7). Let us accumulate the sum

$$\sum_{\substack{i=2\\ \text{Step } 2}}^{n} f(z_{i-1})$$

in the variable **sum_odd** and the sum

$$\sum_{\substack{i=2 \\ \text{Step 2}}}^{n-2} f(z_i)$$

in the variable **sum_even**. The approximate integral is then

```
(h/3.0) * (f(a) + f(b) + 4 * sum_odd + 2 * sum_even)
```

In our function, f is represented by the function parameter **f**.

Function **simpson** in Fig. 12.18 computes an approximate value for

$$\int_a^b f(z)\, dz$$

using Simpson's rule for a given value of a, b, and n. For computational purposes, we rewrite the expressions for **sum_odd** and **sum_even** just given as follows:

$$\text{sum\_odd} = \sum_{\substack{i=2 \\ \text{Step 2}}}^{n} f(z_{i-1}) = f(a+h) + f(a+3h) + \cdots + f(a+(n-1)h)$$

$$\text{sum\_even} = \sum_{\substack{i=2 \\ \text{Step 2}}}^{n-2} f(z_i) = f(a+2h) + f(a+4h) + \cdots + f(a+(n-2)h)$$

Figure 12.18   Computing a Definite Integral Using Simpson's Rule

```
/*
 *  Computes an approximation of the definite integral of function f
 *  from a to b using Simpson's rule with n intervals
 */
double
simpson(double f(double farg),   /*  input - function to integrate       */
        double a,                /*  input - end points of the           */
        double b,                /*             integration region [a, b] */
        int    n)                /*  input - number of intervals         */
```

(continued)

Figure 12.18 (continued)

```
double h, sum_odd, sum_even;
int i;

/*  Compute interval size                                    */
h = (b - a) / n;

/*  Compute sum_odd                                          */
sum_odd = 0;
for  (i = 2;  i <= n;  i += 2) {
    sum_odd  += f(a + (i - 1) * h);
}

/*  Compute sum_even                                         */
sum_even = 0;
for  (i = 2;  i <= n - 2;  i += 2) {
    sum_even += f(a + i * h);
}

/*  Return approximation                                     */
return (h / 3.0 * (f(a) + f(b) + 4.0 * sum_odd + 2.0 * sum_even));
}
```

Applying Simpson's Rule for a Sequence of Values of n

As n increases, the approximate integral becomes closer to the actual integral. However, when we use function simpson, there is a point of diminishing returns because of computational round-off errors. If you try to compute the integral for a sequence of increasing values of n, for example, $n = 2, 4, 8, 16, 32, \ldots$, that point of diminishing returns will become readily apparent. Before that point, successive approximations agree to more and more decimal places; beyond that point, the agreement becomes less and less.

In practice, we apply Simpson's rule for a sequence of n values to identify either the point of diminishing returns or the point at which our result is correct to the desired number of decimal places. Usually we choose a sequence of n values in which n doubles for each iteration of Simpson's rule. A general rule of thumb is that if the integral we get when $n = 2k$ and the integral we get when $n = k$ agree to d decimal places, then the integral we got for $n = 2k$ is correct to $d + 1$ decimal places.

Self-Check

1. Predict the output of the following program, which calls simpson:

```
#include <stdio.h>
#include <math.h>

extern double
simpson(double f(double farg),
        double a, double b, int n);

/*  A function with a simple indefinite integral */
double
f(double x)
{
     return (1.0 / x);
}

/*  A function with no simple indefinite integral */
double
g(double x)
{
     return (sin(x) / x);
}

int
main(void)
{
     printf("\nThe definite integral from 1 to 2 ");
     printf("of f(x)dx is approximately %.4f\n",
           simpson(f, 1.0, 2.0, 2));
     printf("\nThe definite integral from 1 to 3 ");
     printf("of g(x)dx is approximately %.4f\n",
           simpson(g, 1.0, 3.0, 4));

     return (0);
}
```

2. Function f in Exercise 1 is a function for which one would not normally approximate a definite integral. It is quite straightforward to compute the definite integral using the fundamental theorem of the calculus

$$\int_a^b f(x)\,dx = F(b) - F(a)$$

where F is an indefinite integral of f (in this case, $F(x) = \ln(x)$). Calculate the value of the definite integral

$$\int_1^2 f(x)\,dx$$

for function **f** in Exercise 1, and compare this value to the approximation that you predicted.

Programming

1. Write a program that uses function **simpson** with a variety of values of n to approximate

$$\int_1^3 f(x)\,dx$$

for function **f** defined in Self-Check Exercise 1. Try 4, 8, 16, 32, 64, 128, and 256 as values of n, and display a table of these approximations.

12.5 SOLVING FIRST-ORDER DIFFERENTIAL EQUATIONS

Mathematical modeling of the world around us frequently calls for the recovery of a function from knowledge of its rate of change—that is, the solution of a differential equation. Differential equations arise when we study concentration changes in chemical reactions, current flow in circuits, particle motion, population growth, environmental change, and heating and cooling of objects. Many differential equations can and should be solved analytically, using the techniques of calculus. However, for a first-order ordinary differential equation that resists analytical solution, there are numerical methods that we can apply to approximate a solution. In this section, we study the Euler method, and the section's programming exercise presents one of the Runge–Kutta methods—an approach that is both more accurate and more complex than the Euler method.

A differential equation involves the derivative of a function y of x, a derivative that may be a function of x,

$$\frac{dy}{dx} = f(x)$$

or of x and y,

$$\frac{dy}{dx} = f(x, y)$$

or of y,

$$\frac{dy}{dx} = f(y)$$

Examples of first-order ordinary differential equations include

$$\frac{dy}{dx} = \sin x$$

$$\frac{dy}{dx} = 1 - \frac{y}{x}$$

$$\frac{dy}{dx} = x^2 + y^2$$

The first two of these equations can be solved analytically, but there is no closed-form algebraic solution to the third for all values of x and y.

To find a function y that solves a differential equation, we must know the function's value y_0 at some point x_0. Because of the need to know this initial value (x_0, y_0), differential equation problems are also called *initial value problems*.

The Euler Method

The Euler method approximates a solution to an initial value problem of the form

$$\frac{dy}{dx} = f(x, y), \qquad y(x_0) = y_0$$

by "growing" function y one step at a time beginning from the point (x_0, y_0) and using the rate of change computed by the known derivative f. Figure 12.19 illustrates how the Euler method begins from the initial value (x_0, y_0) and takes a step along the tangent to function y's curve, a tangent whose slope can be computed by evaluating $f(x_0, y_0)$. Thus the method approximates

$$y(x_1) = y(x_0 + h) \quad \text{as} \quad y_0 + hf(x_0, y_0)$$

At the point (x_1, y_1), a new tangent is constructed whose slope is $f(x_1, y_1)$, and

$$y(x_2) = y(x_1 + h)$$

**Figure 12.19
Euler Approximation
of Function *y* Given
dy/dx =
f(*x* , *y*) and
y(*x*₀) = *y*₀**

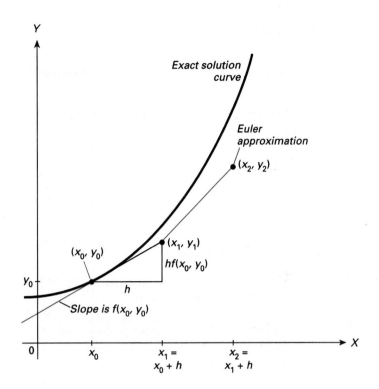

is approximated as

$$y_1 + hf(x_1, y_1)$$

In general, the Euler method computes each new approximation from the previous one by letting

$$x_{n+1} = x_n + h$$
$$y_{n+1} = y_n + hf(x_n, y_n)$$

If *h* is very small, the approximation may closely follow the actual *y*(*x*) curve initially, but errors will accumulate as we take more steps.

EXAMPLE 12.2 ▶ Table 12.4 shows five iterations of the Euler method on the differential equation

$$\frac{dy}{dx} = x + y - 1, \qquad (x_0, y_0) = (0, 1)$$

Table 12.4   Euler Approximation of Function y Given dy/dx = x + y – 1, (x₀, y₀) = (0, 1), h = 0.1

n	x_n	Computation of y_n (approx)	y_n (approx)	y_n (exact)	Error
0	0.0	Given	1.00000		
1	0.1	1.0 + 0.1(0.0 + 1.0 − 1)	1.00000	1.00517	0.00517
2	0.2	1.0 + 0.1(0.1 + 1.0 − 1)	1.01000	1.02140	0.01140
3	0.3	1.01 + 0.1(0.2 + 1.01 − 1)	1.03100	1.04986	0.01886
4	0.4	1.031 + 0.1(0.3 + 1.031 − 1)	1.06410	1.09182	0.02772
5	0.5	1.0641 + 0.1(0.4 + 1.0641 − 1)	1.11051	1.14872	0.03821

with $h = 0.1$. Using

$$y(x) = e^x - x$$

as an analytical solution to the differential equation, the table also shows exact y values to five decimal places for each x, and includes a column showing the error (*exact − approximation*) in the approximations.

Typically, it is not necessary to print all values computed by the Euler method. In our next example, we will compute 100 y values ($h = 0.01$) for every line of output (output interval = 1).

EXAMPLE 12.3

Engineers design power plants and other utilities that make our way of life possible. However, engineers must also plan for the disposal of any toxic waste that results from their enterprises. To assist in this planning, you have been asked to create software that charts in one-year intervals the decay of the radioactive materials that are waste products from nuclear reactors and hospitals.

Radioactive materials decay according to the first-order differential equation

$$\frac{dy}{dx} = -cy$$

where y is the number of radioactive nuclei in a sample, x is time in years, and c is a constant related to the *half-life* of the radioactive material. The half-life is the time at which half of the original nuclei in the sample have decayed to other species. The constant c is related to the material's half-life as follows:

$$c = \frac{\ln(2)}{half\text{-}life}$$

Table 12.5   Half-Life Values for Selected Elements

Cobalt 60	5.26 years
Plutonium 238	87 years
Strontium 90	28 years

Table 12.5 shows the half-life values for some commercially used elements.

The program in Fig. 12.20 gets from the user the half-life of a radioactive material and the number of years of decay to display in the output. The value used as a starting point, $(x_0, y_0) = (0, 1)$, indicates that at time 0, when the material is initially dumped, it contains 100% of its original radioactive nuclei. Subsequent y_n values displayed indicate the fraction of the original radioactive nuclei that remain after h years of decay. Since a step size (h) of 0.01 is used, 100 iterations of the Euler method are necessary to approximate one year of decay. The table displayed by the program also computes an exact value for each year using an analytical solution to the differential equation for radioactive decay:

$$y = e^{-cx}$$

Figure 12.20   Euler Method Program

```
/*
 *  Euler method approximation of solution to initial value problem
 *
 *          dy
 *          ---- =  -cy ,     (x , y ) =  (0, 1)
 *          dx                  0   0
 *
 *  with step size H, output interval = 1 (every STEPS_PER_YEAR steps)
 *
 *  Traces decay of a radioactive material, printing fraction of original
 *  radioactivity remaining for each year.
 */

#include <stdio.h>
#include <math.h>

#define H                0.01    /* step size */
#define STEPS_PER_YEAR   100     /* integer representing 1/H */
```

(continued)

Figure 12.20 (continued)

```
int
main(void)
{
      double halflife;       /* input - half-life of the element
                                         in question               */
      int     years;         /* input - number of years user
                                         requests                  */
      double y,              /* output - approximate result    */
             exact_y,        /* output - actual function value */
             error,          /* output - difference between
                                         actual and approximate values */
             c;              /* ln(2) / half-life               */
      int     x,             /* current year                    */
              i;             /* loop counter                    */

      /* Get half-life from user and compute c                  */
      printf("Half-life in years?> ");
      scanf("%lf", &halflife);
      c = log(2) / halflife;

      /* Get number of years to simulate */
      printf("How many years should I simulate?> ");
      scanf("%d", &years);

      /* Display table heading and first line, which contains
         initial value                                          */
      printf("\nTIME(YEARS)     ACTUAL       APPROX     ");
      printf("ERROR(ACTUAL-APPROX)\n");
      x = 0;   y = 1;
      printf("%5d%18.6f\n", x, y);

      /* Display approximations and exact values for number of
         years requested                                        */
      for  (x = 1;  x <= years;  ++x) {

          /*  Compute one year's approximation  */
          for  (i = 0;  i < STEPS_PER_YEAR;  ++i)
              y += H * -c * y;

          /*  Compute exact value and error for comparison */
          exact_y = exp(-c * x);
```

(continued)

Figure 12.20 (continued)

```
        error = exact_y - y;

        printf("%5d%18.6f%12.6f%19.6e\n", x, exact_y, y, error);
    }

    return (0);
}
```

```
Half-life in years?> 5.26
How many years should I simulate?> 12
```

TIME(YEARS)	ACTUAL	APPROX	ERROR(ACTUAL-APPROX)
0	1.000000		
1	0.876536	0.876460	7.616971e-05
2	0.768316	0.768183	1.335252e-04
3	0.673457	0.673281	1.755520e-04
4	0.590310	0.590104	2.051613e-04
5	0.517428	0.517203	2.247795e-04
6	0.453544	0.453308	2.364226e-04
7	0.397548	0.397306	2.417614e-04
8	0.348465	0.348223	2.421753e-04
9	0.305443	0.305204	2.387996e-04
10	0.267732	0.267499	2.325638e-04
11	0.234676	0.234452	2.242260e-04
12	0.205702	0.205488	2.144004e-04

EXERCISES FOR SECTION 12.5

Self-Check

1. Compute approximations y_1, y_2, y_3, y_4, and y_5 by applying the Euler method with $h = 0.1$ to the initial value problem

$$\frac{dy}{dx} = x^2 + y^2, \qquad (x_0, y_0) = (0, 0)$$

2. The Runge–Kutta[†] method is another numerical approach to recovering a function y from its first derivative

$$\frac{dy}{dx} = f(x, y)$$

[†]There are actually several Runge–Kutta methods. Here we describe the classical fourth-order Runge–Kutta method.

and an initial value. Like the Euler method, the Runge-Kutta method computes each x_{n+1} by adding h to x_n, and it bases its computation of y_{n+1} on the values of x_n and y_n. However, the Runge-Kutta method uses a far more complex formula for y_{n+1}, namely

$$y_{n+1} = y_n + \frac{h}{6}(k_1 + 2k_2 + 2k_3 + k_4)$$

where

$$k_1 = f(x_n, y_n)$$

$$k_2 = f\left(x_n + \frac{h}{2}, y_n + k_1\left(\frac{h}{2}\right)\right)$$

$$k_3 = f\left(x_n + \frac{h}{2}, y_n + k_2\left(\frac{h}{2}\right)\right)$$

$$k_4 = f(x_{n+1}, y_n + k_3 h)$$

Use the Runge–Kutta method to approximate y_1 and y_2 for the initial value problem shown in Table 12.4. Using the exact y_1 and y_2 values from the table, compute the error in the Runge–Kutta approximations. Which method is giving more accurate results—Euler or Runge–Kutta?

Programming

1. Revise the radioactive decay program of Fig. 12.20 so that it uses both Euler and Runge–Kutta methods and prints error values for both methods.

12.6 USING COMMERCIAL OFF-THE-SHELF SOFTWARE

As you are becoming aware, writing software is not easy and can be very time-consuming. When you are a practicing professional, your time is valuable and so writing your own code to solve a problem may not always be the best approach. Fortunately, commercial programs are now available to perform most common tasks, and the majority of these commercial packages are the product of major analysis efforts. Frequently, a user of off-the-shelf software only needs to write some code to reformat data coming into or going out of a commercial package, and sometimes does not need to write any code at all.

The availability of commercial software for engineers is increasing very rapidly. Many programs that not long ago would have required enormous mainframe computers only available at the largest companies are now running on small workstations costing less than \$10,000, or even on laptop computers. There are several distinct types of programs for numerical work. The following is a very brief overview of some of the categories of programs on the market.

Symbolic software packages that perform direct manipulation of equations are available. This means that the programs can solve integrals and equations of certain types without resorting to the numerical approximation techniques addressed earlier in the chapter. Such symbolic mathematics packages often run on a personal computer. For certain problems that require complicated exact solutions, using a symbolic package can save enormous amounts of computation and effort while avoiding problems with round-off and convergence that are associated with methods of numerical approximation.

Visual programming packages contain very large libraries of useful functions. Most packages allow the user to create a specialized solution by selecting with a mouse the necessary library subprograms. The user can write any C functions that might not be supplied with the package and can link these personal functions with the big library and the library display functions. In this way, an engineer can produce a very sophisticated analysis system with minimal effort.

Alternatively, a user might purchase a fairly complete analysis tool to perform some specialized functions such as heat transfer analysis, vibration analysis, and so on. Recent trends have been to have more and more types of analysis software integrated into one package, so that engineers in various disciplines can *concurrently engineer* their products. Such an approach is far less costly than the traditional method of dividing a project into a structural subproblem, a thermal subproblem, and so on, assigning each subproblem to a specialist. Integrating the resulting individual solutions typically required several iterations and was usually quite expensive.

Finally, a user might have a fairly straightforward problem that only requires a certain well-defined numerical function. In this case, instead of writing the solution, the user might call a function from a numerical library. In this book so far, we have introduced a number of functions for performing highly specialized numerical operations. Some functions came with a warning that they would not work in all cases, although other techniques might work. Several commercial libraries of numerical functions have been developed for use by analysts who frequently perform numerical operations on data. In Example 12.4, we walk you through the use of a function from such a library.

EXAMPLE 12.4 ▶

The International Mathematics and Statistics Library (IMSL) is a collection of numerical routines that has been widely used by Fortran programmers for many years. A C version of the IMSL is now available as well. The IMSL comprises coordinated libraries of functions for general applied mathematics, statistics, and other special algorithms. One IMSL function is `imsl_d_lin_sol_gen`, which solves a system of linear algebraic equations. Rather than using an augmented matrix as we did in Section 8.5, `imsl_d_lin_sol_gen` uses separate input parameters for the linear system's $n \times n$ coefficient matrix and the length n vector that represents the system's right-hand side (the final column of our augmented matrix). Figure 12.21 shows a simplified version of part of the documentation of `imsl_d_lin_sol_gen`. You will notice that in the documentation and our example, the $n \times n$ coefficient matrix argument is actually provided as a one-dimensional array. However, use of an $n \times n$ two-dimensional array would also produce correct results, although one would probably receive compiler warnings regarding suspicious pointer conversions.

Figure 12.21 Simplified Documentation of imsl_d_lin_sol_gen

`imsl_d_lin_sol_gen`

PURPOSE: Solve a real general system of linear equations $Ax = b$, returning the solution in an array supplied by the calling function.

REQUIRED DIRECTIVE: `#include <imsl.h>`

USAGE: `imsl_d_lin_sol_gen(n, a, b, IMSL_RETURN_USER, x, 0);`

ARGUMENTS:

`int n`	*(input)*	number of equations
`double a[]`	*(input)*	size $n \times n$ array containing the coefficient matrix of the linear system
`double b[]`	*(input)*	size n array containing the right-hand side of the linear system
`IMSL_RETURN_USER`	*(input)*	library-defined constant
`double x[]`	*(output)*	size n array into which the solution will be stored
`0`	*(input)*	value indicating end of argument list

In Fig. 12.22, we use `imsl_d_lin_sol_gen` to solve the linear system that was our primary example in Section 8.5. ⬅

12.7 COMMON PROGRAMMING ERRORS

The most common errors in programs that perform the numerical techniques discussed in this chapter are caused by inaccuracy in mathematical computations. A small round-off error is often magnified by the repeated computations required

Figure 12.22   Using Function imsl_d_lin_sol_gen

```
/*
 *  Uses IMSL function imsl_d_lin_sol_gen to solve a system of n linear
 *  equations in n unknowns.
 */

#include <imsl.h>
#define  N  3  /* size of coefficient matrix */

int
main(void)
{
      double  coeff[N * N] = {1.0,  1.0,  1.0,  /* coefficient matrix      */
                              2.0,  3.0,  1.0,
                              1.0, -1.0, -1.0},
              rt_side[N] = {4.0,  9.0, -2.0};   /* right-hand side of system */
      double x[N];  /* solution vector */
      int     i;

      imsl_d_lin_sol_gen(N, coeff, rt_side, IMSL_RETURN_USER, x, 0);

      if (x != NULL)
            printf("The values of x are: %10.2f%10.2f%10.2f\n", x[0], x[1],
                   x[2]);
      } else {
            printf("No unique solution\n");
      }
      return (0);
}

The values of x are:      1.00      2.00      1.00
```

in many of these algorithms. This loss of accuracy can cause programs to execute forever instead of converging to a result. If the programs do terminate, the results may be so inaccurate that they would be useless.

Since these programs rely heavily on the use of functions, be very careful when writing argument lists. Make sure each argument list has the correct number of arguments and that the arguments are not misspelled or placed in the wrong position. This same caution applies when calling functions from a commercial library. In addition, you must verify that the types of your arguments match the types expected by the library function you call and that each argument value falls within the valid range for the corresponding parameter.

CHAPTER REVIEW

A number of different numerical techniques were discussed in this chapter, including finding roots (Newton's method), linear regression and correlation, numerical differentiation and integration (Simpson's rule), and solving first-order differential equations. We have just scratched the surface in our discussion of numerical methods. A small sample of the dozens of good references on the subject are listed.

REFERENCES ON NUMERICAL METHODS

John, Peter W. M. *Statistical Methods in Engineering and Quality Assurance.* New York: Wiley, 1990.

Nonweiler, T. R. F. *Computational Mathematics: An Introduction to Numerical Approximation.* New York: Hälsted Press, 1984.

Press, William H., et al. *Numerical Recipes in C: The Art of Scientific Computing.* New York: Cambridge University Press, 1988.

User's Manual: IMSL C/Math/Library™, Version 1.0. Houston: IMSL, Inc., 1991.

QUICK-CHECK EXERCISES

1. Name two methods for finding roots of a function.
2. List the three criteria for converging to a root.
3. A regression line is the _____ _____ line through sample data. It is used to _____ Y values for given X values.
4. How do you declare a parameter that is a function returning a type `int` value and taking two type `int` parameters?
5. The _____ _____ is a statistic that measures how strong a linear relationship exists between the X and Y values of a sample of data points.

6. When approximating $f'(4)$ given that $f(3) = 6.1$, $f(4) = 6.9$, and $f(5) = 7.5$, if we use the central difference formula, our approximation is actually the slope of the line through _____, _____.

7. When applying Simpson's rule, we approximate the definite integral of a function by summing definite integrals of many _____ _____ .

8. The Euler method is a straightforward approach to approximating solutions to _____ _____ problems.

ANSWERS TO QUICK-CHECK EXERCISES

1. Newton's method and the bisection method
2. Assuming that $epsilon_i$ is a very small value, rt is the actual root, x_j is the current guess for a root, and x_{j-1} was the previous guess,

   (1) $|rt - x_j| < epsilon_1$
   (2) $|f(x_j)| < epsilon_2$
   (3) $|x_j - x_{j-1}| < epsilon_3$

3. best fit; predict
4. `int f(int p1, int p2)`
5. correlation coefficient
6. $(3, 6.1)$, $(5, 7.5)$
7. interpolating polynomials
8. initial value or differential equation

REVIEW QUESTIONS

1. What is the name of the field of study concerned with developing methods to use a computer to solve computational problems?

2. When a numerical method for finding a root of a function *diverges*, has it succeeded or failed?

3. If we find a value x_0 such that $f(x_0)$ is within *epsilon* of zero, are we guaranteed that x_0 is within *epsilon* of a root of $f(x) = 0$?

4. What convergence criterion is used by Newton's method?

5. What are linear regression coefficients?

6. Give an example of a situation in which it would be useful to check correlation.

7. In what situation would you be likely to compute a forward or backward difference rather than a central difference when approximating a derivative?

8. When applying Simpson's rule, why must the interval of integration be subdivided into an *even* number of subintervals?
9. Name two numerical methods for approximating solutions to differential equations.

PROGRAMMING PROJECTS

1. The polynomial

$$8x^3 + 2x^2 - 5x + 1$$

has three real zeros.
   a. First, plot the function to determine appropriate initial guesses.
   b. Then, use the function `newton` to find each zero to within a tolerance of 0.0005.
2. Repeat Project 1 for the following functions:
   a. $f(x) = x^4 + 3x^3 - 3x^2 - 6x + 1$
   b. $f(x) = x^4 - 26x^3 + 131x^2 - 226x + 120$
3. If $x^n = c$, then $x^n - c = 0$ and the nth root of c is a zero of the second equation. Use this observation in conjunction with Newton's method to compute
   a. $\sqrt{2}$
   and
   b. $\sqrt[3]{7}$
   to six decimal places.
4. Autonomous systems must monitor and control themselves while being influenced by a variety of external forces. You are writing the on-board control system for a "smart" robot that performs some tasks while being buffeted by several time-varying forces. One time-varying force is steadily increasing and has the value

$$0.55t$$

A second force comes from an oscillating part next to the robot and is represented by

$$-0.3 \sin(t)$$

Finally there is a force f that can be set for a given robot by the robot's operator depending upon external conditions. The force f is applied in a direction opposite to that of the steadily increasing force. Therefore the force F on the robot as a function of time is

$$F = 0.55t - 0.3 \sin(at) - f \quad (\text{kg·m/s}^2)$$

When F is zero, the robot will not need to exercise any countering force of its own, so we can plan some precision motions to happen near that time. Write a program that uses Newton's method to find the earliest time at which the force on the robot is zero. Use an initial guess of $t = 1$ second and use *epsilon* $= 0.001$ and $a = 1$ radian/second. Run the program twice, using an external force of 5 kg·m/s^2 for the first run and an external force of 10 kg·m/s^2 for the second run.

5. Finding out information indirectly about a desired quantity that cannot be measured directly is frequently required of practicing engineers. Engineers can learn many techniques from astronomers, who can directly measure only a few quantities, and who must deduce all other desired information from these few measurements. For example, astronomers are interested in computing the distances to stars from Earth. For most stars, the distance calculation must be based on the star's brightness as observed on Earth. This brightness is proportional to the inverse of the square of the distance from the object and to the object's absolute brightness. Astronomers have discovered certain stars, called Cepheid variables, that vary in a periodic way in brightness. There is a relationship between the period of this variation and the absolute brightness of the star, so Cepheids are very useful as "mile markers" (which astronomers call *standard candles*). If a star that has a very large absolute brightness appears very faint, it must be very far away.

    Astronomers measure brightness in *magnitudes* that form a logarithmic scale ($2.5 \; log(brightness)$). *Absolute magnitude* is the magnitude you would measure if the star were at a distance of 10 parsecs. A smaller magnitude means a brighter object. Consider the following data from G. A. Carlson's article "Sighting Cepheid Variables" in the November 1992 issue of *Scientific American:*

Absolute Magnitude	Logarithm of Period (days)
−3	0.4
−3.5	0.6
−4	0.8
−4.5	1.0
−5.3	1.2
−5.8	1.4
−6.5	1.6
−7.0	1.8
−7.3	2.0

Write a program to find the correlation coefficient and the best fit line for this data. Is there some subset of points that fit the line of best fit less well than the others? (Hand-check by graphing both the points and the line.) If you discard the points farthest from the line, how good is the correlation? Notice that correlating two logarithmic quantities, as we are doing here, is a good way to understand relationships of the form

$$y = x^a$$

since they are equivalent to

$$\log y = a \log x$$

6. An engineer in a laboratory can perform fairly sophisticated tests and repairs on prototype products. In the field, particularly for consumer goods, tests and repairs must be simple or the cost of maintenance will be prohibitive. Machines that self-diagnose failures require especially simple tests.

   You are designing a simple algorithm to be implemented on a chip. The chip will be embedded in a complex machine to diagnose possible incipient failures. The chip will perform its diagnosis based on the knowledge that when all is going well, two measurable quantities x and y will vary as

   $$y = 2x + 3$$

   Write a program that estimates whether a given set of five user-input (x, y) pairs (representing data observed by the self-monitoring machine) fits the "ok" line closely enough. Generate 21 points on the line, using x between 0 and 20. Then combine the field data with these points and compute the correlation coefficient for the entire data set. If the correlation coefficient falls below 0.98, issue a `possible chip failure` message.

7. Write a program that automates the selection of the correlation coefficient cutoff for the self-diagnosing chip problem (Programming Project 6). The new program should process several lists of five (x, y) pairs. Each list is labeled either "fail" or "ok," indicating whether or not the observed data set was accompanied by chip failure. Your program should combine each set of field data with the 21 points on the "all is going well" line and compute the correlation coefficient of the combined data. When all data sets have been processed, display the minimum correlation coefficient associated with an "ok" data set and the maximum correlation coefficient associated with a "fail" data set.

8. Your company is making a series of parts for use in very chemically hostile environments. These parts will be coated with a variety of expensive coatings

so they can survive these environments. You are in charge of one particular scraping part that will have a surface coated on one side with your new proprietary coating, ZeeStop. To find out how much ZeeStop will be required to coat one part, you will need to know the surface area of your part. The part in question is shaped as shown in Fig. 12.23. The surface area is given as

$$A = \int_a^b y \, dx$$

From Fig. 12.23, we can see that the part extends from $x = -3$ to $x = +3$ and that one edge takes the shape of

$$y = (9 - x^2) \, e^{\left(-\frac{x}{3}\right)}$$

Write a program to numerically integrate for A using Simpson's rule to find out how many square centimeters of ZeeStop you will need to apply to each of these parts. Test a variety of even values for n (the number of intervals). Also display exact results computed using the indefinite integral

$$e^{\left(-\frac{x}{3}\right)}(3x^2 + 18x + 27)$$

9. You are deciding whether it is feasible to build a hydroelectric dam to harness the energy in a nearby river. First, you need to determine how much water is flowing in the river. The first piece of information you will need is

Figure 12.23
Tool to Be
Coated with
ZeeStop

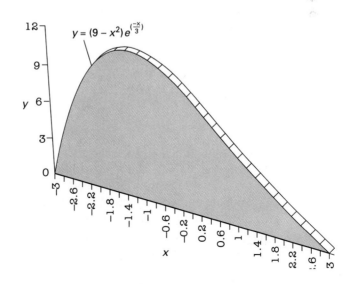

the cross-sectional profile of the river. You have the following depth measurements:

Distance from East Bank (m)	Depth (m)
0	0.0
2	1.0
4	2.1
6	2.5
8	3.3
10	5.0
12	5.2
14	4.0
16	3.0
18	1.2
20	0.5
22	0.0

Use numerical integration to find the cross-sectional area of the river at this point, assuming that the river surface is more or less level across the river and equal to the height of the east bank.

Now you want to determine a very approximate velocity measurement for the river. You do so by tracking the motion of a neutrally buoyant tracer you have placed in the stream.

Time (s)	Distance Downstream (m)
0	0
1	2.0
2	3.95
3	6.15
4	7.99
5	10.06

Compute an average velocity from this data set by finding the velocity at each time, in m/s, and then averaging the results. Multiply the approximate cross section by the approximate average velocity to get an extremely rough estimate of the flow in the river, in cubic meters per second. (Note that to do this problem accurately, it would be necessary to take account of the actual characteristics of the flow both in midriver and near the bottom and sides of the river and then use this velocity profile to calculate the integral of

velocity × area

However it is often useful for engineers to figure out a minimal way to get a rough estimate of a number of interest before spending a lot of salaried time determining an accurate number!)

10. Suppose that a battleship loses power when moving at a speed of 6 m/s. Of course, in reality, ship drag calculations are complex and typically involve drag forces proportional to both the square of the ship velocity and to a geometrically dependent power of velocity (the so-called "wave drag component"). However, for this problem, let us assume that conditions are such that we can approximate the resistance to the ship's motion as proportional to the ship's velocity. Then the ship's distance from the point of power loss is governed by the differential equation

$$\frac{ds}{dt} = v_0 e^{-(k/m)t}$$

with the initial condition $s(0) = 0$. If $k = 44{,}000$ kg/s and $m = 25{,}500{,}000$ kg, what is the total distance that the ship has coasted at $t = 10$ seconds, $t = 20$ seconds, and so on for the first 60 seconds after the power loss? Use both the Euler and Runge–Kutta methods to approximate a solution, and compare your approximations to exact distances computed using

$$s(t) = \frac{v_0 m}{k} (1 - e^{-(k/m)t})$$

After approximating a solution with $h = 10$ seconds, try $h = 5$ and $h = 1$.

11. As one goes higher in the atmosphere, the air becomes colder and thinner. Near the surface of the earth, it is known that the temperature falls off roughly as

$$\frac{dT}{dz} = \beta$$

where β is a constant called the *adiabatic lapse rate*. It is usually expressed as a negative number with units of degrees C per km. Knowing this rate allows meteorologists to make rough estimates of a variety of atmospheric quantities of interest. For example, one can estimate the minimum altitude at which water vapor will begin to condense out of the air and form clouds.

Write a program to approximate dT/dz based on the following data from a weather balloon:

z(km)	T (deg C)
0	15.0
1	8.4
2	2.2
3	−4.3
4	−10.3
5	−17.5
6	−23.0

Average the first derivative values to get an overall estimate of the lapse rate at this location. Where is the worst fit between the average value and the actual behavior?

12. Like Simpson's rule, the *trapezoidal rule* permits numerical approximation of a definite integral. The trapezoidal rule uses line segments to approximate small pieces of the curve

$$y = f(x)$$

The rule then sums the areas of trapezoids created by drawing perpendiculars from the line segment endpoints to the x axis, as shown in Fig. 12.24.

As in Simpson's rule, areas above the axis are viewed as positive; the sign of areas below the axis is negative. The trapezoidal rule approximates

$$\int_a^b f(x)\,dx$$

**Figure 12.24
Approximating
the Area Under
a Curve with
Trapezoids**

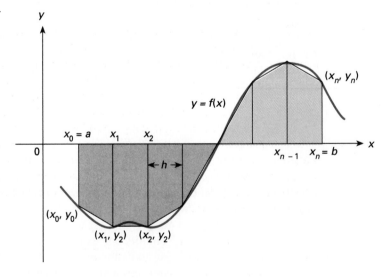

as

$$T = \frac{h}{2}\left(f(a) + f(b) + 2\sum_{i=1}^{n-1} f(x_i) \right)$$

for n subintervals of length

$$h = \frac{b - a}{n}$$

Use the trapezoidal rule in writing a program to approximate a solution to the heat dissipation problem that follows.

Many engineering problems require heat generated by an electrical or mechanical device to be removed from a system before the heat can damage sensitive parts. For example, if we want to find out whether the new heat sink that we have designed will absorb enough heat from the chip internals when our chip warms up, we can use the equation

$$\frac{Q}{m} = \int_{T_1}^{T_2} c\, dT$$

where Q/m is the heat absorbed per unit mass (calories/gram), T_1 is the initial temperature of the chip, T_2 is the final temperature of the chip, and c is the specific heat at constant pressure (cal/g·degK). The value of c can be a function of temperature. Let's say in this case that

$$c = (1.59E{-}11)T^4 - (1.50E{-}8)T^3 + (3.49E{-}6)T^2 + (4.72E{-}4)T - (9.34E{-}3)$$

Write a program that takes as input the initial and final temperatures of a chip and the number of calories of heat that this heat sink must absorb, and computes both the heat absorbed by the heat sink per unit mass and also the heat sink mass needed to absorb the desired number of calories. Note that the sign of the heat into the sink is the opposite of the sign of the heat out of the chip. Use this data for one test: $T_1 = 330°$ K, $T_2 = 300°$ K, $Q = 30$ calories. For a second test try: $T_1 = 110°$ K, $T_2 = 100°$ K, $Q = 15$ calories.

13. Most electronics is based on complex circuits made up of relatively simple elements. Two elements that are used in many circuits are resistors and capacitors. A resistor dissipates energy, and a capacitor stores energy. The equation for the current in a closed circuit consisting of a resistor and capacitor in series with each other is

$$\frac{di}{dT} = \frac{-i}{RC}$$

where i is the current (in amperes), t is time, R is resistance (in ohms), and C is capacitance (in farads.) Write a program to approximate the time behavior for 10 seconds in half-second intervals of a current in this circuit if initially (at $t = 0$) a 1-ampere current is present in the system, $R = 5$ megohms, and $C = 1$ microfarad. Let the initial current, resistance, and capacitance be program inputs.

On physical grounds, what would you expect the time-dependent value of the current to be, given that there is no more current injected into the system, that the resistor dissipates energy, and that the capacitor is an energy storage device? It is always good to first guess an approximate solution and then compare it to the computed solution to see whether the result is reasonable. RC is called the *time constant* of the system: In RC seconds, the current should have fallen to $1/e$ of its initial value. Use this knowledge to check the accuracy of your solution.

14. Compute approximations of the following definite integrals using Simpson's rule:

a. $\int_{1}^{2} \sqrt{2 - (\sin x)^2} \, dx$

b. $\int_{1}^{2} x \cos \frac{x}{2} \, dx$

c. $\int_{1}^{2} (x^3 - 2x^2 + x + 5) \, dx$

d. $\int_{-3}^{1} (1 + x^6) \, dx$

Character Sets

The charts in this appendix show the following character sets: ASCII (American Standard Code for Information Interchange), EBCDIC (Extended Binary Coded Decimal Interchange Code), and CDC[†] Scientific. Only printable characters are shown. The ordinal number for each character is shown in decimal. For example, in ASCII, the ordinal number for 'A' is 65, and the ordinal number for 'z' is 122. The blank character is denoted by □.

Left Digit(s) \ Right Digit	ASCII									
	0	**1**	**2**	**3**	**4**	**5**	**6**	**7**	**8**	**9**
3			□	!	"	#	$	%	&	'
4	(	)	*	+	,	–	.	/	0	1
5	2	3	4	5	6	7	8	9	:	;
6	<	=	>	?	@	A	B	C	D	E
7	F	G	H	I	J	K	L	M	N	O
8	P	Q	R	S	T	U	V	W	X	Y
9	Z	[	/	]	^	–	'	a	b	c
10	d	e	f	g	h	i	j	k	l	m
11	n	o	p	q	r	s	t	u	v	w
12	x	y	z	{			}				

Codes 00–31 and 127 are nonprintable control characters.

[†]CDC is a trademark of Control Data Corporation.

					EBCDIC					
Left Digit(s) \ **Right Digit**	**0**	**1**	**2**	**3**	**4**	**5**	**6**	**7**	**8**	**9**
6					□					
7					¢	.	<	(	+	|
8	&									
9	!	$	*	)	;	¬	_	/		
10							^	,	%	—
11	>	?								
12			:	#	@	'	=	"		a
13	b	c	d	e	f	g	h	i		
14						j	k	l	m	n
15	o	p	q	r						
16			s	t	u	v	w	x	y	z
17								\	{	}
18	[	]								
19				A	B	C	D	E	F	G
20	H	I								J
21	K	L	M	N	O	P	Q	R		
22							S	T	U	V
23	W	X	Y	Z						
24	0	1	2	3	4	5	6	7	8	9

Codes 00–63 and 250–255 are nonprintable control characters.

					CDC					
Left Digit \ **Right Digit**	**0**	**1**	**2**	**3**	**4**	**5**	**6**	**7**	**8**	**9**
0	:	A	B	C	D	E	F	G	H	I
1	J	K	L	M	N	O	P	Q	R	S
2	T	U	V	W	X	Y	Z	0	1	2
3	3	4	5	6	7	8	9	+	−	*
4	/	(	)	$	=	□	,	.	≡	[
5	]	%	≠	⌐	∨	∧	↑	↓	<	>
6	≤	≥	¬	;						

Quick Reference Table: Selected Standard C Library Facilities

Function Name	Description	Number of Parameters	Type(s) of Parameters	Type of Function	Standard Header File
abs	integer absolute value	1	int	int	stdlib.h
acos	arc cosine	1	double	double	math.h
asin	arc sine	1	double	double	math.h
atan	arc tangent	1	double	double	math.h
atan2	arc tangent	2	double	double	math.h
calloc	dynamic array allocation	2	size_t†	void *	stdlib.h
ceil	smallest whole number not less than	1	double	double	math.h
cos	cosine	1	double	double	math.h
cosh	hyperbolic cosine	1	double	double	math.h
exit	program termination	1	int	void	stdlib.h
exp	exponential function (e^x)	1	double	double	math.h
fabs	double absolute value	1	double	double	math.h
fclose	file close	1	FILE *	int	stdio.h

(continued)

† unsigned integer type returned by sizeof operator

Appendix B   (continued)

Function Name	Description	Number of Parameters	Type(s) of Parameters	Type of Function	Standard Header File
fgets	string input from file	3	char * int FILE *	char *	stdio.h
floor	largest whole number not greater than	1	double	double	math.h
fopen	file open	2	char *	FILE *	stdio.h
fprintf	text file formatted output	varies	FILE * const char * types which match conversion specifications	int	stdio.h
fread	binary file input	4	void * size_t[†] size_t FILE *	size_t[†]	stdio.h
free	deallocates dynamically allocated memory	1	void *	void	stdlib.h
fscanf	text file input	varies	FILE * const char * types which match conversion specifications	int	stdio.h
fwrite	binary file output	4	void * size_t[†] size_t FILE *	size_t	stdio.h
getc	character input from text file	1	FILE *	int	stdio.h
getchar	character input from stdin	0		int	stdio.h

(continued)

Appendix B   (continued)

Function Name	Description	Number of Parameters	Type(s) of Parameters	Type of Function	Standard Header File
isalpha	checks for alphabetic character	1	int	int	ctype.h
isdigit	checks for base-10 digit character	1	int	int	ctype.h
islower	checks for lowercase letter	1	int	int	ctype.h
ispunct	checks for punctuation character	1	int	int	ctype.h
isspace	checks for whitespace character	1	int	int	ctype.h
isupper	checks for uppercase letter	1	int	int	ctype.h
log	natural logarithm	1	double	double	math.h
log10	base-10 logarithm	1	double	double	math.h
malloc	dynamic memory allocation	1	size_t†	void *	stdlib.h
memmove	copies given number of characters (bytes)	3	void * const void * size_t†	void *	string.h
pow	exponentiation	2	double	double	math.h
printf	formatted output to stdout	varies	const char * types which match conversion specifications	int	stdio.h
putc	character output to text file	2	int FILE *	int	stdio.h

(continued)

Appendix B   (continued)

Function Name	Description	Number of Parameters	Type(s) of Parameters	Type of Function	Standard Header File
putchar	character output to stdout	1	int	int	stdio.h
rand	pseudorandom number between 0 and RAND_MAX	0		int	stdlib.h
scanf	input from stdin	varies	const char * types which match conversion specifications	int	stdio.h
sin	sine	1	double	double	math.h
sinh	hyperbolic sine	1	double	double	math.h
sprintf	formatted conversion to string	varies	char * const char * types which match conversion specifications	int	stdio.h
sqrt	square root	1	double	double	math.h
srand	initializes pseudo-random number generator	1	unsigned int	void	stdlib.h
sscanf	formatted conversion from string	varies	const char * const char * types which match conversion specifications	int	stdio.h
strcat	string concatenation	2	char * const char *	char *	string.h

(continued)

Appendix B   (continued)

Function Name	Description	Number of Parameters	Type(s) of Parameters	Type of Function	Standard Header File
strcmp	lexical string comparison	2	const char *	int	string.h
strcpy	string copy	2	char * const char *	char *	string.h
strlen	string length (not counting \0)	1	const char *	size_t†	string.h
strncat	string concatenation up to maximum number of characters	3	char * const char * size_t†	char *	string.h
strncpy	string copy up to maximum number of characters	3	char * const char * size_t†	char *	string.h
system	calls operating system with string argument	1	const char *	int	stdlib.h
tan	tangent	1	double	double	math.h
tanh	hyperbolic tangent	1	double	double	math.h
tolower	converts uppercase letter to lowercase	1	int	int	ctype.h
toupper	converts lowercase letter to uppercase	1	int	int	ctype.h

C Operators

Table C.1 shows the precedence and associativity of the full range of C operators, including some operators not previously mentioned. In this table, an ellipsis (. . .) at the beginning of a group of operators indicates that these operators have equal precedence with those on the previous line. The precedence table is followed by a table listing each operator along with its name, the number of operands required, and the section of the text that explains the operator. New operators are marked by lowercase Roman numerals keyed to the descriptions following Table C.2.

Table C.1   Precedence and Associativity of Operations

Precedence	Operation	Associativity
highest	a[..] f(..) . ->	left
(evaluated first)	postfix ++ postfix --	left
	prefix ++ prefix -- sizeof ~ !	right
	... unary + unary - unary & unary *	
	casts	right
	* / %	left
	binary + binary -	left
	<< >>	left
	< > <= >=	left
	== !=	left
	binary &	left
	binary ^	left
	binary |	left
	&&	left
	||	left
	? :	right
	= += -= *= /= %=	right
	... <<= >>= &= ^= |=	
lowest	,	left
(evaluated last)		

Table C.2   Where to Find Operators in Text

Operator	Name	Number of Operands	Where Found
`a[..]`	subscript	1	7.1
`f(..)`	function call	varies	3.4
`.`	direct selection	2	9.1
`->`	indirect selection	2	9.2
`++`	increment	1	5.3
`--`	decrement	1	5.3
`sizeof`	size of memory block	1	10.3
`~`	bitwise negation	1	i
`!`	logical negation	1	4.2
`&`	address of	1	6.3
`*`	indirection	1	6.3
	or multiplication	2	3.2
`( type name )`	cast	1	3.2
`/`	division	2	3.2
`%`	remainder	2	3.2
`+`	unary plus	1	3.2
	or addition	2	3.2
`-`	unary minus	1	3.2
	or subtraction	2	3.2
`<<`	left shift	2	ii
`>>`	right shift	2	ii
`<`	less than	2	4.1
`<=`	less than or equal	2	4.1
`>`	greater than	2	4.1
`>=`	greater than or equal	2	4.1
`==`	equality	2	4.1
`!=`	inequality	2	4.1
`&`	bitwise and	2	iii
`^`	bitwise xor	2	iii
`|`	bitwise or	2	iii
`&&`	logical and	2	4.2
`||`	logical or	2	4.2
`? :`	conditional	3	iv
`=`	assignment	2	2.4
`+=  -=  *=`	compound assignment		
`/=  %=`	(arithmetic)	2	5.2
`<<=  >>=`	(shifts)	2	ii
`&=  ^=  |=`	(bitwise)	2	iii
`,`	sequential evaluation	2	v

Bitwise Operators

In Chapter 3, we studied that positive integers are represented in the computer by standard binary numbers. For example, on a machine where a type int value occupies 16 bits, the statement

n = 13;

would result in the following actual memory configuration:

n | 0 0 0 0 0 0 0 0 0 0 0 0 1 1 0 1 |

Ten of the operators given in Table C.1 take operands of any integer type but treat an operand as a collection of bits rather than as a single number. These operations are described next.

(i) **Bitwise Negation**   Application of the ~ operator to an integer produces a value in which each bit of the operand has been replaced by its negation—that is, each 0 is replaced by a 1, and each 1 is replaced by a 0. Using our n value just shown, we compute ~n as follows:

n | 0 0 0 0 0 0 0 0 0 0 0 0 1 1 0 1 |

~n | 1 1 1 1 1 1 1 1 1 1 1 1 0 0 1 0 |

(ii) **Shift Operators**   The shift operators << (left) and >> (right) take two integer operands. The value of the left operand is the number to be shifted and is viewed as a collection of bits that can be moved. To avoid problems with implementation variations, it is best to use left operands that are nonnegative when right shifting. The right operand is a nonnegative number telling how far to move the bits. The << operator shifts bits left, and the >> operator shifts them right. The bits that "fall off the end" are lost, and the "emptied" positions are filled with zeros. Here are some examples:

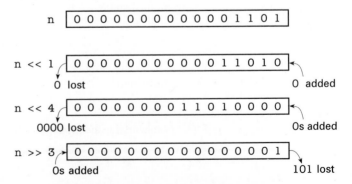

The compound assignment operators <<= and >>= cause the value resulting from the shift to be stored in the variable supplied as the left operand.

(iii) Bitwise and, xor, and or   The bitwise operators & (and), ^ (xor), and | (or) all take two integer operands that are viewed as strings of bits. The operators determine each bit of their result by considering corresponding bits of each operand. For example, if we denote the ith bit of operand n by n_i and the ith bit of operand m by m_i, then the ith bit of result r (r_i) is defined for each operator as shown in Table C.3.

Table C.3   Value of Each Bit of Result r for &, ^, and | with Operands n and m

Operator	Value of r_i	Explanation
&	n_i & m_i	r_i is 1 only if both corresponding operand bits are 1
^	n_i + m_i == 1	r_i is 1 only if the corresponding operand bits *do not* match
|	n_i | m_i	r_i is 1 if at least 1 of the corresponding operand bits is 1

The following is an example of applying each operator:

```
    n   [ 0 0 0 0 0 0 0 0 0 0 0 0 1 1 0 1 ]

    m   [ 0 0 0 0 0 0 0 0 0 0 1 1 1 1 0 0 ]

  n & m [ 0 0 0 0 0 0 0 0 0 0 0 0 1 1 0 0 ]

  n ^ m [ 0 0 0 0 0 0 0 0 0 0 1 1 0 0 0 1 ]

  n | m [ 0 0 0 0 0 0 0 0 0 0 1 1 1 1 0 1 ]
```

The compound assignment operators &=, ^=, and |= cause the result value to be stored in the variable supplied as the left operand.

(iv) Conditional   The conditional operator ? : takes three operands:

c ? r1 : r2

The value of an expression using the conditional is the value of either its second or third operand, depending on the value of the first operand. This evaluation could be pseudocoded as

```
if c
    result value is r1
else
    result value is r2
```

The conditional might be used in defining a macro to find the minimum of two values,

```
#define MIN(x,y)  (((x) <= (y)) ? (x) : (y))
```

(v) **Sequential Evaluation**   The comma operator , evaluates its two operands in sequence, yielding the value of the second operand as the value of the expression. The value of the first operand is discarded. Following are two examples of the comma's use. In the first example, the value of the result of the comma's application is actually used: It is assigned to **x**. In the second example, the comma is merely a device to allow execution of two assignments in a context where only one expression is permitted.

EXAMPLE C.1

The effect of the assignment statement

```
x = (i += 2, a[i]);
```

is the same as the effect of these two statements:

```
i += 2;
x = a[i];
```

Notice that the parentheses around the comma expression in the first version are essential, since the precedence of the assignment operator is higher than the precedence of the comma. Here are "before" and "after" snapshots of memory:

Before		After	
a[0]	4.2	a[0]	4.2
[1]	12.1	[1]	12.1
[2]	6.8	[2]	6.8
[3]	10.5	[3]	10.5
i	1	i	3
x	?	x	10.5

EXAMPLE C.2 In the code fragment that follows, the two loop control variables are initialized to 0. One of these variables is incremented by 2 at the end of each loop iteration while the second variable is incremented by the new value of the first.

```
for  (i = 0, j = 0;
        i < I_MAX  &&  j < J_MAX;
        i += 2, j += i)
     printf("i - %d,  j = %d\n", i, j);
```

The comma operator should be used sparingly, since frequent use greatly increases the code's complexity from the reader's point of view.

C Numeric Types

This text presents the numeric types `int` and `double` and points out that type `char` represents integer character codes. In fact, C provides quite a selection of numeric types for representing integers and for representing numbers that may have fractional parts (*floating-point numbers*).

Integer Types

Table D.1 summarizes the integer types (other than `char`) available in C. Types in the same row of the table require the same amount of memory. For example, `signed int` and `unsigned int` require the same size memory block. However, an unsigned type can represent a value of a magnitude larger than its companion signed type, since the signed type must use one of its binary digits to represent the sign of its number.

Types in a column are arranged so that the size of one type is either the same as or larger than the types above it in the column. Of course, the larger the memory block, the larger the range of values that can be stored.

Table D.1   Integer Types in C (Other Than `char`)

Signed Type	Aliases	Unsigned Type	Aliases
short	short int signed short signed short int	unsigned short	unsigned short int
int	signed int signed	unsigned	unsigned int
long	long int signed long signed long int	unsigned long	unsigned long int

Integer Type char

Type `char` is also an integer type, but C implementations are free to treat type `char` as either signed or unsigned. The full ramifications of this variation are beyond the scope of this appendix. However, even the novice programmer may be affected by this variation when using library facilities such as `getchar` and `getc`, which return type `int` values. It is important to check the value returned to see whether it is a negative integer representing EOF *before* any conversion of type `int` value to type `char`.

Floating-Point Types

Just as there are multiple integer types that differ in their memory require-ments, ANSI C also provides for three floating-point types: `float`, `double`, and `long double`. Values of type `float` must have at least six decimal dig-its of precision; both type `double` and type `long double` values must have at least ten decimal digits. Throughout this text, we use type `double`, the type of constants such as 3.14159 and 2.1E10 and of floating-point parameters of library functions. To use constants of type `float`, we must append the suffix `F`, such as `3.14159F` and `2.1E10F`.

Enumerated Types

ANSI C provides for the definition of an enumerated type with a finite set of integer values represented by identifiers listed in the type definition. For example, a definition of an enumerated type `day_t` is

```
typedef enum
        { sunday, monday, tuesday, wednesday, thursday,
          friday, saturday }
day_t;
```

This type definition has the effect of establishing the type name `day_t` whose valid values are the identifiers `sunday`, `monday`, and so on. These identifiers are automatically associated with the integers 0–6 (`sunday` is 0, `monday` is 1, and so on). An enumerated type serves to create a logical grouping of integer constants that are used to improve program readability.

For example, a declaration of a variable of type `day_t` and an instance of its use as the selector in a `switch` statement follow:

```
day_t current_day;

/*  code that assigns current_day one of the day_t values   */
. . .

/*  selects a day to print */
switch (current_day) {
case sunday:
     printf("Sunday:   ");
     break;

case monday:
     printf("Monday:   ");
     break;

case tuesday:
     printf("Tuesday:   ");
     break;
```

```
    case wednesday:
         printf("Wednesday:   ");
         break;

    case thursday:
         printf("Thursday:   ");
         break;

    case friday:
         printf("Friday:   ");
         break;

    case saturday:
         printf("Saturday:   ");
         break;

    default:
         printf("Invalid day");
    }
```

Variables of an enumerated type may be manipulated just as one would handle any integer variable. The enumerated type values, called *enumeration constants*, may be used in any context where integer constants are valid.

Pointer Arithmetic

C permits application of the addition and subtraction operators to pointer operands if the pointers reference elements of an array. If p is a pointer to an array element, the value of the expression

p + 1

depends entirely on the size of the memory block occupied by one array element. C guarantees that if p is the address of an array's *n*th element, then p + 1 is the address of element *n* + 1.

An example to illustrate the role of context in the evaluation of a pointer expression follows. In Fig. F.1, our example uses two arrays: pl, which is an

Figure F.1   Pointer Arithmetic Example

```
typedef struct {
      char name[STRSIZ];
      double diameter,      /* equatorial diameter in km                */
             dist_sun,      /* average distance from sun in km          */
             orbital_prd,   /* years to orbit sun once                  */
             axial_rot_prd; /* hours to complete one revolution on axis */
} planet_t;

. . .

planet_t pl[2] = {{"Earth", 12713.5, 1.5e+8, 1.0, 24.0},
                  {"Jupiter", 142800.0, 7.783e+8, 11.9, 9.925}};

int nm[5] = {4, 8, 10, 16, 22};
planet_t *p;
int *np;

p = pl + 1;
np = nm + 1;
```

(continued)

AP18

Figure F.1   (continued)

```
printf("sizeof (planet_t) = %d          sizeof (int) = %d\n",
       sizeof (planet_t), sizeof (int));
printf("pl = %d                nm = %d\n", pl, nm);
printf(" p = %d (pl + %d)        \n", p, (int)p - (int)pl);
printf("np = %d (nm + %d)", np, (int)np - (int)nm);
printf(" p - pl = %d\n", p - pl);
```

array of planets, and nm, which is an array of integers. Figure F.2 shows the values of pointers p and np after they are assigned 1 more than pl and nm, respectively. In Fig. F.3, we see possible output produced when our example prints the contents of the four pointer variables as integers. We also see the effect of pointer subtraction on two pointers of the same type.

**Figure F.2
Memory
Snapshot at
Completion
of Pointer
Arithmetic
Example**

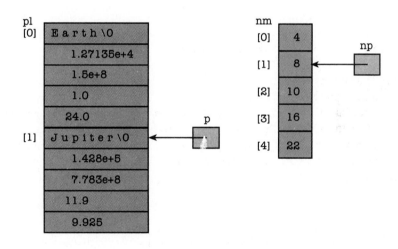

Figure F.3   Output from Pointer Arithmetic Example

```
sizeof (planet_t) = 52        sizeof (int) = 4
pl = 2145835092               nm = 2145835316
 p = 2145835144 (pl + 52)     np = 2145835320 (nm + 4)
 p - pl = 1
```

ANSI C Reserved Words

auto	double	int	struct
break	else	long	switch
case	enum	register	typedef
char	extern	return	union
const	float	short	unsigned
continue	for	signed	void
default	goto	sizeof	volatile
do	if	static	while

ANSWERS

Odd-Numbered Self-Check Exercises

CHAPTER 1

Section 1.2

1. -27.2 in cell 0, 75.62 in cell 999. Cell 998 contains the letter X, cell 2 contains 0.005.

Section 1.4

1. `x = a + b + c;` means "add the values represented by a, b, and c together and save the result in x."

   `x = y / z;` means "divide the value represented by y by the value of z and save the result in x."

   `d = c - b + a;` means "subtract the value represented by b from that in c, then add the value of a, and save the result in d."

   `x = x + 1;` means "add 1 to the value in x."

   `kelvin = celsius + 273.15;` means "add `273.15` to the value represented by `celsius` and save the result in `kelvin`."

Section 1.5

1. A *source file* is created by the programmer and contains a program written in a high-level language. The source file is translated by a compiler into an *object file*. The linker combines the object file with necessary program units from other object files to create a *load file*. The loader then places the load file in main memory.

CHAPTER 2

Section 2.1

1. 1) State the problem clearly (requirements specification).
   2) Determine input/output requirements and relevant formulas (analysis).
   3) Design an algorithm (design).
   4) Implement the algorithm in C (implementation).
   5) Verify the algorithm and test the program (verification and testing).
3. Given the current population at the start of the week and the weekly growth rate, we must compute the population at the end of the week. We are told the growth is a percentage, that is, type `double`. Since the insects are countable items, we will declare the population as an `int`.

Analysis:
```
   Input:   int pop            /* the current population */
            double growth      /* the population growth, percent */
   Output:  int next_week_pop  /* the population at the end of the
                                  week */
```

The population at the end of the week is this week's population plus the additional insects added to the community during the coming week. The additional insects are

```
pop * growth / 100
```

Therefore

```
next_week_pop = pop + pop * growth / 100
```

Design:
Get the population, pop, and growth
```
next_week_pop = pop + pop * growth / 100
```
Output next_week_pop.

Section 2.2

1. The preprocessor; #define and #include.
3. Because it is a universal constant that will not be changed by the program. Furthermore, if the approximation used in a program needed to be changed, all occurrences would have to be changed. Using a constant macro makes this easier.

Section 2.3

1. Reserved words: int, double.
   Conventional constant macros: MAX_ENTRIES, G
   Other valid identifiers: time, this_is_a_long_one, xyz123
   Invalid identifiers: Sue's (' is not allowed), part#2 (# is not allowed), "char" (" is not allowed)

Section 2.4

1. Enter two integers> 5 7
   m = 10
   n = 21
3. My name is Jane Doe.
   I live in Ann Arbor, MI
   and I have 11 years of programming experience.

Section 2.5

1. First comment is terminated by an incorrect comment delimiter (should be * /).
   Second comment includes a nested comment which is not allowed.

3.
```
/*
 *   Calculate and display the sum of two input values
 */

#include <stdio.h>

int
main(void)
{
      int   first,    /* first input value   */
            second,   /* second input value */
            sum;      /* sum of inputs        */

      /* Get input data. */
      scanf("%d%d", &first, &second);

      /* Compute the sum. */
      sum = first + second;

      /* Output the result. */
      printf("\n%d + %d = %d\n", first, second, sum);

      return(0);
}
```

The program displays the first number followed by ' + ' and the second number. Then ' = ' is displayed, followed by the sum of first and second numbers.

Section 2.6

1. `printf("Length is %10.2f cm", length);`
                           ^^^^^^

3. `x#is##12.34##i#is##100`
    `i#is#100`
    `x#is#12.3`

Section 2.7

1. Calls to `printf` to display prompts precede calls to `scanf` to obtain data. Calls to `printf` follow calls to `scanf` when data is echoed. Prompts are used in interactive programs, but not in batch programs. Batch programs should echo input; interactive programs may also echo input.

CHAPTER 3

Section 3.1

1. Type `int` constants: `15`, `-999`
   Type `char` constants: `'*'`, `'x'`, `'9'`
   Type `double` constants: `25.123`, `15.`, `.123`, `32e-4`
   Invalid constants: `'XYZ'`, `$`, `'-5'`
3. Arithmetic underflow

Section 3.2

1. a. 22 / 7 is 3, 7 / 22 is 0, 22 % 7 is 1, and 7 % 22 is 7.
   b. 15 / 16 is 0, 16 / 15 is 1, 15 % 16 is 15, and 16 % 15 is 1.
   c. 3 / 23 is 0, 23 / 3 is 7, 3 % 23 is 3, and 23 % 3 is 2.
   d. −3 / 16 is ??, 16 / −3 is ??, −3 % 16 is ??, and 16 % −3 is ??.
   ?? — The result varies.

3. `PI = 3.14159      MAX_I = 1000      a = 3      b = 4      y = -1.0`

a. `i = a % b;`		`3`
b. `i = (989 - MAX_I) / a;`		`-11/3: ??`
c. `i = b % a;`		`1`
d. `x = PI * y;`		`-3.14159`
e. `i = a / -b;`		`3/-4: ??`
f. `x = a / b;`		`0.0`
g. `x = a % (a / b);`		`Divide by zero`
h. `i = b / 0;`		`Divide by zero`
i. `i = a % (990 - MAX_I);`		`3/-10: ??`
j. `i = (MAX_I - 990) / a;`		`3`
k. `x = a / y;`		`-3.0`
l. `i = PI * a;`		`9`
m. `x = PI / y;`		`-3.14159`
n. `x = b / a;`		`1.0`
o. `i = (MAX_I - 990) % a;`		`1`
p. `i = a % 0;`		`Divide by zero`
q. `i = a % (MAX_I - 990);`		`3`

   ?? — The result varies.

5. `color = 2      black = 2.5      crayon = -1.3      straw = 1`
   `red = 3      purple = 0.3e+1`
   a. `white = 1.666667`
   b. `green = 0.666667`
   c. `orange = 0`
   d. `blue = -3.0`
   e. `lime = 2`
   f. `purple = 0.0`
7. a. 2.1   b. 2.1   c. 10.0   d. 7.2   e. 0.4

Section 3.3

1. The values of WASHER_DIAMETER and OUTER_DIAMETER must be changed.

```
#define WASHER_DIAMETER (5.0/16.0)   /* diameter in inches of
                                      * a flat washer (diameter
                                      * of the hole) */

#define OUTER_DIAMETER (5.0/8.0)     /* diameter of edge of
                                        outer rim of washer */
```

Section 3.4

1. a. `sqrt(u + v) * w * w`   or   `sqrt(u + v) * pow(w, 2)`
   b. `log10(pow(x, y))`
   c. `sqrt(pow(x - y, 2))`
   d. `fabs(x * y - w / z)`

Section 3.5

1.
```
**   **
**   **
******
**   **
**   **

******
  **
  **
  **
******


    *       *
   ***     ***
  ** ** ** **
 **    ***    **
 **     *     **

******
**   **
**   **
**   **
******

    *       *
   ***     ***
  ** ** ** **
 **    ***    **
 **     *     **
```

CHAPTER 4

Section 4.1

1. a. Always
   b. O.K.
3. ans is 2.

Section 4.2

1. x = 15.0
   y = 25.0

   a. x != y   1 (TRUE)
   b. x < x   0 (FALSE)
   c. x >= y - x   1 (TRUE)
   d. x == y + x - y   1 (TRUE)

3. x = 3.0   y = 4.0   z = 2.0   flag = 0

```
! flag          ||       y + z       >=      x - z
   0
       1                              short circuited
                   1
```

```
! ( flag || y + z >= x - z )
     0
                   6.0       1.0
                        1
                1
                0
```

Section 4.3

1.
```
if (x > y) {
      x = x + 10.0;
      printf("x Bigger");
} else {
      printf("x Smaller");
      printf("y is %.2f", y);
}
```

3.
```
if (engine_type == 'J') {
      printf("Jet engine\n");
      speed_category = 1;
} else {
      printf("Propellers\n");
      speed_category = 2;
}
```

Section 4.4

1. 95-decibel noise is very annoying.

Section 4.5

```
1. if (heading > 360.0)
       printf("Error--heading > 360 (%.1f)\n", heading);
   else if (heading >= 270.0)
       printf("The bearing is north %.1f degrees west\n",
              360.0 - heading);
   else if (heading >= 180.0)
       printf("The bearing is south %.1f degrees west\n",
              heading - 180.0);
   else if (heading >= 90.0)
       printf("The bearing is south %.1f degrees east\n",
              180.0 - heading);
   else if (heading >= 0.0)
       printf("The bearing is north %.1f degrees east\n",
              heading);
   else
       printf("Error--negative heading (%.1f)\n", heading);
```

Section 4.6

```
1. red
   blue
   yellow
```

CHAPTER 5

Section 5.1

```
1.  0 10
    1  9
    2  8
    3  7
    4  6
    5  5
```

Section 5.2

```
1. a. Enter an integer> 5
      5
      25
      125
      625
```

b. Enter an integer> 6
  6
  36
  216
  1296
c. Enter an integer> 7
  7
  49
  343
  2401

  In general, this loop displays n, n^2, n^3, and n^4.

3.
```
count = 0;
while (count < 5) {
    count = count + 1;
    printf("Next number> ");
    scanf("%d", &next_num);
    sum = sum + next_num;
}
printf("%d numbers were added; ", count);
printf("their sum is %d.\n", sum);
```

Section 5.3

1.

sum	odd	
0	1	(initial values)
1	3	
4	5	
9	7	
16	9	

Output:
```
 Sum of positive odd numbers less than 8 is 16.
```

3. The answer for both questions is 0.

5.
```
++i;
--j;
n = i * j;
m = i + j;
j--;
p = i + j;
```

7. a.

j	i
10	1
8	2
6	3
4	4
2	5
0	6

Output:
```
    1   10
    2    8
    3    6
    4    4
    5    2
```

b. `j = 10;`
```
   for  (i = 0;   i < 5;   ++i) {
        printf("%d   %d\n", i + 1, j);
        j -= 2;
   }
```

Section 5.4

1. Any initial supply less than 8000 barrels.
3.
```
Number of barrels currently in tank> 8350.8
8350.80 barrels are available.

Enter number of gallons removed> 7581.0
After removal of 7581.00 gallons (180.50 barrels),
8170.30 barrels are available.

Enter number of gallons removed> 7984.2
After removal of 7984.20 gallons (190.10 barrels),
only 7980.20 barrels are left.

*** WARNING ***
Available supply is less than 10 percent of tank's 80000.00-barrel capacity.
```

Section 5.5

1. step a— Initialization of the loop control variable.
   step c— The loop repetition condition, (n is positive.)
   step e— The update of the loop control variable.

Section 5.6

1. a.
```
*
* *
* * *
* * * *
* * * * *
```
   b.
```
* * *
* * *
* * *
* * *
* * *
```

Section 5.7

1. The `for` loop is better because the `do-while` tests the same condition twice on each iteration.

Section 5.8

1.
```
radiation_lev = init_radiation;
while (radiation_lev > min_radiation) {
   if (radiation_lev > SAFE_RAD)
      printf("\n  %3d    %9.4f   Unsafe", day, radiation_lev);
   else
      printf("\n  %3d    %9.4f   Safe", day, radiation_lev);
   day += 3;
   radiation_lev /= 2.0;
}
```

Section 5.9

1.
```
for (count = 0;  count <= n;  ++count) {
   printf("DEBUG*** count=%d\n", count);
   sum += count;
   printf("DEBUG*** sum=%d\n", sum);
}
```

CHAPTER 6

Section 6.1

1. 86

Section 6.2

1. 12.56636

Section 6.3

1.
```
void
sum_n_avg(double  n1,      /* input numbers */
          double  n2,
          double  n3,
          double *sump,    /* output - sum of the three numbers */
          double *avgp)    /* output - average of the numbers   */
```

3.

Reference	Where Legal	Data Type	Value
valp	sub	double *	pointer to color shaded cell
&many	main	int *	pointer to gray shaded cell
code	main	char	'g'
&code	main	char *	pointer to white cell
countp	sub	int *	pointer to gray shaded cell
*countp	sub	int	14
*valp	sub	double	17.1
letp	sub	char *	pointer to white cell
&x	main	double *	pointer to color shaded cell

Section 6.4

1.

Name	Visible in one	Visible in two	Visible in main
one (function)	no	no	yes
var1 (double parameter)	yes	no	no
var2	yes	no	no
alocal	yes	no	no
one (char)	yes	no	no
two	no	yes	yes
one (double parameter)	no	yes	no
var1 (int parameter)	no	yes	no
LARGE	no	no	yes
var1 (char)	no	no	yes

Section 6.5

1. Prototype and first part of function body for **onef**:

```
void
onef(int dat, int *out1p, int *out2p)
{
   int tmp;
   twof(dat, &tmp, out2p);
   . . .
}
```

Prototype of **twof**:

```
void
twof(int indat, int *result1p, int *result2p)
```

Section 6.6

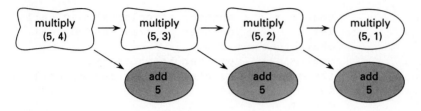

Section 6.7

1. Because `reduce_fraction` takes two input/output parameters.

Section 7.1

1. x3 is a valid variable name.
   x[3] is a reference to the fourth element of array x.
3. `double square_rt[11];`
   `int cube[11];`

Section 7.2

1. Before:

x[0]	x[1]	x[2]	x[3]	x[4]	x[5]	x[6]	x[7]
16.0	12.0	6.0	8.0	2.5	12.0	14.0	-54.5

   After:

x[0]	x[1]	x[2]	x[3]	x[4]	x[5]	x[6]	x[7]
16.0	12.0	6.0	8.0	12.0	14.0	14.0	-54.5

Section 7.3

1. `seg_len = sqrt(pow(x[i + 1] - x[i], 2) +`
   `           pow(y[i + 1] - y[i], 2));`
3. `sum = 0;`
   `for  (i = 0;  i < LIST_SIZE;  i += 2)`
   `    sum += list[i];`

Section 7.4

1. For "conversion code" use

```
int hrs, mins, new;

hrs = time / 100;
mins = time % 100;
new = time_diff + hrs;

if (new < 0) {
        *new_timep = (new + 24) * 100 + mins;
        --(*day_nump);
} else if (new > 24) {
        *new_timep = (new - 24) * 100 + mins;
        ++(*day_nump);
} else {
        *new_timep = new * 100 + mins;
}
```

Section 7.5

1. The value 1 is returned.

```
/*
 *  Searches for target item in first n elements of array arr.
 *  Returns how many times target appears.
 */
int
search(const int arr[],  /*  array to search              */
       int        target, /*  value searched for           */
       int        n)      /*  number of array elements
                              to search                    */
{
   int i,
       cnt; /* Number of times the target is found. */

   /*  Compare each element to target.  */
   cnt = 0;
   for (i = 0; i < n; ++i)
      if (arr[i] == target)
         ++cnt;

   return (cnt);
}
```

Section 7.6

```
1.  /*
     * Gets data to place in dbl_arr until value of sentinel
     * is encountered in the input. Stops input prematurely
     * if there are more than dbl_max data values before the
     * sentinel or if invalid data is encountered.
     *
     *    int     dbl_max  input - declared size of dbl_arr
     *    double  sentinel input - end of data value in input list
     *    double  dbl_arr   output - array of data
     *    double *dbl_sizep output - number of data values stored
     *                               in dbl_arr
     */
    int
    fill_to_sentinel(int dbl_max, double sentinel,
                     double  dbl_arr[], int *dbl_sizep)
    {
       double data;
       int    i, status, result = 1;

       /* Sentinel input loop */
       i = 0;
       for (status = scanf("%lf", &data);
            status == 1 && data != sentinel && i < dbl_max;
            status = scanf("%lf", &data)) {
          dbl_arr[i] = data;
          ++i;
       }

       /* Issue error message on premature exit */
       if (status != 1) {
          printf("***Error in data format ***\n");
          printf("***Using first %d data values ***\n", i);
          result = 0;
       } else if (data != sentinel) {
          printf("***Error: too much data before sentinel***\n");
          printf("***Using first %d data values ***\n", i);
          result = 0;
       }
       /* Send back size of used portion of array */
       *dbl_sizep = i;
       return (result);
    }
```

3.
```
void
bubble(double list[], int n)
{
    int i, pass, sorted;
    double temp;
    . . .
```

Section 7.7

1. b
3.
```
char blanks[]   = "                            ";
    or
char blanks[30] = "                            ";
```

Section 7.8

1.
```
int i, len;
    . . .
/* Gets input data  */
printf("Enter one strand of DNA molecule segment\n"> ");
scanf("%s", strand1);
len = strlen(strand1);
for  (i = 0;  i < len;  ++i) {
    switch (strand1[i]) {
    case 'A':
      strand2[i] = 'T';
      break;

    case 'T':
      strand2[i] = 'A';
      break;

    case 'C':
      strand2[i] = 'G';
      break;

    case 'G':
      strand2[i] = 'C';
      break;
    }
}
strand2[i] = '\0';
    . . .
```

CHAPTER 8

Section 8.1

1.
```c
#include <stdio.h>

#define MAXDEPTH 5

int
main(void)
{
        int soil_type[4][7][MAXDEPTH];        /* Matrix containing soil:
                                                  0 for bedrock, 1 for silt */
        int north_south, east_west, depth;   /* Three indices of soil type */
        int silt;                            /* Number of cells with silt  */
        double percent_silt;                 /* Percent silt               */


        /* Initialize the matrix to all bedrock (values of zero)   */

        for  (north_south = 0;  north_south < 4;  ++north_south)
           for  (east_west = 0;  east_west < 7;  ++east_west)
              for  (depth = 0;  depth < MAXDEPTH;  ++depth)
                   soil_type[north_south][east_west][depth] = 0;
        /*
         *   Self-Check Section 8.1 1a.
         *   Surface cells are at index depth=0. Set
         *   the value of some surface cells (3rd index =0) to silt (value = 1).
         */

        soil_type[2][1][0] = 1;
        soil_type[1][2][0] = 1;
        soil_type[3][1][0] = 1;
        soil_type[1][1][0] = 1;

        /*
         *   Self-Check Section 8.1 1b.
         *   Find percentage of silt cells among cells at depth = 20 m.
         *   the value of some surface cells (3rd index = 2).
         *
         *   Put in four silt cells on top of the initialized-to-zero
         *   part at a depth of 20 meters (third index = 2).
         */

        silt = 0;
        soil_type[2][1][2] = 1;
        soil_type[1][2][2] = 1;
        soil_type[3][1][2] = 1;
```

```
    soil_type[1][1][2] = 1;


    for  (north_south = 0;  north_south < 4;  ++north_south)
       for  (east_west = 0;  east_west < 7;  ++east_west)
             silt += soil_type[north_south][east_west][2];

    percent_silt = (double) silt / (4. * 7.);

    printf("\nPercent silt at depth of 20 m was %.2f\n",
           percent_silt * 100);

     *  Self-Check Section 8.1 1c.
     *  Find surface cells, if any, that have more
     *  than 30 m of silt cells (more than 3 cells with value 1) below
     *  them.
     *
     *  To test this, first set up cell 3,5 to have 40 m of silt.
     *  (Others initialized above have at most 2 cells.)
     */
      soil_type[3][5][0] = 1;
      soil_type[3][5][1] = 1;
      soil_type[3][5][2] = 1;
      soil_type[3][5][3] = 1;

     for  (north_south = 0;  north_south < 4;  ++north_south) {
        for  (east_west = 0;  east_west < 7;  ++east_west) {
            silt = 0;
            for (depth = 0; depth < MAXDEPTH;  ++depth){
                if (soil_type[north_south][east_west][depth] == 1)
                    silt++;
            }
            if (silt > 3)
              printf("Silt greater than 30m deep below %d %d\n",
                        north_south, east_west);
        }
     }

     return(0);
   }
```

Section 8.2

1. The value of a **summed_data** element is set to −1 so that we can keep track of which elements have already been selected and avoid putting two transmitters on one element.

Section 8.3

1. Change the definition of function **f**. Change **NROW** to 30 and **NCOL** to 60.

Section 8.4

1. No.

Section 8.5

1. a. $\begin{aligned} x_1 + x_2 + x_3 &= 4 \\ 2x_1 + 2x_2 + 2x_3 &= 7 \\ x_1 - x_2 + x_3 &= 15 \end{aligned}$ b. $\begin{aligned} x_1 + x_2 + x_3 &= 4 \\ 2x_1 + 2x_2 + 2x_3 &= 8 \\ x_1 - x_2 + x_3 &= 15 \end{aligned}$

   In both cases, the search for a nonzero pivot fails.

CHAPTER 9

Section 9.1

```
1. typedef struct {
         int   degrees,
               minutes;
         char direction;
   } long_lat_t;

3. typedef struct {
        char   authors[50],
               title[50],
               publisher[50];
        int    year;
   } catalog_entry_t;

   catalog_entry_t   book;

   strcpy(book.authors,"Hanly, Koffman, Horvath");
   strcpy(book.title,"C Program Design for Engineers");
   strcpy(book.publisher,"Addison-Wesley");
   book.year = 1995;
```

Section 9.2

```
1. /*
    *  Displays with labels all components of a long_lat_t structure
    */
   void
   print_long_lat(long_lat_t pos) /* input - one long_lat structure */
   {
```

```
        printf("  Degrees:    %d\n", pos.degrees);
        printf("  Minutes:    %d\n", pos.minutes);
        printf("  Direction: %c\n", pos.direction);
}

/*
 *  Determines whether or not the components of pos_1
 *  and pos_2 match
 */
int
long_lat_equal(long_lat_t pos_1,   /* input - positions to      */
               long_lat_t pos_2)   /*              compare      */
{
        return (pos_1.degrees == pos_2.degrees        &&
                pos_1.minutes == pos_2.minutes        &&
                pos_1.direction == pos_2.direction);
}

/*
 *  Fills a type long_lat_t structure with input data.  Integer
 *  returned as function result is success/failure/EOF indicator.
 *      1 => successful input of pos
 *      0 => error encountered
 *      EOF => insufficient data before end of file
 *  In case of error or EOF, value of type long_lat_t output
 *  argument is undefined.
 */
int
scan_long_lat(long_lat_t *pos)  /* output - address of long_lat_t
                                              structure to fill   */
{
        int result;
        char discard;

        result = scanf("%d%d%c%c", &(*pos).degrees,
                                   &(*pos).minutes,
                                   &discard,
                                   &(*pos).direction);
        if (result == 3)
              result = 1;

        return (result);
}
```

Section 9.3

1. When `time_now` is passed as an argument to function `new_time`, the values of its components are copied into `new_time`'s formal parameter `time_of_day`. Assignments to these components just change the function's local copy of the structure.

Section 9.4

1. `(6.50 + j5.00)  +  (3.00 - j4.00)  =  (9.50 + j1.00)`

   `Second result  =  (1.50 + j5.00)`

Section 9.5

1. The & is not applied to `units` because `units` is an array of type `unit_t`, and an array name with no subscript always represents the address of the array's initial element.

CHAPTER 10

Section 10.1

1. a. `n = 123   x = 3.145   str = "xyz"   ch = \n`
   b. `n = 123   x = 3.145   str = "xyz"   ch = \n`
   c. `n = 3     x = 123.0   str = 145     ch = .`
   d. `n = 35    x = ??      str = xyz     ch = z`

Section 10.2

1.
```
/*
 * Complex number file input function returns standard scanning
 * error code
 *    1 => valid scan,  0 => error,  negative EOF value => end of file
 */
int
fscan_complex(FILE *inp,      /* input file pointer */
              complex_t *c) /* output - address of complex variable
                                          to fill  */
{
    int status;

    status = fscanf(inp, "%lf%lf", &(*c).real, &(*c).imag);

    if (status == 2)
          status = 1;
    else if (status != EOF)
          status = 0;

    return (status);
}
```

Section 10.3

```
1. fread(&exec, sizeof (person_t), 1, psn_inp);
3. fwrite(&exec, sizeof (person_t), 1, psn_outp);
5. fread(&num_err[3], sizeof (int), 1, nums_inp);
```

Section 10.4

1. a. Use default values except:
      Low bound for tensile modulus = 135
   b. Use default values except:
      Low bound for name = "vanadium"
      High bound for name = "vanadium"
   c. Use default values except:
      Low bound for melting point = 1400
      High bound for days to delivery = 15
3. `match` does not check the `name` component because it is called from within a `while` loop that only calls it for names that are in range.

 **CHAPTER 11**

Section 11.1

1. a. A microwave oven quickly heats up the objects placed inside of it when the controls are correctly set. It is not necessary to know that the oven is actually emitting energy that is specifically designed to agitate the water molecules in a substance and thus heat up the food.
   b. A television allows one to see various programs simply by turning it on and changing the channels. The user is totally isolated from the electronics used to tune and display the signal the program is riding on.
   c. A calculator allows the user to compute a myriad of numerical calculations without any knowledge of the electronics and logic embedded in the calculator.

Section 11.2

1. A system header file name is surrounded by angular brackets (<>) while a personal header file name would be surrounded by quotes (" ").
3. what, how

Section 11.3

1. It is included in the header file so the user will know the string size for the planet structure.

Section 11.4

```
1. y = DOUBLE(a - b) * c;   ->   y = (a - b) + (a - b) * c;
```

The macro should have been written:

```
#define DOUBLE(x) ((x) + (x))
```

3. `if (DISCRIMINANT(a1, b1, c1) == 0) ->`
    `if (((b1) * (b1) - 4 * (a1) * (c1)) == 0)`
    OK

Section 11.5

1. `unit_max` -- auto; `found` -- auto; `convert` -- extern; `quantity` -- auto;

Section 11.6

1. So that any revision of a type definition or a macro definition will require a change to only one file.

Section 11.7

1.  ```
    #if defined (UNIX)
        printf("Enter <ctrl-d> to quit.");
    #elif defined (VMS)
        printf("Enter <ctrl-z> to quit.");
    #endif
    ```

Section 11.8

1. The following code would be added right after the line `int status;`

    ```
    /* See if arguments were included */
    if (argc < 3) {
        printf("\nPlease include input and output file ");
        printf("names.\n");
        exit(1);
    }
    ```

CHAPTER 12

Section 12.1

1.   1.500
    −0.500
     1.500
    −0.500

    The results make sense. $f(1.5) = 0$ and $f(-0.5) = 0$. We could use the quadratic formula to compute these results.

Section 12.2

1. `a = 0.80, b = 1.15`
    ```

Section 12.3

1.

t	0	1	2	3	4	5	6
$f'(t)$ exact	0.0	0.6	1.2	1.8	1.8	1.8	1.8
$f'(t)$ approx	0.3	0.6	1.2	1.65	1.8	1.8	1.8
error	−0.3	0.0	0.0	0.15	0.0	0.0	0.0

Section 12.4

1. The definite integral from 1 to 2 of f(x)dx is approximately 0.6944.

   The definite integral from 1 to 3 of g(x)dx is approximately 0.8357.

Section 12.5

1. $y_1 = 0$ $y_2 = 0.001000$ $y_3 = 0.005000$ $y_4 = 0.014003$
   $y_5 = 0.030022$